W9-BPL-212

#1800

m

ALSO BY THE EDITORS OF COOK'S ILLUSTRATED

To order any of our books, visit us at
http://www.cooksillustrated.com
1-800-611-0759

THE BEST RECIPE

AMERICAN CLASSICS

THE BEST RECIPE

American Classics

BY THE EDITORS OF

COOK'S ILLUSTRATED

ILLUSTRATIONS BY JOHN BURGOYNE

PHOTOGRAPHY BY CARL TREMBLAY

FRONT COVER PHOTOGRAPH BY CHRISTOPHER HIRSHEIMER

BOSTON COMMON PRESS

BROOKLINE, MASSACHUSETTS

Copyright © 2002 by The Editors of *Cook's Illustrated*

All rights reserved. No part of this book may be reproduced or transmitted in any manner whatsoever without written permission
from the publisher, except in the case of brief quotations embodied in critical articles or reviews.

Boston Common Press
17 Station Street
Brookline, Massachusetts 02445

ISBN 0-936184-55-8
Library of Congress Cataloging-in-Publication Data
The Editors of Cook's Illustrated
The Best Recipe: American Classics—Would you make 28 lemon meringue pies to find the best version? We did.
Here are more than 300 exhaustively tested recipes for America's favorite dishes.
1st Edition

ISBN 0-936184-55-8 (hardback): $29.95
I. Cooking. I. Title
2002

10 9 8 7 6 5 4 3 2

Manufactured in the United States of America

Distributed by Boston Common Press, 17 Station Street, Brookline, MA 02445.

Designed by Amy Klee
Edited by Jack Bishop

Pictured on front of jacket: Lemon Meringue Pie (page 377)
Pictured on back of jacket: Parker House Rolls (page 243)

CONTENTS

PREFACE

I HAVE ATTENDED MY SHARE OF COVERED-
dish suppers, and the offerings have ranged from
sublime mid-August creamed corn to baked beans
so thick and dry that even the local farmers passed
them by. This is why we have a love/hate relation-
ship with American classics. They entice with their
familiarity but often disappoint when we are inti-
mately reacquainted. Recipes that were conceived in
hard times or based on curious local ingredients and
customs often make poor travelers.

Since we are a nation of immigrants, American
classics don't form a unified cuisine. Yet I would
vouch for these timeless recipes from the standpoint
of flavor—each one is packed with it. Clam
chowder, twice-baked potatoes, chicken fricassee,
barbecued brisket, and peach pie don't depend on
culinary nuance—they fill one's mouth with calories
and joy. (Nuts to the low-fat crowd.)

Because such recipes are often in need of reha-
bilitation, our job was to become culinary archae-
ologists, not in the sense of uncovering their cultural
roots but to deconstruct their ingredients and techniques in order to reassemble them in a pleasing and
relatively foolproof new form. Over the years, the
bones of these old recipes have become jumbled
and broken, leaving modern cooks with skeletons
that hardly do justice to the recipes' potential. We
wanted spoon bread, baked beans, and chicken-fried

steak that tasted as good as our memories of them.

Walking the mountains and ridges of my small
Vermont town, I often come across abandoned stone
walls at 2,500 feet, gravestones at the top of Egg
Mountain, where Colonel Shea holed up with his
fellow rebel farmers, and wooded cellar holes where
dance halls and Methodist churches once stood. Yet
the past is not simply a pile of rocks out in the
woods. If you look carefully, you will see that
American classics are very much alive and well—
whether it's the neighbor who defrosts his wind-
shield with a votive candle on the dashboard or the
couple who serve my wife and me spaghetti with
crock-pot squirrel sauce. (Recipe not included.)

For many of us, crab cakes, sticky buns, corn
muffins, lobster rolls, and coconut cream pie are not
out-of-date relics but classics that, with a bit of
sprucing up, are as good as anything served at a four-
star restaurant. After all, there is a reason that we call
them classics. Like the stone walls built hundreds of
years ago, they have stood the test of time. This book
is our way of helping you get reacquainted with
these old favorites so that you can fall in love with
them all over again.

Christopher Kimball
Founder and Editor
Cook's Illustrated

ACKNOWLEDGMENTS

ALL OF THE PROJECTS UNDERTAKEN AT *Cook's Illustrated* are collective efforts, the combined experience and work of editors, test cooks, and writers, all joining in the search for the best cooking methods. This book is no exception.

Editor Jack Bishop spearheaded this project. Dawn Yanagihara supervised the recipe development process. Julia Collin and Matthew Card were the main researchers, recipe developers, and writers for the book. Shannon Blaisdell, Becky Hays, Bridget Lancaster, Raquel Pelzel, Adam Ried, and Meg Suzuki also developed recipes and wrote portions of the text.

Art director Amy Klee and graphic designer Nina Madjid transformed computer files and digital scans into a book. Julia Sedykh designed the cover, and Christopher Hirsheimer photographed the front cover image. Carl Tremblay captured the images at the beginning of each chapter and on the back cover. Daniel van Ackere took step photographs, and John Burgoyne turned these pictures into illustrations.

The following individuals on the editorial, production, circulation, customer service, and office staffs also worked on the book: Ron Bilodeau, Barbara Bourassa, Jana Branch, Rich Cassidy, Sharyn Chabot, Mary Connelly, Cathy Dorsey, Larisa Greiner, India Koopman, Jim McCormack, Jennifer McCreary, Erin McMurrer, Nicole Morris, Henrietta Murray, Juliet Nusbaum, Jessica Quirk, Sumi Selvakumar, and Mandy Shito. And without help from members of the marketing staff, readers might never find our books. Deborah Broide, Steven Browall, Connie Forbes, Jason Geller, Robert Lee, David Mack, Jacqui Valerio, and Jonathan Venier all contributed to marketing and distribution efforts.

1

SOUPS AND STEWS

SOUPS AND STEWS OFFER SOME OF THE best examples of humble yet delicious American cooking. There are literally hundreds of important soups and stews made in kitchens across the country. For this chapter, we have focused on two types of soups and stews: basic recipes that should be in every cook's repertoire as well as regional recipes that enjoy widespread popularity.

The first category includes chicken noodle soup, beef stew, and cream of tomato soup. These recipes are appealing (many are childhood favorites) and generally easy to prepare. But, as with any popular dish, there are plenty of bad versions of these classic recipes. We've all had chicken soup with too little chicken flavor or beef stew that was too thick, too thin, or too bland. Our recipes solve these problems without straying far from tradition.

Regional soups and stews travel well. After all, that's part of the appeal of a soup or stew—that it's easily made with readily available ingredients. We've chosen just a few of our favorite regional soups and stews for this chapter, including New England clam chowder and Texas chili.

Of course, great soups and stews (as well as countless other dishes) begin with good stock. While home cooks can get by without making their own beef stock or fish stock, everyone should know how to turn a chicken into stock. The chapter starts with this essential recipe and then moves on to our favorite soups, chowders, stews, and chilis.

Chicken Stock

MOST STANDARD CHICKEN STOCKS ARE not flavorful enough for a robust chicken soup. They are fine if ladled into risotto or stew but not strong enough for a broth-based chicken soup. Our goal was simple: Create a chicken stock with as much unadulterated chicken flavor as possible. We also wanted to streamline and speed up the process as much as we could.

We started with the most common technique for making stock—the simmering method. We placed all the ingredients (chicken, vegetables, aromatics, and water) in a pot, simmered everything for hours, then strained and defatted the stock. We tested a tremendous number of ingredients—everything from thyme and parsley to carrots and parsnips—and found that we preferred stock with fewer ingredients. Onions, salt, and bay leaves complement the flavor of the chicken; everything else is a distraction.

We tried making stock with a whole cut-up chicken, with whole legs, as well as with the more traditional necks and backs with the simmering method. While the necks and backs yielded a rich stock, tasters preferred stocks made with a cut-up chicken or whole legs, both of which had more flavor and body. Because whole legs are much less expensive, they are our first choice when using the traditional simmering method.

Some other guidelines emerged during testing:

1. Skim any impurities that rise to the surface as the water comes to a boil. Continue to skim any foam, once every hour or so, as the stock simmers. We found that removing the foam gave our stock a clearer appearance.

2. Reduce the heat once the stock comes to a boil. Boiling breaks the fat into tiny droplets that a gravy skimmer will not be able to trap. The result is greasy stock. While refrigerating the stock will allow the fat to congeal, at which point it can be removed, you may not always have time for this step. For the best results, gently simmer the stock (small bubbles will slowly and gently break through the surface).

3. Let the stock simmer as long as possible, up to five hours. We tried simmering stocks from one to six hours. When we tasted the various stocks, it was clear that more time yields a better stock. In fact, our favorite stock simmered for five hours. (After that we could not taste any improvement; evidently the bones were spent, having given up all their flavor to the stock.) A long-cooked traditional chicken stock has a rich, intense chicken flavor, just what you want when making a simple chicken soup with a few dumplings. Although you may be tempted to short-cut this process, don't. While stocks simmered for at least 2½ hours were fine (stocks simmered for less time were insipid), they lacked the intensity and flavor of longer-cooked stocks. Time, and a lot of it, is needed to extract the full flavor from the chicken.

Our testing had produced a great stock, and we had reached some interesting conclusions about traditional stock making, but we wondered if there was a quicker route to good stock. While throwing everything into the pot and letting it simmer for hours is easy (the hands-on work is no more than 10 minutes), you do need to be around the house. There are times when you need stock in a hurry or don't want to hang around the house for five hours. We were willing to try almost anything.

We tried blanching a whole chicken—submerging it briefly in boiling water—based on the theory that blanching keeps the chicken from releasing foam during cooking. The blanched chicken was then partially covered with water and placed in a heatproof bowl over a pan of simmering water. Cooked this way, the chicken never simmered, and the resulting stock was remarkably clear, refined, and full-flavored. The only problem: It took four hours to develop sufficient flavor. We also noted that our 4-pound chicken was good for nothing but the compost heap after being cooked for so long.

A number of recipes promote roasting chicken bones or parts and then using them to make stock. The theory is that roasted parts will flavor stock in minutes, not hours. We tried this several times, roasting chicken backs, necks, and bones—with and without vegetables. We preferred the roasted stock with vegetables. The resulting stock was dark in color and had a nice caramelized onion flavor, but it still wasn't the full-flavored stock we were looking for. While the roasted flavor was quite strong, the actual chicken flavor was too tame.

We tried sautéing a chicken, hacked into small pieces, with an onion until the chicken was slightly browned. The pot was then covered and the chicken and onion allowed to cook over low heat until they released their rich, flavorful juices, which took about 20 minutes. Only at this point did we add water, and the stock was simmered for just 20 minutes more.

We knew we were onto something when we smelled the chicken and onions sautéing, and the finished stock confirmed what our noses had detected. It tasted pleasantly sautéed, not boiled. We had some refining to do, though. For once, we had too much flavor.

We substituted chicken backs and wingtips for the whole chicken and used more water. This stock was less intense but just the right strength to use as a base for some of the best chicken soup we've ever tasted. We made the stock twice more—once without the onion and once with onion, celery, and carrot. The onion added a flavor dimension we liked; the other vegetables neither added nor detracted from the final soup, so we left them out.

After much trial and error, we had a master recipe that delivered liquid gold in just 60 minutes. While this recipe requires some hands-on work (hacking up chicken parts, browning an onion, then simmering), it is ready in a fraction of the time required to make a traditional, long-cooking stock.

The question before us now: How do you come up with these chicken parts for stock? The Buffalo chicken wing fad has made wings more expensive than legs and thighs. For those who can buy chicken backs, this is clearly an inexpensive way to make stock for soup. Our local grocery store usually sells the backs for practically nothing, but in many locations they may be difficult to get. Luckily, we found that relatively inexpensive whole legs make incredibly full-flavored stocks for soup. In a side-by-side comparison of stocks, one made from backs and one from whole legs, we found the whole leg stock to be more full-flavored. Just don't try to salvage the meat once the stock is finished. After 5 minutes of sautéing, 20 minutes of sweating, and another 20 minutes of simmering, the meat is void of flavor.

If you are making a soup that calls for chicken

HACKING UP A CHICKEN FOR STOCK

You can hack up a chicken with a cleaver or use poultry shears. If using a whole chicken, start by removing the whole legs and wings from the body; set them aside. Separate the back from the breast, then split the breast and set the halves aside. Hack or cut the back crosswise into three or four pieces, then halve each of these pieces. Cut the wing at each joint to yield three pieces. Leave the wingtip whole, then halve each of the remaining joints. Because of their large bones, the legs and thighs are the most difficult to cut. Start by splitting the leg and thigh at the joint, then hack or cut each to yield three or four pieces. If using just backs, wingtips, or whole legs, follow the directions outlined above for that part.

meat, such as chicken noodle, use a whole chicken as directed in Quick Chicken Stock with Sautéed Breast Meat (right). The breast is sautéed separately and then set aside while the rest of the bird—legs, back, wings, and giblets—is sautéed and sweated. The breasts are added back to the pot along with the water, and the result is perfectly cooked breast meat, ready to be skinned and shredded when cool. The remaining chicken pieces are discarded. We particularly like the tidiness of this method: One chicken yields one pot of soup.

One note about our recipe for quick stock. We found it necessary to cut the chicken into pieces small enough to release their flavorful juices in a short period of time (see "Hacking Up a Chicken for Stock" on page 3). A cleaver or poultry shears speeds up this process. Don't try to cut through chicken bones with a chef's knife. The blade isn't strong enough to cut through bone, and you may hurt yourself as the knife slips and slides. Even if you do manage to cut through the bone, your knife may become nicked in the process.

Quick Chicken Stock

MAKES ABOUT 2 QUARTS

Chicken pieces are sautéed and then sweated before being cooked in water for a rich but very quick stock. This is our favorite all-purpose stock. It also takes less than an hour to prepare.

I   tablespoon vegetable oil
I   medium onion, chopped medium
4   pounds whole chicken legs or backs and wingtips, cut into 2-inch pieces (see "Hacking Up a Chicken for Stock" on page 3)
2   quarts boiling water
2   teaspoons salt
2   bay leaves

1. Heat the oil in a large stockpot or Dutch oven over medium-high heat. Add the onion; sauté until colored and softened slightly, 2 to 3 minutes. Transfer the onion to a large bowl.

2. Add half of the chicken pieces to the pot; sauté both sides until lightly browned, 4 to 5 minutes. Transfer the cooked chicken to the bowl with the onions. Sauté the remaining chicken pieces. Return the onions and chicken pieces to the pot. Reduce the heat to low, cover, and cook until the chicken releases its juices, about 20 minutes.

3. Increase the heat to high; add the boiling water, salt, and bay leaves. Return to a simmer, then cover and barely simmer until the stock is rich and flavorful, about 20 minutes.

4. Strain the stock; discard the solids. Before using, defat the stock (see page 5). The stock can be refrigerated in an airtight container for up to 2 days or frozen for several months.

Quick Chicken Stock with Sautéed Breast Meat

MAKES ABOUT 2 QUARTS

Choose this stock when you want to have some breast meat in your soup.

I   tablespoon vegetable oil
I   whole chicken (about 4 pounds), breast meat removed on the bone, split, and reserved; remaining chicken cut into 2-inch pieces (see "Hacking Up a Chicken for Stock" on page 3)
I   medium onion, chopped medium
2   quarts boiling water
2   teaspoons salt
2   bay leaves

1. Heat the oil in a large stockpot or Dutch oven over medium-high heat. When the oil shimmers and starts to smoke, add the chicken breast halves; sauté both sides until lightly browned, about 5 minutes. Remove the chicken breast pieces and set aside. Add the onion to the pot; sauté until colored and softened slightly, 2 to 3 minutes. Transfer the onion to a large bowl.

2. Add half of the chicken pieces to the pot; sauté both sides until lightly browned, 4 to 5 minutes. Transfer the cooked chicken to the bowl with the onion. Sauté the remaining chicken pieces. Return the onion and chicken pieces (excluding the breasts) to the pot. Reduce the heat to low, cover, and cook until the chicken releases its juices, about 20 minutes.

3. Increase the heat to high; add the boiling water,

the chicken breasts, salt, and bay leaves. Return to a simmer, then cover and barely simmer until the chicken breasts are cooked through and the stock is rich and flavorful, about 20 minutes.

4. Remove the chicken breasts from the pot; when cool enough to handle, remove the skin from the breasts, then remove the meat from the bones and shred into bite-sized pieces; discard the skin and bone. Strain the stock; discard the solids. Before using, defat the stock (see below). The shredded chicken and stock can be refrigerated separately in airtight containers for up to 2 days.

TWO WAYS TO DEFAT STOCK

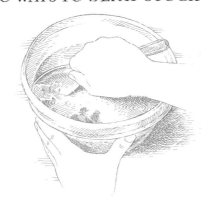

1. Stock should be defatted before being used. The easiest way to do this is to refrigerate it until the fat rises to the surface and congeals. Use a spoon to scrape the fat off the surface of the stock. When skimming chicken stock, you may want to save the fat, which makes a flavorful replacement for oil or butter when cooking. Chicken fat can be refrigerated in an airtight container for several days.

2. If you don't have time to refrigerate the stock and allow the fat to congeal, use a gravy skimmer. Pour the stock into the gravy skimmer, then pour it out through the spout attached to the bottom of the skimmer. The fat floating on top of the liquid will remain behind.

CHICKEN NOODLE SOUP

WITH HOMEMADE CHICKEN STOCK ON HAND, making chicken noodle soup is a relatively easy proposition. Add some vegetables, herbs, and noodles and you've got a great bowl of soup. We did have several questions, though. Which vegetables are best added to this soup? Should the vegetables be sautéed first, or can diced vegetables simply be simmered in chicken stock? As for the pasta, which kind of noodles work best, and should they be cooked in the soup or in a separate pot of boiling water? We wanted to answer all these questions, develop a basic master recipe, then create some more unusual variations.

We tackled the vegetable issue first. We tested a wide range of vegetables, including onions, carrots, celery, leeks, potatoes, zucchini, tomatoes, and mushrooms. We concluded that only the classic ingredients of mirepoix (onion, carrot, and celery) should be part of a basic chicken noodle soup. Other vegetables can work well, but we decided that they are more appropriate for variations. For instance, tomatoes and zucchini give chicken noodle soup an Italian character, and spring vegetables are a natural choice with rice.

To settle the issue of how to cook the vegetables, we prepared two batches of soup. For the first batch, we sautéed the onions, carrots, and celery in a little vegetable oil until softened and then added the chicken stock. For the second batch, we simply simmered the sliced vegetables in stock. As might be expected, we found that sautéing brought out flavors in the vegetables and made a big difference in the finished soup.

We saw a few recipes that suggested saving chicken fat skimmed from homemade stock and using this fat as a cooking medium for the vegetables. We tested this and found that chicken fat does in fact add another level of chicken flavor to the soup. Although not essential, it makes sense to use chicken fat if you have planned ahead and saved what you skimmed from the surface of your stock.

In addition to the vegetables, we found that thyme and parsley brightened flavors. We added dried thyme along with the stock to give it time to soften and permeate the soup. To preserve its freshness, the parsley was best added just before serving.

The noodles were the last (and most important)

element that we needed to investigate. Although dried egg noodles are the most common choice, we ran across several recipes that suggested fresh or dried pasta. Before testing various noodles, we decided to clarify the issue of how to cook them. We simmered egg noodles in the soup as well as in a separate pot of salted water. The noodles cooked in the soup pot shed some starch that somewhat clouded the soup. In contrast, noodles cooked in a separate pot and added to the stock left the finished soup completely clear.

The effect on the soup, however, paled in comparison to the effect on the noodles. Noodles cooked separately tasted bland and did not meld with the soup. The noodles cooked in the soup absorbed some of the chicken stock, giving them a rich, well-rounded flavor. We concluded that you must cook the noodles in the soup.

We identified seven possible noodle choices: dried egg noodles (fine, home-style, and extra-broad), dried linguine, dried spaghetti, fresh fettuccine, and fresh linguine. We cooked 2 ounces of each in a pot of chicken soup. Tasters preferred the egg noodles to both the fresh and dried pastas. The noodles cooked up very soft and yielding. They were tender to the bite and nearly melted in the mouth. Tasters also liked the ridged edges on the noodles, which provided nooks and crannies that trapped pieces of vegetable.

The dried spaghetti and linguine were deemed chewy and the least favorite choices. The fresh fettuccine did have some fans, although the fresh linguine was thought to be too narrow. Fresh fettuccine cooked up fairly soft (but not as soft as the egg noodles), and their width worked better with the vegetables. To make them manageable on a spoon, we recommend cutting them in half and then in half again. Pieces that are 2 to 3 inches long will just fit on a large spoon. (Note that fresh pasta will cook more quickly than dried egg noodles, reducing the simmering time in step 2 of the master recipe to about three minutes.)

Although fresh fettuccine can be used, we think dried egg noodles are the better choice. In addition to their superior texture when cooked, they are more widely available (every supermarket carries them) and less expensive. Tasters liked all three types of dried egg noodles tested. The fine noodles cooked

up no more than 1/16 inch wide and gave the soup a delicate character. The extra-broad and home-style noodles cooked up considerably wider and gave the soup a heartier feeling. Although home-style and extra-broad noodles look pretty much the same in the package, the home-style noodles measure about 1½ inches across when cooked, the extra-broad noodles only an inch across when cooked. In addition, the home-style noodles cooked up a bit flatter, while the extra-broad noodles remained twisted. Each noodle had its partisans in the test kitchen. Choose any one of the three based on your preference.

While the recipes that follow are adaptable, we have carefully timed the addition of vegetables, noodles, grains, and other ingredients to make sure that each item is perfectly cooked—not overcooked. If you make adjustments, keep in mind general cooking times for additional ingredients or substitutions.

Chicken Noodle Soup
SERVES 6 TO 8

The noodles do not hold very well, and this soup is best served as soon as the noodles are tender. If you plan on having leftovers, prepare the recipe through step 1, reserve the portion you want to save for another day, then cook a portion of the noodles in the remaining soup.

- 2 tablespoons chicken fat (reserved from making stock) or vegetable oil
- 1 medium onion, chopped medium
- 1 large carrot, peeled and sliced 1/4 inch thick
- 1 stalk celery, sliced 1/4 inch thick
- 1/2 teaspoon dried thyme leaves
- 2 quarts Quick Chicken Stock with Sautéed Breast Meat (page 4), stock and meat separated
- 2 cups (3 ounces) egg noodles (fine, extra-broad, or home-style)
- 1/4 cup minced fresh parsley leaves
   Salt and ground black pepper

1. Heat the chicken fat in a large stockpot or Dutch oven over medium-high heat. Add the onion, carrot, and celery and sauté until softened, about 5 minutes. Add the thyme, stock, and shredded chicken

meat. Bring the soup to a boil, reduce the heat, and simmer until the vegetables are tender and the flavors meld, 10 to 15 minutes.

2. Stir in the noodles and cook until just tender, about 8 minutes. Stir in the parsley and salt and pepper to taste. Serve immediately.

➤ VARIATIONS

Chicken and Rice Soup with Spring Vegetables

As with noodles, we found that rice tastes best when cooked in the soup rather than a separate pot. Since rice takes more time to soften than do egg noodles, it should be added once the aromatic vegetables have been sautéed.

Follow the recipe for Chicken Noodle Soup, replacing the onion with 1 medium leek, rinsed thoroughly, quartered lengthwise, then sliced thin crosswise. Add ½ cup long-grain rice (omit egg noodles) along with the thyme, stock, and chicken meat in step 1 and cook for 10 minutes. Add ¼ pound trimmed asparagus, cut into 1-inch lengths, and simmer until the asparagus and rice are tender, about 8 minutes. Substitute ¼ cup thawed frozen peas and 2 tablespoons minced fresh tarragon leaves for the parsley. Heat through for 1 minute and serve.

Chicken Soup with Shells, Tomatoes, and Zucchini

Zucchini, tomatoes, and pasta shells give chicken soup an Italian flavor. Pass grated cheese at the table, if desired.

Follow the recipe for Chicken Noodle Soup, adding 1 medium zucchini, chopped medium, along with the onion, carrot, and celery, and increasing the sautéing time to 7 minutes. Add ½ cup diced canned tomatoes along with the stock. Substitute 1 cup small pasta shells or macaroni for the egg noodles and simmer until they are cooked, about 10 minutes. Substitute ¼ cup chopped fresh basil for the parsley.

Chicken Soup with Wild Rice, Leeks, and Mushrooms

Wild rice and wild mushrooms lend a woodsy flavor to this luxurious take on basic chicken noodle soup. Wild rice takes much longer to cook than regular rice, so it is cooked before being added to the soup.

2   quarts Quick Chicken Stock with Sautéed Breast Meat (page 4), stock and meat separated

½   ounce dried wild mushrooms, such as porcini or shiitake

½   cup wild rice

3   tablespoons chicken fat (reserved from making stock) or vegetable oil

I   medium leek, rinsed thoroughly, quartered lengthwise, then sliced thin crosswise

I   large carrot, peeled and sliced ¼ inch thick

⅓   pound sliced fresh button or wild mushrooms

½   teaspoon dried thyme

¼   cup minced fresh parsley leaves
    Salt and ground black pepper

1. Heat 1 cup of the chicken stock in a small saucepan until almost simmering. Remove the pan from the heat, stir in the dried mushrooms, and let stand until the mushrooms have softened, about 20 minutes. Lift the mushrooms from the liquid, rinse if they feel gritty, and chop. Strain the soaking liquid through a sieve lined with a paper towel. Reserve the mushrooms and their liquid separately.

2. While the mushrooms are softening, combine the wild rice and 1 cup water in a small saucepan set over medium-high heat. Bring to a boil, cover, turn the heat to low, and cook until tender, 30 to 35 minutes.

3. Heat the chicken fat in a large stockpot or Dutch oven over medium-high heat. Add the leek and carrot and sauté until softened, about 5 minutes. Add the fresh mushrooms and continue to sauté until the mushrooms are softened, about 5 minutes. Add the dried mushrooms and sauté to release their flavors, about 1 minute.

4. Add the strained soaking liquid from the dried mushrooms, the thyme, and the remaining chicken stock to the pot. Simmer until the vegetables are tender and the flavors meld, 10 to 15 minutes.

5. Add the chicken meat and cooked wild rice and cook for 5 minutes. Stir in the parsley and add salt and pepper to taste. Serve immediately.

CREAM OF TOMATO SOUP

RAINY SATURDAYS IN LATE WINTER BRING
to mind the grilled cheese sandwiches and tomato
soup of childhood. The sandwiches were made with
squishy white bread and cheese from an oblong
box. As for the soup, it came in a can, of course—and
we all know which can. Long after our affection for
other soups sealed in that small red and white icon
has waned, our nostalgia for Campbell's cream of
tomato soup persists. Few of us eat canned tomato
soup these days, but some of us do have a vision of
the perfect tomato soup. Our vision is a soup of
Polartec softness, rich color, and a pleasing balance
of sweetness and acidity.

To get a dose of reality, we opened a can of
Campbell's. Though rich and tomatoey, it was also
cloyingly sweet, not unlike a cream of ketchup soup.
So we moved on to create a soup that would actually
be as good as our childhood memories.

For our first tests, we used fresh out-of-season
tomatoes. Arriving in the test kitchen, the tomatoes
were cosmetically peerless, with gleaming red skins
and crisp upright stems. But their taste was a
different matter. Without exception, the soups they
produced were anemic and completely lacking in
tomato flavor. The soups containing flavor boosters
such as carrots, celery, and onions failed even more
strikingly to suggest a tomato soup. One made with
a roux had the characteristics of a tomato gravy.

Not content to develop a recipe that would be
worth making only during the one or two months
of the year when tomatoes are in prime form,
we turned to canned tomatoes. For our soup we
selected fine canned organic diced tomatoes and
added shallots, a bit of flour to give the finished
product some body, a spoon of tomato paste and
canned chicken broth to enrich the flavor, a splash of
heavy cream and sherry for refinement, and a pinch
of sugar for good measure. Though the resulting
soup was dramatically better than those made with
fresh winter tomatoes, it failed to make the cut; the
flavor simply wasn't robust enough.

How do you get bigger flavor from canned tomatoes? If they were fresh and ripe, you might roast them:
The caramelization of sugar in the skins that occurs
during roasting concentrates and intensifies the flavors.
In the test kitchen, where almost any experiment is

considered worth trying, we decided to roast canned
tomatoes. We hoped that intense dry heat might evaporate the surface liquid and concentrate the flavor.

Leaving our recipe otherwise unchanged, we
switched from diced to whole tomatoes for ease of
handling, drained and seeded them (reserving the
juice for later), then laid them on a foil-covered
rimmed baking sheet and sprinkled them with
brown sugar, which we hoped would induce a surface caramelization. Only minutes after sliding our
tray of tomatoes into a 450-degree oven, the test
kitchen was filled with real tomato fragrance, and we
knew we had done something right. The roasting
made an extraordinary difference, intensifying the
tomato flavor and mellowing the fruit's acidity.
What's more, the rest of the soup could be prepared
while the tomatoes roasted.

Only one minor visual detail marred our efforts.
The intense flavor we'd achieved by roasting the

PREPARING TOMATOES FOR ROASTING

1. With your fingers, carefully open the whole tomatoes over a
strainer set in a bowl and push out the seeds, allowing the juices to
fall through the strainer and into the bowl.

2. Arrange the seeded tomatoes in a single layer on a foil-lined,
rimmed baking sheet. The foil is essential; it keeps the tomatoes
from scorching and sticking to the baking sheet. Let the roasted
tomatoes cool slightly before trying to remove them from the foil.

tomatoes was not mirrored in the soup's color. The deep coronation red we admired while the soup simmered on the stovetop gave way to a faded circus orange during a round in the blender. The mechanical action of combining solids and liquids had aerated the soup and lightened the color. This wouldn't do. We decided to leave the rich tomato broth behind in the saucepan while pureeing the solids with just enough liquid to result in a soup of perfect smoothness. A finish of heavy cream and our vision of tomato soup had come to life.

Cream of Tomato Soup

SERVES 4

Use canned whole tomatoes that are not packed in puree; you will need some of the juice to make the soup. For information on specific brands, see right.

2	(28-ounce) cans whole tomatoes packed in juice, drained, 3 cups juice reserved
1½	tablespoons dark brown sugar
4	tablespoons unsalted butter
4	large shallots, minced
1	tablespoon tomato paste
	Pinch ground allspice
2	tablespoons all-purpose flour
1¾	cups homemade chicken stock or canned low-sodium broth
½	cup heavy cream
2	tablespoons brandy or dry sherry
	Salt and cayenne pepper

1. Adjust an oven rack to the upper-middle position and heat the oven to 450 degrees. Line a rimmed baking sheet with foil. Seed and spread the tomatoes in a single layer on the foil (see the illustrations on page 8). Sprinkle evenly with the brown sugar. Bake until all the liquid has evaporated and the tomatoes begin to color, about 30 minutes. Let the tomatoes cool slightly, then peel them off the foil; transfer to a small bowl and set aside.

2. Heat the butter over medium heat in a large saucepan until foaming. Add the shallots, tomato paste, and allspice. Reduce the heat to low, cover, and cook, stirring occasionally, until the shallots are softened, 8 to 10 minutes. Add the flour and cook, stirring constantly, until thoroughly combined, about 30 seconds. Whisking constantly, gradually add the chicken stock; stir in the reserved tomato juice and the roasted tomatoes. Cover, increase the heat to medium, and bring to a boil. Reduce the heat to low and simmer to blend flavors, stirring occasionally, about 10 minutes.

3. Pour the mixture through a strainer and into a medium bowl; rinse out the saucepan. Transfer the tomatoes and solids in the strainer to a blender; add 1 cup strained liquid and puree until smooth. Place the pureed mixture and remaining strained liquid in the saucepan. Add the cream and warm over low heat until hot, about 3 minutes. Off heat, stir in the brandy and season with salt and cayenne to taste. (Soup can be refrigerated in an airtight container for up to 2 days. Warm over low heat until hot; do not boil.) Serve immediately.

INGREDIENTS:
Canned Whole Tomatoes

Canned whole tomatoes are the closest product to fresh. Whole tomatoes, either plum or round, are steamed to remove their skins and then packed in tomato juice or puree. We prefer tomatoes packed in juice; they generally have a fresher, more lively flavor. Puree has a cooked tomato flavor that can impart a slightly stale, tired flavor to the whole can.

To find the best canned whole tomatoes, we tasted 11 brands, both straight from the can and in a simple tomato sauce. Muir Glen (an organic brand available in most supermarkets and natural foods stores) and Progresso finished at the head of the pack. Either brand is an excellent choice in cream of tomato soup or any recipe that calls for canned whole tomatoes.

CROUTONS

A SHOWER OF CRISP CROUTONS ADDS FLAVOR, crunch, and—yes—elegance to a humble bowl of tomato soup. In fact, most vegetable soups benefit from the addition of a few croutons. We're not talking about the prepackaged croutons sold in the supermarket. Only the real thing will do.

Although croutons are simple fare (cubed bread tossed with fat and toasted in the oven until crisp), we did have some questions. What kind of bread makes the best croutons? Should the crusts be trimmed or left on? Should the bread cubes be coated with butter or oil?

We started with the issue of the bread. We tested several varieties of sliced white bread, Italian bread, and baguette. This test immediately led us to the next variable—the crusts. We quickly determined that croutons are best made with crustless bread cubes. The crusts are already more crunchy and a deeper brown color than the crumb. Including them results in unevenly cooked croutons, with edges that are darker, drier, and harder. Because Italian bread and baguettes have more crust than sliced white bread, we decided that the latter is the best choice for croutons. Avoid thinly sliced bread, which will make meager croutons. Regular or thick-sliced white bread is the best choice.

We found that ½-inch bread cubes create the ideal croutons. Smaller cubes can become too crunchy in the oven and don't absorb soup quite as well. Larger cubes won't fit on a spoon.

We tested both fresh and stale white bread and found that either can be used. Fresh bread is a bit trickier to cut into cubes and takes a bit longer to crisp up in the oven. If you want to use stale bread in our recipe, simply reduce the baking time by about two minutes. Note that croutons made from stale bread will be a bit more crisp than those made from fresh bread.

Fat adds much of the flavor to croutons. Our tasters preferred butter to the various oils we tested, although extra-virgin olive oil was a close second. An oven temperature of 400 degrees browned the croutons nicely without any scorching. Turning the bread cubes at the halfway mark ensures even cooking, as does arranging the bread cubes in a single layer on the baking sheet.

Buttered Croutons

MAKES ABOUT 3 CUPS

The croutons' crisp crunch offers a pleasant contrast with the smooth, velvety texture of a rich pureed soup. Although tasters preferred the flavor of croutons made with butter, olive oil was a close second. If you like, replace the melted butter with an equal amount of extra-virgin olive oil. Be sure to use regular or thick-sliced bread.

6   slices white bread (about 6 ounces), crusts removed and slices cut into ½-inch cubes (about 3 cups)
       Salt and ground black pepper
3   tablespoons unsalted butter, melted

1. Adjust an oven rack to the upper-middle position and heat the oven to 400 degrees. Combine bread cubes and salt and pepper to taste in a medium bowl. Drizzle with the butter and toss well with a rubber spatula to combine.

2. Spread the croutons in a single layer on a rimmed baking sheet or in a shallow baking dish. Bake the croutons, turning at the halfway mark, until golden brown and crisp, 8 to 10 minutes. Cool and then store croutons in an airtight container or plastic bag for up to 3 days.

HAM AND SPLIT PEA SOUP

OLD-FASHIONED RECIPES FOR HAM AND split pea soup start with the bone from a large roast ham that has been nearly picked clean. The bone and some split peas are thrown in a pot with some water and cooked until the meat falls off the bone. By that time, the fat has discreetly melted into the liquid, and the peas have become creamy enough to thicken the soup.

We love split pea soup made this way, but times have changed. Except for the occasional holiday, most cooks rarely buy a bone-in ham, opting more often for the thin-sliced deli stuff. We wondered if we could duplicate this wonderful soup without buying a huge ham.

To confirm or disprove our belief that a ham stock is crucial to split pea soup, we made several pork stocks and pork-enhanced canned chicken broths. In addition to making stock the old-fashioned way from a meaty ham bone, we made stock from smoked pork necks, pork hocks (fresh and smoked), and smoked ham shanks. We also made cheater's stocks: kielbasa simmered in canned chicken broth, kielbasa simmered in water, bacon simmered in chicken broth, and bacon simmered in water.

The stocks based on hocks—fresh as well as smoked—were more greasy than flavorful. In addition, the hocks gave up very little meat, making it necessary to purchase an additional portion of ham to fortify the soup. Ham shanks, which include the hock, made a pleasant but lightweight stock that was a tad greasy and salty—both fixable problems had the stock been more stellar. Pork necks, which are not widely available, made a fairly flavorful but salty stock. All four cheater's stocks failed. Both the kielbasa- and bacon-enhanced chicken broths tasted strongly of overly processed meat, while the water-based versions tasted weak.

Not surprisingly, the stock made from the bone of a big ham was the winner. It was meaty and full-flavored, rich but not greasy, nicely seasoned without being overly salty, and smoky without tasting artificial. Unlike any of the other broths, this one sported bits of meat. And not just good meat—great meat. The tender pieces of ham that fell away from the bone during cooking were not just a nice byproduct

HANDLING A HALF-PICNIC HAM

Half-picnic hams are readily available in supermarkets but contain too much meat for a pot of soup. Our solution is to pull off several meaty sections of the ham and roast them for sandwiches, salads, and egg dishes.

1. With your fingers, loosen the large comma-shaped muscles on top of the picnic half.

2. Use a knife to cut the membrane separating the comma-shaped muscles from the rest of the roast. The remaining meat and bone can be used to make soup.

of the stock. They were the glory of our split pea soup. But was there a way around buying half a ham (with an average weight of about 8 pounds) just to make a pot of soup?

After checking out the ham and smoked pork cases at several different stores, we discovered the picnic cut. Unlike what we generally refer to as ham, which comes from the back legs of the animal, the picnic comes from the shoulder and front legs. Smaller than a ham, the half-picnic weighs only 4½ pounds. After making a couple more pots of soup, we found that the picnic pork shoulder—with its bones, fat, rind, and meat—made outstanding stock, and after two hours of simmering the meat was meltingly tender yet still potently flavorful.

Since we did not need the full picnic half for our pot of soup, we pulled off and roasted two of its meatier muscles for use in other dishes and used the remaining meat, bone, fat, and rind to make the soup. At around 99 cents a pound, a picnic shoulder is usually cheaper than a ham, and often cheaper than pork hocks, shanks, or neck bones as well. Here, we thought, was the modern solution. Rather than buy a ham for eating (and eating and eating) with a leftover bone for soup, instead purchase a picnic for soup, and roast the remaining couple of pounds for eating.

There are several ways to make ham and split pea soup. You can throw all the ingredients—ham bone, peas, and diced vegetables—into a pot and simmer them until everything is tender. Or you can sauté the vegetables, then add the remaining ingredients and cook the soup until the ham and peas are tender. Alternatively, you can cook the ham bone and peas (or give the ham bone a head start) until ham and peas are tender and then add raw, sautéed, or caramelized vegetables to the pot, continuing to cook them until the vegetables are tender and the flavors have blended.

Although we had hoped to keep the soup a straightforward one-pot operation, we found out pretty quickly that dumping everything in at the same time resulted in gloppy, overcooked peas and tired mushy vegetables by the time the ham was tender. For textural contrast in this smooth, creamy soup, we ultimately preferred fully—though not overly—cooked vegetables.

Our best soups were those in which the vegetables spent enough time in the pot for their flavors to blend but not so long that they had lost all of their individual taste. Of the soups with vegetables added toward the end of cooking, we preferred the one with the caramelized vegetables. The sweeter vegetables gave this otherwise straightforward meat-and-starch soup a richness and depth of flavor that made the extra step and pan worth the trouble.

Many pea soup recipes call for an acidic ingredient—vinegar, lemon juice, fortified wine such as sherry or Madeira, Worcestershire sauce, or sour cream—to bring balance to an otherwise rich, heavy soup. After tasting all of the above, we found ourselves drawn to balsamic vinegar. Unlike any of the other ingredients, balsamic vinegar's mildly sweet, mildly acidic flavor perfectly complemented the soup.

Ham and Split Pea Soup

SERVES 6

Use a small 2½-pound picnic ham if you can find one. Otherwise, buy a half-picnic ham and remove some meat, which you can roast and use in sandwiches, salads, or omelets. (See "Handling a Half-Picnic Ham" on page 11.)

1	piece (about 2½ pounds) smoked, bone-in picnic ham
4	bay leaves
1	pound (2½ cups) dried split peas, washed and picked clean of any debris
1	teaspoon dried thyme
2	tablespoons extra-virgin olive oil
2	medium onions, chopped medium
2	medium carrots, chopped medium
2	medium stalks celery, chopped medium
1	tablespoon unsalted butter
2	medium cloves garlic, minced
	Pinch sugar
3	small new potatoes, scrubbed and cut into ½-inch dice (about ¾ cup)
	Ground black pepper
	Minced red onion (optional)
	Balsamic vinegar

1. Place the ham, bay leaves, and 3 quarts water in a large stockpot or Dutch oven. Cover and bring to a boil over medium–high heat. Reduce the heat to low and simmer until the meat is tender and pulls away from the bone, 2 to 2½ hours. Remove the ham meat and bone from the pot. When the ham is cool enough to handle, shred the meat into bite-sized pieces and set aside. Discard the rind, fat, and bone.

2. Add the split peas and thyme to the ham stock. Bring back to a boil, reduce the heat, and simmer, uncovered, until the peas are tender but not dissolved, about 45 minutes.

3. While the ham is simmering, heat the oil in a large skillet over high heat until shimmering. Add the onions, carrots, and celery and sauté, stirring frequently, until most of the liquid evaporates and the vegetables begin to brown, 5 to 6 minutes. Reduce the heat to medium–low and add the butter, garlic, and sugar. Cook the vegetables, stirring frequently, until deeply browned, 30 to 35 minutes; set aside.

4. Add the sautéed vegetables, potatoes, and shredded ham to the pot with the split peas. Simmer, uncovered, until the potatoes are tender and peas dissolve and thicken soup to the consistency of light cream, about 20 minutes more. Season with ground black pepper to taste. (The soup can be refrigerated in an airtight container for up to 2 days. Warm the soup over low heat until hot.) Ladle the soup into bowls, sprinkle with red onion, if using, and serve, passing balsamic vinegar separately.

SCRUBBING POTATOES

Recipes in which potatoes are not peeled usually instruct the cook to "scrub" the potatoes. We like to use a rough-textured "bathing" or "exfoliating" glove for this task. The glove cleans away dirt but is relatively gentle and won't scrub away the potato skin. We keep a glove in the kitchen especially for cleaning potatoes, turnips, carrots, beets, and other root vegetables.

INGREDIENTS: Commercial Chicken Broth

Despite the importance of good chicken stock to a wide array of dishes, few home cooks actually take the time to make it these days. The convenience of commercial chicken broth is inarguable. But the likelihood that it will taste any good at all is questionable.

Like homemade stocks, commercial broths are made from the meat and bones of chickens, only chicken of a kind that's different from what we are accustomed to cooking at home. We mainly cook with meat birds, meaty breeds of chickens raised for about eight weeks and subsequently sold as roasters and broilers in the butcher section of the supermarket. The chickens used in commercial broths are hens, or egg layers. Hens are effectively productive for only one to two years. After that they are not suited to be sold as meat because they are typically skinny birds, having spent all their energy producing eggs. But because they are older and have been more active than young meat birds, they can be more flavorful, and, most important, they have a higher density of the connective tissue known as collagen. When heated with moisture, collagen converts to gelatin and provides broth with body. So, basically, the food industry makes use of retired hens to flavor their broths— much like our grandmothers did.

But they sure must not be using the same ratio of bird to water as our grandmothers did. Few of the commercial broths in our tasting came close to the full-bodied consistency of a successful homemade stock. Many lacked even a hint of chicken flavor. Interestingly, the top four broths are all products of the Campbell Soup Company, of which Swanson is a subsidiary. In order, they were Swanson Chicken Broth, Campbell's Chicken Broth, Swanson Natural Goodness Chicken Broth (with 33 percent less sodium than regular Swanson chicken broth), and Campbell's Healthy Request Chicken Broth (with 30 percent less sodium than regular Campbell's chicken broth). The remaining broths were decidedly inferior and hard to recommend.

We tried to find out more about why Campbell's broths are superior to so many others, but the giant soup company declined to respond to questions, explaining that its recipes and cooking techniques are considered proprietary information. Many of the answers, however, could be found on the products' ingredient labels. As it turned out, the top two broths happened to contain the highest levels of sodium. Salt has been used for years in the food industry to make foods with less than optimum flavor tastier. The top two products also contained the controversial

monosodium glutamate (MSG), a very effective flavor enhancer.

Sadly, most of the products that had lower levels of salt and did not have the benefit of other food industry flavor enhancers simply tasted like dishwater. Their labels did indicate that their ingredients included "chicken broth" or "chicken stock" or sometimes both. But calls to the U.S. Food and Drug Administration and the U.S. Department of Agriculture revealed that there are no standards of definition for chicken broth or stock, so that an ingredient label indicating that the contents include chicken broth or chicken stock could mean anything as long as some chicken is used.

Ingredients aside, we found one more important explanation for why most commercial broths simply cannot replicate the full flavor and body of a homemade stock. Most broths are sold canned, which entails an extended heating process carried out to ensure a sterilized product. The immediate disadvantage of this processing is that heat breaks down naturally present flavor enhancers found in chicken protein. And prolonged heating, which is necessary for canning, destroys other volatile flavors at the same time that it concentrates flavor components that are not volatile, such as salt.

A few national brands of chicken broth have begun to offer the option of aseptic packaging. Compared with traditional canning, in which products are heated in the can for up to nearly an hour to ensure sterilization, the process of aseptic packaging entails a flash heating and cooling process that is said to help products better retain both their nutritional value and their flavor.

We decided to hold another tasting to see if we could detect more flavor in the products sold in aseptic packaging. Of the recommended broths in the tasting, only Swanson broths are available in aseptic packaging, and even these were not yet available nationwide. We tasted Swanson's traditional and Natural Goodness chicken broths sold in cans and in aseptic packages. The results fell clearly in favor of the aseptically packaged broths; both tasted cleaner and more chickeny than their canned counterparts. So if you are truly seeking the best of the best in commercial broths, choose one of the two Swanson broths sold in aseptic packaging. An opened aseptic package is said to keep in the refrigerator for up to two weeks (broth from a can is said to keep refrigerated for only a few days).

➤ VARIATION

Ham and Split Pea Soup with Caraway

Toast 1½ teaspoons caraway seeds in a small skillet over medium-high heat, stirring frequently, until fragrant and browned, about 4 minutes. Follow the recipe for Ham and Split Pea Soup, substituting toasted caraway seeds for the dried thyme.

U.S. Senate Navy Bean Soup

FROM EXPERIENCE, WE KNOW THAT TOO many bean soup recipes result in an unappetizing bowl of gooey gruel punctuated by bits of tough, undercooked beans and mushy, flavorless vegetables. A good bean soup, however, can be a terrific stick-to-the-ribs, cool-weather meal, full of creamy, toothsome beans and deeply flavored with smoked meat and slow-cooked vegetables.

One of the classic homegrown bean soups, U.S. Senate navy bean soup has supposedly been on the menu in the Senate restaurant since 1901. Legend has it that Sen. Fred Dubois of Idaho, who served from 1901 to 1907, demanded that navy bean soup would be on the restaurant menu in perpetuity. The mandate has been attributed to other epicurean senators as well, but all that really matters is that it has been on the menu for more than a century.

The authentic Senate version contains nothing but beans, ham hocks, onion, butter, and water. We tried this version and found it homey but a little too plain. Bucking tradition slightly, we decided we wanted to add some complexity with a few other ingredients and flavors. We figured we would work out the basics of preparing this soup and then figure out how to add more flavor.

We started by testing the accuracy of rule number one in most bean soup recipes: Always soak the beans. We cooked up three batches. Prior to cooking, we soaked one batch overnight and another according to the "quick-soak" method (water and beans simmer for two minutes, then are taken off heat, covered, and allowed to sit in the water for one hour). We didn't presoak the third batch at all. The results were altogether disappointing. Both batches of soaked beans split or exploded. The unsoaked

MAKING A BOUQUET GARNI

A bouquet garni is a classic combination of herbs used to flavor many soups, stews, and sauces. Sprigs of fresh parsley and thyme along with a bay leaf are common ingredients. Tie the herbs together with a piece of kitchen twine so they can be easily removed from the pot when the soup or stew is done.

beans looked better, but their texture was uneven; by the time half of the beans were tender, the other half had overcooked and disintegrated.

From these tests we also learned how to cook the beans. For this soup, tasters responded best to a creamy texture and wanted soft, not firm, beans. Boiling dried beans resulted in uneven cooking; a portion of the beans blew apart and others remained crunchy. But slowly simmering the beans for about two hours yielded soft, barely resilient beans—just what we wanted.

Now we took on rule number two of bean cookery: Never salt the beans during cooking. Recipes that warned against salting stated that it would cause the outer shell of the bean to toughen. We tested beans cooked in salted water and in unsalted water, and the salted beans were indeed slightly more toothsome on the outside. However, these beans were not any less cooked on the inside than the unsalted beans. In addition, the small amount of resistance that the salted beans had developed on the outside seemed to keep them from bursting. The beans were now softly structured on the outside and tender on the inside.

One other advantage of using salted water is flavor. The seasoned beans were simply much tastier than those cooked in unsalted water. We reasoned that by adding other ingredients to the cooking liquid, we could improve the flavor of the beans, that much more. (See "Flavoring Beans" on page 95.) In the end, we chose to infuse the beans with a bit of herbal flavor while they cooked. We added a few thyme sprigs, parsley stems, and two bay leaves all bound together with kitchen twine so they could be easily removed. This bundle is also known as a bouquet garni. (See "Making a Bouquet Garni" on page 14.)

To thicken the soup, we tried various options, including pureeing a portion of the beans in a blender and thoroughly smashing half of the beans in a separate bowl and returning them to the soup. In the end, tasters were most pleased with the rustic look and texture of the simplest method—mashing some of the beans right in the soup pot with a potato masher. The creamy liquid nicely suspended a mixture of whole and broken beans.

For hearty flavor, smoked ham hocks are traditional in this soup. We found that one hock cooked with the beans imparted a deep meatiness without overpowering the bean flavor. Looking for a possible alternative, as ham hocks are not always available, we were surprised to find that diced ham steak delivered a flavor that was almost as good. While this soup wasn't quite as rich tasting, owing to the lack of both fat and the flavorful marrow-filled bone of the hock, tasters were surprised by how good it was. We decided that 6 ounces, or about a cup of diced meat, was just right.

The soup was quite good now, but we wanted a bit more complexity. After testing various possibilities, we decided that sautéed mirepoix (diced onion, carrot, and celery), garlic, and a mixture of herbs would do the trick. The added flavors nicely complemented and enriched the smoky beans without detracting from the soup's rustic charm.

Raw vegetables added to the beans at the beginning of cooking did little for flavor and muddied the color of the ivory-hued beans when they were mashed. Vegetables cooked in the Dutch oven prior to adding the beans lost their texture and also colored the beans. Raw vegetables added toward the end of cooking remained too crunchy. We found that cooking the vegetables separately from the beans was essential to building the soup's deep flavor and maintaining the vegetables' texture. Adding the sautéed vegetables to the beans for just the last half hour of simmering gave the flavors enough time to meld without overcooking the vegetables.

To finish the soup, we decided a little parsley stirred in off the heat would complement the deep flavors. Tasters liked a squeeze of lemon juice, too.

U.S. Senate Navy Bean Soup
SERVES 4 TO 6

The finished texture of the soup should be creamy but not too thick. Eight to 10 strokes with a potato masher should be adequate. If you cannot find a smoked ham hock, a ham steak is almost as good and readily available. We found that 6 ounces of ham steak adds flavor without overwhelming the beans. If using ham steak, cut it into quarter-inch dice and add the meat to the pot when starting the beans.

2	bay leaves
4	sprigs fresh thyme
4	fresh parsley stems plus 1 ½ tablespoons minced parsley leaves
1	pound dried navy beans, washed and picked clean of any debris or dark-colored beans
1	smoked ham hock (about 12 ounces)
	Salt
1	tablespoon unsalted butter
1	medium onion, chopped fine
1	medium carrot, chopped fine
1	medium stalk celery, chopped fine
4	medium cloves garlic, peeled and finely minced
	Ground black pepper
1	teaspoon lemon juice from 1 medium lemon, plus 1 lemon cut into wedges

1. With a 12-inch length of kitchen twine, tie together the bay leaves, thyme sprigs, and parsley stems (see the illustration on page 14).

2. Combine the beans, ham hock, herb bundle, 1½ teaspoons salt, and 4 quarts of cold water in a large Dutch oven. Bring to a boil over medium-high heat, reduce the heat to medium, and simmer until the beans are soft, about 2 hours.

3. While the beans are simmering, heat the butter in a large skillet over medium heat. Add the onion, carrot, and celery and cook, stirring occasionally, until soft and lightly browned, about 10 minutes. Add the garlic and cook until fragrant, about 30

seconds longer. Transfer the sautéed vegetables to a small bowl.

4. Remove the herb bundle and the ham hock from the pot with the beans. Lightly smash some of the beans in the pot with a potato masher until creamy and lightly thickened. Using tongs and a chef's knife, remove and discard the skin, fat, and bones from the hock and mince the meat. Add the meat and the sautéed vegetables to the beans and simmer, uncovered, until the flavors are melded and the soup has thickened, about 30 minutes. (The soup can be refrigerated in an airtight container for several days. Warm over medium-low heat, adding a little water if soup seems too thick.)

5. Just before serving, season the soup with salt and pepper to taste and stir in the parsley and the lemon juice. Ladle the soup into bowls and garnish each with a lemon wedge.

BEEF STEW

BEEF STEW SHOULD BE RICH AND SATISFYING. Our goal in developing a recipe for it was to keep the cooking process simple without compromising the stew's deep, complex flavor. We focused on these issues: What cuts of beef respond best to stewing? How much and what kind of liquid should you use? When and with what do you thicken the stew?

Experts tout different cuts as being ideal for stewing. We browned 12 different cuts of beef, marked them for identification, and stewed them in the same pot. Chuck proved to be the most flavorful, tender, and juicy. Most other cuts were too stringy, too chewy, too dry, or just plain bland. The exception was rib-eye steak, which made good stew meat but is too expensive a cut for this purpose.

Why does chuck make the best stew? Its intramuscular fat and connective tissue make it amenable to long, slow, moist cooking. When cooked in liquid, the connective tissue melts down into gelatin, making the meat tender. The fat in the meat helps as well, in two important ways. Fat carries the chemical compounds that our taste buds perceive as beef, lamb, pork, or veal flavor, and it also melts when cooked, lubricating the meat fibers as it slips between the cells, increasing tenderness.

Our advice is to buy a steak or roast from the chuck and cube it yourself. Precut stewing beef often includes irregularly shaped end pieces from different muscles that cannot be sold as steaks or roasts because of their uneven appearance. Because of the differences in origin, cubes in the same package may not be consistent in the way they cook or taste. Cutting your own cubes from a piece of chuck assures you that all the cubes will cook in the same way and have the flavor and richness of chuck.

The names given to different cuts of chuck vary, but the most commonly used names for retail chuck cuts include boneless chuck-eye roasts, cross-rib roasts, blade steaks and roasts, shoulder steaks and roasts, and arm steaks and roasts. We particularly like chuck-eye roast, but all chuck cuts are delicious when cubed and stewed.

Browning the meat well is another key point to keep in mind. Meat stews generally begin by seasoning the chunks of meat with salt and pepper and then sautéing them in a film of oil. Don't rush this step. In our tests, meat that was only spottily browned didn't taste as good. Browning the meat and some of the vegetables, especially onions, adds flavor to the final dish.

How does browning work? In vegetables it is largely sugars and in meat it is sugars and proteins that caramelize, or brown, making the meat and vegetables taste better. In addition to flavoring the meat, proper browning covers the bottom of the pan with browned bits called fond. When liquid is added to the pot, the fond loosens and dissolves, adding flavor to the stew. This process is called deglazing. Wine and stock are the most common choices for deglazing the pan, but water works, too. Because the foundation of a stew's flavor comes from the fond and deglazing liquid, it is crucial that the meat be browned properly. In most recipes, to ensure proper browning, we sauté the meat in two batches. If all of the meat is put into the pot at once, the pieces crowd one another and steam, thus turning a pallid gray color rather than brown.

Contrary to popular belief, browning does not "seal in" the juices in meat. After browning, when the meat is slow-cooked, more and more juices are expelled as the internal temperature of the meat rises. By the time the meat is fork-tender, it has in fact shed most of its juices. As odd as it sounds, this is the beauty of a stew, since the surrounding liquid, which is served as a sauce, is enriched by these juices.

Having settled on our cut of beef, we started to explore how and when to thicken the stew. Dredging meat cubes in flour is a roundabout way of thickening stew. The floured beef is browned, then stewed. During the stewing process, some of the flour from the beef dissolves into the liquid, causing it to thicken. Although the stew we cooked this way thickened up nicely, the beef cubes had the look of smothered steak.

We also tried two thickening methods at the end of cooking—a beurre manié (softened butter mixed with flour) and cornstarch mixed with water. Both methods are acceptable, but the beurre manié lightened the color of the stew, making it look more like pale gravy than rich stew juices. Also, the extra fat did not improve the stew's flavor enough to justify its addition. For those who prefer thickening at the end of cooking, we found that cornstarch dissolved in water did the job without compromising the stew's dark, rich color.

Pureeing the cooked vegetables is another thickening method. Once the stew is fully cooked, the meat is pulled from the pot and the juices and vegetables are pureed to create a thick sauce. Tasters felt this thickening method made the vegetable flavor too prominent.

Ultimately, we opted for thickening the stew with flour early on, stirring it into the sautéing onions and garlic, right before adding the liquid. Stew thickened this way doesn't taste any better than that thickened at the end with cornstarch, but it is easier. There's no last-minute work; once the liquid starts to simmer, the cook is free to do something else.

We next focused on stewing liquids. We tried water, wine, canned beef broth, canned chicken broth, combinations of these liquids, and beef stock. Stews made with water were bland and greasy. Stews made entirely with wine were too strong. The stew made from beef stock was delicious, but we decided that beef stew, which has many hearty ingredients contributing to its flavor profile, did not absolutely need beef stock, which is quite time-consuming to make. When we turned to canned broths, the chicken outscored the beef broth. (We generally find that canned beef broths have a harsh, chemical flavor.) The stew made entirely with chicken stock was good, but we missed the acidity and flavor provided by the wine. In the end, we preferred a combination of chicken stock and red wine. We tested various kinds and found that fairly inexpensive fruity, full-bodied young wines such as Chianti or Zinfandel to be best. (See page 19 for more information on wine.)

We tested various amounts of liquid and found that we preferred stews with a minimum of liquid, which helps to preserve a strong meat flavor. With

CUTTING STEW MEAT

To get stew meat pieces that are cut from the right part of the animal and regularly shaped, we suggest buying a boneless roast and cutting the meat into cubes yourself. A 3-pound roast, once trimmed, should yield 2¾ pounds of beef, the maximum amount that can be comfortably browned in a Dutch oven in two batches.

1. Pull apart the roast at its major seams (delineated by lines of fat and silver skin). Use a knife as necessary.

2. With a paring knife, trim off excess fat and silver skin.

3. Cut the meat into cubes as directed in specific recipes.

too little liquid, however, the stew may not cook evenly, and there may not be enough "sauce" to spoon over starchy accompaniments. A cup of liquid per pound of meat gave us sufficient sauce to moisten a mound of mashed potatoes or polenta without drowning them.

In our tests, we found the temperature of the stewing liquid to be crucial. We found it essential to keep the temperature of the liquid below 212 degrees. Boiled meat remains tough, and the outside becomes especially dry. Keeping the liquid at a simmer (rather than a boil) allows the internal temperature of the meat to rise slowly. By the time it is fork-tender, much of the connective tissue will have turned to gelatin. The gelatin, in turn, helps to thicken the stewing liquid.

To determine whether stews cook best on the stovetop or in the oven, we tried both, simmering beef stew on the stovetop over low heat (with and without a flame-taming device to protect the pot from direct heat) and in a moderate oven. The flame-tamer device worked too well in distancing the pot from the heat; the stew juices tasted raw and boozy. Putting the pot right on the burner worked better, but we found ourselves constantly adjusting the burner to maintain a gentle simmer, and this method was prone to error. We had the most consistent results in the oven. We found that putting a covered Dutch oven in a 300-degree oven ensures that the temperature of the stewing liquid will remain below the boiling point, at about 200 degrees. (The oven must be kept at a temperature higher than 200 degrees because ovens are not completely efficient in transferring heat; a temperature of 300 degrees allows for the fact that some heat is lost as it penetrates the pot and then the stew.)

To determine when to add the vegetables, we made three different stews, adding carrots, potatoes, and onions to one stew at the beginning of cooking and to another stew halfway through cooking. For our final stew, we cooked the onions with the meat but added steamed carrots and potatoes when the stew was fully cooked.

The stew with vegetables added at the beginning was thin and watery. The vegetables had fallen apart and given up their flavor and liquid to the stew. The beef stew with the cooked vegetables added at the last minute was delicious, and the vegetables were the freshest and most intensely flavored. However, it was more work to steam the vegetables separately. Also, the flavors of vegetables cooked separately from the stew didn't meld well with the flavors from the other ingredients. We preferred to add the vegetables partway through the cooking process. They didn't fall apart this way, and they had enough time to meld with the other ingredients. There is one exception to this rule. Peas should be added just before serving the stew to preserve their color and texture.

One final note: The meat passes from the tough to tender stage fairly quickly. At the 1¾-hour mark, we often found that the meat was still chewy. Fifteen minutes later it would be tender. In another 15 minutes the meat started to dry out. Taste the meat often as the stew nears completion to judge when it's just right.

Hearty Beef Stew
SERVES 6 TO 8

Make this stew in an ovenproof Dutch oven, preferably with a capacity of 8 quarts but not smaller than 6 quarts. Choose one with a wide bottom; this will allow you to brown the meat in just two batches. See page 19 for information about choosing a red wine for use in this dish.

3	pounds beef chuck roast, trimmed and cut into 1½-inch cubes (see the illustrations on page 17)
	Salt and ground black pepper
3	tablespoons vegetable oil
2	medium onions, chopped coarse (about 2 cups)
3	medium cloves garlic, minced
3	tablespoons flour
1	cup full-bodied red wine
2	cups homemade chicken stock or canned low-sodium broth
2	bay leaves
1	teaspoon dried thyme
4	medium red potatoes (about 1½ pounds), peeled and cut into 1-inch cubes
4	large carrots (about 1 pound), peeled and sliced ¼ inch thick
1	cup frozen peas (about 6 ounces), thawed
¼	cup minced fresh parsley leaves

1. Adjust an oven rack to the lower-middle position and heat the oven to 300 degrees. Dry the beef thoroughly on paper towels, then season generously with salt and pepper. Heat 1 tablespoon oil in a large Dutch oven over medium-high heat until shimmering, about 2 minutes. Add half of the meat to the pot so that the individual pieces are close together but not touching. Cook, not moving the pieces until the sides touching the pot are well-browned, 2 to 3 minutes. Using tongs, turn each piece and continue cooking until most sides are well-browned, about 5 minutes longer. Transfer the beef to a medium bowl, add another 1 tablespoon oil to the pot, and swirl to coat the pan bottom. Brown the remaining beef; transfer the meat to the bowl and set aside.

2. Reduce the heat to medium, add the remaining tablespoon oil to the empty Dutch oven, and swirl to coat the pan bottom. Add the onions and ¼ teaspoon salt. Cook, stirring frequently and vigorously, scraping the bottom of the pot with a wooden spoon to loosen browned bits, until the onions have softened, 4 to 5 minutes. Add the garlic and continue

---

INGREDIENTS: Red Wine for Stew

When making a dish that uses red wine, our tendency is to grab whichever inexpensive, dry red is on hand, usually the leftover contents of a recently opened bottle. But we began to wonder what difference particular wines would make in the final dish and decided to investigate.

We called on several wine experts, who gave us some parameters to work with when choosing a red wine for a basic braise such as our Hearty Beef Stew. They suggested a wine that is dry (to avoid a sweet sauce) and that has good acidity (to aid in breaking down the fibers of the meat). They also pointed out that any characteristic found in an uncooked wine would be concentrated when cooked.

From tests we ran, we found that softer, fruity wines such as Merlot yielded a "grape jelly" flavor, which most tasters thought was too sweet for beef stew. We also learned that it's best to avoid wines that have been "oaked," usually older wines; the oak flavor tends to become harsh and bitter as the wine is cooked.

We had the best results with wines made from several types of red wine grapes. Blended wines like Côtes du Rhone produced stews with complex, even flavors. We also had good results with blends from California and Australia.

---

to cook for 30 seconds. Stir in the flour and cook until lightly colored, 1 to 2 minutes. Add the wine, scraping up the remaining browned bits from the bottom and edges of the pot and stirring until the liquid is thick. Gradually add the stock, stirring constantly and scraping the pan edges to dissolve the flour. Add the bay leaves and thyme and bring to a simmer. Add the meat and return to a simmer. Cover and place the pot in the oven. Cook for 1 hour.

3. Remove the pot from the oven and add the potatoes and carrots. Cover and return the pot to the oven. Cook just until the meat is tender, about 1 hour. Remove the pot from the oven. (Stew can be covered and refrigerated for up to 3 days. Bring to a simmer over medium-low heat.)

4. Add the peas, cover, and allow to stand for 5 minutes. Stir in the parsley, discard the bay leaves, adjust the seasonings, and serve immediately.

CHILI CON CARNE

A STRICTLY TEXAN CHILI, KNOWN AS CHILI con carne, depends on either pureed or powdered ancho chiles, uses beef, excludes tomato, onion, and beans, and features a high proportion of meat to chiles. We wanted a chili that would be hearty, heavy on the meat, and spicy but not overwhelmingly hot. We wanted the sauce to have a creamy consistency somewhere between soup and stew. The flavors would be balanced so that no single spice or seasoning stood out or competed with the chile pepper or beef.

Because chiles are the heart of chili con carne, we wanted to learn about the different types. After considerable testing and tasting, we settled on a combination of ancho and New Mexico Red for the dried chiles (see page 20 for more about dried chiles), with a few jalapeños added for their fresh flavor and bite. Chilis made with toasted and ground whole dried chiles tasted noticeably fuller and warmer than those made with chili powder. The two main toasting methods are oven and skillet, and after trying both, we went to the oven simply because it required less attention and effort than skillet toasting. The chiles puff in the oven, become fragrant, and dry out sufficiently after five to six minutes. One caveat, though:

Overtoasted chiles can take on a distinctly bitter flavor, so don't let them go too long.

With the chiles chosen and toasted, the next big question was how best to prepare them. The two options were to rehydrate the toasted chiles in liquid and process them into a puree or to grind them into a powder. It didn't take long for us to select grinding as the preferred method. It was easier, faster, and much less messy than making the puree, which tasters felt produced a chili that was too rich, more like a Mexican enchilada sauce than a bowl of chili.

This felt like the right time to determine the best ratio of chile to meat. Many of the recipes we looked at suggested that a tablespoon of ground chile per pound of meat was sufficient, but we found these chilis to be bland and watery. Two tablespoons per pound of meat, on the other hand, produced chili with too much punch. We compromised: 1½ tablespoons per pound was the way to go.

There was little agreement in the recipes we had collected as to when the chili powder should be added. After running several tests, we found that sautéing the spices, including the chiles, was key to unlocking their flavor. We also discovered that blending the chili powder with water to make a paste kept it from scorching in the pot; this step is strongly advised.

Because we prefer chuck for stews for both its flavor and its texture when slow-cooked, we knew it would work best in chili. Still, there were some aspects of the meat question that had to be settled. Should the chuck be standard hamburger grind, coarser chili grind, hand-cut into tiny cubes, or a combination? The chili made from cubes of beef was far more appealing than those made from either type of ground beef (they both had a grainy, extruded texture). Most of the recipes we looked at specified that the meat should be cut into ¼-inch cubes. However, we found that larger 1-inch chunks gave the chili a satisfying chew. In addition, cutting a chuck roast into larger chunks was much, much faster and easier than breaking it down into a fussy, ¼-inch dice.

Next we set out to determine the best type, or types, of liquid for the chili. The main contenders were water, chicken stock, beef stock, beer, black coffee, and red wine. We tried each one on its own, as well as in any combination we felt made sense. The surprise result was that we liked plain water best, because it allowed the flavor of the chiles to come through in full force. Both stocks, whether on their own or combined in equal parts with each

INGREDIENTS: Dried Chiles

For the most part, chili con carne is based on fairly mild dried chiles. The most common of these are dark, mahogany red, wrinkly skinned ancho chiles, which have a deep, sweet, raisiny flavor; New Mexico Reds, which have a smooth, shiny, brick-red skin and a crisp, slightly acidic, earthy flavor; California chiles, which are very similar to New Mexicos in appearance but have a slightly milder flavor; and long, shiny, smooth, dark brown pasilla chiles. Pasillas, which are a little hotter than the other three varieties, have grapey, herbal flavor notes, and, depending on the region, are often sold as either ancho or mulato chiles.

We sampled each of these chile peppers, as well as a selection of preblended commercial powders, alone and in various combinations in batches of chili. Though the chilis made with individual chiles tasted much more pure and fresh than any of the premixed powders, they nonetheless seemed one-dimensional on their own. When all was said and done, the two-chile combination we favored was equal parts ancho (for its earthy, fruity sweetness and the stunning deep red color it gave the chili) and New Mexico (for its lighter flavor and crisp acidity).

Chile heat was another factor to consider. Hotter dried chiles that appear regularly in chili include guajillo, de árbol, pequín, japónes, and cayenne. Though we did not want to develop a fiery, overly hot chili, we did want a subtle bite to give the dish some oomph. We found that minced jalapeños, added with the garlic to the chili pot, supplied some heat and a fresh vegetable flavor.

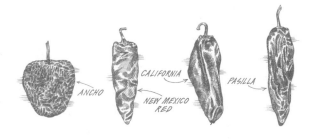

other or with water, muddied the chile flavors. All of the other liquids, used either alone or mixed with an equal part of chicken stock or water, competed with the chile flavor.

Another basic factor to determine was the garlic. Tasters agreed that three cloves were too few and eight were too many, so we settled on five. We found many recipes that called for powdered garlic rather than fresh. Out of obligation, we tested powdered versus fresh garlic and found fresh to be far superior.

Though common in modern recipes, tomatoes and onions are not included in the older, more authentic recipes for Texas chili. Nonetheless, we found both to be essential. The acidity of the tomato

and the sweetness of the onion, both used in small amounts, add interest and dimension to the chili. The batches we tested without them were decidedly dull. We tested various amounts and types of tomato products and determined that more than a cup pushed the flavor of the chili toward that of spaghetti sauce. Products with a smooth consistency, such as canned crushed tomatoes or plain tomato sauce, helped create the smooth sauce we wanted.

We found that bacon lends the chili a subtly sweet, smoky essence. Other "secret" ingredients fell by the wayside. Coca-Cola imparted a sourish, off taste. Brown sugar cut the heat of the chiles. An ounce of unsweetened chocolate did

---

SCIENCE: How Come You Don't Think It's Hot?

One enduring mystery among those partial to spicy food is why people have such varying tolerances for the heat of chile peppers. As it turns out, there are several reasons why your dinner companion may find a bowl of chili only mildly spicy while the same dish causes you to frantically summon a waiter for a glass of milk to cool the heat. (Milk, not water, is the thing to drink when you want to cool the fire in your mouth.)

Your dining partner may be experiencing "temporary desensitization." The phenomenon, discovered by Barry Green of the Monell Chemical Senses Institute in Philadelphia, occurs when you eat something spicy hot, then lay off for a few minutes. As long as you keep eating chiles, their effect keeps building. But if you take a break—even for as few as two to five minutes, depending on your individual susceptibility—you will be desensitized when you go back to eating the chiles. A dish with the same amount of chiles will not seem as hot the second time around.

The more likely explanation, however, is that people who find chiles intensely, punishingly hot simply have more taste buds. According to Linda Bartoshuk, a psychophysicist at the Yale School of Medicine, human beings can be neatly divided into three distinct categories when it comes to tasting ability: unfortunate "nontasters," pedestrian "medium tasters," and the aristocrats of the taste bud world, "supertasters."

This taste-detection pecking order appears to correspond directly to the number of taste buds a person possesses, a genetically predetermined trait that may vary by a factor of 100. Indeed, so radical are the differences between these three types that Bartoshuk speaks of them as inhabiting different "taste worlds."

Bartoshuk and her colleagues discovered the extent of this phenomenon a few years ago when they carried out experiments using a dye that turns the entire mouth blue except for the taste papillae (structures housing taste buds and other sensory receptors). After painting part of subjects' tongues with the dye, they were rather stunned at the differences they saw. One poor taster had just 11 taste buds per square centimeter, while one supertaster had 1,100 in the same area.

Further experiments confirmed that the ability to taste intensely directly corresponds to the number of taste buds. Researchers found that women are twice as likely as men to be supertasters, while men are nearly twice as likely as women to be nontasters.

What does this have to do with how hot you find chiles? It turns out that every taste bud in the mouth has a pain receptor literally wrapped around it. Along with the extra taste buds comes a greater sensitivity to pain. As a result, supertasters have the capacity to experience 50 percent more pain from capsaicin, the chemical that gives chiles their heat.

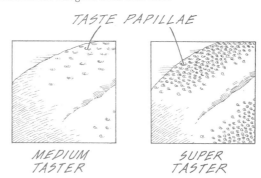

TASTE PAPILLAE

MEDIUM TASTER

SUPER TASTER

give the chili a rounder, deeper flavor, and 2 tablespoons of peanut butter made the sauce more creamy and earthy tasting. Still, much as we liked both chocolate and peanut butter, we decided they were not essential.

Chili is generally thickened to tighten the sauce and make it smoother. Flour, roux (a paste of flour and melted butter), cornstarch, and masa harina (a flour ground from corn treated with lime, or calcium oxide) are the most common options. Dredging the meat in flour before browning and adding a roux along with the liquid were both effective, but these approaches made it more difficult to finesse the consistency of the finished product because both were introduced early in the cooking process. Roux added at the end of cooking left a faint taste of raw flour. We did prefer thickening at the end of cooking, though, because we could add thickener gradually until the chili reached the right consistency. We like chili thick enough to coat the back of a wooden spoon, like the custard base of homemade ice cream.

Our first choice for thickening was masa harina, added at the end of cooking. It both thickened the sauce and imparted a slightly sweet, earthy corn flavor to the chili. If masa harina is not available in your grocery store and you'd rather not mail-order it, use a cornstarch and water slurry. It brings no flavor to the chili, but it behaves predictably and is easy to use, and it gives the gravy a silky consistency and attractive sheen.

One last note: Time and time again, tasters observed that chili, like many stews, always improved after an overnight rest because the flavors blended and mellowed. If possible, cook your chili a day ahead. The result will be worth the wait.

Chili Con Carne

SERVES 6

To ensure the best chile flavor, we recommend toasting whole dried chiles and grinding them in a minichopper (or spice-dedicated coffee grinder), all of which takes only 10 (very well-spent) minutes. Select dried chiles that are moist and pliant, like dried fruit.

To toast and grind dried chiles, place chiles on a rimmed baking sheet in a 350-degree oven until fragrant and puffed, about 6 minutes. Cool, stem, and seed, tearing pods into pieces.

Place pieces of the pods in a spice grinder and process until powdery, 30 to 45 seconds.

For hotter chili, boost the heat with a pinch of cayenne or a dash of hot pepper sauce near the end of cooking. Serve the chili with warm pinto or kidney beans, corn bread or chips, corn tortillas or tamales, rice, biscuits, or plain crackers. Top with chopped fresh cilantro, minced white onion, diced avocado, shredded cheddar or Monterey Jack cheese, or sour cream.

3	tablespoons ancho chili powder, or 3 medium pods (about $1/2$ ounce), toasted and ground (see note above)
3	tablespoons New Mexico Red chili powder, or 3 medium pods (about $3/4$ ounce), toasted and ground (see note above)
2	tablespoons cumin seeds, toasted in a dry skillet over medium heat until fragrant, about 4 minutes, and ground
2	teaspoons dried oregano, preferably Mexican
4	pounds beef chuck roast, trimmed of excess fat and cut into 1-inch cubes (see the illustrations on page 17)
	Salt
7–8	slices bacon (8 ounces), cut into $1/4$-inch dice
1	medium onion, minced
5	medium cloves garlic, minced
4–5	small jalapeño chile peppers, stemmed, seeded, and minced
1	cup canned crushed tomatoes or plain tomato sauce
2	tablespoons lime juice
5	tablespoons masa harina or 3 tablespoons cornstarch
	Ground black pepper

1. Mix the chili powders, cumin, and oregano in a small bowl and stir in $1/2$ cup water to form a thick paste; set aside. Toss the beef cubes with 2 teaspoons salt; set aside.

2. Fry the bacon in a large Dutch oven over medium-low heat until the fat renders and the bacon crisps, about 10 minutes. Remove the bacon with a slotted spoon to a paper towel–lined plate; pour all but 2 teaspoons fat from the pot into a small bowl; set aside. Increase the heat to medium-high; sauté the meat in four batches until well-browned on all sides, about 5 minutes per batch, adding up to

2 more teaspoons bacon fat to the pot as necessary. Set the browned meat aside.

3. Reduce the heat to medium and add 3 tablespoons bacon fat to the now-empty pot. Add the onion and sauté until softened, 5 to 6 minutes. Add the garlic and jalapeños and sauté until fragrant, about 1 minute. Add the chili powder mixture and sauté until fragrant, 2 to 3 minutes. Add the reserved bacon and browned beef, crushed tomatoes, lime juice, and 7 cups water. Bring to a simmer. Continue to cook at a steady simmer until the meat is tender and the juices are dark, rich, and starting to thicken, about 2 hours.

4. Mix the masa harina with ⅔ cup water (or cornstarch with 3 tablespoons water) in a small bowl to form a smooth paste. Increase the heat to medium, stir in the paste, and simmer until thickened, 5 to 10 minutes. Adjust the seasoning generously with salt and ground black pepper to taste. (For the best flavor, refrigerate in an airtight container overnight or for up to 5 days. Bring back to a simmer over medium-low heat.) Serve immediately.

➤ VARIATION

Smoky Chipotle Chili Con Carne

Grill-smoking the meat along with chipotle chiles gives this chili a distinct, but not overwhelming, smoky flavor. Be sure to start with a chuck roast that is at least 3 inches thick. The grilling is not meant to cook the meat but rather to flavor it by searing the surface and smoking it lightly.

1. To SMOKE THE MEAT: Puree 4 medium cloves garlic with 2 teaspoons salt. Rub the intact chuck roast with puree, and sprinkle evenly with 2 to 3 tablespoons New Mexico Red chili powder; cover and set aside. Meanwhile, build a hot fire in the grill. When you can hold your hand 5 inches above the grill surface for no more than 3 seconds, spread the hot coals over an area about the size of the roast. Open the bottom grill vents, scatter 1 cup soaked mesquite or hickory wood chips over the hot coals, and set the grill rack in place. Place the meat over the hot coals and grill-roast, opening the lid vents three-quarters of the way and covering so that the vents are opposite the bottom vents to draw smoke through and around the roast. Sear the meat until all sides are dark and richly colored,

about 12 minutes per side. Remove the roast to a bowl; when cool to the touch, trim and cut into 1-inch cubes, reserving juices.

2. To MAKE THE CHILI: Follow the recipe for Chili Con Carne, omitting the browning of the beef cubes and substituting 5 minced canned chipotle peppers in adobo sauce for the jalapeños. Add the grilled meat and juice with cooked bacon.

NEW ENGLAND CLAM CHOWDER

WE LOVE HOMEMADE CLAM CHOWDER. AFTER all, our test kitchen is located just outside of Boston, in the heart of chowder country. But we must confess that many cooks (including some who work in our test kitchen) don't make their own chowder. While they might never buy chicken soup, they seem willing to make this compromise with chowder. We wondered why.

Time certainly isn't the reason. You can prepare clam chowder much more quickly than you can a pot of good chicken soup. The real reason why many cooks don't bother making their own clam chowder is the clams. First, clams can be expensive. Second, clams are not terribly forgiving—you must cook them soon after their purchase (chickens can be frozen), and then the soup itself must be quickly consumed (again, chicken soup can be frozen or at least refrigerated for another day). Last, chowders are more fragile (and thus more fickle) than other soups. Unless the chowder is stabilized in some way, it curdles, especially if brought to a boil.

Our goals for this soup, then, were multiple but quite clear. We wanted to develop a delicious, traditional chowder that was economical, would not curdle, and could be prepared quickly. Before testing chowder recipes, we explored our clam options (see page 26 for more information). Chowders are typically made with hard-shell clams, so we purchased (from smallest to largest) cockles, littlenecks, cherrystones, and chowder clams, often called quahogs (pronounced *ko-hogs*).

Although they made delicious chowders, we eliminated littlenecks and cockles, both of which were just too expensive to toss into a chowder pot.

Chowders made with the cheapest clams, however, weren't satisfactory, either. The quahogs we purchased for testing were large (4 to 5 inches in diameter), tough, and strong-flavored. Their over-sized bellies (and the contents therein) gave the chowder an overbearing mineral taste, detracting from its smooth, rich flavor.

Though only a little more expensive than qua-hogs, cherrystones offered good value and flavor. The chowder made from these slightly smaller clams was distinctly clam-flavored, without an inky aftertaste. Because there are no industry sizing standards for each clam variety, you may find some small quahogs labeled as cherrystones or large cherrystones labeled as quahogs. Regardless of designation, clams that reach much more than 4 inches in diameter will deliver a distinctly metallic, inky-flavored chowder.

Some recipes suggest shucking raw clams and then adding the raw clam bellies to the soup pot. Other recipes steam the clams open. We tested both methods and found that steaming clams open is far easier than shucking them. After seven to nine minutes over simmering water, the clams open as naturally as budding flowers. Ours did not toughen up as long as we pulled them from the pot as soon as they opened and didn't let them cook too long in the finished chowder.

Although many chowder recipes instruct the cook to soak the clams in salt water spiked with cornmeal or baking powder to remove grit, we found the extra step of purging or filtering hard-shell clams to be unnecessary (see page 26 for more details). All of the hard-shells we tested were rela-tively clean, and what little sediment there was sank to the bottom of the steaming liquid. Getting rid of the grit was as simple as leaving the last few table-spoons of broth in the pan when pouring it from the pot. If you find that your clam broth is gritty, strain it through a coffee filter.

At this point, we turned our attention to texture. We wanted a chowder that was thick but would still qualify as a soup rather than a stew. Older recipes call for thickening clam chowder with crumbled biscuits; bread crumbs and crackers are modern stand-ins.

Bread crumb–thickened chowders failed to impress. We wanted a smooth, creamy soup base for the potatoes, onions, and clams, but no matter how long the chowder was simmered, bread crumbs or crackers never completely dissolved into the cooking liquid. Heavy cream alone, by contrast, did not give the chowder enough body. We discovered fairly quickly that flour was necessary, not only as a thickener but also as a stabilizer, because unthick-ened chowders separate and curdle. Flour can be added at the beginning of cooking to fat that's already in the pan to sauté onion or at the end of cooking as part of a paste made with softened but-ter. Because our final recipe was to be finished with milk or cream rather than butter, we felt the chow-der didn't need the extra butter required to add the flour in a paste to the finished soup. We opted to thicken at the beginning.

STEAMING CLAMS FOR CHOWDER

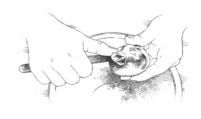

1. Steam clams until they just open (left), not until they open completely (right).

2. Carefully use a paring knife to open the clams, holding each over a bowl to catch any juices that are released.

3. Once open, discard the top shell and use the knife to sever the muscle that connects the clam belly to the bottom shell.

Because most chowders call for potatoes, some recipes suggest that starchy baking potatoes, which tend to break down when boiled, can double as a thickener. In our tests, these potatoes did not break down sufficiently and instead simply became soft and mushy. We found that waxy red boiling potatoes are best for creamy-style chowders. They have a firm but tender texture, and their red skins look appealing.

We now had two final questions to answer about New England clam chowder. First, should it include salt pork or bacon, and, if the latter, did the bacon need to be blanched? Second, should the chowder be enriched with milk or cream?

Salt pork and bacon both come from the pig's belly. Salt pork is cured in salt, while bacon is smoked, and salt pork is generally fattier than bacon. Salt pork is the more traditional choice in chowder recipes, although bacon has become popular in recent decades, no doubt because of its availability. Jasper White writes in *Fifty Chowders* (Scribners, 2000), his definitive book on the subject, that chowders made years ago with salt pork often had a smoky flavor because they were cooked over an open hearth. For modern cooks, bacon achieves both the pork and smoke flavors.

We made clam chowders with both salt pork and bacon, and tasters liked both versions. Frankly, we ended up using such small amounts of pork in our final recipe that either salt pork or bacon works just fine. Bacon is more readily available and, once bought, easier to use up. Blanching the bacon makes it taste more like salt pork, but we rather liked the subtle smokiness of the chowder made with unblanched bacon.

As for the cream versus milk issue, we found that so much milk was required in order to make the chowder look and taste creamy that it began to lose its clam flavor and became more like mild bisque or the clam equivalent of oyster stew. Making the chowder with clam broth (5 cups of the cooking liquid from the steaming clams) then finishing the soup with a cup of heavy cream gave us what we were looking for—a rich, creamy chowder that tasted distinctly of clams.

New England Clam Chowder
SERVES 6

If desired, replace the bacon with 4 ounces of finely chopped salt pork. See page 94 for information about buying salt pork.

7	pounds medium-sized hard-shell clams, such as cherrystones, washed and scrubbed clean (see illustration at left)
4	slices thick-cut bacon (about 4 ounces), cut into ¼-inch pieces
I	large Spanish onion, chopped medium
2	tablespoons flour
I ½	pounds red potatoes (about 4 medium), scrubbed and cut into ½-inch dice
I	large bay leaf
I	teaspoon fresh thyme leaves or ¼ teaspoon dried thyme
I	cup heavy cream
2	tablespoons minced fresh parsley leaves
	Salt and ground black or white pepper

1. Bring 3 cups water to a boil in large stockpot or Dutch oven. Add the clams and cover with a tight-fitting lid. Cook for 5 minutes, uncover, and stir with a wooden spoon. Quickly cover the pot and steam until the clams just open, 2 to 4 minutes (see illustration 1 on page 24). Transfer the clams to a

SCRUBBING CLAMS

Many recipes instruct the cook to scrub clams. Don't skip this step; many clams have bits of sand embedded in their shells that can ruin a pot of soup. We like to scrub clams under cold, running water using a soft brush, sometimes sold as a vegetable brush.

large bowl; cool slightly. Open the clams with a paring knife, holding the clams over a bowl to catch any juices (see illustration 2 on page 24). With the knife, sever the muscle that attaches the clam belly to the shell (see illustration 3 on page 24), and transfer the meat to a cutting board. Discard the shells. Mince the clams; set aside. Pour clam broth into a medium bowl, holding back the last few tablespoons of broth in case of sediment; set the clam broth aside. (You should have about 5 cups. If not, add bottled clam juice or water to make this amount.) Rinse and dry the pot, then return it to the burner.

2. Fry the bacon in the empty pot over medium-low heat until the fat renders and the bacon crisps, 5 to 7 minutes. Add the onion and cook, stirring occasionally, until softened, about 5 minutes. Add the flour and stir until lightly colored, about 1 minute. Gradually whisk in the reserved clam broth. Add the potatoes, bay leaf, and thyme and simmer until potatoes are tender, about 10 to 15 minutes. Add the clams, cream, parsley, and salt (if necessary) and ground pepper to taste; bring to simmer. Remove from the heat, discard the bay leaf, and serve immediately.

➤ VARIATION

Quick Pantry New England Clam Chowder

From late summer through winter, when clams are plentiful, you'll probably want to make fresh clam chowder. But if you're short on time or find clams scarce and expensive, the right canned clams and bottled clam juice will deliver a chowder that's at least three notches above canned chowder in quality. We tested seven brands of minced and small whole canned clams and preferred Doxsee Minced Clams teamed with Doxsee brand clam juice as well as Snow's Minced Clams and Snow's clam juice. These clams were neither too tough nor too soft, and they had a decent natural clam flavor.

Follow the recipe for New England Clam Chowder, substituting 4 cans (6½ ounces each) minced clams for the fresh clams, with juice drained and added to medium bowl along with 1 cup water and 2 bottles (8 ounces each) clam juice. Reserve clam meat in separate bowl. Omit step 1. Add reserved clam meat and juice at same points in step 2 when fresh clam broth and meat would be added.

INGREDIENTS: Clams

Clams are easy enough to cook. When they open, they are done. However, perfectly cooked clams can be made inedible by lingering sand. Straining the juices through cheesecloth after cooking will remove the grit, but it's a pain. Plus, you lose some of the juices to the cheesecloth. Worse still, careful straining will not remove bits of sand still clinging to the clam meat. Rinsing the cooked clams washes away flavor.

That's why so many clam recipes start by soaking clams in cold salt water for several hours. We tried various soaking regimens, such as soaking in water with flour, soaking in water with baking powder, soaking in water with cornmeal, and scrubbing and rinsing in five changes of water. If the clams were dirty at the outset, none of these techniques really worked. Even after soaking, many clams needed to be rinsed and the cooking liquid strained.

However, during the course of this testing, we noticed that some varieties of clams were extremely clean and free of grit at the outset. A quick scrub of the shell exterior and these clams were ready for the cooking pot, without any soaking. The cooked clams were free of grit, and the liquid was clean.

Clams can be divided into two categories—hard-shell varieties (such as quahogs, cherrystones, and littlenecks) and soft-shell varieties (such as steamers and razor clams). Hard-shells live along sandy beaches and bays; soft-shells in muddy tidal flats. This modest shift in location makes all the difference in the kitchen.

When harvested, hard-shells remain tightly closed. In our tests, we found the meat inside to be sand-free. The exterior should be scrubbed under cold running water to remove any caked-on mud, but otherwise these clams can be cooked without further worry about gritty broths.

Soft-shell clams gape when they are alive. We found that they almost always contain a lot of sand. While it's worthwhile to soak them in several batches of cold water to remove some of the sand, you can never get rid of it all. In the end, you must strain the cooking liquid and rinse the cooked clams. Starting with hard-shell clams is a lot easier.

2

SALADS

MAKING SALAD IS ONE OF THE MOST CREATIVE culinary pursuits. Baking requires the cook to follow directions precisely. Roasting a chicken or cooking pasta demands much attention to detail. But salad making allows for a fair amount of improvisation. Watercress can be substituted for arugula, which in turn can be substituted for baby dandelion greens. Many vinegars are interchangeable, and if you want to add cucumber instead of bell pepper, you usually can.

So salad making is creative, but there are some broad guidelines you can observe to get the best possible results. First, choose the right greens (think about both texture and flavor) and make sure they are fresh. (For more information about various salad greens, see page 30.) Second, don't go overboard with too much dressing or too many ingredients.

The recipes that follow represent the best of American salads. The chapter starts with a couple of classic dressings, followed by several leafy salads, and then by more substantial salads made with potatoes, macaroni, tuna, and eggs.

Ranch Dressing

RANCH DRESSING WAS MADE FAMOUS IN the 1950s at the Hidden Valley Guest Ranch in Santa Barbara, California. The recipe was so popular that it was bought and marketed by a large corporation, which proceeded to introduce the herbed buttermilk dressing to the rest of the country in both a powdered and bottled form. Although the stuff made from a powdered mix or picked up in a bottle at the supermarket is still what many of us think of as ranch dressing, it doesn't compare with freshly made.

Most recipes call for buttermilk, thickened with either mayonnaise or sour cream, along with an array of herbs and seasonings. We tried to follow a strictly buttermilk/mayonnaise or buttermilk/sour cream path but found that neither sufficed. While mayonnaise gave the dressing a nice, round sweetness, sour cream was a good thickener and also added tartness to the buttermilk—too much tartness when used alone with the buttermilk. By using all three ingredients, however, we gave the dressing a nice balance of flavors and a pleasing consistency.

To season this buttermilk base, we tried a number of ingredients called for in other recipes, including Worcestershire sauce, Dijon mustard, lime juice, red wine vinegar, celery seeds, and a host of dried herbs. In the end, we found that fresh herbs and seasonings were the keys to a bright, authentic flavor. Fresh parsley and cilantro accented by scallion, shallot, and garlic were the southern California flavors we were looking for. We found it best to mash the garlic into a paste, allowing the garlic flavor to blend quickly and smoothly with the other ingredients. We added minced red pepper for crunch and color and lemon juice to brighten all the flavors.

We found that this dressing worked best over sturdy greens such as romaine, iceberg, green leaf, and spinach. Softer lettuces, such as Boston or Bibb, wilted quickly under the weight of this creamy mixture. Several tasters liked the way the tartness of the buttermilk accented the bitterness of greens such as arugula and radicchio.

INGREDIENTS: Mayonnaise

While homemade mayonnaise is a delicious addition to salads, many cooks prefer the convenience and safety of commercial brands made without raw eggs. In salads such as coleslaw and dressings such as ranch or Thousand Island, good commercial mayonnaise is a fine addition.

Two brands dominate the mayo market: Hellmann's (also known as Best Foods in some parts of the country) and Kraft. Each company makes several products—full fat, reduced fat, and low or no fat. We tasted six kinds of mayonnaise (three from each company); tasters were unanimous in their first choice.

Hellmann's Real Mayonnaise was the creamiest of the bunch, with an excellent balance of flavors. Many tasters felt it was as good, if not better, than most homemade mayonnaise. Hellmann's Light (a reduced-calorie product with about half the fat of Hellmann's Real) took second place. Most tasters thought this product was almost as creamy as the winner.

Kraft Real Mayonnaise finished in third place, right behind Hellmann's Light. It was a bit less creamy and not as flavorful as the top finishers.

The remaining reduced-fat and no-fat products fared poorly in our tasting. Most were too acidic and lacked the sheen of a good mayonnaise. If you want to cut calories and fat, Hellmann's Light is a fine option, but don't try to trim any more fat grams—what you lose in calories just isn't worth what you lose in flavor.

Ranch Dressing
MAKES ABOUT ³/₄ CUP

One recipe of this relatively thick dressing will coat 3 quarts (6 servings) of salad greens. Sturdy greens such as romaine and iceberg are ideal partners with this dressing. See illustrations below for tips on mincing a shallot.

½	small clove garlic, peeled
¼	teaspoon salt
¼	small red bell pepper, minced (about 1 tablespoon)
1	medium scallion, white and green parts, minced
1	small shallot, minced (about ½ tablespoon)
1½	teaspoons minced fresh parsley leaves
½	teaspoons minced fresh cilantro leaves
½	teaspoon lemon juice
	Pinch ground black pepper
¼	cup buttermilk
¼	cup mayonnaise
2	tablespoons sour cream

1. Roughly chop the garlic, then sprinkle it with the salt. With a chef's knife, turn the garlic and salt into a smooth paste (see the illustration on page 31).

2. Mix the garlic paste, bell pepper, scallion, shallot, parsley, cilantro, lemon juice, and black pepper together in a medium bowl. Add the buttermilk, mayonnaise, and sour cream and whisk until smooth. (The dressing can be refrigerated in an airtight container for up to 4 days.)

THOUSAND ISLAND DRESSING

RECIPES SIMILAR TO THOUSAND ISLAND dressing can be found dating back to the 1900s. While the details of its history are sketchy, the recipe seems to have taken its name from the Thousand Islands region in upstate New York and Canada that borders Lake Ontario and the St. Lawrence River. Some sources suggest that Thousand Island is an adaptation of Russian dressing, the difference being in the peppers, olives, and pickles added to Thousand Island (which some say represent the region's thousand islands). This lumpy, salmon-colored dressing is often used as a condiment on sandwiches and burgers as well as a dressing for salads (it can be especially good poured over a wedge of iceberg lettuce and some tomatoes).

Most recipes for Thousand Island dressing call for a mixture of mayonnaise and ketchup garnished with bits of chopped olives, sweet pickles, and hard-boiled egg. We found these dressings too sweet and one-dimensional.

Some recipes called for chili sauce rather than ketchup, and our tasters preferred it for its spicy twang. We also found that mayonnaise rather than ketchup or chili sauce should take the lead. More than 2 tablespoons of chili sauce per ½ cup mayonnaise made the dressing too red and tomatoey. Adding a few aromatics (such as garlic, parsley, and lemon juice) also brightened this otherwise heavy dressing. By mashing the garlic into a paste,

MINCING SHALLOTS

1. Place the peeled shallot flat-side down on a work surface and slice crosswise almost to (but not through) the root end.

2. Make a number of parallel cuts through the top of the shallot down to the work surface.

3. Make very thin slices perpendicular to the lengthwise cuts made in step 2.

INGREDIENTS: Salad Greens

The following glossary starts with the four main varieties of lettuce and then introduces the most commonly available specialty greens. When substituting one green for another, try to choose greens with a similar intensity. For example, peppery arugula could be used as a substitute for watercress or dandelion greens, but not for mild-tasting red leaf lettuce, at least not without significantly altering the flavor of the salad.

All greens should be thoroughly washed and dried (dressing won't cling to damp greens). Large greens should be torn by hand rather than with a knife—we find the latter is more likely to cause bruising and discoloration.

BUTTERHEAD LETTUCES Boston and Bibb are the most common varieties of these very mild-tasting lettuces. A head of butterhead lettuce has a round shape and loose outer leaves. The color of the leaves is light to medium green (except, of course, in red-tinged varieties), and the leaves are extremely tender.

LOOSELEAF LETTUCES Red leaf, green leaf, red oak leaf, and lolla rossa are the most common varieties. These lettuces grow in a loose rosette shape, not a tight head. The ruffled leaves are perhaps the most versatile because their texture is soft yet still crunchy and their flavor is mild but not bland.

ROMAINE LETTUCE The leaves on this lettuce are long and broad at the top. The color shades from dark green in outer leaves (which are often tough and should be discarded) to pale green in the thick, crisp heart. Also called Cos lettuce because it is thought to have originated on the Aegean island of Kos, this variety has more crunch than either butterhead or looseleaf lettuces and a more pronounced earthy flavor. Romaine lettuce is essential in Caesar salad, where the greens must stand up to a thick, creamy dressing.

ICEBERG LETTUCE Iceberg is the best-known variety of crisphead lettuce. Its shape is perfectly round, and the leaves are tightly packed. A high water content makes iceberg especially crisp and crunchy but also robs it of flavor.

ARUGULA Also called rocket, this tender, dark green leaf can be faintly peppery or downright spicy. Larger, older leaves tend to be hotter than small, young leaves, but the flavor is variable, so taste arugula before adding it to a salad. Arugula bruises and discolors quite easily, so try to keep stemmed leaves whole. Very large leaves can be torn just before they are needed.

WATERCRESS With its small leaves and long stalks, watercress is easy to spot. It requires some patience in the kitchen because the stalks are tough and must be removed one at a time. Like arugula, watercress usually has a mildly spicy flavor.

DANDELION GREENS Dandelion greens are tender and pleasantly bitter. The leaves are long and have ragged edges. The flavor is similar to that of arugula or watercress, both of which can be used interchangeably with dandelion. Note that tougher, older leaves that are more than several inches long should be cooked and not used raw in salads.

MIZUNA This Japanese spider mustard has long, thin, dark green leaves with deeply cut jagged edges. Sturdier than arugula, watercress, or dandelion, it can nonetheless be used interchangeably with these slightly milder greens in salads when a strong peppery punch is desired. Note that larger, older leaves are better cooked, so choose small "baby" mizuna for salads.

TATSOI This Asian green has thin white stalks and round, dark green leaves. A member of the crucifer family of vegetables that includes broccoli and cabbage, tatsoi tastes like a mild Chinese cabbage, especially bok choy. However, the texture of these miniature leaves is always delicate.

RADICCHIO This most familiar chicory was almost unknown in this country two decades ago. The tight heads of purple leaves streaked with prominent white ribs are now a supermarket staple. Radicchio has a decent punch but is not nearly as bitter as other chicories, especially Belgian endive.

BELGIAN ENDIVE With its characteristic bitter chicory flavor, endive is generally used sparingly in salads. Unlike its cousin radicchio, endive is crisp and crunchy, not tender and leafy. The yellow leaf tips are usually mild-flavored, while the white, thick leaf bases are more bitter. Endive is the one salad green we routinely cut rather than tear. Remove whole leaves from the head and then slice crosswise into bite-sized pieces.

CHICORY The jagged, curly leaves of chicory, or curly endive, form a loose head that resembles a sunburst. The leaves are bright green, and their flavor is usually fairly bitter. The outer leaves can be somewhat tough, especially at the base. Inner leaves are generally more tender.

ESCAROLE Escarole has smooth, broad leaves bunched together in a loose head. With its long ribs and softly ruffled leaves, it looks a bit like leaf lettuce. As a member of the chicory family, escarole can have an intense flavor, although not nearly as strong as that of endive or chicory.

SPINACH Flat-leaf spinach is better than curly-leaf spinach in salads because the stems are usually less fibrous and the spade-shaped leaves are thinner, more tender, and sweeter. Curly-leaf spinach is often dry and chewy, while flat-leaf spinach, sold in bundles rather than in cellophane bags, is usually tender and moist, more like lettuce than a cooking green.

we were able to release all of its volatile oils, allowing the flavors to blend quickly with the other ingredients.

We discovered that this dressing tasted better when the garnishes (olives, pickles, and egg) were mixed together and seasoned with the garlic, salt, ground black pepper, and lemon juice before being bound with mayonnaise and chili sauce. This ensured that the garnishes, rather than just the mayonnaise, were able to absorb the seasonings, resulting in a more deeply flavored and lively dressing.

Last, we found that most Thousand Island dressings (including our working recipe at this point) are way too thick to pour easily over salad greens. A little water thins the dressing out to the correct consistency.

We tried this dressing on several types of lettuce and liked it best on mild greens such as iceberg and romaine. Spicier greens such as radicchio and chicory clashed with the sweet elements that are part of this dressing's charm.

In the end, we had a fresh-tasting, well-seasoned Thousand Island dressing able to dress everything from the most basic salad greens to a pastrami sandwich and a cheeseburger.

Thousand Island Dressing

MAKES ABOUT I CUP

Because this dressing is thick, one cup of it will coat only about 3 quarts (or about 6 servings) of salad greens. It works best with mild greens such as iceberg and romaine lettuce.

I	small clove garlic, peeled
¼	teaspoon salt
I	tablespoon green olives with pimentos, minced (3 to 4 olives)
¼	cup minced sweet pickle
½	hard-boiled egg (page 44), minced
I	tablespoon minced fresh parsley leaves
I	teaspoon lemon juice
	Pinch ground black pepper
½	cup mayonnaise
2	tablespoons chili sauce

1. Mince the garlic, then sprinkle it with the salt. Use the flat side of a chef's knife to turn the

garlic and salt into a smooth paste (see the illustration below).

2. Mix the garlic paste, olives, pickle, egg, parsley, lemon juice, and ground black pepper together in a medium bowl. Add the mayonnaise, chili sauce, and 1 tablespoon water and stir until uniform. (The dressing can be refrigerated in an airtight container for up to 3 days.)

CHOPPED SALAD

THIS CLASSIC LADIES' LUNCH DISH WAS designed to be easy to eat using only a fork while balancing the plate atop your knees and had its heyday during the 1950s. All the components of the salad are chopped into bite-sized pieces and lightly dressed with oil and vinegar.

There's still much to love about this recipe. When correctly made, this salad combines lettuces and vegetables in a pleasing fashion and offers a range of textures, colors, and flavors. While many recipes for chopped salad call for numerous and lavish vegetable garnishes, we found simpler, more modern salads made with only a few fresh vegetables—cucumber, bell pepper, and radish, as well as tomato—and mild greens tasted best. Although these salads may be simple, we found that a couple

MINCING GARLIC TO A PASTE

Mince the garlic as you normally would on a cutting board with a chef's knife. Sprinkle the minced garlic with salt and then drag the side of the chef's knife over the garlic-salt mixture to form a fine puree. Continue to mince and drag the knife as necessary until the puree is smooth.

of key points distinguish mediocre versions from truly stellar ones.

First, we found that the vegetables should be cut into pieces of similar size. Small pieces (cherry tomatoes cut in half, cucumber and bell pepper cut into ¼-inch dice) are just right. Although this entails slightly more work and attention than rough chopping, the results are worth the extra effort. As for the greens, we found that romaine, Boston, green leaf, and red leaf lettuces were easy to cut into forkable bites and paired well with the vegetables. Tasters did not like spicy greens in this salad. Better to let the tomatoes, cucumbers, and other additions contribute contrasting flavors; our tasters liked mild greens in the background. Finally, it's imperative to use a light hand with the dressing. Too many recipes douse the lettuces and vegetables in dressing, and the resulting salad is limp and heavy.

As for the dressing, we found a light lemon vinaigrette with some fresh herbs set off the fresh vegetables and lettuces best. Heavier dressings made with sour cream or mayonnaise physically swamped the small pieces of vegetable, while more potent vinaigrettes, made with balsamic or red wine vinegar, were overpowering. We also discovered that a little sugar in the vinaigrette helped boost the flavors of the vegetables, making the overall salad much more lively.

When serving the chopped salad, we preferred to use the lettuce as a base for the chopped vegetables. Wanting all the components to be properly dressed, we used half of the vinaigrette to dress the greens and the other half to dress the collective garnishes. This two-step dressing process ensures that everything is properly coated and also allows the salad to be plated in the most attractive fashion.

Chopped Salad
SERVES 4 TO 6

This basic recipe can be altered depending on the vegetables you have on hand. See the variations for some ideas. See illustrations on page 29 for tips on mincing the shallot.

LEMON-HERB VINAIGRETTE

¼	cup olive oil
1	tablespoon lemon juice
2	teaspoons Dijon mustard
½	small shallot, minced (about 1 teaspoon)
1	teaspoon minced fresh parsley leaves
1	teaspoon minced fresh chives
1	teaspoon minced fresh thyme leaves
¼	teaspoon salt
⅛	teaspoon ground black pepper
⅛	teaspoon sugar

PREPARING FENNEL

1. Trim the feathery fronds and stems.

2. Trim a thin slice from the base and remove any blemished outer layers. Cut the bulb in half through the base and use a small knife to remove the pyramid-shaped core in each half.

3. Lay the cored fennel on a work surface and cut in half crosswise. Cut the fennel into ¼-inch-thick strips and then cut the strips crosswise into ¼-inch dice.

SALAD

8   cups mild salad greens (such as romaine, Boston, Bibb, green leaf, or red leaf), cut into 1-inch pieces

½   pint cherry tomatoes, halved

1   small cucumber, peeled, seeded, and cut into ¼-inch dice

1   small yellow bell pepper, stemmed, seeded, and cut into ¼-inch dice

5   medium radishes, stems trimmed, cut in half lengthwise, then sliced thin to create half-moons

1. FOR THE DRESSING: Whisk all the ingredients together in a small bowl and set aside.

2. FOR THE SALAD: Toss the salad greens with half the dressing in a medium bowl. Mix the tomatoes, cucumber, bell pepper, and radishes together in another medium bowl and toss with the remaining dressing.

3. Arrange the salad greens on a serving platter or on individual plates. Spoon the chopped vegetables over the greens and serve immediately.

➤ VARIATIONS

Chopped Salad with Fennel, Green Apple, and Radishes

See illustrations on page 32 for tips on preparing fennel.

Follow the recipe for Chopped Salad, omitting mustard and thyme from the dressing. For the salad, replace tomatoes, cucumber, and bell pepper with 2 medium Granny Smith apples, peeled, cored, and cut into ¼-inch dice, and 1 small head fennel, tops trimmed, cored, and cut into ¼-inch dice.

Chopped Salad with Avocado, Jícama, and Cucumber

Follow the recipe for Chopped Salad, replacing the lemon juice in the dressing with lime juice, omitting the mustard, and replacing the parsley, chives, and thyme with 1 tablespoon minced fresh cilantro. For the salad, replace the tomatoes, bell pepper, and radishes with ½ medium jícama, peeled and cut into ¼-inch dice, and 1 medium avocado, peeled, pitted, and cut into ¼-inch dice.

COBB SALAD

THIS SALAD ORIGINATED IN HOLLYWOOD in 1926 at the Brown Derby, a local restaurant where the stars of the day were known to dine. As the story goes, Bob Cobb, owner of the Brown Derby, made this salad late one night from a bunch of leftovers in the refrigerator and some freshly crisped bacon swiped from a busy chef. The classic version of this main-course salad features chicken, avocado, tomatoes, blue cheese, bacon, and plenty of salad greens.

Since its invention many years ago, Cobb salad has been reproduced and replicated all over the country, with many versions straying far from the original recipe. After tracking down and testing the original version, we found little to change except a few measurements.

The original recipe calls for several types of salad greens. We decided to group the greens into mild and spicy categories, leaving the exact mixture (and shopping list) up to you. In case you don't have leftover chicken in your refrigerator, we found it easiest to broil boneless skinless chicken breasts. While other cuts of chicken tasted fine, the boneless breasts were easy to cut into attractive slices without having to maneuver around any bones. The fact that they were boneless also allowed them cook more quickly under the broiler. By brining the chicken (soaking it in a salty, slightly sweet solution) for about 30 minutes, we were able to ensure that the chicken would remain moist, tender, and flavorful even when chilled.

As for the dressing, the original Cobb salad called for oil, Worcestershire sauce, red wine vinegar, lemon juice, and Dijon mustard. While this combination of ingredients may sound odd, tasters really liked its unique flavor. Not needing to change this authentic dressing too much, we simply altered the ratio of oil to vinegar to 4 to 1, which gave it a more balanced flavor. We found it best to dress the individual components in this composed salad separately, before arranging them on a single platter or individual plates. This method ensured that every element in the salad was seasoned properly and allowed us to assemble the salad in a most attractive fashion. The wedges of hard-boiled egg are the exception to this rule. They are likely to break apart when tossed with vinaigrette. We found it best to arrange the egg wedges (as well as the slices of chicken) over the salad greens and then drizzle some dressing right over them.

Cobb Salad

SERVES 6

If you have 4 cups of leftover chicken on hand, you can omit steps 1 through 3. If mincing garlic to a paste by hand, use the ¼ teaspoon salt in the dressing to help break down the clove (see the illustration on page 31).

BROILED CHICKEN

2   **tablespoons salt**

½   **cup sugar**

3   **boneless, skinless chicken breast halves (about I pound), trimmed, with tenderloins removed and reserved for another purpose**
     Nonstick vegetable spray

DRESSING

½   **teaspoon Dijon mustard**

I   **teaspoon lemon juice**

½   **teaspoon Worcestershire sauce**

I   **small clove garlic, pressed through a garlic press or minced to a paste**

2   **tablespoons red wine vinegar**

½   **cup olive oil**

¼   **teaspoon sugar**

¼   **teaspoon salt**
     Pinch ground black pepper

SALAD

8   **cups mild salad greens (romaine, Boston, Bibb, and/or iceberg)**

4   **cups spicy salad greens (curly endive, watercress, and/or arugula)**

2   **hard-boiled eggs (see page 44), each sliced into eight ⅓-inch-thick wedges**

2   **avocados, peeled, pitted, and cut into ⅓-inch-wide slices (see the illustrations below)**

2   **medium tomatoes, cored and cut into ¼-inch wedges**

6   **slices bacon, fried until crisp and crumbled**

I   **tablespoon minced fresh chives**

2   **ounces Roquefort cheese, crumbled (about ¼ cup)**

1. FOR THE CHICKEN: Dissolve the salt and sugar in 1 quart of cool water in a gallon-sized zipper-lock bag or plastic container. Submerge the chicken in the salt solution and refrigerate for 30 minutes.

2. Adjust an oven rack so it is 6 inches away from the broiler element. Remove the chicken from the brine and dry thoroughly with paper towels. Coat the broiler pan top with vegetable spray and lay the

SLICING AVOCADOS

1. With their dark pebbly skin, Haas avocados are generally creamier and better in salads than larger, smooth-skinned varieties. To remove the flesh in neat slices for salads, start by slicing around the pit and cutting through both ends.

2. Twist to separate the halves and then stick the blade of a large knife sharply into the pit. Lift the blade, twisting if necessary to loosen and remove the pit. (Use a large spoon to pry the pit off the blade and discard the pit.)

3. Use a small paring knife to slice through the avocado, cutting down to but not through the skin.

4. Run a rubber spatula around the circumference, just inside the skin, to loosen the slices, then twist the spatula to pop out the slices.

chicken breasts on top. Place the broiler pan top over the broiler pan bottom and place under the broiler. Broil the chicken until lightly browned, 3½ to 4 minutes. Flip chicken over and broil until cooked fully, 3½ to 4 minutes longer.

3. Place the chicken on a clean plate and cover with plastic wrap. Poke a few vent holes in the plastic wrap and refrigerate the chicken while preparing the other salad ingredients.

4. FOR THE DRESSING: Whisk all ingredients together in a small bowl and set aside.

5. TO ASSEMBLE SALAD: Slice the chicken on the bias into ¼-inch-thick pieces. Toss the mild and spicy salad greens with ⅓ cup dressing in a large bowl. Arrange the dressed salad greens on a large serving platter or on individual plates. Arrange the chicken slices and wedges of hard-boiled egg over the greens and drizzle with 2 tablespoons dressing. Toss the avocados and tomatoes with the remaining tablespoon of dressing in a medium bowl. Arrange the pieces of avocado and tomato over the salad. Sprinkle the bacon, chives, and cheese over the salad and serve immediately.

WALDORF SALAD

WALDORF SALAD WAS CREATED BY OSCAR Tschirky, maître d'hôtel at the Waldorf-Astoria Hotel in New York. Although the original salad (which dates back to 1896) contained only tart apples and crisp celery bound with a little mayonnaise, walnuts and raisins were added into the mix in subsequent years. In recent decades, recipe writers have tried to "update" Waldorf by adding everything from oranges and marshmallows to Cajun spices and whipped cream. After making several of these concoctions, tasters unanimously preferred this crisp, clean salad in its original form, with only walnuts and raisins added to the apples and celery.

Because this simple salad calls for only a few ingredients, it is important that each is fresh and thoughtfully prepared. To start, we found both the apples and celery tasted better when they were peeled. The outer layer of the celery was both stringy and bitter, while the skin on the apples tasted tough and tannic. Granny Smiths are traditional in

this salad, and we liked the crispness and tartness they brought to this dish. Tasters also preferred salads with an equal proportion of celery and apples. Instead of mincing the celery into tiny bits, as if it were a garnish, we sliced it into substantially sized, attractive, half-moon shapes, which made the salad taste more balanced.

Toasting the walnuts is also essential. With so few ingredients, the walnuts add much more punch when toasted in a dry skillet until fragrant. Tossing the apples, celery, walnuts, and celery with mayonnaise yielded a slightly one-dimensional, flat-tasting salad. We found that seasoning the salad ingredients with salt, pepper, and lemon juice before adding the mayonnaise made everything taste brighter. The only liberty we took in updating this recipe was to add a little tarragon, which added a pleasant herbal, anise flavor to this simple salad.

Waldorf Salad

SERVES 4

This salad can be served over a bed of greens as a light main course for lunch or in place of coleslaw as a side dish to sandwiches and grilled foods.

¼	cup walnuts
2	medium Granny Smith apples, peeled, cored, and cut into ½-inch dice (about 2½ cups)
4	stalks celery, peeled and cut crosswise into ¼-inch pieces (about 2½ cups)
⅓	cup raisins
I	tablespoon lemon juice
I	teaspoon minced fresh tarragon
¼	teaspoon salt
	Pinch ground black pepper
⅓	cup mayonnaise

1. Toast the walnuts in a dry skillet over medium heat, stirring frequently, until fragrant, 4 to 5 minutes. Cool the walnuts and then roughly chop them into ⅓-inch pieces.

2. Toss the chopped walnuts, apples, celery, and raisins together in a medium bowl. Season with lemon juice, tarragon, salt, and black pepper and toss again. Stir in mayonnaise and serve immediately.

THREE-BEAN SALAD

IF YOUR MOTHER MADE THREE-BEAN SALAD (and she probably did), it probably featured a sweet, vinegary dressing mixed with canned green, yellow, and kidney beans and a bite of red onion. This salad was good but never great. We wondered if this classic American recipe could be improved with modern ingredients and techniques.

When we began researching the origins of this picnic standby, we discovered that most of the recipes for it have remained essentially unchanged since the 1950s. Given the evolution of the ingredients and cooking techniques used over the last 50 years, we knew this salad could benefit from some updating.

Our goal was a fresh taste (something other than canned beans came to mind) and a light, sweet, and tangy dressing that united the subtle flavors of the beans without overpowering them. To that end, our testing divided itself into three categories: improving the flavor and the texture of the beans; determining the right mix of vinegar and oils for the marinade; and addressing the question of sweetness, which was handled differently in almost every recipe we looked at. (Although we did find a few recipes that did not include a sweetener, sugar in one form or another seemed to differentiate three-bean salad from a simple oil and vinegar vegetable salad.)

We decided to first test boiling, blanching, and steaming the green and yellow beans. Not surprisingly, the less time the beans are cooked, the better they stand up in the dressing. Our 10- and 20-minute boiled beans were soft and flavorless, but those blanched for one and two minutes each weren't cooked enough. We eventually settled on boiling the beans for five minutes. This was long enough to remove their waxy exterior and thereby allow the marinade to penetrate but not long enough to break down their cell structure and make them mushy. After draining the beans, we plunged them into cold water to stop the cooking. Steamed beans held up fairly well, but they didn't have the crunch of the boiled and shocked beans.

Next we moved on to the kidney beans. None of the recipes recommended cooking dried beans—they all called for canned. Just to be sure, we cooked up two batches of beans, then marinated them overnight. Not only were the canned beans a lot easier to use, but they tasted just as good.

With the beans ready for dressing, we moved on to the marinade. Many of the recipes we found were vague: They didn't tell you what type of vinegar to use, or what type of oil. After testing eight oil varieties and seven types of vinegar, we found that we preferred canola oil for its mild flavor and red wine vinegar for its tang.

We were ready to test types of sugar. We also

SEGMENTING AN ORANGE

1. Start by slicing a ¹/₂-inch-thick piece from the top and bottom of the orange.

2. With the fruit resting flat against a work surface, use a very sharp paring knife to slice off the rind, including all of the bitter white pith. Try to follow the contours of the fruit as closely as possible.

3. Working over a bowl to catch the juices, slip the blade between a membrane and one section of fruit and slice to the center, separating one side of the section.

4. Turn the blade of the knife so that it is facing out and is lined up along the membrane on the opposite side of the section. Slide the blade from the center out along the membrane to completely free the section. Continue until all the sections are removed.

wanted to test an idea we had run across in several recipes—cooking the sugar, vinegar, and oil together. We quickly realized that cooking the sugar, vinegar, and oil dramatically improved the flavor of the dressing. We tried cooking vinegar mixed with brown sugar, with honey, and with white sugar over medium heat. The white sugar version won hands down; the cooking process created a syrup with its own unique flavor—sweet and tangy at the same time. It turns out that both heat and the type of sugar used make all the difference between a so-so marinade and a tasty one.

➤ Three-Bean Salad

SERVES 8 TO 10

This recipe is the all-American classic—the variation gives the salad a Southwestern spin. Prepare this salad at least one day before you plan on serving it. The beans taste better after marinating in the dressing.

1	cup red wine vinegar
¾	cup sugar
½	cup canola oil
2	medium cloves garlic, minced
	Salt and ground black pepper
8	ounces green beans, cut into 1-inch-long pieces
8	ounces yellow wax beans, cut into 1-inch-long pieces
1	(15½-ounce) can red kidney beans, drained and rinsed
½	medium red onion, chopped medium
¼	cup minced fresh parsley leaves

1. Heat the vinegar, sugar, oil, garlic, 1 teaspoon salt, and pepper to taste in a small nonreactive saucepan over medium heat, stirring occasionally, until the sugar dissolves, about 5 minutes. Transfer to a large nonreactive bowl and cool to room temperature.

2. Bring 3 quarts water to a boil in a large saucepan over high heat. Add 1 tablespoon salt and the green and yellow beans and cook until the beans are crisp-tender, about 5 minutes. Meanwhile, fill a medium bowl with ice water. When the beans are done, drain and immediately plunge them into the ice water to stop the cooking process; let sit until chilled, about 2 minutes. Drain well.

3. Add the green and yellow beans, kidney beans, onion, and parsley to the vinegar mixture and toss well to coat. Cover and refrigerate overnight to let flavors meld. Let stand at room temperature 30 minutes before serving. (The salad can be covered and refrigerated for up to 4 days.)

➤ VARIATIONS

Three-Bean Salad with Cumin, Cilantro, and Oranges

See the illustrations on page 36 for tips on segmenting the oranges for this salad.

Separate 2 medium oranges into segments, remove membrane from sides of each segment, then cut each segment in half lengthwise. Set aside. Follow the recipe for Three-Bean Salad, substituting ¼ cup lime juice for ¼ cup red wine vinegar, and heating 1 teaspoon ground cumin with vinegar mixture. Substitute minced fresh cilantro leaves for parsley and add halved orange segments to vinegar mixture along with beans.

COLESLAW WITH BUTTERMILK DRESSING

THERE ARE TWO THINGS ABOUT COLESLAW with buttermilk dressing that can be bothersome: the pool of watery dressing that appears at the bottom of the bowl after a few hours and the harsh flavor of buttermilk. Not only did we want to find a way to keep the cabbage from watering down the dressing, but we also wanted to figure out how to make the salad piquant without tasting too sharp and one-dimensional.

To tackle the watery dressing, we tested a number of popular methods for treating cabbage. While most recipes instruct the cook to toss the shredded cabbage immediately with dressing, a few add an extra step. Either the shredded (or merely quartered) cabbage is soaked in ice water for crisping and refreshing, or it is salted, drained, and allowed to wilt.

We soaked cabbage in ice water and found it to be crisp, plump, and fresh. If looks were all that mattered, this cabbage would have scored high next to the limp, salted cabbage in the neighboring colander. But its good looks were deceiving. Even though we drained the cabbage and dried it thoroughly, the dressing didn't really adhere. Furthermore, within minutes, the cabbage shreds started to lose their recently acquired water, making for not a small but a large puddle of water to dilute the creamy dressing. The stiff cabbage shreds were strawlike, making them difficult to fork and even more difficult to get into the mouth without leaving a creamy trail.

Quite unlike the ice-water cabbage, the salted shreds lost most of their liquid while sitting in the salt, leaving the cabbage wilted but pickle-crisp. Since the cabbage had already lost most of its liquid, there was little or no liquid left for the salt to draw into the dressing. We had found the solution to the problem of watery dressing. In addition, we found that this cabbage, having less water in it, took on more of the dressing's flavors, and, unlike the stiff shreds of ice-water cabbage, this limp cabbage was easier to eat.

We did discover that the salting process leaves the cabbage a bit too salty, but a quick rinse washes away the excess salt. After the cabbage has been rinsed, just pat it dry with paper towels and refrigerate until ready to combine it with the dressing. If the coleslaw is to be eaten immediately, rinse it quickly in ice water rather than tap water, then pat it dry. Coleslaw is best served cold.

Having figured out how to keep the cabbage from watering down the dressing, we were ready to tackle the dressing itself. While many recipes simply call for buttermilk seasoned with a few spices and herbs, we found the flavor of the buttermilk itself needed to be tempered. By adding both a little mayonnaise and sour cream, we were able to round out its tart, dairy flavor without losing the buttermilk's distinctive bite. The mayonnaise and sour cream also added body to the dressing, helping it cling to the cabbage.

After trying a variety of flavorings and vegetables, we found fresh carrot, shallot, and parsley seasoned with mustard, vinegar, and a pinch of sugar turned the buttermilk-cabbage mixture into a fresh and authentic-tasting coleslaw that doesn't weep.

Coleslaw with Buttermilk Dressing
SERVES 4

See the illustrations below for tips on shredding cabbage. Serve this tangy slaw with grilled foods, sandwiches, or burgers. See the illustrations on page 29 for tips on mincing the shallot.

1	pound (about ½ medium head) red or green cabbage, shredded fine or chopped (about 6 cups)
	Salt
1	medium carrot, peeled and shredded
½	cup buttermilk
2	tablespoons mayonnaise
2	tablespoons sour cream
1	small shallot, minced (about 2 tablespoons)

SHREDDING CABBAGE

1. Cut a whole head of cabbage into quarters. Cut away the hard piece of the core attached to each quarter.

2. Separate the cored cabbage quarters into stacks of leaves that flatten when pressed lightly.

3. Use a chef's knife to cut each stack of cabbage diagonally into long, thin pieces. Alternatively, roll the stacked leaves crosswise to fit them into the feed tube of a food processor fitted with the shredding disk.

2   tablespoons minced fresh parsley leaves
½   teaspoon cider vinegar
¼   teaspoon Dijon mustard
½   teaspoon sugar
⅛   teaspoon ground black pepper

1. Toss the shredded cabbage and 1 teaspoon salt in a colander or large-mesh strainer set over a medium bowl. Let stand until the cabbage wilts, at least 1 hour or up to 4 hours. Rinse the cabbage under cold running water (or in a large bowl of ice water if serving immediately). Press, but do not squeeze, to drain; pat dry with paper towels. Place the wilted cabbage and the carrot in a large bowl.

2. Stir buttermilk, mayonnaise, sour cream, shallot, parsley, vinegar, mustard, sugar, ¼ teaspoon salt, and pepper in a small bowl. Pour the buttermilk dressing over the wilted cabbage and refrigerate until ready to serve. (Coleslaw can be covered and refrigerated for up to 3 days.)

➤ VARIATIONS

Buttermilk Coleslaw with Green Onion and Cilantro

Follow the recipe for Coleslaw with Buttermilk Dressing, substituting 1 tablespoon minced cilantro for the parsley, 1 teaspoon lime juice for the cider vinegar, omitting the mustard, and adding 2 scallions, sliced thin.

Buttermilk Coleslaw with Lemon and Herbs

Follow the recipe for Coleslaw with Buttermilk Dressing, substituting 1 teaspoon lemon juice for the cider vinegar and adding 1 teaspoon fresh thyme and 1 tablespoon minced chives to the dressing.

POTATO SALAD

WHAT'S A SUMMER PICNIC OR BACKYARD barbecue without potato salad? This dish should be easy to assemble, but all too often the potatoes are bland, and they fall apart under the weight of the dressing.

Potato salads come in numerous styles. Though recipes may seem dramatically different, most have four things in common: potatoes (of course); fat (usually bacon, olive oil, or mayonnaise); an acidic ingredient to perk things up; and flavorings for distinction. We decided to focus on a mayonnaise-based salad with hard-boiled eggs, pickles, and celery.

We first wanted to know what type of potato should be used and how it should be cooked. Recipe writers seemed split down the middle between starchy potatoes (like russets) and waxy potatoes (like Red Bliss), with starchy praised for being more absorbent and waxy admired for their sturdiness. We have always just boiled potatoes with the skin on, but steaming, microwaving, roasting, and baking are all options.

Next, should the potatoes be peeled? If so, when? Some recipes called for cooking potatoes with the skin on, then peeling and seasoning them immediately, working on the assumption that hot potatoes absorb more flavor than cold ones. We wondered if the extra step of seasoning the potatoes with vinegar, salt, and pepper first made any difference. Could we instead just toss all the ingredients together at the same time?

After boiling, steaming, baking/roasting, and microwaving four different varieties of potatoes—Red Bliss, russets, all-purpose, and Yukon Golds—we found Red Bliss to be the potato of choice and boiling to be the cooking method of choice. Higher-starch potatoes—all-purpose and Yukon Golds as well as russets—are not sturdy enough for salad making. They fall apart when cut and look sloppy in salad form.

Next we wanted to see if we could boost flavor at the cooking stage by boiling the potatoes in chicken broth or in water heavily seasoned with bay leaves and garlic cloves. The chicken broth might just as well have been water—there wasn't a hint of evidence that the potatoes had been cooked in broth. The bay leaves and garlic smelled wonderful as the potatoes cooked, but the potatoes were still bland.

The fact that nothing seemed to penetrate the potatoes got us wondering: Does the potato skin act as a barrier? We performed another experiment by cooking two batches of unpeeled potatoes, the first in heavily salted water and the second in unsalted water. We rinsed them quickly under cold running water and tasted. Sure enough, both batches of potatoes tasted exactly the same. We tried boiling potatoes without the skin, but they were water-logged compared with their skin-on counterparts.

We found the paper-thin skin of the boiled red potato not unpleasant to taste and certainly pleasant to look at in what is often a monochromatic salad. Although this saved the peeling step, we found the skin tended to rip when cutting the potato. Because the skin was particularly susceptible to ripping when the potatoes were very hot, we solved the problem in two ways. First, we cut the potatoes with a serrated knife, which minimized ripping, and second, we found it isn't necessary to cut them when they are hot; warm ones are just as absorbent.

To find out if there was any benefit to preseasoning the potatoes, we made two salads. In the first, we drizzled the vinegar on the warm potatoes as soon as they were sliced and seasoned them with salt and pepper. In the second, we let the potatoes cool and then added the vinegar, salt, pepper, and mayonnaise dressing. The results were clear. The salad made with potatoes seasoned when still warm was zesty and delicious. The other salad was bland in comparison.

So here's how you make great potato salad: Boil unpeeled, low-starch, red-skinned potatoes in unsalted water, cool slightly, and then cut with a serrated knife to minimize tearing of the skin. While the potatoes are still warm, drizzle them with vinegar and season with salt and pepper. When cool, add the mayonnaise and other seasonings.

Potato Salad with Hard-Boiled Eggs and Sweet Pickles

SERVES 4 TO 6

Use sweet pickles, not relish, for the best results.

2   pounds Red Bliss potatoes (about 6 medium or 18 new), scrubbed
¼   cup red wine vinegar
    Salt and ground black pepper
3   hard-boiled eggs (see page 44), peeled and cut into ½-inch dice
1   medium stalk celery, minced (about ½ cup)
2   tablespoons minced red onion
¼   cup sweet pickles, minced
½   cup mayonnaise
2   teaspoons Dijon mustard
2   tablespoons minced fresh parsley leaves

1. Cover the potatoes with 1 inch of water in a stockpot or Dutch oven. Bring to a simmer over medium-high heat. Reduce the heat to medium and simmer, stirring once or twice to ensure even cooking, until the potatoes are tender (a thin-bladed paring knife or metal cake tester can be slipped into and out of the center of the potatoes with no resistance), 25 to 30 minutes for medium potatoes or 15 to 20 minutes for new potatoes.

2. Drain; cool the potatoes slightly and peel if you like. Cut the potatoes into ¾-inch cubes (use a serrated knife if they have skins) while still warm, rinsing the knife occasionally in warm water to remove starch.

3. Place the warm potato cubes in a large bowl. Add the vinegar, ½ teaspoon salt, and ¼ teaspoon pepper and toss gently. Cover the bowl with plastic wrap and refrigerate until cooled, about 20 minutes.

4. When the potatoes are cooled, toss with the remaining ingredients and season with salt and pepper to taste. Serve immediately. (Potato Salad can be covered and refrigerated for up to 1 day.)

MACARONI SALAD

MACARONI SALAD IS AN AMERICAN DELI staple. For many people, it's hard to imagine a picnic or summer barbecue without this salad of tender elbow noodles and creamy dressing. Although relatively easy to make, it is also easy to make badly. Few dishes are less appetizing than a bowl of underseasoned, overcooked noodles accompanied by flavorless, limp celery, killer-sweet pickle relish, and an excess of mayonnaise. Good macaroni salad, however, is dreamy when made with perfectly cooked, well-seasoned noodles and crisp vegetables dressed lightly in mayonnaise.

To start, we focused on the pasta. We tried cooking it al dente, and although we prefer a slightly resistant texture in hot pasta, we found it overly toothsome and stiff when cold. Thoroughly cooked pasta, which offered no resistance when eaten hot, took on a pleasantly yielding and bouncy texture when cool and was also able to maintain its shape without becoming mushy. Pasta that was even slightly overcooked tasted mushy and slimy and tore into pieces when tossed with the other ingredients.

We also found that adding more salt than usual to the cooking water made for a more evenly seasoned salad. While the pasta will taste a little salty on its own, it will be perfectly seasoned when mixed with the other salad ingredients and served cold. We found that 2 tablespoons of salt to 4 quarts of water was just right to season one pound of pasta.

Another trick we picked up was how to turn the hot pasta into a cold salad quickly. When the hot pasta was allowed to cool on its own, it clumped together into a starchy mass and began to overcook as the residual heat from the pasta further softened the noodles. Going against all we had learned about how to cook pasta, we rinsed the pasta under cold water, which both stopped it from further cooking and washed away some of the extra starch. (When serving pasta hot with sauce, this starch is a good thing, because it helps the sauce cling to the pasta.) We then spread out the pasta on paper towels to help drain off this extra water (see the illustrations below). If we skipped this step, water was caught in the curves of the macaroni and turned the dressing watery.

DRYING MACARONI

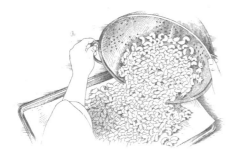

1. Shake the macaroni dry in the colander and spread in an even layer on a rimmed baking sheet lined with paper towels. Let the macaroni dry for 3 minutes.

2. Roll the macaroni in paper towels to blot any remaining moisture and transfer the macaroni to a large bowl.

We found the pasta was best mixed with the classic assortment of fresh vegetables and seasonings: celery, red onion, hard-boiled egg, and sweet pickles. Fresh parsley added a clean, herbal flavor, and a little mustard provided some kick. Wary of burying this fresh-tasting mixture with too much mayonnaise, we started off using only ½ cup per pound of pasta but found the pasta readily soaked up mayonnaise until we hit 1 cup. Although many recipes call for vinegar, we preferred the light, fresh acidity of lemon juice. The salad tastes best when allowed to cool for at least one hour in the refrigerator. The seasonings mellow substantially, so use a liberal hand with salt and pepper.

Macaroni Salad

SERVES 8 TO 10

Make sure to dry the cooked and rinsed pasta thoroughly. See the illustrations at left.

    Salt
1   pound elbow macaroni
1   stalk celery, minced
¼   small red onion, minced (2 to 3 tablespoons)
3   hard-boiled eggs (see page 44), peeled and diced small
¼   cup minced sweet pickles
¼   cup minced fresh parsley leaves
¼   cup lemon juice
1   cup mayonnaise
2   teaspoons Dijon mustard
    Ground black pepper

1. Bring 4 quarts water to a boil in large pot and add 2 tablespoons salt. Stir in the macaroni and cook until thoroughly done, 10 to 12 minutes Drain the macaroni into a colander and rinse with cold water until cool. Shake the macaroni dry in the colander and spread in an even layer on a rimmed baking sheet lined with paper towels. Let the macaroni dry for 3 minutes.

2. Roll the macaroni in paper towels to blot any remaining moisture and transfer the drained macaroni to a large bowl. Toss with the remaining ingredients and season liberally with salt and pepper to taste. Refrigerate the macaroni salad for at least 1 hour or up to 1 day.

➤ VARIATIONS

Macaroni Salad with Curried Apples

Follow the recipe for Macaroni Salad, replacing the hard-boiled eggs, sweet pickles, parsley, and mustard with 1 medium Granny Smith apple, cored and cut into ¼-inch dice (about 1½ cups) and ¼ cup minced fresh basil. Mix 1 tablespoon curry powder into mayonnaise and proceed as directed.

Macaroni Salad with Chipotles and Cilantro

Toast 1½ cups frozen corn kernels and 2 medium unpeeled garlic cloves in a nonstick skillet set over high heat until corn turns spotty brown, about 5 minutes; peel and mince the garlic. Follow the recipe for Macaroni Salad, replacing the hard-boiled eggs, sweet pickles, parsley, and mustard with corn, garlic, 3 scallions, minced (about ¼ cup), and 1 cup cherry tomatoes, quartered. Mix 1 tablespoon minced chipotle chiles in adobo sauce into mayonnaise and proceed as directed.

TUNA SALAD

GRADE-SCHOOL LUNCHES, HOSPITAL CAFETERIAS, and second-rate delis have given tuna salad a bad name with mixtures that are typically mushy, watery, and bland. But these poor examples should not cause cooks to lose hope for this old standard. We tackled tuna salad in the test kitchen and came up with three simple preparation and flavoring tricks that guarantee a tuna salad that is evenly moist, tender, flaky, and well-seasoned every time.

A first-rate tuna salad begins with the best canned tuna. All comers favored solid white tuna over chunk light for its meaty texture and delicate flavor. Among the five brands we tried, StarKist reigned supreme, so we made it the basis of all our subsequent testing. (See page 43 for more details.)

In a dish as simple as tuna salad, the finer points of preparation make a real difference. For instance, most cooks simply squeeze out a bit of the packing water by pressing the detached can lid down lightly on the fish. Tasters consistently deemed all of the salads made with tuna prepared in this manner "soggy" and "watery." Taking the minor extra step of draining the tuna thoroughly in a colander before mixing it with other ingredients gave the salads a toothsome, less watery texture.

Breaking the tuna apart with a fork was another standard procedure we dumped. In salads made with tuna prepared this way, we'd invariably bite into a large, dry, unseasoned chunk that the fork had missed. With the tuna in the colander, we decided to break down the larger chunks with our fingers until the whole amount was fine and even in texture. This gave the finished salad a smooth, even, flaky texture that all of our tasters appreciated.

Seasoning was the last problem we addressed. All too often, tuna salad tastes dull and lifeless because of careless seasoning or, even worse, no seasoning at all. Salt and pepper were critical to making the most of tuna's delicate flavor. An acidic seasoning, such as lemon or lime juice or vinegar, was equally important, adding some much needed brightness to the flavor.

We also found that the order in which we mixed the ingredients made a difference. We first tried mixing the basic seasoning and garnishes with the tuna alone before adding the mayonnaise. Next we tried adding the seasonings, garnishes, and mayonnaise all at once. Our tasters agreed that preseasoning the tuna resulted in a more deeply flavored, lively tuna salad.

After settling on these three basic techniques, we were unanimous in finding mayonnaise to be the binder of choice and found other salad ingredients to be largely a matter of taste. We nonetheless agreed that trace amounts of garlic and mustard added dimension to the overall flavor and that a modest amount of minced pickle provided a touch of piquancy, not to mention a link to tradition. (In fact, tuna takes well to a wide range of flavorings; see some of our variations for inspiration.)

So forget the sopping, mushy salad you ate in your last beleaguered institutional tuna sandwich. The next time the cold cuts run out, or even before, reach for the canned tuna that graces even the emptiest pantry, take a little extra care with the contents, and find out how satisfying a well-made tuna salad sandwich can be.

Classic Tuna Salad

MAKES ABOUT 2 CUPS,
ENOUGH FOR 4 SANDWICHES

See right for information on brands of tuna and the one we recommend.

2	(6-ounce) cans solid white tuna in water
2	tablespoons juice from 1 lemon
¹/₂	teaspoon salt
¹/₄	teaspoon ground black pepper
1	small stalk celery, minced (about ¹/₄ cup)
2	tablespoons minced red onion
2	tablespoons minced dill or sweet pickles
¹/₂	small clove garlic, minced or pressed through garlic press (about ¹/₈ teaspoon)
2	tablespoons minced fresh parsley leaves
¹/₂	cup mayonnaise
¹/₄	teaspoon Dijon mustard

Drain the tuna in a colander and shred with your fingers until no clumps remain and the texture is fine and even. Transfer the tuna to a medium bowl and mix in lemon juice, salt, pepper, celery, onion, pickles, garlic, and parsley until evenly blended. Fold in mayonnaise and mustard until tuna is evenly moistened. (Salad can be covered and refrigerated for up to 3 days.)

➤ VARIATIONS

Tuna Salad with Balsamic Vinegar and Grapes

Follow the recipe for Classic Tuna Salad, omitting the lemon juice, pickles, garlic, and parsley and adding 2 tablespoons balsamic vinegar, 6 ounces halved red seedless grapes (about 1 cup), ¹/₄ cup lightly toasted slivered almonds, and 2 teaspoons minced thyme leaves to tuna along with salt and pepper.

Curried Tuna Salad with Apples and Currants

Follow the recipe for Classic Tuna Salad, omitting the pickles, garlic, and parsley and adding 1 medium firm, juicy apple, cut into ¹/₄-inch dice (about 1 cup), ¹/₄ cup currants, and 2 tablespoons minced fresh basil leaves to tuna along with lemon juice, salt, and pepper; mix 1 tablespoon curry powder into mayonnaise before folding into tuna.

Tuna Salad with Lime and Horseradish

Follow the recipe for Classic Tuna Salad, omitting the lemon juice, pickles, and garlic and adding 2 tablespoons juice and ¹/₂ teaspoon grated zest from 1 lime and 3 tablespoons prepared horseradish to tuna along with salt and pepper.

INGREDIENTS: **Canned Tuna**

We selected the 10 best-selling chunk-light and solid white tunas packed in water and assembled 25 tasters in the test kitchen. We drained each can of tuna and lightly blended it with mayonnaise but added no seasonings.

In most of our blind taste tests, taste has predictably reigned. But when it came to canned tuna, texture set the pace. Most canned tunas are bland—that's why tuna salad is so heavily seasoned. But some brands could be chewed, while others were more suitable to gumming.

Chunk light was the least expensive of the two varieties in our tasting, costing about 41 cents a can less than solid white. This may explain why it is also the top-selling type of canned tuna. Certainly our tasting results do not explain it, since tasters found only one of the five chunk-light samples (Geisha) acceptable. In general, chunk light tuna is made of skipjack tuna or yellowfin tuna or both; skipjack contributes a stronger flavor than yellowfin. Each can contains several small pieces of tuna as well as some flakes.

While our tasters were not wild about the more pronounced flavor of chunk light (which often included an aftertaste of tin), what really upset the balance between the white and light tunas was texture. White tuna you could eat, even pierce, with a fork; the light version was more appropriately scooped with a spoon. When blended with mayonnaise, the small flakes of chunk light tuna quickly broke down even further, taking on a texture that reminded many tasters of cat food. Tasters not only disliked this lack of chew but found that the small shreds of fish held moisture too well, which created a sopping, mushy consistency.

Solid white, on the other hand, consists of one large piece of loin meat from albacore tuna. Though known as "white" tuna, albacore can vary from nearly white to light pink or even beige. Solid white was the tuna of choice among tasters for its mild flavor, milky white appearance, and chunky texture. StarKist took top honors, followed by 3 Diamonds, Chicken of the Sea, Bumble Bee, and Geisha.

Tuna Salad with Cauliflower, Jalapeño, and Cilantro

Follow the recipe for Classic Tuna Salad, omitting the pickles, garlic, and parsley and adding 4 ounces cauliflower florets cut into ½-inch pieces (about 1 cup), 1 medium jalapeño chile, minced (about 2 tablespoons), 2 medium scallions, minced (about ¼ cup), and 2 tablespoons minced fresh cilantro leaves to tuna along with lemon juice, salt, and pepper.

EGG SALAD

EGG SALAD IS ONE OF THOSE SIMPLE, spur-of-the-moment comfort foods that should be easy to make. Yet sometimes it turns out pasty, the overall flavor drab, the mayonnaise excessive, or the onions too biting. The hardest part, though, is cooking the eggs properly.

We have always considered hard-cooking an egg to be a crapshoot. There's no way to watch the proteins cook under the brittle shell of an uncracked egg, and you certainly can't poke it with an instant-read thermometer, as you would with so many other foods. Often the eggs are overcooked, with rubbery whites and chalky yolks. Of course, undercooked eggs without fully set yolks are even more problematic, especially when trying to make egg salad.

There are two general methods for boiling eggs—starting them in cold water and bringing them to a simmer, or lowering them into already simmering water. The first method is not terribly precise. When do you start the clock—when the eggs go into the water or when the water starts to boil? Also, what temperature is right for simmering? Everyone knows what boiling water looks like (and the temperature is always 212 degrees at sea level), but simmering water can be 180, 190, or even 200 degrees. We never developed a reliable timing mechanism with this technique.

Lowering eggs into simmering water is not easy either, because the eggs are likely to crack. Some sources suggest poking a thumb tack through the large end of the egg where the air hole typically sits, but we had inconsistent results with this advice. Again, the issue of defining "simmering water" proved problematic.

Not satisfied with either method, we tried a third method: starting the eggs in cold water, bringing the water to a boil, and then turning off the heat. The pan is covered and the eggs are set aside to cook by residual heat for 10 minutes. There's no need to define "simmer" with this method. As long as you can recognize when water is at a boil and can time 10 minutes, you are guaranteed hard-boiled eggs with bright, creamy yolks and tender whites.

With our eggs perfectly boiled, it was time to make salad. We quickly found that both a fork and a pastry blender mashed the eggs so much that, when blended with mayonnaise, they became unpleasantly pasty. In addition to being reminiscent of baby food, this egg salad was quick to ooze out from between the slices of bread in a sandwich. After experimenting with various options, we found that eggs diced into small cubes (just under one-half inch) gave the salad the full mouthfeel we had been seeking and also held up well in a sandwich.

Foolproof Hard-Boiled Eggs
MAKES 6

You can double or triple this recipe as long as you use a pot large enough to hold the eggs in a single layer, covered by an inch of water.

6   large eggs

1. Place the eggs in a medium saucepan, cover with 1 inch of water, and bring to a boil over high heat. Remove the pan from the heat, cover, and let sit for 10 minutes. Meanwhile, fill a medium bowl with 1 quart of water and 1 tray of ice cubes (or equivalent).

2. Transfer the eggs to the ice bath with a slotted spoon and let sit 5 minutes. Tap each egg all over against the counter surface to crack the shell, then roll it gently back and forth a few times. Begin peeling from the air-pocket (wider) end. The shell should come off in spiral strips attached to the thin membrane.

Classic Egg Salad

MAKES ABOUT 2 1/2 CUPS,
ENOUGH FOR 4 SANDWICHES

A mozzarella slicer turns a boiled egg into perfect ⅜-inch cubes. Place the egg in the slicer and cut through it lengthwise. Turn the egg a quarter turn and slice it crosswise. Then rotate the egg 90 degrees and slice it widthwise.

1	recipe Foolproof Hard-Boiled Eggs (see page 44), peeled and diced medium
¼	cup mayonnaise
2	tablespoons minced red onion
1	tablespoon minced fresh parsley leaves
½	medium stalk celery, chopped fine
2	teaspoons Dijon mustard
2	teaspoons juice from 1 lemon
¼	teaspoon salt
	Ground black pepper

Mix all the ingredients together in a medium bowl, including pepper to taste. Serve. (The egg salad can be refrigerated in an airtight container for up to 1 day.)

➤ VARIATIONS

Egg Salad with Radish, Scallions, and Dill

Follow the recipe for Classic Egg Salad, substituting 1 tablespoon minced fresh dill for the parsley, 1 medium thin-sliced scallion for the red onion, and adding 3 medium radishes, minced.

Creamy Egg Salad with Bacon, Shallots, and Watercress

In a medium skillet over medium heat, fry 4 slices bacon (about 4 ounces, cut into ¼-inch pieces) until brown and crisp, about 5 minutes. Transfer bacon with slotted spoon to plate lined with paper towels; pour off all but 1 tablespoon fat from the pan. Add 2 large shallots, chopped medium, and sauté until softened and browned, about 5 minutes. Follow the recipe for Classic Egg Salad, omitting the celery and salt, substituting sautéed shallots for red onion, and adding the bacon and ¼ cup watercress leaves, chopped coarse.

MOLDED CRANBERRY SALAD

MOLDED JELL-O SALADS HAVE BEEN AROUND since the early 1900s when Knox introduced its "Sparkling Granulated Gelatin." Although this original gelatin was flavorless, fruit-flavored gelatin was soon developed, giving cooks and housewives across America a nifty way to serve salads and leftovers. Although molded gelatin salads have changed through the decades along with culinary fashions, they are still a popular party and picnic staple.

Cranberry salad is probably the most popular molded gelatin salad, and it makes frequent appearances during the holidays in many homes. Most versions don't contain cranberries, using cranberry juice or cranberry gelatin instead.

We compared cranberry-flavored gelatin with flavorless gelatin mixed with cranberry juice. Although tasters were unanimous in preferring the sweet, balanced flavor of the flavored Jell-O to the tinny flavor of gelatinized cranberry juice, the flavored Jell-O needed a little boost. We tried replacing all of the water with cranberry juice, but the flavor was overwhelming. In the end, we found that replacing about half of the water with cranberry juice was enough.

Most cranberry salads have bits of fruits, vegetables, and/or nuts suspended in them. Using some older recipes as a base, we found the presence of most vegetables, such as celery and bell peppers, to be outdated. Although tasters preferred salads made only with fruit, not just any fresh fruit will do. Tropical fruits such as pineapple, papaya, mango, and kiwi contain potent acids that break down the gelatin if they are not cooked or canned. We found most canned fruit to taste subpar, with the exception of canned pineapple chunks and mandarin oranges. We found that fresh grapes added nice texture and crunch to the salad but that fresh cranberry sauce included too many tough, tannic cranberry skins. Many older recipes call for nuts, but none of the tasters were impressed with the little crunchy bits floating in the smooth salad.

The salad can be molded in a wide variety of ways, depending on the shape and size of the molding container used. We found that a 4-quart Bundt pan produced a salad that was especially easy to slice. (The ringlike shape of a Bundt pan provides the salad with a hollow center. In contrast, traditional copper molds turn out a single wobbling mass of salad.) A nonstick Bundt pan is ideal because it's so easy to unmold the salad, but we found that a conventional surface will also release the salad when it is loosened by dipping the mold in hot water.

Molded Cranberry Salad

SERVES 8 TO 10

It is important to allow the Jell-O to set up partially on its own before adding the fruit to ensure that the fruit will "float" throughout the mold. If by chance the Jell-O is too stiff to stir in the fruit, simply pour it back in a saucepan and re-melt it over low heat before partially chilling it again.

5 (3-ounce) packages cranberry Jell-O
3½ cups cold cranberry juice
1 15-ounce can pineapple chunks, drained (about 2 cups)
1 15-ounce can whole mandarin orange segments, drained (about 1 cup)
2 cups red seedless grapes, halved

1. Bring 4 cups of water to a boil in a medium saucepan. Pour the boiling water into a large bowl and sprinkle evenly with Jell-O. Stir to dissolve, about 2 minutes. Stir in the cranberry juice and place the bowl in the refrigerator, allowing the mixture to cool and thicken slightly (but remain in liquid form), about 1 hour.

2. Stir the fruit into the Jell-O mixture. Pour the Jell-O–fruit mixture into a 4-quart Bundt pan or attractive mold of similar size. Refrigerate the mold until the salad has chilled and set up, at least 4 hours or up to 1 day.

3. Unmold the salad on a large serving plate (see the illustrations below). Refrigerate until ready to serve. (If necessary, you can slip the Bundt pan back over the unmolded salad and refrigerate the salad for an hour or two.)

UNMOLDING CRANBERRY SALAD

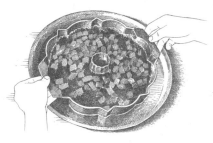

1. Gently lower the bottom of the mold into a bowl filled with hot water and keep it in place for about 5 seconds.

2. With your finger, lightly press the edges of the Jell-O away from the mold to loosen the salad from the pan.

3. Place a large serving plate on top of the mold. Holding the plate securely in place, carefully invert the mold and release the Jell-O salad onto the plate.

3

VEGETABLES

AMERICANS EAT HUNDREDS OF VEGETABLE side dishes. For this chapter, we have gathered two dozen of our favorite recipes—the ones we make over and over again in our own kitchens at home. There are "newer" recipes, such as grilled corn, as well as plenty of old favorites, such as mashed potatoes and Southern-style greens. We've also breathed life into several popular dishes that have fallen on hard times due to the widespread use of convenience products. For instance, our green bean casserole (made with fresh, not frozen, beans and a homemade sauce rather than one from a can) is a revelation. When made right, this dish is worthy of a holiday table.

Boiled and Grilled Corn

DESPITE FARMSTAND SIGNS ACROSS THE COUNTRY announcing "Butter and Sugar" corn for sale, no one really grows old-time butter and sugar corn anymore. Nor does anybody grow most of the other old-fashioned nonhybrid varieties. These bygone varieties of corn have disappeared for a reason. They converted sugar into starch so rapidly once picked that people literally fired up their kettles before going out to gather the corn. Corn has since been crossbred to make for sweeter ears that have a longer hold on their fresh flavor and tender texture.

Basically, there are three hybrid types: normal sugary, sugar enhanced, and supersweet. Each contains dozens of varieties, with fancy names such as Kandy Korn, Double Gem, and Mystique. Normal sugary types, such as Silver Queen, are moderately sweet, with traditional corn flavor. The sugars in this type of corn convert to starch rapidly after being picked. The sugar-enhanced types are more tender and somewhat sweeter, with a slower conversion of sugar to starch. Supersweet corn has heightened sweetness, a crisp texture, and a remarkably slow conversion of sugar to starch after being picked. It is a popular type for growers who supply to distant markets and require a product with a longer shelf life. Any corn sold in your supermarket during the off-season is likely a variety of supersweet.

Beyond the above generalizations, it's impossible to tell which kind of corn you have unless you taste it. With that in mind, we developed cooking methods that would work with all three kinds of corn hybrids. Boiling is probably the most all-purpose cooking method. To increase sweetness, we tried adding milk to the water but found it muddied the corn flavor. Salt toughens the corn up a bit and is best added at the table. Sugar can be added to the water to enhance the corn's sweetness, but when we tried this with supersweet corn it tasted too sweet, almost like dessert.

Grilling is our other preferred method for cooking corn. The ideal grilled corn retains the juiciness of boiled corn without sacrificing the toasty caramelization and smoke-infused graces of the grill. We started our tests with the bare ear cooked directly over a medium-high fire. The outcome seemed too good to be true. The lightly caramelized corn was still juicy, but with a toasty hit of grilled flavor and a sweet essence to chase it down.

In fact, it was too good to be true. The variety of corn we used was fittingly called Fantasy, which is a supersweet variety. When we tried grilling a normal sugary corn variety with the husk off, the outcome was a flavorless, dry, gummy turnoff. The end result was no better with sugar-enhanced corn. The direct heat was just too much for the fleeting flavors and tender texture of the normal sugary and sugar-enhanced corn types.

We went on to test another popular technique: throwing the whole ear on the grill, husk and all, as is. We tried this with all three sweet corn types at various heat levels. Half of the ears of corn were soaked beforehand; the other half were not. In sum, the husk-on method makes for a great-tasting ear of corn, and a particularly crisp, juicy one. But if it were not for the sticky charred husks that must be awkwardly peeled away at the table if you are to serve the corn hot, you would think you were eating boiled corn. The presoaked corn in particular just steamed in the husk and picked up no grilled flavor.

Since grilling with the husk off was too aggressive for non-supersweet varieties and grilling with the husk on was no different from boiled corn, we turned to a compromise approach. We peeled off the outer layers of husk but left the final layer that hugs the ear. This layer is much more moist and delicate than the outer layers, so much so that you can practically see the kernels through the husk. When cooked over a medium-high fire, this gave the corn a jacket heavy enough to prevent dehydration yet light enough to allow a gentle toasting of the kernels. After about eight minutes (rolling the corn one-quarter turn every two minutes), we could be certain that the corn was cooked just right, because the husk picked up a dark silhouette of the kernels and began to pull back at the corn's tip.

Boiled Corn

SERVES 8

If you want to serve more corn, bring a second pot of water to a boil at the same time, or cook the corn in batches in just one pot. If you know that you have supersweet corn, omit the sugar.

> 4   teaspoons sugar, optional
> 8   ears fresh corn, husks and silk removed
>   Salt and ground black pepper
>   Butter (optional)

Bring 4 quarts of water and the sugar, if using, to a boil in a large pot. Add the corn; return to a boil and cook until tender, 5 to 7 minutes. Drain the corn. Season the corn with salt and pepper to taste and butter, if desired. Serve immediately.

Grilled Corn

SERVES 8

While grilling husk-on corn delivers great pure corn flavor, it lacks the smokiness of the grill; essentially, the corn is steamed in its protective husk. By leaving only the innermost layer, we were rewarded with perfectly tender corn graced with the grill's flavor. Prepared in this way, the corn does not need basting with oil.

> 8   ears fresh corn, prepared according to
>   illustrations at right
>   Salt and ground black pepper
>   Butter (optional)

1. Grill the corn over a medium-hot fire (see how to gauge the heat level on page 116), turning the ears every 1½ to 2 minutes, until the dark outlines of the kernels show through the husk and the husk is charred and beginning to peel away from the tip to expose some kernels, 8 to 10 minutes.

2. Transfer the corn to a platter. Carefully remove and discard the charred husk and silk. Season the corn with salt and pepper to taste and butter, if desired. Serve immediately.

> VARIATION

Grilled Corn with Herb Butter

Brush with herb butter just before serving.

Melt 6 tablespoons unsalted butter in a small saucepan. Add 3 tablespoons minced fresh parsley, thyme, cilantro, basil, and/or other fresh herbs and salt and pepper to taste; keep the butter warm. Follow the recipe for Grilled Corn, brushing the herb butter over the grilled corn in step 2.

PREPARING CORN FOR GRILLING

1. Remove all but the innermost layer of the husk. The kernels should be covered by, but visible through, the innermost layer.

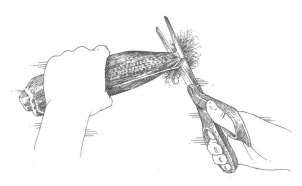

2. Use scissors to snip off the tassel, or long silk ends, at the tip of the ear.

CREAMED CORN

ALTHOUGH CREAMED CORN IS AVAILABLE any time of year out of the can, it doesn't compare with the clean, sweet flavor of late summer corn gently simmered with fresh cream. But if you don't handle the fresh corn and cream correctly, you wind up with that overcooked, just-out-of-the-can flavor you were trying to avoid.

Many recipes start by boiling the corn on the cob, then cutting the kernels off the cob and mixing them with a cream sauce. This technique, however, loses much of the sweet, delicate corn flavor to the cooking water. We quickly rejected this method in favor of recipes that simmer the corn kernels (which are first cut free from the cobs) directly in the cream. This technique releases their sugary, summery flavor into the sauce, which is where you want it to be.

Simply simmering fresh corn kernels in cream, however, wasn't enough. It produced a thin, lumpy mixture that lacked the thickened, spoonable texture we desired. Scraping the pulp out of the spent cobs helped a bit, but we wanted the sauce a bit thicker. Flour and cornstarch just made the sauce gummy and overwhelmed the flavor of the corn. We then tried grating a few of the ears, which broke down some of the kernels into smaller pieces. This did the trick. By grating half of the raw kernels off the cob, we were able to release more of the corn's natural thickener.

After making a few batches of this recipe with different types of corn, we realized that the cooking times can differ, depending on the corn's variety and age. While some corn cooked perfectly in only 10 minutes, others needed five minutes longer. We also found that as the corn and cream cook and thicken, the heat needs to be adjusted to keep the mixture at a simmer to prevent the bottom from burning.

As for the other ingredients, we tried using half-and-half instead of heavy cream, but tasters missed the luxurious flavor and heft provided by the latter. A little shallot, garlic, and fresh thyme complemented the delicate flavor of the corn, while a pinch of cayenne added a little kick.

Creamed Corn

SERVES 6 TO 8

For best texture and flavor, we like a combination of grated corn, whole kernels (cut away from the cobs with a knife), and corn pulp (scraped from the ears with the back of a knife).

5	medium ears fresh corn, husks and silk removed
2	tablespoons unsalted butter
1	medium shallot, minced (about 2 tablespoons)
1	medium clove garlic, minced
1½	cups heavy cream
½	teaspoon minced fresh thyme leaves
	Pinch cayenne pepper
	Salt and ground black pepper

SCIENCE: Corn Storage

While the general rule of thumb is to buy and eat corn the same day it has been harvested (as soon as the corn is harvested the sugars start converting to starches and the corn loses sweetness), most of us have been guilty of breaking that rule. We tried a variety of methods for overnight storage using Silver Queen corn, one of the more perishable varieties.

We found that the worst thing you can do to corn is to leave it sitting out on the counter. Throwing it into the refrigerator without any wrapping is nearly as bad. Storing it in an airtight bag helps, but the hands-down winner entailed wrapping the corn (husk left on) in a wet paper bag and then in a plastic bag (any shopping bag will do). After 24 hours of storage we found the corn stored this way to be juicy and sweet—not starchy—and fresh tasting.

REMOVING KERNELS FROM CORN COBS

Tapered ears of corn can wobble on the cutting board, and kernels can fly around the kitchen. To work safely and more neatly, we cut the ear in half crosswise and then stand the half-ears on their cut surfaces, which are flat and stable.

1. Cut the kernels from 3 ears of corn and transfer them to a medium bowl (see "Removing Kernels from Corn Cobs" on page 50). Firmly scrape the cobs with the back of a butter knife to collect the pulp and milk in the same bowl (see illustration 2 in "Milking Corn" on page 52). Grate the remaining 2 ears of corn on the coarse side of a box grater set in the bowl with the cut kernels (see illustration 1 in "Milking Corn" on page 52). Firmly scrape these cobs with the back of a butter knife to collect the pulp and milk in the same bowl.

2. Heat the butter in a medium saucepan over medium-high heat until the foaming subsides, about 1 minute. Add the shallot and cook until softened but not browned, 1 to 2 minutes. Add the garlic and cook until aromatic, about 30 seconds. Stir in the corn kernels and pulp as well as the cream, thyme, cayenne, ¼ teaspoon salt, and ⅛ teaspoon pepper. Bring the mixture to a simmer and cook, adjusting the heat as necessary and stirring occasionally, until the corn is tender and the mixture has thickened, 10 to 15 minutes. Remove the pan from the heat, adjust the seasonings with salt and pepper to taste, and serve immediately.

➤ VARIATION

Creamed Corn with Red Pepper, Chipotle, and Lime

5	medium ears fresh corn, husks and silk removed
2	tablespoons unsalted butter
½	large red bell pepper, cored, seeded, and cut into ¼-inch dice
1	medium shallot, minced (about 2 tablespoons)
1	medium clove garlic, minced
1	chipotle chile packed in adobo sauce, minced
1½	cups heavy cream
	Salt and ground black pepper
2	teaspoons lime juice
1	tablespoon minced fresh parsley leaves

1. Follow step 1 of the Creamed Corn recipe.
2. Heat the butter in a medium saucepan over medium-high heat until the foaming subsides, about 1 minute. Add the red pepper and shallot and cook until softened but not browned, 1 to 2 minutes. Add the garlic and chile and cook until aromatic, about

30 seconds. Stir in the corn kernels and pulp as well as the cream, ¼ teaspoon salt, and ⅛ teaspoon pepper. Bring the mixture to a simmer and cook, adjusting the heat as necessary and stirring occasionally, until the corn is tender and the mixture has thickened, 10 to 15 minutes. Remove the pan from the heat, stir in the lime juice and parsley, adjust the seasonings with salt and pepper to taste, and serve immediately.

CORN PUDDING

CORN PUDDING IS A COMBINATION OF eggs, milk, and cream—basically, a savory corn custard—graced with a generous helping of freshly cut kernels. We set out to develop a recipe for a tender, creamy custard with lots of corn flavor.

We originally thought that this dish would be a no-brainer. Many American cookbooks include recipes for corn pudding, which invariably boil down to a combination of milk, cream, eggs, and corn. Given the consistency of the recipes, we were quite surprised to find that our first batch of puddings were failures. Each and every one curdled and wept, producing an unwanted pool of watery liquid.

The pudding cooked in a water bath—a large roasting pan filled with hot water—was better than those exposed directly to the oven heat. As with other oven-baked puddings, the water bath tempered the heat and protected the eggs from overcooking. But the water bath alone was not enough to produce a smooth, tender custard. It seemed obvious that the corn in the pudding was the source of the escaping liquid found in every pudding. The question was how to get rid of the moisture in the corn without losing the fresh corn flavor.

After experimenting with various options, we settled on a simple two-step approach. First we cooked the corn kernels in a little butter, just until the moisture in the pan had almost evaporated. Then we eliminated a bit more of the corn's liquid by simmering the kernels in heavy cream. Because heavy cream, unlike milk or even light cream, can be cooked at a boil without curdling, we reasoned that it would be safe to simmer the corn together with the cream that was already part of the recipe. When we tried this method, we were very happy with the results. When we made the pudding with corn that had been briefly sautéed and then simmered with heavy cream to make a thick mixture, we had a dish with great flavor and without any seeping liquid.

Now we were ready to move on to balancing flavors. The first thing we noticed about our now smooth and creamy custard was the corn—there was too much of it. To reduce the corn-to-custard ratio, we cut back from 4 cups of corn to 3. This helped, but there still seemed to be too many large kernels intruding on the tender custard. Perhaps pureeing some of the corn, we thought, would smooth out the texture without sacrificing any of the intense corn flavor. But pureeing did the job too well; we wanted the pudding to have some chew, and now it didn't have enough. Next we tried grating some of the corn directly off the cobs on the coarse side of a box grater. This method gave us just what we were looking for in terms of flavor as well as texture.

MILKING CORN

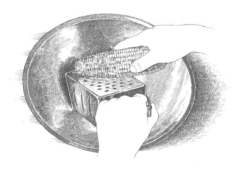

1. Start by grating the ear of corn on the large holes of a box grater.

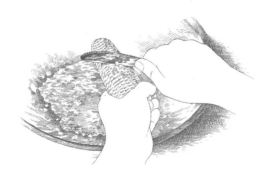

2. Finish by firmly scraping any remaining kernels off the cob with the back of a butter knife.

Creamy Corn Pudding

SERVES 6 AS A SIDE DISH

Corn pudding must be served hot and cannot be reheated, so plan ahead accordingly.

6	medium ears fresh corn, husks and silk removed
3	tablespoons unsalted butter, plus extra for greasing baking dish
⅔	cup heavy cream
1½	teaspoons salt
1	teaspoon sugar
¼	teaspoon cayenne pepper
1⅓	cups whole milk
4	large eggs, beaten lightly
1	tablespoon cornstarch

1. Cut the kernels from 5 ears of corn (see "Removing Kernels from Corn Cobs" on page 50) and transfer them to a medium bowl. Scrape the cobs with the back of a knife to collect the milk in the same bowl (see illustration 2 at left); you should have about 2½ cups kernels and milk. Grate the remaining ear of corn on the coarse side of a box grater set in the bowl with the cut kernels (see illustration 1 at left); you should have about ½ cup grated kernels. Firmly scrape this cob with the back of a butter knife to collect the pulp and milk in the same bowl.

2. Adjust an oven rack to the lower-middle position, place an empty roasting pan or large baking dish on the rack, and heat the oven to 350 degrees. Generously butter an 8-inch square baking dish. Bring 2 quarts water to a boil in a kettle or saucepan.

3. Heat a large heavy-bottomed skillet over medium heat until hot, about 2 minutes. Add the butter; when the foaming subsides, add the contents of the bowl with the corn kernels and pulp. Cook, stirring occasionally, until the corn is bright yellow and the liquid has almost evaporated, about 5 minutes. Add the cream, salt, sugar, and cayenne and cook, stirring occasionally, until thickened and a spoon leaves a trail when the pan bottom is scraped, about 5 minutes. Transfer the corn mixture to a medium bowl. Stir in the milk, then whisk in the eggs and cornstarch. Pour the mixture into the buttered baking dish.

4. Set the dish in the roasting pan or large baking dish already in the oven. Fill the outer pan with boiling water to reach halfway up the inner pan. Bake until the center jiggles slightly when shaken and the pudding has browned lightly in spots, 20 to 25 minutes. Remove the baking dish with the pudding from the water bath. Cool 10 minutes and serve.

CORN FRITTERS

CORN FRITTERS ARE BASICALLY CORN KERNELS (ground, grated, or chopped) enriched with egg and flour and fried until crisp. The ideal fritter is amazingly crisp and golden brown on the outside, creamy and bursting with sweet corn flavor on the inside. As our early tests demonstrated, however, most corn fritters are heavy, dense, greasy cakes with almost no corn flavor.

We started our research by collecting as many fritter recipes, corn or otherwise, as possible, detouring around any that began with "Take one can creamed corn…" or "Heat up the fry-o-later…" We wanted to use fresh corn and a skillet.

We first looked to see how the corn was treated. The main choices were cut, grated, pureed, and chopped. For our first batch we simply cut the kernels off the cob and then stirred them into the egg-and-flour batter. The result was a fritter more like a pancake, with a small amount of corn flavor showing up only if one was lucky enough to bite into a kernel. We went to the other extreme and pureed the kernels, but the amount of flour necessary to make the mixture cohesive produced a very bland, pasty fritter. We knew that we were on to something when we tried grating the corn on a box grater. This time the interior was creamy and flavorful, but the fritters lacked texture. In our next batch we included whole kernels as well as corn pulp. These fritters were packed with fresh corn flavor and texturally interesting.

Next came the binders. It was obvious that the amount of flour added would make the difference between a delicate fritter and a doorstop. We added just enough flour to keep the fritters from falling apart, but even with this small amount of flour the corn flavor was dulled significantly. Cornmeal, another binder found in several recipes, was an option, and the corn flavor that it lent was perfect. When used alone, however, the cornmeal compromised the texture of the fritters, making them unpleasantly grainy. We thought that a mixture of the flour and cornmeal would be perfect, and after trying various ratios, we agreed on equal amounts of each.

These fritters had great corn flavor and a tender texture, but they lacked the creamy richness we desired. We first tried adding melted butter, but the fritters were greasy and the butter seemed to dull the fresh corn flavor. Remembering the creamy consistency of the grated corn pulp, we added in turns a small amount of milk, buttermilk, half-and-half, and heavy cream, hoping to closely emulate the creaminess found in the corn itself. Heavy cream proved to be exactly what the batter needed—the higher amount of fat enriched the fritter yet didn't compromise its sweet corn flavor. At this point we tried baking soda, which some recipes used to lighten the batter. We didn't care for the puffed, tempura-like appearance and texture of these fritters, so we left it out.

Next we tested frying the fritters in butter, oil, and a blend of the two. Butter scorched by the time we got around to frying the second half of our batter. Blending the butter with a bit of oil to prevent burning was not worth the trouble. Vegetable oil proved to be the best cooking medium, both for its reluctance to smoke and its neutral taste; it didn't compete with the corn. At this time we wondered how much oil was really necessary. We found pan-frying in a moderate amount of oil (¼ cup) sufficient to crisp the fritters perfectly.

Finally, we admitted that there are times when we want to make fritters, but fresh sweet corn is not available. We tried our recipe with off-season ears of corn purchased at a local supermarket but found that their moisture content and sweet flavor were greatly diminished. Frozen corn, which is much more flavorful than its canned cousin, was our only option. To obtain a texture similar to the one we got using fresh corn, we pulsed semi-defrosted kernels in the food processor (see our variation). The resulting fritters had great corn flavor and texture—almost as good as those made with fresh corn.

Fresh Corn Fritters

MAKES TWELVE 2-INCH FRITTERS,
SERVING 4 TO 6 AS A FIRST COURSE
OR SIDE DISH

Serve these fritters with tartar sauce, hot pepper sauce, or tomato salsa. For a breakfast treat, drizzle maple syrup over the fritters.

3–4	medium ears fresh corn, husks and silk removed
1	large egg, beaten lightly
3	tablespoons all-purpose flour
3	tablespoons cornmeal
2	tablespoons heavy cream
1	large shallot, minced (about 3 tablespoons)
¾	teaspoon salt
	Pinch cayenne pepper
¼	cup vegetable or corn oil, or more as needed

1. Using a chef's knife, cut the kernels from 1 or 2 ears of corn (see "Removing Kernels from Corn Cobs" on page 50; you should have about 1 cup); transfer the kernels to a medium bowl. Grate the kernels from the remaining 1 or 2 ears of corn on the large holes of a box grater, then firmly scrape any pulp remaining on the cobs with the back of a knife (see illustration 2 in "Milking Corn" on page 52; you should have a generous ½ cup kernels and pulp). Transfer the grated kernels and pulp to the bowl with the cut kernels.

2. Mix the egg, flour, cornmeal, cream, shallot, salt, and cayenne into the corn mixture to form a thick batter. (The batter can be covered and refrigerated for up to 4 hours.)

3. Heat the oil in 12-inch heavy-bottomed skillet over medium-high heat until shimmering, about 2 minutes. Drop heaping tablespoonfuls of batter into the oil (half the batter, or 6 fritters, should fit into the skillet at once). Fry until golden brown, about 50 seconds, then, using a thin metal spatula, turn the fritters and fry until the second side is golden brown, about 50 seconds longer. Transfer the fritters to a paper towel–lined plate. Add more oil to the skillet if necessary and heat until shimmering. Repeat to fry the remaining batter. Serve the fritters immediately.

> VARIATION
Out-of-Season Corn Fritters

When fresh corn is out of season, frozen corn makes a fine substitute. Processing the frozen kernels in a food processor approximates the texture achieved by grating fresh corn.

Use the same ingredient list and quantities as for Fresh Corn Fritters, substituting 2 cups frozen corn kernels thawed at room temperature for 15 minutes for fresh corn. Pulse the corn, egg, flour, cornmeal, cream, shallot, salt, and cayenne in workbowl of food processor fitted with steel blade until mixture forms thick batter with some whole kernels, about ten 1-second pulses. Continue with recipe from step 3.

SUCCOTASH

A STAPLE DISH IN THE DIET OF AMERICAN Indians for centuries, succotash is a delicate summer mixture of fresh corn and lima beans. As simple as it sounds, however, there are plenty of recipes that do it disservice. Some overcook the limas, turning them dry and pasty, while others use too much butter and make the dish greasy. Although we found several recipes that add zucchini, tomatoes, and eggplant to the mix, we wanted a simple succotash that tasted authentic and pure.

Because fresh lima beans can be difficult to find, we tested both dried and frozen. After cooking the two side by side, we found the frozen limas were the way to go, offering a fresher taste and quicker cooking time. As for the corn, we found that kernels scraped from fresh ears tasted much sweeter than bland frozen corn. Fresh kernels also gave succotash a nice crunch; frozen kernels were soggy. We also found extra flavor in the cobs, which we scraped clean using the back of a knife to release any remaining bits of kernels. The limas and corn took only 5 minutes to cook over medium heat. When cooked further, the corn turned too soft while the limas tasted chalky.

To round out the flavor, we found that a small onion and a little garlic did wonders. Many authentic recipes call for green peppers, but our tasters found them unpleasantly bitter. Instead, we liked the sweet, ripe flavor of red peppers; they also added a flourish of color to the mix. We tried sautéing the vegetables in olive oil but preferred the mellow, sweet flavor of butter. Seasoned with salt, black pepper, and a hint of cayenne, our succotash needed only a little fresh parsley to help bring these fresh flavors home. With a total cooking time of about 12 minutes, this quick, summery vegetable sauté is the perfect side dish for an outdoor barbecue or picnic.

Succotash

SERVES 4 TO 6

Although frozen lima beans are fine for succotash, only fresh corn has the proper flavor and texture for this dish.

3	medium ears fresh corn, husks and silk removed
4	tablespoons unsalted butter
I	small onion, minced (about I cup)
½	medium red bell pepper, cored, seeded, and cut into ½-inch dice (about ½ cup)
2	medium cloves garlic, minced
2	cups frozen lima beans (about 10 ounces)
¾	teaspoon salt
⅛	teaspoon ground black pepper
	Pinch cayenne pepper
I	tablespoon minced fresh parsley leaves

1. Using a chef's knife, cut the kernels from the ears of corn (see "Removing Kernels from Corn Cobs" on page 50); transfer the kernels to a medium bowl. Firmly scrape any pulp remaining on the cobs with the back of a knife directly into the bowl with the cut kernels (see illustration 2 in "Milking Corn" on page 52).

2. Melt the butter in a large nonstick skillet over medium-high heat until the foaming subsides, about 1 minute. Add the onion and red pepper and sauté until softened and beginning to brown around the edges, about 5 minutes. Add the garlic and sauté until aromatic, about 30 seconds. Stir in the corn kernels and pulp, frozen lima beans, salt, pepper, and cayenne and turn the heat down to medium. Cook, stirring occasionally, until the limas and corn have cooked through, about 5 minutes. Stir in the parsley and serve immediately.

➤ VARIATIONS

Succotash with Chiles and Cilantro
Follow the recipe for Succotash, adding 1 small jalapeño chile, stemmed, seeded, and minced, along with the onion and red pepper, and replacing the parsley with cilantro.

Succotash with Bacon and Scallions
Follow the recipe for Succotash through step 1. Cook 6 slices of bacon, cut into ½ inch pieces, in a large nonstick skillet over medium-high heat until crisp and brown, about 5 minutes. Transfer bacon to paper towel–lined plate to drain; set aside. To rendered bacon fat in pan (you should have 2 to 3 tablespoons), add 1 to 2 tablespoons of unsalted butter (so that the total amount is 4 tablespoons) and melt over medium-high heat. Proceed as directed in step 2, stirring in 3 minced scallions, both green and white parts, during the final minute of cooking and adding the cooked bacon with the parsley.

BAKED POTATOES

WE BAKED ALL-PURPOSE POTATOES, YUKON Golds, and russets and found that russets produce the fluffiest and, to our mind, the best baked potato. We baked russets at temperatures ranging from 350 to 500 degrees and discovered that traditional slow baking is best, mainly because of the effect it has on the skin. The skin of a potato baked at 350 degrees for an hour and 15 minutes simply has no peer. Just under the skin, a well-baked potato will develop a substantial brown layer. This is because the dark skin absorbs heat during cooking, and the starch just inside the skin is broken down into sugar and starts to brown. If you love baked potato skin, this is the method for you.

If slow baking is essential to good skin, the consistency of the flesh also requires some attention. Letting the potato sit awhile after baking without opening it up will steam the potato and cause the flesh to become more dense. For fluffy potatoes, use a fork to open up the potatoes as soon as they come out of the oven to let the steam escape.

Baked Potatoes

SERVES 4

We found no benefit or harm was done to the potatoes by poking them with the tines of a fork before putting them in the oven. Do use a fork to open the skin as soon as potatoes come out of the oven.

4 medium russet potatoes (7 to 8 ounces each), scrubbed

Heat the oven to 350 degrees. Place the potatoes on a middle rack and bake for 75 minutes. Remove the potatoes from the oven and pierce with a fork to create a dotted X on top of each potato. Press in at the ends of each potato to push the flesh up and out. Serve immediately.

TWICE-BAKED POTATOES

THIS SIMPLE DISH — ESSENTIALLY BAKED russet potatoes from which the flesh has been removed, mashed with dairy ingredients and seasonings, mounded back in the shells, and baked again— offers a good range of both texture and flavor in a single morsel. Done well, the skin is chewy and substantial without being tough, with just a hint of crispness to play off the smooth, creamy filling. In terms of flavor, cheese and other dairy ingredients make the filling rich and tangy, a contrast with the mild, slightly sweet potato shell.

Because twice-baked potatoes are put in the oven twice, we found it best to bake them for just an hour, rather than the usual 75 minutes. Oiling the skins before baking promotes crispness, not something you necessarily want in plain baked potatoes but a trait we came to admire in creamy twice-baked potatoes.

Our baked potato recipe underscores the importance of opening the potatoes right after baking to release as much steam as possible. For twice-baked potatoes, it's advisable to wait a few minutes for the potatoes to cool before slicing them apart and emptying out the flesh; cooled potatoes are much easier to handle, and, because the flesh is mixed with wet ingredients, any compromise to the texture from unreleased moisture is negligible.

Once we had emptied the potato halves of their flesh, we noticed they got a little flabby sitting on the counter waiting to be stuffed. Because the oven was still on and waiting for the return of the stuffed halves, we decided to put the skins back in while we prepared the filling. This worked beautifully, giving the shells an extra dimension of crispness.

Pleased with our chewy, slightly crunchy skins, we now had to develop a smooth, lush, flavorful filling that would hold up its end of the bargain. (Lumpy, sodden, and dull-tasting would not do.) Dozens of further tests helped us refine our filling to a rich, but not killer, combination of sharp cheddar, sour cream, buttermilk, and just 2 tablespoons of butter. We learned to season the filling aggressively with salt and pepper; for herbs, the slightly sharp flavor of scallions or chives was best.

With the filling mixed and mounded back into the shells, our last tests centered on the final baking. We wanted to do more than just heat the filling through; we were intent on forming an attractive

---

INGREDIENTS: Potatoes

Dozens of potato varieties are grown in this country, and at any time you may see as many as five or six in your supermarket. Some potatoes are sold by varietal name (such as Yukon Gold), but others are sold by generic name (baking, all-purpose, etc.). To make sense of this confusion, we find it helpful to group potatoes into three major categories, based on the ratio of solids (mostly starch) to water. The categories are high-starch/low-moisture potatoes (often called starchy), medium-starch potatoes, and low-starch/high-moisture potatoes (often called waxy).

The high-starch/low-moisture category includes baking, russet, and white creamer potatoes. (The formal name for the russet is the russet Burbank potato, named after its developer, Luther Burbank of Idaho. This type of potato is also known as an Idaho. In all of our recipes, we call them russets.) These potatoes are best for baking and mashing. The medium-starch category includes all-purpose, Yukon Gold, Yellow Finn, and purple Peruvian potatoes. These potatoes can be mashed or baked but are generally not as fluffy as the high-starch potatoes. The low-starch/high-moisture category includes Red Bliss, red creamer, new, white rose, and fingerling potatoes. These potatoes are best roasted or boiled and used in salad.

brown crust on it as well. Broiling turned out to be the easiest and most effective method. After 15 minutes, the potatoes emerged browned, crusted, and ready for the table.

Twice-Baked Potatoes

SERVES 6 TO 8

To vary the flavor, try substituting other types of cheese, such as Gruyère, fontina, or feta, for the cheddar. Yukon Gold potatoes, though slightly more moist than our ideal, gave our twice-baked potatoes a buttery flavor and mouth-feel that our tasters liked, so we recommend them as a substitution for the russets.

4	medium russet potatoes (7 to 8 ounces each), scrubbed, dried, and rubbed lightly with vegetable oil
4	ounces sharp cheddar cheese, shredded (about 1 cup)
½	cup sour cream
½	cup buttermilk
2	tablespoons unsalted butter, room temperature
3	medium scallions, thinly sliced
½	teaspoon salt
	Ground black pepper

1. Adjust an oven rack to the upper-middle position and heat the oven to 400 degrees. Bake the potatoes on a foil-lined baking sheet until the skin is crisp and deep brown and a skewer easily pierces the flesh, about 1 hour. Setting the baking sheet aside, transfer the potatoes to a wire rack and let cool slightly, about 10 minutes.

2. Using an oven mitt or folded kitchen towel to handle the hot potatoes, cut each potato in half so that the long, rounded sides rest on a work surface. Using a small spoon, scoop the flesh from each half into a medium bowl, leaving a ⅛ to ¼ inch thickness of flesh in each shell. Arrange the shells on the lined baking sheet and return to the oven until dry and slightly crisped, about 10 minutes. Meanwhile, mash the potato flesh with a fork until smooth. Stir in the remaining ingredients, including pepper to taste, until well combined.

3. Remove the shells from the oven and increase the oven setting to broil. Holding the shells steady on a pan with an oven mitt or towel-protected hand, spoon the mixture into the crisped shells, mounding it slightly at the center, and return the potatoes to the oven. Broil until spotty brown and crisp on top, 10 to 15 minutes. Allow to cool for 10 minutes. Serve warm.

➤ VARIATIONS

Twice-Baked Potatoes with Pepper Jack Cheese and Bacon

Fry 8 strips (about 8 ounces) bacon, cut crosswise into ¼-inch pieces, in medium skillet over medium heat until crisp, 5 to 7 minutes. Remove bacon to paper towel–lined plate to drain; set aside. Follow the recipe for Twice-Baked Potatoes, substituting pepperjack cheese for the cheddar and stirring reserved bacon into the filling mixture.

Twice-Baked Potatoes with Smoked Salmon and Chives

This variation makes a fine brunch dish.

Follow the recipe for Twice-Baked Potatoes, omitting the cheese and scallions and stirring 4 ounces smoked salmon, cut into ½-inch pieces, and 3 tablespoons minced fresh chives into filling mixture. Sprinkle finished potatoes with additional chopped chives as a garnish just before serving.

MASHED POTATOES

MOST OF US WHO MAKE MASHED POTATOES would never consider consulting a recipe. We customarily make them by adding chunks of butter and spurts of cream until our conscience—or a backseat cook—tells us to stop. Not surprisingly, we produce batches of mashed potatoes that are consistent only in their mediocrity.

For us, the consummate mashed potatoes are creamy, soft, and supple, yet with enough body to stand up to sauce or gravy from an accompanying dish. As for flavor, the sweet, earthy, humble potato comes first, then the buttery richness that keeps you coming back for more.

We determined that high-starch potatoes, such as russets, are best for mashing (see page 62 for more information). Next we needed to address the simple matter of the best way to cook the potatoes. We started by peeling and cutting some potatoes into chunks to expedite their cooking while cooking others unpeeled and whole. Even when mashed with identical amounts of butter, half-and-half (recommended by a number of trustworthy cookbooks), and salt, the two batches were wildly different. The potatoes that had been peeled and cut made mashed potatoes that were thin in taste and texture and devoid of potato flavor, while those cooked whole and peeled after cooking yielded mashed potatoes that were rich, earthy, and sweet.

EQUIPMENT: Colanders

A colander is essentially a perforated bowl designed to allow liquid to drain through the holes. It has many uses, such as draining potatoes, pasta, and more. In our initial survey of models, we were not surprised to find colanders made from a range of materials: plastic, enameled steel, stainless steel, anodized aluminum, and wire mesh (which is like a screen). What did surprise us—and how—was the range of prices. Who would have thought that you could drop almost $115 on a simple colander? Especially in light of the price tag on the least expensive contestant, just $3.99. This made the idea of a test even more tantalizing.

As is our fashion in the test kitchen, we put the colanders through a battery of tests to obtain an objective assessment of their performance. We drained pounds and pounds of cooked spaghetti, orzo, and frozen baby peas in each one. Early in testing, we splashed scalding water and hot pasta out of a tiny 3-quart model by pouring it too fast from the cooking pot, so we eliminated that size from the running. The 5- and 7-quart models (10 altogether) performed on par, so we included both in our tests.

Most colanders on the market come with one of two types of bases, either a circular metal ring attached to the bottom, on which the bowl sits pedestal-style, or individual feet soldered to the bottom of the bowl. No matter which type it is, the base should be unfailingly stable to prevent spills. Our research and reading on colanders consistently noted the superiority of the ring over the feet, claiming that a colander on feet is less stable because it touches the ground in only three or four spots. That sounded like a reasonable theory to us until we tested the two models in the group with feet.

These colanders, the Endurance Stainless Steel Footed Colander and the Norpro Expanding Over-the-Sink Colander with Stand, were perfectly stable. During none of the tests did either one tip and spill its contents. (The Norpro can also be suspended between the sides of a sink by extending two metal arms. On our test kitchen sinks, this feature worked just fine, but on some sink designs this colander may be less stable.) In fact, the Endurance remained upright even when we accidentally bumped

it with a heavy stockpot. Similarly, and as we expected, the eight colanders with ring bases also enjoyed total stability. In our experience, then, though most colanders on the market have ring bases, you needn't shy away from a model with feet if that's what you happen to find.

We also expected that the size, placement, and pattern of the drainage holes would be key for quick, efficient draining. Seven of our 10 colanders had the look we expected, that of a metal or plastic bowl with perforations arranged in straight lines, starbursts, or circles; the remaining three had more unusual designs. True to its name, the Endurance Colander/Strainer (not the same as the Endurance footed colander) was a hybrid with a metal bowl that was so thoroughly perforated it almost looked like wire mesh. Two other colanders, the Harold Imports and the Norpro expandable colander, were made from wire mesh, like a strainer. These three colanders had more holes than their more traditional counterparts, and each one performed very well, draining quickly and completely, with no pooling of water and no food—even the wily orzo—slipping through the holes. In truth, though, all of the other colanders also met—or came darn close to meeting—these standards. The traditional colanders with larger holes did allow some orzo to slip through (anywhere from just a few pieces for the Rösle to almost three-quarters of a cup for the Silverstone), but only the Silverstone allowed so much orzo through that it merited a downgrade in the ratings.

When all was said and drained, every colander in the group got the job done, be it the $4 Hoan plastic model or the gleaming $115 Rösle stainless steel model. To make a recommendation, then, we have to be a bit more subjective than usual. So here it is: Based on this testing and our gut feeling, the colander we'd most like to bring home is the Endurance Colander/Strainer. It's reasonably priced at $25, it's solid and comfortable to wield, it drains like a pro and keeps all its contents in check, and many editors here considered it to be an unusually handsome specimen of a colander. When it comes to this basic kitchen utensil, extra money is not well spent.

We talked to several food scientists, who explained that peeling and cutting the potatoes before simmering increases the surface area through which they lose soluble substances, such as starch, proteins, and flavor compounds, to the cooking water. The greater surface area also enables lots of water molecules to bind with the potatoes' starch molecules. Combine these two effects and you've got bland, thin, watery mashed potatoes.

Next were the matters of butter and dairy. Working with 2 pounds of potatoes, which serve four to six, we stooped so low as to add only 2 tablespoons of butter. The potatoes ultimately deemed best in flavor by tasters contained 8 tablespoons. They were rich and full and splendid.

When considering dairy, we investigated both the kind and the quantity. Heavy cream made heavy mashed potatoes that were sodden and unpalatably rich, even when we scaled back the amount of butter. On the other hand, mashed potatoes made with whole milk were watery, wimpy, and washed out. When we tried adding more butter to compensate for the milk's lack of richness, the mixture turned into potato soup. Half-and-half, which we'd used in our original tests, was just what was needed, and 1 cup was just the right amount. The mashed potatoes now had a lovely light suppleness and a full, rich flavor that edged toward decadent.

The issues attending butter and dairy did not end there. We had heard that the order in which they are added to the potatoes can affect texture and that melted butter makes better mashed potatoes than softened butter. Determined to leave no spud unturned, we threw several more pounds into the pot. As it turns out, when the butter goes in before the dairy, the result is a silkier, creamier, smoother texture than when the dairy goes first; by comparison, the dairy-first potatoes were pasty and thick. Using melted rather than softened butter made the potatoes even more creamy, smooth, and light.

With our curiosity piqued by the significant textural differences effected by minor differences in procedure, we again contacted several food scientists, who explained that when the half-and-half is stirred into the potatoes before the butter, the water in it works with the starch in the potatoes to make the mashed potatoes gluey and heavy. When the butter is added before the half-and-half, the fat coats the starch molecules, inhibiting their interaction with the water in the half-and-half added later and thereby yielding silkier, creamier mashed potatoes. The benefit of using melted butter results from its liquid form, which enables it to coat the starch molecules quickly and easily. This buttery coating not only affects the interaction of the starch molecules with the half-and-half, it also affects the starch molecules'

SCIENCE: Stress-Free Spud Storage

Because potatoes seem almost indestructible compared with other vegetables, generally little thought is given to their storage. But problems can result from inadequate storage conditions, so we decided to find out how much difference storage really made. We stored all-purpose potatoes in five environments: in a cool (50–60 degrees), dark place; in the refrigerator; in a basket near a sunlit window; in a warm (70–80 degrees), dark place; and in a drawer with some onions at room temperature. We checked all the potatoes after four weeks.

As expected, the potatoes stored in the cool, dark place were firm, had not sprouted, and were crisp and moist when cut. There were no negative marks on the potatoes stored in the refrigerator, either. Although some experts say that the sugar level dramatically increases in some potato varieties under these conditions, we could not see or taste any difference between these potatoes and the ones stored in the cool, dark, but unrefrigerated environment.

Our last three storage tests produced unfavorable results. The potatoes stored in sunlight, in warm storage, and with onions ended up with a greenish tinge along the edges. When potatoes are stressed by improper storage, the level of naturally occurring toxins increases, causing the greenish tinge known as solanine. Because solanine is not destroyed by heat, any part of the potato with this greenish coloring should be completely cut away before cooking.

The skin of the potatoes stored in sunlight became gray and mottled, while the potatoes stored in a warm place and those stored with onions sprouted and became soft and wrinkled. Sprouts also contain increased levels of solanine and should be cut away before cooking.

interaction with each other. All in all, it makes for smoother, more velvety mashed potatoes. (Melting the butter, as well as warming the half-and-half, also serves to keep the potatoes warm.)

There is more than one way to mash potatoes. In our testing, we had been using either a ricer or a food mill. We preferred the food mill because its large hopper accommodated half of the potatoes at a time. A ricer, which resembles an oversized garlic press, required processing in several batches. Both, however, produced smooth, light, fine-textured mashed potatoes.

A potato masher is the tool of choice for making chunky mashed potatoes, but it cannot produce smooth mashed potatoes on a par with those processed through a food mill or ricer. With a masher, potatoes mashed within an inch of their lives could not achieve anything better than a namby-pamby texture that was neither chunky nor perfectly smooth. Since the sentiment among our tasters was that mashed potatoes should be either smooth or coarse

and craggy, a masher is best left to make the latter.

There are two styles of potato mashers—one is a disk with large holes in it, the other a curvy wire loop. We found the disk to be more efficient for reducing both mashing time and the number of lumps in the finished product.

~~~

Mashed Potatoes

SERVES 4 TO 6

Russet potatoes make slightly fluffier mashed potatoes, but Yukon Golds have an appealing buttery flavor and can be used if you prefer. Mashed potatoes stiffen and become gluey as they cool, so they are best served piping hot. If you must hold mashed potatoes before serving, place them in a heat-proof bowl, cover the bowl tightly with plastic wrap, and set the bowl over a pot of simmering water. The potatoes will remain hot and soft-textured for one hour. This recipe can be increased by half or doubled as needed. This recipe yields smooth mashed potatoes. If you don't mind (or prefer) lumps, use a potato masher, as directed in the variation.

EQUIPMENT: Food Mills

A food mill is no longer a fixture in American kitchens, but it is a terrific tool to have on hand. Think of it as part food processor, because it refines soft foods to a puree, and part sieve, because it separates waste such as peels, seeds, cores, and fiber from the puree. And it accomplishes all of this with the simple turn of a crank, which rotates a gently angled, curved blade. The blade catches the food and forces it down through the holes of a perforated disk at the bottom of the mill. The separation of unwanted material from the puree is the food mill's raison d'être, but another benefit is that it does not aerate the food as it purees, as do food processors and blenders, so you are able to avoid an overly whipped, lightened texture. (In the case of mashed potatoes, a food processor or blender creates a gummy texture.)

Since you can spend as little as $15 and as much as $100 on a food mill (some really huge mills cost as much as $200), we wondered if some were better than others. We gathered six different models (including an electric one) and used them to make mashed potatoes and applesauce. Honestly, there was very little difference in the resulting purees—they were all fine, smooth, and free of unwanted material. Thus, we evaluated the mills more on design factors, such as how easy it was to turn the crank, how efficiently the food was processed, and whether the mills offered

adjustments in the texture of the puree produced.

The best mills in the group were the beautiful stainless steel Cuisipro, the VEV Vigano, and the white plastic Moulinex. Each one was easy to crank and efficient, and they all came with fine, medium, and coarse disks. The top performer of the three was the Cuisipro, but at $80, it was also the most expensive. The $15 Moulinex did nearly as well, so it became the pick of the pack for its combination of low price and high performance. The plastic is surely not as strong as the Cuisipro's stainless steel, but for occasional use, it is just fine.

Both the Foley and the Norpro mills were noticeably less efficient; their blades pushed the food around instead of forcing it though the perforated disk. In addition, neither one offered additional disks for different textures. There was just one medium disk, fixed in place. But the real loser was the Kenwood Passi Electric food mill. Though it was easier than hand-cranking, the power button did not have an "on" position, so the user had to hold it in place. And it took forever to process the food, which went around and around in the hopper. Also, the blade could not be cranked in the reverse direction (as it could on all of the manual models), so there was no way to loosen the food when it got stuck.

2 pounds russet potatoes, scrubbed
8 tablespoons unsalted butter, melted
1 cup half-and-half, warmed
1½ teaspoons salt
   Ground black pepper

1. Place the potatoes in a large saucepan with cold water to cover by about 1 inch. Bring to a boil over high heat, reduce the heat to medium-low, and simmer until the potatoes are just tender when pricked with a thin-bladed knife, 20 to 30 minutes. Drain saucepan and remove potatoes.

2. Set the food mill or ricer over the now empty but still warm saucepan. Spear a potato with a dinner fork, then peel back the skin with a paring knife (see illustration 1 below). Repeat with the remaining potatoes. Working in batches, cut the peeled potatoes

MAKING MASHED POTATOES

1. Hold the drained potato with a dinner fork and peel off the skin with a paring knife.

2. Cut the peeled potato into rough chunks, then drop the chunks into the food mill.

into rough chunks and drop into the hopper of food mill or ricer (see illustration 2 below). Process or rice the potatoes into the saucepan.

3. Stir in the butter with a wooden spoon until incorporated. Gently whisk in the half-and-half, salt, and pepper to taste. Serve immediately.

➤ VARIATIONS

Lumpy Mashed Potatoes
For silky, smooth mashed potatoes, use a food mill or ricer. For chunky mashed potatoes, use a potato masher.

Follow the recipe for Mashed Potatoes, dropping the peeled potato chunks back in the warm saucepan and mashing with a potato masher until fairly smooth. Proceed as directed, reducing the half-and-half to ¾ cup.

Garlic Mashed Potatoes
Toasted garlic contributes the truest, purest garlic flavor imaginable to mashed potatoes. Best of all, the garlic can be peeled after toasting, when the skins will slip right off. Just make sure to keep the heat low and to let the garlic stand off heat until fully softened.

Toast 22 small to medium-large garlic cloves (about ⅔ cup), skins left on, in a small covered skillet over the lowest possible heat, shaking the pan frequently, until the cloves are dark spotty brown and slightly softened, about 22 minutes. Remove the pan from the heat and let stand, covered, until the cloves are fully softened, 15 to 20 minutes. Peel the cloves and, using a paring knife, cut off the woody root end. Follow the recipe for Mashed Potatoes, dropping the peeled garlic cloves into the food mill or ricer with peeled potatoes.

Mashed Potatoes with Root Vegetables
Most root vegetables are more watery than potatoes, so you will need less than the full cup of half-and-half.

Follow the recipe for Mashed Potatoes, replacing 1 pound of potatoes with 1 pound of parsnips, rutabagas, celery root, carrots, or turnips that have been peeled and cut into 1½- to 2-inch chunks. Add the half-and-half ¼ cup at a time until the desired consistency is obtained.

Buttermilk Mashed Potatoes

Buttermilk gives mashed potatoes a pleasing tang and rich texture, even when less butter is used. If you are interested in mashed potatoes with less fat, this is your best option.

Follow the recipe for Mashed Potatoes, reducing the butter to 1 tablespoon and replacing the half-and-half with 1 cup warmed buttermilk.

STEAK FRIES

STEAK FRIES ARE THE RUSTIC, COUNTRY cousin to French fries. With their skin left on and their shape determined largely by the shape of the potato, these wedge-shaped fries are easier to prepare and less wasteful than the typical French fry, where much effort is expended to obtain ruler-perfect consistency. Much like good French fries, however, good steak fries should be crisp on the outside and tender on the inside. They should not be oily, dry, mealy, or soggy.

To start, we needed to find the right potato. Would it be starchy or waxy? (See "Starch in Potatoes" at right.) We tested two of the most popular waxy potatoes, and neither was even close to ideal, both being too watery. During frying, water evaporated inside the potato, leaving hollows that would fill with oil, so the finished fries were greasy. Next we tested the starchy potato most readily available nationwide, the russet. This potato turned out to be ideal, frying up with all the qualities that we were looking for. Its dense, starchy texture cooked to a consistently tender interior while its thick skin fried up good and crisp.

Russets we bought in 5-pound bags, however, came in various sizes and were difficult to cut into uniformly sized wedges. We found russets that are sold loose are more consistent in size and are easier to cut into same-sized wedges for more consistent cooking times. After cooking up fries of various thicknesses, we preferred wedges with an outside edge that measures ¾ inch wide—this works out to one large potato cut into 12 wedges. Any thicker or thinner and the ratio of tender interior to crisp exterior was thrown off.

Many recipes for deep-fried potatoes suggest refrigerating the raw wedges before frying them, and

SCIENCE: Starch in Potatoes

Potatoes are composed mostly of starch and water. The starch is in the form of granules, which in turn are contained in starch cells. The higher the starch content of the potato, the more packed the cells. In high-starch potatoes (russets are a good example), the cells are completely full—they look like plump little beach balls. In medium-starch (Yukon Golds) and low-starch potatoes (Red Bliss), the cells look more like underinflated beach balls. The space between these less-than-full cells is taken up mostly by water.

In our tests, we found that the full starch cells of high-starch potatoes are most likely to maintain their integrity and stay separate when mashed, giving the potatoes a delightfully fluffy texture. In addition, the low water content of these potatoes allows them to absorb milk, cream, and/or butter without becoming wet or gummy. Starch cells in lower-starch potatoes, on the other hand, tend to clump when cooked and break more easily, allowing the starch to dissolve into whatever liquid is present. The broken cells and dissolved starch tend to produce sticky, gummy mashed potatoes.

However, the high moisture content of red potatoes makes them an excellent choice for dishes such as potato salad, where you want the potatoes to hold their shape. Because they contain a fair amount of moisture, they don't absorb much water as they boil. In contrast, low-moisture russets suck up water when boiled and fall apart. The resulting potato salad tastes starchy and looks sloppy.

we found this step to be crucial. Cooling the potatoes down before plunging them in the hot oil allows them to cook more slowly and evenly. By soaking the wedges in a refrigerated bowl of ice water for at least 30 minutes, we were able to ensure that the inner pulp was fully cooked before the outside turned overly brown.

Like most who've fried potatoes before us, we found that simply dunking the chilled, raw fries in hot oil and cooking them until they are done will not produce a good fry. By the time the inside of the fry is cooked and the outside is well browned, the fry itself is wooden and overcooked. Although this technique may work with thinner shoestring-style fries, it doesn't work with thickly cut steak fries. Following the lead of many other recipes, we tried double-frying the potatoes. We first par-fried them at a relatively low temperature to help them cook through without much browning. We then gave them a brief repose to cool off before refrying them quickly in oil at a higher temperature until nicely browned. In combination with the ice water bath, this technique worked like a dream. The thick wedges of potato were evenly cooked, with tender middles and crisp, browned exteriors.

Although many recipes call for par-frying in 350-degree oil and final frying at 375 to 400 degrees, we found these temperatures far too aggressive for thick-cut steak fries. We prefer an initial frying at 325 degrees, with the final frying at 350 degrees. Lower temperatures allowed for easier monitoring; with higher temperatures, the fries can get away from the cook.

Our last test involved different types of frying oils. We experimented with lard, vegetable shortening, canola oil, corn oil, and peanut oil. Lard and shortening make great fries, but we figured that many cooks won't want to use these products. While canola oil produced bland, almost watery fries, we liked the results from both corn and peanut oils. Corn oil offered a clean flavor and rebounded well from temperature fluctuations. Peanut oil, we found, produced light fries, rich but not dense, with an earthy flavor. Although corn oil is fine for frying potatoes, tasters gave the peanut oil a slight edge.

Steak Fries

SERVES 4 TO 6

See illustrations at left for tips on cutting potatoes into wedges.

4   large russet potatoes (about 10 ounces each), scrubbed and cut lengthwise into ¾-inch-thick wedges (about 12 wedges per potato)
2   quarts peanut oil
    Salt and ground black pepper

1. Place the cut fries in a large bowl, cover with cold water by at least 1 inch, and then cover with ice cubes. Refrigerate at least 30 minutes or for up to 3 days.

2. In a 5-quart pot or Dutch oven fitted with a clip-on candy thermometer, or in a large electric fryer, heat the oil over medium-low heat to 325 degrees. (The oil will bubble up when you add the fries, so be sure you have at least 3 inches of room at the top of the pot.)

3. Pour off the ice and water, quickly wrap the potatoes in a clean kitchen towel and thoroughly pat them dry. Increase the heat to medium-high and add the fries, one handful at a time, to the hot oil. Fry, stirring with a Chinese skimmer or large-holed slotted spoon, until the potatoes are limp and soft and have turned from white to gold, about 10 minutes. (The oil temperature will drop 50 to 60 degrees during this frying.) Use a skimmer or slotted spoon to transfer the fries to a triple thickness of paper towels to drain; let rest at least 10 minutes. (The fries can stand at room temperature for up to 2 hours or be wrapped in paper towels, sealed in a plastic zipper-lock bag, and frozen for up to 1 month.)

4. When ready to serve the fries, reheat the oil to 350 degrees. Using the paper towels as a funnel, pour the potatoes into the hot oil. Discard the paper

CUTTING POTATOES INTO WEDGES

1. Cut each potato in half lengthwise. Place the potato half flat-side down and cut into thirds lengthwise.

2. Cut each piece of potato in half lengthwise to yield 12 wedges that measure ¾ inch across on the skin side.

towels and line a wire rack with another triple thickness of paper towels. Fry the potatoes, stirring fairly constantly, until medium brown and puffed, 8 to 10 minutes. Transfer to the paper towel–lined rack to drain. Season to taste with salt and pepper. Serve immediately.

SCALLOPED POTATOES

THINLY SLICED POTATOES LAYERED WITH cream and baked until they are bubbling and browned are a classic accompaniment to a holiday ham or roast beef. Although the supermarket shelves are lined with "add water, heat, and serve" versions of scalloped potatoes, making them from scratch doesn't take much time, and the difference in flavor and texture is tremendous. Our goal was to create a rich but simple version of this classic dish.

To start, we tested three different techniques for "scalloping" potatoes. First, we boiled the potatoes, combined them with a thickened cream sauce (also known as a béchamel), and then finished them in the oven. This method produced a thick, pasty sauce and hollow-flavored potatoes, not to mention several dirty pots. We also tried to combine the raw, sliced potatoes with an unthickened cream sauce, allowing it to cook through and thicken in the oven. While these potatoes had more flavor and the sauce had a better consistency, the cooking time was more than an hour and a half.

Wanting to speed the process up, we tried cooking the potatoes in simmering cream for a few minutes before transferring the potatoes and cream to a casserole dish and finishing the potatoes in the oven. This technique allowed the potatoes to get a head start on cooking and also encouraged them to release some of their starch, which naturally thickened the cream to the consistency of a good sauce. We did find it necessary to cover the pot to prevent the heavy cream and the starch from reducing and thickening too far in advance. By cooking the potatoes in the cream, covered, for about 15 minutes, we were able to reduce the oven time to a mere 20 minutes, resulting in perfectly cooked potatoes and a smooth, lightly thickened cream sauce.

With the technique set, we moved on to the different types of potatoes, testing Yukon Gold, all-purpose, and russet. Although each variety cooked up differently, none was terrible. Yukon Gold and all-purpose potatoes were both a bit too waxy and buttery when mixed with the rich cream. Russet potatoes turned out slightly more tender, and their earthier flavor was the tasters' favorite. The thickness of the potato slices also made a noticeable difference in the final texture of the casserole. We found that potatoes cut into ⅛-inch-thick slices kept their shape but were still flexible enough to form tight layers that stuck together to form a neat casserole. Thicker slices formed a looser, sloppier casserole, while thinner slices melted together and gave the finished dish the texture of mashed potatoes.

Focusing now on the sauce, we noticed that those made with all heavy cream were overbearingly

EQUIPMENT: Vegetable Peelers

You might imagine that all vegetable peelers are pretty much the same. Not so. In our research, we turned up 25 peelers, many with quite novel features. The major differences were the fixture of the blade, either stationary or swiveling; the material of the blade, carbon stainless steel, stainless steel, or ceramic; and the orientation of the blade to the handle, either straight in line with the body or perpendicular to it. The last arrangement, with the blade perpendicular to the handle, is called a harp, or Y, peeler because the frame looks like the body of a harp or the letter Y. This type of peeler, which is popular in Europe, works with a pulling motion rather than the shucking motion of most American peelers.

To test the peelers, we recruited several cooks and asked them to peel carrots, potatoes, lemons, butternut squash, and celery root. In most cases, testers preferred the Oxo Good Grips peeler with a sharp stainless steel blade that swivels. Peelers with stationary blades are fine for peeling carrots, but they have trouble hugging the curves on potatoes.

The Y-shaped peelers tested well, although they removed more flesh along with the skin on potatoes, lemons, and carrots and therefore did not rate as well as the Oxo Good Grips. The one case where this liability turned into an asset was with butternut squash, where these Y-shaped peelers took off the skin as well as the greenish-tinged flesh right below the skin in one pass. With the Oxo Good Grips, it was necessary to go over the peeled flesh once the skin had been removed.

heavy. We tried half-and-half but found that it wasn't rich enough. Even worse, the sauce made with half-and-half curdled in the oven. (Half-and-half simply doesn't have enough fat to keep the dairy proteins from coagulating under high heat, which makes the sauce curdle.) In the end, we simply tempered the heavy cream with a little whole milk, which lightened the rich sauce just enough while keeping its texture smooth.

Now the potatoes needed some seasoning. We started with delicate, fragrant shallots but found their flavor too subtle. A small onion, on the other hand, tasted great when sautéed in the pot with a little butter before adding the cream and potatoes. Garlic added another dimension of flavor, while sprigs of thyme and a few bay leaves infused the cream with the taste of fresh herbs, which was pleasant without being distracting.

Scalloped potatoes also contain cheese. We found that a sprinkling of cheese formed a golden crust on the top of the dish while still allowing the cream to bubble up around the edges and thicken. Cheddar is the classic choice, but we got nice results with other cheeses with good melting properties, including Parmesan, Monterey Jack, and Gruyère.

Scalloped Potatoes

SERVES 8 TO 10

For the fastest and most consistent results, slice the potatoes in a food processor.

2	tablespoons unsalted butter
1	small onion, minced
2	medium cloves garlic, minced
3	cups heavy cream
1	cup whole milk
4	sprigs fresh thyme leaves
2	bay leaves
2	teaspoons salt
1/2	teaspoon ground black pepper
4	pounds russet potatoes, cut into 1/8-inch-thick slices
1	cup shredded cheddar cheese (about 4 ounces)

1. Heat oven to 350 degrees. Meanwhile, melt the butter in a large Dutch oven over medium-high heat until foaming subsides, about 1 minute. Add the onion and sauté until it turns soft and begins to brown, about 4 minutes. Add the garlic and sauté until fragrant, about 30 seconds. Add the cream, milk, thyme, bay leaves, salt, pepper, and potatoes and bring to a simmer. Cover, adjusting the heat as necessary to maintain a light simmer, and cook until the potatoes are almost tender (a paring knife can be slipped into and out of the center of a potato slice with some resistance), about 15 minutes.

2. Transfer the potato mixture to a 3-quart gratin dish and sprinkle with cheese. Bake until the cream has thickened and is bubbling around the sides and the top is golden brown, about 20 minutes. Cool for 5 minutes before serving.

➤ VARIATION

Scalloped Potatoes with Wild Mushrooms
Cover 1/2 ounce dried porcini mushroom pieces with 1/2 cup hot tap water in small microwave-safe bowl; cover with plastic wrap, cut several steam vents in plastic with a paring knife, and microwave on high power for 30 seconds. Let stand until the mushrooms soften, about 5 minutes. Lift the mushrooms from the liquid with a fork and mince, using a chef's knife (you should have about 2 tablespoons). Pour the soaking liquid through a strainer lined with a paper towel and reserve. Follow the recipe for Scalloped Potatoes, adding 3 1/2 ounces fresh shiitake mushrooms, sliced 1/4 inch thick, and 5 ounces fresh cremini mushrooms, sliced 1/4 inch thick, to the foaming butter along with the onions and cook until the mushrooms release their moisture, about 2 minutes. Add minced, rehydrated porcini along with their liquid and cook until all mushrooms are tender and liquid has reduced to about 2 tablespoons, about 3 minutes. Add the garlic and proceed as directed, replacing cheddar with Gruyère or Parmesan.

Candied Sweet Potatoes

CANDIED SWEET POTATOES ARE A TRADITIONAL side dish served alongside a roast ham or Thanksgiving turkey. All too often, however, they turn out watery, overseasoned, and overly sweet, tasting more like a loose, crustless pumpkin pie than a savory side dish. We wanted lightly seasoned and perfectly cooked sweet potatoes soft enough to slice with a fork yet resilient enough not to fall through the fork tines while being eaten.

To start, we followed the method touted in many cookbooks and boiled peeled pieces of sweet potato before tossing them with a brown sugar and butter sauce. Despite the popularity of the method, we found these sweet potatoes to be watery and lacking in flavor. Boiling the sweet potatoes washed away vital flavors and added moisture that was difficult to get rid of. We tried partially cooking the sweet potatoes in the microwave before mixing them with the sauce but found that they overcooked easily while the sauce still lacked substantial flavor. Next we tossed raw, peeled pieces of sweet potato with brown sugar and butter and baked them in a covered casserole dish. This method also produced a watery sauce as well as unevenly cooked potatoes. As the brown sugar and butter began to melt, the potatoes leached some of their liquid, making a watery cooking solution in which the potatoes began to float. It was difficult to keep these floating potatoes completely submerged, and any unsubmerged parts of potato dried out.

We had better luck once we tried cooking the potatoes on the stove top. By cooking the potatoes in a Dutch oven with butter and brown sugar, the flavors of the potatoes and the sauce melded. Lubricated with a little water and covered, the potatoes cooked perfectly in about 50 minutes resulting in the ultimate candied sweet potatoes, with a rich and complex sauce. Although the sauce was still a bit watery when we removed the lid, it was easy to crank up the heat and reduce it quickly to a thicker consistency.

We then tested adding chicken broth, wine, and cider, but tasters preferred the clean taste of the sweet potatoes on their own, seasoned with only a little salt and pepper. While a few tasters preferred the flavor of dark brown sugar to light brown, most found it overpowering. White sugar, on the other hand, was unanimously deemed too bland. We also tried all sorts of spices and herbs, but tasters once again preferred the simple flavors of sweet potatoes

seasoned only with salt and pepper. Several spice and herb concoctions, however, scored well and are offered as variations, as is the classic marshmallow topping.

~

Candied Sweet Potatoes

SERVES 8 TO 10

For a more intense molasses flavor, use dark brown sugar in place of light brown sugar.

- 8 tablespoons unsalted butter, cut into 1-inch pieces
- 6 medium sweet potatoes (about 3¾ pounds), peeled, cut lengthwise into quarters, and then cut crosswise into 1-inch pieces
- 1 cup packed light brown sugar
- 1 teaspoon salt
- ¼ teaspoon ground black pepper

1. Melt the butter in a large Dutch oven over medium-high heat until the foaming subsides, about 1 minute. Add the sweet potatoes, sugar, salt, pepper, and ½ cup water and bring to a simmer. Reduce the heat to medium-low and cover. Cook until the sweet potatoes are tender (a paring knife can be slipped into and out of the center of the potatoes with very little resistance), 45 to 55 minutes, stirring often (every 5 minutes or so).

2. When the sweet potatoes are tender, remove the lid and bring the sauce to a rapid simmer over medium-high heat. Simmer until the sauce has reduced to a glaze, about 10 minutes. Remove the pot from the heat and serve immediately.

➤ VARIATIONS

Candied Sweet Potatoes with Marshmallows

Follow the recipe for Candied Sweet Potatoes through step 1. While the sweet potatoes are simmering, adjust an oven rack so it is 6 inches from the broiler element and heat the broiler. When the sweet potatoes are tender, transfer them to an ovenproof casserole dish and top with 4 cups minimarshmallows. Place the casserole under the broiler until the marshmallows are brown and have melted slightly, 3 to 4 minutes. Serve immediately.

Candied Sweet Potatoes with Orange and Star Anise

Follow the recipe for Candied Sweet Potatoes, replacing water with ½ cup orange juice. Add 2 pieces star anise and 1 teaspoon vanilla extract along with the potatoes in step 1 and proceed as directed, discarding the star anise just before serving.

Candied Sweet Potatoes with Honey, Cardamom, and Ginger

Follow the recipe for Candied Sweet Potatoes, replacing ¼ cup of the light brown sugar with an equal amount of honey. Add 1 teaspoon ground cardamom, 1 teaspoon vanilla extract, and 1 teaspoon grated fresh ginger to the pot along with the sweet potatoes. Proceed as directed.

MASHED TURNIPS

SIMILAR TO MASHED POTATOES, MASHED turnips are smooth and creamy, with an added edge of tangy flavor. When cooked poorly, they are bitter, fibrous, and watery. When cooked well, their light, fluffy texture and unique flavor, accented with a little butter and fresh cream, make a welcome break from the same old dish of potatoes.

To start, we tested both white and yellow turnips. While the white turnips (their skins are blushed with purple) were downright awful, with their harsh, overpowering flavor, the yellow turnips (also known as rutabagas) were pleasantly mild and mellow. Although the flavor of the white turnips can be tempered by mixing them with other root vegetables such as potato or parsnip, we chose to use 100 percent yellow turnips, or rutabagas, which needed no such doctoring.

While the flavor of the yellow turnips was far superior, the puree had an unacceptably starchy and fibrous texture, resembling loose polenta. Wanting a tighter, smoother consistency, we focused on the cooking method. Many recipes simply peel, dice, and boil the turnips before mashing them with cream and butter, but we had little success with this technique. Even when the boiled turnips were thoroughly cooked, dried, and forced through a food mill or ricer, the texture of the puree was mealy and loose.

Next we tried microwaving the turnips whole, a method we often use for stringy sweet potatoes. While this method made a tighter puree, it still had a mealy, tapioca-like quality and the turnips were easy to overcook. Finally, we tried steaming, and although the resulting puree was still slightly mealy, it was not loose, and the cooking process was easy to control. To combat the mealy starchiness, we put the steamed turnips in the food processor. Unlike potatoes, which turn to glue when cooked and processed, the turnips suddenly became a smooth and silky puree.

With a smooth puree in hand, we were ready to add the butter and dairy. Testing heavy cream, half-and-half, and whole milk, tasters preferred the full rich flavor of heavy cream. Because mashed turnips are not nearly as starchy as mashed potatoes, much less cream is required to loosen their texture and add flavor. After testing various amounts of heavy cream and butter, we found 2 pounds of turnips (enough for four people) had the best consistency and flavor when mixed with 4 tablespoons of butter and ½ cup of heavy cream.

Wondering if the order in which the butter and heavy cream are added to the mixture would make a difference (as it does with potatoes), we tasted three batches side by side: one in which the butter was added before the cream, another in which the cream was added before the butter, and the last in which the butter and cream were tossed into the food processor right along with the cooked turnips. As is the case with mashed potatoes, the butter-first batch turned out far lighter and creamier than the other batches. By comparison, the cream-first potatoes were pasty and thick while the all-ingredients-at-once batch was stiff and starchy tasting.

What process was at work here? We learned that when butter is added before cream, the fat coats the starch molecules, inhibiting their interaction with the water in the cream once it is added, yielding a silkier, creamier puree. Melted butter works better than solid butter because the liquid can coat the starch molecules more quickly and easily. This buttery coating also affects the starch molecules' interaction with each other. All in all, it makes for smoother, more velvety mashed turnips.

Our final task was to see if any flavorings or spices

would benefit the mix. We tried nutmeg, allspice, and cinnamon and found the flavor of each to be overpowering, marring the clean, turnip flavor. Instead, tasters preferred the simple, straightforward flavor of turnips seasoned with salt, pepper, and a pinch of sugar (to bring out the turnips' natural sweetness), plus the gentle flavor of fresh thyme when quickly steeped in the heavy cream.

Mashed Yellow Turnips (Rutabagas)

SERVES 4

The hot cream should be ready just as the turnips go into the food processor. If you prepare the cream too far ahead of time a skin will form on the surface. If you start step 2 when the turnips have been steaming for 25 minutes, the timing should work out perfectly.

2	pounds yellow turnips, peeled and cut into ½-inch pieces
½	cup heavy cream
2	sprigs fresh thyme (optional)
	Salt and ground black pepper
	Pinch sugar
4	tablespoons unsalted butter, melted

1. Bring about 1 inch water to boil over high heat in a large soup kettle or saucepan set up with a wire rack, steamer, or pasta insert. Add the turnips, cover, and return the water to a boil. Reduce the heat to medium-high and steam until the turnips are tender, about 30 minutes.

2. Meanwhile, bring the cream, thyme, ¾ teaspoon salt, ¼ teaspoon pepper, and sugar to a simmer in a small saucepan over medium heat. Remove the pan from the heat and discard the thyme.

3. Remove the turnips from the steamer and place in the workbowl of a food processor fitted with a steel blade. Process the hot turnips until smooth, scraping down the sides as necessary, about 1 minute. Transfer the turnip puree to a clean bowl.

4. Stir the melted butter into the turnip puree and gently incorporate with a rubber spatula. Gently stir in the hot cream. Adjust the seasonings with salt and pepper to taste and serve immediately.

STUFFED TOMATOES

OUR PAST EXPERIENCES WITH OVEN-BAKED stuffed tomatoes have not exactly been great. Still, when we are presented with one, the thought of its potential juicy tenderness and warmth is too temping to pass up. We succumb to the hope that maybe this time the stuffed tomato will live up to its potential, only to be let down by the first bite into sodden mediocrity.

What irks us is that the stuffed tomato's singular components hold forth the promise of perfection. What could be better than a ripe, sun-drenched summer tomato, garden-fresh herbs, garlicky bread crumbs, and a sprightly bite of sharp cheese? When these elements are brought together into one vessel, however, their divinity dissipates. The once buxom tomato becomes mealy and bland, and the flavor of the stuffing is drowned within the waterlogged texture of the bread. Determined to save this traditional dish from the bland and watery depths, we set out to prove that an oven-baked stuffed tomato can taste as good as we've always imagined.

We began testing by following the directions called for in most cookbook recipes: stuff a hollowed-out, raw beefsteak tomato with a bread crumb filling and bake it at 375 degrees for 30 minutes. The outcome was a soggy mess. The tomato was bland and watery, and the stuffing tasted dull and overly moist. What's more, the tomato seemed to lack the structural strength to keep the filling intact. We concluded that perhaps the same element that lends majesty to a tomato—water—was the source of our failure.

Ridding the tomato of its excess liquid was our goal. At first we tested oven drying, rationalizing that the slow, low heat would concentrate the tomato's sweetness and vaporize the water. The dried tomato was laden with rich flavor notes, but it was also shriveled and shrunken, a collapsed vessel that was in no condition to hold any stuffing.

We then wondered whether choosing a tomato with a naturally lower water content, such as a plum tomato, might eliminate the water issue altogether. While we did end up with a meaty and sweet stuffed tomato, it lacked the complexity of flavor that the beefsteak possessed, and the effort required to stuff the smaller shell—coupled with the fact that we would have to make twice as many if we were substituting for beefsteak tomatoes—turned us off the plum variety.

Recalling how salt is used to sweat eggplant, we thought it might do the same for a tomato. We cored and seeded a beefsteak, rubbed salt into its interior, and placed it upside down on a stack of paper towels. Within 30 minutes, our dry paper towels had absorbed a tremendous amount of liquid. Dr. Bill Morris, professor in the University of Tennessee's department of food science and technology, explained that when we salted the interior of the tomato, water passed through the cells' semipermeable membranes, moving from the inside of the cells to the outside, in effect, draining the tomato of its excess juices. In addition, the salt brightened and enhanced the tomato's flavor.

Now that we had the moisture problem solved, we moved on to stuffing, baking times, and temperatures. For the stuffing, we tested store-bought bread crumbs, homemade bread crumbs made from stale French bread, and variations in the ratio of crumbs to cheese to herbs. The fine, store-bought crumbs were dry and gritty. Their homemade counterpart, on the other hand, absorbed the tomato's juices yet still provided an interesting chew and crunch, especially when paired with garlic, olive oil, and tangy Parmesan cheese.

Our previous oven-roasting experiment negated a low and long baking period, whereas experiments baking the tomato at an extremely high temperature (450 degrees) for a short time yielded burnt, crusty stuffing and a raw tomato. Baked at 375 degrees for 20 minutes, the tomatoes were tender and topped with a lovely golden crust. The result: a sweet-and-savory-tomato triumph.

Stuffed Tomatoes with Parmesan, Garlic, and Basil

SERVES 6 AS A SIDE DISH

To make bread crumbs, grind any hunk of stale country, Italian, or French bread in the food processor.

6   large (about 8 ounces each) firm, ripe tomatoes, 1/8 inch sliced off stem end, cored, and seeded
1   teaspoon kosher salt
3/4   cup coarse homemade bread crumbs
1   teaspoon plus 3 tablespoons olive oil
1/3   cup grated Parmesan cheese (about 1 1/2 ounces)
1/3   cup chopped fresh basil leaves
2   medium cloves garlic, minced (about 2 teaspoons)
     Ground black pepper

1. Sprinkle the inside of each tomato with salt and place it upside down on several layers of paper towels; let stand to remove any excess moisture, about 30 minutes.

2. Meanwhile, toss the bread crumbs with 1 tablespoon olive oil, Parmesan, basil, garlic, and pepper to taste in a small bowl; set aside. Adjust an oven rack to the upper-middle position, and heat the oven to 375 degrees; line the bottom of a 9 by 13-inch baking dish with foil.

3. Roll up several sheets of paper towels and pat the inside of each tomato dry. Arrange the tomatoes in a single layer in the baking dish. Brush the cut edges of the tomatoes with 1 teaspoon oil. Mound the stuffing into the tomatoes (about 1/4 cup per tomato); drizzle with the remaining 2 tablespoons oil. Bake until the tops are golden brown and crisp, about 20 minutes. Serve immediately.

➤ VARIATION

Stuffed Tomatoes with Goat Cheese, Olives, and Oregano

Follow the recipe for Baked Stuffed Tomatoes with Parmesan, Garlic, and Basil, substituting 3 ounces crumbled goat cheese for Parmesan, omitting basil, and adding 3 tablespoons minced fresh parsley, 1 1/2 teaspoons minced fresh oregano, and 3 tablespoons chopped black olives to bread crumb mixture.

FRIED GREEN TOMATOES

WITH A CRISP COATING AND CLEAN, TART flavor, fried green tomatoes are a classic Southern side dish and snack. Unripe tomatoes are sliced, breaded, and fried to a deep, golden brown and served with hot sauce. When cooked right, these tangy, tomato treats are heavenly. Cooked badly, however, the coating turns greasy while the bland tomato is either undercooked and rock hard or over-cooked and sticky, almost like okra.

Starting with the tomatoes, we noticed they are found in many sizes, measuring anywhere from 2 to 5 inches across. While there were no readily discernible differences in flavor among the tomatoes, we liked the medium-sized tomatoes, which ranged from 2½ to 3½ inches. These tomatoes sliced into good-sized portions that were easy to bread and fry in only a few batches. We fried tomatoes sliced to a variety of thicknesses, and preferred tomatoes cut into ¼-inch-thick slices. Thicker slices refused to cook through, staying tough and crunchy even when the breading was quite brown. Thinner slices over-cooked to a sticky, jam-like consistency. When sliced ¼ inch thick, however, the tomatoes cooked perfectly, turning soft and yielding but not mushy.

Turning our attention to the breading, we tried a number of different methods and ingredients. While some recipes call only for flour, we liked the authentic flavor of cornmeal. Just dipping the tomato in seasoned cornmeal before frying, however, didn't work so well. The coating fell off in places leaving the tomato underneath naked, while the cornmeal itself was too potent in terms of flavor and texture. We then tried using a cornmeal pancake-like batter but found the crust a bit doughy and cakey. The classic breading procedure, dipping into flour, then egg, then a seasoned cornmeal-flour mixture worked well, but this array of ingredients turned somewhat dense and heavy when fried. Taking a cue from our fried chicken recipe, we altered this classic breading by adding some buttermilk and leavener to the egg. This new coating worked easily and tasted great. The leavened buttermilk turned the coating light and supercrisp, while adding a tangy flavor.

After a little more testing, we found that the cornmeal-flour mixture tasted best when seasoned heavily with salt and black pepper as well as a little cayenne. We also liked how the tomatoes tasted when fried in vegetable oil. After frying several batches, we noted that tomatoes fried to a beautiful, golden brown without tasting too greasy when the oil was heated to 350 degrees. Served with hot sauce or wedges of lemon, these crisp delights will have you dreaming of unripe tomatoes.

Fried Green Tomatoes

SERVES 4 TO 6

Any firm, underripe tomato can be used in this recipe. A well-seasoned cast-iron skillet is ideal for frying the tomato slices. We prefer a fine-textured cornmeal for this recipe; coarser cornmeal will make the coating excessively crunchy.

2½	cups unbleached all-purpose flour
1½	cups fine-ground white or yellow cornmeal such as Quaker
	Salt and ground black pepper
¼	teaspoon cayenne pepper
1	large egg
1	cup buttermilk
1	teaspoon baking powder
½	teaspoon baking soda
2	medium green tomatoes (about 12 ounces each), cored and sliced ¼ inch thick (for a total of 12 to 14 slices)
1½–2	cups vegetable oil

1. Measure 1 cup flour into a large shallow dish. Measure remaining 1½ cups flour, cornmeal, 1 table-spoon salt, 1 teaspoon pepper, and cayenne into a second large shallow dish. Beat the egg, buttermilk, baking powder, and baking soda in a medium bowl (mixture will bubble and foam).

2. Working with several slices at a time, drop the tomatoes in the flour and shake the pan to coat. Shake the excess flour from each piece. Using tongs, dip the tomatoes into the buttermilk mixture, turning to coat well and allowing the excess to drip off. Coat the tomato slices with seasoned flour-cornmeal mixture, shaking off any excess. Place the tomatoes on a wire rack set over a rimmed baking sheet. Repeat with remaining tomato slices.

3. Pour enough oil into a 12-inch skillet to measure ⅓ inch in depth. Heat the oil over high heat until it reaches a temperature of 350 degrees, 3 to 4 minutes. Gently lay a single layer of tomato slices in the oil (about 4 or 5 slices) and turn the heat down to medium. Fry until the tomatoes are a deep, golden brown on the first side, 2 to 2½ minutes, adjusting the heat as necessary to maintain the oil at a temperature of 350 degrees. Gently turn the tomato slices over with tongs and fry until the

second side is a deep, golden brown, 2 to 2½ minutes longer. Transfer the fried tomatoes to a rimmed baking sheet lined with paper towels and cool for 1 to 2 minutes. Repeat with the remaining slices, adjusting the heat as necessary to maintain the oil at a temperature of 350 degrees. Serve immediately.

SOUTHERN–STYLE GREENS

UTTERING THE WORDS "COLLARD GREENS" can bring out the Southern drawl in almost anyone. Along with turnip and mustard greens and kale, these tough, leafy greens are the cornerstone of true Southern cooking. Although many old-fashioned recipes tell you to cook greens for hours to make them tender, we found that they are actually easy to overcook. Yet when undercooked, they resemble cheap shoe leather with a tannic bite. We wanted authentic perfectly cooked Southern greens, with lots of flavor and a healthy chew.

While more tender greens (such as spinach) can simply be wilted in a hot pan, tough greens don't have enough moisture to withstand this cooking technique; they scorch before they wilt. Authentic Southern recipes boil collards (as well as kale and turnip or mustard greens) in water for hours, usually with pork. When the greens and pork are done boiling, the remaining cooking liquid is called "pot likker" and is often served as an accompaniment to the greens or as a gravy. We found that this time-consuming traditional method results in greens that are overdone, with a bland, lackluster flavor. The boiling did, however, rid the greens of their harsh tannic flavor. We then tested boiling the greens for shorter amounts of time and found that 7 or 8 minutes was enough for the greens to become tender. This short boiling time also mellowed their flavor without causing them to lose too much of their signature bite.

Wondering if the amount of water mattered, we tested boiling the greens in an abundant quantity of salted water versus a mere 2 quarts of salted water. As was the case with long cooking, we found that greens cooked in an abundance of water diluted their flavor too much. Two quarts of boiling water

removed enough bitterness to make these assertive greens palatable, but not so much as to rob them of their character.

With a quick wring to rid them of extra water, all these greens needed now was some Southern seasoning. In the South greens are typically cooked and served with pork, and we liked the smoky, potent flavor of bacon in our greens. We used the rendered fat from the bacon to sauté some aromatics. We found that red onion, garlic, and brown sugar rounded out the flavor of the greens, while a little chicken stock helped the greens soak up all these new flavors. Finally, we found a little cider vinegar drizzled over the top added a nice, bright punch.

Southern–Style Greens
SERVES 4

Kale, collard greens, and mustard greens can be stemmed by the same method; turnip greens are handled differently (see the illustrations on page 72).

	Salt
2	pounds tough, assertive greens, such as collards, kale, mustard, or turnip, stemmed, washed in several changes of cold water and coarsely chopped
4	slices bacon, cut into ¼-inch dice
2	teaspoons unsalted butter
I	small red onion, minced (about I cup)
2	large cloves garlic, minced
I	teaspoon brown sugar
½–¾	cup homemade chicken stock or canned low-sodium broth
I ½	teaspoons cider vinegar
	Ground black pepper

1. Bring 2 quarts water to a boil in a soup kettle or other saucepan. Add 1½ teaspoons salt and the greens and stir until wilted. Cover and cook until greens are just tender, 7 to 8 minutes. Drain in a colander. Rinse the kettle with cold water to cool, then refill with cold water. Pour the greens into cold water to stop the cooking process. Lift a handful of greens out of the water, and squeeze until only droplets fall from them. Repeat with the remaining greens.

2. Cook the bacon in a large sauté pan over medium heat until lightly browned but not too crisp, 7 to 8 minutes. Transfer the bacon with a slotted spoon to a paper towel–lined plate.

3. Add the butter to the hot bacon fat and heat over medium heat until it has melted and the foaming has subsided, about 1 minute. Add the red onion and sauté until softened and browned, about 10 minutes. Add the garlic, brown sugar, cooked greens, and cooked bacon and toss. Add ½ cup stock and cook over medium-high heat, adding more stock if necessary, until the greens are tender and juicy and most of the stock has been absorbed, about 5 minutes. Add vinegar and season with salt and pepper to taste. Serve immediately.

➤ VARIATIONS

Southern-Style Greens with Andouille Sausage and Red Pepper

Follow the recipe for Southern-Style Greens, replacing the bacon in step 2 with 10 ounces andouille sausage, cut in half lengthwise and then sliced crosswise into ¼-inch pieces. Cook the andouille over medium heat until cooked through, about 5 minutes. Transfer the cooked sausage to a paper towel–lined plate. In step 3, add 4 tablespoons butter to the pan and add ½ large red bell pepper, cut into ½-inch dice, along with the red onion. Proceed as directed, adding the cooked sausage back to the pan along with the greens.

Southern-Style Beans and Greens

Follow the recipe for Southern-Style Greens, adding two 15½-ounce cans white beans, drained and rinsed, and 1 tablespoon minced fresh savory along with the cooked greens in step 3.

STUFFED PEPPERS

MENTION STUFFED PEPPERS TO MOST PEOPLE and they think of a U.S. Army green shell crammed with leftovers from the school cafeteria. Although the classic 1950s sweet pepper filled with rice and beef and topped with ketchup may sound mediocre, this recipe can be delicious if prepared properly.

To get going, we tried a few classic recipes. Although these trial runs produced nothing as bad as what we remembered from the school cafeteria, they were far from perfect. First off, the peppers themselves varied greatly in degree of doneness. Some were so thoroughly cooked that they slumped onto their sides, unable to support their stuffed weight. On the other end of the spectrum, barely cooked peppers added an unfriendly crunch and bitter flavor to the mix. To be a success, the stuffed peppers would have to yield a tender bite yet retain enough structure to stand up proudly on the plate.

None of the fillings hit home, either. An all-rice version was uninteresting, while another stuffed with all meat was leaden and greasy. One recipe called for

PREPARING LEAFY GREENS

TURNIP GREENS
1. Turnip greens are most easily stemmed by grasping the leaf between your thumb and index finger at the base of the stem and stripping it off by hand.

2. When using this method with turnip greens, the very tip of the stem will break off along with the leaves. It is tender enough to cook along with the leaves.

KALE, COLLARDS, AND MUSTARD GREENS
To prepare kale, collards, and mustard greens, hold each leaf at the base of the stem over a bowl filled with water and use a sharp knife to slash the leafy portion from either side of the thick stem.

small amounts of so many varied ingredients that it made us think its creator just wanted to clean out her refrigerator. We came away from this first round of tests wanting a simple yet gratifying filling, neither humdrum nor packed with odd ingredients.

To start, we needed a solid pepper venue with minimal crunch. So we steamed, microwaved, roasted, and blanched a round of peppers and lined them up for everyone in the test kitchen to examine. The steamed and microwaved examples were bland in both color and flavor. We tried roasting in an uncovered dish filled with a little water, an uncovered dish with no water, and a covered dish. Each procedure produced a bitter, subpar pepper. We knew that, allowed to roast a little longer, their sugars would eventually caramelize and the peppers would turn sweet. But at that point their texture would have disintegrated into that of an Italian sandwich ingredient. Tasters unanimously preferred the vibrant color, sturdiness, and overall sweeter flavor of the blanched peppers; the hot water actually seemed to have washed away some of their bitterness.

Usually, a freshly blanched vegetable is plunged immediately into an ice cold water bath in a process known as shocking. The point is to halt the cooking process at just the right moment while stabilizing the vegetable's brightened color. Although the shocked peppers had a slightly brighter hue than those that had been blanched but not shocked, they took much longer to heat through in the oven. So we abandoned shocking and instead fussed with blanching times, being careful to remove the peppers a little early and then allow the residual heat to finish their cooking. We found that a 3-minute dip in boiling water followed by a cooling period on the countertop yielded the perfect balance of structure and chew.

Even with a pepper that's cooked to perfection, everyone knows that in this dish the stuffing is the real star of the show. The options for stuffing ingredients are many, including couscous, polenta, and a number of interesting and unusual grains. But we landed on rice. A universal pantry ingredient, it is a classic in American recipes for stuffed peppers.

Because we wanted these stuffed peppers to work as a quick midweek meal, our goal was to keep the rice-based filling simple and satisfying, with a streamlined ingredient list and preparation method. Tasters did not care much for sausage, heavy seasonings, or a mix of too many ingredients. To our surprise, they were big fans of the classic 1950s version of a pepper stuffed with rice and ground beef. Sautéed onions and garlic rounded out the flavors, while tomatoes added a fresh note and some color. Bound together with a little cheese and topped with ketchup, this retro pepper is a model of "make it from what you have in the pantry" simplicity.

Now we had a pepper, and we had a filling. All we had to do was figure out the best way to get them together.

The first trick is to use the boiling water from the blanched peppers to cook the rice. While the

---

INGREDIENTS: Bell Peppers

Bell peppers spanning the colors of the rainbow are now commonly found sitting side by side in the grocery store, no matter what the season. Wondering if these cheerfully colored peppers had different flavors or were simply cultivated for eye appeal, we conducted a blind tasting. After masking our colleagues' eyes with scarves, we lined them up to taste both raw and blanched examples of red, yellow, orange, green, and purple peppers fresh from the market.

No one guessed all of the colors correctly, but the differences in taste were dramatic. The favorite colors turned out to be red and orange. Without exhibiting much of a pungent pepper flavor, they were both pleasantly sweet. The yellow pepper, with its mildly sweet and slightly tannic flavor, was also well liked. The green pepper, the most easily recognized, was universally disliked for its unripe bitterness. The absolute worst entry, however, was the thin-skinned purple pepper. Its slimy texture and singularly unpleasing flavor elicited comments such as "What we imagine a shoe tastes like" and "Did we just eat a slug?"

As it turned out, these comments weren't far off the mark. As a bell pepper ripens, it turns from green to yellow, orange, or red, depending on the variety. These bright peppers are sweeter simply because they are ripe, whereas the bitter green pepper is unripe. Purple peppers, too, are harvested when immature and would turn an uncommonly dark green if allowed to ripen fully. So unless you're fond of the tannic bitterness of the common green and the purple varieties, we suggest sticking with yellow, orange, or red.

peppers cool and the rice cooks, the onions, garlic, and beef can be sautéed quickly. Then filling and peppers can be assembled and heated through in the oven. The result? Stuffed peppers that take only 45 minutes from start to finish—and that are also truly worth eating.

Stuffed Bell Peppers

SERVES 4 AS A LIGHT MAIN DISH
OR SIDE DISH

When shopping for bell peppers to stuff, it's best to choose those with broad bases that will allow the peppers to stand up on their own. It's easier to fill the peppers after they have been placed in the baking dish because the sides of the dish will hold the peppers steady. See page 73 for guidelines on selecting peppers for this recipe.

	Salt
4	medium red, yellow, or orange bell peppers (about 6 ounces each), ½ inch trimmed off tops, cores and seeds discarded
½	cup long-grain white rice
1½	tablespoons olive oil
1	medium onion, chopped fine (about 1 cup)
12	ounces ground beef, preferably ground chuck
3	medium cloves garlic, minced
1	(14½-ounce) can diced tomatoes, drained, ¼ cup juice reserved
1¼	cups (about 5 ounces) shredded Monterey Jack cheese
2	tablespoons chopped fresh parsley leaves Ground black pepper
¼	cup ketchup

1. Bring 4 quarts water to a boil in a large stockpot or Dutch oven over high heat. Add 1 tablespoon salt and the bell peppers. Cook until the peppers just begin to soften, about 3 minutes. Using a slotted spoon, remove the peppers from the pot, drain off excess water, and place the peppers cut-sides up on paper towels. Return the water to a boil; add the rice and boil until tender, about 13 minutes. Drain the rice and transfer it to a large bowl; set aside.

2. Adjust an oven rack to the middle position and heat the oven to 350 degrees.

3. Meanwhile, heat a 12-inch heavy-bottomed skillet over medium-high heat until hot, about 1½ minutes; add the oil and swirl to coat. Add the onion and cook, stirring occasionally, until softened and beginning to brown, about 5 minutes. Add the ground beef and cook, breaking the beef into small pieces with a spoon, until no longer pink, about 4 minutes. Stir in the garlic and cook until fragrant, about 30 seconds. Transfer the mixture to the bowl with the rice; stir in the tomatoes, 1 cup cheese, parsley, and salt and pepper to taste.

4. Stir together the ketchup and reserved tomato juice in a small bowl.

5. Place the peppers cut-side up in a 9-inch square baking dish. Using a soup spoon, divide the filling evenly among the peppers. Spoon 2 tablespoons ketchup mixture over each filled pepper and sprinkle each with 1 tablespoon of the remaining cheese. Bake until the cheese is browned and the filling is heated through, 25 to 30 minutes. Serve immediately.

GREEN BEAN CASSEROLE

OFTEN REFERRED TO AS THE CLASSIC GREEN Bean Bake, this casserole was developed by Campbell's in 1955 using frozen green beans, canned cream of mushroom soup, and a topping of canned fried onions. Touted by the company as "delicious and easy to make, easy to remember, and leaves room for creativity," the original recipe used only convenient, prepackaged ingredients. We wanted to resurrect this dinosaur and transform it, with fresh instead of prepared ingredients to make it taste better—much better.

Although the original recipe used frozen beans, we found they tasted watery and mushy in this dish. Fresh beans not only offered more flavor, but we were able to cook them to the appropriate doneness and leave a little bit of crunch. We tried sautéing and steaming the green beans but ended up liking the bright green color and seasoned flavor obtained when they were blanched (submerged briefly in boiling water). We found the beans tasted best when blanched in 4 quarts of water heavily seasoned with 2 tablespoons of salt for 4 to 5 minutes. We then plunged the beans into ice water (a process called shocking) to stop them from further cooking. Blanching then shocking allowed us to maximize control over the cooking process, which meant that the beans were perfectly cooked every time.

Our next concern was the cream-based mushroom sauce. We did not want the thick and pasty texture of condensed soup. What we did want was a smooth, velvety sauce filled with true mushroom flavor. We began by testing two popular methods for making a cream sauce: reducing the cream to the proper consistency, and thickening the cream with flour and butter (also known as a roux).

Sauces made by simply reducing cream were too heavy and took too much time for our holiday-size casserole, while sauces thickened with flour tasted pasty and lacked depth of flavor. By combining the methods—using a little flour and reducing the sauce a bit—we got a svelte, flavorful sauce that was neither too rich nor too floury. Briefly testing half-and-half and whole milk, we found neither up to sharing the title ring with the lush, luxurious heft of heavy cream. We tried adding cheese but found the extra flavor to be overpowering and unnecessary.

We had been using white button mushrooms but were disappointed with their lack of flavor. By replacing half of the button mushrooms with cremini and using some dried porcini, we were able to give the sauce a full, earthy, and complex mushroom flavor. While we liked the flavor of portobellos, we found their meaty texture required a different cooking time and made them more difficult to incorporate into our otherwise streamlined recipe.

Onion, garlic, and fresh thyme were great companion flavors for the mushrooms, while chicken stock helped to pull all the flavors in the sauce together. Although we tried adding bacon, white wine, Madeira, and shallots to the sauce, we found their flavors unwelcome and discordant.

With the green beans and mushroom sauce nailed down, all that was left was the fried onion topping. While deep frying our own onions was out of the question because of the time it takes, we found the canned fried onions simply tasted too commercial to use on their own. By mixing the

canned, fried onions with some fresh, seasoned bread crumbs we were able to remove the "from the can" taste of the traditional topping.

Green Bean Casserole

SERVES 8 TO 10

All the components of this dish can be cooked ahead of time. The assembled casserole needs only 15 minutes in a 375-degree oven to warm through and brown.

TOPPING

4 slices sandwich bread with crusts, each slice torn into quarters
2 tablespoons unsalted butter, softened
¼ teaspoon salt
⅛ teaspoon ground black pepper
3 cups canned fried onions (about 6 ounces)

BEANS

Salt
2 pounds green beans, ends trimmed, cut on the diagonal into 2-inch pieces
½ ounce dried porcini mushrooms, rinsed well
6 tablespoons unsalted butter
1 medium onion, minced
12 ounces white button mushrooms, wiped clean, stems trimmed, and sliced ¼ inch thick
12 ounces cremini mushrooms, wiped clean, stems trimmed, and sliced ¼ inch thick
2 tablespoons minced fresh thyme leaves
¼ teaspoon ground black pepper
3 medium cloves garlic, minced
2 tablespoon all-purpose flour
1 cup homemade chicken stock or canned low-sodium broth
2 cups heavy cream

1. FOR THE TOPPING: Pulse the bread, butter, salt, and pepper in the workbowl of a food processor fitted with a steel blade until the mixture resembles coarse crumbs, about ten 1-second pulses. Transfer to a large bowl and toss with the onions; set aside.

2. FOR THE BEANS: Heat the oven to 375 degrees. Bring 4 quarts water to a boil in a large pot. Add 2 tablespoons salt and the beans. Cook until bright green and slightly crunchy, 4 to 5 minutes. Drain the

beans and plunge immediately into a large bowl filled with ice water to stop cooking. Spread the beans out onto a paper towel–lined baking sheet to drain.

3. Meanwhile, cover the dried porcini mushrooms with ½ cup hot tap water in a small microwave-safe bowl; cover with plastic wrap, cut several steam vents with a paring knife, and microwave on high power for 30 seconds. Let stand until the mushrooms soften, about 5 minutes. Lift the mushrooms from the liquid with a fork and mince using a chef's knife (you should have about 2 tablespoons). Pour the liquid through a paper towel–lined sieve and reserve.

4. Melt the butter in a large nonstick skillet over medium-high heat until the foaming subsides, about 1 minute. Add the onion, button mushrooms, and cremini mushrooms and cook until the mushrooms release their moisture, about 2 minutes. Add the porcini mushrooms along with their strained soaking liquid, thyme, 1 teaspoon salt, and pepper and cook until all the mushrooms are tender and the liquid has reduced to 2 tablespoons, about 5 minutes. Add the garlic and sauté until aromatic, about 30 seconds. Add the flour and cook for about 1 minute. Stir in the stock and reduce the heat to medium. Stir in the cream and simmer gently until the sauce has the consistency of a dense soup, about 15 minutes.

5. Arrange the beans in a 3-quart gratin dish. Pour the mushroom mixture over the beans and mix to coat the beans evenly. Sprinkle with the bread crumb mixture and bake until the top is golden brown and the sauce is bubbling around the edges, about 15 minutes. Serve immediately.

STUFFED ZUCCHINI

IN OUR EXPERIENCE, STUFFED ZUCCHINI has either been a healthy but bland attempt at a vegetarian dinner or a thrifty, last-ditch effort to use up some leftovers. Either way, the dish has never garnered any points with us. We prefer the delicate flavor of zucchini in basic preparations: sautéed with a little garlic, thrown on the grill, or lightly roasted in the oven. We wondered, however, if we had been premature in giving this stuffed vegetable a bad rap.

Realizing that a simple summer recipe would make a handy addition to our repertoire (anyone who gardens needs good recipes for zucchini), we set out to create a stuffed zucchini worth making.

To start, we tried several recipes out of favorite cookbooks. One after another, however, each turned out to be a disappointment. Simpler recipes stuffed raw zucchini with rice and vegetables and threw it in the oven. Not only did the zucchini take awhile to cook through, but the filling on top dried out while the filling on the bottom absorbed the zucchini's moisture and became mushy. Other recipes blanched the squash in water or stock before they were stuffed, draining the zucchini of flavor and leaving behind a dull, limp shell. Still others filled the squash raw and baked it in a tomato juice or sauce that succeeded only in imparting a tinned, tomato flavor. As for the fillings, most recipes used precooked rice, which absorbed the moisture in the zucchini, thereby creating a toothless texture and monotonous flavor. The reasons for our longstanding bias against this stuffed vegetable were now more obvious than ever. To make a dish worth eating, we had to figure out how to parcook the zucchini before stuffing it, then find something exciting to stuff it with.

The moisture in the zucchini was clearly the biggest problem. Roasting, with its hot, dry heat, seemed a promising way to lose this moisture while also precooking the squash. We experimented by roasting zucchini whole, roasting it halved, and roasting it halved and seeded. The whole zucchini took too long to cook and steamed itself soggy. Although the halved squash cooked in less time, the seeds still held onto some moisture, leaving behind a soggy shell. The seeded squash, on the other hand, retained the toothsome texture we were looking for and also developed a more concentrated flavor. With the heat of the oven able to hit the flesh of the zucchini directly, more moisture evaporated, intensifying the flavor.

Next we did side-by-side roasting tests. When the zucchini were roasted cut-side up, the moisture that did not evaporate pooled in the hollow space once occupied by the seeds and later seeped into the stuffing, making it watery. When roasted cut-side down, however, the squash dripped moisture onto the hot roasting pan, where it turned to steam. Some of this steam got trapped underneath the overturned squash, speeding up the cooking process. Using a preheated pan further reduced the roasting time while creating a flavorful, golden brown crust along the rim. Salt and pepper brought out flavor, while olive oil prevented sticking. With its lightly browned edges and toothsome texture, the seeded squash, roasted cut-side down on a preheated pan, was by far the best of class. Now we could turn our attention to the filling.

Right off the bat we set up a few guidelines, wanting to use ingredients that most cooks would likely have on hand and to prepare the filling while the squash roasted. We also wanted a filling that would transform the squash into a light meal or an elegant side dish. To start, we tried using a simple combination of sautéed vegetables and cheese, but tasters were left wanting something more substantial. We then tested fillings made with rice, couscous, bread cubes, bread crumbs, and roasted potatoes. The rice and couscous, two predictable choices, tasted fine, but the bread cubes and bread crumbs were mushy and wanting in texture. Somewhat unexpectedly, the roasted potatoes stole the show, giving the dish a satisfying oomph that none of the contenders could match. After trying several varieties of potatoes, including russets, Yukon Gold, and Red Bliss, we found that Red Bliss, a high-moisture/low-starch potato, had the best texture when roasted. Best of all, both the squash and the potatoes roasted at about the same speed when placed on preheated pans in a 400-degree oven.

To get the summery flavor mix we were after, we added some fresh tomatoes, a bit of sautéed garlic, and some slightly caramelized onions along with fresh basil. We also found that a little cheese helped to bind the filling. After trying eight different types of cheese, tasters voted unanimously for Monterey Jack cheese (it edged out even the Parmesan). The flavor of the Jack cheese was evident without being overpowering, and it melted and browned nicely along the top. We finally had a stuffed zucchini worth making; it was even worth serving to company.

Stuffed Zucchini with Tomatoes and Jack Cheese

SERVES 4 AS A MAIN DISH
OR 8 AS A SIDE DISH

Buy firm zucchini with tiny prickly hairs around the stem end; the hairs are a sign of freshness.

4	medium zucchini (about 8 ounces each), washed
	Salt and ground black pepper
4	tablespoons olive oil
3	medium Red Bliss potatoes (about 1 pound), cut into ½-inch cubes
1	medium onion, chopped fine
5	large cloves garlic, minced
3	medium tomatoes (about 1¼ pounds), seeded and chopped
⅓	cup chopped fresh basil leaves
6	ounces Monterey Jack cheese, shredded (about 1½ cups)

1. Adjust one oven rack to the upper-middle position and the second oven rack to the lowest position, then place a rimmed baking sheet on each rack and heat the oven to 400 degrees.

2. Meanwhile, halve each zucchini lengthwise. With a small spoon, scoop out the seeds and most of flesh so that walls of zucchini are ¼ inch thick. Season the cut sides of the zucchini with salt and pepper to taste, and brush with 2 tablespoons oil; set the zucchini halves cut-side down on the hot baking sheet on the lower rack. Toss potatoes with 1 tablespoon olive oil and salt and pepper to taste in a small bowl and spread in a single layer on the hot baking sheet on the upper rack. Roast the zucchini until slightly softened and the skins are wrinkled, about 10 minutes; roast the potatoes until tender and lightly browned, 10 to 12 minutes. Using tongs, flip the zucchini halves over on the baking sheet and set aside.

3. Meanwhile, heat the remaining tablespoon oil in a 12-inch skillet over medium heat until shimmering but not smoking, about 2 minutes. Add the onion and cook, stirring occasionally, until softened and beginning to brown, about 10 minutes. Increase the heat to medium-high; stir in the garlic and cook

until fragrant, about 30 seconds. Add the tomatoes and cooked potatoes; cook, stirring occasionally, until heated through, about 3 minutes. Off heat, stir in the basil, ½ cup cheese, and salt and pepper to taste.

4. Divide the filling evenly among the squash halves on the baking sheet, spooning about ½ cup into each, and pack lightly; sprinkle with the remaining cheese. Return the baking sheet to the upper rack of the oven, and bake the zucchini until heated through and the cheese is spotty brown, about 6 minutes. Serve immediately.

➤ VARIATION

Stuffed Zucchini with Corn, Black Beans, and Chipotle Chiles

4	medium zucchini (about 8 ounces each), washed
	Salt and ground black pepper
4	tablespoons olive oil
1	medium Red Bliss potato (about 5 ounces), cut into ½-inch cubes
1	medium onion, chopped fine
1	cup fresh corn kernels cut from 2 medium ears (see "Removing Kernels from Corn Cobs" on page 50)
5	large cloves garlic, minced
3	medium chipotle chiles en adobo, minced (about 3 tablespoons)
2	medium tomatoes (about 12 ounces), seeded and chopped
1	can (15 ounce) black beans, drained and rinsed (about 1½ cups)
⅓	cup chopped fresh cilantro leaves
6	ounces Monterey Jack cheese, shredded (about 1½ cups)

1. Adjust one oven rack to the upper-middle position and the second oven rack to the lowest position, then place a rimmed baking sheet on each rack and heat the oven to 400 degrees.

2. Meanwhile, halve each zucchini lengthwise. With a small spoon, scoop out the seeds and most of flesh so that walls of zucchini are ¼ inch thick. Season the cut sides of the zucchini with salt and pepper to taste, and brush with 2 tablespoons oil; set the zucchini halves cut-side down on the hot baking sheet on the lower rack. Toss potatoes with 1 tablespoon olive oil and salt and pepper to taste in a small bowl and spread in a single layer on the hot baking sheet on the upper rack. Roast the zucchini until slightly softened and the skins are wrinkled, about 10 minutes; roast the potatoes until tender and lightly browned, 10 to 12 minutes. Using tongs, flip the zucchini halves over on the baking sheet and set aside.

3. Heat the remaining tablespoon oil in a 12-inch skillet over medium heat until shimmering but not smoking, about 2 minutes. Add the onion and cook, stirring occasionally, until softened and beginning to brown, about 10 minutes. Increase the heat to medium-high; stir in the corn and cook until almost tender, about 3 minutes. Add the garlic and chipotle chiles; cook until fragrant, about 30 seconds. Stir in the tomatoes, black beans, and cooked potatoes; cook, stirring occasionally, until heated through, about 3 minutes. Off heat, stir in the cilantro and ½ cup cheese and salt and pepper to taste.

4. Divide the filling evenly among the squash halves on the baking sheet, spooning about ½ cup into each, and pack lightly; sprinkle with remaining

INGREDIENTS: Zucchini

Although the Spanish are credited with introducing squash to Europe, believing them to be melons, it was the Italians who downsized the huge gourds into the delicate, green vegetable they termed *zucchini* in the 18th century. This dainty vegetable, with its elegant flavor and tender flesh, was intended to be eaten before it matured and was immediately popular in France as well as Italy. The English acquired the vegetable through the French and therefore call them *courgettes*, whereas Italian immigrants brought them to America, so we have always called them by their Italian name.

According to Vincent Laurence of White Flower Farms in Litchfield, Conn., there is no noticeable difference in flavor between the different types of zucchini, although different parts of the world prefer different shapes and shades of green. While consumers in the United States prefer straight, dark green zucchini, consumers in Syria prefer a tapered, pale gray zucchini to which the edible blossom is still attached. Although only one type of zucchini is usually available at the grocery store, you can grow more exotic and unusual types from seed.

cheese. Return the baking sheet to the upper rack of the oven, and bake the zucchini until heated through and the cheese is spotty brown, about 6 minutes. Serve immediately.

FRIED ONION RINGS

AMERICANS HAVE GIVEN ONION RINGS THE cold shoulder. And who can blame us? We are served frozen rings of flavorless onions draped in heavy, grease-sodden coats of perfectly smooth, manufactured batter and/or breading. A good homemade onion ring looks far from perfect—its coat is delicately craggy, flaky, and golden brown—but its flavor is just that. The marriage of the seasoned, crispy exterior and the sweet, toothsome onion is one made in heaven.

Some onion ring recipes call for a sticky batter, while others use a thinner batter. A few use baking powder for lift and lightness, while others rely on self-rising flour. Beer, milk, and buttermilk are the standard choices for moistening the onions and getting the dry coating to stick. After testing a variety of recipes and weeding out the duds (which, surprisingly, included beer-battered rings—we liked the flavor but found the texture too tempura-like), we settled on developing a recipe for buttermilk-bound onion rings. Buttermilk added a hint of tang to the rings, and its consistency was perfect for getting the flour coating to adhere.

Using sweet, large Vidalia onions from the outset, we started our testing by concentrating on the onion ring's coating. While we knew we wanted to use buttermilk to fuse a flour mixture to the onion, we had to decide what, exactly, to put in the flour mixture. Flour, salt, and pepper yielded a coating that was on the tough side—too much crackle, not enough crisp. Self-rising flour made a delicate coating that tasters admired. But few of us have self-rising flour in our pantries, so we wanted to duplicate it by adding leavener to regular all-purpose flour. One tablespoon of baking powder to a cup of flour turned out a tissuey coating that was so delicate it flaked right off the onion. Reducing the baking powder to 2 teaspoons was just right. The onion rings fried up crisp, tender, and light, and the coating stayed put.

Now that we had the coating at the right consistency, the flavor needed attention. Salt and pepper were a given, but at modest amounts tasters were disappointed. When they were both upped, tasters complained about the saltiness but loved the pepper level—the rings had a deep, building heat. Salt came down a notch, pepper stayed where it was. But salt and pepper on their own were not enough. Tasters wanted piquancy along with the heat of the pepper, so we tried some cayenne to spice things up. A quarter teaspoon was a bit timid. A half teaspoon was just right.

With only salt, pepper, and cayenne, something was still a little off balance. Some recipes included sugar—perhaps to offset the pungency of the onions—so we gave it a try. Tasters liked the flavor—it tickled their fancy for salty-sweet food, but the sugar wasn't evenly distributed in the flour mixture. Into the buttermilk it went, where it easily distributed itself upon dissolving. The problem of a big bite of sugar was resolved. With a teaspoon of Tabasco sauce in the buttermilk for good measure, the onion rings were a hit. The batter was still perfectly flaky and light, and the flavor was now great. This was not a bland onion ring from a box. Ours were sharp and well-seasoned.

The next order of business was determining which type of fat to fry the rings in. Considering the testing we conducted in the past when developing recipes for steak fries, we figured peanut oil had to be the leading candidate. This recipe had an additional requirement that made peanut oil still more attractive. We found that the best temperature for frying the onion rings was between 380 and 400 degrees; most deep-fried foods get the job done at about 350 degrees. Because peanut oil has a higher smoke point (is less prone to burning) than many other oils typically used for frying, it was the perfect choice for the onion rings. Maintaining the oil's temperature is a tricky task that requires attention, patience (you may have to wait for the temperature of the oil to go down), and an instant-read thermometer that is in good working order and, preferably, quick to produce a reading.

Though we were very happy with our sweet, tender Vidalia rings until now, we wanted to give some other onions a chance. We tested Spanish, white, and red onions against the Vidalias, and the only variety tasters disliked was the Spanish. It was pungent, bitter, and acidic. Red onions had a strange, slightly mushy texture, but their flavor was sweet and interesting. White onions worked very well, holding their shape and sweet flavor in the oil, but Vidalias remained victorious. The sweetest of the group, Vidalias are a perfect match for the sharp, salty coating. Other sweet onions like Walla Wallas and Mauis also fared beautifully in this recipe.

Fried Onion Rings

SERVES 4 TO 6

Maintaining an even oil temperature is key to the success of this recipe. An instant-read thermometer with a high upper range is perfect for checking the temperature of the oil. Our favorite is the Thermapen Digital Thermometer. Don't pile the onions on top of each other in the oil; however, you can fit smaller rings insider larger ones. Plan on at least four batches if you decide to fry the onion rings this way.

1	cup buttermilk
1	teaspoon hot pepper sauce, such as Tabasco
1	teaspoon sugar
1	cup unbleached all-purpose flour
2	teaspoons baking powder
½	teaspoon cayenne pepper
1	teaspoon salt
1½	teaspoons ground black pepper
2	large sweet onions, such as Vidalia, Maui, or Walla Walla (about 1¾ pounds)
3	cups peanut oil

1. Adjust an oven rack to the middle position, set a wire rack over a rimmed baking sheet, place the baking sheet in the oven, and heat the oven to 250 degrees.

2. With a fork, combine the buttermilk, hot pepper sauce, and sugar in a medium bowl until the sugar dissolves. Using a clean fork, combine the flour, baking powder, cayenne, salt, and pepper in a shallow baking dish. Peel and cut the onions into ¼-inch-thick slices. Separate the onion slices into rings.

3. Dip the rings in the buttermilk and shake off the excess liquid. Dredge the rings in the flour mixture, shake off the excess, and gently place the rings on a second wire rack set over a rimmed baking sheet. Repeat until all the rings are coated. Overlap the rings if necessary.

4. Line a large plate with a double layer of paper towels. Meanwhile, heat the oil to 400 degrees (measured with an instant-read thermometer) over medium-high heat in a large, 8-quart, heavy-bottomed Dutch oven with a diameter of approximately 12 inches. Add the onions to form a single layer on the oil's surface and cook until golden brown, no more than 3 minutes. (Oil temperature should not dip below 375 degrees. You may need to adjust stove's heat to maintain the temperature.) Using tongs, transfer the onions to the paper towel–lined plate. Let stand 2 minutes to drain, then carefully transfer to the rack in the warm oven. Replace the paper towels on the plate. Return the oil to 400 degrees and fry the remaining onions, transferring them to the paper towel–lined plate to drain, then to the wire rack in the oven for each batch. Serve onion rings hot from the oven.

4

PASTA, GRAINS, AND BEANS

AMERICANS MAY NOT HAVE A LONG HISTORY of eating pasta, grains, and beans, but certain dishes have become national or, at the very least, regional classics. Certainly pasta has its roots elsewhere (China or Italy, depending on which experts you believe), but the three pasta dishes featured in this chapter—macaroni and cheese, turkey Tetrazzini, and tuna noodle casserole—are as American as apple pie.

Wild rice, grits, and cornmeal are arguably American grains. Wild rice (which is actually a grass that is treated like a grain) is native to this country and relatively unknown in the most of the world. It is often used in poultry stuffings, but we also like wild rice on its own in a pilaf. Ground corn has its origins in Mexico (in the form of masa), but grits and cornmeal are certainly American. Grits and cornmeal are used extensively in Southern cooking. This chapter features two favorites—baked grits with cheese and spoon bread, a cross between corn-bread and a soufflé.

We are often asked what is the difference between grits and cornmeal. Grits are ground skinned corn (also called hominy), while cornmeal is simply ground corn. Why would you skin corn before grinding it? In ancient civilizations in Mexico and other parts of the Americas, corn was boiled with an alkali (such as lye) to loosen the tough outer skins from the kernels and make it possible to grind corn by hand. This process also improved the nutritional quality of the protein in corn. Grinding stones (and later steel rollers) were able to grind corn without first removing the tough outer skins, hence a second type of ground corn, which we call cornmeal.

Sweetened baked beans are another American classic. Either simply flavored (as in Boston baked beans) or spiced up (as in barbecued baked beans), beans become especially creamy when slow-simmered in the oven. Baking beans also creates a lush, richly flavored sauce.

The chapter ends with several Southern rice and bean dishes—red beans and rice, dirty rice, and Hoppin' John. Unlike the other grain and bean recipes in this chapter, these hearty dishes are appropriate as the main course rather than as a side dish.

MACARONI AND CHEESE

THERE ARE TWO DISTINCT STYLES OF MACARONI and cheese. The more common variety is béchamel-based, in which macaroni is blanketed with a cheese-flavored white sauce, usually topped with crumbs, and baked. The other variety is custard-based. In this style, a mixture of egg and milk is poured over layers of grated cheese and noodles. As the dish bakes, the eggs, milk, and cheese set into a custard. This macaroni and cheese is also topped with bread crumbs and baked.

Even though macaroni and cheese is a wonderful, satisfying dish, many of the recipes we tested were tired, leaden, and uninspired. Others attempted to perk up the dish with canned green chiles, scallions, or olives. And, of course, there were attempts to lighten it. No one seemed to really love the dish enough to give it the care it deserves.

Then we ran across a recipe in John Thorne's *Simple Cooking* (Penguin, 1989). "As it happens," he begins, "I'm very fond of macaroni and cheese, and keep a special spot in my heart for cooks who genuinely love it: they are not that many." After reading his four-page essay, we suspected that his recipe for macaroni and cheese was the real thing, the others mere shadows.

Making the dish confirmed what we suspected to be true. John Thorne's macaroni and cheese was the best. His recipe starts with macaroni cooked just shy of al dente. The hot, drained macaroni is then tossed with butter in a heatproof pan or bowl. Evaporated milk, hot pepper sauce, dry mustard, eggs, and a large quantity of cheese are stirred into the noodles. The combination is baked for 20 minutes, with the addition of more cheese and milk additions and a thorough stir every 5 minutes. Frequent stirrings allow the eggs to thicken without setting, which results in an incredibly silky sauce. During cooking, the sauce settles into the tubular openings of the pasta, offering a burst of cheese with each new bite.

Out of curiosity, we baked the two styles of macaroni and cheese defined earlier: one with a cheese-flavored béchamel sauce, the other thickened with eggs, milk, and cheese. Neither compared with Thorne's dish. The béchamel-based version was grainy and tasted exactly as Thorne predicted: not like macaroni and cheese but like "macaroni with cheese sauce." In terms of texture, Thorne's macaroni and cheese was smooth silk, while the béchamel dish was thick velvet.

If we had to choose between the two baked macaroni and cheeses, however, we would pick the cheesier-flavored custard version. Because this custard-based macaroni and cheese was simply a baked version of Thorne's recipe, we thought we might offer it as an alternative to his stirred version. A side-by-side tasting proved the two dishes to be very different, however, and the stirred version remained superior in our minds. The stirred macaroni had a luxuriously silky cheese sauce, while the baked egg, milk, and cheese formed an unappealingly dry custard that set around the noodles.

With the competition ruled out, we moved forward to study Thorne's recipe a little more closely. We wondered if the dish really required evaporated milk or if this was an idiosyncrasy of the late 1930s,

when the recipe was first published in *The Home Comfort Cook Book* (Wrought Iron Range Company, 1937). Wouldn't regular milk or half-and-half work equally well? What other cheeses, besides sharp cheddar, would taste good?

After testing the recipe with whole and low-fat milks and half-and-half, we realized that evaporated milk was indeed an important ingredient. All the macaroni and cheese dishes made with fresh milk curdled a bit, resulting in a chalky, grainy texture. The one made with evaporated milk remained silky smooth. The evaporation and sterilization process stabilizes the milk, which in turn stabilizes the macaroni and cheese.

As for the cheese, we tried Vermont, New York, and Wisconsin cheddars and preferred the less sharp Wisconsin variety. Because the recipe calls for such a large quantity, a slightly milder cheese is preferable. Further testing confirmed this point. Macaroni and

EQUIPMENT: Cheese Graters

In the old days, cheese was grated on the fine teeth of a box grater. Now cheese graters come in several distinct designs. Unfortunately, many of them don't work all that well. With some designs you need Herculean strength to move the cheese over the teeth with sufficient pressure for grating; with others you eventually discover that a large portion of the grated cheese has remained jammed in the grater instead of sitting where it belongs, on your food. Whether you are dusting a plate of pasta or grating a full cup of cheese to use in a recipe, a good grater should be easy to use and efficient.

We rounded up 15 different models and set about determining which was the best grater. We found five basic configurations. Four-sided box graters have different size holes on each side to allow for both fine grating and coarse shredding. Flat graters consist of a flat sheet of metal that is punched through with fine teeth and attached to some type of handle. With rotary graters, you put a small chunk of cheese in a hopper and use a handle to press it down against a crank-operated grating wheel. Porcelain dish graters have raised teeth in the center and a well around the outside edge to collect the grated cheese. We also found a model that uses an electric motor to push and rotate small chunks of cheese against a grating disk.

After grating more than 10 pounds of Parmesan, we came to some conclusions. Success, we learned, was due to a combination

of sharp grating teeth, a comfortable handle or grip, and good leverage for pressing the cheese onto the grater. Our favorite model was a flat grater based on a small, maneuverable woodworking tool called a rasp. Shaped like a ruler but with lots and lots of tiny, sharp raised teeth, the Cheese Grater (as it is called) can grate large quantities of cheese smoothly and almost effortlessly. The black plastic handle, which we found more comfortable than any of the others, also earned high praise. Other flat graters also scored well.

What about traditional box graters? Box graters can deliver good results and can do more than just grate hard cheese. However, if grating hard cheese is the task at hand, a box grater is not our first choice.

We also had good results with rotary graters made from metal but did not like flimsy versions made from plastic. A metal arm is rigid enough to do some of the work of pushing the cheese down onto the grating drum. The arms on the plastic models we tested flexed too much against the cheese, thus requiring extra pressure to force the cheese down. Hand strain set in quickly. A rotary grater can also chop nuts finely and grate chocolate.

The two porcelain dish graters we tested were duds. The teeth were quite ineffective. And the electric grater was a loser of monumental proportions. True, the grating effort required was next to nothing, but so were the results.

cheese made with Gruyère was so strong we couldn't even eat it. To our surprise, highly processed cheeses like American performed quite well in this dish. Much like evaporated milk, the more it is processed, the more stable the cheese and the more creamy the dish. For flavor, use cheddar; for texture, buy American. We also found the dish did not suffer when prepared with only 12 ounces of cheese as opposed to the full pound called for in the original recipe.

Our one final problem to solve concerned the temperature of the macaroni and cheese when served. We found that at the end of the 20 minutes of baking recommended by Thorne, the dish was hot but hardly piping. By the time tasters had consumed their portions, the cheese sauce had cooled and set a bit. This problem, we learned, could not be remedied by leaving the dish in the oven much longer than the suggested 20 minutes. To do so meant running the risk of curdling the eggs, and the dish would develop a subtle grainy texture. We wondered if we could cook the macaroni and cheese on top of the stove instead of in the oven. We found that by using a heavy-bottomed pot and cooking over low heat, it was possible to make the macaroni and cheese on top of the stove in less than five minutes. Not only was this method quicker, it kept the macaroni and cheese piping hot.

Stovetop Macaroni and Cheese

SERVES 4 AS A MAIN COURSE
OR 6 TO 8 AS A SIDE DISH

If you're in a hurry or prefer to sprinkle the dish with crumbled crackers (saltines aren't bad), you can skip the bread crumb step.

TOPPING

1	cup fresh bread crumbs from French or Italian bread
	Pinch salt
1½	tablespoons unsalted butter, melted

MACARONI AND CHEESE

2	large eggs
1	can (12 ounces) evaporated milk
¼	teaspoon hot pepper sauce, such as Tabasco

2	teaspoons salt
¼	teaspoon ground black pepper
1	teaspoon dry mustard, dissolved in 1 teaspoon water
½	pound elbow macaroni
4	tablespoons unsalted butter
12	ounces sharp Wisconsin cheddar, American, or Monterey Jack cheese, grated (about 3 cups)

1. FOR THE TOPPING: Heat the oven to 350 degrees. Mix the bread crumb ingredients together in a small baking pan. Bake until golden brown and crisp, 15 to 20 minutes; set aside.

2. FOR THE MACARONI AND CHEESE: Mix the eggs, 1 cup evaporated milk, hot pepper sauce, ½ teaspoon salt, pepper, and mustard mixture in a small bowl; set aside.

3. Meanwhile, bring 2 quarts water to a boil in a large heavy-bottomed saucepan or Dutch oven. Add the remaining 1½ teaspoons salt and macaroni; cook until almost tender but still a little firm to the bite. Drain and return macaroni to the pan over low heat. Add the butter; toss to melt.

4. Pour the egg mixture over the buttered noodles along with three-quarters of the cheese; stir until thoroughly combined and the cheese starts to melt. Gradually add the remaining milk and cheese, stirring constantly, until the mixture is hot and creamy, about 5 minutes. Serve immediately, topped with toasted bread crumbs.

➤ VARIATION

"Baked" Macaroni and Cheese

This dish is for those who prefer their macaroni and cheese topped with crumbs and served out of a baking dish. Smooth and creamy like the stovetop version, this version is broiled just long enough to brown the crumb topping.

TOPPING

2	tablespoons unsalted butter
1	cup fresh bread crumbs from French or Italian bread
	Pinch salt
1	ounce sharp Wisconsin cheddar, American, or Monterey Jack cheese, grated (about ¼ cup)

MACARONI AND CHEESE

2   large eggs

1   can (12 ounces) evaporated milk

¼   teaspoon hot pepper sauce, such as Tabasco

2   teaspoons salt

¼   teaspoon ground black pepper

1   teaspoon dry mustard, dissolved in 1 teaspoon
     water

½   pound elbow macaroni

4   tablespoons unsalted butter

11   ounces sharp Wisconsin cheddar, American, or
     Monterey Jack cheese, grated (about 2¾ cups)

1. FOR THE TOPPING: Heat the butter in a large skillet over medium heat until foam subsides. Add the bread crumbs; cook, tossing to coat with the butter, until crumbs just begin to color. Season to taste with salt; set aside. When cool, stir in the cheese.

2. FOR THE MACARONI AND CHEESE: Mix the eggs, 1 cup evaporated milk, hot pepper sauce, ½ teaspoon salt, pepper, and mustard mixture in a small bowl; set aside. Adjust an oven rack so it is about 6 inches from the broiler element and heat the broiler.

3. Meanwhile, bring 2 quarts water to a boil in a large heavy-bottomed saucepan or Dutch oven. Add 1½ teaspoons salt and the macaroni; cook until almost tender but still a little firm to the bite. Drain and return macaroni to the pan over low heat. Add the butter; toss to melt.

4. Pour the egg mixture over the buttered noodles along with three-quarters of the cheese; stir until thoroughly combined and the cheese starts to melt. Gradually add the remaining milk and cheese, stirring constantly, until the mixture is hot and creamy, about 5 minutes.

5. Pour the cooked macaroni and cheese into a 9-inch-square baking dish (or other ovenproof dish of similar surface area). Spread the crumbs evenly over the top. Broil until crumbs turn deep brown, 1 to 2 minutes. Let stand to set a bit, about 5 minutes, and serve immediately.

TURKEY TETRAZZINI

TURKEY TETRAZZINI CAN BE AN INTERESTING blend of toasted bread crumbs, silky sauce, and a modicum of turkey meat, all bound together by one of our favorite foods, spaghetti. Or it can taste like cafeteria food. The downside of most casseroles—in which the fusion of individual tastes and textures diminishes them all—can hold true here as well. We wondered if a basic noodle casserole could be reengineered so that this eminently practical American dish could be made worthy of a well-laid table.

A bit of culinary sleuthing solved the most pressing problem, the fact that the ingredients are double-cooked. (Most casserole recipes are two-step affairs: Cook the ingredients, mix them together, and then bake them in a casserole.) In *American Cookery* (Little, Brown & Co., 1972), James Beard suggests using a shallow baking dish rather than a deep casserole. Paired with a very hot (450-degree) oven, this reduces the baking time to a mere 15 minutes, a fraction of the time suggested by most cookbooks. Tasted against longer baking times and slower ovens, this quick method won hands down. With its fresher-tasting vegetables, it easily avoided the wretched, overcooked dullness of cafeteria cuisine.

Next we adjusted the sauce. The traditional choice is béchamel, a sauce in which milk is added to a roux, a paste made from flour and hot fat. We decided to use a velouté, a sauce based on chicken stock rather than dairy. This brightened up both the texture and the flavor, since dairy tends to dampen other flavors. We also played around with the amount of sauce, trying larger and smaller quantities, and found that more sauce overran the taste of the other ingredients. In this case, less was more. It still needed a burst of flavor, however, so we spruced it up with a shot of sherry and a little lemon juice and nutmeg; a bit of Parmesan cheese provided tang and bite; and a full 2 teaspoons of fresh thyme also helped freshen the flavor.

Most recipes do not toast the bread crumbs before baking. Doing so does complicate things by adding an extra step (in a pinch, you can skip the toasting), but it also adds to the flavor and texture of the dish; it's worth the minimal effort required. Tossing the toasted bread crumbs with a bit of grated Parmesan also helps to boost the flavor.

Turkey Tetrazzini

SERVES 8

Tetrazzini is also great with leftover chicken. Using a shallow baking dish without a cover and a very hot oven benefits both texture and flavor. Don't skimp on the salt and pepper; this dish needs aggressive seasoning.

TOPPING

½	cup fresh bread crumbs
	Pinch salt
1 ½	tablespoons unsalted butter, melted
¼	cup grated Parmesan cheese

FILLING

6	tablespoons unsalted butter, plus extra for greasing baking dish
8	ounces white button mushrooms, cleaned and sliced thin
2	medium onions, chopped fine
	Salt and ground black pepper
¾	pound spaghetti or other long-strand pasta, strands snapped in half
¼	cup flour
2	cups homemade chicken stock or canned low-sodium chicken broth
3	tablespoons dry sherry
¾	cup grated Parmesan cheese
¼	teaspoon grated nutmeg
2	teaspoons juice from 1 lemon
2	teaspoons minced fresh thyme leaves
2	cups frozen peas
4	cups leftover cooked boneless turkey or chicken meat, cut into ¼-inch pieces

1. FOR THE TOPPING: Adjust an oven rack to the middle position and heat the oven to 350 degrees. Mix the bread crumbs, salt, and butter in a small baking dish; bake until golden brown and crisp, 15 to 20 minutes. Cool to room temperature and mix with Parmesan in a small bowl. Set aside.

2. FOR THE FILLING: Increase the oven temperature to 450 degrees. Heat 2 tablespoons butter in a large skillet over medium heat until the foaming subsides; add the mushrooms and onions and sauté, stirring frequently, until the onions soften and the liquid from the mushrooms evaporates, about 10 to 12 minutes. Season with salt and ground black pepper to taste; transfer to a medium bowl and set aside.

3. Meanwhile, bring 4 quarts water to a boil in a large pot. Add 1 tablespoon salt and the pasta and cook until al dente. Reserve ¼ cup cooking water, drain the spaghetti, and return to the pot with reserved liquid.

4. Melt 4 tablespoons butter in a clean skillet over medium heat. When the foam subsides, whisk in the flour and cook, whisking constantly, until the flour turns golden, 1 to 2 minutes. Whisking constantly, gradually add the chicken stock. Turn the heat to medium-high and simmer until the mixture thickens, 3 to 4 minutes. Off heat, whisk in the sherry, Parmesan, nutmeg, lemon juice, thyme, and ½ teaspoon salt. Add the sauce, sautéed vegetables, peas, and meat to the spaghetti and mix well; adjust seasonings to taste.

5. Turn the mixture into a buttered 9 by 13-inch baking dish (or other shallow, ovenproof dish of similar size), sprinkle evenly with the reserved bread crumbs, and bake until the bread crumbs brown and the mixture is bubbly, 13 to 15 minutes. Serve immediately.

TUNA NOODLE CASSEROLE

IS TUNA NOODLE CASSEROLE AN AMERICAN institution or national nightmare? In most cases, the answer is both, no doubt because most versions of this dish are so bad. Most often made from a canned soup base—cream of mushroom, cream of celery, and cream of chicken are the usual choices—mixed with soggy noodles, canned tuna, and a few stray vegetables from the crisper drawer, tuna noodle casserole delivers little in flavor or texture, save for the sometimes crunchy topping of bread crumbs. We wanted our tuna noodle casserole to possess a silky sauce, tasty, firm chunks of vegetables, and properly cooked noodles. We also wanted to figure out how to add some brightness to the dish.

First the vegetables. Many recipes use a lot of celery, which adds crunch but almost no flavor. Interestingly enough, our tasters preferred no celery at all. Bell peppers held a similar fate. Green peppers were rejected immediately, and while red peppers performed slightly better, tasters preferred to do without them altogether. Onions were included for their subtle aromatic flavor; in fact, two were necessary to make their presence known. Mushrooms, a must in any tuna noodle casserole, were also included. After testing cremini and white button mushrooms, tasters could find no appreciable difference, so we went with the more available white button. We sautéed both the onions and the mushrooms to give them a slightly caramelized flavor and to allow the moisture in the mushrooms to evaporate so as not to water down the sauce. Peas were added for color and the sake of tradition. We found that frozen peas would not turn soggy if we added them right before baking. A little fresh thyme and parsley brought out even more freshness and color.

On to the tuna. Many of the oil-packed tunas tested had little textural appeal out of the can. Imported olive oil–packed tuna was a little better but didn't hold much of its shape when mixed in the casserole. Water-packed solid white tuna was much better. Right out of the can we were able to flake it into big chunks that held their shape in the casserole. (For information on specific brands of tuna, see page 43.)

While many recipes call for elbow macaroni, we found it too starchy and thick. We chose fettuccine instead for its toothsome texture and big structural presence. To make the dish easier to eat, we broke the fettuccini in thirds so that there was no need to wind the pasta around a fork.

If not using a canned soup base, most cooks turn to a béchamel, a sauce made from a roux (hot fat and flour) and milk. Tasters thought that this sauce deadened any hope of a bright-tasting casserole. Next we tried a velouté, a similar sauce based on chicken stock instead of dairy (we used canned low-sodium chicken broth as a substitute). This produced the velvety sauce we were looking for, with plenty of chicken flavor to enrich the dish. We added a small amount of milk to give the sauce a little creaminess and just enough lemon juice to wake up the other ingredients.

As for the topping, we learned that store-bought bread crumbs, which are too often stale and sandy, did not work. Instead we used fresh bread crumbs, which we tossed with a little butter and toasted in the oven. Finally, a tuna noodle casserole to be proud of.

Tuna Noodle Casserole
SERVES 6

See page 43 for the results of our tasting of various brands of canned tuna.

TOPPING

1	cup fresh bread crumbs
	Pinch salt
1 ½	tablespoons unsalted butter, melted

FILLING

	Salt
¾	pound dried fettuccine, noodles broken into thirds
6	tablespoons unsalted butter, plus extra for greasing baking dish
10	ounces white button mushrooms, wiped clean, stems trimmed, sliced ¼-inch thick
2	medium onions, minced
	Ground black pepper
¼	cup all-purpose flour
2	cups homemade chicken stock or canned low-sodium chicken broth
¾	cup whole milk
1	tablespoon lemon juice
¼	cup minced fresh parsley leaves
1 ½	tablespoons chopped fresh thyme leaves
2	(6-ounce) cans solid white tuna in water, drained and flaked into 1-inch pieces with a fork
1 ½	cups frozen peas, thawed

1. Set an oven rack to the middle position and heat the oven to 350 degrees. Mix the bread crumbs, salt, and butter in a small baking dish; bake until golden brown and crisp, 15 to 20 minutes. Cool to room temperature and transfer to a bowl.

2. Increase the oven temperature to 450 degrees. Butter a shallow casserole or baking dish that measures about 9 by 13-inches.

3. Meanwhile, bring 4 quarts water to a boil in a large pot. Add 1 tablespoon salt and the pasta and

cook until al dente. Reserve ¼ cup of the cooking water, drain the pasta, and return to the pot with reserved liquid.

4. Heat 2 tablespoons butter in a large skillet over medium heat until foaming subsides. Add the mushrooms and onions, season with salt and pepper to taste, and sauté, stirring frequently until onions soften and mushroom liquid evaporates, about 10 to 12 minutes. Check the seasonings, transfer to a medium bowl, and set aside.

5. Melt 4 tablespoons butter in a clean skillet over medium heat. When the foam subsides, whisk in the flour and cook, whisking constantly, until the flour turns golden, 1 to 2 minutes. Whisking constantly, gradually add the chicken stock and milk. Raise the heat to medium-high and cook until the mixture thickens, about 5 minutes. Off heat whisk in ½ teaspoon salt, lemon juice, parsley, and thyme.

6. Add the sauce, mushroom mixture, tuna, and peas to the pasta and mix well. Check the seasonings and adjust to taste.

7. Turn the mixture into the buttered baking dish, sprinkle evenly with the reserved bread crumbs, and bake until the bread crumbs brown and the mixture is bubbly, about 10 minutes. Serve immediately.

WILD RICE PILAF

WILD RICE, IN EITHER A STUFFING OR A side dish, finds its way onto many holiday tables. It can be both delicious and visually appealing, but, quite frankly, it rarely is. It tends to be over- or undercooked and poorly seasoned, especially in side dishes like pilafs, where the rice has not been graced with the bird's flavorful juices. Most pilafs also lack enough supporting flavors and contrasting textures, such as vegetables, dried fruit, or nuts. We wanted to overcome these problems and devise a full-flavored, attractive side dish worthy of the holiday table.

By itself, wild rice is overwhelming in both nutty flavor and chewy texture. We are most fond of wild rice when it is mixed with another variety of rice. (Technically, wild rice is not a rice at all but a grain harvested from a variety of marsh-growing grass that is only distantly related to rice.)

After some early tests, we determined that wild rice should be slowly simmered in seasoned water or broth for a minimum of 45 minutes. There simply is no way to cut back on the cooking time and properly soften this tough grain. And to prevent sticking (a common problem in many of the recipes we tested), we found it best to cook the rice in slightly more liquid than it will absorb and then drain the excess once the grains have softened.

Given this long cooking, we knew we would run into trouble when trying to add another grain. Most long-grain rice is best steamed until it absorbs all the liquid in the pot, a process that takes just 15 to 20 minutes. Brown rice is the exception, cooking in about the same time as wild rice. When we tried cooking wild and brown rice together, however, we had poor results. The brown rice was overdone and glutinous, and the wild rice was unevenly cooked; some grains had exploded and others were still crunchy. And tasters thought that the flavor of brown rice was too similar to that of the wild rice and did not offer an interesting contrast. Our one-pot cooking idea was not meant to be.

Having accepted that we would need to cook the wild rice and another rice independently, we tried a variety of rices, this time with no concern for their required cooking time. Instant rice was mushy and flavorless, as was converted rice. Gently scented basmati rice was delicious on its own, but its fragrance and delicate flavor were lost when combined with the wild rice. Regular long-grain white rice proved the winner, its soft but firm texture and pale color contrasting sharply with the wild rice. We found the best way to cook the white rice so that it was not sticky was to rinse it of excess starch and sauté the raw rice in butter for a few minutes before adding the liquid. This is a classic pilaf technique that guarantees glossy, plump grains of rice—we could not find a way to improve it.

It was an easy step to cook vegetables to flavor the pilaf prior to cooking the rice. We were keen on flavorings that would complement a holiday table. Sautéed carrots, onion, and celery seemed natural. Tasters enjoyed the combination, but a few thought that the celery made the pilaf taste too much like a stuffing. We removed the celery and replaced it with more carrot, which added color and a pleasing sweetness. Thyme and parsley tossed into the rice added a pleasing freshness and lightened the pilaf.

While we love dried fruit in pilafs, we were cautious about adding it because the fruit is often tough and leathery. Tart dried cranberries seemed ideal for our pilaf, but their chewy texture was unpleasant in the pilaf with chewy wild rice. Plumping the fruit in hot water helped, but it did little for flavor. Then we added them to the white rice as it steamed and were pleased with the soft texture of the cranberries. And the fruit imparted some flavor to the rice.

To reemphasize the wild rice's nuttiness and add a different texture to the pilaf, we tried different kinds of nuts. Hazelnuts and walnuts were overpowering, and almonds lacked enough flavor. Pecans, with their rich buttery flavor, were the favorite in the test kitchen.

After a dozen batches, we were pleased, and everyone in the kitchen was ready to add the pilaf to their holiday tradition. The flavors were deep, the variety of textures was pleasing, and the autumnal colors fit right in next to the turkey.

Wild Rice Pilaf

SERVES 6 TO 8

To toast the pecans, place them in a dry skillet set over medium heat. Cook, shaking pan occasionally to turn the nuts, until fragrant, 4 to 5 minutes.

4	cups homemade chicken stock or canned low-sodium chicken broth (add up to 1/4 cup water to bring total up to 32 ounces if using two 14 1/2-ounce cans)
2	bay leaves
1	cup wild rice, washed and picked clean of any debris
1 1/2	cups long-grain white rice
	Salt
3	tablespoons unsalted butter
1	medium onion, diced fine
1	large carrot, diced fine
3/4	cup dried cranberries
2	teaspoons minced fresh thyme leaves
1	tablespoon minced fresh parsley leaves
3/4	cup pecans, toasted and coarsely chopped
	Ground black pepper

1. Bring the stock and the bay leaves to a boil in a medium saucepan. Add the wild rice, cover, and reduce the heat to low. Simmer until the rice is plumped and fully cooked, 40 to 45 minutes. Transfer the rice to a fine-mesh strainer to remove any excess liquid from the rice.

2. Meanwhile, place the white rice in a medium bowl and add enough water to cover by 2 inches. Using your hands, gently swish the grains to release excess starch. Carefully pour off the water, leaving the rice in the bowl. Repeat 4 or 5 times, or until the water runs almost clear. Using a fine-mesh strainer, drain the remaining water from the rice.

3. Bring 2 1/4 cups water and 1 teaspoon salt to a boil in a small saucepan. Remove the pan from the heat and cover. Meanwhile, heat the butter in a medium saucepan over medium heat until the foam begins to subside. Add the onion and the carrot and cook until softened but not browned, about 4 minutes. Add the white rice and stir to coat the grains with butter. Cook until the grains begin to turn translucent, about 3 minutes. Stir the hot seasoned water into the rice and return to a boil. Reduce the heat to low, sprinkle the cranberries evenly across the rice, and cover. Simmer until all the liquid is absorbed, 16 to 18 minutes. Remove the pan with the rice from the heat and fluff with a fork. To keep warm until the wild rice is finished, place a kitchen towel folded in half over the saucepan and replace the lid.

4. Toss the wild rice, white rice, herbs, and toasted pecans in a large bowl and mix well. Season to taste with salt and pepper. Serve immediately.

SPOON BREAD

SPOON BREAD IS A SOUTHERN SPECIALTY made from a cornmeal batter that is poured into a baking dish and placed in a hot oven until set. The texture is somewhere between rich cornbread and a soufflé (because spoon bread is soft—and must be served with a spoon—it's probably closer to a soufflé). Spoon bread is a side dish that can be served in place of rice or potatoes or for breakfast.

To make spoon bread, you first whisk cornmeal into a simmering liquid and let it thicken to a "mush," as if you were cooking oatmeal or farina. To the cooled mush you add eggs, salt, butter, and other ingredients. The mixture is poured into a baking dish and baked for 35 to 45 minutes. The resulting dish should be light as air, with a tender, rich crumb.

As with many traditional dishes, ingredients and cooking techniques for spoon bread vary enormously. We began to develop the recipe for our ideal spoon bread by figuring out the best way to make the cornmeal mush.

The proportion of liquid to solids differed wildly in the recipes we consulted. After trying various ratios, we eventually settled on a medium-thick batter, using 3 cups liquid to 1 cup cornmeal. It was harder to incorporate beaten egg whites into heavier mushes, which baked up, well, somewhat heavy. Lighter versions simply did not gel adequately.

The act of stirring cornmeal into simmering milk can be tricky; if you don't do it properly, the meal can separate from the liquid and turn into a bunch of lumps rather than a smooth mush. Plenty of recipes call for the use of a double boiler to prevent lumping, but our suggestion is to focus intently on the job at hand. Start whisking like crazy and don't stop until the mush is thickened, two to four minutes later. It's not much of a time investment when you consider the alternative: 20 to 30 minutes of gentle stirring in a double boiler. Keep the cooking temperature low rather than high, because you want the cornmeal to soften as it cooks.

Having settled on the mush-making method, we moved on to consider the individual ingredients of the dish. Spoon bread made with water is like cornbread made with water: lean. Because spoon bread is often an accompaniment to a special meal, we prefer to splurge on the real article and cut fat and calories somewhere else. Half-and-half was our liquid of choice, supplying just the right amount of richness; cream provided too much, and milk not quite enough.

The oldest recipes for spoon bread call for whole eggs, not separated. A later trend called for separating the eggs and beating them to produce a light, high soufflé. Now we are beginning to see inroads into that procedure, with chemical leaveners compensating for the work the eggs would do. After tasting several dozen of these spoon breads, we found those made with baking powder or baking soda to taste plainly of chemicals. Beaten whites are the best leavener.

Finally, we considered the important question of what type of cornmeal to use. Yellow corn is more common in the North, and Southerners choose white for the same reason. We found that both made good spoon bread, the major difference being that the white produced a bread that was slightly milder in flavor.

A more important variation came with grinds. We prefer a fine grind because it produces a considerably smoother texture. Yellow Quaker cornmeal has a texture akin to table salt and is the proper grind. If you can't get fine-ground cornmeal in your local store, it's no problem. You can approximate a fine grind by putting a medium-ground cornmeal in the food processor or, even better, the blender. The processing will take several minutes, but eventually you will have little clouds of powder-fine meal in the bottom of the workbowl or blender jar.

Spoon Bread
SERVES 6 TO 8

A standard 8-inch soufflé dish works beautifully, but any straight-sided, heavy pan will work, even a cast-iron skillet. Because the spoon bread falls fast from its spectacular height, serve it as quickly as possible; even in its deflated state, though, spoon bread still tastes delicious. Serve leftovers with maple syrup.

3   cups half-and-half

I   teaspoon salt

I   cup fine-ground white or yellow cornmeal, such as Quaker

2   tablespoons unsalted butter, plus extra for greasing soufflé dish

3   large eggs, warmed to room temperature, then separated

1. Heat the oven to 350 degrees. Butter a 1½-quart soufflé dish.

2. Bring the half-and-half and salt to a simmer in a large, heavy saucepan. Reduce the heat to low. Slowly whisk in the cornmeal. Continue whisking until the cornmeal thickens and develops a satin sheen, 2 to 4 minutes. Turn off the heat and stir in the butter; set the mush aside to cool slightly.

3. Whisk the yolks and 1 to 2 teaspoons water together in a small bowl until lemon-colored and very frothy. Stir them into the cooled mush, a little at a time to keep the yolks from cooking. Beat the egg whites to stiff but not dry peaks; gently fold them into the mush mixture.

4. Pour the mixture into the buttered soufflé dish. Bake until the spoon bread is golden brown and has risen above the rim of the dish, about 45 minutes. Serve immediately.

➤ VARIATION

Spoon Bread with Cheddar Cheese
Follow the recipe for Spoon Bread, adding ½ cup (2 ounces) grated sharp cheddar cheese along with the butter.

BAKED CHEESE GRITS

A STAPLE OF THE SOUTHERN BREAKFAST table, grits are a nutritious and substantial start to the day. They appear in many guises, including simmered and sweetened with maple syrup or molasses; cooked to a thick consistency, cooled, and fried in slices; and, our favorite, enriched with cheese and spices and baked until brown on the top and creamy in the middle. From experience, however, we have found that baked cheese grits are often far from perfect. They are either bland and watery or too weighted down with ham, sausage, and other potent flavorings. For our recipe, we wanted a compromise—hearty, robust flavor that did not overwhelm the subtlety of the grits.

We started by cooking the grits. There are two kinds of grits: instant, which cook in five minutes; and old-fashioned, which cook in 15 minutes. In a side-by-side tasting, most tasters thought the instant grits were too creamy and tasted overprocessed. The old-fashioned grits were creamy yet retained a slightly coarse texture that tasters liked. They are called grits for a reason.

To add richness without relying solely on butter, as many recipes do, we cooked the grits in milk rather than water. The grits tasted good, but more in a hot breakfast cereal way—not the flavor we were hoping for. And the flavor of the grits disappeared

behind the lactose-heavy milk flavor. Even when we diluted the milk significantly, the grits tasted too heavily of cooked milk. We then tried a small amount of heavy cream and water mixed together. Everyone liked this batch—the grits were rich but without an overwhelming dairy flavor. We were surprised to find that cooked cream does not develop same strong "cooked" flavor as milk. This is because the extra fat in cream keeps the milk proteins from breaking down when heated. After a few more batches of varying proportions, we found that 1 part cream to 3 parts water provided the best flavor.

To improve things, we tried a few simple additions that would deepen the flavor of the grits without being overpowering. A small diced onion cooked in the saucepan before adding the liquid brought depth and a touch of sweetness. Many tasters liked a little garlic as well, but others thought the garlic overwhelmed the other flavors, so we left it out. Hot pepper sauce added piquancy that cut through the richness.

With the grits cooked, we needed some cheese to fold in before baking. Recipes we found included everything from pasteurized cheese slices to a Spanish cheese called Manchego. A Spanish cheese seemed too far afield for such a humble dish, but we were ready to try just about anything. Monterey Jack and Pepper Jack cheeses made the grits taste sour, although the jalapeños were appreciated and made us increase our amount of hot sauce. Regular cheddar was bland, but the flavor was getting there. Extra-sharp cheddar proved to be the winner. The flavor was assertive and complemented the subtle corn flavor. Everyone in the test kitchen also liked smoked cheddar, but thought that it might be a little strong for the breakfast table.

Now it was time to bake our grits. We knew we wanted a dense texture, more akin to baked polenta than custardy spoon bread. We started off by adding two lightly beaten eggs to the grits before baking, and this provided an airy, almost soufflé-like texture that most tasters found unpleasant. We needed more eggs (and the eggs' coagulating proteins) to bind the grits and give the dish the dense texture we desired. Four eggs made the grits too heavy, and the egg flavor predominated. Three eggs, on the other hand, provided just enough structure without making the grits taste too eggy.

Forty-five minutes in a 350-degree oven (with a little more cheese sprinkled on after 30 minutes to help brown the top) finished off our testing. We had attained our ideal baked grits, rich and flavorful, with a clear corn flavor. And they are neutral enough to pair perfectly with eggs and sausage for breakfast or with roast chicken for dinner.

Baked Cheese Grits

SERVES 4 TO 6

Old-fashioned grits are well worth the extra 10 minutes of cooking; instant grits will bake up too smooth and have an overprocessed flavor. Grits are ready when they are creamy and smooth but retain a little fine-textured coarseness. We preferred a very sharp aged cheddar, but feel free to use any extra-sharp cheddar you like. Or, for a heartier flavor more suitable to brunch or a dinner side dish, substitute smoked cheddar or smoked gouda.

2	tablespoons plus 1 teaspoon unsalted butter
1	small onion, diced fine
1	cup heavy cream
½	teaspoon hot pepper sauce, such as Tabasco
½	teaspoon salt
1⅛	cups old-fashioned grits
8	ounces extra-sharp cheddar cheese, grated (about 2 cups)
3	large eggs, lightly beaten
	Ground black pepper

1. Adjust an oven rack to the lower-middle position and heat the oven to 350 degrees. Grease a 9 by 9-inch baking dish with 1 teaspoon butter.

2. Heat the remaining butter in a large saucepan over medium heat until the foam begins to subside. Add the onion and cook until softened but not browned, about 4 minutes.

3. Add 3 cups water, the cream, hot pepper sauce, and salt and bring to a boil. Whisk in the grits and reduce the heat to low. Cook, stirring frequently, until the grits are thick and creamy, about 15 minutes.

4. Off the heat, thoroughly stir in 1½ cups cheese, the eggs, and pepper to taste. Pour the mixture into the greased baking dish, smooth the top with a rubber spatula, and place the grits in the oven.

5. Bake for 30 minutes. Remove the dish from the oven, sprinkle the remaining ½ cup cheese evenly over the top, and return to the oven. Continue baking until the top is browned, about 15 minutes. Let rest 5 minutes and serve.

BOSTON BAKED BEANS

THERE IS NO DISH MORE CENTRAL TO NEW England cuisine than Boston baked beans, which are white navy beans traditionally flavored with nothing but molasses, salt pork or bacon, and dried mustard. While spare in ingredients, the beans are robust and complexly flavored because of the long, slow simmer they get in the oven. Unfortunately, a lot of the baked beans we have tried are flavorless, under-cooked, or saccharine sweet. Although the recipes we tried were easy enough to put together, arriving at the best-tasting, most efficient recipe for Boston baked beans had its challenges.

The first was the lengthy cooking time. We hoped to shortcut the all-day simmer that most recipes required. To begin, we pitted dried beans against canned beans. Given the long cooking time, it's no surprise that canned beans turned out mushy. They were also unable to absorb flavors like dried beans. (See page 95 for more information on how beans absorb flavors.) This is one dish in which the ease of canned beans was definitely not worth it.

INGREDIENTS: **Molasses**

Molasses is a byproduct of the cane sugar-refining process—it is the liquid that is drawn off after the cane juice has been boiled and undergone crystallization. The resultant molasses is then subjected to subsequent boilings. With each boiling, the molasses grows increasingly dark, bitter, and potent, as more sugar is extracted from it.

There are three types of molasses. Light molasses comes from the first boiling, dark molasses from the second, and black-strap from the third. In the past, sulfur dioxide was often added to molasses to clarify it. Although this process made molasses more attractive, it also added an unappealing flavor. Today, most molasses, including all major brands, is unsulfured.

Thus decided on dried beans, we tried hastening their cooking time by means of a variety of techniques and supposed shortcuts, but they all proved futile. Beans soaked overnight and then simmered cooked unevenly—they were either tough or broke apart. Rapidly boiled beans also cooked unevenly. Even a moderate increase in oven temperature, from the standard recommendation of 300 degrees up to 350 degrees—failed. Defeated, we accepted that the navy beans would have to take their full five hours in a 300-degree oven if they were to have a creamy texture with a slight resiliency. The good news is that once the beans are in the oven, they require no more than an occasional stir, so the cook is free for other activities.

With the cooking method set, we attacked the seasonings. Fat and pork flavoring traditionally come from a healthy amount of salt pork (see page 94 for more information) simmered with the beans. We diced the pork and, over the long cooking time, most of the fat was rendered from the meat, leaving chewy bits of salty pork to punctuate the creamy beans. Most of our testers enjoyed the lush texture the rendered fat contributed to the beans, but the pork did not provide quite enough meaty flavor. This led us to bacon, which is meatier than salt pork. We replaced the salt pork with bacon, but the flavor of the bacon was so strong that it overpowered the more delicate flavor of the beans. We then tried salt pork along with just a small amount of bacon, and this proved the right combination to boost the meatiness without taking over the dish.

While it is traditional to simmer the meat with the beans (some recipes ask the cook to simply throw a big chunk of salt pork in the bottom of the pot), some tasters were put off by the occasional unrendered chunk of fat nestled in the finished beans. We saw several recipes in which the meat was first sautéed, so that the fat was rendered prior to simmering. This batch of beans was the unanimous favorite in the kitchen; the flavors were deeper and meatier because the meat had been browned, and the fat was uniformly distributed throughout the dish.

While most baked bean recipes call for powdered mustard, we hoped to use prepared mustard—something everyone has in their refrigerator. Jarred mustard also provides a perk—vinegar—which we thought might balance some of the sweetness in the

---

INGREDIENTS: "Fresh" Dried Beans

As one of our test cooks stood over pots of beans during the testing for baked beans, she began to wonder if there was a way to tell if the beans were fresh. Noticing a pile of raw beans shriveling in a bowl of water, a colleague observed that beans shrivel when they are old. The test cook herself became aware that some of the beans she cooked were old when, instead of being creamy, their interiors were gritty or mealy. Because bean bags contain no "sell by" date, however, we weren't sure how to determine if the beans we pulled off the supermarket shelves were fresh.

For more information, we contacted legume expert Dr. Barry Swanson at Washington State University. Yes, shriveling during soaking is generally a sign of age, he told us. That is because beans should absorb moisture only through their hilum, the part of the bean that attaches to the pod. But beans are not handled with much care, Swanson said: "People think of them as piles of rocks or gravel." Beans that have been knocked around can develop holes in their seed coats. These holes subsequently admit water, shriveling the bean. Dr. Swanson counsels that apart from soaking, there is no way to tell if the beans you buy are fresh. His advice: "If you find some fresh beans, buy some more."

---

recipe. Dijon-style mustard such as Grey Poupon was too strong tasting, and the texture of whole-grain mustard was wrong. Everyday brown mustard—Gulden's, in particular—provided just the right tangy but mellow flavor.

When it came to molasses, we found a little of that rich mineral tang goes a long way. Much more than a half a cup took over the whole dish, whereas anything less was hard to taste. Just a tablespoon stirred in right before serving helped brighten all of the flavors, much like a squirt of lemon juice would.

While we adhered to tradition for the most part and were relatively pleased with our recipe, some tasters felt the beans lacked body. When we added more molasses, mustard, or meat, the dish became unbalanced. In our research, we had found a few recipes that included raw onion simmered with the beans, which we had initially tried and found unsatisfying. But in the search for more flavor, are thoughts returned to onion. We had cooked the meat already, rendering out the fat, so cooking the onion required only a few more minutes. The onion gave us the flavor we had been looking for. Our beans now tasted deeply flavored.

We followed the instructions of many of the recipes we had found which suggested removing the lid for the last hour of cooking for a little browning. After five hours of cooking, we were rewarded with perfectly tender, rich beans with a syrupy sauce loaded with complex flavors.

Boston Baked Beans
SERVED 4 TO 6

We usually use a relatively mild molasses, but feel free to use a stronger molasses if you want a richer flavor. A couple of tasters preferred versions made with the very potent black-strap molasses. (For more information on types of molasses, see page 92.)

4	ounces salt pork, trimmed of rind and diced
2	ounces bacon (about 2 slices), diced
1	medium onion, diced
1 ½	tablespoons prepared brown mustard
½	cup, plus 1 tablespoon molasses
1	pound dried navy beans, washed and picked clean of any debris or dark-colored beans
	Salt
	Ground black pepper

1. Adjust an oven rack to the lower-middle position and heat the oven to 300 degrees. Heat a 6-quart Dutch oven over medium heat for 2 minutes, add the salt pork and bacon, and cook until lightly browned and most of the fat is rendered, 5 to 6 minutes. Add the onion and continue to cook until the onion has softened, about 8 minutes. Add the mustard, ½ cup molasses, beans, 2 teaspoons salt, and 9 cups water and increase the heat to medium-high. Once boiling, cover the pot and place it in the oven.

2. Cook, stirring once every hour, until the beans are thoroughly soft, about 4 hours. Remove the lid and continue to cook until the liquid has thickened to a syrupy consistency, 1 to 1½ hours. Remove the beans from the oven and stir in the remaining tablespoon of molasses and salt and pepper to taste. (The beans can be refrigerated in an airtight container for up to several days. Warm over medium-low heat before serving.)

INGREDIENTS: Salt Pork

Some confusion exists about the difference between fatback and salt pork, a confusion we experienced at several markets where these products were not correctly labeled.

Salt pork comes from the belly of the pig (like bacon), and it has been cured or preserved in salt. It has streaks of meat running through it and is often rendered to make cracklings. Salt pork is fattier and chewier than bacon, but the two can often be used interchangeably. One significant difference is that bacon is usually smoked, while salt pork is not.

As its name implies, fatback comes from the back of the animal. Unlike salt pork, fatback is not smoked or cured; it is simply fresh fat. Fatback is generally used to lard meat—that is, to run strips of fat through lean meat to improve its flavor when roasted. Fatback doesn't contain meat and cannot be used as a substitute for salt pork or bacon.

BARBECUED BAKED BEANS

BARBECUED BAKED BEANS ARE SLOW-SIMMERED, oven-cooked beans that are similar to Boston baked beans. Barbecued baked beans are bit brasher in flavor, however, so they stand up better to the big flavors of grilled and barbecued foods. Unfortunately, any recipe with the word "barbecue" in its title tends to inspire cooks to toss a pantry's worth of flavorings into the dish; we have tasted "barbecued" beans overloaded with odd seasonings and incendiary with chili heat. We wanted barbecued beans heady with flavor, but we also wanted the seasonings to be balanced enough so that we could taste the beans.

We borrowed certain elements from our Boston baked bean recipe, including the type of bean (navy beans), the long and slow cooking method, and the cooked onion. The flavorings, however, needed to be more substantial. Tasters favored bacon for its smoky, assertive flavor, excluding salt pork altogether (in our Boston baked beans, salt pork takes the lead, with just a hint of bacon added for a meatier flavor). We also added a hefty amount of garlic to the diced onion to further boost the flavor.

As far as seasonings beyond the bacon, onion, and garlic, we wanted to keep it simple. We tried recipes that included everything from diced tomatoes to

Worcestershire sauce, but the flavors were muddy— too much was going on. To get the most potent flavor from the fewest ingredients, we turned to barbecue sauce, and to Bulls-Eye Brand Original Barbecue sauce in particular, the favorite sauce in our blind taste test (see page 128 for details). The sauce's flavors paired well with beans: sweet and tangy, with a potent hickory kick. A little went a long way—a half cup of sauce was enough to flavor the whole pot of beans. Some tasters wanted a slightly stronger hickory taste (which mellowed during the long simmer). A tablespoon stirred in at the end of cooking did the job. The sauce's vinegar tang also cut through the sweetness of this recipe.

While delicious, the barbecue sauce was a little one-dimensional, so we tried adding a little prepared brown mustard (Gulden's is our favorite). As little as 1½ tablespoons did the trick; the mustard added body and balanced the sharp and acrid flavors of the barbecue sauce. As mustard cooks, the compounds that give it its potent kick break down, developing a mellow, nutty flavor.

To sweeten the beans, we thought we could use the molasses that tasted so good in our Boston baked beans. Unfortunately, the mineral bitterness of molasses competed with the hickory tang of the barbecue sauce. We switched to brown sugar, which has some of the earthy flavors of molasses but none of the bitterness, and the results were good. Most tasters, however, wanted just a little more body in the sauce, so we added a tablespoon of molasses back into the mix.

While the beans were flavorful, tasters wanted a little more depth and complexity. We pored over a slew of barbecue sauce and chili recipes looking for that secret ingredient to finish our beans and found something we thought might work: coffee. We replaced part of the water with strong black coffee and were rewarded with delicious, complexly flavored beans. While undetectable in the finished beans, coffee added depth, and its bitterness balanced the sweet and tangy flavors of the sauce. With just a few ingredients and very little preparation, we had beans that would make a great complement to just about any grilled food or backyard party.

SCIENCE: Flavoring Beans

How does flavor get into a bean? We found out that at least two processes are going on as flavor develops in a bean. First, the bean itself develops flavor as it cooks. Beans are full of starch granules made up of layers of tightly packed starch molecules, arranged something like the layers of an onion. As the bean cooks, liquid seeps into the bean through the tiny white area on its side, the hilum, where the bean was originally connected to the pod. (The rest of the seed coat is impermeable unless it has been damaged in handling.) As the liquid leaks in, slowly at first and then more quickly, it gets in between the layers of starch, and the starch granules begin to swell. Eventually, the granules swell to the point of cracking, and the starch rushes into the bean in a process called gelatinization. This process not only alters the texture of a bean but improves its flavor. So, in cooking terms, a fully cooked bean has more flavor than an undercooked bean.

We went back into the kitchen to test this theory, tasting beans cooked in plain water every 10 minutes after the first hour

of cooking until the beans burst. We found that the beans changed over time from a starchy, acrid taste with a chalky texture to a less acrid, rounder flavor with a velvety texture. Once the beans burst, they actually lost flavor, as if it were being washed away by the water.

So cooking itself changes the flavor and texture of the bean. But how do flavors outside the bean get infused into it? When you cook beans with vegetables and herbs, the water-soluble flavor compounds in those ingredients dissolve and flavor the water and then enter and swell the bean, thus flavoring it.

We wondered if it was necessary to introduce the flavorings at the outset of the cooking process. We cooked two batches of beans—one in plain water with bay leaves, garlic, and onions added to the pot once the beans were tender, the other in water with bay leaves, garlic, and onions added at the outset. The beans cooked with the flavorings from the outset tasted much better. Once the starch molecule has totally swollen, it ceases to take in water and therefore cannot absorb any flavorings.

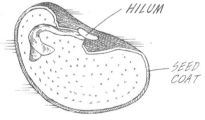

HILUM

SEED COAT

Barbecued Baked Beans

SERVES 4 TO 6

Black coffee is not such a strange companion to beans. It often appears in chili recipes, "cowboy" cooking, and barbecue sauce recipes. If you do not have time to make freshly brewed coffee, instant will do. If using a barbecue sauce other than Bull's-Eye, you may have to adjust the amounts of sugar and hot sauce. If you don't have our preferred brown mustard, Gulden's, on hand, any brand will do.

¼	pound bacon, diced
1	medium onion, diced
4	medium cloves garlic, minced
1	pound dried navy beans, washed and picked clean of any debris or dark-colored beans
1	cup strong black coffee
¼	cup dark brown sugar
1	tablespoon molasses
1½	tablespoons prepared brown mustard
½	cup plus 1 tablespoon barbecue sauce, preferably Bull's-Eye
½	teaspoon hot pepper sauce, such as Tabasco
	Salt
	Ground black pepper

1. Adjust an oven rack to the lower-middle position and heat the oven to 300 degrees. Heat a 6-quart Dutch oven over medium heat for 2 minutes, add the bacon, and cook until lightly browned and most of the fat has rendered, 5 to 6 minutes. Stir in the onion and continue to cook until softened, about 8 minutes. Add the garlic and cook until fragrant, about 30 seconds. Add the beans, coffee, brown sugar, molasses, mustard, ½ cup barbecue sauce, hot pepper sauce, 2 teaspoons salt, and 8 cups water. Increase the heat to high; once boiling, cover the pot and place it in the oven.

2. Cook, stirring once every hour, until the beans are thoroughly soft, about 4 hours. Remove the lid and continue to cook until the liquid has thickened to a syrupy consistency, 1 to 1½ hours. Remove from the oven and stir in the remaining tablespoon of barbecue sauce and salt and pepper to taste. (The beans can be refrigerated in an airtight container for up to several days. Warm over medium-low heat before serving.)

RED BEANS AND RICE

AS NEW ORLEANS LEGEND HAS IT, RED beans and rice was made on Mondays, with the remnants of the Sunday ham, and allowed to simmer slowly, unattended, while the woman of the house busied herself with laundry. From a simple dish of leftovers and pantry staples, it became one of the defining dishes of the bayou.

Red beans and rice, as made nowadays, consists of kidney beans flavored with pork (in one of its many guises), aromatic vegetables (usually onion, celery, and bell pepper), and herbs and spices, all served over white rice and topped off with a garnish consisting of anything from fresh sliced onions to pickled peppers. Like any venerated dish, however, this one has been treated badly at the hands of some cooks and recipe writers. We have had gooey concoctions that come close to bean dip in consistency and other versions laced with such improbable ingredients as cloves, Worcestershire sauce, flour, and ketchup. We wanted a version of red beans and rice that was close to its simple roots, with a pleasing texture and full, rich, spicy flavor but without a mile-long shopping list.

The traditional ham bone can be hard to come by, so we tried both bacon and a smoked pork hock in its place. Tasters all voted for the bacon, which, while lacking the rich tasting marrow of the ham bone, provided good flavor. The pork hock contributed surprisingly little flavor in comparison to the bacon. We cooked a scant 2 ounces of bacon (about two strips) until the fat was rendered. Tasters all enjoyed the deep pork flavor and felt it was the right amount of bacon (any more made the beans taste greasy). We also wanted to add sausage to our beans—the Cajun andouille sausage in particular, which is an authentic element we hoped would add complexity and meatiness, rounding out the now somewhat one-dimensional flavor of the bacon.

We often have a hard time finding andouille in local markets and have used Polish kielbasa in the past. In a taste test comparing four possible sausages, tasters liked the andouille the best, but the kielbasa was the runner-up. Linguiça, a spicy Portuguese sausage, and Mexican chorizo were too pungent and overwhelmed the other flavors.

The vegetables were next. Not out to reinvent the wheel, we stuck close to the trinity of Cajun cooking: onion, celery, and green bell pepper. Most of our tasters, however, disliked the green pepper's bitterness. When we substituted red bell pepper, everyone liked the flavor. We also added a healthy dose of garlic—never a stranger to Cajun cooking—to stand up to the hearty sausage. Bay leaves, dried thyme, and dried oregano—the classic seasonings for red beans—rounded out the flavor. Most tasters thought all three herbs were necessary for depth and complexity.

For spiciness, hot pepper sauce or cayenne pepper is traditional. Tasters liked each on its own but were most fond of the flavor and spiciness when both were used. We found that the heat of cayenne pepper built slowly, while the heat of hot sauce hit instantly. The vinegar in the hot sauce also helped to balance the other flavors in the dish.

Plain long-grain white rice is the authentic accompaniment. A few recipes we found actually mix the beans and rice together, but none of the tasters found that presentation appetizing. Brick-red beans nestled on a bed of fluffy white rice made the best appearance.

To top the beans, recipes suggested a variety of garnishes, including sliced spring onions, pickled onions, pickled pepper sauce, and more sausage. Most tasters enjoyed the way the liveliness of the onion and vinegar contrasted with the rich and creamy beans, so we tried combining pickled onions and pickled chile peppers. We chose red onions for their natural sweetness and color and added fresh jalapeño slices for heat.

Red Beans and Rice

SERVES 4 TO 6 AS A MAIN COURSE

It is worth looking for both small kidney beans and andouille sausage for an authentic texture and flavor. We were pleased with readily available Goya dried "small red beans."

- 2 ounces bacon (about 2 slices), diced
- 1 medium onion, diced fine
- 1 medium red bell pepper, stemmed, seeded, and diced fine
- 1 medium stalk celery, diced fine
- 4 medium cloves garlic, minced
- 1 teaspoon ground black pepper
- ½ teaspoon cayenne pepper
- 1 teaspoon hot pepper sauce, such as Tabasco, plus more to taste
- 1 teaspoon dried oregano
- 1 teaspoon dried thyme
- 4 bay leaves
  Salt
- 1 pound dried small red kidney beans, washed and picked clean of any debris
- ½ pound andouille or kielbasa sausage, halved lengthwise and then cut crosswise into ¼-inch half circles
- 6 cups cooked long-grain white rice (from 3 cups raw rice)
- 1 recipe Pickled Red Onions (recipe follows)

1. Heat an 8-quart Dutch oven over medium heat for 2 minutes, add the bacon, and cook until lightly browned and the fat has rendered, 5 to 6 minutes. Add the onion, bell pepper, and celery, and continue to cook, stirring frequently, until the vegetables have softened, about 8 minutes more. Stir in the garlic and cook until fragrant, about 30 seconds. Add the black pepper, cayenne, hot pepper sauce, oregano, thyme, bay leaves, 1 teaspoon salt, beans, and 12 cups water and bring to a boil over medium-high heat. Reduce the heat to low and simmer, stirring occasionally, until the beans are soft and the liquid thickens, about 2½ hours.

2. Stir in the sausage and cook until the sauce is thick and creamy, about 30 minutes. Adjust the seasonings, adding more salt or hot pepper sauce as desired. Serve the beans in a shallow bowl over the cooked rice and garnish with the pickled onions.

Pickled Red Onions

MAKES ABOUT 1 CUP

You can add more jalapeños if you want more heat.

- ½ cup white vinegar
- 4 bay leaves
- ½ teaspoon salt
- 1 tablespoon sugar
- 12 black peppercorns
- 1 medium red onion, halved and sliced thin
- 1 jalapeño chile, stemmed, seeded, and sliced thin

Bring the vinegar, bay leaves, salt, sugar, peppercorns, and ½ cup water to a boil in a small saucepan over medium-high heat. Stir in the onion and jalapeño, return to a boil, and remove the pan from the heat. Cool to room temperature and remove and discard the bay leaves and the peppercorns. (The pickled onions can be refrigerated in an airtight container for up to 1 week.) Serve at room temperature, lifting onion and chile slices from the liquid with a fork.

DIRTY RICE

DIRTY RICE, ONE OF THE MORE COLORFULLY named Cajun dishes, is a delicious combination of chicken livers, vegetables, sausage, and white rice. The dubious name was derived from how the cooked chicken livers crumble into the rice and give it a "dirty" grayish hue. A lot of recipes seem to take the name literally and add everything but the kitchen sink to the rice, including chicken innards and necks, ground beef, ground pork, and a whole list of vegetables and spices. For our dirty rice, we wanted to keep the flavors abundant but clean; we didn't want a dish with so many ingredients that it tasted muddy or would take all day to prepare.

Like most savory Cajun dishes, dirty rice is built on a foundation of onions, celery, and bell peppers sautéed in lard or bacon grease. We used this combination in our red beans and rice and were pleased with the body and flavor the vegetables and pork fat contributed. A quarter pound of browned bacon—more convenient and more flavorful than lard—provided enough fat to adequately cook the vegetables. Contrary to our recipe for red beans and rice, where we substituted red bell pepper for the traditional green, here we included both green and red for visual appeal. Tasters did not object to the mild bitterness of the green pepper, as they had in red beans and rice. A substantial amount of garlic added a lot of body to the vegetables and a characteristic Cajun zing.

While both chicken gizzards and livers are traditional ingredients in dirty rice, we chose livers because they are more available and because most tasters disliked the intense organ flavor of gizzards. We tried sautéing and simmering the livers and were struck by the difference in taste. Dry heat-sautéing the livers with the vegetables proved the best method. The rich, slightly earthy liver flavor married well with the sweet and savory vegetables. When the livers were simmered, however, the earthiness increased and overwhelmed the other ingredients.

Finding out that moist heat adversely affected the flavor of the chicken livers changed our whole approach to cooking the dish. We had planned on cooking the rice like a pilaf—sautéing the vegetables and chicken livers, adding the rice and water, and then simmering everything together until the rice was tender. But our tests with chicken livers convinced us to cook the aromatic vegetables and meat independent from the rice. We did find that if we used a pot large enough for the rice, we could cook the livers in it first and then deglaze the fond (the browned bits left in the pan after sautéing) with the liquid used to cook the rice. This not only saved us from washing one pot but gave the resulting cooked rice both color and a good bit of flavor.

While the dirty rice was delicious with just bacon and chicken livers, tasters hankered for more meat. We added a bit of andouille sausage, the spicy Cajun pork sausage, and there was no going back. The flavor was deep, rich, and smoky, and even confirmed liver haters were coming back for seconds and thirds.

To finish the dish, it was a simple step to fold the vegetables and meat into the cooked rice in the large pot. This rice may not be the "dirtiest" you'll ever see, but it does pack a lot of well-balanced flavor.

Dirty Rice

SERVES 4 TO 6 AS A MAIN COURSE

While an 8-quart Dutch oven may seem excessive, we found it allowed the vegetables to cook without "sweating" too much and losing their texture and flavor. If you can't find spicy andouille sausage, kielbasa makes a decent, if not terribly authentic, alternative.

2	cups long-grain white rice
4	ounces bacon (about 4 slices), diced
I	medium onion, diced
I	large stalk celery, diced
I	medium red bell pepper, stemmed, seeded, and diced

1 medium green bell pepper, stemmed, seeded, and diced

4 medium cloves garlic, minced

8 ounces chicken livers, rinsed, any veins and fat removed, and chopped coarse

4 ounces andouille or kielbasa sausage, halved lengthwise and then cut crosswise into ¼-inch half circles

½ teaspoon ground black pepper

½ teaspoon cayenne pepper

½ teaspoon hot pepper sauce, such as Tabasco, plus more to taste

Salt

1¾ cups homemade chicken stock or canned low-sodium chicken broth

2 bay leaves

2 teaspoons minced fresh thyme leaves

2 teaspoons minced fresh oregano leaves

2 teaspoons minced fresh parsley leaves

1. Place the rice in a medium bowl and add enough water to cover by 2 inches; using your hands, gently swish the grains to release the excess starch. Carefully pour off the water, leaving the rice in the bowl. Repeat the process 4 or 5 times, until the water is almost clear. Using a fine-mesh strainer, drain the water from the rice and set the rice aside.

2. Heat an 8-quart Dutch oven over medium heat for 2 minutes. Add the bacon and cook until lightly browned and the fat has rendered, 5 to 6 minutes. Add the onion, celery, and bell peppers and continue to cook, stirring frequently, until the vegetables have softened, about 10 minutes. Stir in the garlic and cook until fragrant, about 30 seconds, and then add the chicken livers, sausage, black pepper, cayenne, hot pepper sauce, and ½ teaspoon salt. Continue to cook, stirring occasionally, until the chicken livers are no longer pink and have given off most of their liquid, 8 to 9 minutes. Transfer the vegetables and meat to a medium bowl and cover with aluminum foil to keep warm.

3. Increase the heat to high and add the chicken stock, bay leaves, and 1¼ cups water (3 cups total liquid). With a wooden spoon, scrape the bottom of the pot to remove any browned bits, and then add the rice. Once boiling, stir, reduce the heat to low, and cover. After 17 minutes, remove the rice from the

heat, fluff with a fork, and remove the bay leaves. With a rubber spatula, gently fold in the meat and vegetable mixture and the herbs, and season to taste with salt and hot pepper sauce. Serve immediately.

HOPPIN' JOHN

WHILE GENERALLY SERVED ON NEW YEAR'S Day for good luck during the upcoming year, Hoppin' John is good anytime as a robust meal. Authentic Hoppin' John, as made in the Carolinas, is a white rice pilaf or casserole flavored with smoked pork, black-eyed peas, herbs, and spices. There are different suggestions as to the origin of its odd name, but some researchers believe it is derived from the Creole-inflected French *pois à pigeon*, or pigeon pea, the original bean used in the dish.

Whatever the name may mean, we find that too often Hoppin' John is chockfull of pithy or overcooked peas and soggy, wet rice. Often the dish is strangely bland—necessitating the use of great quantities of hot sauce. We wanted to devise a recipe that did not overcook the peas or rice and that was both highly flavored and balanced. We also wanted to cook it in the oven, like a casserole, to free up the stovetop for other uses.

Hoppin' John is usually made with black-eyed peas (more readily available than the authentic pigeon pea), although field peas are sometimes substituted. We were unable to find a source for field peas north of the Mason-Dixon line, so we stuck with black-eyed peas. We tried peas in different forms and were surprised by what we discovered. Canned peas were out of the question. They were slimy and did not hold up well to any further cooking. Dried peas cooked unevenly; sometimes the peas were tough and wrinkled (a sure sign of a stale pea), while other times they were tender to a fault. Luckily, we found precooked black-eyed peas in the frozen foods aisle. These peas retained their shape and pleasing texture and need only minutes to cook as opposed to the hours of cooking dried peas require.

We found that Hoppin' John's deep flavor rested squarely on the pork. Smoked ham hock is authentic but problematic. Tasters enjoyed the flavor but disliked the texture of the meat, which we shredded and returned to the pot after the dish had simmered. Salt pork was vetoed for its overwhelmingly "chewy" texture. Diced, cooked ham was the favorite for its pleasing texture, but it lacked the smokiness of the ham hock. A small amount of bacon, in addition to the ham, added the requisite smokiness and also supplied ample fat in which to sauté the vegetables.

From the many options for vegetables we selected only aromatics, onions and garlic, which added body, sweetness, and pungency. Other vegetables, like celery and bell pepper, detracted from the simple flavors of the pork, peas, and rice. For herbs, thyme and bay leaves are traditional, and everyone in the kitchen liked them. We decided to stir in parsley at the end for color and freshness.

With the flavors settled, we were ready to cook the rice. We wanted rice that was fluffy, not sodden or sticky, as it is in too many rice casseroles. We knew that the choice of rice and the ratio of liquid to rice were crucial to success. After cooking numerous pots of rice, we found that 3½ cups liquid to 1½ cups rice provided the texture we desired. We also substituted chicken stock for some of the water to add a little more flavor. A casserole dish (covered with aluminum foil to keep the rice from drying out) and the regulated heat of the oven proved to best way to cook the rice. On top of the stove, a saucepan became overfilled with ingredients and the rice cooked very unevenly.

Hoppin' John

SERVES 4 TO 6 AS A MAIN COURSE

Frozen black-eyed peas have a surprisingly good texture and flavor. Do not use canned peas in this recipe; they are too mushy and can't withstand baking in the oven.

	Butter for greasing baking dish
1	tablespoon vegetable oil
6	ounces cooked ham, cut into ½-inch dice (about 1¼ cups)
4	ounces bacon (about 4 slices), cut into ½-inch dice

1	medium onion, diced
3	medium cloves garlic, minced
1½	cups long-grain white rice
1½	teaspoons minced fresh thyme leaves
½	teaspoon hot red pepper flakes
2	bay leaves
2	cups homemade chicken stock or canned low-sodium chicken broth
1	teaspoon salt
	Ground black pepper
1	(10-ounce) package frozen black-eyed peas, thawed and rinsed
2	tablespoons minced fresh parsley leaves

1. Preheat the oven to 375 degrees. Butter a 9 by 13-inch baking dish and set it aside.

2. Heat the oil until shimmering in a heavy, 12-inch skillet over medium-high heat. Add the ham and cook until fat has rendered, about 6 minutes. Add the bacon and cook until slightly crisp, about 3 minutes. Use a slotted spoon to remove the ham and bacon from the pan and set aside on a paper towel–lined plate.

3. Spoon off and discard all but 2 tablespoons of the fat from the skillet and return to the heat. Reduce the heat to medium; add the onion and sauté, stirring frequently, until softened, 3 to 4 minutes. Add the garlic and sauté until fragrant, about 30 seconds longer. Stir in the rice, thyme, and red pepper flakes and cook, stirring frequently, until the rice is coated and glistening, about 1 minute longer. Transfer the rice mixture to the baking dish and add the bay leaves.

4. Return the skillet to the heat; add the chicken stock, 1½ cups water, salt, and pepper to taste. Increase the heat to medium-high, scraping the browned bits off the bottom of pan with a wooden spoon. Add the black-eyed peas, ham, and bacon, bring to a boil, and pour over the rice mixture, stirring to combine.

5. Cover the baking dish tightly with aluminum foil and bake for 20 minutes. Remove from the oven, stir the rice (if the rice appears too dry, add ¼ cup water), re-cover with foil, and cook until the rice is fully tender, 20 to 25 minutes more. Remove the dish from the oven. Stir in the parsley, re-cover the dish, and allow it to rest for 5 to 10 minutes. Serve immediately.

5

BEEF

AS A NATION, AMERICANS CERTAINLY LOVE beef. Our cattle industry has a long, proud history, and many connoisseurs believe that our beef is the world's finest. For most of our history, home cooks have relied on inexpensive offerings and ground beef. Many of these cuts come from the chuck or brisket (see the illustration below) and are quite tough unless cooked for long periods of time. (Think pot roast or brisket.) Expensive cuts, such as prime rib or New York strip steaks, come from the rib or short loin and were once eaten mainly at restaurants. But in recent years, home cooks have been attracted to these tender cuts. Many can be grilled and ready to serve in a matter of minutes.

For this chapter, we have decided to focus on down-home favorites made with relatively affordable cuts of beef. Seared filet mignon has its place in every cook's repertoire, but we suspect that home cooks prepare more meat loaf than filet.

CHICKEN-FRIED STEAK

ALTHOUGH THIS TRUCK-STOP FAVORITE often gets a bad rap, chicken-fried steak can be delicious when cooked just right. When cooked wrong, the dry, rubbery steaks snap back with each bite and are coated in a damp, pale breading and topped with a bland, pasty white sauce. When cooked well, however, thin cutlets of beef are breaded and fried until crisp and golden brown. The creamy gravy that accompanies the steaks is well seasoned and not too thick.

The first question we encountered on the road to good chicken-fried steak was what type of steak to use. By design, chicken-fried steak is a technique used with only the cheapest of cuts. No one would use strip steaks or filet mignon in this recipe, but steaks from the round, chuck, and sirloin are all contenders. We tested cube, Swiss, top-round, bottom-round, eye-round, chuck, and top sirloin steaks and came up with one winner. The cube steak was our favorite. This steak is lean yet tender; most of the other cuts tested were either fatty or difficult to chew.

Cube steak is usually cut from the round and tenderized (cubed) by the butcher, who uses a special machine to give the steak its unique, bumpy texture. We found that this lean, tender steak required little trimming and was easy to pound out to a thin cutlet, about ⅓ inch thick. Regular top-, bottom-, and eye-round steaks, on the other hand, were thick and tough, requiring lots of muscle to pound out and chew. Swiss and chuck steaks, which come from the shoulder, were slightly less tough but still chewy and resilient. Top sirloin tasted great and had a nice texture, but the meat was laced with wide strips of gristle. Trimming the gristle turned this steak into small, awkwardly sized pieces, making for unusual portions and cooking times.

What really makes chicken-fried steak great is the coating and subsequent frying. But what kind of coating is best? To find out, we tested straight flour against various contenders, including cornflakes, Melba toast, cornmeal, matzo crumbs, ground saltines, and panko (Japanese bread crumbs). Straight flour was light and clung well to the steak but was simply too delicate for the toothsome meat and cream gravy. Cornflakes and Melba toast both burned and became tough, while the grittiness of cornmeal was simply out of place. Matzo, saltines, and panko all tasted great but quickly grew soggy under the rich cream gravy.

We figured our single-breading technique might to be blame and decided to try double (or bound) breading. With single breading, meat is dipped into egg and then into flour, while double breading starts

THE EIGHT PRIMAL CUTS OF BEEF

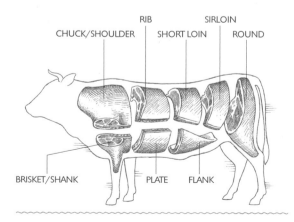

off with an initial dip in flour, then into egg, and again into flour (or into a coating such as those we tried with the steak). In side-by-side tests, we were surprised to discover that single breading was actually messier than double. When initially dipped in flour, the meat becomes dry and talcum-smooth, allowing the egg to cling evenly to the surface. The double breading also offered a more substantial base coat on the meat that didn't become overly thick or tough. Seasoned flour and a double-breading technique yielded a much improved crust.

Although this double breading was far superior to any other breading so far, we were still left wanting a heartier and crunchier crust. We wondered if we could bolster the egg wash with some buttermilk, baking soda, and baking powder, something that we knew worked well with fried chicken. Sure enough, these ingredients turned the egg wash into a thick, foamy concoction. This created a wet yet airy layer into which both layers of flour were able to stick and hydrate. This wet-looking, skin-like coating fried up to an impressive, dark mahogany color with a resilient texture that didn't weaken under the gravy. Because the coating is such a big part of the dish, we found it necessary to season it heavily using salt, black pepper, and cayenne.

After frying a few batches of these steaks, we found the flavor of peanut oil preferable to that of vegetable oil or even shortening. Because the steaks are thin, they fry evenly in just one inch of oil. To keep splattering to a minimum, we used a deep Dutch oven. We also noted that the steaks fried to a dark, beautiful brown without tasting too greasy when the oil was heated initially to 375 degrees. Although the thick breading offers substantial protection from the hot oil, the steaks usually cook through completely within the time it takes for the crust to brown, about 2½ minutes per side.

Equally important to the crust is the cream gravy made from the fried drippings. Not wanting to waste any time while the fried steaks were kept warm in the oven, we found it easy to strain the small amount of hot oil used to fry the steaks right away. Adding the strained bits of deep-fried crumbs back to the Dutch oven, we were ready to make gravy. Most recipes simmer the drippings with some milk and thicken it with flour. To avoid making a floury-

tasting sauce, we decided to cook the flour in the fat (that is, make a roux) and then add the milk, along with a splash of chicken stock. We found this technique quick and easy, and it produced an authentic-tasting sauce.

We tested recipes using cream, half-and-half, and evaporated milk, but tasters preferred the fresh, clean flavor and lighter texture of whole milk. Onions and cayenne are traditional seasonings for the gravy, but tasters also liked small additions of thyme and garlic (neither of which is authentic). Topped with the light, well-seasoned gravy, this chicken-fried steak is the best any trucker has ever tasted.

Chicken-Fried Steak

SERVES 6

Getting the initial oil temperature to 375 degrees is key to the success of this recipe. An instant-read thermometer with a high upper range is perfect for checking the temperature; a clip-on candy/deep-fry thermometer is also fine. If your Dutch oven measures 11 inches across (as ours does), you will need to fry the steaks in two batches.

STEAK

3 cups unbleached all-purpose flour
Salt and ground black pepper
⅛ teaspoon cayenne pepper
1 large egg
1 teaspoon baking powder
½ teaspoon baking soda
1 cup buttermilk
6 cube steaks, about 5 ounces each, pounded to ⅓-inch thickness
4–5 cups peanut oil

CREAM GRAVY

1 medium onion, minced
⅛ teaspoon dried thyme
2 medium cloves garlic, minced
3 tablespoons all-purpose flour
½ cup homemade chicken stock or canned low-sodium chicken broth
2 cups whole milk
¾ teaspoon salt
¼ teaspoon ground black pepper
Pinch cayenne pepper

1. FOR THE STEAKS: Measure the flour, 5 teaspoons salt, 1 teaspoon pepper, and cayenne into a large shallow dish. In a second large shallow dish, beat the egg, baking powder, and baking soda; stir in the buttermilk (the mixture will bubble and foam).

2. Set a wire rack over a rimmed baking sheet. Pat the steaks dry with paper towels and sprinkle each side with salt and pepper to taste. Drop the steaks into the flour and shake the pan to coat. Shake excess flour from each steak, then, using tongs, dip the steaks into the egg mixture, turning to coat well and allowing the excess to drip off. Coat the steaks with flour again, shake off the excess, and place them on the wire rack.

3. Adjust an oven rack to the middle position, set a second wire rack over a second rimmed baking sheet, and place on the oven rack; heat the oven to 200 degrees. Line a large plate with a double layer of paper towels. Meanwhile, heat 1 inch of oil in a large (11-inch diameter) Dutch oven over medium-high heat to 375 degrees. Place three steaks in the oil and fry, turning once, until deep golden brown on each side, about 5 minutes (oil temperature will drop to around 335 degrees). Transfer the steaks to the paper towel–lined plate to drain, then transfer them to the wire rack in the oven. Bring the oil back to 375 degrees and repeat the cooking and draining process (use fresh paper towels) with the three remaining steaks.

4. FOR THE GRAVY: Carefully pour the hot oil through a fine-mesh strainer into a clean pot. Return the browned bits from the strainer along with 2 tablespoons of frying oil back to the Dutch oven. Turn the heat to medium, add the onion and thyme, and cook until the onion has softened and begins to brown, 4 to 5 minutes. Add the garlic and cook until aromatic, about 30 seconds. Add the flour to the pan and stir until well combined, about 1 minute. Whisk in the stock, scraping any browned bits off the bottom of the pan. Whisk in the milk, salt, pepper, and cayenne; bring to a simmer over medium-high heat. Cook until thickened (gravy should have a loose consistency—it will thicken as it cools slightly), about 5 minutes.

5. Transfer the chicken-fried steaks to individual plates. Spoon a generous amount of gravy over each steak. Serve immediately, passing any remaining gravy in a small bowl.

MEAT LOAF

NOT ALL MEAT LOAVES RESEMBLE MAMA'S. In fact, some ingredient lists look like the work of a proud child or defiant adolescent. Canned pineapple, cranberry sauce, raisins, prepared taco mix, and even goat cheese have all found their way into published recipes. Rather than feud over flavorings, though, we decided to focus on the meatier issues.

To begin with, we narrowed our testing to red meat. We had plenty of questions to answer: What meat or mix of meats delivers good mouthfeel and flavor? Which fillers offer unobtrusive texture? Should the loaf be cooked free-form or in a standard loaf pan, or are the new perforated pans designed for meat loaves worth the money? Should the loaf be topped with bacon, ketchup, both, or neither? Is it better to sauté the onions and garlic before adding them to the meat mix, or are they just as good raw and grated?

To determine which ground meat or meat mix makes the best loaf, we used a very basic meat loaf recipe and made miniature loaves with the following meat proportions: equal parts beef chuck and pork; equal parts veal and pork; equal parts beef chuck, pork, and veal; 2 parts beef chuck to 1 part ground pork and 1 part ground veal; 3 parts beef chuck and 1 part ground bacon; equal parts beef chuck and ham; all ground beef chuck; and all ground veal.

We found out that meat markets haven't been selling meat loaf mix (a mix of beef, pork, and veal, usually in equal proportions) all these years for nothing. As we expected, the best meat loaves were made from the combinations of these three meats. Straight ground veal was tender but overly mild and mushy, while the all-beef loaf was coarse-textured, liver-flavored, and tough. Though interesting, neither the beef/ham nor the beef/bacon loaves looked or tasted like classic meat loaf. Both were firm, dense, and more terrine-like. Also, as bacon lovers, we preferred the bacon's smoky flavor and crispy texture surrounding, not in, the loaf.

Although both of the beef/pork/veal mixtures were good, we preferred the mix with a higher proportion of ground chuck. This amount gave the loaf a distinct but not overly strong beef flavor. The extra beef percentage also kept the loaf firm, making it easier to cut. Mild-tasting pork added another flavor dimension, while the small quantity of veal kept it tender. For those who choose not to special-order this mix or mix it themselves at home, we recommend the standard meat loaf mix of equal parts beef, pork, and veal.

After comparing meat loaves made with and without fillers or binders, we realized that starch in a meat loaf offers more than economy. Loaves made without filler were coarse-textured, dense, and too hamburger-like. Those with binders, on the other hand, had that distinctive meat loaf texture.

But which binder to use? Practically every hot and cold cereal box offers a meat loaf recipe using that particular cereal. We made several meat loaves, each with a different filler. Though there was no clear-cut winner, we narrowed the number from 11 down to three.

After tasting all the meat loaves, we realized that

INGREDIENTS: Ketchup

For many people, a burger isn't done until it has been coated liberally with ketchup. Ketchup is also an essential ingredient in many meat loaf recipes, including ours. This condiment originated in Asia as a salty, fermented medium for pickling or preserving ingredients, primarily fish. Early versions were made with anchovies and generally were highly spiced.

Tomato-based ketchup has its origins in nineteenth-century America. We now consume more than 600 million pints of ketchup every year, much of it landing on top of burgers. But as any ketchup connoisseur knows, not all brands are created equal. To find out which is the best, we tasted 13 different samples, including several fancy mail-order ketchups and one we made in our test kitchen.

It wasn't much of a surprise that the winner was Heinz. For all tasters but one, Heinz ranked first or second, and they described it with words like "classic" and "perfect." A tiny bit sweeter than Heinz, Del Monte took second place, while Hunt's (the other leading national brand, along with Heinz and Del Monte) rated third.

What about the mail-order, organic, fruit-sweetened, and homemade ketchups? Most tasters felt these samples were overly thick and not smooth enough. Some were too spicy, others too vinegary. Our homemade ketchup was too chunky, more like "tomato jam" than ketchup. In color, consistency, and flavor, none of these interlopers could match the archetypal ketchup, Heinz.

a good binder should help with texture but not add distinct flavor. Cracker crumbs, quick-cooking oatmeal, and fresh bread crumbs fit the bill.

Just as we found that we liked the less distinctly flavored fillers, so we preferred sautéed—not raw—onions and garlic in the meat mix. Because the meat loaf cooks to an internal temperature of just 160 degrees, raw onions never fully cook. Sautéing the vegetables is a five-minute detour well worth the time.

We found our meat loaves in need of some liquid to moisten the filler. Without it, the filler robs the meat dry. As with the fillers, we ran across a host of meat loaf moisteners and tried as many as made sense.

Tomato sauce made the loaf taste like a meatball with sauce. We liked the flavor of ketchup but ultimately decided that we preferred it baked on top rather than inside.

Beer and wine do not make ideal meat moisteners, either. The meat doesn't cook long enough or to a high enough internal temperature to burn off the alcohol, so the meat ends up with a distinctly raw alcohol taste.

As with many other aspects of this home-cooked favorite, we found that there is a good reason why the majority of meat loaf recipes call for some form of dairy for the liquid—it's the best choice. We tried half-and-half, milk, sour cream, yogurt, skim and whole evaporated milk, and even cottage cheese. Whole milk and plain yogurt ended up as our liquids of choice, with the yogurt offering a complementary subtle tang to the rich beef.

Cooks who don't like a crusty exterior on their meat loaf usually prefer to bake it in a loaf pan. We found that the high-sided standard loaf pan, however, causes the meat to stew rather than bake. Also, for those who like a glazed top, there is another disadvantage: The enclosed pan allows the meat juices to bubble up from the sides, diluting and destroying the glaze. Similarly, bacon placed on top of the meat loaf curls and doesn't properly attach to the loaf, and if tucked inside the pan, the bacon never crisps.

For all these reasons, we advise against the use of a standard loaf pan. If you prefer a crustless, soft-sided meat loaf, invest in a meat loaf pan with a perforated bottom and accompanying drip pan. The enclosed pan keeps the meat soft while the perforated bottom allows the drippings to flow to the pan below.

While still not ideal for a crispy bacon top, it at least saves the glaze from destruction.

We ultimately found that baking a meat loaf free-form on a rimmed baking sheet gave us the results we wanted. The top and sides of the loaf brown nicely, and basting sauces, like the brown sugar and ketchup sauce we developed, glaze the entire loaf, not just the top. Bacon, too, covers the whole loaf. And because its drippings also fall into the pan, the bacon crisps up nicely.

Meat Loaf with Brown Sugar–Ketchup Glaze

SERVES 6 TO 8

If you like, you can omit the bacon topping from the loaf. In this case, brush on half of the glaze before baking and the other half during the last 15 minutes of baking. If you choose not to special-order the mix of meat below, we recommend the standard meat loaf mix of equal parts beef, pork, and veal, available at most grocery stores.

GLAZE

½	cup ketchup or chili sauce
4	tablespoons brown sugar
4	teaspoons cider or white vinegar

MEAT LOAF

2	teaspoons vegetable oil
1	medium onion, chopped
2	cloves garlic, minced
2	large eggs
½	teaspoon dried thyme leaves
1	teaspoon salt
½	teaspoon ground black pepper
2	teaspoons Dijon mustard
2	teaspoons Worcestershire sauce
¼	teaspoon hot pepper sauce, such as Tabasco
½	cup whole milk or plain yogurt
2	pounds meat loaf mix (50 percent ground chuck, 25 percent ground pork, 25 percent ground veal)
⅔	cup crushed saltine crackers (about 16) or quick oatmeal or 1⅓ cups fresh bread crumbs
⅓	cup minced fresh parsley leaves
6–8	ounces thin-sliced bacon (8 to 12 slices, depending on loaf shape)

1. FOR THE GLAZE: Mix all ingredients in a small saucepan; set aside.

2. FOR THE MEAT LOAF: Heat the oven to 350 degrees. Heat the oil in a medium skillet. Add the onion and garlic; sauté until softened, about 5 minutes. Set aside to cool while preparing the remaining ingredients.

3. Mix the eggs with the thyme, salt, black pepper, mustard, Worcestershire sauce, hot pepper sauce, and milk in a medium bowl. Add the egg mixture to the meat in a large bowl along with the crackers, parsley, and cooked onion and garlic; mix with a fork until evenly blended and the meat mixture does not stick to the bowl. (If mixture sticks, add more milk, a couple tablespoons at a time, until the mix no longer sticks.)

4. Turn the meat mixture onto a work surface. With wet hands, pat the mixture into a loaf shape approximately 9 by 5 inches. Place on a foil-lined (for easy cleanup) rimmed baking sheet. Brush with half the glaze, then arrange the bacon slices, crosswise, over the loaf, overlapping slightly, to completely cover the surface of the loaf. Use a spatula to tuck the bacon ends underneath the loaf.

5. Bake the loaf until the bacon is crisp and the internal temperature of the loaf registers 160 degrees, about 1 hour. Cool at least 20 minutes. Simmer the remaining glaze over medium heat until thickened slightly. Slice the meat loaf and serve with extra glaze passed separately.

TAMALE PIE

TAMALE PIE HAS ITS ROOTS IN SOUTHWESTERN cooking. A mildly spicy ground meat filling is layered between a cornmeal crust and baked. Versions of this dish have been made throughout the past century. Although time and fashion have altered the recipe from decade to decade, the basic idea remains the same. A good pie contains a juicy, spicy mixture of meat and vegetables encased in a cornmeal crust that is neither too stiff nor too loose. Bad tamale pies, however, are dry and bland and usually have too much or too little filling.

Modern recipes often use cornbread for the crust. Many of these cornbread recipes skip the bottom layer of crust all together and just bake cornbread batter on top of the ground meat filling. More traditional recipes use cornmeal mush (cornmeal cooked with liquid, not unlike polenta) for both the bottom and top crusts. After several tests, we came to prefer a more traditional pie fully encased in cornmeal mush. Not only was this kind of tamale pie easier to serve, but its soft, polenta-like texture mixed nicely with the meat filling and was easier to eat.

We did have a number of questions about how to prepare the cornmeal mush. For starters, we tested finely ground cornmeal (such as Quaker, which is sold in most supermarkets) against coarser meals. As expected, the crust made with fine-ground cornmeal was slightly smoother, but it was also bland in comparison with the toothsome crust made with coarse ground cornmeal. (For more information on cornmeal, see page 268.) We made the mush with water and stock as well as with and without butter. Tasters preferred the clean, simple flavor of mush made with just water, salt, and cornmeal. The stock and butter added more flavor and fat to the crust than was necessary. We found 4 cups of water to 1½ cups cornmeal yielded a spoonable texture with enough structure to contain the meat filling.

Authentic and modern recipes use a variety of techniques to make the mush; some cook it slowly over low heat to keep it from burning, while others use the microwave. We found it difficult to keep an eye on the mush in the microwave, while cooking it low and slow was unnecessary. Using medium-high heat and a heavy-duty whisk, the mush took only 3 minutes to thicken to the right consistency.

With the cornmeal mush crust in place, we moved on to the filling. Most recipes use either ground beef or ground pork as the base, but we liked the flavors of both when mixed together. An all-beef pie turned out boring and tough, while an all-pork pie was light and mealy. A pie made with equal amounts of beef and pork turned out flavorful and nicely textured.

Most tamale pie fillings call for tomatoes, corn, and black beans. We found that this simple recipe easily accommodates canned and frozen vegetables with no ill effect on the final flavor. Seasoned with onion, garlic, jalapeño, and a little fresh oregano, the tamale filling tasted fresh and spicy.

Putting together the crust and filling was simple. We found that a deep-dish pie plate held the volume of this pie perfectly, and the sloped edges made it easy to spread the cornmeal mush over the bottom and up the sides evenly. A layer of cheese just under the top crust melts nicely without turning the top crust soggy or mixing prematurely with the filling. Sealed with a top layer of cornmeal mush, the pie needs only 30 minutes on the lowest oven rack in a 375-degree oven for the cornmeal to set and the pie to heat through. The pie will be easier to serve if you allow it to cool slightly before digging in.

Tamale Pie
SERVES 6 TO 8

We like coarse cornmeal (about the texture of kosher salt) for the crust. We had good results with Goya Coarse Yellow Cornmeal. To keep the cornmeal mush at a spreadable consistency, cover it while assembling the pie. If the mush does get too dry, simply loosen it with a little hot water.

FILLING

	Butter for greasing pie plate
1	tablespoon vegetable oil
½	pound 90 percent lean ground beef
½	pound ground pork
1	large onion, chopped fine
1	medium jalapeño chile, minced
2	medium cloves garlic, minced
1	teaspoon ground cumin
¼	teaspoon cayenne pepper
1	tablespoon chili powder
1	teaspoon salt
1	(14½-ounce) can diced tomatoes in juice
1	(15-ounce) can black beans, drained and rinsed
1	cup fresh or frozen corn
1	tablespoon minced fresh oregano
	Ground black pepper
2	ounces shredded Monterey Jack cheese (about ½ cup)

CRUST

4	cups water
¾	teaspoon salt
1½	cups coarse cornmeal

1. FOR THE FILLING: Butter a 10-inch deep-dish pie plate (or similar casserole dish with 3-quart capacity) and set it aside. Adjust an oven rack to the lowest position and heat the oven to 375 degrees.

2. Heat the oil in a large skillet over high heat until hot, about 1 minute. Add the ground beef and pork and cook, breaking up large clumps of meat with a wooden spoon, until no longer pink and beginning to brown, about 4 minutes. Add the onion and jalapeño and cook until just softened, about 3 minutes. Add the garlic, cumin, cayenne, chili powder, and salt and cook until aromatic, about 30 seconds. Add the tomatoes with their juice along with the black beans and corn. Simmer until most of the liquid has evaporated, about 3 minutes. Remove the pan from the heat and stir in the oregano and pepper to taste. Set aside.

3. FOR THE CRUST: Bring the water to a boil in a heavy-bottomed, large saucepan over high heat. Add the salt and then slowly pour in the cornmeal while whisking vigorously to prevent lumps from forming. Reduce the heat to medium-high and cook, whisking constantly, until the cornmeal begins to soften and the mixture thickens, about 3 minutes. Remove the pan from the heat.

4. TO ASSEMBLE AND BAKE: Spread two-thirds of the cornmeal mixture (about 2½ cups) over the bottom and up the sides of the buttered pie plate. Place the lid back on top of the pan with the remaining cornmeal mixture to prevent the mixture from drying out. Spoon the beef mixture evenly into the dish and sprinkle with the cheese. Spread the remaining cornmeal mixture evenly on top of the cheese, spreading it out to the edges of the pie plate to seal in the filling.

5. Bake until the crust has set and the pie is heated through, 25 to 30 minutes. Remove the pie plate from the oven and let cool for 10 minutes. Spoon portions onto individual plates or into bowls and serve immediately.

POT ROAST

POT ROAST, A SLOW-FOOD SURVIVOR OF generations past, has stubbornly remained in the repertoire of Sunday-night cookery, but with few good reasons. The meat is often tough and stringy and so dry that it must be drowned with the merciful sauce that accompanies the dish. Perhaps the longevity of pot roast lies in the fact that it is difficult to get it right the first (or 30th) time.

Pot roast by definition entails the transformation of a tough (read cheap), nearly unpalatable cut of meat into a tender, rich, flavorful main course by means of a slow, moist cooking process—braising. It should not be truly sliceable; the tension of a stern gaze should be enough to break it apart. It is never pink or rosy in the middle—save that for prime rib or steak.

The meat for pot roast should be well marbled with fat and connective tissue to provide the dish with the necessary flavor and moisture. Recipes typically call for roasts from the sirloin (or rump), the round (leg), or the chuck (shoulder). (See the illustration on page 102.) When all was said and done, we roasted a dozen cuts of meat to find the right one.

The sirloin roasts tested—the bottom rump roast and the top sirloin—were the leanest of the cuts. A long cooking time was needed to break down this meat to a palatable texture. The round cuts—top round, bottom round, and eye of round—had more fat running through the meat than the sirloin cuts, but the meat was chewy. The chuck cuts—shoulder roast, boneless chuck roast, cross rib, chuck mock tender, seven-bone pot roast, top-blade roast, and chuck-eye roast—cooked up the most tender, although we gave preference to three of these cuts (see "Three Good Chucks" on page 110). The high proportion of fat and connective tissue in these chuck cuts gave the meat much-needed moisture and superior flavor.

Tough meat can also benefit from the low, dry heat of oven roasting, and it can be boiled. With pot roast, however, the introduction of moisture by means of a braising liquid is thought to be integral to the breakdown of the tough muscle fibers. (We also tried dry-roasting and boiling pot roast just to make sure. See page 112 to find out why braising was the winner.) It was time to find out what kind and how much liquid was needed to best cook the roast and supply a good sauce.

Before we began the testing, we needed to deal with the aesthetics of the dish. Because pot roast is traditionally cooked at a low temperature, the exterior of the meat will not brown sufficiently if it is not first sautéed in a Dutch oven on the stovetop. High heat and a little oil were all that were needed to brown the crust of the beef and boost both the flavor and appearance of the dish.

Using water as the braising medium, we started with a modicum—½ cup—as suggested in a few recipes. This produced a roast that was unacceptably fibrous, even after hours of cooking. After increasing the amount of liquid incrementally, we found the moistest meat was produced when we added liquid halfway up the sides of the roast. Depending on the cut, this would be between two and four cups of liquid. The larger amount of liquid also accelerated the cooking process, shaving nearly one hour off the cooking time needed for a roast that was cooked in just ¼ cup of liquid. Naively assuming that more is always better, we continued to increase the amount of water but found that this produced no additional benefit. We also found that it was necessary to cover the Dutch oven with a piece of aluminum foil before placing the lid on top. The added seal of foil kept the liquid from escaping through the cracks of a loose-fitting lid via steam and eliminated any need for additional liquid.

Next we tested different liquids, hoping to add flavor to the roast and sauce. Along with the old standby, water, we tested red wine, canned low-sodium chicken broth, and canned low-sodium beef broth. The red wine had the most startling effect on the meat, penetrating it with a distinctively sour wine flavor that most tasters agreed was "good, but not traditional pot roast." However, tasters did like the flavor of a little red wine added to the sauce after the pot roast was removed from the pan. Each of the broths on their own failed to win tasters over completely—the chicken broth was rich but gave the dish a characteristic poultry flavor, while the beef broth tasted sour when added solo. In the end, we found an equal proportion of each did the job, with the beef broth boosting the depth of flavor and chicken broth tempering any sourness. Because different amounts of liquid would have to be added to the pot depending on the size and shape of each individual roast, we decided to be consistent in the amount of chicken and beef broth used—1 cup each—and to vary the amount of water to bring the liquid level up to the halfway mark on the meat.

Trying to boost the flavor of the sauce even further,

we added the basic vegetables—carrot, celery, onion, garlic—to the pot as the meat braised. Unfortunately, the addition of raw vegetables made the pot roast taste more like a vegetable stew. We then tried sautéing them until golden brown and found that their caramelized flavor added another layer of flavor to the sauce. Tomato paste, an ingredient found in several recipes, was not a welcome addition. Tasters appreciated the sweetness it added but not the "tinny" flavor. We added a little sugar (2 teaspoons) to the vegetables as they cooked, and this gave the sauce the sweetness that tasters were looking for.

Some recipes thicken the sauce with a mixture of equal parts butter and flour; others use a slurry of cornstarch mixed with a little of the braising liquid. Both techniques made the sauce more gravy-like than we preferred, and we didn't care for the dilution of flavor. We chose to remove the roast from the pot, then reduce the liquid over high heat until the flavors were well concentrated and the texture more substantial.

When it comes to how to cook the roast, the schools of thought are divided neatly into two camps: on the stove and in the oven. After a few rounds of stovetop cooking, we felt that it was too difficult to maintain a steady, low temperature, so we began pot-roasting in the oven, starting out at 250 degrees. This method required no supervision, just a turn of the meat every 30 to 40 minutes to ensure even cooking. We then tested higher temperatures to reduce the cooking time. Heat levels above 350 degrees boiled the meat to a stringy, dry texture because the exterior of the roast overcooked before the interior was cooked and tender. The magic number turned out to be 300 degrees—enough heat to keep the meat at a low simmer while high enough to shave a few more minutes off the cooking time.

As we've said, pot roast is well-done meat—meat cooked to an internal temperature above 165 degrees. Up to this point, we were bringing the meat to an internal temperature of 200 to 210 degrees, the point at which the fat and connective tissue melt. In a 300-degree oven, we found the roast came up to that temperature in a neat 2½ hours, by no means a quick meal but still a relatively short time in which to cook a pot roast. But we still had not achieved the fall-apart-tender pot roast that we wanted, so we went back and reviewed our prior testing to see what we might have missed.

Once in a great while in the test kitchen we happen upon a true "Eureka!" moment, when a chance test result leads the way to a breakthrough cooking technique. Some days before, we had forgotten to remove one of the roasts from the oven, allowing it to cook one hour longer than intended. Racing to the kitchen with an instant-read thermometer, we found the internal temperature of this roast was still 210 degrees, but the meat had a substantially different appearance and texture. The roast was so tender that it was starting to separate along its muscle lines. A fork poked into the meat to test tenderness met with no resistance and nearly disappeared into the flesh. We carefully took the roast out of the pot and "sliced" into it. Nearly all the fat and connective tissue had dissolved into the meat, giving each bite a soft, silky texture and rich, succulent flavor. The conclusion? Not only do you have to cook pot roast until it reaches 210 degrees internally, but the meat has to remain at that temperature for a full hour. (We tried additional oven time with no improvement.) In other words, cook the pot roast until it's done—and then keep on cooking.

Simple Pot Roast
SERVES 6 TO 8

For pot roast, we recommend a chuck-eye roast. Seven-bone and top-blade pot roasts are also good, but they are thinner cuts. Remember to add only enough water to come halfway up the sides of the roast, and begin checking the roast for doneness after 2 hours. If using a top-blade roast, tie it before cooking (see the illustrations on page 111) to keep it from falling apart. Mashed or boiled potatoes are good accompaniments to pot roast.

1	boneless chuck-eye roast (about 3½ pounds)
	Salt and ground black pepper
2	tablespoons vegetable oil
1	medium onion, chopped medium
1	small carrot, chopped medium
1	small rib celery, chopped medium
2	medium cloves garlic, minced
2	teaspoons sugar
1	cup canned low-sodium chicken broth
1	cup canned low-sodium beef broth
1	sprig fresh thyme
1–1½	cups water
¼	cup dry red wine

THREE GOOD CHUCKS

THE SEVEN-BONE POT ROAST is a well-marbled cut with an incredibly beefy flavor. It gets its name from the bone found in the roast, which is shaped like the number seven. Because it is only 2 inches thick, less liquid and less time are needed to braise this roast. Do not buy a seven-bone pot roast that weighs more than 3½ pounds, as it will not fit into a Dutch oven.

THE TOP-BLADE POT ROAST is also well-marbled with fat and connective tissue, which make this roast very juicy and flavorful. Even after thorough braising, this roast retains a distinctive strip of connective tissue, which is not unpleasant to eat. This roast is also sold as a blade roast.

THE CHUCK-EYE ROAST is the fattiest of the three roasts and the most commonly available. The high proportion of fat gives pot roast great flavor and tenderness. Because of its thicker size, this roast takes the longest to cook. Most markets sell this roast already tied. If necessary, do this yourself.

1. Adjust an oven rack to the middle position and heat the oven to 300 degrees. Thoroughly pat the roast dry with paper towels; sprinkle generously with salt and pepper.

2. Heat the oil in a large heavy-bottomed Dutch oven over medium-high heat until shimmering but not smoking. Brown the roast thoroughly on all sides, reducing the heat if the fat begins to smoke, 8 to 10 minutes. Transfer the roast to a large plate; set aside. Reduce the heat to medium; add the onion, carrot, and celery to the pot and cook, stirring occasionally, until beginning to brown, 6 to 8 minutes. Add the garlic and sugar; cook until fragrant, about 30 seconds. Add the chicken and beef broths and thyme, scraping the bottom of the pan with a wooden spoon to loosen the browned bits. Return the roast and any accumulated juices to the pot; add enough water to come halfway up the sides of the roast. Place a large piece of aluminum foil over the pot and cover tightly with a lid; bring the liquid to a simmer over medium heat, then transfer the pot to the oven. Cook, turning the roast every 30 minutes, until fully tender and a meat fork or sharp knife

easily slips in and out of the meat, 3½ to 4 hours.

3. Transfer the roast to a carving board; tent with foil to keep warm. Allow the liquid in the pot to settle about 5 minutes, then use a wide spoon to skim the fat off the surface; discard the thyme. Boil over high heat until reduced to 1½ cups, about 8 minutes. Add the wine and reduce again to 1½ cups, about 2 minutes. Season to taste with salt and pepper.

4. Using a chef's or carving knife, cut the meat into ½-inch-thick slices, or pull apart into large pieces; transfer the meat to a warmed serving platter and pour about ½ cup sauce over the meat. Serve, passing the remaining sauce separately.

➤ VARIATION

Pot Roast with Root Vegetables

In this variation, carrots, potatoes, and parsnips are added near the end of cooking to make a complete meal.

1. Follow the recipe for Simple Pot Roast. In step 2, when the roast is almost tender (a sharp knife should meet little resistance), add 1½ pounds (about 8 medium) carrots, sliced ½ inch thick (about 3

HOW TO TIE A TOP-BLADE ROAST

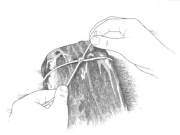

1. Slip a 6-foot piece of twine under the roast and tie a double knot.

2. Loop the long end of twine under and around the roast.

3. Run the long end through the loop.

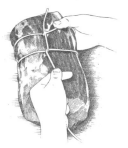

4. Repeat this procedure down the length of the roast.

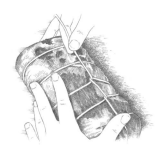

5. Roll the roast over and run the twine under and around each loop.

6. Wrap the twine around the end of the roast, flip roast, and tie to original knot.

cups); 1½ pounds small red potatoes, halved if larger than 1½ inches in diameter (about 5 cups); and 1 pound (about 5 large) parsnips, sliced ½ inch thick (about 3 cups) to the Dutch oven, submerging them in the liquid. Continue to cook until the vegetables are almost tender, 20 to 30 minutes.

2. Transfer the roast to a carving board; tent with foil to keep warm. Allow the liquid in the pot to settle for about 5 minutes, then use a wide spoon to skim the fat off the surface; discard the thyme sprig. Add the wine and salt and pepper to taste; boil over high heat until the vegetables are fully tender, 5 to 10 minutes. Using a slotted spoon, transfer the vegetables to a warmed serving bowl or platter. Using a chef's or carving knife, cut the meat into ½-inch-

thick slices or pull apart into large pieces; transfer to the bowl or platter with the vegetables and pour about ½ cup sauce over. Serve, passing the remaining sauce separately.

CORNED BEEF AND CABBAGE

CORNED BEEF AND CABBAGE, THE VENERABLE one-pot meal composed of boiled corned beef, cabbage, and other winter vegetables (also known in parts of the country as New England boiled dinner), has struck us less as a dish with big flavor and genuine dinner-table appeal than as a symbol of the

SCIENCE: The Mystery of Braising

Braising—searing meat, partially submerging it in liquid in a sealed pot, and then cooking it until fork-tender—is a classic technique used with, among other things, tough cuts of meat such as pot roast. A variety of cooks have put forward theories about why and how braising works (as opposed to roasting or boiling), but no food scientist of our acquaintance has offered a definitive explanation of the science behind the technique. We set out to devise a series of experiments that would finally explain the mystery of braising.

Before kitchen testing began, we researched the meat itself to better understand how it cooks. Meat (muscle) is made up of two major components: muscle fibers, which are the long thin strands visible as the "grain" of meat, and connective tissue, the membranous, translucent film that covers the bundles of muscle fiber and gives them structure and support. Muscle fiber is tender because of its high water content (up to 78 percent). Once meat is heated beyond about 120 degrees, the long strands of muscle fiber contract and coil, expelling moisture in much the same way as it's wrung out of a towel. In contrast, connective tissue is tough because it is composed primarily of collagen, a sturdy protein that is in everything from the cow's muscle tendons to its horns. When collagen is cooked at temperatures exceeding 140 degrees, it starts to break down to gelatin, the protein responsible for the tender meat, thick sauces, and rich mouthfeel of braised dishes.

In essence, then, meat both dries out as it cooks (meat fibers lose moisture) and meat becomes softer (the collagen melts). That is why meat is best either cooked rare or pot-roasted—cooked to the point that the collagen completely dissolves.

Anything in between is dry and tough, the worst of both worlds.

This brings us to why braising is an effective cooking technique for tough cuts of meat. To determine the relative advantages of roasting, braising, and boiling, we constructed a simple test. One roast was cooked in a 250-degree oven, one was braised, and one was simmered in liquid to cover. The results were startling.

The roasted meat never reached an internal temperature higher than 175 degrees, even after four hours, and the roast was tough and dry. To our surprise, both the braised and boiled roasts cooked in about the same amount of time, and the results were almost identical. Cutting the roasts in half revealed little difference—both exhibited nearly full melting of the thick bands of connective tissue. As far as the taste and texture of the meat, tasters were hard pressed to find any substantial differences. Both roasts yielded meat that was exceedingly tender, moist, and infused with rich gelatin.

The conclusion? Both water and steam are effective conductors of heat and can bring a roast up to the temperature necessary to melt collagen. Dry heat (roasting) is ineffective because the meat never gets hot enough. In addition, it does not appear that steam heat (braising) enjoys any special ability to soften meat over boiling. Any tough cut of meat will soften if maintained at 210 degrees for one hour. It's simply a matter of physics and meat chemistry.

One final note. Braising has one advantage over simmering or boiling. Half a pot of liquid reduces much faster to a sauce than a full pot. Since just about every braising recipe calls for making a sauce out of the cooking liquid, this is a real advantage.

stalwart Yankee ethics of hard work and thrift. That misconception, however, was the first of several to be busted during our testing. In the course of tasting umpteen dishes of corned beef and cabbage, we came to realize that this dish needn't be mushy, overwhelmingly salty, or one-dimensional, as it had always seemed. Instead, it can be a full-flavored medley of meaty, tender, well-seasoned beef, subtle spice, and sweet, earthy vegetables, each distinct in flavor and texture.

We commenced our research and testing with the usual spate of recipes, most of which were based on a four- to six-pound piece of corned beef. The term corned refers to the curing of meat with salt, often used as a method of preservation before refrigeration became widespread. Legend has it that the salt grains were roughly the same size as corn kernels, hence the name corned beef. The cut of beef most commonly corned is boneless brisket, which is a trimmed, 12 to 13-pound piece taken from the front part of the cow's breast. For retail sale, the whole brisket is usually split into two parts, called the first, or flat, cut and the second, or point, cut. Of the two, the point cut is thicker, fattier, and, to our taste, more flavorful and more tender than the flat cut. Both cuts can be trimmed further into smaller pieces of meat, and both are available as commercially corned beef.

At the supermarket, we found more commercial corned beef options than we had anticipated from reading the recipes we had researched. In addition to "low-sodium" corned beef, there were regular and "gray," each in both flat and point cuts in sizes ranging from three to six pounds. We were told by a representative from Mosey's, a national producer of corned beef, that the gray style is popular only in, and therefore limited to, New England. The difference between regular and gray is made clear on the package. The brine for gray corned beef contains only water and salt, whereas the "regular" corned beef brine also contains sodium nitrite, which helps the meat retain its red color by reacting with purple color pigments and turning them to pink and red.

We brought home an example of each type and took to the stove. Cooking directions on the packages and in our research recipes did not vary by much. Generally, instructions were to cover the meat with one to three inches of water and simmer until tender, anywhere from 2½ to 3½ hours, depending on the size of the brisket.

To our surprise, the regular corned beef choices disappointed us across the board. Though they remained an appealing pink even when cooked, our tasters described the flavor of both the full- and low-salt versions as "sharp and somewhat chemical," most likely from the nitrite. In addition, the texture was deemed grainy, with a noticeably chalky mouthfeel. By comparison, the gray corned beef looked, well, gray, because it lacked the color boost given to regular brisket by the nitrite. The flavor, however, was superior, and for that, we'll gladly trade the pink color. Whereas the chemical qualities we noted in the regular versions obscured the flavor of the beef, the gray corned beef tasted cleaner and beefier. The salt had a stronger presence than we preferred, and the spice we look for in ideal corned beef was nonexistent, but we knew we wanted to stick with the gray for further testing.

But because the gray corned beef we preferred is a product limited to a small region of the country, we decided to try corning our own brisket. We figured that this would also make it easier to control the saltiness. Our research turned up two methods of corning—the wet cure and the dry cure. Both methods require close to a week, but they are also mindlessly easy. All you need to do is prepare the meat and its cure. Beyond that, there is no work whatsoever. We tested each method, using 5-pound fresh briskets in both flat and point cuts.

Because meat preservative is readily available in drugstores in the form of the potassium nitrate called saltpeter, we still had the option of producing regular and gray corned beef. Even in our home-corned beef, though, the preservative added a harshness to the flavor that competed with the taste of the beef. Because the color of the meat was less important to us than the flavor, we dropped the saltpeter from further testing.

Testing the wet method for our gray corned beef involved tasting briskets cured in a brine of 2 cups of salt and 3 quarts of water for 14, 12, 10, 7, and 5 days. Among all of them, we liked the 5-day brisket best, noting a pleasing saltiness alongside the distinctive flavor of beef. We also confirmed our preference for the fattier point cut of brisket.

Fat carries flavor in all cuts of meat, and beef brisket is no different. The flat cut is especially lean and therefore less flavorful and moist than the point cut.

At this point, we also gave the dry-cure method a go. Adapting a recipe from Julia Child's *The Way to Cook* (Knopf, 1989), we rubbed our 6-pound, point-cut brisket with ½ cup salt and a few crushed herbs and spices, placed it in a two-gallon zipper-lock bag, weighted the meat with a brick, and let it sit for five days in the fridge. Lo and behold, the result was the best corned beef of them all, even better than the five-day wet-cured corned beef, with a concentrated beef flavor, assertive yet not overpowering saltiness, and a pleasant spiciness. Curing the brisket for two extra days, seven in total, brought out the flavor of the spices a little more, without affecting the saltiness.

Julia Child's recipe suggested desalting the dry-cured meat by soaking it in several changes of water for at least 24 hours or up to three days, depending on the size of the brisket. To be honest, we initially overlooked this step; we simply rinsed the surface of the meat to remove shards of crumbled bay leaf and cracked peppercorns and went ahead with the cooking. When we finally did try the full desalting, we found that the meat

LOCATING THE BRISKET

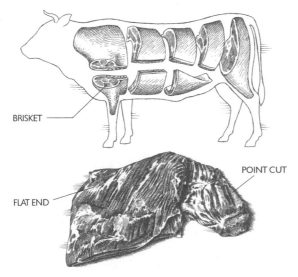

BRISKET

FLAT END

POINT CUT

Butchers often separate the whole brisket into two parts, the flat end (left portion) and the point cut (right portion). The point cut is a bit thicker and contains more fat. It is more tender than the flat end.

tasted slightly richer because of the diminished salt presence, but not so much better that it justified a 24-hour soak as opposed to a quick rinse.

With the corned beef tasting just the way we wanted it, we turned our attention to the cooking method, then to the vegetables. Though most recipes call for cooking corned beef and cabbage on the stove, we did try a couple of tests in the oven. Our advice is to stick to the stove, on which the meat cooked faster and was easier to monitor. Also, we found that adding the vegetables and adjusting the heat to compensate was easier with the pot on top of the stove.

On the stove, we noticed that the meat emerged from the pot tender and flaky if cooked at a lively simmer, as opposed to tight and tough when cooked at a full boil. We also preferred to cook the meat covered to prevent water evaporation and a resulting overconcentration of salt in the broth. We experimented with different quantities of water in the pot, covering the corned beef by ½ inch to 3 inches and found that it makes no difference in terms of the meat or vegetables. The amount of water does matter to the broth, though. The broth produced from covering the meat by ½ inch to an inch (8 to 10 cups over a 4½ pound brisket in our 8-quart pot) and cooking it with the pot lid on was nicely seasoned and suitable for use on its own or in a soup.

The last, though not insignificant, variable was the vegetables. We tested a wide variety of vegetables, from the familiar to the exotic, and settled on the traditional green cabbage, with the added interest of carrots, parsnips, potatoes, turnips, rutabagas, onions, and Brussels sprouts, all borrowed from the New England boiled dinner, as our favorites. We tried cooking the vegetables along with the meat, but there were two distinct disadvantages to this approach. First, it was difficult to judge when the vegetables were properly done. Second, it would require a pot larger than any we had in the test kitchen or in our own homes.

The best method turned out to be removing the meat from the broth when done, then cooking the vegetables in the broth. This not only benefited the vegetables, giving them a full, round flavor from the salt and rendered fat in the broth, but it also allowed us time to let the meat rest before cutting it.

Home-Corned Beef Brisket and Cabbage, New England Style

SERVES 8 WITH LEFTOVERS

If you prefer a leaner piece of meat, feel free to use the flat cut. In fact, we found more flat-cut than point-cut briskets in supermarket meat cases, so you'll probably have to ask the meat department attendant or butcher to bring you a point cut. Leave a bit of fat attached for better texture and flavor. The meat is cooked fully when it is tender, the muscle fibers have loosened visibly, and a skewer slides in with minimal resistance. Serve this dish with horseradish, either plain or mixed with whipped or sour cream, or with grainy mustard.

½	cup kosher salt
1	tablespoon black peppercorns, cracked
¾	tablespoon ground allspice
1	tablespoon dried thyme
½	tablespoon paprika
2	bay leaves, crumbled
1	fresh beef brisket (4 to 6 pounds), preferably point cut (see illustration on page 114), trimmed of excess fat, rinsed and patted dry
7-8	pounds prepared vegetables of your choice (see below)

1. Mix the salt and seasonings in a small bowl.

2. Spear the brisket about 30 times per side with a meat fork or metal skewer. Rub each side evenly with the salt mixture; place in a 2-gallon zipper-lock bag, forcing out as much air as possible. Place in a pan large enough to hold it (a rimmed baking sheet works well), cover with a second, similar-size pan, and weight with two bricks or heavy cans of similar weight. Refrigerate 5 to 7 days, turning once a day. Rinse the meat and pat dry.

3. Bring the brisket to a boil with water to cover by ½ to 1 inch in a large Dutch oven or stockpot (at least 8 quarts), skimming any impurities that rise to

---

Vegetables for Corned Beef and Cabbage

The vegetables listed below are some of our favorites. However, if you love potatoes but cannot abide parsnips, choose vegetables to suit your tastes. To make sure that the vegetables are evenly cooked, we trim them all to sizes appropriate for their density and cooking characteristics and add them to the pot in two batches.

CATEGORY 1

Once the meat has been removed from the pot, add the desired selection and quantity of vegetables from this category. Return the liquid to a boil and simmer for 10 minutes before adding vegetables from category 2.

VEGETABLE	PREPARATION
Carrots	Peeled and halved crosswise; thin end halved lengthwise, thick end quartered lengthwise.
Rutabagas (small)	Peeled and halved crosswise; each half cut into six chunks.
White turnips (medium)	Peeled and quartered.
New potatoes (small)	Scrubbed and left whole.

CATEGORY 2

At the 10-minute mark, add selected vegetables from this category, return cooking liquid to boil, then continue to simmer until all vegetables are just tender, 10 to 15 minutes longer.

VEGETABLE	PREPARATION
Boiling onions	Peeled and left whole.
Green cabbage, uncored (small head)	Blemished leaves removed and cut into six to eight wedges.
Parsnips	Peeled and halved crosswise; thin end halved lengthwise, thick end quartered lengthwise.
Brussels sprouts, whole	Blemished leaves removed, stems trimmed, and left whole.

the surface. Cover and simmer until a skewer inserted in the thickest part of the brisket slides out with ease, 2 to 3 hours.

4. Heat the oven to 200 degrees. Transfer the meat to a large platter, ladling about 1 cup cooking liquid over it to keep it moist. Cover with aluminum foil and set in the oven.

5. Add the vegetables from category 1 to the pot and bring to a boil; cover and simmer until the vegetables begin to soften, about 10 minutes. Add the vegetables from category 2 and bring to a boil; cover and simmer until all the vegetables are tender, 10 to 15 minutes longer.

6. Meanwhile, remove the meat from the oven and cut it across the grain into ¼-inch slices. Return the meat to the platter.

7. Transfer the vegetables to the meat platter, moisten with additional broth, and serve.

Grilling Basics

GRILLING IS THE QUICK COOKING (OR searing) of foods over an open fire. Relatively thin cuts such as steaks as well as delicate foods like seafood and vegetables can be grilled. Once the food is seared on both sides, it's probably done. True grilling (as opposed to barbecuing with the cover on) is hot and fast. (See page 122 for a definition of barbecuing.)

To put a good crust on foods, especially grilled meats, you must use enough charcoal. Because heat is so important, we prefer irregularly shaped chunks of lump hardwood charcoal rather than pillow-shaped briquettes when grilling. Hardwood charcoal burns hotter than briquettes and is well suited to this kind of outdoor cooking.

When grilling, we always leave the cover off. Over time, soot and resinous compounds can build up on the inside of a kettle grill lid, which can then impart an off flavor reminiscent of stale smoke to the food. This effect is most noticeable in fish and poultry. When we want to trap heat on an open charcoal grill to make sure the food cooks through, we prefer to cover it with a disposable aluminum roasting pan or pie plate. (Note that for barbecuing, the grill cover must be kept on to trap heat. However, the use of wood chips and chunks overpowers the off flavor the lid can impart.)

Grilling on gas requires slightly different (but similar) procedures. We find that gas grills work best with the lid down in all instances. They put out a lot less heat than a charcoal fire, and foods won't brown properly if the lid is left open. Because gas burns cleanly, there's no buildup of soot on the inside of the lid and thus no danger that foods cooked in a covered gas grill will pick up an off flavor.

Whether cooking on charcoal or gas, it's imperative to use the right level of heat. To make our recipes easy to follow, we have devised a system that quantifies the heat level by measuring the amount of time you can comfortably hold your hand above the cooking grate (see below for details). If you use this system, the cooking times in our recipes will be excellent guidelines. However, we recommend that you test foods often for doneness when grilling.

TAKING THE TEMPERATURE OF THE FIRE

Use the chart below to determine the intensity of the fire. The terms *hot fire, medium-hot fire, medium fire,* and *medium-low fire* are used in all our grilling and barbecuing recipes. When using a gas grill, ignore dial readings such as medium or medium-low in favor of actual measurements of the temperature, as described here.

INTENSITY OF FIRE	TIME YOU CAN HOLD YOUR HAND 5 INCHES ABOVE GRATE
Hot fire	2 seconds
Medium-hot fire	3 to 4 seconds
Medium fire	5 to 6 seconds
Medium-low fire	7 seconds

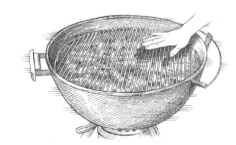

Once the coals have been spread out in the bottom of the grill, put the cooking grate in place and put the cover on for five minutes to heat up the grate. (On gas grills, preheat with the lid down and all burners on high for 15 minutes.) Scrape the cooking grate clean and then take the temperature of the fire by holding your hand 5 inches above the cooking grate and counting how long you can comfortably leave it in place.

Grilling over a live fire is not like cooking in a precisely calibrated oven. Be prepared to adjust the timing, especially if grilling in cool or windy weather. An instant-read thermometer is the best way to gauge the progress of most foods on the grill. The other option is to remove a test piece and peek into the food with the tip of a knife.

HAMBURGERS

AMERICANS PROBABLY GRILL MORE HAMBURGERS than any other food. Despite all this practice, plenty of hamburgers seem merely to satisfy hunger rather than give pleasure. Too bad, because making an exceptional hamburger isn't that hard or time-consuming. Fast-food chains no doubt had good reasons when they decided against selling hand-formed, 100 percent ground-chuck burgers; home cooks, however, do not. If you have the right ground beef, the perfect hamburger can be ready in less than 15 minutes, assuming you season, form, and cook it properly. The biggest difficulty for many cooks, though, may be finding the right beef.

To test which cut or cuts of beef would cook up into the best burgers, we called a butcher and

LIGHTING A CHARCOAL FIRE

Our favorite way to start a charcoal fire is with a chimney starter, also known as a flue starter. To use this simple device, fill the bottom section with crumpled newspaper, set the starter on the grill grate, and fill the top with charcoal. (Most starters can hold about five quarts of charcoal.) When you light the newspaper, flames will shoot up through the charcoal, igniting it. When the coals are well-lit and covered with a layer of gray ash, dump them onto the charcoal grate. (If you need more than five quarts of charcoal, add some unlit charcoal. Continue heating until all the coals are gray.)

ordered chuck, round, rump, sirloin, and hanging tenderloin, all ground to order with 20 percent fat. (Although we would question fat percentages in later testing, we needed a standard for these early tests. Based on experience, this percentage seemed right.) After a side-by-side taste test, we quickly concluded that most cuts of ground beef are pleasant but bland when compared with robust, beefy flavored ground chuck. Pricier ground sirloin, for example, cooked up into a particularly boring burger.

So pure ground chuck—the cut of beef that starts where the ribs end and travels up to the shoulder and neck, ending at the foreshank—was the clear winner. We were ready to race ahead to seasonings, but before moving on we stopped to ask ourselves whether cooks buying ground chuck from the grocery store would agree with our choice. Our efforts to determine whether grocery-store ground chuck and ground-to-order chuck were even remotely similar took us along a culinary blue highway from kitchen to packing plant, butcher shop, and science lab.

According to the National Livestock and Meat Board, the percentage of fat in beef is checked and enforced at the retail level. If a package of beef is labeled 90 percent lean, then it must contain no more than 10 percent fat, give or take a point. Retail stores are required to test each batch of ground beef, make the necessary adjustments, and keep a log of the results. Local inspectors routinely pull ground beef from a store's meat case for a fat check. If the fat content is not within 1 percent of the package sticker, the store is fined.

Whether a package labeled ground chuck is, in fact, 100 percent ground chuck is a different story. First, we surveyed a number of grocery store meat department managers, who said that what was written on the label did match what was in the package. For instance, a package labeled "ground chuck" would have been made only from chuck trimmings. Same for sirloin and round. Only "ground beef" would be made from mixed beef trimmings.

We got a little closer to the truth, however, by interviewing a respected butcher in the Chicago area. At the several grocery stores and butcher shops where he had worked over the years, he had never known a store to segregate meat trimmings. In fact, in his present butcher shop, he sells only two kinds of ground beef: sirloin and chuck. He defines ground sirloin as ground beef (mostly but not exclusively sirloin) that's labeled 90 percent lean, and chuck as ground beef (including a lot of chuck trimmings) that's labeled 85 percent lean.

Only meat ground at federally inspected plants is guaranteed to match its label. At these plants, an inspector checks to make sure that labeled ground beef actually comes from the cut of beef named on the label and that the fat percentage is correct. Most retailers, though, cannot guarantee that their ground beef has been made from a specific cut; they can only guarantee fat percentages.

Because the labeling of retail ground beef can be deceptive, we suggest that you buy a chuck roast and have the butcher grind it for you. Even at a local grocery store, we found that the butcher was willing to grind to order. Some meat always gets lost in the grinder, so count on losing a bit (2 to 3 percent).

Because commercially ground beef is at risk for contamination with the bacteria E. coli, we thought it made theoretical sense for home cooks to grind their beef at home, thereby reducing their odds of eating tainted beef. It doesn't make much practical sense, though. Not all cooks own a grinder. And even if they did, we thought home grinding demanded far too much setup, cleanup, and effort for a dish meant to be so simple.

To see if there was an easier way, we tried chopping by hand and grinding in the food processor. The hibachi-style hand-chopping method was just as time-consuming and even more messy than the traditional grinder. In this method, you must slice the meat thin and then cut it into cubes before going at it with two chef's knives. The fat doesn't distribute evenly, meat flies everywhere, and, unless your knives are razor sharp, it's difficult to chop through the meat. What's worse, you can't efficiently chop more than two burgers at a time. In the end, the cooked burgers can be mistaken for chopped steak.

The food processor did a surprisingly good job of grinding meat. We thought the steel blade would raggedly chew the meat, but the hamburger turned out evenly chopped and fluffy. (For more information, see "Food Processor as Grinder," page 119.)

We figured the average chuck roast to be about 80 percent lean. To check its leanness, we bought a chuck roast—not too fatty, not too lean—and ground it in the food processor. We then took our ground chuck back to the grocery store and asked the butcher to check its fat content in the Univex Fat Analyzer, a machine the store uses to check each batch of beef it grinds. A plug of our ground beef scored an almost perfect 21 percent fat when tested.

Up to this point, all of our beef had been ground with approximately 20 percent fat. A quick test of burgers with less and more fat helped us to decide that 20 percent fat, give or take a few percentage points, was good for burgers. Any more fat and the burgers are just too greasy. Any less starts to compromise the beef's juicy, moist texture.

When to season the meat with salt and pepper may seem an insignificant detail, but when making a dish as simple as a hamburger, little things matter. We tried seasoning the meat at four different points in the process. Our first burger was seasoned before the meat was shaped, the second burger was seasoned right

SHAPING HAMBURGERS

1. With cupped hands, toss one portion of meat back and forth from hand to hand to shape it into a loose ball.

2. Pat lightly to flatten the meat into a ¾-inch-thick burger that measures about 4½ inches across. Press the center of the patty down with your fingertips until it is ½ inch thick, creating a well in the center. Repeat with the remaining portions of meat.

Food Processor as Grinder

Even though we have a meat grinder in our test kitchen, we don't regularly grind meat ourselves. The setup, breakdown, and cleanup required for a 2-pound chuck roast is just not worth the effort. Besides, hamburgers are supposed to be impromptu, fast, fun food.

To our surprise, the food processor does a respectable grinding job, and it's much easier to use than a grinder. The key is to make sure the roast is cold, that it is cut into small chunks, and that it is processed in small batches. For a 2-pound roast, cut the meat into 1-inch chunks. Divide the chunks into four equal portions. Place one portion of meat in the workbowl of a food processor fitted with a steel blade. Pulse the cubes until the meat is ground, fifteen to twenty 1-second pulses. Repeat with the remaining portions of beef. Then shape the ground meat as directed in the recipe.

---

before cooking, the third after each side was seared, and the fourth after the burger had been fully cooked.

Predictably, the burger that had been seasoned throughout was our preference. All the surface-seasoned burgers were the same. Tasters got a hit of salt up front, then the burger went bland. The thin surface area was well seasoned while the interior of the burger was not.

Working with fresh-ground chuck seasoned with salt and pepper, we now moved on to shaping and cooking. To defy the overpacking and overhandling warning you see in many recipes, we thoroughly worked a portion of ground beef before cooking it. The well-done burger exterior was nearly as dense as a meat pâté, and the less well-done interior was compact and pasty.

It's pretty hard to overhandle a beef patty, though, especially if you're trying not to. Once the meat has been divided into portions, we found that tossing each portion from one hand to the other helped bring the meat together into a ball without over-working it.

We made one of our most interesting discoveries when we tested various shaping techniques for the patties. A well in the center of each burger ensured that they came off the grill with an even thickness instead of puffed up like a tennis ball. (See "Shaping

Hamburgers" on page 118.) To our taste, a four-ounce burger seemed a little skimpy. A six-ounce portion of meat patted into a nicely sized burger fit perfectly in a bun.

Now nearly done with our testing, we needed only to perfect our grilling method. Burgers require a real blast of heat if they are to form a crunchy, flavorful crust before the interior overcooks. While many of the recipes we looked at advise the cook to grill burgers over a hot fire, we suspected we'd have to adjust the heat because our patties were quite thin in the middle. Sure enough, a superhot fire made it too easy to overcook the burgers. We found a medium-hot fire formed a crust quickly, while also providing a wider margin of error for properly cooking the center. Nonetheless, burgers cook quickly—needing only 2½ to 3½ minutes per side. Don't walk away from the grill when cooking burgers.

To keep the burgers from sticking to the grill, we coated it with oil. All you need to do is dip a wad of paper towels in some vegetable oil, hold the wad with long-handled tongs, and rub it on the hot grate just before adding the burgers.

One last finding from our testing: Don't ever press down on burgers as they cook. Rather than speeding their cooking, pressing on the patties serves only to squeeze out their juices and make the burgers dry.

Charcoal-Grilled Hamburgers
SERVES 4

For those who like their burgers well-done, we found that poking a small hole in the center of the patty before cooking helped the burger cook through to the center before the edges dried out. See the illustrations on page 118 for tips on shaping burgers. See above left for details about grinding your own meat with a food processor.

1½ pounds 100 percent ground chuck
1 teaspoon salt
½ teaspoon ground black pepper
Vegetable oil for grill rack
Buns and desired toppings

1. Light a large chimney starter filled with hardwood charcoal (about 2½ pounds) and allow to burn

until all the charcoal is covered with a layer of fine gray ash. Spread the coals out evenly over the bottom of the grill. Set the cooking rack in place, cover the grill with the lid, and let the rack heat up, about 5 minutes. Use a wire brush to scrape clean the cooking grate. The grill is ready when the coals are medium-hot. (You should be able to hold your hand 5 inches above the cooking grate for 3 to 4 seconds; see the illustration on page 116.)

2. Meanwhile, break up the chuck to increase the surface area for seasoning. Sprinkle the salt and pepper over the meat; toss lightly with your hands to distribute the seasonings. Divide the meat into four equal portions (6 ounces each); with cupped hands, toss one portion of meat back and forth to form a loose ball. Pat lightly to flatten the meat into a ¾-inch-thick burger that measures about 4½ inches across. Press the center of the patty down with your fingertips until it is about ½ inch thick, creating a well, or divot, in the center of the patty. Repeat with the remaining portions of meat.

3. Lightly dip a small wad of paper towels in vegetable oil; holding the wad with tongs, wipe the grill rack. Grill the burgers, divot-side up, uncovered and without pressing down on them, until well seared on the first side, about 2½ minutes. Flip the burgers with a wide metal spatula. Continue grilling to the desired doneness, about 2 minutes for rare, 2½ minutes for medium-rare, 3 minutes for medium, and 4 minutes for well-done. Serve immediately in buns with desired toppings.

Gas-Grilled Hamburgers

SERVES 4

See the illustrations on page 118 for tips on shaping burgers.

- 1½   pounds 100 percent ground chuck
- 1   teaspoon salt
- ½   teaspoon ground black pepper
-   Vegetable oil for grill rack
-   Buns and desired toppings

1. Preheat the grill with all burners set to high and the lid down until the grill is very hot, about 15 minutes. Use a wire brush to scrape clean the cooking grate. Leave both burners on high.

2. Meanwhile, break up the chuck to increase the surface area for seasoning. Sprinkle the salt and pepper over the meat; toss lightly with your hands to distribute the seasonings. Divide the meat into four equal portions (6 ounces each); with cupped hands, toss one portion of meat back and forth to form a loose ball. Pat lightly to flatten the meat into a ¾-inch-thick burger that measures about 4½ inches across. Press the center of the patty down with your fingertips until it is about ½ inch thick, creating a well, or divot, in the center. Repeat with the remaining portions of meat.

3. Lightly dip a small wad of paper towels in vegetable oil; holding the wad with tongs, wipe the grill rack. Grill the burgers, divot-side up, covered and without pressing down on them, until well seared on

---

SCIENCE: No More Puffy Burgers

All too often, burgers come off the grill with a domed, puffy shape that makes it impossible to keep condiments from sliding off. Fast-food restaurants produce burgers that are even, but they are also extremely thin. We wondered if we could find a way to produce a meatier burger that would have the same thickness from edge to edge, giving the condiments a nice, flat top to sit on.

We shaped 6-ounce portions of ground beef into patties that were 1 inch, ¾ inch, and ½ inch thick. Once cooked, all of these burgers looked like tennis balls, and it was nearly impossible to anchor ketchup and other goodies on top. After talking to several food scientists, we understood why this happens.

The culprit behind puffy burgers is the connective tissue, or collagen, that is ground up along with the meat. When the connective tissue in a patty heats up to roughly 130 degrees, it shrinks. This happens first on the flat top and bottom surfaces of the burger and then on the sides, where the tightening acts like a belt. When the sides tighten, the interior meat volume is forced up and down, so the burger puffs.

One of the cooks in the test kitchen suggested a trick she had picked up when working in a restaurant. We shaped patties ¾ inch thick but then formed a slight depression in the center of each one so that the edges were thicker than the center. On the grill, the center puffed up to the point where it was the same height as the edges. Finally, a level burger that could hold onto toppings.

the first side, about 3 minutes. Flip the burgers with a wide metal spatula. Continue grilling, covered, to the desired doneness, about 3 minutes for rare, 3½ minutes for medium-rare, 4 minutes for medium, and 5 minutes for well-done. Serve immediately in buns with desired toppings.

➤ VARIATIONS

Grilled Cheeseburgers

We suggest grating cheese into the raw beef as opposed to melting it on top. Because the cheese is more evenly distributed, a little goes much farther than a chunk on top. Also, there's no danger of overcooking the burgers while you wait for the cheese to melt.

Follow the recipe for Charcoal-Grilled Hamburgers or Gas-Grilled Hamburgers, mixing 3½ ounces cheddar, Swiss, Jack, or blue cheese, shredded or crumbled as necessary, into the ground chuck along with the salt and pepper. Shape and cook the burgers as directed.

Grilled Hamburgers with Garlic, Chipotles, and Scallions

Toast 3 medium unpeeled garlic cloves in a small dry skillet over medium heat, shaking the pan occasionally, until the garlic is fragrant and the color deepens slightly, about 8 minutes. When cool enough to handle, skin and mince the garlic. Follow the recipe for Charcoal-Grilled Hamburgers or Gas-Grilled Hamburgers, mixing garlic, 1 tablespoon minced chipotle chile in adobo sauce, and 2 tablespoons minced scallions into the meat along with the salt and pepper.

Grilled Hamburgers with Cognac, Mustard, and Chives

Mix 1½ tablespoons cognac, 2 teaspoons Dijon mustard, and 1 tablespoon minced fresh chives in a small bowl. Follow the recipe for Charcoal-Grilled Burgers or Gas-Grilled Burgers, mixing the cognac mixture into the meat along with the salt and pepper.

COOKING BURGERS INDOORS

Nothing beats a grilled hamburger, but weather and circumstance (like living in a high-rise apartment) may not always permit outdoor cooking. So what's the best way to cook hamburgers in the kitchen?

Broiling and pan-searing are the two obvious choices. Even with the burgers very close to the heating element, we found that broiling did not create the kind of thick crust we wanted. We had much better results in a very hot pan (cast iron is ideal). And we didn't even need any fat in the pan to keep the burgers from sticking. All of the variations above and on page 122 can be cooked according to the recipe that follows.

Pan-Seared Hamburgers

SERVES 4

A well-seasoned cast-iron pan is our first choice for this recipe, but any heavy-bottomed skillet can be used.

1½	pounds 100 percent ground chuck
1	teaspoon salt
½	teaspoon ground black pepper
	Buns and desired toppings

1. Break up the chuck to increase the surface area for seasoning. Sprinkle the salt and pepper over the meat; toss lightly with your hands to distribute the seasonings. Divide the meat into four equal portions (6 ounces each); with cupped hands, toss one portion of meat back and forth to form a loose ball. Pat lightly to flatten the meat into a ¾-inch-thick burger that measures about 4½ inches across. Press the center of the patty down with your fingertips until about ½ inch thick, creating a well, or divot, in the center. Repeat with the remaining portions of meat.

2. Heat a 12-inch skillet over medium-high heat. When the skillet is hot (drops of water flicked into it should evaporate immediately), add the patties, divot-side up. Cook the burgers, turning once, to the desired doneness, about 3 minutes per side for rare, 3½ minutes per side for medium-rare, 4 minutes per side for medium, and 5 minutes per side for well-done. Serve immediately in buns with desired toppings.

Grilled Hamburgers with Porcini Mushrooms and Thyme

Cover ½ ounce dried porcini mushroom pieces with ½ cup hot tap water in a small microwave-safe bowl; cover with plastic wrap, cut several steam vents with a paring knife, and microwave on high power for 30 seconds. Let stand until the mushrooms soften, about 5 minutes. Lift the mushrooms from the liquid with a fork and mince, using a chef's knife (you should have about 2 tablespoons). Follow the recipe for Charcoal-Grilled Hamburgers or Gas-Grilled Hamburgers, mixing the porcini mushrooms and 1 teaspoon minced fresh thyme leaves into the meat along with the salt and pepper.

BARBECUE BASICS

BARBECUE IS ONE OF THE GREAT AMERICAN pastimes. But when we say barbecue, we don't mean cooking a few steaks on the grill out back. We mean true barbecue, where ribs, brisket, or pork roasts are cooked low and slow (not hot and fast, which is what happens with most grilling) until the meat is extremely tender and permeated with smoke flavor. The following pages explain basic barbecue techniques as well as the results of our kitchen tests with the woods (both chunks and chips), spice rubs, and sauces that give barbecued foods their unique character and flavor.

Most cooks intuitively understand how to grill. You build the biggest fire possible and place the food right over the coals. Once the food is nicely seared on both sides, it's done. Steaks, chops, and other relatively thin foods can be grilled this way because the interior will be cooked by the time the exterior is nicely browned.

But what about a thick pork roast or brisket? If grilled directly over a hot fire, the exterior will be charred and ashen well before the interior of such a large piece of meat has a chance to cook through. The solution is indirect cooking. While grilling calls for filling the grill with charcoal or lighting all the gas burners, indirect cooking on the grill relies on a smaller fire. The lit coals are banked on one side of the grill, or one of the gas burners is turned off. Foods cooked by indirect heat are placed over the "cool" part of the grill. With the lid on to trap the heat, both the exterior and interior of the food cook slowly and evenly, much as they do in an oven.

Why bother with indirect cooking on the grill when you can roast in the oven? The smoky flavor we associate with ribs and pulled pork comes only from the grill.

Barbecuing is the traditional low-and-slow cooking method used with ribs, pulled pork (shredded Boston butt), and brisket. Because the goal is to impart as much smoke flavor as possible, a long cooking time over a relatively low fire is required. Barbecuing also provides ample time for fatty, tough cuts to become more tender.

Although there is much debate among barbecue experts as to the proper cooking temperature, we found in our testing that barbecuing should take place between 250 and 300 degrees. While some chefs and pit masters might argue that ribs are best barbecued at 180 degrees, we found it very difficult to maintain such a low fire. Also, such low temperatures allow bacteria to multiply and increase the risk of food-borne illnesses.

Our tests also revealed a common misunderstanding about barbecuing. Despite its name, barbecue sauce is generally not applied to barbecued foods as they cook. Barbecued foods are best flavored with

BARBECUING ON A GAS GRILL

Remove part or all of the cooking grate. Place a foil tray with soaked wood chips on top of the primary burner. Make sure the tray is resting securely on the burner so it will not tip. Replace the grill rack. Light all burners and cover the grill. When you see a lot of smoke (after about 20 minutes), turn off the burner (or burners) without the chips and place the food over it (or them). If the chips flame, douse the fire with water from a squirt bottle. Cover the grill.

spice rubs prior to cooking. Barbecue sauce applied to ribs before cooking will burn. If you want to use barbecue sauce on barbecued foods, apply it during the last minutes of cooking or pass some at the table.

A kettle-style grill with a cover is a must for barbecuing with charcoal. The deep bowl shape allows air and smoke to circulate. A large grill, with a cooking surface that measures 22 inches across, is best for indirect cooking. On smaller grills, the "cool" part of the grill may be too cramped to hold large cuts of meat. Regular briquettes are best here because they burn more slowly than hardwood charcoal.

As with a charcoal grill, size matters when trying to barbecue many foods on a gas grill. Unless the cooking surface is at least 400 square inches, you might have trouble with large, flat cuts such as ribs or brisket. In addition to size, the number of burners is critical. It's not possible to cook indirectly on a grill with only one burner because the burner is usually positioned in the center of the grill and the "cool" parts of the grill are too small to fit most foods. You must use a grill with at least two burners. With one burner on and one burner off, at least half of the grill will be cool enough for indirect cooking.

It's just as important for a gas grill to have a thermometer. You can stick an oven thermometer on the cooking grate near the food, but then you have to open the lid to find out what the temperature is. Opening the lid causes heat to dissipate and prolongs the total cooking time.

To set up a gas grill for indirect cooking, remove all warming shelves attached to the hood or the back of the grill. (Leave the racks in place when making ribs on a small grill.) You want to position the wood chips over the primary burner. With some gas grills, one burner must be turned on first. This is the primary burner. With other grills, you may designate a primary burner yourself.

WOOD CHUNKS AND CHIPS

ONE OF THE BEST REASONS TO BARBECUE is to flavor foods with smoke. Charcoal itself has some flavor (gas adds none), but the real smoky flavor of good ribs or brisket comes from wood chunks or chips. Chips will work on either a charcoal or gas grill, but chunks are suited to charcoal fires only,

BARBECUING ON A CHARCOAL GRILL

1. Arrange the coals in the grill: Pile the lit coals on one half of the grill and leave the other half free of coals. Place soaked and drained wood chunks or a foil packet filled with wood chips on top of the coals. Set the top grate in position, heat briefly, and then scrape the grate clean with a wire brush. You are now ready to cook over the cool part of the fire. Put the food on the grill and set the lid in place. Open the air vents as directed in individual recipes.

2. Monitor the heat level: We like to have some idea of the temperature inside a kettle grill as foods cook. A grill thermometer inserted through the vents on the lid can tell you if the fire is too hot or if the fire is getting too cool and you need to add more charcoal. You will get different readings depending on where the lid vents are and thus the thermometer is in relation to the coals. Because you want to know the temperature where the food is being cooked, rotate the lid so that the thermometer is close to the food. Make sure, however, that the thermometer stem does not touch the food.

3. Adjust the heat level: You can control the heat level to some extent by adjusting the vents on the lid and base of the grill. Opening the vents gives the fire more oxygen and will cause the coals to burn hotter at first, but then the fire will cool down more quickly as the coals peter out. Closing the vents partially (don't close the vents all the way or the fire will die) lowers the heat but keeps the coals from burning up too fast and helps the fire last longer.

since they must rest in a pile of lit coals to work. (If placed on the bottom of a gas grill they will not get hot enough to smoke.)

Chips and chunks come from the same source— a tree. The only differences are size and shape. Chunks are usually the size of a lemon or small orange; chips are thinner shards, more like the fine wood chips you might spread over a garden bed. (That said, it's also the case that pieces within the same bag can vary greatly in size.)

Wood chips and chunks are made from hardwoods because they burn more slowly than softer woods, such as apple. The most common choices are hickory, mesquite, and alder, although some stores may carry cherry or oak. Resinous woods, like pine, are not used for grilling because they give foods an off flavor.

Hickory is the most traditional wood used for outdoor cooking, but mesquite and oak have their partisans. In our tests, we found that any hardwood chunks or chips can be used. Frankly, the differences in flavor are minimal, especially if the food has been coated with spices. The difference between hickory and mesquite, for instance, is hard to taste on spice-rubbed ribs or brisket. Feel free to use whatever wood is available.

Using wood chunks is the easiest way to add smoke flavor when cooking over charcoal. You don't want the wood to catch fire and give up all its smoke at once. Ideally, the chunks should smolder slowly, releasing smoke for as long as possible. We found that soaking chunks adds enough moisture to the wood to keep it from catching fire as soon as it is placed on the charcoal. Soak as many 3-inch chunks (each about the size of a tennis ball) as directed in each recipe in cold water to cover for one hour, then drain the chunks and place them directly on the lit pile of charcoal.

As might be expected, the amount of wood added to the fire will affect the amount of resulting smoke flavor. For maximum wood flavor, add several chunks at the outset (just before heating up the cooking grate) and then again at the halfway point in the barbecuing process.

If you can't find wood chunks, wood chips may be used. We tried soaking the chips and throwing them directly onto the coals, but they caught fire immediately. The same thing happened when we placed the chips in an open foil tray on top of the coals— an open tray does not provide enough protection for the chips and can tip over if placed on an uneven pile of charcoal. To keep the chips from burning up too quickly, we found it best to wrap them in a foil packet (see the illustrations below). There's no need to soak these chips; the foil protects them from catching fire too quickly.

Chips are the only choice for gas grills since chunks are hard to position right over a lit burner and may not get hot enough to smoke. Therefore, foods barbecued over gas will never taste as smoky as foods cooked over charcoal. Still, we wanted to maximize the amount of smoke the chips would give off in a gas grill. We tried various methods for adding chips before we hit upon the best solution.

Both soaked and unsoaked chips thrown directly into the bottom of a gas grill burned much too quickly, giving up their smoke all at once. We tried wrapping the chips in a foil packet, which had worked for us with charcoal, but found that in this case the packet actually was too effective a shield; not enough smoke was being released.

USING WOOD CHIPS ON A CHARCOAL GRILL

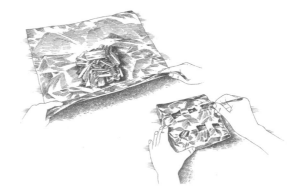

1. Place the amount of wood chips called for in the recipe in the center of an 18-inch square of heavy-duty aluminum foil. Fold in all four sides of the foil to encase the chips.

2. Turn the foil packet over. Tear about six large holes (each the size of a quarter) through the top of the foil packet with a fork to allow smoke to escape. Place the packet, with holes facing up, directly on a pile of lit charcoal.

When barbecuing with a gas grill, we prefer to place the chips in an open foil tray. (See the illustrations below for information on constructing a tray from heavy-duty aluminum foil.) The tray shields the chips from direct contact with the burner but is open on top to allow the smoke to flow freely. The tray also makes it possible to spread out the chips so that they are not piled on top of each other, as they are inside a smaller foil packet. When we placed unsoaked chips in the tray they caught fire immediately. Soaking the chips for 15 minutes prevents them from igniting and allows them to smolder slowly and produce a lot of smoke.

Is there a difference in the flavor imparted by wood chunks and wood chips? To find out, we tested the same amount of wood chips and wood chunks by weight (8 ounces) under the same conditions in a charcoal fire.

The wood chips were placed in a heavy-duty foil packet with holes cut into the packet to allow the smoke to escape, while the wood chunks were soaked for an hour and then drained. Each was then placed in a separate grill on top of 40 ignited coals. On each grill the lid was closed, the lid vents were opened half way, and all other vents were left completely open. The chips smoked for 30 to 35 minutes, while the chunks smoked twice as long, for one hour. The food exposed to the smoke for twice the amount of time had a greater concentration of smoky, grilled flavor.

If you have a choice between wood chips and wood chunks, use the wood chunks for the grill. They deliver more smoky flavor. If you don't have a choice and must use wood chips, they make a perfectly acceptable substitute for chunks. You may even find them preferable if you prefer a lighter smoke flavor in barbecued food.

Barbecue Rubs

A MIXTURE OF DRY SPICES, CALLED A RUB, is often used to coat foods before barbecuing. Rubs encourage the formation of a deeply browned crust filled with complex, concentrated flavors. Like marinades, spice rubs add flavor to foods before cooking, but we think rubs and pastes have several advantages over marinades.

Because rubs are composed almost solely of spices and herbs, they provide stronger flavors than marinades. (Marinades are mostly oil and an acidic liquid, such as lemon juice or vinegar.) Rubs also stick better to foods than marinades—after all, they are massaged directly into foods before grilling. Better sticking means better flavor. Finally, marinades almost always contain a lot of oil, which can cause flare-ups. Spice rubs

USING WOOD CHIPS ON A GAS GRILL

1. Start with a 12 by 18-inch piece of heavy-duty foil. Make a 1-inch fold on one long side. Repeat three more times, then turn the fold up to create a sturdy side that measures about an inch high. Repeat the process on the other long side.

2. With a short side facing you, fold in both corners as if wrapping a gift.

3. Turn up the inside inch or so of each triangular fold to match the rim on the long sides of the foil tray.

4. Lift the pointed end of the triangle over the rim of foil and fold down to seal. Repeat the process on the other short side.

EQUIPMENT: Spice Grinder

You can buy a specialized tool designed just for grinding spices, but most cooks will find it easier to invest in a cheap coffee mill that they use exclusively for grinding spices. (Don't try to grind coffee beans in a mill that has been used for spices. Mills are impossible to clean thoroughly, and cumin-flavored coffee isn't the best way to start your day.) Don't use an expensive burr coffee grinder; spices can be ground perfectly well in the blade-type grinder that has a small hopper on top. To get an even grind, see the illustration below.

Hold the coffee mill in one hand and place the other hand over the hopper on top. Lift the whole unit off the counter and grind, shaking the unit gently to move the spices around the blade and grind them evenly and finely.

can be left on foods for several hours without causing fires.

Spice rubs can be used on just about any type of food you want to barbecue, and, in general, you can mix and match rubs and pastes on different foods with abandon. Still, it's worth following a couple of guidelines. First, consider matching the strength of the rub or paste with the nature of the food being cooked. For example, earthier spices are better with meat, lighter spices and herbs with fish and chicken. Also keep in mind that spices like cumin and paprika are good "bulk" spices, while aromatic spices like cinnamon and cloves should be used lightly.

We find that bare hands—not brushes—are the best tools for applying rubs. Use a bit of pressure to make sure the spices actually adhere to the food. Although the rubs can be applied right before cooking, we find that the flavor of the spices penetrates deeper into the food if given some time. In general, we like to refrigerate rubbed meats for at least a few hours (and sometimes a few days) to allow the flavor to develop.

Dry Rub for Barbecue
MAKES ABOUT 1 CUP

You can adjust the proportions of spices in this all-purpose rub or add or subtract a spice, as you wish. For instance, if don't like spicy foods, reduce or eliminate the cayenne. Also, if you are using hot chili powder, you may want to eliminate the cayenne. This rub works well with ribs and brisket as well as with Boston butt if you want to make pulled pork.

4	tablespoons sweet paprika
2	tablespoons chili powder
2	tablespoons ground cumin
2	tablespoons dark brown sugar
2	tablespoons salt
1	tablespoon dried oregano
1	tablespoon granulated sugar
1	tablespoon ground black pepper
1	tablespoon ground white pepper
1–2	teaspoons cayenne pepper

Mix all ingredients together in a small bowl. (The rub can be stored in an airtight container at room temperature for several weeks).

BARBECUE SAUCES

BARBECUE SAUCE IS THE MOST COMMON sauce used for grilling. Almost all sauces contain ingredients such as tomatoes or a sweetener that will cause them to burn if left on grilled foods for any length of time. For this reason, these sauces are usually brushed on grilled foods during the last few minutes of cooking and also served at the table.

Classic barbecue sauce is relatively easy to make. We found that the combination of tomato sauce and whole tomatoes in juice cooks down to a thick, glossy texture. Vinegar, brown sugar, and molasses add the sour and sweet notes, while spices (paprika, chili powder, black pepper, and salt) round out the flavors. For some brightness, we add a little fresh orange juice as well. The only downside to this sauce is that it takes at least two hours of gentle simmering for the flavors to come together and for the tomatoes to break down into a sauce of the proper consistency.

We wondered if there was a way to shortcut the process. The first thing we had to do was get rid of the canned whole tomatoes—they took too long to cook down into a thick sauce. All tomato sauce (and no fresh tomatoes) made a sauce that seemed more appropriate for pasta. We had better luck with ketchup, which is already sweet, tart, and thick.

The only other major obstacle we encountered when developing our quick barbecue sauce was the onion. After two hours of simmering in our classic barbecue sauce, the onions became very soft and lost their texture. In our quick-cooked sauce, they remained crunchy. We tried pureeing the quick sauce after it had cooked, as we did with our classic sauce, but the quick sauce lost its glossy texture when pureed and became grainy. One of our test cooks suggested using onion juice—made by pureeing raw onion with water—to give the sauce some onion flavor. This worked liked a charm.

At this point, it was only a matter of adding flavors. Worcestershire sauce and Dijon mustard added instant depth to a quick-cooked sauce. The usual spices—chili powder, cayenne, black pepper—provided more flavor and heat.

Classic Barbecue Sauce

MAKES 3 CUPS

Brush this sauce onto chicken parts during the last minute or two of grilling or serve at the table with ribs, brisket, or pulled pork.

2	tablespoons vegetable oil
I	medium onion, minced
I	(8-ounce) can tomato sauce
I	(28-ounce) can whole tomatoes with juice
¾	cup distilled white vinegar
¼	cup firmly packed dark brown sugar
2	tablespoons molasses
I	tablespoon sweet paprika
I	tablespoon chili powder
2	teaspoons liquid smoke (optional)
I	teaspoon salt
2	teaspoons ground black pepper
¼	cup orange juice

1. Heat the oil in a large, heavy-bottomed saucepan over medium heat until hot and shimmering (but not smoking). Add the onion and sauté until golden brown, 7 to 10 minutes, stirring frequently. Add the remaining ingredients. Bring to a boil, then reduce the heat to the lowest possible setting and simmer, uncovered, until thickened, 2 to 2½ hours.

2. Puree the sauce, in batches, if necessary, in a blender or the workbowl of a food processor. Transfer to a bowl and use immediately or cover in an airtight container. (The sauce can be refrigerated for up to 2 weeks or frozen for several months.)

Quick Barbecue Sauce

MAKES ABOUT 1½ CUPS

Classic barbecue sauce must simmer for a long time to break down the tomatoes. However, we found that starting with ketchup can shortcut the process. Use this sauce as you would any another barbecue sauce—either brushed on foods during the last minutes of grilling or served at the table as a dipping sauce with ribs or brisket.

I	medium onion, peeled and quartered
I	cup ketchup
2	tablespoons cider vinegar
2	tablespoons Worcestershire sauce
2	tablespoons Dijon mustard
5	tablespoons molasses
I	teaspoon hot pepper sauce, such as Tabasco
¼	teaspoon ground black pepper
I½	teaspoons liquid smoke (optional)
2	tablespoons vegetable oil
I	medium clove garlic, minced
I	teaspoon chili powder
¼	teaspoon cayenne pepper

INGREDIENTS: **Liquid Smoke**

What gives homemade or bottled barbecue sauce its smoky flavor? It's a compound called liquid smoke. Many home cooks avoid this product because they assume it's full of unhealthful compounds. Actually, liquid smoke is an all-natural product made by burning hickory hardwood, condensing the smoke, and then filtering it to remove impurities. Look for liquid smoke in supermarkets and other places that sell grilling paraphernalia.

1. Process the onion and ¼ cup water in the workbowl of a food processor fitted with a steel blade until pureed and the mixture resembles slush, about 30 seconds. Strain the mixture through a fine-mesh strainer into a liquid measuring cup, pressing on the solids with a rubber spatula to obtain ½ cup juice. Discard the solids in the strainer.

2. Whisk the onion juice, ketchup, vinegar, Worcestershire, mustard, molasses, hot pepper sauce, black pepper, and liquid smoke (if using) together in a medium bowl.

3. Heat the oil in a large nonreactive saucepan over medium heat until shimmering but not smoking. Add the garlic, chili powder, and cayenne; cook until fragrant, about 30 seconds. Whisk in the ketchup mixture and bring to a boil; reduce the heat to medium-low and simmer gently, uncovered, until the flavors meld and the sauce is thickened, about 25 minutes. Cool the sauce to room temperature before using. (The sauce can be refrigerated in an airtight container for up to 1 week.)

Sweet-Sour-Spicy Barbecue Sauce

MAKES ABOUT 1½ CUPS

We developed this highly acidic sauce for beef ribs. The vinegar, tomato paste, and spices balance the richness of the beef. It is quite strong, so brush only a little bit of the sauce onto the ribs to begin with. If you like your sauce especially spicy, add another ½ teaspoon of cayenne pepper.

1	cup distilled white vinegar
¼	cup tomato paste
2	tablespoons salt
½	cup sugar
2	tablespoons sweet paprika
2	teaspoons dried mustard
2	teaspoons ground black pepper
½	teaspoon cayenne pepper
½	teaspoon onion powder
½	teaspoon garlic powder
½	teaspoon chili powder
4	tablespoons vegetable oil

1. Mix the vinegar, tomato paste, salt, and sugar together in a medium bowl. In another bowl, combine the paprika, dried mustard, black pepper, cayenne pepper, onion powder, garlic powder, and chili powder.

2. Heat the oil in a small saucepan over medium heat. Add the spice mixture and cook until sizzling and fragrant, 30 to 45 seconds. Stir in the vinegar mixture and increase the heat to high. Bring to a boil, reduce the heat to low, and simmer for 5 minutes. Remove the pan from the heat and cool to room temperature. (The sauce can be refrigerated in an airtight container for up to 1 week.)

INGREDIENTS: Bottled Barbecue Sauces

Despite the best of intentions, there's not always time to make barbecue sauce. Even our quick recipe requires 10 minutes of prep time and a half hour of cooking time. It's no surprise that many cooks turn to bottled sauces.

We wondered if some brands of bottled barbecue sauce were much better than others. Are the "gourmet" brands worth the extra money, or will a supermarket brand suffice? We tasted 11 samples to find out.

Our panel preferred the more expensive sauces because they were the spiciest and had the strongest flavors. Tasters loved Mad Dog, Gates, and Stubb's, three boutique brands with distinctive flavors. All provided good hits of vinegar and spice.

Sweet, ketchupy sauces landed at the bottom of the ranking. Most of the supermarket brands were in this group. The one exception was Bull's-Eye, which was sweet, but not overly so. It also had a fair amount of smoke. Heinz, KC Masterpiece, and Kraft rated much lower. When we checked the ingredient labels after the tasting, we found that most of the low-rated sauces contained corn syrup and starch. These ingredients were associated with gooey, syrupy sweet sauces.

As with our homemade recipes, bottled sauces are finishing sauces, not basting sauces. They all contain sugar and tomatoes, which will cause foods to burn within minutes after application. Don't marinate food destined for the grill in barbecue sauce. The food will burn and taste awful. Just brush a little sauce on during the last two or three minutes of the cooking time and then brush again just before serving. Or just bring the sauce to the table and let everyone add sauce to taste.

Eastern North Carolina–Style Barbecue Sauce

MAKES 2 CUPS

This sauce contains no tomato but is rich with heat and vinegar. It is traditionally served with pulled pork (page 153) but can also be brushed onto ribs or brisket.

I   cup distilled white vinegar
I   cup cider vinegar
I   tablespoon sugar
I   tablespoon hot red pepper flakes
I   tablespoon hot pepper sauce, such as Tabasco
     Salt and ground black pepper

Mix all ingredients, including salt and pepper to taste, together in a medium bowl. (The sauce can be refrigerated in an airtight container for up to several days.)

Mid–South Carolina Mustard Sauce

MAKES 2 1/2 CUPS

Another classic sauce for pulled pork (page 152) that works well with most any cut of grilled pork.

I   cup cider vinegar
6   tablespoons Dijon mustard
2   tablespoons maple syrup or honey
4   teaspoons Worcestershire sauce
I   teaspoon hot pepper sauce, such as Tabasco
I   cup vegetable oil
2   teaspoons salt
     Ground black pepper

Mix all ingredients, including black pepper to taste, in a medium bowl. (The sauce can be refrigerated in an airtight container for up to several days.)

BARBECUED BEEF RIBS

IN MOST PARTS OF THE COUNTRY, WHEN people say "ribs," they mean spareribs. However, beef ribs are another option worth considering. Barbecuing beef ribs is basically the same as barbecuing pork ribs (see page 148). The goal is to get tender, smoky, red-tinged meat that almost falls off the bone. Because beef ribs are the bones included in prime rib, they are already tender and flavorful, so they require less cooking time than pork ribs. However, you don't want to cut the cooking time too much, because you still need to render excess fat and infuse the ribs with smoke flavor.

Butchers generally cut beef rib bones from the prime rib to make either boneless rib roasts or rib-eye steaks. If you don't see beef ribs in the meat case, ask your butcher if there are some unpackaged ribs in the back.

Prime rib has seven bones. Sometimes we found an entire slab of beef ribs with seven bones, but often we saw just a couple of ribs packaged together. As long as there are at least four ribs in a row, it's fine to barbecue them. These bones are quite large, so just a few make a serving. We think that 12 bones (in either two or three partial slabs) are enough to feed four. When shopping, get the meatiest bones you can. We found that even the leanest ribs have more than enough fat to keep them moist during barbecuing. If you can only find ribs that are really fatty, trim away some surface fat before cooking them.

You will need a large kettle or gas grill to cook 12 beef ribs. It's fine if the ribs overlap slightly at the outset; we found that the meat quickly shrinks and that the ribs will fit in a single layer within 30 minutes or so. Don't try to cook more than 12 ribs at once; they just don't brown properly when stacked on top of each other.

Although some sources say that beef ribs can be quick-cooked on the grill, we thought ribs cooked this way were bland. Yes, they were tender, but we wanted more smoke as well as that red tinge you get from slow cooking on the grill. We ended up using the same method that worked with pork, with some modifications.

At first, we lit the same amount of coal we had used for pork spareribs, but we found that the beef ribs were getting too dark too quickly and that the ends were getting a touch burnt and dried out. So we reduced the number of briquettes from 40 to 30, with great results. The ribs were able to cook longer without burning, and some of the interior layers of fat now had time to render and drip off the ribs.

129

When we let the ribs cook for only 1 hour and 15 minutes, we found them to be a little too fatty still. Barbecuing for 1 hour and 45 minutes to 2 hours produced better results.

As we had done with spareribs, we tested wrapping the beef ribs in aluminum foil and a paper bag for an hour; this method worked for us again. The wrapped beef ribs were more tender and moist throughout. When the ribs were taken straight off the grill and eaten, they were still delicious, but some of the meat on the ends of the ribs was a little dry and tough. Letting them rest in the foil and paper bag redistributed the moisture throughout the ribs, making them more appealing.

Barbecued Beef Ribs on a Charcoal Grill

SERVES 4

Beef rib bones are quite large, so you may need to carefully arrange them on the grill to make them fit. (You will need a large kettle grill for this recipe.) Don't worry if the ribs overlap a bit—they will shrink while cooking to fit comfortably in the grill. While a classic barbecue sauce can be used with beef ribs, tasters felt that a more acidic sauce best complemented the richness of beef.

12	beef ribs in 2 or 3 slabs (about 5 pounds total), trimmed of excess fat if necessary
½	cup plus 2 tablespoons Dry Rub for Barbecue (page 126)
2	(3-inch) wood chunks or 2 cups wood chips Heavy-duty aluminum foil Brown paper grocery bag
1½	cups Sweet-Sour-Spicy Barbecue Sauce (page 128)

1. Rub both sides of the ribs with the dry rub and let stand at room temperature for 1 hour. (For stronger flavor, wrap the rubbed ribs in a double layer of plastic wrap and refrigerate for up to 1 day.)

2. Soak the wood chunks in cold water to cover for 1 hour and drain, or place the wood chips on an 18-inch square of aluminum foil, seal to make a packet, and use a fork to create about six holes to allow the smoke to escape (see the illustrations on page 124).

3. Meanwhile, light a large chimney filled one-third with charcoal briquettes (about 1¾ pounds, or 30 coals) and allow to burn until covered with a thin layer of gray ash. Empty the coals into one side of the grill, piling them up in a mound two briquettes high. Keep the bottom vents completely open. Place the wood chunks or the packet with the chips on top of the charcoal. Put the cooking grate in place, open the grill lid vents completely, and cover, turning the lid so that the vents are opposite the wood chunks or chips to draw smoke through the grill. Let the grate heat for 5 minutes and then clean it with a wire brush.

4. Position the ribs over the cool part of the grill. Barbecue, turning the ribs every 30 minutes, until the meat starts to pull away from the bones and has a rosy glow on the exterior, 1¾ to 2 hours. (The initial temperature inside the grill will be about 325 degrees and will drop to 250 degrees after 2 hours.)

5. Remove the ribs from the grill and completely wrap each slab in foil. Put the foil-wrapped slabs in a brown paper bag and crimp the top of the bag to seal tightly. Allow to rest at room temperature for 1 hour.

6. Unwrap the ribs and brush with some sauce. Serve, passing extra sauce at the table.

BEEF RIBS

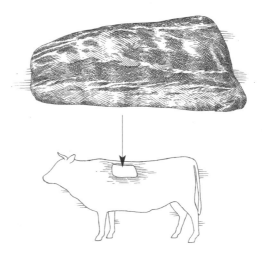

Conventional beef ribs are cut from the rib roast along the back of the animal. These bones are sold in partial or full slabs (a full slab has seven bones) about eight inches long.

Barbecued Beef Ribs on a Gas Grill

SERVES 4

Beef rib bones are quite large, so you may need to carefully arrange them on the grill to make them fit. (You will need a large grill for this recipe.) Don't worry if the ribs overlap a bit—they will shrink while cooking to fit comfortably in the grill. Keep an eye on the grill thermometer and adjust the lit burner as necessary to prevent the ribs from browning too quickly. While a classic barbecue sauce can be used with beef ribs, tasters felt that a more acidic sauce best complemented the richness of beef.

12	beef ribs in 2 or 3 slabs (about 5 pounds total), trimmed of excess fat if necessary
½	cup plus 2 tablespoons Dry Rub for Barbecue (page 126)
2	cups wood chips
	Heavy-duty aluminum foil
	Brown paper grocery bag
1½	cups Sweet-Sour-Spicy Barbecue Sauce (page 128)

1. Rub both sides of the ribs with the dry rub and let stand at room temperature for 1 hour. (For stronger flavor, wrap the rubbed ribs in a double layer of plastic wrap and refrigerate for up to 1 day.)

2. Soak the wood chips for 15 minutes in a bowl of water to cover. Place the wood chips in a foil tray (see the illustrations on page 125). Place the foil tray with the soaked wood chips on top of the primary burner (see the illustration on page 122). Turn all burners to high and preheat with the lid down until the chips are smoking heavily, about 20 minutes.

3. Scrape the grate clean with a wire brush. Turn the primary burner down to medium and turn off the other burner(s). Position the ribs over the cool part of the grill. Barbecue, turning the ribs every 30 minutes, until the meat starts to pull away from the bones and has a rosy glow on the exterior, 2 to 2½ hours. (The temperature inside the grill should be a constant 275 degrees; adjust the lit burner as necessary.)

4. Remove the ribs from the grill and completely wrap each slab in foil. Put the foil-wrapped slabs in a brown paper bag and crimp the top of the bag to seal tightly. Allow to rest at room temperature for 1 hour.

5. Unwrap the ribs and brush with some sauce. Serve, passing extra sauce at the table.

BARBECUED BRISKET

OUR FAVORITE WAY TO COOK BRISKET IS to barbecue it. When prepared correctly, the meat picks up a great smoky flavor and becomes fork-tender. Unfortunately, many a barbecued brisket ends up burnt, tough, or chewy. This is because brisket is so tough to begin with. Unless it is fully cooked, the meat is very chewy and practically inedible. Because brisket is so large (a full cut can weigh 13 pounds), getting the meat "fully cooked" can take many hours. Our goal was to make the meat as tender as possible as quickly as possible.

What does "fully cooked" mean when talking about brisket? To find out, we roasted four small pieces to various internal temperatures. The pieces cooked to 160 and 180 degrees were dry and quite tough. A piece cooked to 200 degrees was slightly less tough, although quite dry. A final piece cooked to 210 degrees had the most appealing texture and the most pleasant chew, despite the fact that it was the driest.

So what's going on here? Heat causes muscle proteins to uncoil and then rejoin in a different formation, which drives out juices in the same way that wringing removes moisture from a wet cloth. This process starts in earnest at around 140 degrees, and by the time the meat reaches 180 degrees, most of its juices have been expelled. This explains why a medium-rare steak (cooked to 130 degrees) is much juicier than a well-done steak (cooked to 160 degrees).

With tender cuts, like steak, the lower the internal temperature of the meat, the juicier and less tough the meat will be. However, with cuts that start out tough, like brisket, another process is also at work. Brisket is loaded with waxy-looking connective tissue called collagen, which makes the meat chewy and tough. Only when the collagen has been transformed into gelatin will the meat be tender. Collagen begins to convert to gelatin at 130 to 140 degrees, but the conversion process occurs most rapidly at temperatures above 180 degrees.

When cooking brisket, the gelatinization of collagen must be the priority. Thus, the meat should be cooked as fully as possible, or to an internal temperature of 210 degrees. The muscle juices will be long gone (that's why the sliced meat is served with barbecue sauce), but the meat will be extremely tender because all the collagen will have been converted to gelatin.

It is important to point out that moist-heat cooking methods (such as braising) are appropriate for cooking meats to such high internal temperatures because water is a more efficient conductor of heat than air. Meats cooked in a moist environment heat up faster and can be held at high internal temperatures without burning or drying out.

Given the fact that brisket must be fully cooked and that it can be so big, the meat needs 10 or 12 hours of barbecuing to reach the fork-tender stage. Even when butchers separate the brisket into smaller pieces, as is often the case, the cooking time is astronomical. Most cooks are not prepared to keep a fire going that long. To get around this tending-the-fire-all-day-long problem, we found it necessary to commit barbecue heresy. After much testing, we decided to start the meat on the grill but finish it in the oven, where it could be left to cook unattended.

We wondered how long the meat would have to stay on the grill to pick up enough smoke flavor. In our testing, we found that two hours allowed the meat to absorb plenty of smoke flavor and created a dark brown, crusty exterior. At this point, the meat is ready for the oven. We found it best to wrap the meat in foil to create a moist environment. (Unwrapped briskets cooked up drier, and the exterior was prone to burning.) After barbecuing, a whole brisket requires three hours or so in a 300-degree oven to become fork-tender. Barbecue purists might object to our use of the oven, but this method works, and it doesn't require a tremendous commitment of hands-on cooking time.

Some further notes about our testing. Although many experts recommend basting a brisket regularly as it cooks on the grill to ensure moistness, we disagree. Taking the lid off wreaked havoc with our charcoal fire, and the meat didn't taste any different

despite frequent basting with sauce. Likewise, we don't recommend placing a pan filled with water (we also tried beer) on the grill. Some barbecue masters believe that the liquid adds moisture and flavor to the meat, but we couldn't tell any difference between brisket cooked with and without the pan of liquid.

Brisket comes with a thick layer of fat on one side. We tried turning the brisket as it cooked, thinking this might promote even cooking, but we had better results when we barbecued the brisket fat-side up the entire time. This way, the fat slowly melts, lubricating the meat below.

Barbecued Beef Brisket on a Charcoal Grill
SERVES 18 TO 24

Cooking a whole brisket, which weighs about 10 pounds, may seem like overkill. However, the process is easy, and the leftovers keep well in the refrigerator for up to four days. (Leave leftover brisket unsliced, and reheat the foil-wrapped meat in a 300-degree oven until warm.) Don't worry if your brisket is a little larger or smaller; split-second cooking times are not critical because the meat is eaten very well-done. Still, if you don't want to bother with a big piece of meat, barbecuing brisket for less than a crowd is easy to do. Simply ask your butcher for either the point or flat portion of the brisket (we prefer the point cut; see page 114), each of which weighs about half as much as a whole brisket. Then follow this recipe, reducing the spice rub by half and barbecuing for just 1½ hours. Wrap the meat tightly in foil and reduce the time in the oven to 2 hours. No matter how large or small a piece you cook, it's a good idea to save the juices the meat gives off while in the oven to enrich the barbecue sauce. Hickory and mesquite are both traditional wood choices with brisket.

¾ cup Dry Rub for Barbecue (page 126)
1 whole beef brisket (9 to 11 pounds), fat trimmed to ¼ inch thickness
2 (3-inch) wood chunks or 2 cups wood chips
   Heavy-duty aluminum foil
2 cups barbecue sauce (see pages 127 to 129)

1. Apply the rub liberally to all sides of the meat, pressing down to make sure the spices adhere and completely obscure the meat. Wrap the brisket

tightly in plastic wrap and refrigerate for 2 hours. (For stronger flavor, refrigerate the brisket for up to 2 days.)

2. About 1 hour prior to cooking, remove the brisket from the refrigerator, unwrap, and let it come up to room temperature. Soak the wood chunks in cold water to cover for 1 hour and drain, or place the wood chips on an 18-inch square of aluminum foil, seal to make a packet, and use a fork to create about six holes to allow smoke to escape (see the illustrations on page 124).

3. Meanwhile, light a large chimney filled a bit less than halfway with charcoal briquettes (about 2½ pounds, or 40 coals) and allow to burn until covered with a thin layer of gray ash. Empty the coals into one side of the grill, piling them up in a mound two or three briquettes high. Keep the bottom vents completely open. Place the wood chunks or the packet with the chips on top of the charcoal. Put the cooking grate in place, open the grill lid vents completely, and cover, turning the lid so that the vents are opposite the wood chunks or chips to draw smoke through the grill. Let the grate heat for 5 minutes and then clean it with a wire brush.

4. Position the brisket, fat-side up, on the side of the grill opposite the fire. Barbecue, without removing lid, for 2 hours. (The initial temperature will be about 350 degrees and will drop to 250 degrees after 2 hours.)

5. Adjust an oven rack to the middle position and preheat the oven to 300 degrees. Attach two pieces of heavy-duty foil, 48 inches long, by folding the long edges together two or three times, crimping tightly to seal well, to form an approximate 48 by 36-inch rectangle. Position the brisket lengthwise in the center of the foil. Bring the short edges over the brisket and fold down, crimping tightly to seal. Repeat with the long sides of the foil to seal the brisket completely. (See illustrations 1 and 2 on page 134.) Place the brisket on a rimmed baking sheet. Bake until the meat is fork-tender, 3 to 3½ hours.

6. Remove the brisket from the oven, loosen the foil at one end to release steam, and let rest for 30 minutes. If you like, drain the juices into a bowl (see illustration 3 on page 134) and defat the juices in a gravy skimmer.

7. Unwrap the brisket and place it on a cutting board. Separate the meat into two sections and carve it against the grain on the diagonal into long, thin slices (see illustrations 4 and 5 on page 134). Serve with plain barbecue sauce or with barbecue sauce that has been flavored with up to 1 cup of defatted brisket juices.

Barbecued Beef Brisket on a Gas Grill

SERVES 18 TO 24

You will need a pretty large grill to cook a whole brisket. If your grill has fewer than 400 square inches of cooking space, barbecue either the point or flat end, each of which weighs about half as much as a whole brisket. Then follow this recipe, reducing the spice rub by half and barbecuing for just 1½ hours. Wrap the meat tightly in foil and reduce the time in the oven to 2 hours. No matter how large or small a piece you cook, it's a good idea to save the juices the meat gives off while in the oven to enrich the barbecue sauce.

¾   cup Dry Rub for Barbecue (page 126)
1   whole beef brisket (9 to 11 pounds), fat trimmed to ¼ inch thickness
2   cups wood chips
     Heavy-duty aluminum foil
2   cups barbecue sauce (see pages 127 to 129)

1. Apply the rub liberally to all sides of the meat, pressing down to make sure the spices adhere and completely obscure the meat. Wrap the brisket tightly in plastic wrap and refrigerate for 2 hours. (For stronger flavor, refrigerate the brisket for up to 2 days.)

2. About 1 hour prior to cooking, remove the brisket from the refrigerator, unwrap, and let it come up to room temperature.

3. Soak the wood chips for 15 minutes in a bowl of water to cover. Place the wood chips in a foil tray (see the illustrations on page 125). Place the foil tray with the soaked wood chips on top of the primary burner (see the illustration on page 122). Turn all burners to high and preheat with the lid down until chips are smoking heavily, about 20 minutes.

4. Scrape the grate clean with a wire brush. Turn the primary burner down to medium and turn off the other burner(s). Position the brisket, fat-side up,

over the cool part of the grill. Cover and barbecue for 2 hours. (The temperature inside the grill should be a constant 275 degrees; adjust the lit burner as necessary.)

5. Adjust an oven rack to the middle position and preheat the oven to 300 degrees. Attach two 48-inch pieces of heavy-duty foil by folding the long edges together two or three times, crimping tightly to seal well, to form a rectangle of about 36 by 48 inches. Position the brisket lengthwise in the center of the foil. Bring the short edges over the brisket and fold down, crimping tightly to seal. Repeat with the long sides of the foil to seal the brisket completely. (See illustrations 1 and 2 below.) Place the brisket on a rimmed baking sheet. Bake until the meat is fork-tender, 3 to 3½ hours.

6. Remove the brisket from the oven, loosen the foil at one end to release steam, and let rest for 30 minutes. If you like, drain the juices into a bowl (see illustration 3 below) and defat the juices in a gravy skimmer.

7. Unwrap the brisket and place it on a cutting board. Separate the meat into two sections and carve it against the grain on the diagonal into long, thin slices (see illustrations 4 and 5, below). Serve with plain barbecue sauce or with barbecue sauce that has been flavored with up to 1 cup of defatted brisket juices.

KEYS STEPS TO BARBECUED BRISKET

1. After barbecuing, place the brisket on two 4-foot sections of heavy-duty aluminum foil that have been sealed together to make a 4 by 3-foot rectangle. Bring the short ends of the foil up over the brisket and crimp tightly to seal.

2. Seal the long sides of the foil packet tightly up against the sides of the meat. Put the brisket on a rimmed baking sheet and in the oven.

3. After the brisket comes out of the oven, use oven mitts to lift the rimmed baking sheet and carefully pour the juices into a bowl. Reserve the juices and defat if you like. They make a delicious addition to the barbecue sauce.

4. Since the grain on the two sections of the brisket goes in opposite directions, separate the two cuts before slicing.

5. Carve the brisket into long, thin slices, cutting against the grain on the diagonal.

THREE-BEAN SALAD WITH CUMIN, CILANTRO, AND ORANGES **PAGE 37**

CORN MUFFINS **PAGE 280**

STUFFED TOMATOES WITH PARMESAN, GARLIC, AND BASIL **PAGE 69**

CHILI CON CARNE **PAGE 22**

FRESH CORN FRITTERS **PAGE 54**

WILD RICE PILAF **PAGE 89**

SPIRAL-SLICED HAM **PAGE 143**

CRISP BREADED PORK CUTLET SANDWICH **PAGE 138**

BROILED SALMON WITH MUSTARD AND CRISP POTATO CRUST **PAGE 203**

CRANBERRY NUT BREAD **PAGE 273**

MOLASSES SPICE COOKIES WITH ORANGE ESSENCE **PAGE 320**

COCONUT LAYER CAKE **PAGE 355**

NEW YORK CHEESECAKE WITH FRESH STRAWBERRY TOPPING   **PAGE 361**

SWEET POTATO PIE **PAGE 379**

LEMON POUND CAKE **PAGE 340**

6

PORK AND LAMB

AMERICANS HAVE LONG BEEN FOND OF pork. We cook almost every cut and regularly eat pork for breakfast (bacon), lunch (cutlet sandwiches), and dinner (ham, chops, ribs). Lamb is far less popular, but there is at least one lamb dish, shepherd's pie, that regularly shows up in American homes.

Up until World War II, pigs were raised as much for their fat as for their meat. A pig with four to five inches of exterior fat (equivalent to about 60 pounds of lard) at slaughter was the norm. After the war, vegetable sources of fat (oil, shortening, margarine) became preferred over animal, and lard was no longer an asset. This trend, coupled with concerns for healthy eating over the past two or three decades that generally discourage intake of animal fat, caused the industry to "lean up" its pork, largely through genetic engineering. Today, many processors penalize producers for pigs that carry an exterior layer of fat of more than four-fifths inch (or more than eight pounds). All told, today's pork has about 30 percent less fat than it did 20 years ago.

The industry's success in eliminating the pig's surface fat, however, has resulted in the loss of intramuscular fat as well. Known as marbling, this fat traps and retains juices during cooking and gives the meat flavor and body. This reduction in fat poses the greatest challenges for the cook in the loin, the area that extends from the back of the shoulder down to the hip and is home to chops as well as the tenderloin crown roast of pork. Because they are so lean, these cuts require special treatment to prevent them from becoming tough and chewy when cooked.

Although health experts recommend cooking all meat (including pork) to an internal temperature of 160 degrees, we find that most pork cuts cooked to this temperature are dry and tough. An internal temperature of 145 to 150 degrees is our preference. At this temperature the meat, when cut, is ivory in color and reveals a distinct grain, but the juices still run pale pink.

Fear of trichinosis should not prompt anyone to overcook pork. The trichinae parasite is killed at 137 degrees, when pork is still medium-rare. What's more, trichinosis is now quite uncommon in the United States. Only 230 cases were reported nationwide between 1991 and 1996, and the source of contamination in some 40 percent of these cases was wild game. If you are unalterably opposed to pinkish pork juices (or are concerned about salmonella from cross-contamination with other foods), you should cook pork to 160 degrees, but the meat will be quite dry.

Cuts from the shoulder, belly, and leg are less prone to drying out. Meat from these areas tends to be not only much fattier but also quite tough, requiring long, slow cooking if it is to become fork-tender. The shoulder is divided into two cuts, the picnic roast and Boston butt. The leg is sold as ham, and the belly is the part bacon and spareribs come from.

THE FOUR PRIMAL CUTS OF PORK

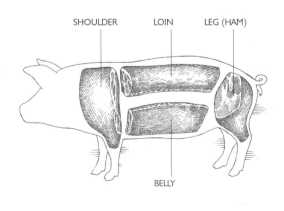

SHOULDER   LOIN   LEG (HAM)

BELLY

PORK CUTLETS

TO MANY AMERICANS, A PORK DINNER usually means chops or a roast. But denizens of the Midwestern heartland, particularly Iowa, Indiana, and Missouri, might think instead of pan-fried breaded pork cutlets. Or they might think of tough disks of meat shrouded in a greasy, pale crust, which is how these cutlets can turn out if they're not cooked properly. If things go well, though, the pork is tender and the breading crisp, golden, and substantial.

Testing started with the basics: the pork itself. The two suitable cuts of pork we found in the supermarket, boneless loin chops and tenderloin, were also the two cuts cited most consistently in the recipes we researched. We tried both and tasters favored cutlets from the tenderloin by a wide margin. They were remarkably tender and mildly flavored.

The next issue was thickness. When the cutlets were too thick, the breading overbrowned by the time the interior cooked through; when too thin, the meat was done long before the breading had taken on enough color. We ended up preferring cutlets pounded to a thickness of ½ inch. They were thick enough to offer some chew and a cushion against overcooking as the crust developed to an even, golden brown. At first, we simply cut the tenderloin crosswise into ½-inch slices. But the tenderloin is a slender muscle, so these slices were rarely more than 2½ inches in diameter (and often smaller), making a skimpy presentation. Our solution—to divide the tenderloin into six pieces (about 2 inches each in thickness) and then pound them to the desired thickness—both increased the diameter of the cutlets so they looked more attractive and standardized the yield of the recipe. One tenderloin now yielded six broad cutlets, enough for three servings.

As we often do in the test kitchen, we tried brining the cutlets, soaking them in a solution of water, salt, and often sugar as well. After several tests and considerable debate, we decided to skip this step since it did not improve the texture of the meat (pork tenderloin is almost always tender and supple unless overcooked). Seasoning the cutlets with salt and pepper was a much easier way to add flavor. To provide a good baseline flavor, liberal doses of salt and ground black pepper on the cutlets themselves were essential; experiments with seasoning only the breading components with different herb and spice combinations were less effective.

Many classic Midwestern recipes call for a cornmeal coating mixture. Here our tasters broke with tradition, selecting a thick coat of fresh bread crumbs (made by grinding high-quality white sandwich bread in the food processor) over a cornmeal-flour combination, dried bread crumbs, or cracker crumbs. The fresh bread crumbs were light, crisp, and flavorful, whereas the cornmeal was gritty, the dried crumbs stale, and the crackers pasty. A thin coat of beaten egg (with a bit of oil added to help it slide off the meat more easily) acted as a glue between the meat and crumbs, and a sheer film of flour applied to

MAKING PORK CUTLET SANDWICHES

Breaded pork cutlets are often used in sandwiches. They take well to a range of garnishes, traditional and not. Try any combination of the following: lettuce, thin-sliced tomato or red onion (raw or pickled), coleslaw, mustard, barbecue sauce, tartar sauce, pickle relish, or prepared chutney. Mayonnaise is also traditional; if you feel adventurous, flavor it by mixing ½ cup mayonnaise with 1 minced anchovy fillet (about ½ teaspoon) or 1 small minced chipotle chile en adobo (about 1 teaspoon). Or, for an Asian-inspired mayo, add 2 teaspoons soy sauce and ½ teaspoon each grated ginger and minced garlic. Soft white sandwich bread or hamburger buns are the breads of choice.

the meat just beforehand allowed the egg to cling. We tried to do without the initial flour coating, but the egg would not adhere to the meat without it, leading to a flimsy coating.

The glory of these cutlets is the crust, which is, alas, the component that can most easily go awry. One bad habit of many cooks we know, skimping on the oil when they pan-fry, deals the crust a fatal blow. We tried cooking a batch of cutlets in just 4 tablespoons of oil, and the results—poor, splotchy browning—confirmed our hunch that using enough oil is critical. To develop their hallmark golden, crunchy crust, the cutlets must be pan-fried in oil that reaches roughly halfway up their sides, about ½ cup per batch in a 12-inch skillet.

Heat, or lack thereof, is another problem that most cooks encounter when pan-frying. When we failed to heat the oil enough before adding the cutlets to the skillet, several problems arose. First, the breading absorbed too much oil, so the finished cutlets were greasy. Second, the breading took too long to brown properly, and that extended stay in the pan caused the meat to toughen slightly. These pitfalls are avoided easily enough, though, if the oil is hot enough for the cutlets to sizzle briskly upon entering the pan and to continue cooking at a moderate pace that allows the breading to brown evenly without burning at the edges. We found that the pan must be preheated over medium-high heat until the oil starts to shimmer—about 2½ minutes. (Time may vary depending on your particular pan and stovetop.) Taking care not to overcrowd the skillet with more than three cutlets per batch, we tested cooking times and learned that 2½ minutes per side browned the breading to a gorgeous golden hue without overcooking the meat within.

So if you don't skimp on either the oil or the heat, you can produce beautifully browned pork cutlets in just minutes that are crisp on the outside and tender and juicy on the inside. And they make great sandwiches to boot.

Crisp Breaded Pork Cutlets

SERVES 3

Pork tenderloins, which are sometimes sold in pairs, can weigh anywhere from 12 to 24 ounces. For this recipe, it is best to use a tenderloin that weighs at least 16 ounces. If you have two skillets, you can use both at once to cut the time it takes to fry. Our favorite accompaniments for breaded pork cutlets are applesauce, mashed potatoes, or coleslaw. If your cutlets are destined for a sandwich, check out "Making Pork Cutlet Sandwiches" on page 137 for garnish ideas.

- 6   slices high-quality white bread, such as Pepperidge Farm, crusts removed and bread torn into rough 1½-inch pieces
- ½   cup all-purpose flour
- 2   large eggs
- 1   tablespoon plus 1 cup vegetable oil
- 1   pork tenderloin (about 1 pound), trimmed of silver skin, cut crosswise into 6 pieces, and pounded to thickness of ½ inch, following illustrations below
      Salt and ground black pepper

1. Process the bread in a food processor until evenly fine-textured, 10 to 15 seconds (you should have about 3 cups fresh bread crumbs); transfer the crumbs to a pie plate or shallow baking dish.

2. Adjust an oven rack to the lower-middle position, set a large heatproof plate on the rack, and heat the oven to 200 degrees. Spread the flour in a second pie plate. Beat the eggs with 1 tablespoon oil in a third pie plate. Position the flour, egg, and bread crumb plates in a row on the work surface.

3. Blot the cutlets dry with paper towels and set aside. Sprinkle the cutlets liberally with salt and pepper. Working one at a time, dredge the cutlets thoroughly in flour, shaking off excess. Using tongs, dip both sides of the cutlets in the egg mixture, allowing the excess to drip back into the pie plate to ensure a very thin coating. Dip both sides of the cutlets in the bread crumbs, pressing the crumbs with your fingers to form an even, cohesive coat. Place the breaded cutlets in a single layer on a wire rack set over a baking sheet and allow the coating to dry about 5 minutes.

4. Meanwhile, heat ½ cup oil in a heavy-

TURNING ONE TENDERLOIN INTO SIX CUTLETS

1. Slip a knife under the silver skin, angle it slightly upward, and use a gentle back-and-forth motion to remove the silver skin.

2. Cut the tenderloin crosswise into six equal pieces, including the tapered tail end.

3. Stand one piece of tenderloin on cut side on a piece of plastic or parchment, cover with a second piece, and pound gently with a mallet or meat pounder to an even thickness of ½ inch.

4. The thin tail piece of the tenderloin requires some finessing to produce a cutlet. Fold the tip of the tail under the cut side and pound between two sheets of parchment or plastic.

bottomed 12-inch nonstick skillet over medium-high heat until shimmering but not smoking, about 2½ minutes. Lay 3 cutlets in the skillet; fry until deep golden brown and crisp on the first side, gently pressing down on the cutlets with a wide metal spatula to help ensure even browning and checking browning partway through, about 2½ minutes (smaller cutlets from the tail end of the tenderloin may cook faster). Using tongs, flip the cutlets, reduce the heat to medium, and continue to cook until the meat feels firm when pressed gently and the second side is deep golden brown and crisp, again checking browning part way through, about 2½ minutes longer. Line the warmed plate with a double layer of paper towels and set the cutlets on top; return the plate to the oven.

5. Discard the oil in the skillet and wipe the skillet clean using tongs and a large wad of paper towels. Repeat step 4 using another ½ cup oil and the now-clean skillet and preheating the oil just 2 minutes to cook the remaining 3 cutlets. Serve.

SMOTHERED PORK CHOPS

MANY OF US IN THE TEST KITCHEN HAVE fond memories from our youth of pork chops swimming in a hearty sauce, packed with big onion flavor. Our mothers gave the dish different names, but it was clearly a variation on smothered pork chops. Southern at heart, authentic smothered pork chops are browned pork chops simmered under a blanket of onions (and hence "smothered") and a thick brown gravy. The pork chops share equal billing with the sauce, which should be thick and heady with sweet onions. In addition to flavoring and moistening the chops, the sauce is made in sufficient quantity to moisten egg noodles, mashed potatoes, or rice.

In our fuzzy nostalgia, we forgot that the chops were probably tough and bland and the sauce gelatinous or floury. No doubt some of our harried mothers relied on canned soup to get dinner to the table quickly. Could we make smothered chops without Campbell's prepackaged help?

The most obvious first test was what type of pork chop worked best. We tend to favor thick-cut rib loin chops because they have a higher fat content than other chops, which is important to the chop's flavor. We also usually brine our chops (soak them in a solution of water, salt, and often sugar) to ensure moist and tender meat. For our first batch of smothered chops, we brined 1½-inch-thick rib loin chops in our standard brine, and then browned and braised the chops for half an hour (the standard braising time for all the smothered chop recipes we culled). Surprisingly, the meat was tough, dry, and flavorless. In a subsequent test, we doubled our braising time to one hour and the chops were still bland and dry. The braising liquid, however, was almost intolerably saline from the brine that leached out of the meat. We figured that brining was unnecessary for braised meat because it is a moist cooking method and the meat does not undergo the kind of moisture loss that is associated with grilling or sautéing. So we switched tactics completely and tried unbrined chops from ½ inch to more than an inch thick. Tasters were all

INGREDIENTS: Pork Chops

In many supermarkets, all pork chops from the loin are simply labeled "loin chops." However, there are significant differences in the four types of chops that come from the loin. Two—the blade chop and the sirloin chop—are less common and more likely to be labeled correctly. The two chops that you are most likely to run into labeled simply "loin chop" are the center-cut chop and the rib chop (see page 140).

As the name implies, center-cut chops are cut right out of the center of the loin. You can pick them out by the bone that divides them into two sections, giving them a close resemblance to a T-bone steak. Like a T-bone, they have meat from the loin on one side of the bone and a small portion of the tenderloin muscle on the other side. Some people prefer these center-cut chops because the tenderloin portion in particular is extremely tender.

However, our top choice is the rib chop, cut from the rib section of the loin, which is slightly closer to the shoulder. It has a somewhat higher fat content, which makes it both more flavorsome and less likely to dry out during cooking. The rib pork chop can be distinguished by the section of rib bone along one side. Sometimes rib and center-cut chops are sold boneless, making it much more difficult to tell them apart. But since we find bone-in meat juicier when cooked, we suggest you look for bone-in chops.

impressed by the substantial pork flavor and the tenderness of the meat. Tasters all favored the skinnier chops (½ inch thick), which were more tender than the inch-thick chops.

Because we were using thin chops, we tried shortening the braising time, but with little success. After 15 minutes, they were cooked through, but tough. After 30 minutes, they were more tender and flavorful. Extending the braise for another 15 minutes did little for either texture or flavor, so we left it at half an hour.

We found that adequately browning the chops was essential to developing richness and depth in the meat and the sauce. We were surprised by how quickly the chops browned; about two minutes per side in a very hot pan gave the chops a thick golden crust. A thorough drying of the chop with paper towels and a generous coating of salt and black pepper on the chop prior to browning helped promote a thick crust. While the crust is partially washed away during the slow braise, it enriches the flavor and color of the sauce.

A hefty amount of yellow onions is crucial to the sauce's richness. To add a little sweetness and more color to the sauce, we cooked the onions until they browned a bit and started to soften, about five minutes. We knew adding a little salt to the onions while they cooked would help break them down faster, but we were amazed at how efficiently the salt worked. The onions released enough liquid to deglaze (or lift) the fond (the browned bits adhered to the pan after browning the chops).

We tried a variety of liquids for braising, including water, beef stock, chicken stock, and wine blended with chicken stock. Water tasted thin and flavorless. Beef stock overwhelmed the other flavors and tasted tinny and salty. Wine and chicken stock combined in equal parts toughened the meat and tasted sour. All chicken stock was the winner. It provided a supportive background for the onion and pork flavors.

To thicken the sauce, we embraced tradition and used a roux, flour cooked in some type of fat. Many of the recipes we found avoided using roux as a thickener, probably to keep the dish to one pan, but we were displeased with the options. Flour sprinkled into the onions while they cooked made the gravy taste of raw flour, and cornstarch turned the sauce gelatinous and translucent, making it visually unappealing. Dusting the pork chops with flour turned the exterior of the meat gummy, and the sauce tasted of raw flour again. Roux, on the other hand, did not taste of flour, it adequately thickened the sauce, and it added a mildly nutty flavor to the dish. Yes, it involved another pot, but the nominal hassle was well worth it. We cooked the roux for about five minutes, or just long enough to turn light brown. We found adding room-temperature stock to the hot roux and stirring constantly helped prevent lumps from forming.

Borrowing a Southern technique, we tried making the roux with rendered bacon fat instead of bland vegetable oil. The sauce tasted fantastic; the smokiness accented the sweet onions and the meatiness reemphasized that of the pork chops. And the crisp bacon bits served well as a crunchy, visually appealing garnish.

After a half hour of braising, we were surprised by how much liquid the onions released. We did not want to reduce the onion amount, so we tried reducing the sauce after braising to concentrate it. A mere four to five minutes of cooking over medium-high heat, after removing the chops from

CENTER-CUT CHOP

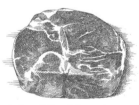

A bone runs through the middle of the center-cut chop with meat on either side. The meat on the left side of the bone is from the tenderloin.

RIB CHOP

The bone on a rib chop runs along one edge of the chop, with all the meat on just one side of the bone.

the pan, thickened the sauce to a velvety gravy. A little minced parsley perked up the deep flavors.

Our mothers would be proud. We had an easy, richly flavored dish perfect for a weeknight meal, and there wasn't a can of soup in sight.

Smothered Pork Chops

SERVES 4

Make sure the chops are quite dry before browning them to prevent sticking and to promote the best crust. The pork chops pair well with a variety of starches, which you will want to soak up the rich gravy. We liked them best with simple egg noodles, but rice or mashed potatoes also taste great.

4	ounces bacon, diced (about 4 slices)
3	tablespoons all-purpose flour
1¾	cups homemade chicken stock or canned low-sodium broth
1	tablespoon vegetable oil
4	bone-in rib loin pork chops, ½ to ¾ inch thick
	Salt and ground black pepper
2	medium onions, halved and sliced thin
2	medium cloves garlic, minced
1	teaspoon minced fresh thyme leaves
2	bay leaves
1	tablespoon finely minced parsley leaves

1. Fry the bacon in a medium saucepan over medium heat until lightly browned and the fat is rendered, 6 to 7 minutes. Remove the browned bacon from the pan with a slotted spoon and set aside on a small plate. Reduce the heat to medium-low and gradually stir in the flour with a wooden spoon, making sure to work out any lumps that may form. Continue stirring constantly, reaching into the corners of the pan, until the mixture is light brown, 4 to 5 minutes. Add the chicken stock in a slow, steady stream while vigorously stirring. Reduce the heat to low and keep the sauce warm.

2. Heat the oil in a 12-inch skillet over high heat until shimmering, 2 to 3 minutes. Meanwhile, pat the chops dry with paper towels and season generously with salt and pepper. Place the chops in the pan in a single layer and cook until a deep brown crust forms, about 2 minutes. Turn the chops over

and cook for another 2 minutes. Remove the chops from the pan and set aside on a plate.

3. Reduce the heat to medium and add the onions and ½ teaspoon salt. Cook, stirring frequently and scraping any browned bits off the bottom of the pan, until the onions soften and begin to brown around the edges, about 5 minutes. Stir in the garlic and thyme and cook until fragrant, about 30 seconds longer. Return the chops to the pan in a single layer and cover each chop with onions. Pour in the warm sauce, add the bay leaves, and cover with a tight-fitting lid. Reduce the heat to low and cook until the meat is tender, about 30 minutes.

4. Transfer the chops to a warmed plate and cover with foil. Increase the heat to medium high and, stirring frequently, cook until the sauce thickens to a gravy-like consistency, 4 to 5 minutes. Stir in the parsley and adjust the seasonings. Cover each chop with a portion of the sauce, sprinkle with the reserved bacon, and serve immediately.

➤ VARIATIONS

Smothered Pork Chops Braised in Cider with Apples

Follow the recipe for Smothered Pork Chops, replacing the chicken stock with an equal amount of apple cider and replacing one of the onions with 1 large or 2 small Granny Smith apples, peeled, cored, and cut into ⅓-inch slices. Proceed as directed.

Smothered Pork Chops with Spicy Collard Greens

Follow the recipe for Smothered Pork Chops, increasing the oil to 2 tablespoons, reducing the onions to 1, and increasing the garlic to 4 cloves. Once the onion and garlic are cooked, add 4 cups thinly sliced collard greens and ½ teaspoon crushed red pepper flakes. Return the browned chops to the pan and proceed as directed.

SPIRAL-SLICED HAM

WE'VE ALWAYS BEEN FOND OF HAM. WE love its toothy, meaty chew and its unique combination of sweetness, saltiness, and smokiness. Despite this devotion to ham, we have to admit that the versions that appear on most holiday tables are far from ideal. Very often they are dry as dust or mushy as a wet paper towel. We decided to find the best possible way to prepare a precooked supermarket ham so that it could live up to its full potential.

Our tasting of the hams available in the average supermarket revealed spiral-sliced ham as the favorite. As for "cooking" (really, only heating) these fully cooked hams, it's a no-brainer—which is why, we'll bet, hams are so popular around the holidays. The problem is that heating instructions for spiral-sliced hams differ from package to package. To add to the confusion, there are discrepancies in recommended final internal temperatures. Such imprecision wouldn't be such an issue if these hams didn't readily dry out and turn to jerky when improperly heated.

One factor that had to be decided at the outset was the internal temperature to which the ham should be heated. Spiral-sliced hams are fully cooked, and so long as the sell-by date hasn't come and gone, the ham can be served straight out of the package. While most cooks would still elect to heat the ham before serving, there is no consensus as to what temperature it should reach before being brought to the table. The label of one package said 120 degrees. The National Pork Producers Council said 140 degrees. Two manufacturers didn't include a temperature in their heating directions, so we called to inquire and were told 150 degrees by one and 155 degrees by the other. This discrepancy is unfortunate, because heating the ham to the proper internal temperature is critical to helping it retain its juices.

When we heated a ham to 140 degrees it lost a large amount of liquid and was dry. Heating to 130 degrees was an improvement, but we found that taking the ham to only 100 degrees was better yet. The outer inch of the ham registered at about 145 degrees, and residual heat caused the internal temperature to continue rising as the ham rested, covered, after coming out of the oven. After 40 minutes it peaked at 115 to 120 degrees, which had been our original goal. Though this may sound like a low temperature, the ham was warm to the touch and, most important, had remained moist and juicy. And, after all, we are dealing with a precooked cut of meat.

Having settled on the final temperature, we needed to figure out exactly how to get there. Our first task was to determine the proper oven temperature. We quickly found that a high (400 degrees) or even a moderate (325 degrees) oven was no good. Though the hams were covered with foil for protection, when subjected to these temperatures they lost an astounding amount of liquid (up to 2 cups); the meat was leathery and the slices torqued and splayed.

We then began experimenting with low oven temperatures. These worked much better, but cooking time now became an issue. At the low end of the scale, an average 9-pound ham heated in a 225-degree oven was juicy and held its shape, but it took a grueling 3¼ hours to heat up. In a 250-degree oven, the ham was just as good, but it heated in 2¾ hours, shaving 30 minutes off the cooking time.

Although easy, this was still a long process, so we sought means to speed it up. We tried different combinations of high and low temperatures, but they were either detrimental to the moistness of the ham or effected no improvement in the cooking time. Someone in the test kitchen then suggested a plastic oven bag instead of the foil cover. Quite to our astonishment, this simple, flimsy looking accouterment—relatively new to supermarket shelves—cut off a few minutes per pound. It may sound insignificant, but this can translate into a 20- to 30-minute

TRIMMING THE OVEN BAG

Use scissors to trim the oven bag, leaving 1 inch above the tie.

difference when cooking a piece of meat the size of a ham. We posited that the oven bag, wrapped tightly around the ham, eliminated the air space—an insulation of sorts—that is formed between the foil and the ham, thereby giving the ham direct exposure to heat and speeding its heating. A call to food scientist Shirley O. Corriher confirmed this. Corriher explained that the oven bag forms a tight seal that helps encapsulate the heat, whereas the heat easily escapes through the loose seal between baking dish and foil. Another step that speeds the heating process is letting the ham stand at room temperature for 90 minutes before putting it in the oven. This, too, takes off a couple of minutes per pound. By using an oven bag and letting the ham stand at room temperature we had whittled the heating time down to about 2¼ hours, with a 40-minute rest out of the oven. Protracted though this process may seem, it's great in that it frees the oven for other tasks.

In addition to proper heating technique, two other important factors come into play in getting the ham you really want: what you use for sauce and which half of the ham you buy.

Most spiral-sliced hams come with an enclosed packet of glaze. We tossed them all aside because we have found that glazes, whether prepackaged or homemade, do little to enhance this kind of ham. Instead, they tend to sit on the surface like a layer of gooey candy. Although this may appeal to children, we much prefer to make an interesting, flavorful sauce to accompany the ham. The sauce, since it doesn't use any pan drippings, can be made ahead

and reheated. It dresses up the ham, making it look and taste more elegant, and it also adds moisture to carved ham slices, which tend to dry out somewhat as they sit uncovered on a serving platter.

We also discovered that the shank end of the ham is substantially easier to carve than the sirloin, or butt, end because of the bone configuration. The packages aren't labeled as such, but the shank can be identified by the tapered, more pointed end opposite the cut side. The sirloin, on the other hand, has a very blunt, rounded end. (See illustration on page 147.) If you can't find a shank half, however, don't despair; both halves taste equally good. Your knife will just encounter a few more bumps and curves while carving.

Spiral-Sliced Ham

SERVES 20 TO 30

You can put the ham in the oven cold, bypassing the 90-minute standing time. If you do, add a couple of minutes per pound to the heating time. If using an oven bag, cut slits in the bag so it does not burst. Allow about 3 to 4 servings per pound for a bone-in ham. We recommend buying a shank portion because the bone configuration makes it easier to carve; look for the half ham with a tapered, pointed end.

1   spiral-sliced half ham (7 to 10 pounds),
    preferably shank end

1. Unwrap the ham and remove and discard the plastic disk covering the bone. Place the ham in a

CARVING A SPIRAL-SLICED HAM

1. With the tip of a paring or carving knife, cut around the bone to loosen the attached slices.

2. Using a long carving knife, slice horizontally above the bone and through the spiral-cut slices, toward the back of the ham.

3. Pull the cut portion away from the bone and cut between the slices to separate them fully.

4. Beginning at the tapered end, slice above the bone to remove the remaining chunk of meat. Flip the ham over and repeat the procedure for the other side.

plastic oven bag, tie the bag shut, and trim the excess plastic (see the illustration on page 142). Set the ham cut-side down in a 9 by 13-inch baking dish and cut four slits in the top of the bag with a paring knife. Alternatively, place the unwrapped ham cut-side down in the baking dish and cover tightly with foil. Let stand at room temperature 90 minutes.

2. Meanwhile, adjust an oven rack to the lowest position and heat the oven to 250 degrees. Bake the ham until the center of the ham registers about 100 degrees on an instant-read thermometer, 1½ to 2½ hours (about 14 minutes per pound if using a plastic oven bag, about 17 minutes per pound if using foil), depending on the size of the ham.

3. Remove the ham from the oven and let it rest in the baking dish in the oven bag or with the foil cover until the internal temperature registers 115 to 120 degrees on an instant-read thermometer, 30 to 40 minutes. Cut open the oven bag or remove the foil, place the ham on a carving board, and slice according to the illustrations on page 143. Serve immediately with one of the following sauces, if desired.

Dried Cherry and Stout Sauce with Brown Sugar and Allspice

MAKES ABOUT 4 CUPS

Stout is a strong, dark beer made from toasted barley. It makes a rich sauce with smoky notes and a bitter finish.

1	cup homemade chicken stock or canned low-sodium broth
2	tablespoons cornstarch
2	tablespoons unsalted butter
3	medium shallots, chopped fine
⅛	teaspoon ground allspice
4	cups stout
⅓	cup packed brown sugar
1	cup dried tart cherries (about 5 ounces)
1½	tablespoons balsamic vinegar
	Salt and ground black pepper

1. Whisk together the chicken stock and cornstarch in a small bowl; set aside. Heat the butter in a 12-inch skillet over medium heat until foaming; add the shallots and sauté until softened, about 3 minutes. Stir in the allspice; cook until fragrant, about 30 seconds. Add the stout, brown sugar, and dried cherries; increase the heat to medium-high, bring to a simmer, and cook until slightly syrupy, about 10 minutes.

2. Whisk the chicken stock and cornstarch mixture to recombine, then gradually whisk it into the simmering liquid; return to a simmer to thicken the sauce, stirring occasionally. Off heat, stir in the balsamic vinegar; season to taste with salt and pepper. (The sauce can be cooled to room temperature and refrigerated for up to 2 days. Reheat in a medium saucepan over medium-low heat.) Serve with ham.

Mustard Sauce with Vermouth and Thyme

MAKES ABOUT 3½ CUPS

The Dijon mustard lends a creaminess to this sauce, while the whole-grain mustard adds texture and visual appeal.

1½	cups homemade chicken stock or canned low-sodium broth
2	tablespoons cornstarch
2	tablespoons unsalted butter
3	medium shallots, chopped fine
2	cups dry vermouth
1	tablespoon packed brown sugar
½	cup Dijon mustard
¼	cup whole-grain mustard
1	tablespoon chopped fresh thyme leaves
	Salt and ground black pepper

1. Whisk together the chicken stock and cornstarch in a small bowl; set aside. Heat the butter in a 12-inch skillet over medium heat until foaming; add the shallots and sauté until softened, about 3 minutes. Stir in the vermouth and sugar; increase the heat to medium-high and simmer until the alcohol vapors have cooked off, about 4 minutes.

2. Whisk the chicken stock and cornstarch mixture to recombine, then gradually whisk it into the simmering liquid; return the sauce to a simmer to thicken, stirring occasionally. Off heat, whisk in the Dijon and whole-grain mustards and thyme; season to taste with salt and pepper. (The sauce can be cooled to room temperature and refrigerated for up to 2 days. Reheat in a medium saucepan over medium-low heat.) Serve with ham.

Coca-Cola Fresh Ham Roast

ROASTED FRESH HAM GLAZED WITH COKE is a Southern tradition. For many cooks, though, this recipe will seem quite foreign. First, there's the meat. Although this roast is called a ham, it's not really a ham at all—or at least not what most of us understand the term to mean. It's not cured in the fashion of a Smithfield ham or salted and air-dried like prosciutto. It's not pressed or molded like a canned ham, and it's not smoked like a country ham. In fact, the only reason this cut of pork is called a ham is because it comes from the pig's hind leg.

The other thing that makes cola ham unique is the glaze. Few serious cooks would consider Coke as a recipe ingredient. Yes, you might drink Coke, but to cook with it seemed a bit strange. But we figured tradition couldn't be all wrong and that something about Coke's sweet but acidic flavor might just work. We decided to develop a recipe for roast fresh ham and then begin work on the cola glaze.

Even before we began roasting, we had decided that a full fresh ham, weighing in at about 20 pounds, was too much for all but the very largest feast. So we decided to use one of the two cuts into which the leg is usually divided—the sirloin, or butt, which comes from the top of the leg, and the shank, from the bottom of the leg. We also decided that we wanted our ham skin-on (we couldn't see giving up the opportunity for cracklings). Fortunately, this is how these roasts are typically sold.

From our experiences with other large roasts, we knew what the big problem would be: making sure the roast cooked all the way through while the meat stayed tender and moist. In our first set of tests, then, we wanted to assess not only the relative merits of sirloin and shank but also the best oven temperature and cooking time.

Early on in this process, we determined that the roast needed to be cooked to a lower final internal temperature than some experts recommend. We found that we preferred the roast pulled from the oven at 145 to 150 degrees; at this point, the meat is cooked to about medium and retains a slight blush. While the roast rests, its residual heat brings the temperature up to approximately 155 to 160 degrees.

With the internal temperature determined, we started testing for the best oven temperature to get it there. First to come out of the oven was a ham from the sirloin end of the leg that we had roasted at a high temperature, 400 degrees, for its entire stay in the oven. Carving this ham was akin to whittling wood—Olympics-worthy agility with the carving knife was required to gut around the aitchbone (pronounced H-bone, a part of the hip), the cracklings were more suited for tap shoes than consumption, and the meat was dry, dry, dry. We moved on to roasting a shank-end ham at low heat the whole way through. This ham tasted like a wrung-out washcloth, with no cracklings in sight. What we did appreciate was the straightforward bone composition of the shank end, which simplified carving and convinced us to use this end of the fresh ham for the remainder of our tests.

Next we roasted a shank-end ham by starting it at a low temperature (325 degrees) and finishing it at a higher one (400 degrees), hoping to end up with both moist meat and crispy cracklings. To our dismay, this ham was also rather dry, which we attributed to the ham's long stay in the oven, made necessary by the low cooking temperature. What's more, the brief hike in the temperature at the end of cooking didn't help to crisp the skin.

Again, we figured we ought to try the opposite: starting the ham at a high temperature to give the meat a head start and get the skin on its way to crisping, then turning down the heat for the remainder of the roasting time to cook the meat through. Although meat cooked according to this method was slightly chalky and dry, the skin was close to our goal, crispy enough to shatter between our teeth yet tender enough to stave off a trip to the dentist. We decided that this would be our roasting method.

Hoping to solve the dry meat dilemma, we brined a shank-end ham, immersing it in a solution of saltwater and spices to tenderize and flavor it. More than slightly biased from the positive results we achieved in past brining experiments with turkey, chicken, shellfish, and other cuts of pork, we expected brining to make the meat incredibly juicy. The salt in a brine causes the proteins in meat to unravel and recombine, tenderizing the meat and forming a network that traps the water, effectively sealing in moisture. This effect allows the cook to increase the roasting temperature, thus speeding the roasting process, without fear of drying out the meat. Our estimations proved accurate: The brined shank emerged from the oven succulent and flavorful, with meat tender enough to fall apart in your mouth.

Just when we thought the ham couldn't possibly get any better, we decided to try roasting one shank face-down on a rack set in a roasting pan rather than letting it sit directly in the pan. This adjustment kept the cut end from becoming tough and leathery from direct contact with the hot pan. Rack roasting also allowed the heat to circulate around the ham constantly, promoting faster and more even cooking.

With our timing and temperature firmly in place, we turned to tweaking the flavor of the roast and obtaining the type of cracklings we had heard of but never really tasted. Not content with the infusion of flavor from the brine, we turned to spice pastes to further develop the flavor of the roast. Fresh thyme, sage, rosemary, garlic, brown sugar, cloves, dried mustard, juniper berries, peppercorns, and salt were all given an equal opportunity to complement the pork. We liked the combination of sage's earthy sweetness and garlic's pungent bite as well as the edge of fresh parsley, peppercorns, and kosher salt.

It now came time to prepare the glaze. While some recipes we tried called for simply basting the roast in its own drippings, we veered in the direction of sugary glazes, opting for sugar's ability to crisp, caramelize, and sweeten the skin. Our standard glaze calls for 1 cup orange juice and 2 cups brown sugar. When we replaced the juice with Coke, the results were cloying. The glaze needed some acidity and maybe some heat. Lime juice added to the mix balanced the intense sweetness of the brown sugar and Coke. As for heat, our tasters like the fresh flavor of minced jalapeños.

The question now: Exactly when should we apply the glaze? Throughout the roasting period? If so, at what intervals? Since part of the beauty of this pork roast is that it can be left in the oven mostly unattended, we didn't want glazing to complicate the process. Starting the ham at 500 degrees negated glazing it at the outset—the sugary glaze would definitely char black before the roast had been in the oven very long. We decided to let the roast cook unglazed at 500 degrees for the first 20 minutes. We then turned the oven temperature down to 350 degrees and began to brush it liberally with glaze. We continued to do so in 45-minute intervals, which amounted to three bastings during the roasting period. This ham was the one: flavorful meat with sweetened, crunchy skin.

At this point, our ham was pretty darn good. Just when we thought our work was done, one staff member joked that we should try brining the meat in Coke. After giving this joke fair consideration, we dumped 6 liters of Coca-Cola Classic into a brine bucket, added kosher salt, and let the ham soak in this foamy concoction overnight. The next day we cooked it according to our recipe. The outcome was the talk of the kitchen. It was juicy, it was unusual, it was fantastic. The Coke had added its own unique flavor to the ham while tenderizing the meat even more than our regular brine. The meat was falling off the bone and unbelievably tender throughout.

We turned to food scientist Dr. Eric Decker from the University of Massachusetts at Amherst to find out just what the Coke brine was doing. While Coke has about the same amount of sugar as orange or apple juice, he explained, it has roughly 27 times that of our standard brine. This higher sugar concentration flavors the meat. Coke is also considerably more acidic than our brine; it has a pH level of 3.3, while our brine is relatively neutral, hovering around 7. The acid, like the salt in the brine, helps to tenderize the roast by untangling the protein strands. Luckily, this sour, acidic flavor is balanced by the sugar and that unique Coca-Cola flavor, resulting in a ham you won't soon forget.

More than one person in the test kitchen proclaimed this ham the best roast pork they'd ever eaten. Rich and tender, with an underlying hint of sweetness, the meat had the power to quiet a room full of vocal, opinionated cooks and editors. Perhaps even better is the sweet, slightly salty, crisp and crunchy skin that intensifies to a deep crimson by the time the roast is done. It was attacked with precision and swiftness during our trials in the test kitchen. Unbelievably succulent, tender, and uncomplicated, this culinary gem will leave you wondering how you could have gotten along without it.

Fresh Ham with Cola Glaze

SERVES 8 TO 10

Fresh ham comes from the pig's hind leg. Because a whole leg is too large for most occasions, it is usually cut into two sections. The sirloin, or butt, end is harder to carve than our favorite, the shank end. If you don't have room in your refrigerator, you can brine the ham in a large insulated cooler or a small plastic garbage can; add five or six freezer packs to the brine to keep it well cooled.

HAM AND BRINE

1	bone-in fresh half ham with skin, 6 to 8 pounds, preferably shank end, rinsed
3	cups kosher salt or 1 ½ cups table salt
6	liters Coke Classic
2	heads garlic, cloves separated, lightly crushed, and peeled
10	bay leaves
½	cup black peppercorns, crushed

GARLIC AND HERB PASTE

1	cup lightly packed sage leaves from 1 large bunch
½	cup parsley leaves from 1 bunch
8	medium cloves garlic, peeled
1	tablespoon kosher salt or 1 ½ teaspoons table salt
½	tablespoon ground black pepper
¼	cup olive oil

GLAZE

1	cup Coke Classic
¼	cup juice from 2 limes
2	cups packed dark or light brown sugar
2	medium jalapeño chiles, cut crosswise into ¼-inch-thick slices

1. FOR THE HAM AND BRINE: Carefully slice through the skin and fat with a serrated knife, making a 1-inch diamond pattern on ham. Be careful not to cut into meat.

2. In a large (about 16-quart) bucket or stockpot, dissolve the salt in the Coke. Add the garlic, bay leaves, and crushed peppercorns. Submerge the ham in the brine and refrigerate 8 to 24 hours.

3. Set a large disposable roasting pan on a baking sheet for extra support; place a flat wire rack in the roasting pan. Remove the ham from the brine; rinse under cold water and dry thoroughly with paper towels. Place the ham, wide cut-side down, on the rack. (If using the sirloin end, place the ham skin-side up.) Let the ham stand, uncovered, at room temperature for 1 hour.

4. FOR THE PASTE: Meanwhile, adjust the oven rack to the lowest position and heat the oven to 500 degrees. In the workbowl of a food processor fitted with a steel blade, process the sage, parsley, garlic, salt, pepper, and oil until the mixture forms a smooth paste, about 30 seconds. Rub all sides of the ham with the paste.

5. FOR THE GLAZE: Bring the Coke, lime juice, brown sugar, and jalapeños to a boil in a small nonreactive saucepan over high heat; reduce the heat to medium-low and simmer until syrupy and reduced to about 1⅓ cups, 5 to 7 minutes. (Glaze will thicken as it cools between bastings; heat over medium heat about 1 minute, stirring once or twice, before using.)

6. TO COOK THE HAM: Roast the ham at 500 degrees for 20 minutes. Reduce the oven temperature to 350 degrees and continue to roast, brushing the ham with glaze every 45 minutes, until the center of the ham registers 145 to 150 degrees on an instant-read thermometer, about 2½ hours longer. Tent the ham loosely with foil and let stand until the center of the ham registers 155 to 160 degrees on the thermometer, 30 to 40 minutes. Carve, following illustrations on page 148, and serve.

CHOOSING A HAM

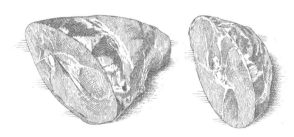

For easy carving, look for a shank-end ham (left), which has a tapered pointed end opposite the cut side. The sirloin, or butt, end (right) has a rounded, blunt end.

BARBECUED SPARERIBS

WHEN PEOPLE USE THE WORDS "RIBS" AND "barbecue" in the same sentence, they are usually talking about pork spareribs. We wanted to know whether it is possible to produce authentic ribs (the kind you get at a barbecue joint) at home.

We started our tests by cooking one slab of ribs over indirect heat (the ribs on one side of the grill, the coals on the other), parboiling and then grilling another slab over direct heat, and cooking a third on our grill's rotisserie attachment (although reluctant to use this unusual bit of equipment, we thought, in the name of science, that we should give it a shot). All three tests were conducted over charcoal with hickory chips in a covered grill.

The ribs cooked over indirect heat were the hands-down favorite. Those cooked on the rotisserie were not nearly as tender, and the parboiled ribs retained the unappealing flavor of boiled meat. While the indirect method needed some refinement, we were convinced that it is the best way to cook ribs at home. It also comes closest to replicating the method used by barbecue pit masters.

We tested a number of popular techniques for barbecuing ribs. Some experts swear by placing a source of moisture in the grill, most often an aluminum pan filled with water or beer. We filled a pan with water and put it next to the coals to create some steam. We couldn't taste the difference between the ribs cooked with and without the water. Next, we tested turning and basting. We found that for the even melting of the fat, it is best to turn ribs every half-hour. Turning also ensures even cooking. It's important, though, to work as quickly as possible when turning the ribs to conserve heat in the grill. Basting proved to be a bust. Tomato-based sauces burned over the long cooking time, and we didn't find the basted meat any more moist than meat without basting.

Under normal weather conditions, we found the ribs were done in two to three hours. Signs of doneness include the meat starting to pull away from the ribs (if you grab one end of an individual rib bone and twist it, the bone will actually turn a bit and separate from the meat) and a distinct rosy glow on the exterior. Because the ribs require a relatively short cooking time, there is no need to replenish the coals. A fire that starts out at 350 degrees will drop back to around 250 degrees at the end of two hours.

At this point in our testing, we had produced good ribs, but they were not quite as moist and tender as some restaurant ribs. We spoke with several pit masters, and they suggested wrapping the ribs when they come off the grill. We wrapped the ribs in foil and then placed them in a brown paper bag to trap any escaping steam. After an hour, we unwrapped the ribs and couldn't believe the difference. The flavor, which was great straight off the grill, was the same, but the texture was markedly improved. The meat on the wrapped ribs literally fell off the bone.

We spoke with several food scientists, who explained that as the ribs rest, the juices redistribute throughout the meat, making the ribs more

CARVING THE TWO CUTS OF HAM

SHANK END

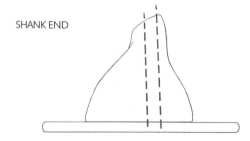

1. Transfer the ham to a cutting board and carve it lengthwise alongside the bone, following the two dotted lines in the illustration above.
2. Place the large boneless pieces that you have just carved flat on the cutting board and slice into ½-inch pieces.

SIRLOIN END

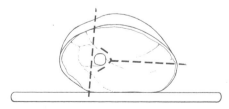

1. Transfer the ham to a cutting board and carve into three pieces around the bones, following the dotted lines in the illustration above.
2. Place the large boneless pieces that you have just carved flat on the cutting board and slice into ½-inch pieces.

moist and tender. In fact, these ribs are so flavorful and tender that we consider sauce optional.

Several kinds of pork ribs are available in most markets. Spareribs come from the underbelly, or lower rib cage, of the pig. A full slab contains 13 ribs and weighs about three pounds. Baby back ribs don't come from a young pig. Rather, they are from the upper front end of the rib cage and are smaller than spareribs. Country-style ribs come from the upper rear end of the rib cage (opposite the lean tenderloin). (See the illustration on page 151.)

We prefer regular spareribs to either baby back ribs or country-style ribs. The latter ribs are leaner, but the extra fat on spareribs helps keep the meat tender and moist during the long cooking process. Baby back ribs are especially prone to drying out, as are country-style ribs, though to a lesser extent.

❧ Barbecued Spareribs on a Charcoal Grill

SERVES 4

Hickory is the traditional wood choice with ribs, but some of our tasters liked mesquite as well. If you like, serve the ribs with barbecue sauce, but they are delicious as is.

2	full slabs pork spareribs (about 6 pounds total)
¾	cup Dry Rub for Barbecue (page 126)
2	(3-inch) wood chunks or 2 cups wood chips
	Heavy-duty aluminum foil
	Brown paper grocery bag
2	cups barbecue sauce (see pages 127 to 129), optional

1. Rub both sides of the ribs with the dry rub and let stand at room temperature for 1 hour. (For stronger flavor, wrap the rubbed ribs in a double layer of plastic wrap and refrigerate for up to 1 day.)

2. Soak the wood chunks in cold water to cover for 1 hour and drain, or place the wood chips on an 18-inch square of aluminum foil, seal to make a packet, and use a fork to create about six holes to allow smoke to escape (see illustrations on page 124).

3. Meanwhile, light a large chimney filled a bit less than halfway with charcoal briquettes (about 2½ pounds, or 40 coals) and allow to burn until covered with a thin layer of gray ash. Empty the coals into one side of the grill, piling them up in a mound two or three briquettes high. Keep the bottom vents completely open. Place the wood chunks or the packet with the chips on top of the charcoal. Put the cooking grate in place, open the grill lid vents completely, and cover, turning the lid so that the vents are opposite the wood chunks or chips to draw smoke through the grill. Let the grate heat for 5 minutes and clean it with a wire brush.

4. Position the ribs over the cool part of the grill. Barbecue, turning the ribs every 30 minutes, until the meat starts to pull away from the bones and has a rosy glow on the exterior, 2 to 3 hours. (The initial temperature inside the grill will be about 350 degrees; it will drop to 250 degrees after 2 hours.)

5. Remove the ribs from the grill and completely wrap each slab in aluminum foil. Put the foil-wrapped slabs in a brown paper bag and crimp the top of the bag to seal tightly. Allow to rest at room temperature for 1 hour.

6. Unwrap the ribs and brush with barbecue sauce, if desired (or serve with sauce on the side). Cut between the bones and serve the ribs immediately.

❧ Barbecued Spareribs on a Gas Grill

SERVES 4

If working with a small grill, cook the second slab of ribs on the warming rack.

2	full slabs pork spareribs (about 6 pounds total)
¾	cup Dry Rub for Barbecue (page 126)
2	cups wood chips
	Heavy-duty aluminum foil
	Brown paper grocery bag
2	cups barbecue sauce (see pages 127 to 129), optional

1. Rub both sides of the ribs with the dry rub and let stand at room temperature for 1 hour. (For stronger flavor, wrap the rubbed ribs in a double layer of plastic wrap and refrigerate for up to 1 day.)

2. Soak the wood chips for 15 minutes in a bowl of water to cover. Place the wood chips in a foil tray (see illustrations on page 125). Place the foil tray with the soaked wood chips on top of the primary burner

(see illustration on page 122). Turn all burners to high and preheat with the lid down until the chips are smoking heavily, about 20 minutes.

3. Scrape the grate clean with a wire brush. Turn the primary burner down to medium and turn off the other burner(s). Position the ribs over the cool part of the grill. Barbecue, turning the ribs every 30 minutes, until the meat starts to pull away from the bones and has a rosy glow on the exterior, 2 to 3 hours. (The temperature inside the grill should be a constant 275 degrees; adjust the lit burner as necessary.)

4. Remove the ribs from the grill and completely wrap each slab in aluminum foil. Put the foil-wrapped slabs in a brown paper bag and crimp the top of the bag to seal tightly. Allow to rest at room temperature for 1 hour.

5. Unwrap the ribs and brush with barbecue sauce, if desired (or serve with sauce on the side). Cut between the bones and serve the ribs immediately.

OVEN-ROASTED RIBS

BARBECUED SPARERIBS STRIKE A PRIMITIVE chord deep within all of us, excluding perhaps the most ardent vegetarian (although we suspect they have secret longings). The sweet and spicy crust and smoky, lush meat tempts us as few foods do. But we are the first to admit that hauling out the grill and stoking the slow fire necessary for sublime ribs can be inconvenient. And forget about barbecuing ribs during the winter in many parts of the country. Is there another way to achieve such bliss?

Most oven-roasted rib recipes we have tried turned out tough, stringy, and relatively flavorless meat, completely devoid of all the merits of barbecued ribs. Driven by the haunting flavor of great ribs, we thought we might create a recipe for oven-roasted spareribs that placed a close second to our barbecued ribs.

For the meat, there was little choice in the matter. Plain-old spareribs provided the best flavor and were the most economical. Baby back ribs cooked only nominally faster and were very tough. Country-style ribs were flavorless. Two slabs of spareribs, about three pounds each, was enough to abundantly feed four people, and they went into the oven on one rack. We found that the meat needed little preparation outside of trimming any excessive fat.

One of the charms of indoor cooking is that the only equipment necessary is a pan in which to cook the ribs. After roasting several batches of ribs in roasting pans and on baking sheets, we favored suspending the ribs on a sturdy flat rack above the more shallow baking sheet so that the ribs would not rest in the rendered fat. The baking sheet also allowed for the best circulation of heat.

To flavor the meat, we employed our Dry Rub for Barbecue (page 126). We found that the ribs needed to sit for a minimum of an hour coated in the rub for the spices to penetrate the meat. Refrigerating the spice-rubbed ribs overnight gave the meat the best flavor. If you can plan ahead, letting the rubbed meat rest in the refrigerator overnight is the best way to build flavor.

As any barbecue pit master will tell you, the key to tender, falling-of-the-bones ribs is a steady fire and slow cooking. On a grill, the ribs are placed on the opposite side of the cooking grate from a small pile of banked coals. The temperature will fluctuate between 250 and 350 degrees—the lower the better. We experimented with oven temperatures ranging from 250 degrees to 350 degrees and found 300 degrees to be best. At 250 degrees, the ribs cooked for close to five hours before the meat had separated from the bone, and the outer meat was leathery. At 350 degrees, the ribs cooked too quickly and were tough and flabby with unrendered fat. At 300 degrees, they were fully done in three and a half hours; the meat had separated from the bone and was quite juicy. A lot of the fat had rendered out, too.

With an ideal oven temperature selected, we experimented with a variety of techniques to see if we could improve on the texture of the meat, if at all. Blanching, or parboiling, the ribs is a commonly employed technique that hastens cooking, but we found it yielded surprisingly tough, dry meat. We also tried adding a pan of water to the oven to increase the oven's humidity, but again the meat was tough in comparison with the dry-cooked meat. We then tried wrapping the ribs in foil to trap the steam. The wrapped ribs were paler but juicier than unwrapped ribs. This inspired us to try wrapping the ribs for part of the cooking time and then uncovering them to attain the characteristic dark crust. We found that covering them for only the first hour of cooking yielded moist ribs with a thick flavorful crust.

The meat was sweet, savory, and succulent, but it lacked the smoky flavor and aroma essential to great ribs. We tried substituting ground chipotle chiles (smoked jalapeño peppers) for the cayenne pepper in our spice rub, but the smokiness of the chiles mysteriously disappeared among the other flavors. We then thought about adding barbecue sauce for its hickory flavor—a sensitive issue considering how quickly sugar-laden sauce burns. We first tried slathering sauce on after we took the foil off, one hour into cooking, and the sauce blackened and turned bitter. We then tried basting the ribs after three hours of cooking, and they remained wet and gummy when pulled from the oven half an hour later. Splitting the difference proved just right. When applied to the ribs after two hours of cooking (so the sauce cooked for one and a half hours), the sauce darkened but did not burn and reduced to a sticky, satisfying glaze.

The ribs disappeared from the test kitchen within minutes of coming out of the oven, but we were able to save a few and tried wrapping the ribs in foil and sealing them in a paper bag—the trick that had worked so well with our barbecued ribs. As we had expected, the ribs wrapped for an hour were juicier

and more tender than ribs that were not wrapped.

While our oven-roasted ribs may not be quite as rarefied as those from a roadside shack in Kansas City, they are pretty close and infinitely easier than a trip to the Midwest.

Oven-Roasted Spareribs
SERVES 4

While the final step of wrapping the ribs in foil and the paper bag may seem eccentric, it is well worth it. We found the meat prepared this way to be extraordinarily succulent and tender.

2	full slabs pork spareribs (about 6 pounds total), trimmed of excess fat
¾	cup Dry Rub for Barbecue (page 126)
3	cups barbecue sauce (see pages 127 to 129)

1. Rub both sides of the ribs with the dry rub and let stand at room temperature for 1 hour. (For stronger flavor, wrap the rubbed ribs in a double layer of plastic wrap and refrigerate for up to 1 day.)

2. Adjust an oven rack to the middle position and heat the oven to 300 degrees. Place the ribs meaty-side up on a heavy rack in a rimmed baking sheet and then wrap the pan with aluminum foil. Cook for 1 hour and then remove the foil. Cook for another hour and then liberally brush the meaty side of the ribs with the barbecue sauce, about ¾ cup per slab. Cook for another 1½ hours, or until the bones have separated from the meat.

3. Remove the ribs from the oven and completely wrap each slab in foil. Put the foil-wrapped slabs in a brown paper bag and crimp the top of the bag to seal tightly. Allow to rest at room temperature for 1 hour.

4. Unwrap the ribs, cut in between the bones, and serve immediately with more barbecue sauce on the side.

THREE KINDS OF PORK RIBS

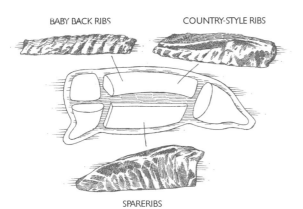

BABY BACK RIBS   COUNTRY-STYLE RIBS

SPARERIBS

Spareribs come from the underbelly of the pig, or the lower rib cage, and have the most fat, making them the best choice for barbecuing. Baby back ribs (sometimes called back ribs or loin back ribs) come from the loin, or upper front end of the rib cage, where the bones are shorter. Country-style ribs are cut from the upper rear end of the rib cage (closer to the legs). These ribs are quite large and meaty.

PULLED PORK

PULLED PORK, ALSO CALLED PULLED PIG or sometimes just plain barbecue, is slow-cooked pork roast that is shredded, seasoned, and then served on a hamburger bun (or sliced white bread) with just enough of your favorite barbecue sauce, a couple of dill pickle chips, and a topping of coleslaw.

Our goal was to devise a procedure for cooking this classic Southern dish that was both doable and delicious. The meat should be tender, not tough, and moist but not too fatty. Most barbecue joints use a special smoker. We wanted to adapt the technique for the grill. We also set out to reduce the hands-on cooking time, which in some recipes can stretch to eight hours of constant fire tending.

There are two pork roasts commonly associated with pulled pork sandwiches: the shoulder roast and the fresh ham. In their whole state, both are massive roasts, anywhere from 14 to 20 pounds. Because they are so large, most butchers and supermarket meat departments cut both the front and back leg roasts into more manageable sizes. The part of the front leg containing the shoulder blade is usually sold as either a pork shoulder roast or a Boston butt and runs from 6 to 8 pounds. The meat from the upper portion of the front leg is marketed as a picnic roast and runs about the same size. The meat from the rear leg is often segmented into three or four separate boneless roasts called a fresh ham or boneless fresh ham roast (see illustration on page 154).

For barbecue, we find it best to choose a cut of meat with a fair amount of fat, which helps keep the meat moist and succulent during long cooking and adds considerably to the flavor. For this reason, we think the pork shoulder roast, or Boston butt, is the best choice. We found that picnic roasts and fresh hams will also produce excellent results, but they are our second choice.

To set our benchmark for quality, we first cooked a Boston butt using the traditional low-and-slow barbecue method. Using a standard 22-inch kettle grill, we lit about 30 coals, or close to 2 pounds, and cooked the roast over indirect heat (with the coals on one side of the grill and the roast on the other), adding about eight coals every half-hour or so. It took seven hours to cook a 7-pound roast. While the meat was delicious, tending a grill fire for seven hours is not something many people want to do.

In our next test we tried a much bigger initial fire, with about five pounds of charcoal. After the coals were lit, we placed the pork in a small pan and set it on the grate. The trick to this more intense method is not to remove the lid for any reason until the fire is out three hours later. Because you start with so many coals, it is not necessary to add charcoal during the cooking time.

Unfortunately, the high initial heat charred the exterior of the roast, while the interior was still tough and not nearly fork-tender when we took it off the grill. So we tried a combination approach: a moderate

KEY STEPS TO PULLED PORK

1. If using fresh ham or a picnic roast (shown here), cut through the skin with the tip of a chef's knife. Slide the knife blade just under the skin and work around to loosen the skin while pulling it off with your other hand. Boston butt does not need to be trimmed.

2. Set the unwrapped roast, which has been placed in a disposable pan barely larger than the meat itself, on the grill grate opposite the coals and the wood.

3. After cooking, as soon as the meat is cool enough to handle, remove the meat from the bones and separate the major muscle sections with your hands.

4. Remove as much fat as desired and tear the meat into thin strips.

amount of charcoal (more than in the low-and-slow method but less than in the no-peek procedure), cooking the pork roast for three hours on the grill and adding more charcoal four times. We then finished the roast in a 325-degree oven for two hours. This method produced almost the same results as the traditional barbecue, but in considerably less time and with nine fewer additions of charcoal.

We find it helpful to let the finished roast rest wrapped in foil in a sealed paper bag for an hour to allow the meat to reabsorb the flavorful juices. In addition, the sealed bag produces a steaming effect that helps break down any remaining tough collagen. The result is a much more savory and succulent roast. Don't omit this step; it's the difference between good pulled pork and great pulled pork.

As with most barbecue, pork roast benefits from being rubbed with a ground spice mixture. However, because the roast is so thick, we find it best to let the rubbed roast "marinate" in the refrigerator for at least three hours and preferably overnight. The salt in the rub is slowly absorbed by the meat and carries some of the spices with it. The result is a more evenly flavored piece of meat.

Barbecued Pulled Pork on a Charcoal Grill

SERVES 8

Preparing pulled pork requires little effort but lots of time. Plan on nine hours from start to finish: three hours with the spice rub, three hours on the grill, two hours in the oven, and one hour to rest. Hickory is the traditional choice with pork, although mesquite can be used if desired. Serve the pulled pork on plain white bread or warmed buns with the classic accompaniments of dill pickle chips and coleslaw.

I	bone-in pork roast, preferably Boston butt, 6 to 8 pounds
¾	cup Dry Rub for Barbecue (page 126)
4	(3-inch) wood chunks or 4 cups wood chips
	Heavy-duty aluminum foil
	Disposable aluminum roasting pan (about 8 by 10 inches)
	Brown paper grocery bag
2	cups barbecue sauce (see pages 127 to 129)

1. If using a fresh ham or picnic roast, remove the skin (see illustration 1 on page 152). Massage the dry rub into the meat. Wrap the meat tightly in a double layer of plastic wrap and refrigerate for at least 3 hours. (For stronger flavor, the roast can be refrigerated for up to 3 days.)

2. At least 1 hour prior to cooking, remove the roast from the refrigerator, unwrap, and let it come up to room temperature. Soak the wood chunks in cold water to cover for 1 hour and drain, or place the wood chips on an 18-inch square of aluminum foil, seal to make a packet, and use a fork to create about six holes to allow smoke to escape (see illustrations on page 124).

3. Meanwhile, light a large chimney filled a bit less than halfway with charcoal briquettes (about 2½ pounds, or 40 coals) and allow to burn until covered with a thin layer of gray ash. Empty the coals into one side of the grill, piling them up in a mound two or three briquettes high. Open the bottom vents completely. Place the wood chunks or the packet with the chips on top of the charcoal.

4. Set the unwrapped roast in the disposable pan and place it on the grate opposite the fire (see illustration 2 on page 152). Open the grill lid vents three-quarters of the way and cover, turning the lid so that the vents are opposite the wood chunks or chips to draw smoke through the grill. Cook, adding about 8 briquettes every hour or so to maintain an average temperature of 275 degrees, for 3 hours.

5. Adjust an oven rack to the middle position and heat the oven to 325 degrees. Wrap the pan holding the roast with heavy-duty foil to cover completely. Place the pan in the oven and bake until the meat is fork-tender, about 2 hours.

6. Slide the foil-wrapped pan with the roast into a brown paper bag. Crimp the top shut. Let the roast rest for 1 hour.

7. Transfer the roast to a cutting board and unwrap. When cool enough to handle, "pull" the pork by separating the roast into muscle sections, removing the fat, if desired, and tearing the meat into thin shreds with your fingers (see illustrations 3 and 4 on page 152). Place the shredded meat in a large bowl. Toss with 1 cup barbecue sauce, adding more to taste. Serve, passing the remaining sauce separately.

Barbecued Pulled Pork on a Gas Grill

SERVES 8

Preparing pulled pork requires little effort but lots of time. Plan on nine hours from start to finish: three hours with the spice rub, three hours on the grill, two hours in the oven, and one hour to rest. The key to using the gas grill is maintaining the proper temperature so that the pork cooks slowly. Adjust the lit burner as necessary. Serve the pulled pork on plain white bread or warmed buns with the classic accompaniments of dill pickle chips and coleslaw.

I	bone-in pork roast, preferably Boston butt, 6 to 8 pounds
¾	cup Dry Rub for Barbecue (page 126)
4	cups wood chips
	Heavy-duty aluminum foil
	Disposable aluminum roasting pan (about 8 by 10 inches)
	Brown paper grocery bag
2	cups barbecue sauce (see pages 127 to 129)

1. If using a fresh ham or picnic roast, remove the skin (see illustration 1 on page 152). Massage the dry rub into the meat. Wrap the meat tightly in a double layer of plastic wrap and refrigerate for at least 3 hours. (For stronger flavor, the roast can be refrigerated for up to 3 days.)

2. At least 1 hour prior to cooking, remove the roast from the refrigerator, unwrap, and let it come up to room temperature.

3. Soak the wood chips for 15 minutes in a bowl of water to cover. Place the wood chips in a foil tray (see illustrations on page 125). Place the foil tray with the soaked wood chips on top of the primary burner (see illustration on page 122). Turn all burners to high and preheat with the lid down until the chips are smoking heavily, about 20 minutes.

4. Turn the primary burner down to medium and turn off the other burner(s). Set the unwrapped roast in the disposable pan and position the pan over the cool part of the grill. Barbecue for 3 hours. (The temperature inside the grill should be a constant 275 degrees; adjust the lit burner as necessary.)

5. Adjust an oven rack to the middle position and heat the oven to 325 degrees. Wrap the pan holding the roast with heavy-duty foil to cover completely. Place the pan in the oven and bake until meat is fork-tender, about 2 hours.

6. Slide the foil-wrapped pan with the roast into a brown paper bag. Crimp the top shut. Let the roast rest for 1 hour.

7. Transfer the roast to a cutting board and unwrap. When cool enough to handle, "pull" the pork by separating the roast into muscle sections, removing the fat, if desired, and tearing the meat into thin shreds with your fingers (see illustrations 3 and 4 on page 152). Place the shredded meat in a large bowl. Toss with 1 cup barbecue sauce, adding more to taste. Serve, passing the remaining sauce separately.

THREE PORK ROASTS

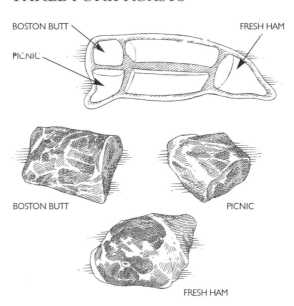

Although all three cuts make good pulled pork, Boston butt is our first choice because it has enough fat to keep the meat moist and succulent throughout the long cooking process.

HAM LOAF

ALTHOUGH LESS POPULAR THAN ITS KIN, meat loaf, ham loaf is traditional in many parts of the country. In our test kitchen library, homespun cookbooks from Down-East Maine to southern California all contain variations. Like red beans and rice, ham loaf supposedly originated as a Monday night dinner based on Sunday's leftovers. And like too many recipes based on leftovers, there are some pretty poor versions out there—from greasy, over-seasoned logs to sticky-sweet creations closer to dessert in flavor. We were not sure what our ideal ham loaf would be, but we knew we could do better than most of the recipes we tested.

Heading into testing, we knew there were two ways to approach ham loaf: We could use flavors associated with baked ham, like fruit or warm spices, or we could choose ingredients common in meat loaf recipes, such as garlic, herbs, and bread crumbs. We tried loaves topped with fruit, loaves enriched with nuts and spices, and simple pork variations on meat loaf. The meat loaf style won unanimously. Tasters agreed that fruit flavorings and lots of spices belong on whole hams, not in ham loaves.

Ham loaf provides the perfect use for the leftover bits and trimmings of a ham that might otherwise linger in the refrigerator. If you do not have leftovers and still hanker for a ham loaf, ham steaks work well, too. We discovered that about a pound of ham supplied enough flavor for one loaf without making the loaf too salty or overwhelmingly "hammy." We chose readily available standard ground pork to mix with the ham. A blend of half ham and half ground pork delivered good flavor and yielded a loaf that could serve six to eight.

Ground pork can go into the ham loaf as is, but the ham needs to be broken down somehow. We found that grinding the ham to the proper size in a food processor proved crucial to the loaf's texture. If it was too coarse—¼ inch and larger bits—the loaf was marred by an unpleasant chewiness. When the ham was ground too fine—almost to a paste—the loaf was mealy. About 1/16-inch bits, or bread-crumb size, provided the best texture, reminiscent of meat loaf.

For seasonings, we were able to apply findings from our meat loaf recipe (see page 106). Sautéed onions and garlic tasted as good in the ham loaf as in

the meat loaf, adding a pleasing sweetness and depth. A little mustard and hot pepper sauce added piquancy that cut the ham's richness, and parsley and thyme brought freshness and color. A pinch each of allspice and cloves reaffirmed the ham flavor.

To bind the loaf, tasters favored fresh bread crumbs above cracker crumbs and oatmeal, both of which had worked well in our meat loaf recipe. In ham loaf, the cracker crumbs and oatmeal adversely affected the texture of the loaf, making it too loose. We found that the ham loaf required more crumbs than meat loaf because the ham, which is already cooked, does not bind the way uncooked beef does. Bread crumbs, and lots of them, are the best binder for the job.

To keep the meat moist while cooking, we tried a variety of liquids, including wine, stock, and different dairy products. Wine lent the loaf a decidedly acidic flavor, and stock took over. Whole milk yogurt was the crowd pleaser for the way its lactic tang offset the ham's potent smokiness.

Although we liked the terrine-like formality of the ham loaf baked in a standard loaf pan, it did not have the crispy exterior we desired. And fat and juices rendered from the loaf pooled in the pan, effectively steaming the meat. Unless you have a dedicated meat loaf pan with holes permeating the bottom, we think the best way to cook a ham loaf (or meat loaf, for that matter) is freeform on a rimmed baking sheet lined with aluminum foil. Excess juices and fat run off the loaf and allow the sides and top to crisp nicely.

To add a little more crispness to the ham loaf, we appropriated the bacon topping from our meat loaf recipe. Tasters liked the texture and the way it introduced a third pork flavor to the loaf.

We also loved the sweet tomato-based glaze on our meat loaf and wanted a similar glaze that would complement the pork. Ham and mustard are a natural combination, and honey has a unique flavor that works well with both. A healthy dose of freshly ground black pepper cut the honey's sweetness. We put the glaze underneath the bacon, the same technique we use for the meat loaf, but we also added more glaze at the end of cooking to "candy" the bacon and make the loaf look glossier.

The results were stunningly attractive. The bacon

picked up a mahogany glow, and the interior, in stark contrast to meat loaf, retained an attractive rosy pink flecked with herbs.

Baked Ham Loaf

SERVES 6 TO 8

Use either a pound of boneless ham (from a leftover roast) or ham steaks. If using the latter, we had good results with ham steaks from Cook's, a company that also makes a favorite spiral-cut ham.

1/2	cup honey
1/4	cup plus 2 teaspoons Dijon mustard
3/4	teaspoon ground black pepper
2	teaspoons vegetable oil
1	medium onion, diced
2	medium cloves garlic, minced
2	large eggs, lightly beaten
1/4	cup minced fresh parsley leaves
1	teaspoon minced fresh thyme leaves
1/4	teaspoon hot pepper sauce, such as Tabasco
	Pinch ground cloves
	Pinch ground allspice
1/2	cup whole milk plain yogurt
1	pound ground pork
1	pound ham, ground to 1/16-inch bits (resembling bread crumbs) in a food processor
2	cups fresh bread crumbs
6–8	ounces thin-sliced bacon (8 to 12 slices, depending on loaf shape)

1. Adjust an oven rack to the middle position and heat the oven to 350 degrees.

2. For the glaze, mix together the honey, 1/4 cup mustard, and 1/4 teaspoon pepper in a small saucepan over low heat just until combined; set aside.

3. Heat the oil in a medium skillet over medium heat. Add the onion and cook until softened, about 5 minutes. Add the garlic and cook until fragrant, about 30 seconds longer. Remove the pan from the heat.

4. In a large bowl, mix together the eggs, remaining 2 teaspoons mustard, remaining 1/2 teaspoon pepper, parsley, thyme, hot pepper sauce, cloves, allspice, and yogurt. Add the ground pork, ham, bread crumbs, and cooked onion and garlic, and mix

everything together until it no longer sticks to the side of the bowl (if it does stick, add another 1 to 2 tablespoons yogurt). Turn the mixture onto a foil-lined rimmed baking sheet and pat into a roughly 5 by 9-inch loaf shape. Brush the loaf with half of the glaze, then arrange the bacon slices, crosswise, over the loaf, overlapping slightly, to cover the surface of the loaf completely. With a spatula, tuck the bacon ends underneath the loaf.

5. Bake the loaf until the bacon is crisp and the internal temperature of the loaf registers 160 degrees, about 1 hour. Remove the loaf from the oven, increase the oven temperature to 450 degrees, and coat the loaf with the remaining glaze. Return the loaf to the oven and cook until glaze bubbles and turns golden, about 5 minutes. Cool at least 20 minutes and serve.

SHEPHERD'S PIE

NOTHING MORE THAN A RICH LAMB STEW blanketed under a mashed potato crust, shepherd's pie is a hearty casserole originally from the cool climes of sheep-centric northern Britain. Today, it is as much a part of American cookery as British, best eaten on a blustery winter day sidled up to a roaring fire with a frothy pint of stout. It's arguably America's favorite lamb dish.

Like numerous other dishes in this book, shepherd's pie was a meal made Monday with Sunday night's leftovers—the remnants of the roast, vegetables, and mashed potatoes. In this day and age, few of us have such delicious Sunday dinners, much less leftovers, so we aimed to create an assertively flavored shepherd's pie from scratch.

Our first step was to figure out what cut of lamb worked best. To save on prep time, we hoped to use ground lamb. Shepherd's pie made with ground lamb tasted OK, but it was somewhat bland. If pinched for time, ground lamb is a decent choice, but we prefer our favorite cut of lamb for stewing, shoulder chops. It is easy to cut the meat off the bone and into cubes, and, after searing, the meat delivers a rich lamb flavor without tasting gamey or greasy, as lamb often does. While many of the recipes we gathered specified minced lamb, we preferred larger, more toothsome chunks.

Choosing vegetables to flavor the lamb proved easy. Sautéed carrots and onions added sweetness and depth. A touch of garlic added a little zest, and sweet frozen peas—characteristic of many British-style meat stews—brought bright color to an otherwise drab-looking dish. For herbs, we wanted big flavors strong enough to stand up to the lamb's richness. Rosemary and thyme are traditional lamb flavorings, and they tasted great in this instance. Fresh, not dried, herbs provided the best flavor.

As for the liquid in the stew, we settled on chicken stock enriched with red wine. Beef broth clashed with lamb's earthy flavors, while chicken stock was neutral. After testing a variety of red wines, we liked a medium-bodied Côtes-du-Rhone best because it is well rounded, low in tannins, and not oaky, all traits that allowed it to marry well with all the flavors in the dish. In addition to the stock and wine, we added a little Worcestershire sauce for its sweetness and savory tang.

With the stew assembled and cooked, we were ready to top it off with a mashed potato crust. We quickly found out that simple mashed potatoes would not do; they crumbled and broke down while baking. We started our adjustments by reducing the amount of butter and dairy we usually add to mashed potatoes. To give the potatoes some structure, we then added egg yolk to the potatoes, turning the mashed potatoes into what the French call Duchess potatoes. The yolks did the trick; the potatoes retained their shape and texture and picked up a little more richness in the bargain. (Given the added richness of the yolks, we felt that whole milk, rather than half-and-half, was the better dairy choice.) The yolks also gave the potatoes a slight golden hue that complemented the deep brown of the stew beneath.

We tried a variety of methods for assembling the casserole and were most pleased with the simplest route. The stew fit into either a 9 by 13-inch baking dish or, more snugly, into a 10-inch pie plate, which made for a more attractive presentation than the rectangular dish. A large, rubber spatula was the best tool for spreading the potatoes evenly across the top of the stew. It was important to completely cover the stew and seal the edges of the pan with the potato topping; otherwise the stew sometimes bubbled out of the pan.

Because the lamb is already tender when it goes into the casserole, the baking time is short. Once the potato crust turns golden brown, the shepherd's pie is ready to come out of the oven.

Shepherd's Pie
SERVES 6 TO 8

Diced lamb shoulder chops give the filling a much richer flavor than ground lamb. If you prefer to use ground lamb, see the variation that follows. This recipe includes basic assembly instructions in a 9 by 13-inch baking dish. For a fancier presentation in a 10-inch pie plate, see the illustrations on page 158.

FILLING

3 pounds lamb shoulder chops (4 chops), boned and cut into 1-inch pieces (should yield about 1½ pounds meat)
1½ teaspoons salt
1 teaspoon ground black pepper
3 tablespoons vegetable oil
2 medium onions, chopped coarse
2 medium carrots, cut into ¼-inch slices
1 medium clove garlic, minced
2 tablespoons all-purpose flour
1 tablespoon tomato paste
2¼ cups homemade chicken stock or canned low-sodium broth
¼ cup full-bodied red wine
1 teaspoon Worcestershire sauce
1 teaspoon chopped fresh thyme leaves
1 teaspoon chopped fresh rosemary
1 cup frozen peas, thawed

TOPPING

2 pounds large russet potatoes, peeled and cut into 2-inch cubes
1 teaspoon salt
6 tablespoons unsalted butter, softened
¾ cup whole milk, warmed
2 large egg yolks
Ground black pepper

1. FOR THE FILLING: Season the lamb with salt and pepper. Heat 2 tablespoons oil in a 12-inch skillet over medium-high heat until shimmering. Add half of the lamb and cook, stirring occasionally, until well browned on all sides, 5 to 6 minutes. Remove the lamb from the pan and set aside in a medium bowl. Heat the remaining tablespoon of oil in the pan. Add the remaining lamb and cook, stirring occasionally, until well browned on all sides, 5 to 6 minutes. Transfer the lamb to the bowl.

2. Reduce the heat to medium and add the onions and carrots to the fat in the now-empty pan. Cook until softened, about 4 minutes. Add the garlic, flour, and tomato paste and cook until the garlic is fragrant, about 1 minute. Whisk in the stock, wine, and Worcestershire sauce. Stir in the thyme, rosemary, and browned lamb. Bring to a boil, reduce the heat to low, cover, and simmer until the lamb is just tender, 25 to 30 minutes.

3. FOR THE TOPPING: Meanwhile, put the potatoes in a large saucepan; add water to cover and ½ teaspoon salt. Bring to a boil and continue to cook over medium heat until the potatoes are tender when pierced with a knife, 15 to 20 minutes. Drain the potatoes well and return them to the pan set over low heat. Mash the potatoes, adding butter as you mash. Stir in the warm milk and then the egg yolks. Season with the remaining ½ teaspoon salt and pepper to taste.

4. TO ASSEMBLE AND BAKE: Adjust an oven rack to the middle position and heat the oven to 400 degrees. Stir the peas into the lamb mixture and check the seasonings. Pour the lamb mixture evenly into a 9 by 13-inch baking dish. With a large spoon, place the mashed potatoes over the entire filling. Starting at the sides to ensure a tight seal, use a rubber spatula to smooth out the potatoes and anchor them to the sides of the baking dish. (You should not see any filling.) Bake until the top turns golden brown, 20 to 25 minutes. Let rest for 5 to 10 minutes and serve.

➤ VARIATION

Shepherd's Pie with Ground Lamb

Follow the recipe for Shepherd's Pie, substituting 1½ pounds ground lamb for the shoulder chops. Cook, one half at a time, until well browned, about 3 minutes for each batch of lamb. Proceed as directed, reducing the simmering time in step 2 to 15 minutes.

MAKING PIE-SHAPED SHEPHERD'S PIE

The filling and potato topping for our shepherd's pie fit nicely in a standard 9 by 13-inch baking dish. But for a fancier presentation, we like to bake the pie in a 10-inch pie plate. The mashed potato topping rises high above the filling, much like a lemon meringue pie or baked Alaska. If you want to try this presentation, follow the steps below.

1. Place the filling in a 10-inch pie plate and then drop spoonfuls of mashed potatoes around the perimeter of the pie plate.

2. Use a rubber spatula to attach the potatoes to the rim of the pie plate. It's important to seal the edges this way to prevent the filling from bubbling out of the pie plate in the oven.

3. Drop the remaining mashed potatoes in the center of the pie plate and then smooth the top with a spatula. Because the topping rises so high, we recommend baking the pie on a rimmed baking sheet to catch any leaks.

7

POULTRY

CHICKEN HAS BECOME AMERICA'S FAVORITE weeknight entrée, and turkey remains the top choice for holiday gatherings. That said, these birds can be extremely hard to cook, and results are often disappointing. Who hasn't served a turkey with sawdust-dry breast meat or a chicken with soggy skin?

These problems derive from the structure of these birds. Breast meat has very little fat and is prone to drying out. Overcooking is a constant threat for white meat. Dark meat, on the other hand, takes more time to cook; it has a fair amount of fat that must be rendered, or melted and released from the bird, if the meat is to be palatable. In addition to these competing interests, you have to deal with the skin. In most cases, you want the skin all over the bird to crisp.

With these challenges in mind, we offer our favorite chicken and turkey recipes, along with the accompaniments (stuffings, gravies, and sauces) that go with these birds.

Basic Roast Chicken

COOKING A CHICKEN WOULD APPEAR TO be a simple task. The meat is not tough by nature. The dark meat is relatively forgiving in terms of cooking time. The breast meat is not particularly thick, which means that the outer layers are less likely to dry out while you are attempting to properly cook the center of the bird.

Yet when you are served a perfectly roasted chicken, the experience is not only unusual, it is extraordinary. The skin is perfectly crisp and well-seasoned. The white meat is juicy and tender, but with a hint of chew. The dark meat is fully cooked all the way to the bone. There is clearly more to chicken cookery than one would imagine, because most home-cooked chickens are either grossly overcooked or so underdone that they resemble an avian version of steak tartar.

To solve this problem once and for all, we decided to devise a series of tests based on a few simple observations. The first observation is that chicken is made up of two totally different types of meat: white and dark. The white meat is inevitably overcooked and dry even as the dark meat is still little more than raw next to the bone. The second observation is that chicken, unlike beef, has skin, which should be nicely browned and crispy. As we found during the testing process, crisp skin is not always consistent with perfectly cooked meat. Finally, chicken is an odd amalgam of meat and bones. The drumsticks and wings stick out, the thigh meat is on the side of the bird, and the breast meat is on the top (at least when the chicken is roasted). The home cook is dealing with a complex three-dimensional structure, quite different from a brisket or a pot roast. The chicken's anatomy requires a more complex set of cooking instructions. In search of these instructions, we ended up roasting chickens 14 different ways.

We started our tests with the most pertinent question: What is the best oven temperature for roasting a chicken? Our first bird went into a 450-degree oven and cooked for 44 minutes. When it emerged, the skin was dark and crispy, but we encountered the classic problem with high-heat meat cookery. While the dark meat was fine, the outer portion of the white meat was overcooked and on the tough side even as the internal thigh temperature registered 160 degrees, the temperature we generally consider best for white meat. (Dark meat really tastes best cooked to 165 to 170 degrees.)

We then went to the other extreme and tested a bird in a 275-degree oven for an hour and 35 minutes, raising the heat to 425 degrees for the last 10 minutes to crisp up the skin. The white meat was not quite as juicy as the dark, but not dry either. The skin, however, was a light gold, not a rich sienna, and it was chewy and not very tasty—obviously, not browned enough.

Finally, we tried a simple, classic approach. We roasted the bird at 375 degrees for one hour. The skin was golden and slightly crispy. At 160 degrees internal temperature, the juices ran clear, but the dark meat was still not properly cooked near the bone. We continued cooking until the thigh meat reached an internal temperature of about 170 degrees. At this point, the breast meat was close to 180 degrees, but it was still juicy. This was an interesting discovery. While the breast meat of chicken roasted at 450 degrees was a bit dry when the thigh registered 160 degrees, the bird roasted at 375 degrees still had juicy breast meat when the thigh registered close to 170 degrees. We also found that "until the juices run clear" is an imprecise measure of doneness—the white meat will be cooked, but the dark meat can still be a little bloody at the bone, a sight that we would prefer to leave to B movies rather than the dinner plate.

In an attempt to get crispier skin, we tried preheating the oven to the higher temperature of 450 degrees and turning the heat down to 350 degrees upon putting in the chicken. The bird cooked in 53 minutes, and the skin was pale gold and slightly chewy—not much difference from the chicken roasted at 375 degrees and not quite as good overall. Next, we roasted a bird at 375 degrees for 30 minutes, then raised the heat to 450 degrees. This method delivered the best results—perfectly cooked meat and crisp skin.

We were happy with these results, but there remained a couple of techniques often recommended for roasting chicken that we wanted to test. The first was basting. Is basting really a good idea, or is it just another one of those hand-me-down cookbook directions that really makes no sense? We started with butter and basted every 15 minutes. The results were appalling. Despite a nice brown color, the skin was chewy and greasy. The next bird was basted with oil, which turned out a crispier skin, but the color was off—a pale gold. We then brushed a bird with butter before roasting and shoved it in the oven without any further basting. This was the best method. Great color and great crispy texture.

Basting may have made sense when cooking a large piece of meat on a spit over an open fire. The outer layers would be prone to overcooking, and the basting may have prevented burning or scorching. But a 3-pound chicken is a different matter entirely. The skin will not scorch or burn (in fact, if you leave it alone, it will cook rather nicely on its own), and the basting liquid is not going to penetrate the meat, making it more tender. Juiciness has nothing to do with the external application of liquid. The only reason to brush a chicken with butter is to advance the color of the skin. The oven heat turns the milk solids in the butter brown and, in the process, the skin develops more flavor as well.

The second often-recommended technique we wanted to test was trussing, which is said to promote more even cooking. We trussed a bird according to the best French method and cooked it for what seemed a long time, 1½ hours. The white meat overcooked, but the dark meat was just right. It was also interesting to note that the cooking time was so long. We concluded that trussing makes it more difficult to properly cook the inner part of the thigh. (Because it is less exposed to the heat, it needs more oven time. Voilà! Overcooked white meat.) An untrussed bird took only one hour to cook, and the white and dark meat were both nicely cooked.

Having figured out that continuous basting and trussing were both unnecessary, we were hoping to find that the bird need not be turned, either. But even cooking is crucial to chicken cookery, and a couple of tests were in order.

First we roasted a bird for 15 minutes on each side and then put it on its back. This chicken, weighing close to 3¼ pounds, took just 50 minutes to cook. The skin was golden and crunchy, the white and dark meat perfectly cooked, and the overall presentation superb. To make this process a bit easier, we tried roasting another bird breast-side down for 20 minutes and then turned it breast-side up. This chicken was good, but the skin was less crispy, and at the point the white meat was perfect the dark meat was a bit undercooked. Thus, unfortunately, two turns proved crucial.

After we had roasted a half-dozen birds according to our basic method (375 degrees for 30 minutes, then 450 degrees for the rest of cooking, with two turns for even cooking), we made an interesting discovery. The thigh that was facing up during the second 15 minutes of roasting ended up lower in temperature than the thigh that started off facing up. At first we thought this was just a random occurrence, but after measuring the temperature in four or five birds, it became clear that this was a trend. After thinking about this phenomenon for a few days, we seem to have figured it out. The thigh that started off facing the roasting pan was facing a cold pan that reflected little heat. When the thigh that started by facing up was turned face down, the pan was hot and was radiating plenty of heat. To even this out, we decided to preheat the roasting pan.

One final test we wanted to make was to cook a chicken in a clay roaster. We had heard a lot of good

INGREDIENTS: Chicken

Picking out a quality chicken at the supermarket is a guessing game. The terms fresh, organic, free-range, all natural, and lean rarely indicate good flavor or texture, and neither does price. In our 1994 chicken tasting the only dependable sign of quality we found was brand, with Bell & Evans and Empire taking top honors. Eight years later, we wondered if these companies would win a second tasting and if, at long last, we could find a reliable, non-branded measure of quality.

We identified and investigated a long list of genetic and environmental factors that might help the consumer purchase a high-quality, tasty bird. Our first stop was genetic engineering. Birds are bred to meet the goals of a particular producer. Murray's chickens, for example, are engineered for a high yield of breast meat and a low yield of fat. (Tasters found them "tough" and "dry.") Perdue chickens are bred for a high ratio of meat to bone. (We found this means big breasts but scrawny legs.) It seemed to us, at least at first pass, that few, if any, producers were engineering birds for flavor.

More toothsome meat can simply be the result of a chicken's age. The older the chicken (an older broiler/fryer is seven to nine weeks old rather than the more typical six to seven weeks), the more distinct its flavor. Free-range birds, whose diet is less intense and less controlled than that of indoor chickens (because free-range birds have unrestricted access to the outdoors, they can eat random grasses and insects), take longer to reach their proper weight and are older when they are processed. Yet the "free-range" moniker is no indication of superior flavor. The two free-range birds we tasted, Eberly and D'Artagnan, had both fans and critics.

Processing factors that can affect the flavor and appearance of a chicken include how the chicken was rinsed and chilled prior to packaging. Antimicrobial agents, such as sodium triphosphates, are sometimes added to the final rinse water to cut down on contamination by bacteria like salmonella. (Some tasters can detect traces of this chemical. It is usually described as "metallic.") Some rinsing methods cause excess water to build up under the skin, and this can lead to a shriveled appearance after cooking.

After slaughtering and rinsing, the chickens are quickly chilled to a temperature of about 28 degrees, or just above their freezing point. If the chickens are chilled too quickly, their meat can get spongy and watery. If chilled too slowly, the meat can dry out and develop an off color. None of these effects could be confirmed in our tasting because we could not be certain how a particular bird was processed.

Our first solid clue to any possible connection between processing method and flavor emerged when we discovered that Empire, the only kosher chicken in our tasting, was also the best tasting. (Murray birds are processed under similar conditions in accordance with Muslim law.) Both Empire and Murray birds are hand-slaughtered rather than killed by machine, which ensures both a clean kill and a quick and efficient "bleed-out." Industry experts indicated that machine-processed chickens are more likely to be subject to improper slaughtering, which can cause blood to clot, resulting in tough meat or a livery flavor.

Because tasters far preferred the Empire chicken to Murray's, however, it followed that more was at work here than slaughtering technique. For one thing, kosher chickens like Empire's are dunked in cold water to remove feathers after slaughter. Cold water firms both the skin and the fat layer beneath it. In contrast, most other producers scald birds in hot water to remove the feathers. The experts we talked to said that scalding can "solubilize" the chicken's fat, leading to excessive moisture loss and a wrinkled appearance in the chicken skin after cooking. Uneven scalding can also cause "barking," or a blotchy appearance in the skin.

Appearance aside, perhaps the most noticeable difference between the Empire bird and the others we tasted is that the Empire bird tasted juicy and well-seasoned. In keeping with Jewish law, the chickens are buried in salt for one hour to draw out impurities and are then rinsed in cold spring water. The combination of salt and water acts like a brine, encouraging the fiber in the meat to open and trap the salt and water, leading to a juicier, more flavorful bird. This single factor, more than any other, seems to put the Empire bird ahead of the pack.

If you are looking for advice on purchasing a high-quality, good-tasting chicken, we recommend kosher. All the other adjectives—free-range, natural, lean, organic, and the like—don't necessarily translate into a better-tasting chicken. Empire, the brand that won our contest, was followed by Bell & Evans, winner of our 1994 tasting. You can't go wrong with either. Let it also be noted that Tyson, a mass-produced bird priced at just $1.29/lb, came in third, ahead of birds costing more than twice as much. One last word of advice. Out of eight birds in the tasting, Perdue finished dead last, with tasters describing the meat as "pithy," "chalky," and "stringy," with sour notes as well.

things about these roasters and tried La Cloche, a bell-shaped clay cooker intended for bread but that works well with other recipes. We followed the directions and roasted the bird enclosed in the clay cooker in a 425-degree oven. The directions suggested cooking for 90 minutes (with no specification of how large a bird to use), which seemed absurd—the bird was done in just an hour (the internal temperature of the thigh registering 168 degrees), and this was a large chicken, weighing about 3½ pounds. The good news is that the white and dark meat cooked equally, and the meat was quite juicy. The bad news is that the skin was pale and, although moist, chewy rather than crispy. If you are a skin fanatic, you probably don't want to roast your chicken in a clay cooker.

Having roasted 14 chickens, we had finally arrived at the best method: Roast the chicken on its side untrussed at 375 degrees in a preheated pan, turning it on its other side after 15 minutes. After another 15 minutes, turn the chicken breast-side up and cook at 450 degrees until the thigh has reached an internal temperature of 165 to 170 degrees and the breast registers 160 degrees. Easy, straightforward, and guaranteed (or as guaranteed as cooking methods can be) to produce a truly satisfying roast chicken.

Basic Roast Chicken

SERVES 4

A 3½-pound bird should roast in 55 to 60 minutes, while a 4-pound bird requires 60 to 65 minutes. If using a basket or V-rack, be sure to grease it so the chicken does not stick to it. If you don't have a basket or V-rack, set the bird on a regular rack and use balls of aluminum foil to keep the roasting chicken propped up on its side.

- I whole chicken (about 3 pounds; see page 162 for guidelines on selecting the best-tasting chicken), giblets removed and reserved for another use, chicken rinsed and patted dry with paper towels
- 2 tablespoons unsalted butter, melted
   Salt and ground black pepper
   Oil for basket or V-rack

1. Place a shallow roasting pan in the oven and heat the oven to 375 degrees. Brush the chicken with butter and sprinkle liberally with salt and pepper to taste.

2. Remove the heated pan from oven and set the oiled basket or V-rack in it. Place the chicken on the rack, wing-side up. Roast 15 minutes, then rotate the chicken, other wing-side up. Roast 15 minutes, then rotate the chicken, breast-side up. Turn the oven to 450 degrees. Roast until an instant-read thermometer inserted in the breast registers 160 degrees and in thigh registers between 165 and 170 degrees, 20 to 25 minutes longer. Transfer the chicken to a cutting board; let rest 10 minutes. Carve and serve.

HIGH-ROAST CHICKEN

AT THE PINNACLE OF SIMPLE FOOD IS roast chicken. With an oven and a chicken as the only requisites, it's an easy answer to the weeknight cooking conundrum. Our basic roast chicken fits the bill perfectly.

But occasionally we want something different. We'd heard mentioned the "high-roasting" technique for chicken in which the bird is roasted at temperatures in excess of 450 degrees. It's reputed to produce a better bird, with skin that is crisp and tanned to a deep golden hue. The only drawback we could foresee was that the breast meat might be prone to overcooking at such high temperatures.

In *Roasting: A Simple Art* (Morrow, 1995), Barbara Kafka suggests roasting a 5- to 6-pound bird at 500 degrees for about an hour. While it seemed to us rather pyromaniacal, we have heard several people swear by her method. So along with roasting birds at 425 and 450 degrees, we gave it a go. However, we decided to use 3½- to 4-pound birds because they are the size most commonly found in grocery stores.

When the birds came out of the oven, the differences between them were marked. The 500-degree bird was a looker, with beautiful, deep brown, crisp skin. The other two were splotchy and only mildly attractive. And, of course, the inevitable had occurred. The breast meat on all the birds had been torched; as the thighs sauntered up to the finish line, the more delicate breast meat overcooked. And, worst of all, with 450- and 500-degree oven temperatures, we chased everyone, coughing and hacking, out of the kitchen with billows of smoke.

To remedy the uneven cooking, we tried several adjustments, from preheated roasting pans to different configurations of oven temperatures, all to no avail. The obvious solution was to rotate the bird so that the breast would spend some time shielded from the intense oven heat while the thighs would receive the exposure they needed to catch up. After trying this technique, however, we vetoed it. We were after deep browning and crisp skin, neither of which were produced by this method. For that, the bird needs to spend all or at least most of the roasting time breast up.

We suspected that the fix lay in butterflying the chicken—that is, removing the backbone, then opening and flattening the bird. That would give the thighs greater exposure to the heat, increasing the odds that they would cook at the same rate as the breast. In addition, all areas of skin would be face-up to facilitate even browning and crisping. We tried it, and it worked like a charm. The thighs actually raced ahead of the breast meat and finished first.

While butterflying a chicken is actually an easy task—it takes all of a couple of minutes—we worried that it was too much to ask of the home cook on a weeknight. And yet the results had been so good. Tasters concurred that roast butterflied chicken was roast chicken elevated to a whole new level in terms of both appearance and doneness. Consequently, we put our hesitations aside and concentrated on determining the best roasting temperature for the butterflied bird. Again, for the best-browned, most crispy, and nicest looking bird, 500 degrees was the optimal temperature.

But there was still that smoking problem. We tried putting water in the pan beneath the bird (which was set on a rack), but this steamed the chicken and prevented the skin from crisping. We tried bread slices, soaked wood chips, and even uncooked rice to catch the drippings, but they all turned to charcoal before the chicken was done. Then we tried potatoes. They burned in spots, dried out in others, and stuck to the pan, but they also showed mouthwatering potential; tasters lined up for any morsel of crispy potato that could be salvaged. Even better, by creating a buffer and absorbing some of the

drippings, the potatoes kept the fat from hitting the hot pan bottom, where it would normally sizzle and burn on contact. We knew that with some finessing, the answer to the smoking problem could also provide a great side dish.

We assumed that the potatoes would need some protection as they cooked to keep them from burning and drying out. A broiler pan came to the rescue. With its slotted top and its ample bottom pan, which nicely accommodated the potatoes, it was just what the chicken and potatoes needed. The potatoes in the broiler pan had turned a deep brown and were as crisp as potato chips but far tastier. A foil lining on the pan bottom helped with potato removal and cleanup, and that was that. Not surprisingly, the potatoes won their own fans, who, waiting for the daily potato call, began to regard the chicken as the side dish.

Now that we had solved the major problems of high-roast chicken, we began to wonder if we could take this method to further heights. Though the butterflied chickens had been emerging from the oven with crisp skin, we noticed that as they sat waiting to be carved, the breast skin would become soggy. We began searching for a way to keep it crisp. We tried basting with oil, basting with butter, putting butter under the skin, putting chicken fat under the skin, and finishing the cooking under the broiler, but we found only one thing that worked. When other colleagues heard what it was, they rolled their eyes: drying the chicken uncovered overnight in the refrigerator. We borrowed the technique from recipes for crispy-skin Chinese roasted duck. Letting the bird dry uncovered in the fridge allows surface moisture to evaporate; the skin becomes dry and taut and so crisps more readily in the heat of the oven. It took a couple of side-by-side tastings to convince tasters that air drying worked and was worth the effort. And even though we agreed that it is worth the trouble, it remains an option—that is, you can skip it and still have a great roast chicken.

The other step in preparation for roasting that makes a significant improvement in the flavor and texture of the bird is brining. The salt in the brine permeates the chicken, so the meat is evenly seasoned and full-flavored. Brining also keeps the breast meat moist and tender, providing a cushion if it overcooks a bit (though there's little chance of that happening with a butterflied bird). Brining solutions are formulated in concentrations to fit the duration of the brine; we chose to go with a very concentrated one-hour brine that can be done the evening you intend to roast the bird or, if you plan ahead, the night before, so that the bird can dry overnight in the refrigerator. But there is also a quick solution. In the course of testing different types of birds we were glad to discover that kosher chickens, which are salted during processing to draw out fluids, provide an excellent pre-brined bird for those cooks with time constraints.

With technique resolved, we wanted to work flavorings into the roast chicken. Clearly, anything on the surface of the chicken would burn at 500 degrees. Instead, garlic, herbs, and other bold flavors mixed with some softened butter and placed under the chicken skin before roasting added subtle, welcome flavor not only to the chicken but to the potatoes below as well.

When all was said and done, we had roasted four dozen chickens and more than 60 pounds of potatoes. But we had accomplished what we set out to do. We had four-star, perfectly browned roast chicken with spectacular skin—and potatoes, too.

Crisp-Skin High-Roast Butterflied Chicken with Potatoes

SERVES 4

If you prefer not to brine, use a kosher chicken—it is salted and has a taste and texture similar to a brined bird. For extra crisp skin, after applying the flavored butter (if using), let the chicken dry uncovered in the refrigerator for 8 to 24 hours. For this cooking technique, russet potatoes offer best potato flavor, but Yukon Golds develop a beautiful color and better retain their shape after cooking. Either works well in this recipe. A food processor makes quick and easy work of slicing the potatoes.

I   cup kosher salt or ½ cup table salt (for brine)

½   cup sugar

I   whole chicken (3½ to 4 pounds; see page 162 for guidelines on selecting the best-tasting chicken), giblets removed and reserved for another use, fat around cavity removed and discarded

I   recipe flavored butter for placing under skin, optional (recipes follow)

2½   pounds (4 or 5 medium) russet or Yukon Gold potatoes, peeled and sliced ⅛ to ¼ inch thick

1½   tablespoons olive oil

¾   teaspoon salt (for potatoes) Ground black pepper

1. Dissolve the salt and sugar in 2 quarts cold water in a large container. Immerse the chicken and refrigerate until fully seasoned, about 1 hour. Meanwhile, adjust an oven rack to the lower-middle position and heat the oven to 500 degrees. Line the bottom of a broiler pan with foil and spray with nonstick vegetable cooking spray. Remove the chicken from the brine and rinse thoroughly under cold running water. Following the illustrations on page 166, butterfly the chicken, flatten the breastbone, apply the flavored butter (if using), and position the chicken on a broiler pan rack; thoroughly pat dry with paper towels.

2. Toss the potatoes with 1 tablespoon oil, salt, and pepper to taste in a medium bowl. Spread the potatoes in an even layer in the foil-lined broiler pan bottom. Place the broiler pan rack with the chicken on top. Rub the chicken with the remaining 1½ teaspoons oil and sprinkle with pepper to taste.

3. Roast the chicken until spotty brown, about 20 minutes. Rotate the pan and continue to roast until the skin has crisped and turned a deep brown and an instant-read thermometer registers 160 degrees in the thickest part of the breast, 20 to 25 minutes longer. Transfer the chicken to a cutting board. With potholders, remove the broiler pan rack; soak up excess grease from the potatoes with several sheets of paper towels. Remove the foil liner with the potatoes from the broiler pan bottom and invert the foil and potatoes onto a baking sheet or second cutting board. Carefully peel back the foil, using a metal spatula to help scrape the potatoes off the foil as needed. With additional paper towels, pat off the remaining grease. Cut the chicken into serving pieces and serve with potatoes.

Chipotle Butter
with Lime and Honey
MAKES ABOUT 3 TABLESPOONS

2   tablespoons unsalted butter, softened
1   medium clove garlic, finely minced or pressed
    through garlic press
1   teaspoon honey
1   teaspoon very finely grated lime zest
1   medium chipotle chile en adobo, seeded and
    minced to a paste, with 1 teaspoon adobo sauce

Mash together all ingredients in a small bowl.

Mustard-Garlic Butter
with Thyme
MAKES ABOUT 3 TABLESPOONS

2   tablespoons unsalted butter, softened
1   medium clove garlic, finely minced or pressed
    through garlic press
1   tablespoon Dijon mustard
1   teaspoon minced fresh thyme leaves
    Ground black pepper

Mash together all ingredients, including pepper to taste, in a small bowl.

BUTTERFLYING A CHICKEN

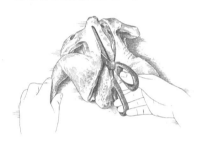

1. Cut through the bones on either side of the backbone, then remove and discard the backbone.

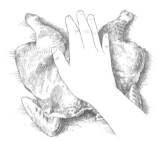

2. Flip the chicken over as shown and use the heel of your hand to flatten the breastbone.

3. If using a flavored butter, slip your fingers between skin and breast, loosening the membrane.

4. Scoop some of the butter onto a spoon, slide it under the breast skin, and push it off with your fingers.

5. Work the butter under the skin to cover the breast evenly. Repeat steps 4 and 5 with each drumstick and thigh.

6. Transfer the chicken to a broiling rack and push each leg up to rest between thigh and breast.

FRIED CHICKEN

WHAT MAKES FRIED CHICKEN GREAT? FIRST come, first served: the crust. Crisp and crackling with flavor, the crust must cleave to the chicken itself, not balloon away or flake off in chips like old radiator paint. In addition, it should carry a deep, uniform mahogany without spots or evidence of greasiness. As for the chicken itself, tender, moist, and flavorful are the descriptors of the day. Served hot, it should be demonstrably juicy; served room temperature, it should be moist. On no account should it be punishingly dry or require a salt shaker as a chaperone.

The truth is that frying chicken at home is a daunting task, a messy tableau of buttermilk dip and breading, hot fat, and splatters one hopes will end at the stove's edge. The results are often tantamount to the mess: greasy, peeling chicken skin and dry, unseasoned meat that's a long way from Grandma's.

It was no surprise to us that the chicken we were frying had to be premium quality to be worth the effort. Packaged chicken parts were irregular and disappointing, containing mismatched pieces in shabby dress with tattered skin, cut without a nod to basic anatomy. Given this situation, we thought it wise to spend a few minutes cutting a whole 3½-pound broiler into 12 manageable pieces (see page 170).

In our first stove-side excursion, we fried up several batches of chicken with different coatings, oils, and so on. But our real interest resided beneath the skin. Half of the chickens had been brined for two hours; the other half had not. A brine is at minimum a mixture of salt and water; sugar is often added as well. When soaked in a brine, chicken (as well as other poultry and meat) absorbs some of the salt and some of the water, thereby becoming more flavorful and more juicy once cooked. The tasting results bore out these benefits of brining. However glorious the crust, however perfectly fried the piece, the unbrined chicken earned marks far below its brined competition. Who wants to bite through a crisp, rich, seasoned crust only to hit dry, white Styrofoam? Another benefit of brining presented itself during cooking. Our brined chicken parts fried at equal rates, relieving us of the need to baby-sit the white meat or pull the wings out of the fat early.

While brining per se may not be common practice when preparing fried chicken, soaking the chicken pieces in some kind of liquid—particularly buttermilk—is traditional. This process is thought to tenderize the meat (a mistaken assumption) and add flavor. We examined a number of soaking solutions and found the bright acidic flavor and clinging viscosity of buttermilk to produce the best flavor accents and richest browning during cooking.

Appreciating the tang of a buttermilk soak but unwilling to forgo the succulence of brined chicken, we found ourselves whispering "buttermilk brine." Instead of soaking the chicken in buttermilk alone, why not add the saline blast of a brine, doubling the

---

SCIENCE: How Brining Works

Why are some roast chickens and turkeys dry as sawdust while others boast meat that's firm, juicy, and well seasoned? The answer is brining. Soaking a chicken or turkey in a brine—a solution of salt (and often sugar) and a liquid (usually water)—provides it with a plump cushion of seasoned moisture that will sustain it throughout cooking. The chicken or turkey will actually gain a bit of weight—call it, for lack of a better term, water retention—that stays with it throughout cooking. This weight gain translates into moist flesh; the salt and sugar in the brine translate into seasoned, flavorful flesh.

Brining works under the auspices of two rules of nature, diffusion and osmosis, that like things to be kept in equilibrium. For instance, when brining a turkey, there is a greater concentration of salt and sugar outside of the turkey (in the brine) than inside the turkey (in the cells that make up its flesh). The law of diffusion states that the salt and sugar will naturally flow from the area of greater concentration (the brine) to lesser concentration (the cells). There is also a greater concentration of water, so to speak, outside of the turkey than inside. Here, too, the water will naturally flow from the area of greater concentration (the brine) to lesser concentration (the cells). When water moves in this fashion, the process is called osmosis.

Once inside the cells, the salt, and, to a lesser extent, the sugar, cause the cell proteins to unravel, or denature. As the individual proteins unravel, they become more likely to interact with one another. This interaction results in the formation of a sticky matrix that captures and holds moisture. Once exposed to heat, the matrix gels and forms a barrier that keeps much of the water from leaking out as the meat cooks. Thus you have meat that is both better seasoned and much more moist than when you started.

---

rewards and minimizing the number of steps? To get a leg up on the idea, we made it a flavored brine, adding not only salt and sugar but a mountain of crushed garlic, a couple of crushed bay leaves, and some sweet paprika.

This remarkable "twofer" won high marks indeed, well above those garnered by a unilateral soak or brine. The buttermilk and paprika showed spirit, garlic and bay crept into the crust, and the meat was tender and seasoned. We also spiked the brine with ¼ cup of sugar—not enough to sweeten but enough to bring other flavors out of hiding.

Fried foods taste irresistibly good when dressed in crumbs or flour not only because their insides are protected from damaging temperatures but also because hot, enveloping fat performs minor miracles on the flavor of the flour or crumbs. But what kind of coating is best?

To find out, we tested straight flour against a panoply of contenders: matzo crumbs, ground saltines, cornflakes, Melba toast, cornmeal, and panko (Japanese) bread crumbs. In the end, plain flour—requiring in this instance no seasoning whatsoever since the chicken had been brined—surpassed all other options for the integrity and lightness of the crust it produced.

Many fried chicken recipes use a single breading process in which the chicken is dipped first into beaten egg, then into flour or crumbs. A double, or bound, breading dips the chicken into flour first, then into egg, and finally into flour or crumbs. In side-by-side tests, we found that the double breading offered a superior base coat—more tenacious in its grip, more protective in its bearing—without being overly thick or tough.

Another practice that has made its way into many fried chicken recipes is that of air-drying the breaded chicken before frying it. Rather than becoming soggy in the refrigerator, as might be expected, the breading toughens up over time to produce a fried chicken of superior crispiness. We were also curious about the effect of air-drying on unbreaded chicken. We have come to favor the laser-crisp and taut skin of roasted birds that have been air-dried and wanted to see if an analogous effect could be achieved by refrigerating our brined, unbreaded chicken on a rack for a couple of hours.

We were reasonably confident this would allow the buttermilk to dry just enough to maintain a protective and flavorful posture and the chicken to bread nicely without first being dabbed or dried, frying up dry and crisp.

We tested the effects of air-drying the chicken before and after breading and compared the results with chicken that underwent no air-drying. Both air-dried versions were superior in terms of crust, but each was distinctly different from the other. The chicken that was breaded and then air-dried had a heartier, more toothsome crust—crunchy to some, hard to others. The chicken that was air-dried and then breaded was lighter and crispier, flaky, more shattery. We preferred this traditionally Southern crust. Though it initially seemed ideal, we noticed that its delicate crispiness succumbed to sandiness and porosity over the course of a few hours. This was not acceptable.

The memory of a particularly light but resilient crust on a chicken-fried steak recipe we had made persuaded us to add baking soda and baking powder to an egg wash bolstered with buttermilk. We hoped the sandiness in the crust that developed over time might thus be offset. Stirred into the wash, ½ teaspoon of baking soda and 1 teaspoon of baking powder produced just enough carbon dioxide to lighten the breading to perfection. Not only did it bronze to a shattery filigree in the hot fat, it also remained crisp as it cooled.

One of the most important requirements of fat as a frying medium is that it offer nothing of its own flavor—and, in fact, have none to offer. This means that the oil must be refined—in other words, cleansed and sanitized. Another requirement is that the oil perform at temperatures below its smoke point (the temperature at which it emits smoke and acrid odors) to maintain thermal stability. With the relatively moderate temperatures required by our recipe, all refined vegetable oils stayed well below their smoke points. In the end, peanut oil edged out Crisco shortening by virtue of its marginally more neutral and clean flavor.

A cast-iron Dutch oven covered during the first half of the frying reduced splatters to a fine spray, maintained the oil temperature impeccably, and fried the chicken through in about 15 minutes total versus the 20 minutes per side recommended in many recipes.

Drying the gleaming, bronzed statuettes was the most satisfying test. Paper bags are simply not porous enough to keep the chicken out of a gathering pool of grease. We found that paper towels absorbed excess fat quickly and that rolling the pieces over onto a bare rack thereafter kept them crisp.

Crispy Fried Chicken
SERVES 4 TO 6

Maintaining an even oil temperature is key to the success of this recipe. An instant-read thermometer with a high upper range is perfect for checking the temperature; a clip-on candy/deep-fry thermometer is fine, though it can be clipped to the pot only for the uncovered portion of frying.

CHICKEN

1¼	cups kosher salt or ½ cup plus 2 tablespoons table salt
¼	cup sugar
2	tablespoons paprika
3	medium heads garlic, cloves separated
3	bay leaves, crumbled
2	quarts low-fat buttermilk
1	whole chicken (about 3½ pounds; see page 162 for guidelines on selecting the best-tasting chicken), giblets discarded, cut into 12 pieces (see the illustrations on page 170)

COATING

4	cups all-purpose flour
1	large egg
1	teaspoon baking powder
½	teaspoon baking soda

3–4	cups refined peanut oil or vegetable shortening

1. FOR THE CHICKEN: In a large zipper-lock plastic bag, combine the salt, sugar, paprika, garlic cloves, and bay leaves. With a rubber mallet or flat meat pounder, smash the garlic into the salt and spice mixture thoroughly. Pour the mixture into a large plastic container or nonreactive stockpot. Add 7 cups buttermilk and stir until the salt is completely dissolved. Immerse the chicken, cover with plastic wrap, and refrigerate until fully seasoned, 2 to 3 hours. Remove the chicken from the buttermilk brine and shake off any excess; place it in a single layer on a large wire rack set over a rimmed baking sheet. Refrigerate uncovered for 2 hours. (After 2 hours, the chicken can be covered with plastic wrap and refrigerated up to 6 hours longer.)

2. FOR THE COATING: Measure the flour into a large shallow dish. Beat the egg, baking powder, and baking soda in a medium bowl; stir in the remaining 1 cup buttermilk (mixture will bubble and foam). Working in batches of three, drop the chicken pieces in the flour and shake the pan to coat. Shake the excess flour from each piece, then, using tongs, dip the chicken pieces into the egg mixture, turning to coat well and allowing the excess to drip off. Coat the chicken pieces with flour again, shake off the excess, and return to a wire rack.

3. Adjust an oven rack to the middle position, set a second wire rack over a second rimmed baking sheet, and place it on the oven rack; heat the oven to 200 degrees. Line a large plate with double layer of paper towels. Meanwhile, heat the oil (which should have a depth of 2½ inches in the pan) to 375 degrees over medium-high heat in a large 8-quart cast-iron Dutch oven with a diameter of about 12 inches. Place half of the chicken pieces skin-side down in the oil, cover, reduce the heat to medium, and fry until deep golden brown, 6 to 8 minutes; after about 3 minutes, lift the chicken pieces with tongs to check for even browning; rearrange if some pieces are browning faster than others. (Spot-check the oil temperature; after the first 6 minutes of frying the oil should be about 325 degrees. Adjust the burner if necessary.) Turn the chicken pieces over and continue to fry, uncovered, until they are deep golden brown on the second side, 6 to 8 minutes longer. Using tongs, transfer the chicken to the paper towel–lined plate; let stand 2 minutes to drain, then transfer to the rack in the warm oven. Replace the paper towel lining on the plate. Return the oil to 375 degrees and fry the remaining pieces, transferring the pieces to the paper towel–lined plate to drain. Remove the wire rack with the other chicken pieces from the oven, and transfer the just-cooked chicken from the plate to the rack. Let cool about 5 minutes, and serve.

CUTTING UP A CHICKEN FOR FRYING

Chicken destined for frying should be cut into fairly small pieces. Instead of the standard eight pieces (two breasts, two wings, two thighs, and two legs), we cut each breast piece in half and sever the wing at the main joint (the skin cooks better when thus separated, and the wing pieces are easier to eat) to yield a total of 12 pieces.

1. With a sharp chef's knife, cut through the skin around the leg where it attaches to the breast.

2. Using both hands, pop the leg joint out of its socket.

3. Use a chef's knife to cut through the flesh and skin to detach the leg from the body.

4. A line of fat separates the thigh and drumstick. Cut through the joint at this point. Repeat steps 1 through 4 with the other leg.

5. Bend the wing out from the breast and use a boning knife to cut through the joint. Repeat with the other wing.

6. Cut through the cartilage around the wingtip to remove it. Discard the tip. Cut through the joint to split. Repeat with the other wing.

7. Using poultry shears, cut along the ribs to completely separate the back from the breast. Reserve the backbone for another use.

8. Place the knife on the breastbone, then apply pressure to cut through and separate the breast into halves.

9. Cut each breast in half crosswise into two pieces.

OVEN-FRIED CHICKEN

WE'VE ALWAYS THOUGHT OF OVEN-FRIED chicken as ersatz fried chicken—only for those who were afraid to mess up their kitchen or consume too much fat. Depending on the liquid or crumb coating, this chicken could be bland, soggy, rubbery-skinned, greasy, artificially flavored, dry, or crumbly. Was it possible, we wondered, to make a decent alternative to the real thing?

After looking at scores of recipes, we realized that the coatings—both the moist one that helps the crumbs stick and the dry one that provides texture and crunch—were the key issues to examine.

Since the moist coating comes first, we started there. Before testing, we assumed this wet dunk did little more than help the crumbs adhere to the chicken. After testing, however, it became clear that this initial coat plays a larger role. A good first coat, we discovered, should offer flavor, attract the right proportion of crumbs to form an impressive, uniform crust, and, finally, help the crust stay crunchy during baking.

To find the best moist coating, we baked 13 drumsticks, keeping the dry coating constant while varying the moist coating: water, whole milk, evaporated milk, cream, buttermilk, yogurt, sour cream, milk beaten with egg, egg beaten with lemon juice, and egg with Dijon mustard. In addition, we tried legs coated with ranch dressing, mayonnaise, and butter.

Because many recipes for oven-fried chicken start by rolling chicken parts in butter, we thought the fat coatings would perform well. Not so. All of them—butter, mayonnaise, and ranch dressing—created a slick surface that prevented the crumbs from adhering properly. In addition, none of the fats did anything to crisp the crumbs.

Moreover, with the exception of buttermilk and evaporated milk, none of the dairy coatings impressed us. Buttermilk and evaporated milk did attract decent crusts and give a subtle flavor dimension to the chicken, but they didn't result in the crispness we wanted.

The egg beaten with lemon did result in a crisp coating. Unfortunately, it also contributed too much lemon flavor with an overcooked egg aftertaste. But

SCIENCE: Secret to Successful Frying

Many cooks shy away from frying, thinking that the technique adds loads of fat to their food. Taking nothing for granted, we put this notion to the test. We heated 3 cups of peanut oil to 375 degrees in an 8-quart Dutch oven and pan-fried a whole cut-up chicken in two batches. To our delight, we poured back almost exactly 3 cups of fat after frying. Each time the test was repeated, we ended up with virtually the same amount of fat before and after.

The explanation is simple: If the water in the food you are frying is kept above the boiling point (212 degrees), the outward pressure of the escaping water vapor keeps oil from soaking into the hot food. If the frying oil is not hot enough, on the other hand, the oil will seep into the food, making it greasy. The key is to get the oil hot enough before adding food (375 degrees worked well) so that you can maintain a temperature (around 325 degrees) that keeps the moisture within the food at a boil.

a change of just one ingredient made all the difference. Chicken coated with beaten egg and Dijon mustard was our favorite. This not-too-thick, not-too-thin moistener not only attracted a uniform, impressive layer of crumbs, it also gave the meat a wonderfully subtle flavor. Unlike many of the wet coatings, which made the crumbs either soggy or barely crisp, this one took the crumbs to an almost crunchy level.

Up until this point, we had been using dry bread crumbs in our tests. With our tests of wet coatings concluded, it was time to focus on other dry coating options. We started with 20 dry coatings or combinations thereof, all from published recipes. After baking and tasting them all, there wasn't a single one we thought was perfect.

Of the cereal coatings, cornflakes were the best, offering good color and crunch, but they also had too much sweet corn flavor. Ditto for bran flakes, but their distinct flavor was even more pronounced. Unprocessed bran looked like kitty litter, while Grape-Nuts looked like hamster food.

Crackers didn't work, either. Both saltines and Ritz were too soft; the Ritz, in addition, were too sweet. Cracker meal delivered a bland blond shell. In the bread department, stuffing mix scored well in crunch but struck out in flavor. Fresh bread crumbs, on the other hand, tasted great but lacked the crunch we had come to like.

The meals and flours, as to be expected, did not show well. Cornmeal tasted raw, and it chipped off the chicken like flecks of old paint. Our grocery store's house brand of Shake 'n Bake was vile, tasting of liquid smoke and bad hot dogs.

Although this first round of tests did not produce a strong winner, it did help us to clarify what it was that we wanted—a coating that was crunchy (not just crisp) and flavorful (but not artificial tasting) and that baked up a rich copper brown.

With a clear ideal in mind, we found a whole new range of coating possibilities in the specialty/international cracker section of our grocery store, including Melba toast, pain grillé (French crisp toast), Swedish crisps, lavash (crisp flat bread), bread sticks, bagel chips, Italian toasts, and pita chips. This series of tests delivered oven-fried chicken that was much closer to our ideal. The rather surprising winner, it turned out, was Melba toast. It scored the best in all three major categories—texture, flavor, and color.

Over the course of testing, we found that we much preferred legs and thighs to breasts because they don't dry out as quickly. As expected, the buttermilk brine that worked so well in our crispy fried chicken recipe did wonders here, too. The meat was more moist and better seasoned after a two-hour brine. We also discovered that we didn't like the skin on oven-fried chicken. Unlike fried chicken, in which hot oil causes the fat to render and the skin to crisp, oven heat simply softens the skin and makes it rubbery. We decided to remove the skin before coating the pieces.

Oven temperature was a simple matter. We started baking at 400 degrees, and all of the chicken pieces were cooked through and rich golden brown in about 40 minutes. A wire rack set over a foil-covered rimmed baking sheet or shallow baking pan allows heat to circulate around the chicken during baking, letting the chicken crisp without being turned. The foil, of course, protects the pan, making cleanup a breeze.

In the end, this "fried" chicken was pretty darn good. Perhaps not as crispy as the real thing, but certainly a close runner-up.

Oven-Fried Chicken
SERVES 4

To make Melba toast crumbs, place the toasts in a heavy-duty plastic freezer bag, seal, and pound with a meat pounder or other heavy blunt object. Leave some crumbs in the mixture the size of pebbles, but most should resemble coarse sand.

CHICKEN
1 1/4	cups kosher salt or 1/2 cup plus 2 tablespoons table salt
1/4	cup sugar
2	tablespoons paprika
3	medium heads garlic, cloves separated
3	bay leaves, crumbled
7	cups low-fat buttermilk
4	whole chicken legs, separated into drumsticks and thighs (see illustration 4 on page 170) and skin removed

COATING
1/4	cup vegetable oil
1	box (about 5 ounces) plain Melba toast, crushed (see note)
2	large eggs
1	tablespoon Dijon mustard
1	teaspoon dried thyme
3/4	teaspoon salt
1/2	teaspoon ground black pepper
1/2	teaspoon dried oregano
1/4	teaspoon garlic powder
1/4	teaspoon cayenne pepper (optional)

1. FOR THE CHICKEN: In a large zipper-lock plastic bag, combine the salt, sugar, paprika, garlic cloves, and bay leaves. With a rubber mallet or flat meat pounder, smash the garlic into the salt and spice mixture thoroughly. Pour the mixture into a large plastic container or nonreactive stockpot. Add the buttermilk and stir until salt is completely dissolved. Immerse the chicken and refrigerate until fully seasoned, 2 to 3 hours. Remove the chicken from the buttermilk brine and shake off the excess; place the chicken pieces in a single layer on a large wire rack set over a rimmed baking sheet. Refrigerate uncovered for 2 hours. (After 2 hours, the chicken

can be covered with plastic wrap and refrigerated up to 6 hours longer.)

2. Adjust an oven rack to the upper-middle position and heat the oven to 400 degrees. Line a baking sheet with foil and set a large flat wire rack over the pan.

3. FOR THE COATING: Drizzle the oil over the Melba toast crumbs in a shallow dish or pie plate; toss well to coat. Mix the eggs, mustard, thyme, salt, pepper, oregano, garlic powder, and cayenne, if using, with a fork in a second shallow dish or pie plate.

4. Working one piece at a time, coat the chicken on both sides with the egg mixture. Set the chicken in Melba crumbs, sprinkle the crumbs over the chicken, and press to coat. Turn the chicken over and repeat on the other side. Gently shake off the excess and place the chicken on the rack in the pan. Bake until the chicken is deep nutty brown and juices run clear, about 40 minutes. Serve.

BUFFALO WINGS

FIRST CONCEIVED OF AT THE ANCHOR BAR in Buffalo, New York, in the 1960s, Buffalo wings are now found throughout the country at any bar or Super Bowl party worth its salt. The odd combination of chicken wings slathered with hot sauce and blue cheese dipping sauce may seem like a drunken concoction best forgotten about in the morning, but it is actually a harmonious union. The sauce's bright heat is tamed by the soothing, creamy dip. Under the right circumstances, even bad wings (and we have had our share of flabby, tough wings in greasy sauce)

are pretty good. But we wanted to come up with a recipe for really good wings: juicy meat with a crisp coating; a spicy (but not incendiary), slightly sweet, and vinegary sauce; and a creamy but pungent blue cheese dip.

For Buffalo wings, the raw chicken wing itself is almost always cut in two segments and the relatively meatless wingtip removed. The wings come packaged as whole wings or as pre-cut segments affectionately referred to as drumettes. We found that pre-cut wings were often poorly cut and unevenly sized, so we chose to buy whole wings and cut them ourselves, which was easy and economical. With kitchen shears or a sharp chef's knife, the wing is halved at the main joint and the skinny tip of the wing is lopped off and discarded (or saved for stock).

While the wings were easy to prepare, cooking them proved a little trickier because of their high fat content. At the Anchor Bar, Buffalo wings are deep-fried, which renders the fat and leaves the skin crisp and golden. But deep-frying can be a daunting project in a home kitchen. We hoped that oven-roasting might be a viable alternative. Roasting at a fairly low temperature is a common cooking method for fatty fowl like duck and goose; it leaves the skin bronzed and crispy and the meat moist from the slowly rendered fat. We placed the wings skin-side down on a rack resting on a rimmed baking sheet so that the chicken would not be sitting in fat. At 300 degrees, the wings cooked for an hour and were wan and dry. At 375 degrees, the chicken was still a little flabby after 45 minutes of cooking, and the meat was on the dry side.

CUTTING UP CHICKEN WINGS

1. With a chef's knife, cut into the skin between the larger sections of the wing until you hit the joint.

2. Bend back the two sections to pop and break the joint.

3. Cut through the skin and flesh to completely separate the two meaty portions.

4. Hack off the wingtip and discard.

We decided to switch gears and try the stovetop. Sautéing the wings did little for their flavor or texture. And they were still greasy because the fat was not rendered. Pan-frying, or cooking the chicken partially submerged in fat, yielded much better results, but turning the chicken midway through cooking prompted hot fat to spatter. We decided that if we were going to pan-fry, we might as well try deep-frying. Maybe there was something to tradition after all. We found that if we used a deep Dutch oven and kept the oil at a constant 360 degrees, spattering oil was minimal and cleanup easy.

We tossed the wings with salt, pepper, and cayenne and then fried them for about 12 minutes until golden. While these wings were juicy and crisp, most tasters wanted an even crispier exterior. We did not want to resort to a batter, so we tried dredging the wings, testing one batch dredged in flour and another in cornstarch. The cornstarch provided a thin and brittle coating, not unlike tempura, that was the tasters' favorite. We found thoroughly drying the chicken with paper towels prior to tossing with the cornstarch and seasonings ensured crisp skin and no gumminess.

With the wings fried and placed in the oven to keep warm, we were ready to tackle the sauce. Most recipes we found agreed that authentic Buffalo wing sauce, as made at the Anchor Bar, is nothing but Frank's Louisiana Hot Sauce and butter or margarine, blended in a 2-to-1 ratio. Most recipes also suggest intensifying the sauce's heat with a bit of Tabasco or other hot pepper sauce, because on its own Frank's is not quite spicy enough. While we liked this simple sauce, most tasters wanted something a little more dynamic. We included brown sugar to round out the flavors. A little cider vinegar balanced out the sugar and added a pleasing sharpness.

Creamy blue cheese dressing and carrot and celery sticks are the classic accompaniments to Buffalo wings. For our dressing, we picked a mild blue cheese and combined it with buttermilk and sour cream for tang and richness and with mayonnaise for creaminess. A little white wine vinegar brightened the flavors and a pinch of sugar brought everything together. While we normally stay away from garlic powder, here it blended well with the other ingredients and added a subtle background note rather than the assertive bite that comes with fresh garlic. Our final Buffalo wings buck tradition just a bit, but only in the service of delivering a close to foolproof crowd-pleasing favorite.

~

Buffalo Wings

SERVES 6 TO 8 AS AN APPETIZER

Frank's Louisiana Hot Sauce is vinegary and not terribly spicy. Combine this sauce with a more potent hot sauce, such as Tabasco, to give the wings the proper heat.

4	tablespoons unsalted butter
½	cup Frank's Louisiana Hot Sauce
2	tablespoons hot pepper sauce, such as Tabasco, plus more to taste
1	tablespoon dark brown sugar
2	teaspoons cider vinegar
1–2	quarts peanut oil, for frying
1	teaspoon cayenne pepper
1	teaspoon ground black pepper
1	teaspoon salt
3	tablespoons cornstarch
18	chicken wings (about 3 pounds), wingtips removed and remaining wings separated into 2 parts at the joint (see the illustrations on page 173)
4	stalks celery, cut into thin sticks
2	carrots, peeled and cut into thin sticks
1	recipe Blue Cheese Dressing (recipe follows)

1. Melt the butter in a small saucepan over low heat. Whisk in the hot sauces, brown sugar, and vinegar until combined. Remove from the heat and set aside.

2. Preheat the oven to 200 degrees. Line a baking sheet with paper towels. Heat 2½ inches of oil in a large Dutch oven over medium-high heat to 360 degrees. While the oil heats, mix together the cayenne, black pepper, salt, and cornstarch in a small bowl. Dry the chicken with paper towels and place in a large mixing bowl. Sprinkle the spice mixture over the wings and toss with a rubber spatula until evenly coated. Fry half the chicken wings until golden and crisp, 10 to 12 minutes. With a slotted spoon, transfer the fried chicken wings to the baking sheet. Keep this first batch warm in the oven while frying the remaining wings.

3. Pour the sauce mixture in a large bowl, add the chicken wings, and toss until the wings are uniformly coated. Serve immediately with the carrot and celery sticks and Blue Cheese Dressing on the side.

Blue Cheese Dressing

MAKES ABOUT 1 ½ CUPS

Use a mild blue cheese such as Danish blue or Stella Blue cheese from Wisconsin. Both of these cheeses are widely available in supermarkets.

5	ounces crumbled blue cheese (about 1 cup)
6	tablespoons buttermilk
6	tablespoons sour cream
4	tablespoons mayonnaise
4	teaspoons white wine vinegar
½	teaspoon sugar
¼	teaspoon garlic powder
	Salt and ground black pepper

Mash the blue cheese and buttermilk in a small bowl with a fork until the mixture resembles cottage cheese with small curds. Stir in the sour cream, mayonnaise, vinegar, sugar, and garlic powder. Adjust seasoning with salt and black pepper to taste. (The dressing can be refrigerated in an airtight container for up to 1 week.)

CHICKEN POT PIE

MOST EVERYONE LOVES A GOOD CHICKEN pot pie, though few seem to have the time or energy to make one. Not surprising. Like a lot of satisfying dishes, traditional pot pie takes time. Before the pie even makes it to the oven, the cook must poach a chicken, take the meat off the bone and cut it up, strain the stock, prepare and blanch vegetables, make a sauce, and mix and roll out biscuit or pie dough. Given the many time-consuming steps it can take to make a pot pie, our goal was to make the best one we could as quickly as possible. Pot pie, after all, was intended as weeknight supper food.

Our experiences with making pot pie also made us aware of two other difficulties. First, the vegetables tend to overcook. A filling that is chockfull of bright,

fresh vegetables going into the oven looks completely different after 40 minutes of high-heat baking under a blanket of dough. Carrots become mushy and pumpkin-colored, while peas and fresh herbs fade from fresh spring green to olive drab. We wanted to preserve the vegetables' color as long as it didn't require any heroic acts to do so.

We had also made a number of pot pies that were too juicy. Before baking, the filling was thick and creamy. When cut into after baking, the pie looked like chicken soup en croute. Although we wanted the pie moist and saucy, we also wanted it thick enough to eat with a fork.

We began by determining the best way to cook the chicken. In addition to making pies with roast chicken and poached chicken, we steamed and roasted whole chickens and braised chicken parts.

Steaming the chicken was time-consuming, requiring about one hour, and the steaming liquid didn't make a strong enough stock for the pot pie sauce. Roast chicken also required an hour in the oven, and by the time we took off the skin and mixed the meat in with the sauce and vegetables, the roasted flavor was lost. We had similar results with braised chicken. It lost its delicious flavor once the browned skin was removed.

Next we tried poaching, the most traditional cooking method. Of the two poaching liquids we tried, we preferred the chicken poached in wine and stock to the one poached in stock alone. The wine infused the meat and made for a richer, more full-flavored sauce. To our disappointment, however, the acidity of the wine sauce caused the green peas and fresh herbs to lose their bright green color in the oven. Vegetables baked in the stock-only sauce kept their bright color, though the bland sauce needed perking up—a problem we'd have to deal with later. Now we were ready to test this method against quicker-cooking boneless, skinless chicken breasts.

Because boneless, skinless breasts cook so quickly, sautéing was another possible cooking method for them. Before comparing our liking for poached parts versus poached breasts, we tried cooking the breasts three different ways. We cut raw breast meat into bite-sized pieces and sautéed them; we sautéed whole breasts, shredding the breast meat once it was cool enough to handle; and we poached whole breasts in stock, also shredding the meat.

Once again, poaching was our favorite method. The resulting tender, irregularly shaped chicken pieces mixed well with the vegetables and, much like textured pasta, caused the sauce to cling. The sautéed chicken pieces, however, floated independently in the sauce, their surfaces too smooth to attract sauce. For simplicity's sake, we had hoped we would like the sautéed whole breasts. Unfortunately, sautéing caused the outer layer of meat to turn crusty, a texture we did not like in the pie.

Our only concern with the poached boneless, skinless breasts was the quality of the stock. In earlier tests, we found that bone-in parts could be poached in canned broth (rather than homemade stock) without much sacrifice of flavor. We surmised that the bones and skin improved the flavor of the broth during the long cooking time. But how would quick-cooking boneless, skinless breasts fare in canned broth? The answer: not as bad as we feared. In our comparison of the pies made with boneless breasts poached in homemade stock and canned broth, we found little difference in quality. Evidently, it's not the cooking time of the chicken but the abundance of ingredients in a pot pie that makes it possible to use canned broth with no ill consequences. Ultimately, we were able to shave half an hour off the cooking time (10 minutes to cook the breasts compared with 40 minutes to cook the parts). For those who like either dark or a mix of dark and white meat in the pie, boneless, skinless chicken thighs can be used as well.

A good pot pie with fresh vegetables, warm pastry, and full-flavored sauce tastes satisfying. One with overcooked vegetables tastes stodgy and old-fashioned. So we made pies with raw vegetables, sautéed vegetables, and parboiled vegetables. After comparing the pies, we found that the vegetables sautéed before baking held their color and flavor best, the parboiled ones less so. The raw vegetables were not fully cooked at the end of the baking time and gave off too much liquid, watering down the flavor and thickness of the sauce.

EQUIPMENT: Cutting Boards

What separates good cutting boards from bad ones? Is it material? Size, thickness, or weight? Whether the board warps or retains odors with use? And what about the issue of bacteria retention?

To sort all of this out, we gathered boards made from wood, polyethylene (plastic), acrylic, glass, and Corian (the hard countertop material) and used them daily in our test kitchen for eight weeks. We found the two most important factors to be size and material.

In terms of size, large boards provide ample space for both cutting and pushing aside cut foods and waste. The disadvantage of really large boards is that they may not fit in the dishwasher. We are willing to make that sacrifice for the extra work area. If you are not, buy the largest board that will fit in your dishwasher. No matter the dimensions, a board should be heavy enough for stability but not so heavy (or thick and bulky) to impede its easy movement around the kitchen. We found boards in the range of 3 to 4 pounds to be ideal.

Material is important primarily in terms of the way the board interacts with the knife, but it is also relevant to odor retention and warping. We disliked cutting on hard acrylic, glass, and Corian boards because they don't absorb the shock of the knife strike. Plastic and wood boards are softer and therefore cushion the knife's blow, making for more controlled cutting. The pebbly surface texture of the acrylic and glass boards was another point against them. We found that a rough texture promotes knife slide.

There is one advantage to hard boards—they don't retain odors like plastic and wood can. A dishwasher will remove odors from plastic boards as well as specially treated dishwasher-safe wood boards. (Unless treated by the manufacturer with a waterproof coating, wood boards should never go in the dishwasher.)

If your boards are too large to fit in the dishwasher, use one for onions, garlic, and the like; another for raw poultry and meat; and a third for other foods. To remove most odors and bacteria, wash with hot soapy water after each use and then sanitize with a light bleach solution (1 tablespoon of bleach to 1 gallon of water).

Many plastic and wood boards warp over time. Makers of wood boards advise consumers to season their boards with mineral oil to build up water resistance and, thereby, resist warping. As none of the cooks we know will go this extra mile, plastic boards probably make the most sense for home cooks. Keep them away from the heating element in the dishwasher to prevent warping.

Our final task was to develop a sauce that was flavorful, creamy, and of the proper consistency. Chicken pot pie sauce is traditionally based on a roux (a mixture of butter and flour sautéed together briefly), which is thinned with chicken broth and often enriched with cream.

Because of the dish's inherent richness, we wanted to see how little cream we could get away with using. We tried three different pot pie fillings, using ¼ cup cream, ¼ cup half-and-half, and 1½ cups milk, respectively. Going into the oven, all of the fillings seemed to have the right consistency and creaminess; when they came out, however, it was a different story. Vegetable and meat juices diluted the consistency and creaminess of the cream and half-and-half sauces. To achieve a creamy-looking sauce, we would have needed to increase the cream dramatically. Fortunately, we didn't have to try it, because we actually liked the milk-enriched sauce. The larger quantity of milk kept the sauce creamy and tasted delicious.

To keep the sauce from becoming too liquidy, we simply added more flour. A sauce that looks a little thick before baking will become the perfect consistency after taking on the chicken and vegetable juices released during baking.

We had worked out the right consistency, but because we had been forced to abandon the wine for the vegetables' sake, the sauce tasted a little bland. Lemon juice, a flavor heightener we had seen in a number of recipes, had the same dulling effect on the color of the vegetables as the wine. We tried sherry, and it worked perfectly. Because sherry is more intensely flavored and less acidic than wine, it gave us the flavor we were looking for without harming the peas and carrots.

Chicken Pot Pie

SERVES 6 TO 8

You can make the filling ahead of time, but remember to heat it on top of the stove before topping it. Mushrooms can be sautéed along with the celery and carrots, and blanched pearl onions can stand in for the onion.

1	recipe pie dough or biscuit topping (pages 178–179)
1½	pounds boneless, skinless chicken breasts and/or thighs
2	cups canned low-sodium chicken broth
1½	tablespoons vegetable oil
1	medium-large onion, chopped fine
3	medium carrots, peeled and cut crosswise ¼ inch thick
2	small stalks celery, cut crosswise ¼ inch thick
	Salt and ground black pepper
4	tablespoons unsalted butter
½	cup flour
1½	cups milk
½	teaspoon dried thyme
3	tablespoons dry sherry
¾	cup frozen green peas, thawed
3	tablespoons minced fresh parsley leaves

1. Make the pie dough or biscuit topping and refrigerate it until ready to use.

2. Adjust an oven rack to the lower-middle position and heat the oven to 400 degrees. Put the chicken and broth in a small Dutch oven or stockpot over medium heat. Cover, bring to a simmer; simmer until the chicken is just done, 8 to 10 minutes. Transfer the chicken to a large bowl, reserving the broth in a measuring cup.

3. Increase the heat to medium-high; heat the oil in the now-empty pan. Add the onion, carrots, and celery; sauté until just tender, about 5 minutes. Season to taste with salt and pepper. While the vegetables are sautéing, shred the meat into bite-sized pieces. Transfer the cooked vegetables to a bowl with the chicken; set aside.

4. Heat the butter over medium heat in the empty pan. When the foaming subsides, add the flour; cook about 1 minute. Whisk in the chicken broth, milk, any accumulated chicken juices, and thyme. Bring to a simmer, then continue to simmer until the sauce fully thickens, about 1 minute. Season to taste with salt and pepper; stir in the sherry.

5. Pour the sauce over the chicken mixture; stir to combine. Stir in the peas and parsley. Adjust the seasonings. (Can be covered and refrigerated overnight; reheat before topping with the pastry.) Pour the mixture into a 9 by 13-inch pan (or shallow baking dish of similar size) or six 12-ounce ovenproof dishes. Top with desired pastry dough; bake until the

pastry is golden brown and filling is bubbly, 30 minutes for large pie and 20 to 25 minutes for smaller pies. Serve hot.

➤ VARIATIONS

Chicken Pot Pie with Spring Vegetables

Follow the recipe for Chicken Pot Pie, replacing the celery with 18 thin asparagus stalks that have been trimmed and cut into 1-inch pieces. Increase the peas to 1 cup.

Chicken Pot Pie with Wild Mushrooms

The soaking liquid used to rehydrate dried porcini mushrooms replaces some of the broth used to poach the chicken and then to enrich the sauce.

Follow the recipe for Chicken Pot Pie, soaking 1 ounce dried porcini mushrooms in 2 cups warm tap water until softened, about 20 minutes. Lift the mushrooms from the liquid, strain the liquid, and reserve 1 cup. Use the soaking liquid in place of 1 cup of canned chicken broth. Proceed with the recipe, cooking the rehydrated porcini and 12 ounces sliced button mushrooms with the vegetables. Finish as directed.

Chicken Pot Pie with Corn and Bacon

This Southern variation with corn and bacon works especially well with the biscuit topping.

Follow the recipe for Chicken Pot Pie, replacing the oil with ¼ pound bacon, cut crosswise into ½-inch-wide strips. Cook over medium heat until fat is rendered and bacon is crisp, about 6 minutes. Remove the bacon from the pan with a slotted spoon and drain on paper towels. Cook the vegetables in the bacon fat. Add the drained bacon to the bowl with the chicken and cooked vegetables. Proceed with the recipe, replacing the peas with 2 cups fresh or frozen corn.

Savory Pie Dough Topping

MAKES ENOUGH FOR
1 RECIPE CHICKEN POT PIE

If you like a bottom crust in your pot pie, you can duplicate that soft crust texture by tucking the overhanging dough down into the pan side rather than fluting it.

1½	cups (7½ ounces) unbleached all-purpose flour
½	teaspoon salt
8	tablespoons (1 stick) unsalted butter, chilled and cut into ¼-inch pieces
4	tablespoons vegetable shortening, chilled
3–4	tablespoons ice water

1. Mix the flour and salt in a food processor fitted with a steel blade. Scatter the butter pieces over the flour mixture, tossing to coat the butter with a little of the flour. Cut the butter into the flour with five 1-second pulses. Add the shortening and continue cutting it in until the flour is pale yellow and resembles coarse cornmeal, with butter bits no larger than small peas, about four more 1-second pulses. Turn the mixture into a medium bowl.

2. Sprinkle 3 tablespoons ice water over the mixture. With the blade of a rubber spatula, use a folding motion to mix it in. Press down on the dough mixture with the broad side of a spatula until the dough sticks together, adding up to 1 tablespoon more ice water if the dough will not come together. Shape the dough into a ball, then flatten into a 4-inch-wide disk. Wrap in plastic wrap and refrigerate 30 minutes, or up to 2 days, before rolling.

3. When the pie filling is ready, roll the dough on a floured surface to approximate an 11 by 15-inch rectangle, about ⅛-inch thick. If making individual pies, roll the dough ⅛ inch thick and cut 6 dough rounds about 1 inch larger than the dish circumference. Place the dough over the pot pie filling, trimming the dough to within ½ inch of the pan lip. Tuck the overhanging dough back under itself so the folded edge is flush with the pan lip. Flute the edges all around. Alternatively, don't trim dough and tuck the overhanging dough down into the pan side. Cut at least four 1-inch vent holes in a large pot pie or one 1-inch vent hole in smaller pies. Proceed with Chicken Pot Pie recipe.

Fluffy Buttermilk Biscuit Topping

MAKES ENOUGH FOR 1 RECIPE
CHICKEN POT PIE

For more information about biscuit making, see page 281.

1	cup (5 ounces) unbleached all-purpose flour
1	cup (4 ounces) plain cake flour
2	teaspoons baking powder
¼	teaspoon baking soda
1	teaspoon sugar
½	teaspoon salt
8	tablespoons (1 stick) unsalted butter, chilled, quartered lengthwise, and cut crosswise into ¼-inch pieces
¾	cup cold buttermilk, plus 1 to 2 tablespoons if needed

1. Pulse the dry ingredients in the workbowl of a food processor fitted with a steel blade. Add the butter pieces; pulse until the mixture resembles coarse cornmeal with a few slightly larger butter lumps.

2. Transfer the mixture to a medium bowl; add the buttermilk; stir with a fork until the dough gathers into moist clumps. Transfer the dough to a floured work surface and form into a rough ball, then roll dough ½-inch thick. Using 2½- to 3-inch pastry cutter, stamp out 8 rounds of dough. If making individual pies, cut the dough slightly smaller than the circumference of each dish. (Dough rounds can be refrigerated on a lightly floured baking sheet covered with plastic wrap up to 2 hours.)

3. Arrange the dough rounds over the warm filling and proceed with Chicken Pot Pie recipe.

CHICKEN AND DUMPLINGS

DESPITE AMERICA'S ONGOING LOVE AFFAIR with comfort food, chicken and dumplings, unlike its baked cousin, chicken pot pie, hasn't made a comeback. After making several dozen batches of dumplings, we think we know why.

As tricky as it can be to make pie pastry or biscuits for pot pie, dumplings are far more temperamental.

With pot pie, dry oven heat and a rich sauce camouflage minor flaws in biscuits or pastry, whereas moist, steamy heat highlights gummy or leaden dumplings. What's more, pot pie, with its meat, vegetables, crust, and sauce, is a complete meal. Chicken and dumplings is, well, chicken and dumplings. A few hearty vegetables would make it a complete meal—just the selling point to attract today's busy cook.

Our mission in developing a recipe for chicken and dumplings was twofold. First, we wanted a recipe that was as foolproof and complete as that for a good chicken pot pie. Second, we wanted a dumpling that was light yet substantial, tender yet durable. But which style of dumpling to explore?

In different parts of the country, dumplings come in different shapes. They may be rolled thin and cut into strips, rolled thick and stamped out like biscuits, or shaped into round balls by hand. Could these three styles come from the same dough, or would we need to develop separate doughs to accommodate each style? Most flour-based dumplings are made of flour, salt, and one or more of the following: butter, eggs, milk, and baking powder. Depending on the ingredient list, dumplings are usually mixed in one of three ways. The most common is a biscuit or pastry style in which cold butter is cut into the dry ingredients, then cold milk and/or eggs are stirred in until just mixed. Other dumplings are made by simply mixing wet into dry ingredients. Finally, many of the eggier dumplings are made pâte-à-choux (or puff-pastry) style, adding flour to hot water and butter, then whisking in eggs, one at a time.

We spent a full day making batch after batch of dumplings in some combination of the above ingredients and following one of the three mixing methods. By the end of the day, we hadn't made a single dumpling that we really liked.

We finally made progress after looking at a recipe in *Master Recipes* (Ballantine, 1987), in which author Stephen Schmidt cuts butter into flour, baking powder, and salt. Then, instead of adding cold liquid to the dry ingredients, he adds hot liquid to the flour-butter mixture. Dumplings made according to this method were light and fluffy, yet they held up beautifully during cooking. These were the firm yet tender dumplings we were looking for. This type of dumpling is a success because hot liquids, unlike cold ones, expand and set the starch in the flour, keeping it from absorbing too much of the cooking liquid. Now that we had the technique down, it was time to test the formula.

We thought that cake flour dumplings would be even lighter-textured than those made with all-purpose. In fact, just the opposite was true. They were tight, spongy little dumplings with a metallic, acidic aftertaste. The process by which cake flour is chlorinated leaves it acidic. One of the benefits of acidic flour is that it sets eggs faster in baking, resulting in a smoother, finer texture. This acidic flavor, less distracting in a cake batter rich with butter, sugar, and eggs, really comes through in a simple dumpling dough.

Although we were pretty sure that dumplings made with vegetable shortening wouldn't taste as good as those made with butter, we had high hopes for the ones made with chicken fat. After a side-by-side tasting of dumplings, one batch made with butter, one with shortening, and one with chicken fat, we selected those made with butter. The shortening-based dumplings tasted flat, like cooked flour and chicken stock, while those made with chicken fat tasted like flour and stronger-flavored chicken stock. The butter gave the dumplings that extra flavor dimension they needed.

Liquids were simple. Dumplings made with chicken stock, much like those made with chicken fat, tasted too similar to the stewing liquid. Those made with water were pretty dull. Because buttermilk tends to separate and even curdle when heated, buttermilk dumplings felt a little wrong. Whole milk dumplings were tender, with a pleasant biscuity flavor—our first choice.

Up to this point, we had made all of our dumplings by cutting the fat into the dry ingredients, then adding hot liquid. Because we were adding hot milk, we questioned why it was necessary to cut in the cold butter. Why couldn't we simply heat the milk and butter together and dump the mixture into the dry ingredients? A side-by-side tasting of dumplings made according to the two different mixing techniques made us realize that cutting the butter into the flour was indeed an unnecessary step. The simpler route of adding hot milk and melted butter to the dry ingredients actually yielded more substantial, better-textured dumplings.

Having decided on dumplings made with all-purpose flour, butter, milk, baking powder, and salt, we tested the formula by shaping them into balls, cutting them into biscuit shapes, and rolling them thin and cutting them into strips. Regardless of shape, we got the same consistent results: tender, sturdy dumplings.

We now turned our energies to updating the chicken part of the dish. Our first few attempts were disastrous. To make the dish clean and sleek, we left the chicken pieces on the bone, cut the vegetables into long, thin strips, and thickened the stewing liquid slightly. As we ate the finished product, we realized that we needed a knife (to cut the chicken off the bone), a fork (to eat the vegetables, dumplings, and meat), and a spoon (for the liquid). Although we wanted the dish to look beautiful, it

SHAPING DUMPLINGS

1. For flat, noodlelike dumplings, roll the dough ⅛ inch thick and cut it into 2 by ½-inch strips.

2. For biscuitlike dumplings, roll the dough ½ inch thick. Use a 2-inch biscuit cutter or a round drinking glass top to cut rounds.

3. For round, puffy dumplings, divide the dough into 18 pieces. Roll each piece into a rough round.

had to be eater-friendly. This meant that the chicken had to come off the bone, the vegetables needed to be cut a little smaller, and the liquid would have to be reduced and thickened. As the dish evolved, we worked toward making it not only a one-dish but also a one-utensil meal.

Boneless, skinless chicken breasts just didn't seem right for this dish. We wanted large, uneven chunks of light and dark meat. Only a whole chicken would work. Because we wanted this dish to serve six to eight and because we preferred bigger chunks of meat, we chose the larger oven roasters over the small fryer hens. Because we had already developed a method for making rich, flavorful chicken stock and perfectly poached chicken parts (see page 4), we simply adapted the technique to this recipe.

Our updated chicken and dumplings now needed vegetables, but where and how to cook them? In an attempt to streamline the process, we tried cooking the vegetables along with the poaching chicken parts. After fishing out hot, slightly overcooked vegetables from among the chicken parts and pieces, we decided this little shortcut wasn't worth it. So we simply washed the pot, returned it to the stove, and let the vegetables steam for 10 minutes while removing the meat from the bone, straining the stock, and making the dumpling dough. Because the vegetables would cook again for a short time in the sauce, we wanted them slightly undercooked at this point. Steaming them separately gave us more control.

With our meat poached and off the bone, our stock degreased and strained, and our vegetables steamed, we were ready to complete the dish—almost like someone ready to stir-fry. We chose to thicken the sauce at the beginning of this final phase rather than at the end of it because once our chicken, vegetables, and dumplings were added to the pot, thickening became virtually impossible.

To a roux (or paste) of flour and chicken fat (using every bit of the chicken to make the dish), we added our homemade stock and stirred until it thickened. Although we needed 6 cups of stock to poach the chicken parts, we found this quantity of liquid made the dish much too saucy, more like chicken and dumpling soup. Pouring off 2 cups of stock to reserve for another use solved the problem.

We added the chicken and vegetables to the thickened sauce, then steamed the dumplings. The dumplings thus remained undisturbed while the chicken and vegetables had an opportunity to marry and mingle with one another and the sauce. A few peas and a little parsley made the dish beautiful, and a little dry sherry or vermouth, as we found with chicken pot pie, heightened the flavor. A touch of cream enriches and beautifies, but the dish is equally good without it.

Chicken and Dumplings with Aromatic Vegetables
SERVES 6 TO 8

A touch of heavy cream gives this dish a more refined look and rich flavor, but it can be omitted. If you are in a hurry, you can poach boneless chicken breasts in low-sodium canned broth, pull the breast into large pieces, and skip step 1 below. This compromise saves time, but the results are not nearly as delicious.

CHICKEN AND VEGETABLES
- 1 large roasting chicken (6 to 7 pounds; see page 162 for guidelines on selecting the best-tasting chicken), cut into 2 drumsticks, 2 thighs, and 2 breast pieces, each with skin removed; back, neck, and wings hacked with cleaver into 1- to 2-inch pieces to make stock
- 1 large onion, unpeeled and cut into large chunks
- 2 bay leaves
- Salt
- 3 stalks celery, trimmed and cut into 1 by ½-inch pieces
- 4 medium carrots, peeled and cut into 1 by ½-inch pieces
- 6 boiling onions, peeled and halved
- 4 tablespoons unsalted butter or chicken fat from the cooked chicken
- 6 tablespoons all-purpose flour
- 1 teaspoon dried thyme
- 2 tablespoons dry sherry or vermouth
- ¼ cup heavy cream (optional)
- ¾ cup frozen peas, thawed
- ¼ cup minced fresh parsley leaves
- Ground black or white pepper

DUMPLINGS

2	cups all-purpose flour
1	tablespoon baking powder
¾	teaspoon salt
3	tablespoons butter
1	cup milk

1. FOR THE CHICKEN: Heat a large Dutch oven over medium-high heat. Add the hacked-up chicken pieces (back, neck, and wings) and onion chunks; sauté until onion softens and chicken loses its raw color, about 5 minutes. Reduce the heat to low, cover, and continue to cook until the chicken pieces give up most of their liquid, about 20 minutes. Increase the heat to medium-high, add 6 cups hot water, skinned chicken parts (legs, thighs, and breasts), bay leaves, and ¾ teaspoon salt, and bring to a simmer. Reduce the heat; continue to simmer, partially covered, until the stock is flavorful and chicken parts are just cooked through, about 20 minutes longer. Remove the chicken parts and set aside. When cool enough to handle, remove the meat from the bones in 2- to 3-inch chunks. Strain the stock, discarding the chicken pieces. Skim and reserve fat from stock and set aside 4 cups of stock, reserving extra for another use.

2. Meanwhile, bring ½-inch water to a simmer in the cleaned Dutch oven fitted with steamer basket. Add the celery, carrots, and boiling onions; cover and steam until just tender, about 10 minutes. Remove and set aside.

3. FOR THE DUMPLINGS: Mix the flour, baking powder, and salt in a medium bowl. Heat the butter and milk to a simmer and add to the dry ingredients. Mix with a fork or knead by hand two or three times until mixture just comes together. Following the illustrations on page 180, form the dough into desired shape; set aside.

4. TO FINISH THE DISH: Heat the butter or reserved chicken fat in cleaned Dutch oven over medium-high heat. Whisk in the flour and thyme; cook, whisking constantly, until flour turns golden, 1 to 2 minutes. Continuing to whisk constantly, gradually add the sherry or vermouth, then the reserved 4 cups chicken stock; simmer until the gravy thickens slightly, 2 to 3 minutes. Stir in optional cream and chicken and vegetables; return to a simmer.

5. Lay the formed dumplings on the surface of the chicken mixture; cover and simmer until the dumplings are cooked through, about 10 minutes for strip dumplings and 15 minutes for balls and biscuit rounds. Gently stir in the peas and parsley. Adjust the seasonings, including generous amounts of salt and pepper. Ladle a portion of meat, sauce, vegetables, and dumplings into soup plates and serve immediately.

➤ VARIATION

Chicken and Herbed Dumplings with Aromatic Vegetables

Follow the recipe for Chicken and Dumplings with Aromatic Vegetables, adding ½ cup minced soft fresh herb leaves such as parsley, chives (or scallion greens), dill, and tarragon to the dumpling mixture along with the dry ingredients. If other herbs are unavailable, parsley alone can be used.

CHICKEN FRICASSEE

CHICKEN CAN BE ROASTED, SAUTÉED, grilled, fried, stir-fried, oven-fried, baked, poached, and smoked, but these days we rarely think about a simple fricassee. Why? Well, for one thing, most of us mistake it for some outdated Cordon Bleu preparation. In fact, a chicken fricassee is nothing more than a whole cut-up chicken poached in stock, after which a simple sauce is made from the liquid. It's simple, it's flavorful, and it's easy. So why has it been forgotten? As in the case of many recipes for other traditional dishes, the answer is quite simple. They are either too time-consuming or no longer appeal to the modern palate. But this is not the case with chicken fricassee, which is neither time-consuming nor worthy of disdain. It seemed high time to resurrect chicken fricassee.

The process did involve solving some problems, however. The first was to define the parameters of the recipe. The fricassee has had a long history and many different interpretations. (For more information, see page 184.) In short, though, a French fricassee meant chicken (or sometimes vegetables) cooked in a white sauce. Over time, this dish evolved to become chicken poached in a clear liquid, usually chicken stock but sometimes water and/or wine. When the chicken was done, it was removed from the pan and a sauce was made from the poaching liquid. This simple definition was our starting point.

But we had other considerations as well. We did not want an overly acidic sauce or an extremely rich sauce, preferring instead something flavorful but lighter and more modern. We were also keen on developing a recipe that could be put together as quickly and simply as possible, making it a candidate for weeknight cooking. This would mean shortening cooking times and using the minimum number of pans and ingredients. We also wanted to make sure that the skin was appealing, which would require sautéing; otherwise we would opt for skinless pieces of chicken. Producing moist chicken was also going to be important.

We started off with a blind taste test, choosing the lightest, most promising fricassee recipes we could find. The first was a classic French preparation in which the chicken pieces were lightly sautéed in butter and then simmered in equal amounts of chicken stock and white wine; the dish was then finished with a bit of heavy cream. The resulting sauce was judged too acidic, and the chicken's skin was unappealing. The second recipe was similar to the first except that the cooking liquid was a combination of water and chicken stock. This recipe also called for three large carrots and two large celery stalks. The sauce was thin and vegetal, with a carrot flavor so strong that it was unwelcome. The third recipe, the worst of the lot, called for 45 minutes of cooking in chicken stock, much too long to produce moist meat. After these initial forays, we made three decisions: to use chicken stock rather than water or wine for the poaching liquid, to use a light hand when finishing the sauce with cream, and to exercise a high degree of parsimony when added the remaining ingredients.

Now we were ready to create our own recipe. First, though, we had to decide on a brown or white fricassee, the difference being a matter of whether the chicken is sautéed before being poached. A quick test confirmed that sautéing develops flavor and renders fat from the skin, some of which is used to flavor the sauce. We preferred a full-fledged sauté to the light sauté used in some of the recipes selected for the blind tasting; the higher heat made the skin crispier and the dish more flavorful.

At this point we had a working recipe. A whole chicken is cut up, seasoned liberally with salt and pepper, and sautéed in olive oil and butter. The chicken is then simmered in stock for about 20 minutes and removed from the liquid. Meanwhile, onions and mushrooms are sautéed in a second pan, and a sauce is then made with the poaching liquid, the vegetables, and a bit of heavy cream to finish. We decided to thicken the sauce using a basic roux, which is simply melted butter and flour whisked together over high heat.

The first test of this master recipe produced very good results. The sauce had a nice, rich flavor; by poaching the chicken in stock we had created a wonderful double stock. But there were still some problems. The sauce was a bit too fatty, and it was also a bit flat, in need of some bite and contrast. We substituted a half cup of white wine for the same amount of stock, using the wine to deglaze the pan after sautéing the onions and mushrooms. This helped, but we found that an additional squirt of lemon juice just before serving was also necessary for balance. We then tried substituting half-and-half for the cream, a change that made the sauce more balanced as well as lighter. We also tried making the sauce with no dairy. This version was acceptable, but the sauce lacked the silky feeling provided by the half-and-half and did not balance as nicely with the wine and lemon juice.

Because we like diners to have a choice of white or dark meat, we usually buy a whole chicken and cut it up in the test kitchen, but chicken thighs work well, too. You can use skinless chicken parts if you like, but if you do so we suggest that you eliminate the sautéing step, simply starting the recipe by poaching the chicken in the stock. This will result in a very good but somewhat less flavorful dish. We also learned that it was best to let the cooked chicken rest in a covered bowl rather than keeping it warm in the oven. A great deal of liquid escapes from the meat when left in a warm oven, resulting in dry chicken. Finally, be sure to add back to the sauce any accumulated juices from the resting chicken.

Chicken Fricassee with Mushrooms and Onions

SERVES 4

We have divided the task of browning the chicken parts between a Dutch oven and a medium skillet that is later used to sauté the vegetables. This eliminates the need to brown in batches in one pot and shortens the cooking time by about 10 minutes. Dark meat fans can substitute eight bone-in, skin-on thighs for the whole chicken.

1	whole chicken (3 to 4 pounds; see page 162 for guidelines on selecting the best-tasting chicken), cut into 2 wings, 2 drumsticks, and 2 thighs, with breast quartered (see illustrations 1–5 and 7–9 on page 170)
	Salt and ground black pepper
2	tablespoons olive oil
4	tablespoons unsalted butter
2½	cups homemade chicken stock or canned low-sodium chicken broth
1	medium onion, chopped fine
10	ounces white mushrooms, left whole if small, halved if medium, quartered if large
½	cup dry white wine
3	tablespoons flour
1	cup half-and-half
1	teaspoon minced fresh thyme leaves
1½	tablespoons lemon juice
¼	teaspoon freshly grated nutmeg
¼	cup minced fresh parsley leaves

1. Season the chicken with salt and pepper to taste. Heat 1 tablespoon each olive oil and butter in both a large Dutch oven and a medium skillet over medium-high heat. When foam subsides, add the chicken pieces, skin-side down, and cook until well-browned, 4 to 5 minutes on each side. Spoon off all but 2 tablespoons fat from the Dutch oven. Add the chicken from the skillet, arranging pieces in a single layer as much as possible. Add the stock, partially cover, and bring to a boil. Reduce the heat to low and simmer until the chicken is fully cooked, 20 to 25 minutes. Remove the Dutch oven from the heat, transfer the chicken to a bowl, cover the bowl with foil, and set aside.

2. While the chicken is simmering, drain off all but 1 tablespoon fat from the now-empty skillet. Add the onion, mushrooms, and ¼ teaspoon salt and sauté over medium-high heat, stirring occasionally, until the mushroom liquid evaporates and the vegetables begin to brown, 6 to 8 minutes. Add the wine and cook until almost all of the liquid evaporates, 2 to 3 minutes. Transfer the vegetables to a small bowl and set aside.

3. Set the Dutch oven with the chicken cooking liquid back over medium heat. Heat the remaining 2 tablespoons butter in the now-empty skillet over medium heat until foaming. Add the flour and whisk until golden in color, about 1 minute. Add the half-and-half, whisking vigorously until smooth. Immediately whisk this mixture into the hot chicken cooking liquid in the Dutch oven and bring to a boil over medium-high heat. Reduce the heat to medium-low and simmer, stirring frequently, until thickened to the consistency of heavy cream, 6 to 8 minutes.

WHAT IS A FRICASSEE?

The dictionary defines a fricassee as poultry stewed in sauce. This rather spare explanation is not incorrect, but it is less than complete. In the recipe contained in the 1915 edition of *The Fannie Farmer Cookbook,* the chicken is cooked in cream, removed, and a sauce is then made in the pot using chicken stock and additional cream. This method is quite close to the original interpretation of the French fricassee, which, according to *Larousse Gastronomique,* refers to chicken cooked in a white sauce, not merely poached in a liquid. So, at least until recently, a fricassee was poultry stewed in a cream sauce.

As times changed, so did the recipe. James Beard, for example, offers a white fricassee in which he starts by poaching the chicken in water and then makes a white sauce fortified with cream and egg yolks. This is still no recipe for a modern cook. But he also offers a brown fricassee recipe (in a brown fricassee, the chicken is sautéed before poaching) that is significantly lighter, the sauce finished with cream but no eggs. We think this kind of fricassee has the most appeal today.

These days, modern cookbooks usually define a fricassee as chicken poached in stock from which a sauce is then made. The sauce can be merely a reduction, in which the stock is simmered down to a more concentrated state, or it can be enriched with cream or other ingredients.

Stir in the mushroom mixture, thyme, lemon juice, and nutmeg and season with salt and pepper to taste.

4. Add the chicken to the Dutch oven and simmer until heated through, 2 to 3 minutes. Stir in 2 tablespoons parsley. Transfer the chicken pieces to serving or individual plates. Spoon the sauce over the chicken and sprinkle with remaining parsley. Serve immediately.

➤ VARIATION

Chicken Fricassee with Peas and Carrots
Follow the recipe for Chicken Fricassee with Mushrooms and Onions, substituting 1 small carrot, diced small, for the mushrooms. Sauté until the vegetables begin to brown, 3 to 4 minutes. Reduce the heat to low, add wine, cover, and cook until the carrots are tender, 10 to 12 minutes. Stir in ½ cup thawed frozen peas, increase the heat to medium-high, and cook until almost all of the liquid evaporates, 1 to 2 minutes. Transfer to a small bowl; set aside. Continue with the recipe, substituting peas and carrots for the mushroom mixture in step 3.

COUNTRY CAPTAIN CHICKEN

FOLKLORE ABOUT COUNTRY CAPTAIN CHICKEN abounds. Some claim that a sea captain toting spices brought the recipe from India in the early 1800s. The captain is said to have introduced the recipe (and the necessary spices) to residents of Savannah, Georgia, which was then an important shipping port for the spice trade. Others say it is named for the captain of Indian troops (called country troops) who served the dish to British soldiers, also in the 1800s.

Whatever its origin, it is universally recognized as a favorite of President Franklin D. Roosevelt. In the 1940s, he enjoyed the stew at the Little White House at Warm Springs, Georgia, where he underwent treatment for paralysis. He liked it so much that he instructed his chef to serve it to Gen. George Patton when he visited the Little White House.

It is understandable that the comforting, curried flavor of country captain was such a favorite of F.D.R. The chicken dish is at once spicy, sweet, and fragrant, but not overpoweringly so. Almost all recipes call for tomatoes, garlic, onions, green peppers, curry powder, and raisins or currants, and cooks vary the dish with additional spices. With its playful name, colorful look, and bright flavors, it has become a well-known dish, particularly in Georgia and other parts of the South.

Before beginning our tests, we narrowed the field a bit by choosing to make the stew with chicken thighs. While some recipes call for cut-up whole chickens, we opted to use thighs only—their dark, rich meat is flavorful and well suited to stewing. After making this decision, we prepared three different versions of the recipe. The differences between the three were significant.

The first recipe intrigued us with its unusual additions of bacon and orange juice, but tasters found it unbalanced in flavor. The bacon took over, and the orange juice was lost behind the curry powder. The stewing liquid reduced during cooking but was still quite thin—not very stewlike. In this recipe, raisins appeared as a garnish, but tasters agreed that the raisins were more pleasant when plumped while stewing rather than added at the table. The second recipe was the simplest of the three, made with the most basic of ingredients, and it left tasters wanting more flavor, sweetness, and spice. We liked the appearance, texture, and taste of the third recipe. The tender bites of stewed chicken, raisins, mango, and tomato with a final sprinkling of parsley won us over. The addition of flour made for a nicely thickened sauce. Another advantage of this recipe was that it removed the chicken skin after browning, while both of the other recipes left the skin on. Tasters unilaterally disliked chicken skin in the stew. The soft, flabby skin was always left behind, and stews made with the skin on were described as greasy. The technique of quickly cooking the thighs with the skin on and later removing it proved best.

Many of the recipes that we looked at did not specify a type of curry powder, though varieties of curry are infinite. We tested standard yellow curry powder (the kind most frequently spotted on supermarket shelves) against hotter Madras-style curry powder as well as a homemade curry powder, ground just before cooking. Tasters

GARNISHES FOR COUNTRY
CAPTAIN CHICKEN

These garnishes are optional, but they are an easy way to
dress up this stew. Use them singly or in combination.

· ½ cup sliced almonds, toasted
· 1 banana, peeled and cut into ¼-inch dice
· ½ cup sweetened shredded coconut
· 1 Granny Smith apple, cored and cut into ¼-inch dice
  and tossed in lemon juice
· 4 to 5 scallions, sliced thin

preferred the Madras-style curry powder for the
heat it offered up in contrast with the sweet, round
flavors of the stew. The stew made with standard
curry powder was bland in comparison. The one
made with homemade curry powder was good, but
it didn't seem worth the effort given how much we
liked the version made with the premixed Madras-
style curry.

During testing, tasters consistently enjoyed the
traditional garnish of toasted almonds. Since the stew
looks and tastes like party food, we also tested a host
of traditional curry garnishes to serve along with it.
Mango chutney is suggested in many recipes, but we
found it too strong in flavor. Bananas, shredded
coconut, green apple, and scallions complemented
the sweet/hot flavors of the stew perfectly.

Country Captain Chicken

SERVES 6

*For this recipe, we like to use Madras-style curry powder,
which is hotter than standard curry powder. Toasted almonds
are a traditional garnish, but it's fun to pass a variety of
garnishes at the table (for other ideas see left). Serve with
long-grain rice.*

8	bone-in chicken thighs (about 3 pounds), trimmed of excess skin and fat
	Salt and ground black pepper
1	teaspoon vegetable oil
2	large onions, chopped coarse
1	medium green bell pepper, stemmed, seeded, and chopped coarse
2	medium cloves garlic, minced
1½	tablespoons sweet paprika
1	tablespoon Madras-style curry powder
¼	teaspoon cayenne pepper
3	tablespoons flour
1½	cups homemade chicken stock or canned low-sodium chicken broth
1	(14½-ounce) can diced tomatoes
1	bay leaf
½	teaspoon dried thyme
½	cup raisins
1	ripe mango, peeled, pitted, and cut into ¼-inch dice (see the illustrations below)
¼	cup minced fresh parsley leaves

HANDLING A MANGO

1. Mangoes are notoriously hard
to peel, owing to their odd
shape and slippery texture. We
start by removing a thin slice
from one end of the mango so it
can sit flat on a work surface.

2. Hold the mango cut-side
down and remove the skin in
thin strips with a sharp paring
knife or serrated knife, working
from top to bottom.

3. Once the peel has been
removed, cut down along one
side of the flat pit to remove the
flesh from one side of the
mango. Do the same thing on
the other side of the pit.

4. Trim around the pit to
remove any remaining flesh. The
flesh can now be sliced or diced
as desired.

1. Adjust an oven rack to the lower-middle position and heat the oven to 300 degrees. Season the chicken liberally with salt and pepper to taste. Heat the oil in a large Dutch oven over medium-high heat until shimmering but not smoking, about 2 minutes. Add four chicken thighs, skin-side down, and cook, not moving them until the skin is crisp and well-browned, about 5 minutes. Using tongs, flip the chicken and brown on the second side, about 5 minutes longer. Transfer the browned chicken to a large plate. Brown the remaining chicken thighs, transfer them to the plate, and set aside. When the chicken has cooled, remove and discard the skin. With a spoon, remove and discard all but 1 tablespoon fat from the pan.

2. Add the onions and bell pepper to the empty Dutch oven and sauté over medium heat until softened, 4 to 5 minutes. Stir in the garlic, paprika, curry powder, and cayenne and cook until the spices are fragrant, about 30 seconds. Stir in the flour and cook for 1 to 2 minutes. Add the stock, scraping up any browned bits stuck to the pot. Add the tomatoes, bay leaf, thyme, raisins, and mango, and bring to a boil. Reduce the heat and simmer for 10 minutes. Add the chicken pieces and accumulated juices, submerging the chicken in the liquid. Return to a simmer, cover, and place the pot in the oven. Cook until the chicken is done, about 30 minutes. Remove the pot from the oven. (The stew can be covered and refrigerated for up to 3 days. Bring to a simmer over medium-low heat before serving.)

3. Stir in the parsley, discard the bay leaf, and adjust the seasonings. Serve immediately, with garnishes if desired.

ROAST TURKEY

IS IT POSSIBLE TO ROAST A TURKEY PERFECTLY? Usually juicy breast meat comes at a price—shocking pink legs and thighs. You have some leeway with the dark meat, which is almost impossible to dry out during normal roasting times. The problem is that the breast, which is exposed to direct heat and finishes cooking at a lower temperature, becomes parched, while the legs and thighs take their time creeping to doneness. Nearly every roasting method in existence tries to compensate for this; very few succeed.

We tested dozens of different methods for roasting a turkey, from traditional to idiosyncratic. Our goals were to end up with an attractive bird, to determine the ideal internal temperature, and to find a method that would finish both white and dark meat simultaneously.

Our first roasting experiments used the method most frequently promoted by the National Turkey Federation, the U.S. Department of Agriculture (USDA), and legions of cookbook authors and recipe writers. This method features a moderately low roasting temperature of 325 degrees, a breast-up bird, and an open pan. We tried this method twice, basting one turkey and leaving the other alone. The basted turkey acquired a beautifully tanned skin, while the unbasted bird remained quite pale. Both were cooked to 170 degrees in the leg/thigh. Despite the fact that this was 10 degrees lower than recommended by the USDA and most producers, the breasts still registered a throat-catchingly dry 180 degrees.

We quickly determined that almost all turkeys roasted in the traditional breast-up manner produced breast meat that was 10 degrees ahead of the leg/thigh meat (tenting the breast with heavy-duty foil was the exception; read on). Because white meat is ideal at 160 degrees, and dark thigh meat just loses its last shades of pink at about 170 degrees, you might conclude, as we did, that roasting turkeys with their breasts up is a losing proposition.

We also discovered that stuffing a bird makes overcooked meat more likely. Because it slows interior cooking (our tests showed a difference of nearly 30 degrees in internal temperature after an hour in the oven), stuffing means longer oven times, which can translate to bone-dry surface meat. We eventually developed a method for roasting a stuffed turkey (see page 193), but if the turkey is your priority, we recommend cooking the dressing separately.

Of all the breast-up methods, tenting the bird's breast and upper legs with foil, as suggested by numerous authors, worked the best. The foil deflects some of the oven's heat, reducing the ultimate temperature differential between white and dark meat from 10 to 6 degrees. The bird is roasted at a consistent 325-degree temperature, and during the last 45 minutes of roasting the foil is removed, allowing enough time for lovely browning. If you're partial to open-pan roasting and don't care to follow the technique we developed, try the foil shield; it certainly ran second in our tests.

Amidst all these failures and near-successes, some real winners did emerge. Early on, we became fans of brining turkey in a saltwater bath before roasting. When we first removed the brined turkey from the refrigerator, we found a beautiful, milky-white bird. When roasted, the texture of the breast was different from that of the other birds we had cooked; the meat

INGREDIENTS: Turkey

Many people purchase a turkey just once during the year. Thanksgiving, of course, would be that occasion. When the moment of purchase arrives, however, the buyer may be somewhat befuddled. The options are many—this brand or that brand, fresh or frozen, flavor-enhanced or not. Then there is the growing number of product disclaimers to weed through—no antibiotics, no animal byproducts, minimal processing, and on and on it goes.

Everyone has priorities and standards when it comes to purchasing turkey. But what it all comes down to for most every cook is whether friends or relatives drive away after the big meal murmuring "That was the best turkey I've ever had" or "Thank goodness there was plenty of gravy and cranberry sauce."

To try to ensure the former response, we decided to do a blind turkey tasting. We corralled as many turkeys as we have ovens and cooked them all up. We roasted them using exactly the same method (starting breast-side down in a 400 degree oven, then rotating to one side, then the other side, and finally back to breast-side up to finish) and determined doneness at exactly the same internal temperature (175 degrees measured at the thigh). We then held a blind tasting, rating each of the nine birds for flavor, texture, and overall likeability.

Because turkey is for the most part a regionally distributed product, few national brands are available. Consequently, our lineup consisted primarily of brands found on the East Coast. We selected them carefully, however, in order to represent the range of the types of turkeys found in stores nationwide. This included birds that were fresh and frozen, flavor-enhanced (or "basted," to use the industry term) and minimally processed.

We have found that the best way to cook a turkey is to brine it first—that is, to immerse the turkey overnight in a strong solution of water and salt. Recognizing that not everyone brines their turkey, though, we did not brine any of the turkeys for the tasting. But a few of the turkeys in the tasting came prepared in a manner that is similar to brining. These had either been injected with a salt solution or, in the case of the kosher bird, rubbed with salt, left to rest so that the salt penetrates, and then rinsed during processing.

All the turkeys in the tasting that were basted or rubbed with salt as part of their manufacturer's processing method were remarkably moist and tender and placed high in our ratings. The reason? As the basting solution penetrates the turkey, the salt unravels the coiled proteins in the uncooked muscle, trapping water between the protein strands. As the meat cooks, the proteins set and form a barrier that prevents moisture from leaking out. The salt also helps to enhance the natural flavors of the turkey.

Commercially basted turkeys can also "fool" you into thinking a turkey is juicier than it is. This is because the basting solutions often contain some kind of fat—usually butter or oil. "In small amounts, fat makes the salivary glands produce saliva, which tricks you into thinking there's more juiciness in the meat," says Dr. Sarah G. Birkhold, assistant professor of poultry science at Texas A & M University.

While the success of the basted and kosher turkeys was not unexpected, what did surprise us was that tasters found no discernible difference between frozen and fresh birds. That came as no surprise to Birkhold, however. She explained that improved technology permits manufacturers to "flash freeze" birds in freezers where temperatures range around 30 degrees below zero and cold air is blasted at about 60 miles per hour. This prevents the development of large ice crystals that can damage the tissue, causing moisture loss. Home freezers, of course, cannot replicate this process. So if you are buying a turkey in advance of Thanksgiving, you are much better off buying a frozen one than buying and freezing a fresh one.

While prebasted birds might conveniently deliver juicy, tender meat, we still advocate brining a turkey on your own whenever possible. As our results show, a standard U.S. Department of Agriculture (USDA) grade A turkey is a good choice; it can only get better with brining. Note, however, that when brining at home, you should avoid kosher or "basted" birds, which have already been treated with salt. A final advantage to brining your turkey at home is that you can avoid the additives often contained in basted birds.

was firm and juicy at the same time. And the turkey tasted fully seasoned; others had required a bite of skin with the meat to achieve the same effect. We experimented with the brining time and found that 8 hours in the refrigerator produces a nicely seasoned turkey without overly salty pan juices. Brining was our first real breakthrough; we now believe it to be essential to achieving perfect taste and texture. But we had yet to discover the way to roast.

Our most successful attempt at achieving equal temperatures in leg and breast came when we borrowed James Beard's technique of turning the turkey as it roasts. In this method, the bird begins breast-side down on a V-rack, then spends equal time on each of its sides before being turned breast-side

up. The V-rack is important not just to hold the turkey in place but also to elevate it, affording it some protection from the heat of the roasting pan. This combination of rack and technique produced a turkey with a breast temperature that ran only a few degrees behind the leg temperature.

Because we were using smaller turkeys than Beard had used, we had to fine-tune his method. Large turkeys spend enough time in the oven to brown at 350 degrees; our turkeys were in the 12-pound range and were cooking in as little as two hours, yielding quite pale skin. Clearly, we needed higher heat.

Reviewing our notes, we noticed that the basted birds were usually the evenly browned, beautiful ones.

PREPARING A ROAST TURKEY

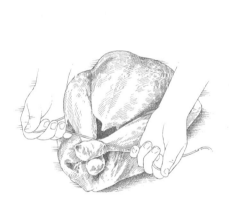

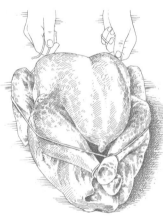

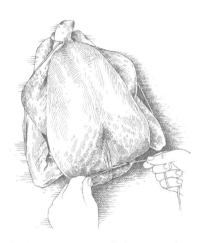

1. Using the center of a 5-foot length of kitchen twine, tie the legs together at the ankles.

2. Run the twine around the thighs and under the wings on both sides of the bird and pull it tight.

3. Keeping the twine pulled snug, tie a firm knot around the excess flesh at the neck of the bird. Snip off the excess twine.

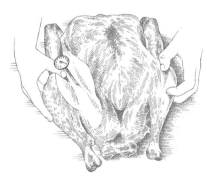

4. When using an instant-read thermometer, make sure that you measure the temperature of the thickest part of the thigh.

5. This cutaway drawing shows the actual point to which the tip of the thermometer should penetrate.

So we turned up the heat to 400 degrees, basted faithfully, and got what we wanted. In an effort to streamline, we tried to skip the leg-up turns, roasting only breast-side down, then breast-side up. But in order for the turkey to brown all over, these two extra turns were necessary. Brining, turning, and basting are work, yes, but the combination produces the best turkey we've ever had.

During our first few tests, we discovered that filling the cavity with aromatic herbs and vegetables made for a subtle but perceptible difference in flavor. This was especially noticeable in the inner meat of

EQUIPMENT: Electric Carving Knives

Often overlooked since their heyday in the 1960s, electric knives remain eminently useful for cutting every course of a holiday meal, from appetizers right on through to dessert. Just to prove this point, we gathered seven models in a single sweep through local discount and hardware stores and put them through their paces on a variety of foods.

Electric knives operate by the quick mechanized sawing action of two serrated blades. Clipped together at one end, the blades fit so snugly against each other that they function, in effect, as a single blade. With the two blades thus connected, you insert their bases into the motor unit (which also serves as the handle), switch on the motor, and let the slices fall where they may.

Contemporary electric knives are supposed to offer improved comfort and balance and more efficient performance than their predecessors. To see if this was really the case, we got our hands on a 1960s vintage electric knife, a pristine Riviera Electric Slicing Knife. At 26.6 ounces, the Riviera weighed a full 6 ounces more than our leading knife, making it much harder to use. In addition, its balance was terrible because the motor was positioned at the far rear of the unit, making the grip much less comfortable than any of the current models in our lineup.

This group included units from Black & Decker, White Westinghouse, Rival, Hamilton Beach, Sanyo, Toastmaster, and Krups. We tested each of them by carving large holiday roasts (stuffed pork loin and roast turkey, in our case) and by serving up a number of delicate dishes.

We quickly came to some general conclusions about the usefulness of these knives. We found, for example, that they are better suited for uniformly shaped roasts than for poultry. None of our contestants was nimble enough to negotiate the curves and inner spaces of a whole roasted turkey, so we judged them on how well they sliced the breast alone. We used our preferred carving strategy of removing the breast as a whole, laying it flat on the carving board, and cutting it crosswise into thin slices, each with a small piece of crisp skin still attached. Just try that with a regular knife.

Where electric knives really excel, however, is in cutting foods made up of different layers with distinctly firm and soft textures. Consider pecan pie, for example. The top layer is all crunchy, caramelized nuts. Beneath that is a soft, custardy gel. In a well-executed slice of pecan pie, the soft bottom layer should not become mashed and oozy because of the pressure exerted to cut through the firm, nutty, top layer. If everything goes right, both layers will remain separate and defined so that each slice has a crisp, neat presentation. Just try that with a regular knife.

Other delicate, layered foods with the same dynamic at play include quesadillas (like a Mexican grilled cheese sandwich made with tortillas) and roulade, a rolled cake with a soft, creamy filling. We tested the knives on them all, and in every case they outperformed nonelectric knives. Another quick point: For a holiday party, when presentation really counts, there's nothing like a good electric knife for cutting small, uniform, neat pieces of appetizers such as a savory phyllo pastry.

Although most of the electric knives we tested proved very useful, there were clear differences among them. To begin with, some were far more comfortable to use than others. There were two different grip configurations among the knives. The Hamilton Beach, Toastmaster, and Sanyo all had loop handles molded into the top of their motor units. On the Black & Decker, White Westinghouse, Rival, and Krups knives, the motor unit itself served as the grip. This arrangement allowed users to choke up on the grip, which led to a better feeling of balance—and therefore improved control—while cutting. Without exception, all testers preferred the more "natural feel" of the integrated handles in this group, in part because the way you hold them comes closer to the way you hold a regular knife.

The placement of the power switch was another design consideration. All but one of the knives with our preferred grip, the Krups, had trigger-type power switches located on the bottom of their handles. Users favored this position over top-mounted power buttons, especially when the top-mounted buttons were positioned near the blade-release buttons, which could lead to some dangerous confusion. The knives with both integrated handles and trigger-type power switches—Black & Decker, White Westinghouse, and Rival—were our top three picks.

the leg and thigh; turkeys with hollow cavities, by contrast, tasted bland. Roasted alongside the turkey, the same combination of carrot, celery, onion, and thyme also did wonders for the pan juices.

Best Roast Turkey
SERVES 10 TO 12
We prefer to roast small turkeys, no more than 14 pounds gross weight, because they cook more evenly than large birds. If you must cook a large bird, see the variation below.

4	cups kosher salt or 2 cups table salt
4	cups sugar
1	turkey (12 to 14 pounds gross weight; see page 188 for guidelines on selecting a turkey), rinsed thoroughly; giblets, neck, and tailpiece removed and reserved to make gravy (see page 192)
3	medium onions, chopped coarse
1½	medium carrots, chopped coarse
1½	stalks celery, chopped coarse
6	sprigs thyme
3	tablespoons unsalted butter, melted

1. Dissolve the salt and sugar in 2 gallons of cold water in a large stockpot or clean bucket. Add the turkey and refrigerate or set in a very cool spot (40 degrees or colder) for 8 hours.

2. Remove the turkey from the brine and pat dry the inside and outside with paper towels. Place the turkey on a meat rack (or sturdy flat rack) set over a rimmed baking sheet. Place the turkey in the refrigerator, uncovered, and air-dry for at least 8 hours or overnight.

3. Adjust an oven rack to the lowest position and heat the oven to 400 degrees. Toss one-third of the onion, carrot, celery, and thyme with 1 tablespoon of the melted butter and place this mixture in the body cavity. Bring the turkey legs together and perform a simple truss (see the illustrations on page 194).

4. Scatter the remaining vegetables and thyme over a shallow roasting pan. Pour 1 cup water over the vegetables. Set a V-rack in the pan. Brush the entire breast side of the turkey with half of the remaining butter, then place the turkey, breast-side down, on the V-rack. Brush the entire backside of the turkey with the remaining butter.

5. Roast for 45 minutes. Remove the pan from

oven (close the oven door); baste with the juices from the pan. With a wad of paper towels in each hand, turn the turkey, leg/thigh-side up. If the liquid in the pan has totally evaporated, add another ½ cup water. Return the turkey to the oven and roast for 15 minutes. Remove the turkey from the oven again, baste, and again use paper towels to turn the other leg/thigh-side up; roast for another 15 minutes. Remove the turkey from the oven one last time, baste, and turn it breast-side up; roast until the breast registers about 165 degrees and the thigh registers 170 to 175 degrees on an instant-read thermometer, 30 to 45 minutes (see illustrations 4 and 5 on page 189). Remove the turkey from the pan and let it rest until ready to carve, at least 20 minutes. Serve with gravy.

VARIATION
Large Roast Turkey
SERVES 18 TO 20
Smaller turkeys cook faster and are generally more tender, but sometimes you need a bigger bird for a large holiday crowd. By tinkering with our original recipe, we were able to produce a beautiful large turkey without sacrificing juiciness and flavor. When roasting a large turkey, it's not necessary to roast the bird on each side.

Follow the recipe for Best Roast Turkey, roasting a 18- to 20-pound turkey breast-side down in 250-degree oven for 3 hours, basting every hour. Then turn breast-side up and roast another hour, basting once or twice. Increase the oven temperature to 400 degrees and roast until done, about 1 hour longer.

GRAVY

TO A TRADITIONALIST, THE THOUGHT OF A gravyless Thanksgiving dinner is culinary heresy. Good gravy is no mere condiment; it's the tie that binds. But too often gravy is a last-minute affair, thrown together without much thought. The result: either dull, greasy gravy or thin, acidic pan juices that are one-dimensional, lacking the body and stature that we expect from a good American gravy. So we set out to produce a rich, complex sauce with as much advance preparation as possible to avoid that last-minute time pressure, when space is at a premium and potatoes need to be mashed, turkey sliced, water goblets filled, and candles lit.

We began our tests by experimenting with thickeners. In a blind taste test we tried four different options, including cornstarch, beurre manié (a paste made from equal parts by weight of flour and butter), and two flour-based roux, one regular (a mixture of melted butter and flour stirred together over heat) and one dark (in which the butter-flour paste is cooked until it is dark brown).

Although most tasters were pretty sure before the tasting began that the cornstarch-thickened gravy would have inferior texture and flavor, it actually turned out to be quite good. Admittedly, it was a bit thinner in body and more acidic in flavor than the roux-based sauces, but it was acceptable. Overall, though, the dark roux proved to be the best thickener. It added a subtle depth and complexity to the sauce not found with the other options. A roux-based gravy can also be made ahead of time, a slight advantage over the cornstarch and beurre manié options, which require last-minute whisking.

To the dark roux, we added turkey stock made from the neck and giblets. Cooking the sauce over low heat for half an hour or more helped develop the flavor, but the resulting gravy was still pale and lacked punch. We then tried using a bulb baster to remove fat from the roasting turkey and using this as the base for the roux, instead of the butter. This tasted fine but was not an improvement over the butter version. We soon discovered, however, that the trick was to take this basic brown sauce—prethickened—and enrich it with pan drippings.

Pan drippings are the source of gravy's allure and also its difficulties. That gorgeous mahogany-colored goo that congeals at the bottom of a roasting pan is one of the best-tasting things on earth, a carnivore's ambrosia. But we found that to get dark brown pan drippings with a complex range of flavors, you need to roast your turkey over aromatic vegetables—onions, carrots, and celery—as well as some fresh thyme sprigs. We also found it necessary to keep an eye on the pan, adding water whenever things started looking too dry.

After deglazing the pan with wine and simmering off the alcohol, we strained the resulting wine sauce into the roux, smashing the remaining herbs and vegetables into the strainer with a wooden spoon to wring the taste out of them. The result was worth the effort. After a quick simmer and an adjustment of the seasonings, we had an intense and richly flavored sauce that had the familiarity and comfort of traditional American gravy but hinted at the sophistication of a fine French brown sauce.

Giblet Pan Gravy
MAKES ABOUT 6 CUPS

The gravy is best made over several hours. Complete step 1 while the turkey is brining. Continue with step 2 once the bird is in the oven. Start step 3 once the bird has been removed from the oven and is resting on a carving board.

1	tablespoon vegetable oil
	Reserved turkey giblets (heart and gizzard), neck, and tailpiece
1	onion, unpeeled and chopped
1½	quarts homemade turkey or chicken stock or 1 quart canned low-sodium chicken broth plus 2 cups water
2	sprigs thyme
8	stems parsley
3	tablespoons unsalted butter
¼	cup flour
1	cup dry white wine
	Salt and ground black pepper

1. Heat the oil in a stockpot; add the giblets, neck, and tail, then sauté until golden and fragrant, about 5 minutes. Add the onion; continue to sauté until softened, 3 to 4 minutes longer. Reduce the heat to low; cover and cook until the turkey and onion release their juices, about 20 minutes. Add the stock and herbs, bring to a boil, then adjust the heat to low. Simmer, uncovered, skimming any impurities that may rise to the surface, until the broth is rich and flavorful, about 30 minutes longer. Strain the broth (you should have about 5 cups) and reserve the neck, heart, and gizzard. When cool enough to handle, shred the neck meat, remove the gristle from the gizzard, then dice the reserved heart and gizzard. Refrigerate the giblets and broth until ready to use.

2. While the turkey is roasting, return the reserved turkey broth to a simmer. Heat the butter in a large heavy-bottomed saucepan over medium-low heat. Vigorously whisk in the flour (the roux will froth and then thin out again). Cook slowly, stirring constantly, until nutty brown and fragrant, 10 to 15 minutes. Vigorously whisk all but 1 cup of hot broth into the roux. Bring to a boil, then continue to simmer until the gravy is lightly thickened and very flavorful, about 30 minutes longer. Set aside until the turkey is done.

3. When the turkey has been transferred to a carving board to rest, spoon out and discard as much fat as possible from the roasting pan, leaving the caramelized herbs and vegetables. Place the roasting pan over two burners at medium-high heat (if the drippings are not dark brown, cook, stirring constantly, until they caramelize.) Return the gravy to

a simmer. Add the wine to the roasting pan of caramelized vegetables, scraping up any browned bits with a wooden spoon and boiling until reduced by half, about 5 minutes. Add the remaining 1 cup broth, then strain the pan juices into the gravy, pressing as much juice as possible out of the vegetables. Stir the giblets into the gravy; return to a boil. Adjust the seasonings, adding salt and pepper to taste if necessary. Serve with carved turkey.

EQUIPMENT: Roasting Pan

Roasting pans can cost $2 or $200, or even more once you start talking about copper. Most roasting pans are made of aluminum because it heats quickly. Some pans are lined with stainless steel, which is easier to clean than aluminum. We find that material is less important than size, depth, and weight.

A roasting pan should be large enough to hold a turkey or leg of lamb. A 9 by 13-inch baking pan is fine for a chicken, but you will need something considerably larger for most roasts. For most recipes in this book, including turkey, a 12 by 15-inch pan will work just fine.

In addition to size, you want a roasting pan that is deep enough to keep fat from splattering onto the walls of the oven. Since many roasts are cooked on racks, a shallow pan may prove problematic. On the other hand, a really deep pan will discourage browning. We find a depth of 2½ inches to be ideal.

We also prefer roasting pans with handles, which make it easy to lift the pan in and out of the oven. Last, you should consider buying a roasting pan with a heavy bottom. Some recipes, including our recipe for turkey with gravy, end by placing the empty pan on top of the stove for deglazing. A thin pan may buckle or scorch.

We know that many cooks rely on disposable aluminum pans for holiday roasts and birds. They are large and cheap and require no cleanup. The downside is that these pans are flimsy and can fall apart. If you insist on using them, fit two pans together to support heavy roasts and birds. Also, buy disposable pans with handles and support the bottom of the filled pan when lifting it.

ROAST TURKEY WITH STUFFING

THERE IS SOMETHING UNDENIABLY FESTIVE about a stuffed roast turkey, and for many people the holidays just aren't the holidays without one. Every year, though, we are warned that for health and safety reasons, turkeys are best roasted unstuffed. Despite these warnings, many cooks continue to stuff their holiday bird. For the sake of flavorful, moist, turkey infused stuffing, these cooks sacrifice perfectly cooked breast meat and risk food-borne illness from underdone stuffing.

There must be a way, we thought, to safely and successfully roast a stuffed turkey, keeping the breast meat succulent and ensuring that the stuffing is fully cooked. Before we began, we decided to limit our turkey to a maximum of 15 pounds, because it is just too difficult to safely stuff and roast larger birds.

Our objectives were clear. For health reasons, we wanted to find a means of minimizing the amount of time our stuffing would spend in the danger zone of 40 to 140 degrees, in which bacteria grows most quickly. In addition, we sought to coordinate the cooking of the breast and the thigh. We knew that the breast meat cooks faster than the thigh by about 10 degrees, and because the breast is done at 165 degrees and the thigh at 170-175, this usually results in choke-quality white meat. Introducing stuffing into this equation, we thought, was just asking for trouble; testing had demonstrated that stuffing the turkey slows interior cooking significantly, requiring longer cooking times and producing even drier surface meat.

After a few introductory tests, it became clear that this was exactly the problem we would face. Using high heat or low, the stuffing lagged behind the meat, remaining 5 degrees shy of the 165 we were aiming for, even when both breast and thigh were about 15 degrees higher than we wanted them.

In desperation, we toyed with the idea of sticking hot skewers or a ball of foil into the stuffing in the cavity to help conduct some heat. Suddenly, it occurred to us that if we heated the stuffing for a few minutes in the microwave before filling the cavity, we might give it a head start on cooking. This technique worked for roasting Cornish hens, so why wouldn't it work for a turkey?

We tested the prewarmed stuffing hypothesis on a turkey that we roasted at a constant 325 degrees. We heated the stuffing in the microwave to about 120 degrees before stuffing the bird. We opted to roast the bird one hour breast-side down, one hour on each side, then finish with the breast up. As we monitored the temperature of the stuffing, the outlook seemed grim. The stuffing temperature dropped and bottomed out in the first hour at 89 degrees. Gradually it climbed back up and hit 140 degrees, also free of the danger zone, in 2¼ hours, the best time yet. Most impressively, this time we were waiting for the thigh to finish cooking, not the stuffing! The breast was long gone at 178 degrees, but we knew we were onto something. This was an enormous improvement over the 3½ hours it had taken for the cold stuffing used in previous tests to dawdle its way to 165, while the breast and thigh meat overcooked.

We pursued the prewarming technique and found that the stuffing usually hits its lowest temperature in the bird at the one-hour mark, dropping approximately 20 degrees. In the microwave we were able to heat it to 130 degrees; starting at such a high temperature helps it get out of the danger zone in 2¼ to 2¾ hours. We checked with food scientists to see if this half an hour differential in times presented a bacterial growth problem. We were told no, since very little occurs above 110 degrees. No longer did we have to wait for the stuffing to finish cooking while the breast and thigh overcooked.

With the stuffing issue resolved, we focused on the best way to roast the turkey. It had become clear to us that high heat and even constant moderate heat wreak havoc on the turkey, resulting in parched breast meat. The low-and-slow method is, well, too low and slow—not a safe method for a stuffed turkey. A combination of low heat with high or moderate heat seemed to be the answer.

We also determined that no matter what the cooking temperature, roasting the bird breast-side down for only one hour was not sufficient. In this position, the breast is shielded and its cooking slowed while the thighs are exposed to the heat needed to speed their cooking. If we rotated the breast up after one or even two hours, the breast was guaranteed to overcook in the remaining time. We abandoned roasting with each leg side up to afford the breast more "downtime."

We then roasted two turkeys, both started breast-side down. One cooked at a low 250 degrees for

STUFFING A TURKEY

1. Use a measuring cup to place the preheated stuffing in the cavity of the bird. Remember, it's imperative that the stuffing be heated before it is placed in the bird.

2. To keep the stuffing in the cavity, use metal skewers (or cut bamboo skewers) and thread them through the skin on both sides of the cavity.

3. Center a 2-foot piece of kitchen twine on the top skewer and then cross the twine as you wrap each end of the string around and under the skewers. Loosely tie the legs together with another short piece of twine.

4. Flip bird over onto its breast. Stuff the neck cavity loosely with approximately 1 cup of stuffing. Pull the skin flap over and use a skewer to pin the flap to the turkey.

three hours, was rotated breast-side up, cooked for an additional 15 minutes, and then the temperature was increased to 400 degrees. The breast overcooked as the thigh crept up to 175 degrees. The other turkey we roasted at 400 degrees for one hour, reduced the oven temperature to 250 degrees, flipped it breast-side up after a total of three hours, then turned the heat back up to 400 degrees and roasted until done. This bird finished as close to perfection as possible: 163 degrees in the breast, 175 degrees in the thigh, and 165 degrees in the stuffing. Clearly, the thigh meat benefited from the initial blast of heat. The only disappointment was the spotty browning of the skin. A few minor adjustments to the time spent breast-side up, and we arrived at a safe, perfectly roasted stuffed turkey.

Roast Stuffed Turkey

SERVES 10 TO 12

A 12- to 15-pound turkey will accommodate about half of the stuffing. Bake the remainder in a casserole dish while the bird rests before carving.

4	cups kosher or 2 cups table salt
4	cups sugar
1	turkey (12 to 15 pounds gross weight; see page 188 for guidelines on selecting a turkey), rinsed thoroughly; giblets, neck, and tailpiece removed and reserved to make gravy (see page 192)
2	medium onions, chopped coarse
1	medium carrot, chopped coarse
1	stalk celery, chopped coarse
4	sprigs thyme
12	cups prepared stuffing (pages 196–198)
3	tablespoons unsalted butter, plus extra to grease casserole dish and foil
1/4	cup homemade turkey or chicken stock or canned low-sodium chicken broth

1. Dissolve the salt and sugar in 2 gallons of cold water in a large stockpot or clean bucket. Add the turkey and refrigerate or set in a very cool spot (40 degrees or colder) for 8 hours.

2. Remove the turkey from the brine and pat dry inside and out with paper towels; set aside. Place the turkey on a meat rack (or sturdy flat rack) set over a rimmed baking sheet. Place the turkey in the refrigerator, uncovered, and air-dry for at least 8 hours or overnight.

3. Adjust an oven rack to the lowest position and heat the oven to 400 degrees. Scatter the onions, carrot, celery, and thyme over a shallow roasting pan. Pour 1 cup water over the vegetables. Set a V-rack in the pan.

4. Place half of the stuffing in a buttered medium casserole dish, dot the surface with 1 tablespoon butter, cover with buttered foil, and refrigerate until ready to use. Microwave the remaining stuffing on full power, stirring two or three times, until very hot (120 to 130 degrees), 6 to 8 minutes (if you can handle the stuffing with your hands, it is not hot enough). Spoon 4 to 5 cups of stuffing into the turkey cavity until very loosely packed (see illustration 1 on page 194). Secure the skin flap over the cavity opening with turkey lacers or skewers (see illustrations 2 and 3 on page 194). Melt the remaining 2 tablespoons butter. Tuck the wings behind the back, brush the entire breast side with half of the melted butter, then place the turkey breast-side down. Fill the neck cavity with the remaining heated stuffing and secure the skin flap over the opening (see illustration 4 on page 194). Place on the V-rack and brush the back with the remaining butter.

5. Roast 1 hour, then reduce the temperature to 250 degrees and roast 2 hours longer, adding more water if the pan becomes dry. Remove the pan from the oven (close the oven door) and, with a wad of paper towels in each hand, turn the bird breast-side up and baste (the temperature of the breast should be 145 to 150 degrees). Increase the oven temperature to 400 degrees; continue roasting until the breast registers about 165 degrees, the thigh registers 170 to 175 degrees, and the stuffing registers 165 degrees on an instant-read thermometer, 1 to 1½ hours longer. Remove the turkey from the oven and let rest until ready to carve.

6. Add ¼ cup stock to the dish of reserved stuffing, replace the foil, and bake at 400 degrees until hot throughout, about 20 to 25 minutes. Remove the foil; continue to bake until the stuffing forms a golden brown crust, about 15 minutes longer.

7. Carve the turkey; serve with stuffing and gravy.

Industry standards developed by the U.S. Department of Agriculture and the National Turkey Federation call for whole birds to be cooked to an internal thigh temperature of 180 to 185 degrees. The breast temperature, according to these standards, should be 170 degrees. However, our kitchen tests showed that no meat is at its best at a temperature of 180 or 185 degrees. And breast meat really tastes best closer to 160 to 165 degrees.

While the USDA might have us believe that the only safe turkey is a dry turkey, this just isn't true. The two main bacterial problems in turkey are salmonella and campylobacter. According to USDA standards, salmonella in meat is killed at 160 degrees, as is campylobacter. Turkey is no different. So why the higher safety standard of 180 degrees?

Part of the problem is that stuffing must reach an internal temperature of 165 degrees to be considered safe. (Carbohydrates such as bread provide a better medium for bacterial growth than do proteins such as meat; hence the extra safety margin of 5 degrees.) The USDA also assumes that most cooks don't own an accurate thermometer.

The final word on poultry safety is this: As long as the temperature on an accurate instant-read thermometer reaches 160 degrees when inserted in several places, all unstuffed meat (including turkey) should be bacteria-free. Dark meat is undercooked at this stage and tastes better at 170 or 175 degrees. With our turning method, the breast will reach about 165 degrees when the leg is done.

A temperature of 165 degrees also guarantees that stuffed turkeys are safe. Bacteria in meat cooked to 180 or 185 degrees is certainly long gone—but so is moistness and flavor.

BREAD STUFFING FOR TURKEY

IN OUR TESTS, WE FOUND THAT DRY BREAD cubes are essential when making stuffing because they do a better job of absorbing seasonings and other flavors than fresh cubes. To dry bread, cut a fresh loaf of French or other white bread into half-inch slices, place the slices in a single layer on baking sheets or cooling racks, and allow the slices to sit out overnight. The next day, cut the slices into half-inch cubes and allow them to dry in a single layer for an additional night.

If you're in a hurry, place half-inch slices of bread in a 225-degree oven for 30 to 40 minutes, or until dried but not browned. Remove the bread from the oven and cut into half-inch cubes. You will need a 1-pound loaf of bread to obtain the 12 cups of bread cubes necessary for the following recipes.

All of these stuffings can be covered and refrigerated for up to one day. Store the mixture in a 9 by 13-inch or comparably sized microwave-safe pan and reheat in a 325-degree oven or microwave until stuffing is heated through before packing it into a bird. Place any stuffing that won't fit in the bird in a greased 8-inch-square baking dish. Drizzle ¼ cup stock over the stuffing, dot with pats of butter, and cover with a piece of foil smeared with butter. Bake in a 400-degree oven for 20 to 25 minutes, remove the foil, and continue to bake until the stuffing forms a golden brown crust, about 15 minutes longer.

Bread Stuffing with Sausage, Pecans, and Dried Apricots

MAKES ABOUT 12 CUPS

High-quality sausage is the key to this recipe. Toast the pecans in a 350-degree oven until fragrant, 6 to 8 minutes.

1	pound sweet Italian sausage, removed from casings and crumbled
6	tablespoons unsalted butter
1	large onion, chopped (about 1½ cups)
4	medium stalks celery, chopped (about 1½ cups)
½	teaspoon each dried sage, dried thyme, and dried marjoram
½	teaspoon ground black pepper
½	cup fresh parsley leaves, chopped fine
2	cups pecans, toasted and roughly chopped
1	cup dried apricots, cut into thin strips
1	teaspoon salt
12	cups dried French or other white bread cubes (see the instructions under "Bread Stuffing for Turkey" at left)
1	cup homemade turkey or chicken stock or canned low-sodium chicken broth
3	large eggs, lightly beaten

1. Cook the sausage in a large skillet over medium heat until browned, about 10 minutes. Transfer the sausage to a large bowl with a slotted spoon. Discard the fat and in the same pan melt the butter.

2. Add the onion and celery and cook, stirring occasionally, over medium heat until soft and translucent, 6 to 7 minutes. Add the dried herbs and pepper and cook for another minute. Transfer the contents of the pan to the bowl with the sausage. Add the parsley, pecans, apricots, and salt and mix to combine. Add the bread cubes to the bowl.

3. Whisk the stock and eggs together in a small bowl. Pour the mixture over the bread cubes. Gently toss to evenly distribute the ingredients. Follow the instructions in the recipe Roast Stuffed Turkey on page 195 to stuff the bird and bake extra stuffing.

Bread Stuffing with Ham, Pine Nuts, Mushrooms, and Fennel

MAKES ABOUT 12 CUPS

Cremini mushrooms have more flavor than regular white button mushrooms, but the latter can be used in this recipe.

6	tablespoons unsalted butter
1	large onion, chopped (about 1½ cups)
1	large fennel bulb, fronds and stems removed (see page 32), bulb chopped (about 1½ cups)
10	ounces cremini mushrooms, cleaned and sliced thin
1½	teaspoons dried basil
½	teaspoon ground black pepper
1	cup pine nuts, toasted
¼	pound thinly sliced prosciutto, cut into thin strips
¼	pound thinly sliced smoked ham, cut in half and then crosswise into thin strips
½	cup grated Parmesan cheese
½	cup fresh parsley leaves, chopped fine
½	teaspoon salt
12	cups dried French or other white bread cubes (see the instructions under "Bread Stuffing for Turkey" on page 196)
1	cup homemade turkey or chicken stock or canned low-sodium chicken broth
3	large eggs, lightly beaten

1. Melt the butter in a large skillet or Dutch oven. Add the onion and fennel and cook, stirring occasionally, over medium heat until soft and translucent, 6 to 7 minutes. Add the mushrooms and cook until the liquid they release has evaporated, about 10 minutes. Add the basil and pepper and cook for another minute. Transfer the contents of the pan to a large bowl.

2. Add the pine nuts, prosciutto, smoked ham, Parmesan, parsley, and salt to the bowl and mix to combine. Add the bread cubes.

3. Whisk the stock and eggs together in a small bowl. Pour the mixture over the bread cubes. Gently toss to evenly distribute the ingredients. Follow the instructions in the recipe Roast Stuffed Turkey on page 195 to stuff the bird and bake extra stuffing.

Bread Stuffing with Bacon, Apples, Sage, and Caramelized Onions

MAKES ABOUT 12 CUPS

1	pound bacon, cut crosswise into ¼-inch strips
6	medium onions, sliced thin (about 7 cups)
1	teaspoon salt
2	Granny Smith apples, peeled, cored, and cut into ½-inch cubes (about 2 cups)
½	teaspoon ground black pepper
½	cup fresh parsley leaves, chopped fine
3	tablespoons fresh sage leaves, cut into thin strips
12	cups dried French or other white bread cubes (see the instructions under "Bread Stuffing for Turkey" on page 196)
1	cup homemade turkey or chicken stock or canned low-sodium chicken broth
3	large eggs, lightly beaten

1. Cook the bacon in a large skillet or Dutch oven over medium heat until crisp and browned, about 12 minutes. Remove the bacon from the pan with a slotted spoon and drain on paper towels. Discard all but 3 tablespoons of the rendered bacon fat.

2. Increase the heat to medium-high and add the onions and ¼ teaspoon salt. Cook the onions until golden in color, stirring occasionally and

scraping the sides and bottom of the pan, about 20 minutes. Reduce the heat to medium and continue to cook, stirring more often to prevent burning, until the onions are deep golden brown, another 5 minutes. Add the apples and continue to cook another 5 minutes. Transfer the contents of the pan to a large bowl.

3. Add the remaining ¾ teaspoon salt, pepper, parsley, and sage to the bowl and mix to combine. Add the bread cubes.

4. Whisk the stock and eggs together in a small bowl. Pour the mixture over the bread cubes. Gently toss to evenly distribute the ingredients. Follow the instructions in the recipe Roast Stuffed Turkey on page 195 to stuff the bird and bake extra stuffing.

CORNBREAD STUFFING

CORNBREAD STUFFING IS A SOUTHERN classic. We set out to make a cornbread stuffing with a toasted top, moist interior, and satisfyingly rich flavor. After a few initial batches, we became aware of the principal problems with this dish. We found that most cornbread stuffings are much too dry. The cornbread turns into stale, loose nuggets that refuse to bind with any of the other ingredients. On the other end of the spectrum are stuffings that are too wet. They simply turn into a damp, sloppy mass. We wanted a moist and cohesive stuffing that wasn't soggy or greasy. While most recipes use stock, butter, and eggs to bind the stuffing ingredients together and add moisture, we wondered if there were other options. Finally, there was quantity. None of the stuffings we had tried made nearly enough to handle a Thanksgiving crowd of 8 to 10 hungry people and provide ample allowance for leftovers.

We decided to begin by finding out which type of cornbread is best suited for stuffing and then figure out how it should be prepared. Although there were differences of opinion, tasters generally preferred the rather fluffy, slightly sweet Northern-style cornbread.

Next we focused our attention on what to do with the cornbread once it was made. We made stuffings from cornbread that was whacked into small crumbs, cut into even-sized cubes, and torn into bite-sized pieces. The crumbs had a potent cornbread flavor, but the texture was mealy and unattractive. Although the cubed cornbread looked very tidy, it didn't carry the same flavorful punch as the crumbs. Tearing cornbread in bite-sized pieces, however, created enough crumbs to release the cornbread flavor, while the bigger pieces were toothsome and made for the most attractive dish.

We now made stuffings using fresh, toasted, and stale cornbread. The fresh cornbread turned soggy and bland, while the flavor of the toasted bread was overpowering. The hands-down winner of the lot was the stuffing made with stale bread, with its potent but not bullish flavor and pleasingly moist texture. (Drying fresh cornbread in a warm oven accomplishes the same thing.) With the main ingredient in the bag, we turned next to the binders.

Turkey or chicken stock, eggs, and pan drippings are the classic ingredients used to help moisten and bind a stuffing. After ruling out turkey drippings, which we use to make gravy, we tested stuffings made with stock and eggs on their own to see exactly how each would fare. As expected, the eggs thoroughly bound the ingredients so that each forkful of stuffing was cohesive. The stock added the necessary moisture and distinct poultry flavor. Obviously, a mixture of these two ingredients was key, but we also wanted to add something to the stuffing that would make it a bit richer and softer without turning it greasy or wet. Recalling an old cornbread pudding recipe, we tried pouring a little half-and-half into the mix. This was the missing link, turning a second-rate side dish into a medal winner. The stuffing took on an extraordinarily full, rich flavor without being oily or sodden.

Soaking stale bread is a classic technique. You are replacing the bread's lost moisture with something more flavorful. Wondering if an adaptation of this idea would move our stuffing along, we soaked the stale cornbread in the egg, stock, and cream mixture overnight. We then baked it and compared it with stuffings baked after an hour-long soak, a 30-minute soak, and no soaking at all.

The differences in the stuffings were remarkable. The unsoaked stuffing tasted absolutely dull and lifeless when compared with the overnighter, and the 30-minute soaker was not nearly as good as the

60-minute one. While there was an obvious difference between the overnighter and the 60-minute version, it was far less than we had expected. Because overnight soaking can be inconvenient, we settled on one hour.

Now all we needed to do was round out the final flavors. Onions, celery, and fresh thyme and sage were a shoo-in. As we had expected, they all needed to be sautéed slightly before being mixed in with the cornbread. We tried adding a little wine or whiskey but found that their boozy flavor meddled with the rich flavor of the cornbread. Finally, some bulk pork sausage added nice pockets of texture and a meaty punch without overpowering the balance of flavors. Here was a cornbread stuffing that would match that of any Southern grandmother. It almost seems a shame to hide it under a stream of gravy.

Cornbread and Sausage Stuffing

MAKES ABOUT 12 CUPS, SERVING 10 TO 12

In this recipe, the stuffing is baked outside of the turkey in a baking dish. If you want to stuff your turkey with it, prepare the stuffing through step 2, then follow the directions in step 4 on page 195 for microwaving stuffing. To make the stuffing a day in advance, increase both the chicken stock and half-and-half by ¼ cup each and refrigerate the unbaked stuffing 12 to 24 hours; before transferring it to the baking dish, let the stuffing stand at room temperature for about 30 minutes so that it loses its chill.

12	cups cornbread broken into 1-inch pieces (include crumbs), spread in even layer on 2 baking sheets, and dried in 250-degree oven 50 to 60 minutes (recipe follows)
3	cups homemade turkey or chicken stock or canned low-sodium chicken broth
2	cups half-and-half
2	large eggs, beaten lightly
8	tablespoons (1 stick) unsalted butter, plus extra for greasing baking dish
1½	pounds bulk pork sausage, broken into 1-inch pieces
3	medium onions, chopped fine (about 3 cups)
3	stalks celery, chopped fine (about 1½ cups)
2	tablespoons minced fresh thyme leaves
2	tablespoons minced fresh sage leaves
3	cloves garlic, minced
1½	teaspoons salt
2	teaspoons ground black pepper

1. Place the cornbread in a large bowl. Whisk together the stock, half-and-half, and eggs in a medium bowl; pour over the cornbread and toss very gently to coat so that the cornbread does not break into smaller pieces. Set aside.

2. Heat a heavy-bottomed, 12-inch skillet over medium-high heat until hot, about 1½ minutes. Add 2 tablespoons butter to the pan and swirl to coat the pan bottom. When the foam subsides, add the sausage and cook, stirring occasionally, until the sausage loses its raw color, 5 to 7 minutes. With a slotted spoon, transfer the sausage to a medium bowl. Add about half the onions and celery to the fat in the skillet; sauté, stirring occasionally, over medium-high until softened, about 5 minutes. Transfer the onion mixture to the bowl with the sausage. Return the skillet to the heat and add the remaining 6 tablespoons butter; when the foam subsides, add the remaining celery and onions and

INGREDIENTS: Boxed Cornbread Mixes

We're always on the lookout for shortcuts around the holidays, and we were not about to overlook cornbread mixes. We tried our stuffing recipe with six well-respected mixes and liked the results we got with one of them.

Martha White's Yellow Cornbread Mix was the champion, achieving a beautiful, golden crust, well-balanced cornbread flavor, and toothsome texture. Betty Crocker's Golden Corn Muffin and Bread Mix and Jiffy's Corn Muffin Mix were the sweetest of the bunch, inspiring comments such as "candy sweet" and "dessert stuffing." The other Martha White entries, including the Buttermilk and Cotton Pickin' Cornbread Mixes, along with White Lily White Cornbread Mix, resembled one another closely, with their sweet, pale crust and soggy, cakelike texture.

The problem with Martha White's Yellow Cornbread Mix is that it is sold only in a few lucky states. Unless it graces the shelves of your local store, you'd best roll up your sleeves and put together a batch of our Golden Cornbread (see page 200).

sauté, stirring occasionally, until softened, about 5 minutes. Stir in the thyme, sage, and garlic; cook until fragrant, about 30 seconds; add the salt and pepper. Add this mixture along with the sausage and onion mixture to the cornbread and stir gently to combine so that cornbread does not break into smaller pieces. Cover the bowl with plastic wrap and refrigerate to blend flavors, at least 1 hour or up to 4 hours.

3. Adjust an oven rack to the lower-middle position and heat the oven to 400 degrees. Butter a 10 by 15-inch baking dish (or two 9-inch square or 7 by 11-inch baking dishes). Transfer the stuffing to the baking dish; pour any liquid accumulated in the bottom of the bowl over the stuffing and, if necessary, gently press the stuffing with a rubber spatula to fit it into the baking dish. Bake until golden brown, 35 to 40 minutes.

➤ VARIATION

Spicy Cornbread Stuffing with Red Peppers, Chipotle Chiles, and Andouille Sausage

Andouille is a spicy smoked Cajun sausage. If you cannot find any, chorizo makes a fine substitute.

Follow the recipe for Cornbread and Sausage Stuffing through step 1. In step 2, melt 4 tablespoons butter in a heated skillet; when foam subsides, add 2 red bell peppers, cut into ¼-inch pieces, to skillet along with a third of the onions and celery. Sauté until softened, about 5 minutes, and transfer to a medium bowl. Return the skillet to the heat and add the remaining 4 tablespoons butter; when foam subsides, add the remaining onion and celery and sauté, stirring occasionally, until softened, about 5 minutes. Stir in 4 or 5 chipotle chiles en adobo, chopped (about 4 tablespoons), along with the thyme, sage, and garlic. Add this mixture, along with the sautéed onions and celery and 1½ pounds andouille sausage, cut into ½-inch pieces, to the cornbread and mix gently so that the cornbread does not break into

smaller pieces. Cover and refrigerate as directed in step 2; proceed with step 3 to bake stuffing.

~✦~

Golden Cornbread

MAKES ABOUT 16 CUPS CRUMBLED CORNBREAD

If you are using this cornbread for your stuffing, you will use about three-quarters of the recipe—the rest is for nibbling.

4	tablespoons unsalted butter, melted, plus extra for greasing baking dish
4	large eggs
1⅓	cups buttermilk
1⅓	cups milk
2	cups yellow cornmeal, preferably stone-ground
2	cups all-purpose flour
4	teaspoons baking powder
1	teaspoon baking soda
2	tablespoons sugar
1	teaspoon salt

1. Adjust an oven rack to the middle position and heat the oven to 375 degrees. Grease a 9 by 13-inch baking dish with butter.

2. Beat the eggs in a medium bowl; whisk in the buttermilk and milk.

3. Whisk the cornmeal, flour, baking powder, baking soda, sugar, and salt together in a large bowl. Push the dry ingredients up the sides of the bowl to make a well, then pour the egg and milk mixture into the well and stir with a whisk until just combined; stir in the butter.

4. Pour the batter into the greased baking dish. Bake until the top is golden brown and the edges have pulled away from the sides of the pan, 30 to 40 minutes.

5. Transfer the baking dish to a wire rack and cool to room temperature before using, about 1 hour.

8

FISH AND SHELLFISH

BUYING FISH AND SHELLFISH IS AS TRICKY (if not more so) than cooking it. A general point to keep in mind: You must buy from a trusted source, preferably one with a high turnover that will ensure freshness. While cooking can hide imperfections in meat and poultry, there is little the cook can do to salvage a tired piece of salmon or over-the-hill lobsters.

So what should you look for at the seafood shop? Fish should smell like the sea, not fishy or sour. The flesh should look bright, shiny, and firm, not dull or mushy. When possible, try to get your fishmonger to slice steaks and fillets to order rather than buying precut pieces that may have been sitting for some time and lost some fluids. Avoid fish that is shrink-wrapped, since the packaging makes it difficult to examine and smell the fish. No matter how you buy fish, make sure it has been kept chilled until the minute you buy it; get fish home quickly and into the refrigerator.

Many shellfish are sold alive. This means lobsters should be moving around in the tank, and oysters, clams, and mussels should be tightly shut. If the shellfish doesn't smell fresh or look fresh, it probably isn't. Given the perishability of fish and shellfish, we suggest shopping and cooking on the same day.

The recipes that follow are our takes on America's favorite seafood dishes, both humble (baked scrod and pan-fried catfish) and elegant (crab cakes and lobster Newburg).

BROILED SALMON

SALMON IS A SUREFIRE CROWD PLEASER (it's America's favorite fish for dinner), but it's not always easy to make for a crowd. Many cooks shy away from poaching, and our favorite indoor cooking method—pan-searing individual portions—can get cumbersome with too many pieces of fish. Our preferred outdoor cooking techniques—hot-smoking and straightforward grilling—can accommodate larger pieces of fish, but for denizens of the North, among whom we count ourselves, cooking outside is impractical, if not impossible, for almost half the year.

So we set out to beat the odds and find the best way of cooking a whole side of salmon, enough to feed eight or more guests, in the oven. We wanted fish that was moist but not soggy, firm but not chalky, and nicely crusted, with golden, flavorful caramelization over its flesh. If we could work some interesting flavors and contrasting textures into the bargain, all the better.

Creating some flavorful caramelization on the flesh of the fish was a key goal, so we focused right away on high-heat cooking. Baking, though it seemed like a natural choice, was out because it implies cooking in a moderate, 350-degree oven, which would never brown the fish. Heating things up from there, we tested roasting at oven temperatures of 400, 450, and 500 degrees. To our surprise, none of them worked well. Even at 500 degrees, on a preheated pan, the fish remained pale owing to the necessarily short 16-minute cooking time; any more time in the oven and the fish would overcook. Another source of consternation was moisture—not the lack of it, as we might have expected, but an excess. The abundance of fat and collagen in the farmed Atlantic salmon we were using melted during cooking, giving the fish an overly wet, slippery texture and fatty mouthfeel.

Broiling was the next step up in heat, and here we met with some success. The salmon browned nicely under the intense broiler heat and, as a result, also developed better flavor. Some of the copious moisture evaporated, leaving the fish with a much-improved texture, drier and more firm, yet still juicy. None of the broiling and roasting combinations we went on to try topped broiling from start to finish. We were on the right track to be sure, but plain broiled salmon was not terribly inspiring. If we were going to serve this to a crowd of people at a weekend dinner party, a flavor boost and some textural interest would be absolutely necessary.

The addition of an interesting topping for the fish could, we thought, achieve both goals. Dried bread crumbs came immediately to mind—and left almost as quickly once we tasted them. The flavor was lackluster, and the texture akin to sawdust. Our favorite Japanese panko bread crumbs were judged too light of flavor and feathery of texture. Fresh bread crumbs were a crisp improvement, and toasted fresh bread crumbs laced with garlic, herbs, and butter were better still. But there were more avenues to explore.

Dry spice rubs, similar to what we might apply to the fish if grilling, met with mixed results. Glazes and spice pastes won praise for their flavor, but since they themselves were wet, they added little in the way of texture.

Potatoes were another topping possibility. Potato crusts on fish are typically engineered by laying paper-thin slices of potato on the fish and sautéing it on the stovetop. Testing proved that the slices would not form a cohesive crust without the direct heat of a hot pan. In addition, we couldn't slice them thin enough without the help of a mandoline. But because tasters loved the potato flavor, we tried some other methods. A crust of grated raw potatoes remained too loose and crunchy. Sautéing the grated potato before applying it to the fish helped some, but not enough, while completely precooking the potatoes robbed them of both flavor and texture.

Clinging tenaciously to the notion of potato flavor while groping for another way to build a crisp, crunchy texture, one test cook smirked and suggested, half in jest, that we try crushed potato chips. Everyone in the test kitchen laughed, but after settling down we looked at one another and said, practically in unison, "Let's try it." Imagine our astonishment, then, at the chips' overwhelming success. Though a bit greasy and heavy on their own, they offered just what we were looking for in a crust: great potato flavor and crunch that wouldn't quit. After lightening the chips up by mixing in some fresh toasted bread crumbs and adding dill for complementary flavor, we found ourselves with an excellent, if unorthodox, topping. We also found that the chips made a rich foil for some of the other flavors we wanted to add.

Because the chips brown under the broiler in just a minute—literally—we broiled the fish until it was almost cooked through before adding the topping. This gave us just the texture we wanted. After adding a flavorful wet element (mustard) to help the crumbs adhere to the fish, we knew we had it: a quick, oven-cooked, well-flavored, texturally interesting—and rather surprising—salmon dinner for a crowd.

PREPARING SALMON

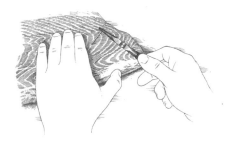

1. Run your fingers over the surface to feel for pinbones, then remove them with tweezers or needle-nosed pliers.

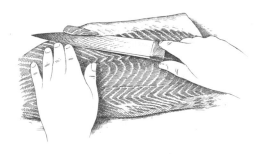

2. Hold a sharp chef's knife at a slight downward angle to the flesh and cut off the whitish, fatty portion of the belly.

Broiled Salmon with Mustard and Crisp Potato Crust
SERVES 8 TO 10

Heavy-duty foil measuring 18 inches wide is essential for creating a sling that aids in transferring the cooked fillet to a cutting board. Use a large baking sheet so that the salmon will lie flat. If you can't get the fish to lie flat, even when positioning it diagonally on the baking sheet, trim the tail end. If you prefer to cook a smaller 2-pound fillet, ask to have it cut from the thick center of the fillet, not the thin tail end, and begin checking doneness a minute earlier.

3	slices high-quality sliced sandwich bread, such as Pepperidge Farm, crusts removed
4	ounces plain high-quality potato chips, crushed into rough ⅛-inch pieces (about 1 cup)
6	tablespoons chopped fresh dill
1	whole side of salmon fillet, about 3½ pounds, pinbones removed and belly fat trimmed (see illustrations at left)
1	teaspoon olive oil
¾	teaspoon salt
	Ground black pepper
3	tablespoons Dijon mustard

INGREDIENTS: Potato Chips

We tried thick-cut Yukon Gold (Terra brand), kettle-cooked (Kettle brand), ridged (Ruffles), thin (Lay's), and molded (Pringles) in our broiled salmon recipe. The thick-cut and kettle-cooked were the best, offering superior potato flavor and the sturdiest crunch. In a pinch, ridged chips will suffice.

1. Adjust one oven rack to the uppermost position (about 3 inches from the heat source) and the second rack to the upper-middle position; heat the oven to 400 degrees.

2. Pulse the bread in the workbowl of a food processor fitted with the steel blade until processed into fairly even ¼-inch pieces about the size of Grape-Nuts cereal (you should have about 1 cup), about ten 1-second pulses. Spread the crumbs evenly on a rimmed baking sheet; toast on the lower rack, shaking the pan once or twice, until golden brown and crisp, 4 to 5 minutes. Toss together the bread crumbs, crushed potato chips, and dill in a small bowl; set aside.

3. Increase the oven setting to broil. Cut a piece of heavy-duty foil 6 inches longer than the fillet. Fold the foil lengthwise in thirds and place lengthwise on a rimmed baking sheet; position the salmon lengthwise on the foil, allowing the excess foil to hang over the baking sheet. Rub the fillet evenly with oil; sprinkle with salt and pepper to taste. Broil

the salmon on the upper rack until the surface is spotty brown and the outer ½ inch of the thick end is opaque when gently flaked with a paring knife, 9 to 11 minutes. Remove the fish from the oven, spread evenly with the mustard, and press the bread crumb mixture onto the fish. Return to the lower rack and continue broiling until the crust is deep golden brown, about 1 minute longer.

4. Following the illustrations below, transfer the salmon and foil sling to a cutting board, remove the sling, and serve the salmon from the board.

➤ VARIATIONS

Broiled Salmon with Barbecue Sauce and Crisp Potato Crust

Follow the recipe for Broiled Salmon with Mustard and Crisp Potato Crust, replacing the mustard with 3 tablespoons barbecue sauce.

Broiled Salmon with Horseradish and Crisp Potato Crust

Heat 3 tablespoons unsalted butter in a small skillet over medium heat until foaming; sauté ½ cup minced shallots (about 4 medium) until softened and translucent, about 2 minutes. Off heat, add ½ cup prepared horseradish and 1 tablespoon sugar; set aside. Follow the recipe for Broiled Salmon with Mustard and Crisp Potato Crust, substituting 1 tablespoon fresh thyme leaves for the dill and horseradish mixture for the Dijon mustard.

SERVING THE SALMON

 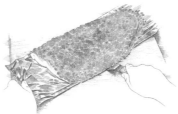 

1. Grasp the foil overhang at both ends; lift carefully and set the fish on the cutting board.

2. Slide an offset spatula under the thick end. Grasp the foil, press the spatula down against the foil, and slide it under the fish down to the thin end, loosening the entire side of fish.

3. Grasp the foil again, hold the spatula perpendicular to the fish to stabilize it, and pull the foil out from under the fish. Use a moist paper towel to clean up the board, and serve immediately.

SALMON CAKES

WE ARE, IN MANY WAYS, LUCKY NOT TO BE frugal 19th-century New Englanders. One reason, which may have eluded you until now, is that we can use fresh, raw fish in our salmon cakes if we choose. In America, fish cakes started out as thrifty New England fare, designed to use up salt-preserved or leftover cooked fish and potatoes. Back in the 1800s, the use of fresh fish would certainly have been regarded as a suspicious extravagance, if not down-right odd.

Even today, the overwhelming majority of salmon cake recipes we researched started with cooked, or in some cases canned, salmon and used the traditional binder of cooked potato. The occasional recipe that did call for raw fish was usually titled Salmon Burgers. It was to these burgers that all of the tasters gravitated when we cooked up six different recipes for salmon cakes, patties, croquettes, and burgers to kick off our recipe development process. The chunky texture, the moistness, and the direct salmon flavor of the burgers appealed to all.

From there, we thought, we could easily extrapolate our ideal salmon cake: toothsome, tender, and moist on the inside; crisp and golden brown on the outside; shapely; and firm and cohesive throughout. But we encountered many potholes on the road to that ideal. Salmon cakes often suffer from a texture that is either dry, overprocessed, and mushy or wet, loose, and underbound. Fresh salmon flavor may be close to absent, replaced by a distracting cacophony of ill-placed seasonings. The exterior coating may be lackluster. It was clear that to come up with the best possible recipe we would have to thoroughly test binders, seasonings, coatings, cooking mediums, and timing.

Based on our experience with three different brands of canned salmon, we wouldn't for a minute consider using that product as a base for our cakes. Full of bones and skin that made cleaning a real hassle, all three brands were utterly unappealing in terms of appearance, smell, taste, and texture. When it came to considering leftover cooked fish, we asked around among home cooks. Everyone we interviewed reported buying only as much fish as could be eaten in a single meal; leftover cooked fish is simply not something most people have on hand these days.

That was the first good reason we found to make these salmon cakes with fresh fish.

Despite the break with both tradition and the dictate of most current recipes, it was easy to find other good reasons for using fresh fish. The savings of time and effort were high on the list. We simply couldn't see the point of bringing home a beautiful, fresh salmon fillet and then going to the trouble of cooking it twice, once to make "leftovers" and then again to make the cakes. On top of that, we wanted to take advantage of the collagen, a structural protein found in raw fish (and meat) that melts when cooked and provides natural moisture and binding capacity. Both characteristics would be boons to the cakes' texture that precooking the salmon would eliminate. Last, the raw fish would provide a hedge against overcooking the cakes and, consequently, drying them out.

Having decided to use fresh fish, we next tried a couple of methods for breaking it down. Predictably, the food processor ground the fish too finely for our tastes, even when we proceeded with the greatest care. As it turned out, chopping the fish by hand was not difficult, and it provided a far greater margin of error in terms of overprocessing than did the food processor.

The collagen in the fish gave us a great head start in binding the cakes, but it couldn't do the job entirely on its own. Without additional binders the cakes had a chunky, heavy texture and such strong salmon flavor that some tasters were overwhelmed. Common choices for binders included eggs, either whole or yolks alone, and mayonnaise. Of the many egg combinations we tried, the yolks alone worked best. But when we tried mayonnaise, everyone preferred it over the egg yolks. Just 2 tablespoons of mayonnaise for the 1¼ pounds of chopped fish we were using added a noticeable creaminess to the cakes' texture and a welcome tang to the flavor. Any more, though, and the cakes began to get a little greasy.

Starchy products—including cooked potato, crushed crackers, dry and fresh bread crumbs, and bread soaked in milk—made up another category of binders worth testing. The cooked potato produced cakes that were rubbery and dry, and both the crushed crackers and dried bread crumbs became leaden and mushy by absorbing too much moisture from the fish, not to mention the fact that they gave the cakes a stale flavor. The milk-soaked bread showed well, but best overall was the fresh bread crumbs we made by simply mincing a piece of sturdy, white sandwich bread from which we had removed the crusts. The bread lightened and softened the texture of the cakes, making them smoother and more refined. Their flavor also benefited. On its own, the bread tasted slightly sweet, so it helped to balance out the strong flavor of the salmon and the creamy tang of the mayonnaise.

With the binding just right, we tried the various flavorings listed in our stack of test recipes. Maybe we're just purists, but the herbs, scallions, garlic, mustard, Worcestershire sauce, hot pepper sauce, and Old Bay seasoning all tasted out of place. In the end, the basic combination of onion, lemon juice, and parsley prevailed by providing simple, bright, fresh flavors. Some tasters objected to the crunch of the minced onion, but we quickly solved that problem by grating it to allow for better integration into the fish mixture.

The next step was to find the crisp, light, golden coating of our dreams. Some recipes left out the coating altogether, but the resulting cakes lacked interest and tasted too fishy. Flour alone soaked right into the fish mixture and became pasty when cooked. Dried bread crumbs alone were OK, but uninspiring. Our stellar coating involves a full breading treatment, called anglaise, which consists of flour, beaten egg, and bread crumbs, applied in sequence. Although making the coating does entail some extra work as well as more dirty dishes, the result is well worth it: a thin, toasty—even gorgeous—coating. A 15-minute stay in the freezer prior to breading, we found, firms the cakes slightly for easier handling and causes some of the surface moisture to evaporate, which helps the breading to adhere.

Perfecting the cooking procedure was our last step. Temperature and timing were crucial to ensure that the breading browned but did not burn and that the cakes cooked through to the center without overcooking and drying out. Stovetop cooking over a medium-high flame in a large, heavy-bottomed skillet (at least 12 inches in diameter to accommodate eight cakes) proved to be our answer. Cooking the cakes in a generous quantity of vegetable oil—it should reach halfway up the cakes in the pan—for just two minutes per side produced a perfect golden crust and moist fish within, cooked just barely to medium. We tried the oven finish called for in many recipes and found it to be a useless extra step.

We also experimented with other fats as a cooking medium, including olive oil, butter, clarified butter, and a combination of butter and vegetable oil. But for its safety, ease of use, and convenience, vegetable oil alone remained our cooking medium of choice. Its neutral flavor allowed the balanced flavor of the fish mixture, bright seasonings, and toasty breading of these salmon cakes to really shine.

Pan-Fried Fresh Salmon Cakes
SERVES 4

A big wedge of lemon is the simplest accompaniment to salmon cakes, but any of the dipping sauces on page 221 are an excellent embellishment. If possible, use supercrisp panko (Japanese bread crumbs) to coat the salmon cakes.

1 1/4	pounds salmon fillet
1	slice high-quality white sandwich bread, such as Pepperidge Farm, crusts removed and white part chopped very fine (about 5 tablespoons)
2	tablespoons mayonnaise
1/4	cup finely grated onion
2	tablespoons chopped fresh parsley leaves
3/4	teaspoon salt
1 1/2	tablespoons juice from 1 lemon
1/2	cup all-purpose flour
2	large eggs, lightly beaten
1 1/2	teaspoons plus 1/2 cup vegetable oil
3/4	cup plain dried bread crumbs, preferably panko Lemon wedges or one of the dipping sauces on page 221

1. Following the illustration on page 203, locate and remove any pinbones from the salmon flesh. Using a sharp knife, cut the flesh off the skin, then discard the skin. Chop the salmon flesh into 1/4- to 1/3-inch pieces and mix with the chopped bread, mayonnaise, onion, parsley, salt, and lemon juice in a medium bowl. Scoop a generous 1/4-cup portion

salmon mixture from the bowl and use your hands to form into a patty measuring roughly 2½ inches in diameter and ¾ inch thick; place on a parchment-lined baking sheet and repeat with the remaining salmon mixture until you have 8 patties. Place the patties in the freezer until the surface moisture has evaporated, about 15 minutes.

2. Meanwhile, spread the flour in a pie plate or shallow baking dish. Beat the eggs with 1½ tea-spoons vegetable oil and 1½ teaspoons water in a second pie plate or shallow baking dish, and spread the bread crumbs in a third. Dip the chilled salmon patties in the flour to cover; shake off excess. Transfer to the beaten egg and, using a slotted spat-ula, turn to coat; let the excess drip off. Transfer to the bread crumbs; shake the pan to coat the patties completely. Return the now-breaded patties to the baking sheet.

3. Heat the remaining ½ cup vegetable oil in a large, heavy-bottomed skillet over medium-high heat until shimmering but not smoking, about 3 minutes; add the salmon patties and cook until medium golden brown, about 2 minutes. Flip the cakes over and continue cooking until medium golden brown on the second side, about 2 minutes longer. Transfer the cakes to a plate lined with paper towels to absorb excess oil on surface, if desired, about 30 seconds, and then serve immediately with lemon wedges or dipping sauce.

➤ VARIATIONS
Pan-Fried Smoked Salmon Cakes
Follow the recipe for Pan-Fried Fresh Salmon Cakes, substituting 8 ounces smoked salmon or lox, chopped into ¼- to ⅓-inch pieces, for 8 ounces of fresh salmon and reducing the salt to ½ teaspoon.

Pan-Fried Fresh Salmon Cakes with Cheese
Follow the recipe for Pan-Fried Fresh Salmon Cakes, adding 2 tablespoons grated Parmesan or Asiago cheese to the salmon mixture and reducing the salt to ½ teaspoon.

PAN-FRIED TROUT

ALTHOUGH THIS CAMPSITE FAVORITE MAY seem simple and straightforward, pan-frying trout can easily turn ugly. When perfectly cooked, the sweet, delicate flavor of trout is protected by a crisp layer of cornmeal fried until golden brown. When things go wrong, which seems to happen more often than not, the cornmeal remains pale and turns soggy while the trout underneath leaches out sticky, white foam, a sure sign it is overdone and dry.

Unless you've been successful on a recent fishing trip, you'll be buying trout at your local supermarket or fish shop. Most markets sell farm-raised trout cut into fillets. While the varieties of trout taste different, we found only the size of the fillets made a difference when cooking. Fillets weighing five to seven ounces were the easiest to bread, fry, and serve, with each fillet serving as one portion. Although sev-eral recipes we found instructed us to remove the skin, we found it necessary to keep the skin intact to help the flesh from falling apart, and our tasters considered the crispy fried skin a treat. Trout also has many little pinbones that can be difficult to remove before cooking. In the end, tasters did not mind eating around them or plucking them occasionally from their fork.

We dusted trout with several different types of cornmeal mixtures. Fine-ground cornmeal fried up smooth and crisp, while coarser cornmeal was too chewy and thick to cook through. Coatings made only of cornmeal, however, turned out extremely dense and chewy. By tempering the cornmeal with flour, we were able to make the coating crisp and light without losing any cornmeal flavor. Equal parts cornmeal to flour turned out the most balanced crust, neither too dense nor too floury. Because trout is mildly flavored, it is important to season the coating heavily with salt, pepper, and cayenne.

Simply dusting the trout with the seasoned corn-meal mixture wasn't enough to make great fried trout. This simple, one-layer coating went soggy only moments out of the pan. Dipping the fish in an egg wash before dusting with the seasoned cornmeal mixture (a two-stage breading) offered a thicker, more substantial crust, but it was still not hearty enough. We then tried dusting the fish with flour, dipping it in an egg wash, then dusting it with cornmeal (known as a three-stage or bound bread-ing). This produced a crisp, crackling crust that held up long enough for us to serve and eat the fish.

The term pan-frying is defined by the amount of oil in the pan. As opposed to a deep fry, in which the food is submerged completely in hot oil, pan-fried food is cooked one side at a time in oil that measures part of the way up the side of the food. When pan-frying chicken or pork cutlets, it is possible to use a relatively small amount of oil. When we tried to use a modest amount of oil with trout fillets, however, the results were quite poor. The cornmeal crust was undercooked and raw-tasting—we needed more oil and more heat.

We increased the oil to a depth of ½ inch and switched from a skillet to a Dutch oven to minimize splatters. With the oil temperature at 350 degrees, the fillets still fried up pale. Only when we cranked up the oil to 400 degrees did the crust turn golden and crisp in a mere 4 minutes. Served with tartar sauce, this picture perfect, cornmeal-fried trout remains crisp long out of the pan and breaks open to reveal tender, flaky flesh that might be improved only by a lakeside campsite and a good sunset.

Pan-Fried Trout

SERVES 4

Although we used an 11-inch sauté pan with sides 2½ inch high during our tests with no problem, we recognize the danger in heating oil to 400 degrees on the stovetop. Just to be safe, we recommend using a Dutch oven with sides at least 5 inches high. The oil will still splatter, how-ever, and should not be left unattended. Use any variety of trout available. We had good luck with red rainbow, white rainbow, and golden trout.

I	cup unbleached all-purpose flour
½	cup fine-ground cornmeal
	Salt and ground black pepper
⅛	teaspoon cayenne pepper
2	large eggs
2–3	cups vegetable oil
4	trout fillets with skin on (5 to 7 ounces each)
	Lemon wedges or one of the dipping sauces on page 221

1. Set a wire rack over a rimmed baking sheet, place the sheet on the middle oven rack, and heat the oven to 200 degrees. Place ½ cup flour in a wide, shallow dish. In a separate wide, shallow dish, mix together the remaining ½ cup flour, cornmeal, 1 tea-spoon salt, ¼ teaspoon pepper, and cayenne. In a third shallow dish, whisk the eggs with 1 tablespoon of oil until uniform.

2. Pat the fish fillets dry with paper towels and sprinkle each side with salt and pepper to taste. Drop the fish into the flour and shake the dish to coat. Shake the excess flour from each piece, then, using tongs, dip the fillets into the egg mixture, turning to coat well and allowing the excess to drip off. Coat the fillets with the cornmeal mixture, shake off excess, and lay on another wire rack set over a rimmed baking sheet.

3. Heat ½ inch of oil in a large, heavy-bottomed Dutch oven over high heat until the oil reaches a temperature of 400 degrees. (The oil should not smoke but it will come close.) Lay two trout fillets in the oil and fry, turning once, until golden brown, about 4 minutes. Adjust the heat as necessary to keep the oil between 385 and 390 degrees. Remove the fillets from the oil with a slotted spoon and lay them on a plate lined with several layers of paper towel; blot to help remove any excess oil. Transfer the fried fish to the wire rack in the warm oven. Bring the oil back to 400 degrees and repeat the cooking process with the remaining fish fillets. Serve the fried fish immedi-ately with either lemon wedges or dipping sauce.

PAN-FRIED CATFISH

CATFISH NEVER USED TO BE CONSIDERED the making of a fancy meal. Thought by many to be a junk fish, pan-fried catfish was common in the Low Country (the coastal areas of South Carolina and Georgia), where it flourished in local waters. Today, however, catfish is highly sought after and expensive. Although we found pan-frying catfish to be very similar to pan-frying trout, we did stumble across elements of the task that are unique to catfish.

First off, most catfish found at the store is farm-raised in fresh water, although ocean catfish (also known as wolffish) can occasionally be found. While the oddly sized fillets of ocean catfish (some are mammoth and others tiny) don't easily lend themselves to pan-frying, we found the average farm-raised, fresh-water fillets usually weigh in around three quarters of a pound. Two fillets of farm-raised catfish will easily serve four people, and we found it best to cut each fillet in half, making it easier to both cook and serve. We found it best to cut the fillets down the middle so that each portion has both a thin tail end and a thicker middle. This ensure that each half fillet will cook at the same rate and that each person will have the same ratio of crisp, fried tail to tender, flaky flesh. We also found it necessary to remove the skin and the dark, fatty tissue that lies directly underneath it. While the skin offended no one, the dark fatty tissue was very fishy tasting and unappealing.

As with trout, these fillets benefited from being dredged in flour, dipped in an egg wash, and finally coated with a seasoned cornmeal/flour mixture. Also like the trout, they browned beautifully and cooked through in only four minutes in ½ inch of 400-degree oil.

Pan-Fried Catfish

SERVES 4

To minimize splatters and maximize safety, use a Dutch oven with sides at least 5 inches high (not a regular skillet) when pan-frying the fish.

1	cup unbleached all-purpose flour
½	cup fine-ground cornmeal
	Salt and ground black pepper
⅛	teaspoon cayenne pepper
2	large eggs
2–3	cups vegetable oil
2	catfish fillets (about 12 ounces each), skin and dark fatty flesh just below skin trimmed, fillets cut in half lengthwise
	Lemon wedges or one of the dipping sauces on page 221

1. Set a wire rack over a rimmed baking sheet, place the sheet on the middle oven rack, and heat the oven to 200 degrees. Place ½ cup flour in a wide, shallow dish. In a separate wide, shallow dish, mix together the remaining ½ cup flour, cornmeal, 1 teaspoon salt, ¼ teaspoon pepper, and cayenne. In a third shallow dish, whisk the eggs with 1 tablespoon oil until uniform.

2. Pat the fish fillets dry with paper towels and sprinkle each side with salt and pepper to taste. Drop the fish into the flour and shake the dish to coat. Shake the excess flour from each piece, then, using tongs, dip the fillets into the egg mixture, turning to coat well and allowing the excess to drip off. Coat the fillets with the cornmeal mixture, shake off the excess, and lay them on another wire rack set over a rimmed baking sheet.

3. Heat ½ inch of oil in a large, heavy-bottomed Dutch oven over high heat until the oil reaches a temperature of 400 degrees. (The oil should not smoke, but it will come close.) Place two catfish fillets in the oil and fry, turning once, until golden brown, about 4 minutes. Adjust the heat as necessary to keep the oil between 385 and 390 degrees. Remove the fillets from the oil with a slotted spoon and lay them on a plate lined with several layers of paper towel; blot to help remove any excess oil. Transfer the fried fish to the wire rack in the warm oven. Bring the oil back to 400 degrees and repeat the cooking process with the remaining fish fillets. Serve the fried fish immediately with either lemon wedges or dipping sauce.

BOSTON BAKED SCROD

NAMED FOR THE OLD BEANTOWN RESTAURANTS that made this dish famous, Boston baked scrod is now a seafood restaurant standard across the country. Every once in a while this simple recipe turns out great, with sweet, tender pieces of cod lightly seasoned with butter and lemon and topped with crisp, toasted crumbs. More often than not, however, it's rubbery and bland and topped off with a soggy crust. Knowing how good it can be and how awful it usually is, we set out to discover what makes Boston baked scrod worth the effort.

The term scrod, as we quickly found out when shopping, is somewhat controversial and may be used to refer to several types of small fish (weighing fewer than 2½ pounds or so). It is more accurate to use the term scrod cod when buying fish at the local market to make sure the fish you are getting is really cod. A scrod cod fillet weighs about 1 pound and is enough for two portions. For easy cooking and serving, we found it helpful to cut the strangely shaped fillets in half crosswise. These two pieces, however, are much different in shape and thickness. Knowing that they would not cook at the same rate, we found it necessary to fold the thin tailpiece in half to make it as thick as the piece from the head end of the fish.

After fitting four pieces of cod in a glass casserole dish, we baked and broiled up several batches. After testing a variety of oven temperatures and positions, we preferred the 14 minutes it took to cook the fish under the broiler. Positioned 6 inches from the element (ours is electric), the fish cooked through evenly with no ill effect on texture or flavor. Because cod is a relatively wet fish, it stands up well to the broiler's intense heat. We did have decent results in a hot (450-degree oven), but the baking time was longer than the broiling time, and we still needed to switch the broiler on to brown the crumbs, and so broiling it was.

Although we had now developed a good cooking method, these initial tests drove home how bland the flavor of cod really is. No amount of lemon juice squeezed onto the fish at the table could turn it into a tasty meal. In an effort to zip up the bland cod, we tried broiling the fish with both butter and lemon juice. As the fish broiled, it soaked up some of these flavors and released some of its moisture. The fish not only turned out a bit more seasoned, but a flavorful little sauce was created in the pan. By adding some sautéed shallot, garlic, and fresh parsley to the butter and lemon juice, we brought the cod to a new level, where it tasted both impressive and clean. With a heavy-handed dose of salt and black pepper, we had discovered a quick and easy way to make scrod worth eating.

The final component of Boston baked scrod is the toasted crumbs of bread that garnish the top of each portion. Adding both texture and flavor, these crumbs are not only an authentic part of the recipe but help to raise it above the humdrum. Prepackaged bread crumbs were disappointingly bland and heavy, adding only a sandy crunch. Fresh bread crumbs, on the other hand, simply absorbed moisture as the fish cooked, turning wet and sodden instead of toasting. Only toasted, homemade bread crumbs contributed the seasoning and texture we were after. Made by processing and toasting several slices of high-quality sandwich bread and then seasoning them with salt, black pepper, and fresh parsley, these crumbs needed only a minute under the broiler to adhere to the fish and heat through. Topped with crunchy, flavorful crumbs, these well-seasoned fillets of cod and their impromptu sauce are the best representatives of Boston baked scrod we've ever tasted.

Boston Baked Scrod
SERVES 4

Cod fillets average about one pound at most markets. If you cut each fillet in half crosswise, you will have enough for four servings. To keep the thinner pieces from the tail end from overcooking, fold these pieces in half before placing them in the casserole dish.

TOPPING

2	slices high-quality sandwich bread, such as Pepperidge Farm, quartered
1	tablespoon minced fresh parsley leaves
1/4	teaspoon salt
1/8	teaspoon ground black pepper

SCROD

5	tablespoons unsalted butter, melted
1	medium shallot, minced
1	small clove garlic, minced very fine
1 1/2	tablespoons lemon juice
1	tablespoon minced fresh parsley leaves
	Salt and ground black pepper
2	skinless cod fillets (each about 1 pound), cut in half crosswise

1. FOR THE TOPPING: Adjust one oven rack to the upper-middle position (about 6 inches from heat source) and the second rack to the middle position; heat the oven to 400 degrees.

2. Pulse the bread in the workbowl of a food processor fitted with the steel blade until processed into fairly even 1/4-inch pieces about the size of Grape-Nuts cereal, about ten 1-second pulses.

Spread the crumbs evenly on a rimmed baking sheet; toast on the lower rack, shaking the pan once or twice, until golden brown and crisp, 4 to 5 minutes. Toss together the bread crumbs, parsley, salt, and pepper in a small bowl; set aside.

3. FOR THE SCROD: Increase the oven setting to broil. Melt the butter in a small skillet over medium-high heat until the foaming has subsided. Reduce the heat to medium and add the shallot and garlic and sauté until slightly softened, about 1 minute. Remove the pan from the heat, add the lemon juice, parsley, ¼ teaspoon salt, and ⅛ teaspoon pepper, and swirl to incorporate. Remove the pan from the heat and set aside.

4. Season the scrod liberally with salt and pepper. Fold the thin tailpieces in half to increase their thickness. Place the fillets in a shallow 9 by 13-inch casserole dish and pour the melted butter mixture over. Broil until the fish is completely opaque when gently flaked with a paring knife, 14 to 15 minutes. Baste the fish with the pan drippings and top with the bread crumbs. Continue broiling until the crumbs are golden brown, about 1 minute. Using a metal spatula, transfer the fish to individual plates and pour the basting juices around the edges of the fish (not on top, or the bread crumbs will become soggy). Serve immediately.

STEAMED LOBSTERS

AS WITH MOST SEAFOOD, WE FIND THAT knowing how to shop for lobster is just as important as knowing how to cook it. Lobsters must be purchased alive. Choose lobsters that are active in the tank, avoiding listless specimens that may have been in the tank too long. Maine lobsters, with their large claws, are meatier and sweeter than clawless rock or spiny lobsters, and they are our first and only choice. Size is really a matter of preference and budget. We found it possible to cook large as well as small lobsters to perfection as long as we adjusted the cooking time (see page 213).

During the initial phase of testing, we confirmed our preference for steamed lobster rather than boiled. Steamed lobster did not taste better than boiled, but the process was simpler and neater, and

the finished product was less watery when cracked open on the plate. Steaming the lobster on a rack or steamer basket kept it from becoming waterlogged. (If you happen to live near the ocean, seaweed makes a natural rack.) We found that neither beer nor wine in the pot improved the lobster's flavor, nor did any herbs, spices, or other seasonings. It seems that nothing can penetrate the hard lobster shell.

Although we had little trouble perfecting our cooking method, we were bothered by the toughness of some of the lobster tails we were eating. No matter how we cooked them, most of the tails were at least slightly rubbery and chewy.

We spent six months talking to research scientists, chefs, seafood experts, lobstermen, and home cooks to see how they tackled the problem of the tough tail. The suggestions ranged from the bizarre (petting the lobster to "hypnotize" it and thus prevent an adrenaline rush at death that causes the tail to toughen or using a chopstick to kill the lobster before cooking) to the sensible (avoiding really old, large lobsters). But after testing every one of these suggestions, we still didn't have a cooking method that consistently delivered a tender tail.

Occasionally, we would get a nice tender tail, but there did not seem to be a pattern. We then spoke with several scientists who said we were barking up the wrong tree. The secret to tender lobster was not so much in the preparation and cooking as in the selection.

Before working on this topic in the test kitchen, the terms hard-shell and soft-shell lobster meant nothing to us. Unlike crabs, lobsters are not clearly

HARD-SHELL VERSUS SOFT-SHELL LOBSTERS

To determine whether a lobster has a hard or soft shell, squeeze the side of the lobster's body. A soft-shell lobster will yield to pressure, while a hard-shell lobster will feel hard, brittle, and tightly packed.

distinguished in this way at the retail level. Of course, we knew from past experience that some lobster claws rip open as easily as an aluminum flip-top can, while others won't crack until you take out your shop tools. We also noticed the small, limp claw meat of some lobsters and the full, packed meat of others. We attributed these differences to the length of time the lobsters had been stored in the tank. It seems we were wrong. These variations are caused by the particular stage of molting that the lobster was in at the time it was caught.

As it turns out, most of the lobsters we eat during the summer and fall are in some phase of molting. During the late spring, as waters begin to warm, lobsters start to form new shell tissue underneath their old shells. As early as June off the shores of New Jersey and in July or August in colder Maine and Canadian waters, the lobsters shed their hard exterior shell. Because the most difficult task in molting is pulling the claw muscle through the old shell, the lobster dehydrates its claw (hence the smaller claw meat).

Once the lobster molts, it emerges with nothing but a wrinkled, soft covering, much like that on a soft-shell crab. Within 15 minutes, the lobster inflates itself with water, increasing its length by 15 percent and its weight by 50 percent. This extra water expands the wrinkled, soft covering, allowing the lobster plenty of room to grow long after the shell starts to harden. The newly molted lobster immediately eats its old shell, digesting the crucial shell-hardening calcium.

Understanding the molt phase clarifies the deficiencies of soft-shell summer lobster. It explains why it is so waterlogged, why its claw meat is so shriveled and scrawny, and why its tail meat is so underdeveloped and chewy. There is also far less meat in a 1-pound soft-shell lobster than in a hard-shell lobster that weighs the same.

During the fall, the lobster shell continues to harden, and the meat expands to fill the new shell.

REMOVING MEAT FROM STEAMED LOBSTERS

1. Twist the tail to separate it from the body.

2. Twist off the tail flippers.

3. Use a fork or your finger to push the tail meat up and out through the wide end of the tail.

4. Twist the claw appendages off the body.

5. Twist the claw from the connecting joint.

6. Remove the pincer of the claw. Use a gentle motion; the meat will often stay attached to the rest of claw. Otherwise, use a cocktail fork to pick out the meat.

7. Use lobster crackers to break open the claw and, if possible, remove the meat in a single piece.

8. Crack open the connecting joint and remove the meat with a cocktail fork.

By spring, lobsters are at their peak, packed with meat and relatively inexpensive since it is easier for fishermen to check their traps than it is during the winter. As the tail grows, it becomes firmer and meatier and will cook up tender, not tough. Better texture and more meat are two excellent reasons to give lobsters a squeeze at the market and buy only those with hard shells. As a rule of thumb, hard-shell lobsters are reasonably priced from Mother's Day through the Fourth of July.

Steamed Lobsters

SERVES 4

Hard-shell lobsters are much meatier than soft-shell lobsters, which have recently molted. To determine whether a lobster has a hard or soft shell, see the illustration on page 211. Because hard-shell lobsters are packed with more meat than soft-shell lobsters, you may want to buy slightly larger lobsters if the shells appear to be soft.

1   live lobsters
8   tablespoons unsalted butter, melted until hot
     (optional)
     Lemon wedges

Bring about 1 inch of water to a boil over high heat in a large stock pot set up with a wire rack, pasta

Approximate Steaming Times and Meat Yields for Lobster

LOBSTER SIZE	COOKING TIME (IN MINUTES)	MEAT YIELD (IN OUNCES)
1 lb		
SOFT-SHELL	8 to 9	about 3
HARD-SHELL	10 to 11	4 to 4½
1¼ lbs		
SOFT-SHELL	11 to 12	3½ to 4
HARD-SHELL	13 to 14	5½ to 6
1½ lbs		
SOFT-SHELL	13 to 14	5½ to 6
HARD-SHELL	15 to 16	7½ to 8
1¾ –2 lbs		
SOFT-SHELL	17 to 18	6¼ to 6½
HARD-SHELL	about 19	8½ to 9

insert, or seaweed bed. Add the lobsters, cover, and return the water to a boil. Reduce the heat to medium-high and steam until lobsters are done (see the table below). Serve immediately with warm butter and lemon wedges.

LOBSTER NEWBURG

THIS RICH LOBSTER DISH IS NAMED AFTER Ben Wenberg, a West Indies sea captain who gave the recipe to the chef at Delmonico's in New York City in 1876. Lobster Newburg was originally known as Lobster Wenberg. But when Ben got into a drunken brawl, he and his name were stricken from the restaurant and "Wenberg" became "Newburg." Considered one of the most luxurious dishes of the day, it consisted of lobster meat in a slightly spicy cream sauce served over rice, puff pastry, or toast points. Today, however, this dish is too heavy to sit well with most palates. Our goal in developing this recipe to its well-deserved place in modern cooking was to lighten and rejuvenate it, making it more appropriate for the modern age.

To begin, we tried several prominent recipes and focused on the trickiest and most important aspect of Newburg: the sauce. The sauce starts with cream that must be thickened with either egg yolks, a combination of flour and butter (a roux), or cornstarch. We tasted sauces made with all three options side by side. The yolk-based sauce had a near perfect consistency with an attractive, yellow hue, but was incredibly rich. The roux produced a thick, pasty sauce with a dull flavor, while the cornstarch contributed a fuzzy sheen and starchy mouthfeel. Throwing out the roux and cornstarch, we decided to work with the egg yolks. By reducing the number of yolks from six to four (for 1½ cups heavy cream), the sauce remained lush without being overly rich. We tried using three yolks but found the sauce lacking in both flavor and body.

Working with 4 yolks to 1½ cups of heavy cream, we tried replacing either part or all of the cream with half-and-half, milk, or chicken stock in an effort to further lighten the sauce. Although the half-and-half and milk did not fare well with our tasters, we liked a combination of chicken stock and cream. The stock added a savory note and helped mitigate the heavy dairy flavor of the sauces made with just cream or cream and either half-and-half or milk. By replacing ½ cup of the heavy cream with chicken stock, we were able to create a balanced and approachable base that was ready for seasoning.

Not wanting to load down the sauce with heavy aromatics, we found the perfumed flavor of shallot along with the gentle bite of sautéed garlic added just enough nuance. Many recipes called for either sherry or brandy, but we found the distinct flavor of both were necessary to balance the richness of the cream and egg. We cooked some of the liquor with the sauce but found that adding a fresh splash of liquor again at the end made the finished sauce more lively. Seasoned with a little nutmeg and a pinch of cayenne, the sauce also benefited from additions of freshly minced parsley and tarragon.

With the sauce in place, we moved on to the lobster. Steaming (rather than boiling) works especially well in this recipe. Not only does an inch of water come to a boil faster than an entire pot, but, when cooked, the lobsters retain less water, making the removal of meat from shell less messy. Four 1½-pound hard-shell lobsters (or five soft-shell lobsters) will yield the appropriate amount of meat to serve six people.

Lobster Newburg
SERVES 6

Serve over rice, a decorative puff pastry shell, or simple toast points. See the illustration on page 211 to learn how to tell if a lobster is a hard-shell or a soft-shell.

4	live 1½-pound hard-shell lobsters (or 5 soft-shell lobsters)
2	tablespoons unsalted butter
4	tablespoons minced shallots
2	medium cloves garlic, minced
3	tablespoons plus 1 teaspoon dry sherry
3	tablespoons plus 1 teaspoon brandy
½	cup homemade chicken stock or canned low-sodium chicken broth
1	cup heavy cream
	Pinch grated nutmeg
	Pinch cayenne pepper
	Salt and ground black pepper
4	large egg yolks
1½	tablespoons minced fresh parsley leaves
1½	teaspoons minced fresh tarragon leaves

1. Bring about 1 inch of water to a boil over high heat in a large stockpot set up with a wire rack, pasta insert, or seaweed bed. Add the lobsters, cover, and return the water to a boil. Reduce the heat to medium-high and steam until the lobsters are done, 15 to 16 minutes for hard-shell lobsters, 13 to 14 minutes for soft-shell lobsters. Off heat, remove the lobsters from the pot and let sit on a rimmed baking sheet until cool enough to handle. Following the illustrations on page 212, remove the lobster meat from the shells and cut it into 1-inch pieces. Set the lobster meat aside.

2. Melt the butter in a large skillet over medium heat until the foaming subsides. Add the shallots and cook until softened, 1½ to 2 minutes. Stir in the garlic and sauté until fragrant, about 30 seconds. Add 3 tablespoons sherry, 3 tablespoons brandy, and the chicken stock, bring to a simmer, and cook, stirring occasionally, until the sauce has reduced to ¾ cup, 3 to 4 minutes. Add the cream, nutmeg, cayenne, ¼ teaspoon salt, and ⅛ teaspoon pepper and bring back to a simmer. Cook until the sauce has thickened slightly and reduced to 1½ cups, to 4 minutes. Turn the heat to low.

REMOVING TENDONS FROM SCALLOPS

The small, rough-textured, crescent-shaped muscle that attaches the scallop to the shell will toughen when cooked. Use your fingers to peel the tendon away from the side of each scallop before cooking.

3. Whisk the yolks in a large bowl until they are broken up and combined. Whisk ¼ cup of the hot cream mixture into the yolks until loosened and combined. Whisk the tempered egg mixture back into the simmering cream mixture. Whisk constantly until evenly colored and thoroughly combined, about 30 seconds. Add lobster meat, parsley, tarragon, remaining 1 teaspoon sherry, and remaining 1 teaspoon brandy. Allow lobster to heat through, about 1 minute. Remove pan from the heat, season with salt and pepper to taste, and serve immediately.

➤ VARIATION

Seafood Newburg

Replacing some of the lobster with shrimp and scallops cuts some of the work associated with the recipe.

2	live 1½-pound hard-shell lobsters (or 2 soft-shell lobsters)
4	teaspoons vegetable oil
¾	pound medium shrimp, peeled and deveined
¾	pound sea scallops, tendons removed (see illustration on page 214)
2	tablespoons unsalted butter
4	tablespoons minced shallots
2	medium cloves garlic, minced
3	tablespoons plus 1 teaspoon dry sherry
3	tablespoons plus 1 teaspoon brandy
½	cup homemade chicken stock or canned low-sodium chicken broth
1	cup heavy cream
	Pinch grated nutmeg
	Pinch cayenne pepper
	Salt and ground black pepper
4	large egg yolks
1½	tablespoons minced fresh parsley leaves
1½	teaspoons minced fresh tarragon leaves

1. Bring about 1 inch of water to a boil over high heat in a large stockpot set up with a wire rack, pasta insert, or seaweed bed. Add the lobsters, cover, and return the water to a boil. Reduce the heat to medium–high and steam until the lobsters are done, 15 to 16 minutes for hard-shell lobsters, 13 to 14 minutes for soft-shell lobsters. Off heat, remove the lobsters from the pot, and let sit on a rimmed baking sheet until cool enough to handle. Following the illustrations on page 212, remove the lobster meat from the shells and cut into 1-inch pieces. Set the lobster meat aside.

2. Heat 2 teaspoons oil in a large skillet over high heat. Add the shrimp and sauté until curled, pink, and cooked through, 1 to 1½ minutes. Remove the shrimp from the pan and set aside in a medium bowl. Heat the remaining 2 teaspoons oil in the empty skillet. Lay scallops flat-side down in a single layer in the pan and cook until the bottoms are browned, 1 to 1½ minutes. Using a spatula, flip the scallops and cook on the second side until lightly browned, about 1½ minutes longer. Transfer the scallops to the bowl with the shrimp.

3. Set the empty pan over medium heat and add the butter. When the foaming subsides, add the shallots and cook until softened, 1½ to 2 minutes. Stir in the garlic and sauté until fragrant, about 30 seconds. Add 3 tablespoons sherry, 3 tablespoons brandy, and the chicken stock, bring to a simmer, and cook, stirring occasionally, until the sauce has reduced to ¾ cup, 3 to 4 minutes. Add the cream, nutmeg, cayenne, ¼ teaspoon salt, and ⅛ teaspoon pepper and bring back to a simmer. Cook until the sauce has thickened slightly and reduced to 1½ cups, 3 to 4 minutes. Turn the heat to low.

4. Whisk the yolks in a large bowl until they are broken up and combined. Whisk ¼ cup of the hot cream mixture into the yolks until loosened and combined. Whisk the tempered egg mixture back into the simmering cream mixture. Whisk constantly until evenly colored and thoroughly combined, about 30 seconds. Add the lobster meat, shrimp, scallops, parsley, tarragon, remaining 1 teaspoon sherry, and remaining 1 teaspoon brandy. Allow the lobster to heat through, about 1 minute. Remove the pan from the heat, season with salt and pepper to taste, and serve immediately.

SOFT-SHELL CRABS

THERE ARE DOZENS OF SPECIES OF CRABS, but the blue crab, which is found in waters along the East Coast, is the most common variety. Soft-shell crabs are blue crabs that have been taken out of the water just after they have shed their shells. At this brief stage of its life, the whole crab, with its new, soft, gray skin, is almost completely edible and fabulously delicious.

For the cook, soft-shells are a wonderfully immediate experience. Once cleaned, they demand to be cooked and eaten on the spot, so they offer a very direct taste of the sea. Because they must be cooked so quickly after they are killed and cleaned, home cooks have an advantage over restaurants. We're convinced that the best way to enjoy soft-shells is to cook them at home, where you can be sure to eat them within minutes of their preparation.

The whole point of preparing soft-shells is to get them crisp. The legs should crunch delicately, while the body should provide a contrast between its thin, crisp outer skin and the soft, rich interior that explodes juicily in the mouth. Deep-frying delivers these results, but this method is better suited to restaurants, since air pockets and water in the crab cause a lot of dangerous splattering. For optimum safety, soft-shell crabs should be deep-fried in a very large quantity of oil in a very deep pot, which is not practical at home.

We wanted to develop an alternative method for home cooks. We tried roasting, but the crabs did not get crisp enough. Grilling is not always practical, and broiling did not work well. In the end, we found that pan-frying produces a satisfyingly crisp crab. Crabs still splatter hot fat when cooked this way, but there is less fat to splatter than in deep-frying. To avoid the mess and danger of the splattering fat, we recommend sliding a splatter screen (see page 218) over the pan as the crabs cook.

A coating of some kind helps crisp the crab. We tried flour, cornmeal, bread crumbs, and even Cream of Wheat coatings and ended up choosing flour. It's a shame to hide the unique, essential flavor of the crab with a heavy coating, and flour provides a crisp crust without adding flavor. It also has the advantage of being on hand most of the time.

We also tried soaking the crabs in milk for two hours before applying the coating, as we had read that this process sweetens the crab. To the contrary, we found that milk takes away from the just-out-of-the-water flavor that we like.

The type of fat you use for frying is largely a matter of personal preference. We tried frying floured crabs in whole butter, clarified butter, vegetable and peanut oils, and a combination of whole butter and olive oil. Whole butter gave the crabs a delicious, nutty taste and browned them well. Clarified butter didn't brown them significantly better and was more work, so it offers no advantage over whole butter. (Clarified butter can be brought to higher temperatures than whole butter because the easily burnt milk solids have been removed.) Vegetable and peanut oils got the crab a hair crisper than butter and added no flavor; peanut oil crisped the crabs particularly well because it fries very hot without burning. The combination of butter and oil didn't give a

CLEANING A SOFT-SHELL CRAB

 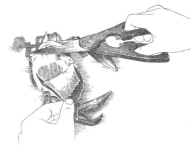 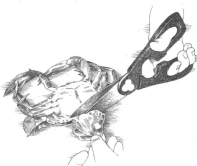

1. Cut off crab's mouth with kitchen scissors; the mouth is the first part of the shell to harden. You can also cut off the eyes at the same time, but this is for purely aesthetic purposes; the eyes are edible.

2. Lift the pointed sides of the crab, and cut out the spongy off-white gills underneath; the gills are fibrous and watery and unpleasant to eat.

3. Finally, turn the crab on its back and cut off the triangular, or T-shaped, "apron flap."

better result than either fat used separately, and we were surprised to find that the flavor of butter and even the flavorlessness of the other oils complement the crab better than the olive oil. Our preference is to fry with peanut oil or butter, depending on the taste we want and the kind of sauce we are making.

Whether you opt for peanut oil, vegetable oil, or butter, crabs fry best in quite a lot of fat. Count on at least one tablespoon of butter per crab depending on the size of the pan; the crabs actually seem to absorb the butter as they cook. When cooking with oil, we add the oil to a depth of ⅛ to ¼ inch. You can cook in any kind of pan, but a cast-iron pan holds heat particularly well and practically guarantees a crispy critter.

Once you've cooked the crabs, they should be sauced and served immediately. In a pinch, you can hold crabs for a few minutes in a 300-degree oven, but they're really better eaten practically out of the pan. Therefore, if you're serving a main course for four (count on two crabs per person), you'll need two pans, each at least 11 inches in diameter, if you expect everyone to sit down to eat together. If you have only one pan, your best bet is to let two people start on the first batch of crabs when they're cooked, while you start cooking the second batch. Or serve crabs as an appetizer—one per person is plenty. Because they're fried, the crabs don't need much of a sauce, just a drizzle of something acidic such as lemon juice or vinegar.

Pan-Fried Soft-Shell Crabs

SERVES 4

A splatter screen is essential if you want to minimize the mess and the danger to your arms and face. For maximum crispness, cook the crabs in two pans, each covered with a splatter screen, so you can serve the crabs as soon as they are cooked. If you are working with just one splatter screen and pan, cook four crabs in 4 tablespoons of butter, transfer them to a platter in a 300-degree oven, wipe out the pan, add 4 more tablespoons of butter, and cook the remaining crabs.

1 cup unbleached all-purpose flour
8 medium-to-large soft-shell crabs, cleaned (see illustrations on page 216) and patted dry with paper towels

10 tablespoons unsalted butter
¼ cup lemon juice
2 tablespoons minced fresh parsley leaves
   Salt and ground black pepper

1. Place the flour in a wide, shallow dish. Dredge the crabs in flour; pat off excess. Heat two 11- or 12-inch heavy-bottomed skillets over medium-high heat until the pans are quite hot, about 3 minutes. Add 4 tablespoons butter to each pan, swirling the pans to keep the butter from burning as it melts. When the foam subsides, add four crabs, shell-side down, to each pan. Cover each pan with a splatter screen and cook, adjusting the heat as necessary to keep the butter from burning, until the crabs turn reddish brown, about 3 minutes. Turn the crabs with a spatula or tongs and cook until the second side is browned, about 3 minutes more. Drain the crabs on a plate lined with paper towels.

2. Set one pan aside for cleaning. Pour off the butter from the other pan and remove from the

INGREDIENTS: Soft-Shell Crabs

Considering how perishable they are, it is not surprising that soft-shells can be quite difficult to locate. Fresh soft-shells are available only "in season," which used to mean a few short months during the summer. Now the "season" can extend from February all the way through to September and maybe even into October, depending on the weather. Frozen crabs may also be available, but they are not nearly as good.

Once you buy the crabs, your fishmonger will probably offer to clean them for you. If you like the crabs juicy, you'll be happier if you clean them yourself. The reason is that a crab, like a lobster, grows by shedding its hard shell periodically. After shedding, the crab swells with water to fill out its new skin, and the skin immediately begins to harden into a new, larger shell. When you clean a live crab, juice pours out of it. The longer the crab sits before cooking, the more liquid it loses. We found that a crab that is cooked immediately after cleaning is much plumper and juicier than a crab cleaned several hours before cooking. To clean a live crab, follow the illustrations on page 216.

We advise against storing soft-shells. Even a live crab won't stay that way very long in your refrigerator; because they can die from the cold temperature in your refrigerator, they're better off at the fish store, where they are kept not cold, but cool.

heat. Add the lemon juice to deglaze the hot pan. Cut the remaining 2 tablespoons butter into pieces and add to the skillet. Swirl the pan to melt the butter. Add the parsley and salt and pepper to taste. Arrange two crabs on each of four plates. Spoon some sauce over each plate and serve immediately.

➤ VARIATION

Pan-Fried Soft-Shell Crabs with Lemon, Capers, and Herbs

The pan sauce is tart and powerfully flavored; you need only about one tablespoon per serving.

Follow the recipe for Pan-Fried Soft-Shell Crabs, reducing the lemon juice to 3 tablespoons and adding 2 teaspoons sherry vinegar, 1½ teaspoons chopped capers, and 1 medium scallion, sliced thin, to the pan with the lemon juice in step 2. Proceed as directed, adding 2 teaspoons minced fresh tarragon with parsley, salt, and pepper.

CRAB BOIL

THE SCENE AT A CRAB BOIL ALWAYS LOOKS the same. Picnic tables are covered with layers of newspaper, towering stacks of napkins, and piles of mallets and other utensils for extracting meat from cooked crabs. A large tub of ice-chilled beer is somewhere nearby. Usually made for a crowd or party, a traditional crab boil simply throws sausage, corn, potatoes, and crabs together in a huge pot of spicy boiling broth set over an outdoor propane burner. When cooked through, the contents of the pot are strained and dumped over the newspaper-clad tables, and with the help of the mallets, the meal begins. Although we found a few recipes that tried to pare down the party-sized crab boil to an indoor, weeknight dinner, they either turned out bland or were complicated, requiring several pots of boiling broth to cook the components separately. We wanted to find a way to bring the party indoors without losing the authentic flavor, simple cooking method, and rustic charm of a true crab boil.

Although several types of crabs are edible, most boils call for blue crabs. Both male and female blue crabs are available, and although the males offer more meat, they are harder to find and more expensive.

EQUIPMENT: Splatter Screen

EQUIPMENT: Splatter Screen

Because they are full of water, soft-shell crabs spit hot fat when they are pan-fried. To protect your hands and face (and to keep your stovetop from becoming covered with grease), we recommend that you slide a splatter screen—a round, flat wire net with a handle—over the skillet with the crabs as they cook. Steam escapes through the netting so the crabs stay crisp (a lid would trap steam and make the crabs soggy), but the fat stays in the pan.

A splatter screen can be used whenever you are pan-frying. Just make sure to use a screen that is slightly larger than the skillet. Also, because the handle on many splatter screens is metal, it will become hot and should be handled with a pot holder or oven mitt.

Many markets sell bushels of male and female crabs separately; buy male crabs if you can. Blue crabs also come in a variety of sizes, with prices increasing along with the weight. As we found out, if you've never cooked crabs before, they are wily, little animals that can pinch the cook. Keep the crabs cool and accessible to circulating air, but contained, until you are ready to cook them. Although some recipes call for washing and scrubbing the crabs in cool water, we found this to be a nearly impossible as well as unnecessary task, as the crabs are "washed" when plunged into the boiling broth.

With the wily crabs confined to the refrigerator, we amassed the other ingredients and began to work on the method. The traditional boil includes sausage, potatoes, and corn, all of which are cooked in the same spicy broth as the crabs. Although these ingredients are usually cooked at once in the same pot, we couldn't find a pot large enough to accommodate them all. Because the crabs are quite voluminous and take up most of the room in a large stockpot, we quickly realized that they would have to be cooked separate from the other ingredients, but we still planned on cooking the potatoes, corn, and sausage together in the pot at the same time.

We found that small red potatoes were flavored nicely by the sausage. We tested several varieties and preferred the toothsome, dense texture and sweet flavor of Red Bliss. Tasters liked the potatoes when they were cooked whole rather than cut into pieces, which became messy. The corn, however, was more appropriately sized when cut in half. Tying the potatoes and sausage loosely in a cheesecloth sack and adding the corn in the last five minutes of cooking, we found, made them extremely easy to remove from the pot, leaving the broth ready for the crabs. Depending on the size of the crabs, we found they took anywhere from 7 to 15 minutes to turn dark red and cook through.

With the method in place, we focused our attention on the spices. We found several types of prepackaged crab boil mixtures, such as Old Bay to Zatarain's, along with many recipes for creating a mixture. Although the idea of creating our own spice mixture sounded appealing, the ingredient list quickly became very long and involved. More important, we liked the results (and ease) of Old Bay and Zatarain's just as well. Zatarain's comes in a "boil-in-bag" pouch, and we found its flavor milder than that of Old Bay. Tasters preferred the free-floating, fuller flavor of Old Bay as it clung to potatoes and worked its way into the crevices of the corn and crabs. We found 8 quarts of water seasoned with ½ cup of Old Bay (along with a little extra cayenne) made just the right amount of well-seasoned broth.

We tested adding onions and garlic to the pot and found the onions did very little while the garlic added a nice flavor. Other recipes call for either lemon or cider vinegar, and we liked the stronger flavor of vinegar. But because the vinegar did not agree with the potatoes and corn, we found it best to add it to the boil along with the crabs.

For the first few tests, we brought the water to a boil with the seasoning and then added the sack of potatoes and sausage. With an eye toward efficiency, however, we tried bringing the cold water, potatoes, sausage, spices, and garlic to a boil at the same time. The result was fantastic, as the gently heated water evenly cooked the potatoes alongside the flavorful sausage. By the time it hit a boil, the potatoes were almost done and the sausage was heated through, lending its smoky flavor to the broth along with the Old Bay.

Made in 45 minutes using only one pot, this recipe looks and tastes absolutely authentic when dumped out over a newspaper-covered kitchen table and served with melted butter, lemon wedges, and rolls of paper towels.

Crab Boil

SERVES 4

Make sure to buy crabs that are alive; don't cook any crabs that appear to be dead or whose eyes do not react to a gentle blow of breath. Handle the crabs with gloves or tongs, as their small, sharp claws are agile and can pinch. You will need a large pot (at least 12 quart capacity) for this recipe. Mallets, paring knives, meat pounders, hammers, and small frying pans are among the utensils that may be employed to help retrieve bits of crab meat from the shell. See the illustrations below for tips on extracting the meat.

EATING WHOLE BLUE CRABS

 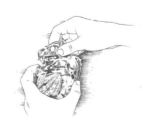 

1. Twist off the claws and legs and break them open with a mallet to expose the meat. Turn the crab upside down and insert a paring knife into the front. Twist the knife to loosen the bottom shell from the body.

2. Remove the knife and pry the bottom shell (at left above) away from the top shell. Discard the top shell.

3. Use your fingers to remove the feathery white gills on either side of the crab.

4. Use your hands to break the crab in half front to back. Break each piece in half again to expose the meat of the crab.

<table>
<tr><td>1</td><td>pound small red potatoes (about 1 inch in diameter)</td></tr>
</table>

1   pound small red potatoes (about 1 inch in
     diameter)

1   pound kielbasa sausage, cut into 1-inch lengths

½   cup Old Bay seasoning

1   medium head garlic, smashed with a mallet
     (with skins on)

1½   teaspoons cayenne pepper

⅓   cup salt

4   medium ears corn, husks and silk removed,
     ears cut in half

¼   cup cider vinegar

20   live blue crabs, preferably males, about
     6 ounces each (if smaller, use 28 to 32 crabs)

½   pound salted butter, melted

1   lemon, cut into wedges

1. Loosely tie potatoes and kielbasa in a large single layer of cheesecloth. Bring 8 quarts of water, Old Bay, garlic, cayenne, salt, potatoes, and kielbasa to a boil over high heat in a large stockpot. Cook until the potatoes are almost tender (a paring knife can be slipped into and out of the center of a potato with slight resistance), 10 to 15 minutes. Add the corn and cook until both the corn and potatoes are tender, about 5 minutes longer.

2. Remove the corn and the sack of potatoes with long tongs and transfer them to a large colander set in the sink to drain. Bring the spiced water back to a boil; add the vinegar and the crabs. Cook until the crabs are dark red, 7 to 15 minutes, depending on their size.

3. Meanwhile, remove the potatoes and sausage from the cheesecloth and place on a platter with the corn; cover to keep warm. When the crabs are fully cooked, carefully drain the entire pot into a colander set in a sink and allow to drain thoroughly. Spread several layers of newspaper over a large table and dump the crabs onto the paper. Serve immediately with butter, lemon wedges, crab cracking utensils (see note), and a large empty bowl for the empty shells.

CRAB CAKES

GOOD CRAB CAKES TASTE FIRST AND FOREmost of sweet crabmeat. Too many restaurants serve crab-flecked dough balls. That's why the crab cake is especially suited to home cooking.

Great crab cakes begin with top-quality crabmeat. We tested all the various options, and the differences are stark. Canned crabmeat is horrible; like canned tuna, it bears little resemblance to the fresh product. Fresh pasteurized crabmeat is watery and bland. Frozen crabmeat is stringy and wet. There is no substitute for fresh blue crabmeat, preferably "jumbo lump," which indicates the largest pieces and highest grade. This variety costs a couple of dollars a pound more than other types of fresh crab meat, but, since a 1-pound container is enough to make crab cakes for four, in our opinion, it's money well spent.

Fresh lump blue crab is available year-round but tends to be most expensive from December to March. The meat should never be rinsed, but it does need to be picked over to remove any shells or cartilage the processors may have missed.

Once we figured out what type of crab to use, our next task was to find the right binder. None of the usual suspects worked. Crushed saltines were a pain to smash into small-enough crumbs, potato chips added too much richness, and fresh bread crumbs blended into the crabmeat a little too well. We finally settled on fine dry bread crumbs. They have no overwhelming flavor and are easy to mix in. The trickiest part is knowing when to stop; crab cakes need just enough binder to hold them together but not so much that the filler overwhelms the seafood. We started out with ¾ cup crumbs but ended up reducing it down to just 2 tablespoons for our final recipe. Cooks who economize by padding out their pricey seafood with bread crumbs will end up with dough balls, not crab cakes.

The other ingredients we adopted are equally basic. Good, sturdy commercial mayonnaise (we like Hellmann's) keeps the crabmeat moist (a homemade blend can be too liquidy), and a whole egg, unbeaten, makes the crab, crumbs, and seasonings meld together both before and during cooking.

Classic recipes call for spiking crab cakes with everything from Tabasco to Worcestershire sauce, and those are both fine. But we've decided the best blend of tradition and trendiness is Old Bay seasoning combined with freshly ground white pepper and a tablespoon or more of chopped fresh herbs.

Just as essential as careful seasoning is careful mixing. We found a rubber spatula works best, used in a folding motion rather than stirring. This is important because you want to end up with a chunky consistency. Those lumps aren't cheap.

We were pleased with our basic recipe on most fronts, but we still had trouble keeping the cakes together as they cooked. Our last breakthrough came when we tried chilling the shaped cakes before cooking. As little as half an hour in the refrigerator made an ocean of difference. The cold firmed up the cakes so that they fried into perfect plump rounds without falling apart. We found that formed cakes can be kept, refrigerated and tightly wrapped, for up to 24 hours.

We also tried different cooking methods. After baking, deep-frying, and broiling, we settled on pan-frying in a cast-iron skillet over medium-high heat. This method is fast and also gives the cook complete control over how brown and how crisp the cakes get. We first tried frying in butter, but it burned as it

---

DIPPING SAUCES FOR SEAFOOD

These sauces work especially well with salmon cakes (page 206), trout or catfish fillets (pages 208 to 209), crab cakes (page 222), and fried oysters (page 224). You might also serve one of these sauces with steamed lobsters (page 213).

Tartar Sauce

MAKES GENEROUS ³/₄ CUP

The classic sauce for fried seafood.

- ³/₄ cup mayonnaise
- 1¹/₂ tablespoons minced cornichons (about 3 large), plus 1 teaspoon cornichon juice
- 1 tablespoon minced scallion
- 1 tablespoon minced red onion
- 1 tablespoon capers, minced

Mix all ingredients in a small bowl. Cover and refrigerate until the flavors blend, at least 30 minutes. (The sauce can be refrigerated for up to several days.)

Creamy Lemon Herb Sauce

MAKES GENEROUS ¹/₂ CUP

This sauce is flavorful, but it won't overpower delicate seafood.

- ¹/₂ cup mayonnaise
- 2¹/₂ tablespoons juice from 1 lemon
- 1 tablespoon minced fresh parsley leaves
- 1 tablespoon minced fresh thyme leaves

- 1 large scallion, white and green part, minced
- ¹/₂ teaspoon salt
- Ground black pepper

Mix all ingredients in a small bowl; season to taste with pepper. Cover and refrigerate until flavors blend, about 30 minutes. (The sauce can be refrigerated for up to several days.)

Creamy Chipotle Chile Sauce

MAKES ABOUT ¹/₂ CUP

This sauce is the richest and most complex of the three.

- ¹/₄ cup mayonnaise
- ¹/₄ cup sour cream
- 2 teaspoons minced canned chipotle chiles in adobo sauce
- 1 small clove garlic, minced
- 2 teaspoons minced fresh cilantro leaves
- 1 teaspoon juice from 1 lime

Mix all ingredients in a small bowl. Cover and refrigerate until the flavors blend, about 30 minutes. (The sauce can be refrigerated for up to several days.)

saturated the crab cakes. Cut with vegetable oil, it was still too heavy and made a mess of the pan. The ideal medium turned out to be plain old vegetable oil. It can be heated without burning and smoking, it creates a crisp crust, and it never gets in the way of the crab flavor.

Pan-Fried Crab Cakes

SERVES 4

The amount of bread crumbs you add will depend on the crabmeat's juiciness. Start with the smallest amount, adjust the seasonings, then add the egg. If the cakes won't bind at this point, then add more bread crumbs, 1 tablespoon at a time.

I	pound jumbo lump crabmeat, picked over to remove cartilage or shell
4	scallions, green part only, minced (about ¹/₂ cup)
I	tablespoon chopped fresh herb, such as cilantro, dill, basil, or parsley
I¹/₂	teaspoons Old Bay seasoning
2–4	tablespoons plain dry bread crumbs
¹/₄	cup mayonnaise
	Salt and ground white pepper
I	large egg
¹/₄	cup all-purpose flour
¹/₄	cup vegetable oil
	Lemon wedges or one of the dipping sauces on page 221

1. Gently mix the crabmeat, scallions, herb, Old Bay, 2 tablespoons bread crumbs, and mayonnaise in a medium bowl, being careful not to break up the lumps of crab. Season with salt and white pepper to taste. Carefully fold in the egg with a rubber spatula until the mixture just clings together. Add more crumbs if necessary.

2. Divide the crab mixture into four portions and shape each into a fat, round cake, about 3 inches across and 1¹/₂ inches high. Arrange on a baking sheet lined with waxed or parchment paper; cover with plastic wrap and chill at least 30 minutes. (The crab cakes can be refrigerated up to 24 hours.)

3. Put the flour on a plate or in a pie tin. Lightly dredge the crab cakes in the flour. Heat the oil in a large, preferably nonstick skillet over medium-high heat until hot but not smoking. Gently lay chilled crab cakes in the skillet; pan-fry until the outsides are crisp and browned, 4 to 5 minutes per side. Serve immediately with lemon wedges or dipping sauce.

FRIED OYSTERS

OYSTERS ARE AMONG THE FEW FOODS THAT are perfectly delicious with no preparation (apart from being pried from their shells). But as with many foods, they taste still better when deep-fried. Dusted with cornmeal, these little morsels make for mouth-watering hors d'oeuvres, an authentic New Orleans po' boy sandwich (see page 266), or simply an exotic snack. But there is nothing more disappointing than fresh oysters fried in a batter so dense it obscures the delicately flavored interior. In search of a reliable recipe that could successfully produce fried oysters at home, we were giddy with anticipation at the thought of perfecting this bayou classic.

As tasters jockeyed for a position close to the hot oil, we fried up a few different recipes. Most recipes we found used a bound breading—the oysters were dipped in flour, then an egg wash, then flour again—sometimes swapping the flour for either cornmeal or cornstarch. A few recipes, however, called for a tempura-like batter lightened with beer or club soda. Oysters fried in a bound breading turned out dense and heavy with minimal oyster flavor shining through. The tempura batters, on the other hand, were light and crisp but lacked the satisfaction of a cornmeal crunch. While none of these recipes was right on, it helped to narrow our focus. We now knew that we wanted a fried oyster with a little cornmeal flavor, a satisfying crunch, and a potent yet tender interior. With unwavering enthusiasm, the tasters lined up again around the bubbling oil and waited.

First we tried a cornmeal-tempura batter, hoping to combine disparate methods and flavors for a perfect crust. When fried, however, the batter turned cake-like, with a soggy inner layer that sloshed around the oyster. Realizing this would never work, we moved on to different breading methods, downgrading the dense, heavy three-stage bound breading to a two-stage and a one-stage. A two-stage breading includes a dip in egg, then into cornmeal, while a one-stage is a simple dusting of cornmeal. After drying off more oysters, we dipped, dusted, and fried another round. While the two-stage turned out much lighter than the three-stage, the coating was still too thick and overpowering. The one-stage, on the other hand, was nearly perfect. The coating was crisp and light with a good, mild flavor, but we found it fell off the oyster as it fried, leaving the oysters naked in spots.

While giving the oysters the old one-two in the previous round, a bell went off in our heads. Why were we drying off the oysters? Although it is a common practice to dry off pieces of chicken and fish before breading and frying, we wondered what would happen if we left the oysters a bit wet. Using their natural juices (also known as liquor) in place of an egg wash, we simply lifted them from the bowl, letting the excess liquor run off before tossing them with cornmeal. It took only one bite of these perfectly coated and fried oysters to know we were on to something. The oyster liquor was slightly more loose than the egg wash, helping a light layer of cornmeal cling to the oyster. This liquor also boosted the oysters' natural flavor.

Moving on to the cornmeal mixture itself, we found coarse cornmeal too hearty for delicate oysters and preferred finely ground cornmeal. We then tried mixing equal parts cornmeal and all-purpose flour and found that this crust had the perfect balance of crispness and crunch. Although some recipes add cornstarch, we found its powdery texture and talc-like flavor all wrong. After frying up many batches, we noted the importance of seasoning the cornmeal/flour mixture amply with salt, pepper, and cayenne, as their flavors dissipate rapidly in the hot oil.

We briefly tested frying the oysters at different temperatures and realized that their small size called for a high temperature that would give the cornmeal coating a chance to brown before the oysters became overcooked and tough. In 400-degree oil, the oysters needed only 2 minutes in the pot to cook perfectly, remaining moist and tender inside and developing a thin, crisp coating outside. We drained the fried oysters onto paper towels to rid them of excess oil, then transferred them to an elevated wire rack in a warm oven to keep them crisp while the remaining oysters hit the hot oil.

Finally, while tasters showed a slight preference for oysters that we shucked ourselves, it was not enough to cause us to take on the extra work and expense involved with unshucked oysters. Using the perishable, half-pound containers of freshly shucked oysters sold at the fish counter, all we had to do was check for renegade bits of shell before breading.

INGREDIENTS: Shucked Oysters

Although you can shuck your own oysters (see page 226 for tips on buying an oyster knife), we strongly recommend that you leave this job to your fishmonger when frying oysters. If at all possible, buy freshly shucked oysters at a reputable fish market rather than purchasing oysters packed and shipped in a plastic container or in a tin with a plastic lid.

There are several advantages to having your oysters shucked to order. First, you'll know that the oysters were just taken out of their shells, which is an indicator of freshness. Second, you'll be able to control the number of oysters per pint. When we purchased already packed pints, we found that the number of oysters per pint ranged from 25 to 50!

If you can find only packed oysters, make sure that the lid on the container is tightly sealed, and avoid containers that are swelling or blown up—this happens when the oysters are releasing gas and indicates that they are old. Packed oysters should be clearly dated so that you can judge their freshness. Some oysters will be packed with a "pull" date—the date after which the oysters can no longer be sold. Look for a pull date that is as far in the future as possible.

The oysters themselves should be fairly uniform in size and plump, with a smooth, creamy color. They should also be shiny, but not slimy. Slime indicates that the oysters are way past their prime. The oyster liquor should be clear (it might have a very slight gray tinge), not milky or cloudy. If you can, smell the oysters—superfresh oysters will have a very fresh, salty, ocean-like smell. Never buy oysters that have a fishy or "low tide" odor.

It's best to use oysters on the same day that you buy them, but, if necessary, oysters can be refrigerated (in a closed container, in their liquor) for up to two days. Store the container in a bowl of ice to keep the oysters well-chilled.

Served with tartar sauce or wedges of lemon, these fried oysters are among the best we've ever tasted. And the recipe couldn't be simpler.

Fried Oysters

MAKES 45, SERVING 6 TO 8

Although fried oysters are usually made for a party, this recipe can easily be reduced by half or even a third. When reducing the recipe, use an appropriately sized pot with fairly high sides to prevent excess splattering, and cover the bottom with an inch of oil for frying. We found a Chinese wire skimmer made quick and easy work of gathering the hot, fried oysters from the oil, while letting most of the hot oil fall back into the pot.

¾	cup fine-ground cornmeal
¾	cup unbleached all-purpose flour
1½	teaspoons salt
¾	teaspoon ground black pepper
¼	teaspoon cayenne pepper
1	pound shucked oysters in their liquor (about 45 oysters)
5–6	cups peanut or vegetable oil
	Lemon wedges or one of the dipping sauces on page 221

1. Set a wire rack over a rimmed baking sheet and place on the middle rack in the oven; warm the oven to 200 degrees. In a large, shallow dish, mix together the cornmeal, flour, salt, pepper, and cayenne. In a separate, medium bowl, combine all oysters with their liquor (juices) and check for bits of shell. Using a slotted spoon, scoop up about 8 oysters, briefly allowing the excess liquor to drip off, and scatter them across the cornmeal mixture. Shake the dish to coat the oysters evenly with cornmeal mixture. Transfer the oysters to a second wire rack set over a rimmed baking sheet. Repeat with the remaining oysters.

2. Heat 1 inch of oil in a large, heavy-bottomed Dutch oven over high heat until the oil reaches a temperature of 400 degrees. Drop ⅓ of the breaded oysters (about 15 oysters) in the hot oil. Using a wire skimmer, stir and poke at the oysters as they fry to prevent them from fusing together. Adjust the heat as necessary to keep the oil at 400 degrees. Remove the oysters from the hot oil with the wire skimmer

when they have turned golden brown and the frying has slowed, about 2 minutes. Transfer the oysters to a plate lined with several layers of paper towel, then to the clean wire rack set over the rimmed baking sheet in the oven to keep warm. Return the oil to 400 degrees and repeat with remaining oysters. Serve with lemon wedges or dipping sauce.

OYSTERS ROCKEFELLER

ABUNDANT AND INEXPENSIVE, OYSTERS have long been the fancy of chefs developing recipes for the American dining public. Oysters Rockefeller—which was first served at Antoine's Restaurant in New Orleans in 1899—is probably the most famous of these recipes. Although the original concoction is still a "secret," according to Antoine's, most recipes call for oysters on a half-shell dolloped with spinach puree, topped with bacon, and run under the broiler. Very often these recipes suffocate the sweet, ethereal flavor of the oyster with a heavy, dense spinach mixture and overly smoky bacon. Looking to enhance the oyster's gentle flavor, we set out to develop a recipe for oysters Rockefeller that would live up to its elegant namesake.

Starting with the oysters, we tested the main varieties native to waters off the United States. Although these varieties range in flavor from sweet to flinty, mild to potent, and soft to toothsome, the only requirement for oysters Rockefeller is size. Small oysters, such as Olympia and Kumamoto, simply don't offer enough surface area to hold the spinach puree. Using large Atlantic oysters (Pacific oysters are another good option), we began to shuck our way through the first batch and immediately learned a few tricks.

First off, oysters are very gritty and need to be well scrubbed, using an abrasive sponge and plenty of water. Shucking, we soon found out, takes a little practice but is a straightforward procedure requiring only time and a little muscle (see the illustrations on page 225). Once opened, the oyster contains meat as well as a liquid, known as oyster liquor. When oysters are eaten raw, this liquor is carefully kept in the half-shell and served with the meat. When making

Rockefeller, however, it is necessary to pour this liquor off. If left in the shell, it puts a slippery barrier between the spinach puree and the oyster, allowing the puree to slide around. But knowing that the liquor is full of valuable flavor, we decided to reserve it and see if we could use it later.

With shucked oysters at the ready, we turned our attention to the spinach puree. Most recipes we looked at used spinach, bread crumbs, shallots (or scallions), butter, and bacon, but the remaining ingredients are not as standard. Some use heavy cream or Hollandaise sauce, while others include fennel, watercress, celery, a variety of herbs, Pernod (a licorice-flavored liquor), Worcestershire sauce, cayenne, and Parmesan or Gruyère cheese. Setting these variables aside, we worked with the standard ingredients and easily nailed down the technique. It became immediately obvious that sautéing the vegetables in butter before turning them into a puree was necessary. Otherwise, the puree tasted harsh and bitter.

With technique in hand, we focused on the standard ingredients beginning with spinach. We tried frozen spinach, regular fresh spinach, and baby spinach in side by side batches. The frozen spinach was stringy and tasted like an old freezer, while the regular spinach released lots of moisture and had a harsh, tannic flavor. The baby spinach, however, was delicate both in texture and flavor, wilting quickly in the sauté pan and releasing much less liquid. Sold pre-washed in tidy bags, baby spinach needed no preparation and added plenty of earthy, green flavor without overpowering the delicate oysters.

We tested both shallots and scallions but found the perfumed shallot superior to the harsher scallion. Omitting the bread crumbs altogether, the puree turned loose and soupy, but store-bought crumbs were heavy, with a stale flavor. Instead, we liked the sweet flavor and absorbent texture of freshly processed sandwich bread. Although many recipes call for crisp bites of bacon to garnish the top of each oyster, we found the smoky pork flavor only bullied the fine flavor of oyster out of the limelight. Deciding to omit the bacon, we began to look into the other seasonings as well as binders.

Using the reserved oyster liquor from shucking, we tried adding it to the puree (about 2 tablespoons) and were amazed at the boost in oyster flavor. The liquor added an undeniable oyster essence that permeated the spinach. While many recipes add a splash of cream to help enrich the puree, we found it simply muted the clean, light spinach and oyster flavors. Adding several herbs and greens, we liked only the fresh flavor of parsley. Chives and chervil had flavors that were difficult to notice, while watercress and fennel were too overpowering. Tasters liked a bit of tarragon in the mix, although it did not compare to the impressive flavor of Pernod, which has a similar flavor. Just a splash of Pernod perfectly complemented the oyster, adding both complexity and nuance to the puree. A little garlic furthered this complexity, while red pepper flakes added a nice, gentle kick. Finally, we found the flavor of Gruyère, rather than Parmesan, paired well with both the oyster and the Pernod, while helping

SHUCKING OYSTERS

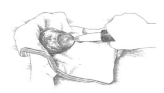   

1. Start by holding the oyster cupped-side down in a kitchen towel. Keep the oyster flat as you work to keep the flavorful juices from spilling out of the shell. Locate the hinge with the tip of the knife.

2. Push between the edges of the shells, wiggling back and forth to pry them open.

3. Detach the meat from the top shell and discard the shell.

4. To make eating easier, sever the muscle that holds the meat of the oyster to the bottom shell. As you do all of this, work over a bowl to catch the precious oyster liquor that is released.

the puree cling to the oyster in the oven.

One tablespoon of this simple puree evenly covered one Atlantic oyster, offering the best ratio of oyster to spinach. Most recipes call for pans filled with rock salt to hold the oysters level as they cook. Several recipes even call for heating the salt through beforehand, claiming it helps the oysters to cook evenly. Not only did we find placing the filled oysters in hot salt a hassle, but the extra heat actually overcooked the oysters, turning them rubbery. Instead, we simply placed the shucked oysters and their shells directly into a wide shallow dish filled with ½ inch of rock salt. The rock salt held the oysters level as they were filled, allowing the meat and puree to nestle safely in the deep curve of the shell. We tried table and kosher salt instead of rock salt but found that these small granules made their way into the oyster, much like unwelcome beach sand onto a clean blanket. It is necessary to use low-sided dishes to allow the heat of the broiler quick and easy access to the filled oysters. When placed under the broiler, it took only 10 minutes for the spinach puree to heat through and the cheese to brown, at which point the oysters were gently cooked through, with their edges slightly ruffled.

With the oysters fresh out of the oven, tasters eagerly gathered around and simultaneously burned their mouths. After allowing the oysters to cool for several minutes, we agreed that they tasted rich and refined, with multiple layers of complex flavor. Finally, a dish able to live up to the name Rockefeller.

Oysters Rockefeller
SERVES 4

We found that the oysters were easy to manage and looked attractive when broiled in two 9-inch pie plates. They can also be cooked all together in a shallow dish large enough to hold the 12 oysters with ample space between (roughly 9 by 13 inches). Depending on your broiler, cooking times may vary.

3	cups rock salt
12	large oysters, well scrubbed (preferably Atlantic or Pacific oysters)
2	tablespoons unsalted butter
2	large shallots, minced (about ¼ cup)
¼	teaspoon salt
⅛	teaspoon ground black pepper
	Pinch hot red pepper flakes

EQUIPMENT: Oyster Knives

Shucking oysters is a difficult task best left to the fishmonger when possible. But if you want to serve oysters on the half-shell or oysters Rockefeller at home, you must open them yourself. We decided to investigate oyster knives and see if the choice of utensil could make this job any easier.

What should you look for when choosing an oyster knife? First and foremost, an oyster knife must be safe to use. The handle should be easy to grip, even when your hands become slippery or wet. An oyster knife should also be efficient. If it takes five minutes to open every oyster, the knife is nearly useless.

Most knives specifically designed for opening oysters have short handles and short, flat blades that taper to a point. Some models have a round piece of metal that separates the blade from the handle. The guard at the base of the blade is designed to reduce the risk of injury. Many experts claim that an old-fashioned church-key can opener can be used on oysters. These sources suggest using the pointed tip designed for punching holes in cans, not the flat end designed for opening bottles.

We rounded up seven oyster knives, a church-key can opener, and several hundred oysters. We had both experienced shuckers and complete novices open several oysters with each knife. There was unanimous consensus about which knives made this difficult task easier.

Everyone agreed that it's worth spending the money on an oyster knife. Yes, you may eventually open a few oysters with a can opener, but the task will be frustrating and time-consuming. Among oyster knives, testers preferred models with sharp, pointed tips that were angled slightly upward. This design made it surprisingly easy to make that first penetration into the hinge between the top and bottom shells. Testers also preferred plastic handles that were contoured and textured. These handles felt more secure and comfortable than wooden ones. A blade guard between the blade and handle is a useful feature, but it should not come at the expense of blade length. We found that longer blades are better able to detach the oyster meat from the shells.

2   medium cloves garlic, minced

4   ounces baby spinach (5 cups loosely packed)

1   slice high-quality white sandwich bread,
     such as Pepperidge Farm, crusts removed,
     torn into 4 pieces

1/4   cup loosely packed fresh parsley leaves

2   tablespoons Pernod

2   tablespoons grated Gruyère cheese

1   lemon, cut into wedges

1. Adjust one oven rack so that it is 6 inches from the broiler element. Spread ½ inch of rock salt into two 9-inch pie plates or cake pans or other appropriate dish (see note). Following the illustrations on page 225, shuck the oysters, reserving the oyster liquor in a small bowl. Gently nestle 12 half-shells holding one oyster each into the rock salt.

2. Heat the butter in a large nonstick skillet over medium heat until the foaming subsides. Add the shallots, salt, pepper, and red pepper flakes and sauté until the shallots soften, about 2 minutes. Add the garlic and sauté until fragrant, about 30 seconds. Add the spinach and sauté, tossing occasionally, until the spinach has fully wilted, about 1½ minutes. Remove the pan from the heat and set aside.

3. Pulse the bread in the workbowl of a food processor fitted with a steel blade until it turns to coarse crumbs (resembling Grape-Nuts), about ten 1-second pulses. Add the reserved spinach mixture, the reserved oyster liquor, parsley, Pernod, and Gruyère. Pulse, scraping the sides of the workbowl down as necessary, until the mixture forms a smooth paste, about ten 1-second pulses. Spoon 1 tablespoon of the spinach mixture on top of each oyster.

4. Broil the oysters until spotty brown, about 10 minutes. Allow the oysters to cool for several minutes before serving them straight from the hot, salted dish with lemon wedges.

CLAMBAKE

A CLAMBAKE IS A RITE OF SUMMER ALONG the East Coast. At this festive beach party, loads of shellfish and a variety of vegetables are steamed in a wide, sandy pit using seaweed and rocks warmed from a nearby campfire. This feast usually takes a day or more to prepare—digging the pit is no small chore—and hours to cook. We wanted to re-create the great flavors of the clambake indoors. Though some may mock the idea of a kitchen clambake, it is nonetheless a simple and efficient way (taking a mere half-hour) to prepare a fantastic shellfish dinner—complete with corn, potatoes, and sausage—for a hungry crowd.

An indoor clambake is not a novel idea. We found dozens of recipes in our cookbook library. While the methods used to put together an indoor clambake vary dramatically, the ingredients, in keeping with tradition, are fairly consistent, including clams, mussels, lobsters, potatoes, corn, onions, and spicy sausage. Some recipes tell the cook to partially cook each ingredient separately and then finish things together on the grill, while others recommend specific systems for layering the ingredients in a stockpot. Some recipes use seaweed or corn husks for extra flavor, while others tout the importance of smoky bacon. The common goal of all these recipes, however, is to manage the process such that the various components are cooked perfectly and ready to serve at the same time. Taking note of these different clambake styles, we began our testing.

It soon became apparent which methods were worthwhile and which simply made a mess. Partially cooking the ingredients separately before combining them on the grill was time-consuming and produced a clambake without that authentic clambake flavor. Layering the various ingredients in a stockpot, on the other hand, was both easy to do and produced tasty results. With the stockpot set over high heat, the components steamed and infused one another with their flavors. This method was not without problems, however, as the onions turned out slimy, and half the ingredients wound up submerged in shellfish-flavored water. Using this pot method as a point of departure, we began to tinker with the method and the ingredients.

Although all of the recipes we uncovered called

for adding water to the pot to create steam for cooking, we found the shellfish released enough of their own liquid to make adequate steam. When placed over high heat, the shellfish took only a few minutes to release the moisture needed to steam the whole pot, with a cup or more left over to use as a sauce for the clams and mussels. We took advantage of those first few minutes when the pot was dry by lining it with sliced sausage, giving it a chance to sear before the steam was unleashed. We tested several kinds of sausage, and tasters preferred mild kielbasa. The light smoke flavor of this sausage works well with seafood, and the sausage is fairly juicy and fatty, making it perfectly suited to this cooking method.

With the sausage layered on the bottom, we played with the order in which to add the remaining ingredients. We found it best to lay the clams and mussels right on top of the sausage because they provide most of the necessary liquid for the steam and needed to be close to the heat source. Wrapping them loosely in a cheesecloth sack makes them easy to remove when done. Although potatoes actually take the longest to cook, they were best laid on top of the clams and mussels, close to the heat source yet easily accessible with a prodding knife to test their doneness. We shortened their cooking time by cutting the potatoes into 1-inch pieces.

Corn, with a layer of husk left on, was placed on top of the potatoes. The husk, we found, protects the delicate corn from becoming infused with too much shellfish flavor. The husk also protects the corn from any foam released by the lobsters, which we placed on top of the corn. We decided to omit the onions, which no one ate; the bacon, which smoked out the delicate flavor of the shellfish; and the seaweed, which was hard to find and unnecessary for flavor.

Layered in this fashion, the clambake took just 17 to 20 minutes to cook through completely over high heat. Surprisingly, the shellfish liquid is quite salty and naturally seasons all the ingredients. After taking a couple of minutes to remove the ingredients from the pot and arrange them attractively on a platter, we had a feast that had been made from start to finish in half an hour.

Indoor Clambake

SERVES 4 TO 6

Choose a large, narrow stockpot in which you can easily layer the ingredients. The recipe can be cut in half and layered in an 8-quart Dutch oven, but it should cook in the same amount of time.

2	pounds littleneck or cherrystone clams, scrubbed
2	pounds mussels, shells scrubbed and beards removed
1	pound kielbasa, sliced into $1/3$-inch-thick rounds
1	pound small new or red potatoes, scrubbed and cut into 1-inch pieces
2	live lobsters (about 1 $1/2$ pounds each)
4	medium ears corn, silk and all but the last layer of husk removed (see illustrations on page 49)
8	tablespoons salted butter, melted

1. Place the clams and mussels on a large piece of cheesecloth and tie the ends together to secure; set aside. In a large, heavy bottomed, 12-quart stockpot, layer the sliced kielbasa, the sack of clams and mussels, the potatoes, the corn, and the lobsters on top of one another. Cover with the lid and place over high heat. Cook until the potatoes are tender (a paring knife can be slipped into and out of the center of a potato with little resistance), and the lobsters are bright red, 17 to 20 minutes.

2. Remove the pot from the heat and remove the lid (watch out for scalding steam). Remove the lobsters and set aside until cool enough to handle. Remove the corn from the pot and peel off the husks; arrange the ears on a large platter. Using a slotted spoon, remove the potatoes and arrange them on the platter with the corn. Transfer the clams and mussels to a large bowl and cut open the cheesecloth with scissors. Using a slotted spoon, remove the kielbasa from the pot and arrange it on the platter with the potatoes and corn. Pour the remaining steaming liquid in the pot over the clams and mussels. With a kitchen towel in your hand, twist and remove the lobster tails, claws, and legs (if desired). Arrange the lobster parts on the platter. Serve immediately with melted butter and an ample amount of napkins.

9

YEAST BREADS, ROLLS, AND PIZZAS

THIS CHAPTER COVERS BASIC LOAF BREADS, rolls, sticky buns, and pizza. Although ingredients vary among these recipes, there are two constants. All of these favorite baked goods are made with yeast, and the doughs must be kneaded.

Several kinds of yeast are available to home cooks. All yeast begins as a small, cultured, purified sample that feeds and multiplies continuously in a liquid medium until it reaches the desired volume and stage of development. This liquid yeast is sold by the tankerful to commercial food manufacturers. For bakeries, yeast companies remove some of the moisture from liquid yeast to create a product called crumbled yeast, which is sold in 50-pound bags. The next processing step extrudes the yeast to make a product that remains fully hydrated yet fine enough to press into the small cakes you see for sale in supermarkets, labeled cake yeast. Further processing yields dried, powdered yeast, called active dry yeast. (The same process is used to make other dry yeasts, including rapid-rise and instant yeasts, although these products start with different strains of yeast. For more information on rapid-rise and instant yeast, see page 235.)

Starting with the correct ingredients is part of the puzzle when making good breads, rolls, and pizzas. Proper technique is equally important. Our experience in the test kitchen has revealed the importance of several issues.

MEASURING FLOUR

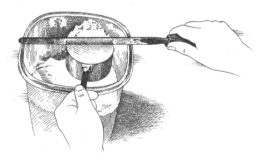

No matter the type or brand, we measure all flour by the dip-and-sweep method. Dip a metal or plastic dry measure into a bag of flour so that the cup is overflowing. Then use the flat side of a knife or an icing spatula to level off the flour, sweeping the excess back into the bag. Short of weighing flour (which is what professional bakers do), this measuring method is your best guarantee of using the right amount of flour. Spooning the flour into the measuring cup aerates it, and you might end up with as much as 25 percent less flour by weight.

First of all, most bread doughs do not require lengthy kneading. In fact, we have found that kneading bread for 10 to 15 minutes can often produce an inferior loaf. Often the kneading that occurs in a standing mixer or food processor (coupled with a minute or two on a floured surface to bring the dough together in a ball) will suffice.

If you are kneading by hand, resist the temptation to add too much flour to the dough or you risk a dry texture. (This temptation is one reason why we prefer to knead bread dough in a standing mixer or food processor when possible.) In many recipes, the dough will at first seem very sticky, as if it needs more flour. However, as it rises, the dough hydrates—that is, the water becomes more evenly distributed as the flour absorbs it—and the texture becomes very soft and smooth. So do not add more flour unless the dough seems much too wet. One way to avoid adding more flour is to slightly moisten your hands to prevent sticking.

On rare occasions, you may find that a loaf does not rise properly. Check to make sure that the expiration date on your yeast has not passed. Another possibility is that the water was too hot and killed the yeast. (Water used to make bread should be no hotter than 115 degrees.) A poor rise may also mean that you have added too much flour or placed the bread in a cool, drafty spot. To remedy the latter situation, heat your oven for 10 minutes at 200 degrees and turn it off; the oven can now be used as a proofing box. A microwave oven can also be used as a proofing box. All that's involved is to nearly fill a 2-cup Pyrex measure with water, place it in the microwave, and bring the water to a boil; the dough (which should be in a bowl covered with plastic wrap) is then placed in the microwave oven with the measuring cup. The preheated water will keep the microwave oven at the proper temperature for rising.

It should also be noted that the length of time the bread is in the oven has a tremendous effect on texture and quality. Most cookbooks tell you to tap the bottom of a loaf of bread to see if it is done. (Supposedly, a loaf will sound hollow when done.) This is, at best, an inexact method. We find it is much better to use an instant-read thermometer. For bread baked in a loaf pan, insert the thermometer into one end of the loaf, angling it down

INGREDIENTS: All-Purpose Flour

We wanted to know if there was a single all-purpose flour that would be best for those who keep only one kind of flour in the pantry. So we stocked our test kitchen shelves with nine brands of all-purpose flour and started a bake-off that eventually stretched over some six months. We ended up preparing two kinds of cookies, pie pastry, biscuits, cake, muffins, and bread with each brand of flour, often making several batches of each item.

When milling all-purpose flour, a flour company must make a number of choices that will influence the way its product performs in recipes. For starters, there is the essence of the flour, the wheat itself. All-purpose flour is typically made from hard red winter wheat, soft red winter wheat, or a combination of the two. Of the flours we used in the taste tests, five were made from hard winter wheat, one was made of soft wheat, and three were a mix of soft and hard.

Perhaps the primary difference between these types of wheat—and, consequently, the flours made from them—is the variation in protein content. Hard winter wheat is about 10 to 13 percent protein, soft wheat about 8 to 10 percent. Mixtures of the two wheats are somewhere in between. You can actually feel this difference with your fingers; the hard wheat flours tend to have a subtle granular feel, while soft wheat flours feel fine but starchy, much like cornstarch.

High-protein flours are generally recommended for yeasted products and other baked goods that require a lot of structural support. The reason is that the higher the protein level in a flour, the greater the potential for the formation of gluten. The sheets that gluten forms in dough are elastic enough to move with the gas released by yeast yet sturdy enough to prevent that gas from escaping, so the dough doesn't deflate. Lower-protein flours, on the other hand, are recommended for chemically leavened baked goods. This is because baking powder and baking soda are quick leaveners. They lack the endurance of yeast, which can force the naturally resistant gluten sheets to expand. Gluten can overpower quick leaveners, causing the final baked product to fall flat.

A second important difference in flours is whether they are bleached or not. Technically, all all-purpose flours are bleached. Carotenoid pigments in wheat lend a faint yellowish tint to freshly milled flour. But in a matter of about 12 weeks, these pigments oxidize, undergoing the same chemical process that turns a sliced apple brown. In this case, yellowish flour changes to a whiter hue (though not stark white). Early in this century, as the natural bleaching process came to be understood, scientists identified methods to chemically expedite and intensify it. Typically, all-purpose flours are bleached with either benzoyl peroxide or chlorine gas. The latter not only bleaches the flour but also alters the flour proteins, making them less inclined to form strong gluten. Today consumers prefer chemically bleached flour over unbleached because they associate the whiter color with higher quality. In our tests, some of the baked goods made with bleached flour were such a pure white that they actually looked startlingly unnatural and "commercial" versus homemade.

Of all the product taste tests we have run, these flour tastings were undoubtedly the most difficult. The differences in flavor between the various versions of the selected recipes were usually extremely subtle. For example, tasting nine different plain muffins in which the only ingredient difference was the brand of flour required shrewd discrimination on the tasters' part. The most obvious differences were often in appearance.

That is not to say, however, that the tests were inconclusive. As difficult as it was for tasters to pick up differences, they were remarkably consistent in their observations. The performance of each of the flours tested, however, was not so consistent. All of the flours baked up well enough in most of the recipes. And some baked up better than that—at times. Failure also occurred, sometimes without apparent reason.

While the protein guidelines make eminently good sense, to our surprise, the results of our tests did not always correspond. The biscuit test did reveal a certain progression from light, cake-like biscuits produced by the lowest-protein flours to coarser, heavier biscuits produced by the higher-protein flours. But our tasters liked all of the biscuits, except for one that had stale flavors. Another trend we noticed was that lower-protein flours spread more in tests of chocolate chip cookies and muffins.

As an overall category, the four bleached flours in our tests in fact did not perform as well as the unbleached flours and were regularly criticized for tasting flat or carrying "off" flavors, often described as metallic. These characteristics, however, were more difficult to detect in recipes that contained a high proportion of ingredients other than flour. Coincidentally, our cake tests and chocolate chip cookie tests (both sugary recipes) were the two tests in which off flavors carried by the bleached flour went undetected or were considered faint.

Despite the variations and subtleties, however, the good news is that we did end up with two flours we can recommend wholeheartedly. Both King Arthur and Pillsbury unbleached flours regularly made for highly recommended baked goods, producing a more consistent range of preferred products than the other seven flours in the taste tests. If you are going to have only one flour in the house, our advice is to choose one of these two.

toward the middle. This method produces the same reading as poking through the bottom of the loaf without having to remove the bread from the pan. Note that different types of bread should be baked to different internal temperatures.

SANDWICH BREAD

AMERICAN LOAF BREADS ARE QUITE DIFFERENT from their European cousins, primarily because they contain fat in the form of milk and melted butter. This produces a more tender crumb and a softer loaf that is particularly well-suited to sandwiches. These home-style loaves are baked in metal loaf pans, and their crust is thin. As we discovered during the testing process, this is not just an exercise in convenience. American loaf bread is every bit as inspiring as those toothier imports. There is nothing like a fresh-from-the-oven loaf cut into slabs and slathered with butter and honey.

These days, many home cooks might choose to use a bread machine to make this type of bread. In our experience, this method produces a crust that is mediocre at best and an interior of unpredictable quality—that is, all too often, cakelike. As for purchasing this type of bread at the store, it's actually not that easy. Most gourmet shops don't carry a basic sandwich bread. Of course, many people who might enjoy making terrific sandwich bread at home don't even try it because they think it takes most of a day. We set out to develop a good, solid recipe that could be done in two hours, start to finish, including baking time.

For many home cooks, the other great impediment to making bread at home is the notion of kneading by hand. To find out if this was essential, we used a standard American loaf bread recipe and tested hand-kneaded bread against bread kneaded by machine—both in a standing mixer and a food processor—to find out if hand kneading makes better bread. The results were eye-opening. The hand-kneaded loaf was not as good as the two loaves kneaded by machine. It was denser, did not rise as well, and the flavor lacked the pleasant yeastiness found in the other loaves. After some additional testing and discussion, we hit on a reasonable explanation: When kneading by hand, most home cooks cannot resist adding too much additional flour, because bread dough is notoriously sticky. In a machine, however, you add no additional flour, and the resulting bread has the correct proportion of liquid to flour.

Now that we knew that kneading this kind of bread by machine was actually preferable to doing it by hand, we set out to refine the techniques. We wanted to include separate recipes for a standing mixer and a food processor, given that many home kitchens have one or the other, but not both.

Starting with the standing mixer, we tested the dough hook versus the paddle attachment. (Some recipes use the paddle for part or all of the kneading process.) The hook turned out to be vastly preferable, as dough quickly got caught in the paddle, requiring frequent starting and stopping to free it. We also found that a medium-speed setting is better than a slow setting. Although the hook appears to move at an alarming rate, the resulting centrifugal force throws the dough off the hook, resulting in a more thorough kneading. At slower speeds, the dough has a tendency to cling to the hook like a child on a tire swing.

Next we turned to the food processor. This method, to our surprise, was very successful, although the dough did require about four minutes of hand kneading at the finish. (A food processor does not knead as thoroughly as a standing mixer.) Using a metal blade, we pulsed the dry ingredients to combine them. Then, with the machine running, we added the liquid ingredients through the feed tube and processed the dough until it formed a rough ball. After a rest of two minutes, we processed the dough a second time, for about 30 seconds, and then removed it to a lightly floured counter for hand kneading. We also tested the recipe without any hand kneading and found the resulting bread inferior— coarser in texture, with less rise.

We also noted that the action of the food processor was quite different from that of the standing mixer. A relatively dry dough had worked well in the mixer because it was less likely to stick to the dough hook. However, in the food processor a slightly wetter dough seemed preferable, as the metal blade stretched and pulled it better than a dry dough, which ended up simply being cut into pieces. Therefore, to improve the performance of the food processor, we added 2 tablespoons of water to the dough.

With our dough and kneading methods set, we turned to oven temperatures and baking times. When we baked our bread at oven temperatures of 350, 375, and 400 degrees, the two higher temperatures overcooked the crust by the time the inside of the loaf was done. Again, unlike most European breads, this American loaf is prone to quick browning because it contains milk, butter, and honey.

To determine the proper baking time, you have to figure out how to decide when your bread is done. After testing bread taken from the oven at internal temperatures of 190, 195, and 200 degrees, the loaf producing a reading of 195 degrees was clearly the winner. The lower temperature produced

dense bread, and the higher temperature produced dry, overcooked bread.

As stated above, one of our objectives in developing this recipe was to produce bread as quickly as possible. Our first thought was to use rapid-rise or instant yeast, even though we were certain that they would produce inferior (less flavorful) bread—another example of technology run amok. To our surprise, not only did the rapid-rise yeast greatly reduce rising times, but, in a blind tasting, the bread tasted better than loaves made with regular active dry yeast. (For details on these tests, see page 235.)

To further speed the rising process, we preheated the oven to 200 degrees for 10 minutes, turned it off, then used it as our proofing box, allowing the dough to rise in a very warm, draft-free environment. Next we tried heating the milk and water to jump-start the yeast. When the liquids were too hot, well above 130 degrees, we had some failures because the yeast

---

EQUIPMENT: Digital Scales

Every serious cook needs an accurate scale for weighing fruits, vegetables, and meats. When making bread, a scale is even more critical. Professional bakers know that measuring flour by volume can be problematic. A cup of flour can weigh between 4 and 6 ounces, depending on the type of flour, the humidity, whether or not the flour has been sifted, and the way the flour has been put into the cup. Weight is a much more accurate way to measure flour.

There are two basic types of kitchen scales. Mechanical scales operate on a spring and lever system. When an item is placed on the scale, internal springs are compressed. The springs are attached to levers, which move a needle on the scale's display (a ruler with lines and numbers printed on a piece of paper and glued to the scale). The more the springs are compressed, the farther the needle moves along the ruler.

Electronic, or digital, scales have two plates that are clamped at a fixed distance. The bottom plate is stationary, the top plate is not. When food is placed on the platform attached to the top plate, the distance between the plates changes slightly. The movement of the top plate (no more than one thousandth of an inch) causes a change in the flow of electricity through the scale's circuitry. This change is translated into a weight and expressed in numbers displayed on the face of the scale.

We tested 10 electronic scales and 9 mechanical scales. As a

group, the electronic scales were vastly preferred. Their digital displays are much easier to read than the measures on most mechanical scales, where the lines on the ruler are so closely spaced it's impossible to nail down the precise weight within half an ounce. Also, many mechanical scales could weigh items only within a limited range—usually between 1 ounce and 5 pounds. What's the point of owning a scale that can't weigh a large chicken or roast? Most electronic scales can handle items that weigh as much as 10 pounds and as little as 1/4 ounce. Among the electronic scales we tested, we found that several features make the difference between a good electronic scale and a great one. Readability is a must. The displayed numbers should be large. Also, the displayed numbers should be steeply angled and as far from the weighing platform as possible. If the display is too close to the platform, the numbers can hide beneath the rim of a dinner plate or cake pan.

An automatic shut-off feature will save battery life, but this feature can be annoying, especially if the shut-off cycle kicks in at under two minutes. A scale that shuts off automatically after five minutes or more is easier to use. A large weighing platform (that detaches for easy cleaning) is another plus. Last, we preferred electronic scales that display weight increments in decimals rather than fractions. The former are more accurate and easier to work with when scaling a recipe up or down.

SCIENCE: How Yeast Works

Yeast is a plant-like living organism. Its function in a bread dough is to consume sugars and starches in the flour and convert them into carbon dioxide and alcohol, which give bread its lift and flavor. This process is known as fermentation. Flavor compounds and alcohol—byproducts of fermentation—give yeasted bread its characteristic aroma and flavor.

A small amount of honey or sugar is sometimes added to bread dough to enhance the fermentation process—yeast grows faster and better when it has enough food (sugar) to feed on. Warm water (about 110 degrees) is also necessary to activate dry yeast—very hot or cold water may impair its functioning. In fact, very warm water (in excess of 130 degrees) will kill the yeast, and yeast will not activate well in cool water.

Heat is generated during fermentation and rising, and punching the dough down mixes the warmer dough (in the center) with the cooler dough (on the outside edges), thus normalizing the overall temperature. Punching down also releases any excess carbon dioxide, breaks apart yeast particles that are clinging together, and redistributes the sugars, giving the yeast a refreshed food source. After punching down, the dough is often given a second rise, which happens more quickly since there is more yeast at work.

During the first few minutes of baking, the alcohol (formed earlier during fermentation) evaporates, gasses expand, and bubbles enlarge, fostering more rise. This is referred to as oven spring. The yeast cells are killed off during the first few minutes in the oven.

was killed by the excessive heat. We did find, however, that when we warmed the liquids to about 110 degrees, the rising times were reduced by 5 to 10 minutes. These three changes brought the first rise down to 40 minutes and the second rise to a mere 20. Now we could make homemade bread in two hours, including kneading, both risings, and the baking time, which for this bread took no more than 40 minutes.

At the end of two months of testing, we had produced a terrific loaf of bread in just two hours, start to finish. Using rapid-rise yeast, we kneaded the dough in a standing mixer for 10 minutes (and then by hand for a mere 15 seconds). We then let it rise in a warmed oven for 40 to 50 minutes, at which point we gently shaped it and placed it in a loaf pan. The

second rise took 20 to 30 minutes, after which we baked the dough at a moderate 350 degrees for about 40 minutes, or until the internal temperature reached 195 degrees.

Sandwich Bread

MAKES ONE 9-INCH LOAF

This recipe uses a standing electric mixer; a variation below gives instructions for using a food processor. You can hand-knead the dough, but we found it's easy to add too much flour during this stage, resulting in a somewhat tougher loaf. To promote a crisp crust, we found it best to place a loaf pan filled with boiling water in the oven as the bread bakes.

3½–3¾ cups (17½ to 18¾ ounces) unbleached all-purpose flour, plus extra for work surface
2 teaspoons salt
1 cup warm milk (about 110 degrees)
⅓ cup warm water (about 110 degrees)
2 tablespoons unsalted butter, melted
3 tablespoons honey
1 package (about 2¼ teaspoons) rapid-rise or instant yeast

1. Adjust an oven rack to the lowest position and heat the oven to 200 degrees. Once the oven temperature reaches 200 degrees, maintain the heat for 10 minutes, then turn off the oven.

2. Mix 3½ cups flour and the salt in the bowl of a standing mixer fitted with the dough hook. Mix the milk, water, butter, honey, and yeast in a 1-quart Pyrex liquid measuring cup. Turn the machine to low and slowly add the liquid. When the dough comes together, increase the speed to medium and mix until the dough is smooth and satiny, stopping the machine two or three times to scrape dough from the hook, if necessary, about 10 minutes. (After 5 minutes of kneading, if the dough is still sticking to the sides of the bowl, add flour, 1 tablespoon at a time and up to ¼ cup total, until the dough is no longer sticky.) Turn the dough onto a lightly floured work surface; knead to form a smooth, round ball, about 15 seconds.

3. Place the dough in a very lightly oiled large mixing bowl, rubbing the dough around the bowl to lightly coat. Cover the bowl with plastic wrap and

place in the warmed oven until the dough doubles in size, 40 to 50 minutes.

4. Gently press the dough into a rectangle 1 inch thick and no longer than 9 inches. With a long side facing you, roll the dough firmly into cylinder, pressing with your fingers to make sure the dough sticks to itself. Turn the dough seam-side up and pinch it closed. Place the dough in a greased 9 by 5 by 3-inch loaf pan and press it gently so it touches all four sides of the pan. Cover with plastic wrap; set aside in a warm spot until the dough almost doubles in size, 20 to 30 minutes.

5. Keep one oven rack at the lowest position and place the other at the middle position and heat the oven to 350 degrees. Place an empty loaf pan on the bottom rack. Bring 2 cups of water to a boil in a small saucepan. Pour the boiling water into the empty loaf pan in the oven and set the loaf onto the middle rack. Bake until an instant-read thermometer inserted at an angle from the short end just above the pan rim into the center of the loaf reads 195 degrees, 40 to 50 minutes. Remove the bread from the pan, transfer to a wire rack, and cool to room temperature. Slice and serve.

INGREDIENTS: Rapid-Rise and Instant Yeast

We taste-tested our recipe for sandwich bread with eight different brands of yeast, including several active dry, instant, and rapid-rise entries. We placed the doughs made with rapid-rise and instant yeast in a warmed oven for just 40 minutes, whereas breads made with the regular active dry yeast took about two hours when left to rise on the counter.

Although we expected slower-rising active dry yeast to promote more flavor in the finished loaves, this was not the case. Our tasters actually preferred the loaves made with instant and rapid-rise yeasts. The faster rise, in fact, yielded more flavor and produced a noticeably sweeter bread. One theory is that a rapid rise provides less time for the creation of the acidic byproducts of fermentation, hence a sweeter loaf. It is also true that rapid-rise and instant yeast have superior enzyme activity, which converts starches to sugar faster than regular-rise varieties.

But even taking all of these factors into account, it still seems logical that a longer, gentler rise would give the dough more time to produce complex flavors. This may be true for a European style loaf that contains nothing more than flour, yeast, salt, and water. But our American-style sandwich bread (see our recipe on page 234) contains both fat (milk and butter) and sugar (honey) so that the complexity of flavors, which would be evident in a plainer loaf, is easy to miss. Even more to the point, though, is the fact that rapid-rise and instant yeasts are not necessarily an inferior product.

Yeast is a plant, and different varieties have quite different qualities, as do different varieties of, say, roses. Rapid-rise and instant yeasts have been genetically engineered to reproduce the best characteristics of yeasts from around the world. Although genetic engineering often results in loss of flavor, our blind taste tests confirmed that in this case it produced an excellent product.

As for why these yeasts work faster, there are two primary reasons. Besides the more rapid enzyme activity described above, rapid-rise and instant yeast also have an open, porous structure, which means that they absorb liquid instantly. When these yeasts were introduced for home use, consumers had some difficulty with them; this is because home cooks continued to follow habit and proofed the yeast—that is, dissolved it in water to see if it bubbled, which was "proof" that the yeast was alive and could do its work—rather than mixing it directly into the flour, as instructed by the manufacturer. Because of its efficiency, this new yeast dissolved in water rapidly and ran out of food (starch) and died before the rising process was complete. To correct this problem, scientists went back and added more starch to the mix, giving the yeast enough food to survive proofing.

Today, however, most yeast does not need to be dissolved in water before being used in a recipe. For one thing, yeast is now marked with an expiration date for freshness, so there's no need to proof, or test, the yeast as long as the expiration date hasn't passed. (Note that these expiration dates should be taken seriously. We tried baking a loaf with yeast that was one month past expiration, and the rising times were double those experienced with fresh yeast. The resulting loaf was denser, with a smaller rise. For our sandwich bread, we opted not to proof the yeast in water but to mix it directly into the warm liquid to speed up preparation time.

Keep in mind that whether you dissolve yeast directly in liquid or add it to the flour, the temperature of the water or milk used is crucial. Dry yeast will die in ice water or in liquids at 125 degrees or higher. When testing recipes, we found that hot milk often killed off the yeast and therefore suggest using warm milk (about 110 degrees). We also use warm water at the same temperature in many recipes.

➤ VARIATIONS

Sandwich Bread Kneaded in a Food Processor

Add an extra 2 tablespoons of water so the food processor blade can knead the dough more effectively. During the hand-kneading phase, you may need to add a little flour to make a workable dough. To ensure a tender bread, however, add as little as possible.

Follow the recipe for Sandwich Bread, increasing the warm water by 2 tablespoons. Mix the flour and salt in the workbowl of a food processor fitted with a steel blade. Add the liquid ingredients; process until a rough ball forms. Let the dough rest 2 minutes. Process 35 seconds. Turn the dough onto a lightly floured work surface and knead by hand until dough is smooth and satiny, 4 to 5 minutes. Proceed as directed.

Slow-Rise Sandwich Bread

If you do not have rapid-rise yeast on hand, try this slow-rise variation.

Follow the recipe for Sandwich Bread, substituting an equal amount of active dry yeast for the rapid-rise yeast. Let the dough rise at room temperature, instead of in the warm oven, until almost doubled (about 2 hours for first rise and 45 to 60 minutes for the second rise).

Buttermilk Sandwich Bread

Buttermilk gives the bread a slight tang.

Follow the recipe for Sandwich Bread, bringing the water to a boil rather than to 110 degrees. Substitute cold buttermilk for the warm milk, adding it to the hot water. (The mixing of hot water and cold buttermilk should bring the liquid to the right temperature, about 110 degrees, for adding the yeast.) Increase the first rise to 50 to 60 minutes.

Oatmeal Sandwich Bread

To turn this loaf into oatmeal-raisin bread, simply knead ¾ cup raisins, tossed with 1 tablespoon flour, into the dough after it comes out of the food processor or mixer.

Bring ¾ cup water to a boil in a small saucepan. Add ¾ cup rolled oats; cook to soften slightly, about 90 seconds. Follow the recipe for Sandwich Bread, decreasing the flour from 3½ cups to 2¾ cups, adding the cooked oatmeal to the flour, and omitting the warm water from wet ingredients.

ANADAMA BREAD

ANADAMA IS AN ECCENTRIC NAME FOR what amounts to sandwich bread enriched with cornmeal and molasses. Most sources attribute the unique name to an ornery New England farmer "damning" his wife "Anna" for the unwavering diet of cornmeal mush she provided for him. Whatever the case, anadama bread has deep roots in rustic New England cookery. As we found, however, this bread can suffer from a variety of ills, including gritty texture, denseness, and saccharine sweetness. We hoped to overcome these problems and make a great loaf, ideal for toasting and sandwiches.

Because anadama is similar to a basic loaf bread, we started off by trying to manipulate our sandwich loaf into anadama bread. We quickly learned that we would have to make some major adjustments. Incorporating the cornmeal into the dough was the first step. Adding raw cornmeal to the dough resulted in gritty bread without much corn flavor. Soaking the cornmeal in the lukewarm milk and water also produced a gritty loaf. We realized that the cornmeal had to be cooked to soften it, but what was the best method? The amount of water in our sandwich bread recipe (⅓ cup) was too little; the cornmeal solidified into a thick paste punctuated with lumps that remained hard in the dough. Simmering the cornmeal in the milk in our sandwich bread recipe (1 cup) worked much better. After a mere minute of cooking, the cornmeal softened and developed the texture of soft polenta. We decided to melt the butter with the milk to save a step.

We tried various methods to mix the dough. Adding everything together—flour, water, yeast, molasses, and mush—yielded unevenly combined dough flecked with lumps of cornmeal mush. The mush had to be combined with the flour prior to the other ingredients for the best integration. As little as a minute of mixing adequately blended the cornmeal mush and flour. With the cornmeal mush incorporated, the water, yeast, and molasses were easily added to form a uniform dough.

We found that it was tricky gauging when and if the dough needed more flour during kneading. The molasses made the dough quite sticky, and it looked as if it needed more flour, but when we felt the dough, it rarely needed any flour. Feeling the dough is the best way to tell; if you can touch it without it tenaciously sticking to your hands, the dough probably does not need any more flour. When it did stick, we added flour a tablespoon at a time until it reached the right texture. Occasionally scraping the dough off the dough hook and the sides of the workbowl during kneading helped as well. After 10 minutes of machine kneading and a quick turn by hand, the dough was smooth, shiny, and elastic.

Because this dough is sticky, we had trouble kneading it by hand or in a food processor. When we tried to knead it by hand, the dough stuck to our hands and the counter unless we added more flour, but more flour made the finished loaf tough. As for the food processor, the dough stuck to the blade and could not be properly kneaded. The larger bowl of a standing mixer and the dough hook are the best tools for kneading this dough.

Unfortunately, we found that this dough rose quite a bit more slowly than the dough in our sandwich bread recipe. Even in the warmed oven, it took a full hour and a half for the first rise to double in bulk. We figured that the heavy cornmeal and molasses weighed down the dough. Adding more yeast made the dough rise faster, but the flavor was adversely affected. After shaping, the dough took another hour and a half to double in bulk—a small inconvenience, but well worth it for the flavor.

We baked the risen loaf according to the sandwich bread recipe with a pan of water underneath. In a slight alteration, we brushed the top of the loaf

---

EQUIPMENT: Standing Mixer

Years ago, free-standing mixers were a kitchen staple. Your grandmother probably had a "mixmaster," which is a generic term for a free-standing mixer, though it is actually a brand name for units manufactured by Sunbeam. For a while, these large machines went out of favor as new food processors and more powerful hand mixers, which were better suited for many of the tasks of standing mixers, became available. If all you want to do is whip egg whites or cream, or if you only make cakes from a mix, you don't really need a heavy-duty standing mixer.

However, if you like to bake, a standing mixer permits maximum flexibility. Models with the most options, such as a whisk, paddle, and dough hook, will open up the most possibilities for baking everything from cakes and cookies to breads.

Perhaps the best use for standing mixers is for mixing and kneading bread dough. Standing mixers knead perfectly in about one-third the time of hand kneading, and with far more control and satisfaction than bread machines. (Hand-held mixers lack the stability and power to do a good job.) Some large food processors can knead bread dough, but they can handle only relatively small batches of dough.

Unfortunately, not all brands of standing mixers are helpful kitchen allies. In the process of testing seven of the top-selling standing mixers, we found that some models are simply too difficult and frustrating to work with to make them worthwhile purchases. Outdated engineering and poorly designed beaters and bowls made it a challenge, rather than a pleasure, to prepare baked goods in several of the models we used.

On the other hand, three of the seven models were outstanding, and making cakes, cookies, and bread with them was enjoyable and gratifying. The Rival Select was exceptional, performing every task flawlessly. The two KitchenAid models we tested were outstanding as well, although the Rival's dough hook is better designed and kneaded bread dough more quickly. These three models are also the most expensive of the group, costing $300 to $400. Are they worth it? Plainly and simply, yes. Each is designed for endurance, so it makes sense to spend the money up front, since you will derive years of use and pleasure from these models.

Both the Rival Select and the two KitchenAid mixers operate by "planetary action," in which a wide, flat beater (called the paddle) moves around a stationary bowl. This proved the most effective way of blending ingredients, since the paddle reaches the sides as well as the center of the bowl and gathers particles quickly. As a result, there is little need to stop the machine and scrape the sides of the bowl.

Another critical point of comparison among the mixers was stability. The Rival and KitchenAid models are heavy and barely vibrate even when put to the test of mixing stiff cookie and bread dough. A standing mixer you have to hold with one or two hands is not a labor-saving device. The Rival and the KitchenAids were the best at kneading bread dough, performing the task quickly, smoothly, and efficiently, with the motors showing not the slightest sign of strain and without spilling any flour. All three models had the weight, stability, and power needed to make smooth, elastic, tender dough.

with butter and sprinkled a little cornmeal across it to emphasize the nutty corn flavor. The resulting loaf was everything we hoped for: an appealing dark and chewy crust yielding to a moist and dense crumb.

With our technique mastered, we tried different types of cornmeal and molasses. Tasters unanimously favored coarse, stone-ground cornmeal over finer cornmeal. Even after baking, the coarser meal retained a deep corn flavor and a pleasing texture. Fine commercial cornmeal disappeared behind the strong flavor of the molasses. We tried different coarse cornmeals, both local and nationally available, and they all worked well. As far as molasses, dark or "robust" flavored molasses was the winner, adding depth and a mild bitterness that complemented the sweet corn flavor. The dark molasses also lent the loaf a rich ebony color reminiscent of pumpernickel.

We loved this loaf both as toast and sandwich bread, especially with ham and cheese, leftover barbecued pork, or even peanut butter and jam.

Anadama Bread
MAKES ONE 9-INCH LOAF

We think it is worth searching out high-quality, stone-ground cornmeal for this hearty bread; the deep corn flavor is well worth the effort. If you cannot find stone-ground cornmeal, use the coarsest meal you can find. We were pleased with Goya brand coarse cornmeal, which is readily available in most markets, often in the Latin foods section. (See page 268 for more information on cornmeal.) We liked Grandma's brand "robust" molasses in this recipe, but any dark molasses will do the job. Just stay away from black-strap; its dark, bitter flavor is overpowering. (See page 92 for information on molasses.)

1	cup whole milk
4	tablespoons unsalted butter
½	cup (2¾ ounces) plus 2 teaspoons stone-ground cornmeal
3–3¼	cups (15 to 16¼ ounces) unbleached all-purpose flour
2	teaspoons salt
⅓	cup warm water (110 degrees)
1	package (about 2¼ teaspoons) rapid-rise or instant yeast
5	tablespoons dark molasses

1. Adjust an oven rack to the lowest position and heat the oven to 200 degrees. Once the oven reaches 200 degrees, maintain the heat for 10 minutes, then turn off the heat.

2. Combine the milk and 2 tablespoons butter in a small saucepan and bring almost to a simmer over medium heat. Whisk in ½ cup of cornmeal and continue to stir for 1 minute. Transfer the mixture to a small bowl and cool until just warm to the touch, about 100 degrees.

3. Mix 3 cups flour and salt in the bowl of a standing mixer fitted with a dough hook. Mix the water, yeast, and molasses in a measuring cup. On low speed, briefly mix together the flour and salt, and then add the cornmeal and milk mixture to the flour, processing on low speed until the cornmeal mixture is roughly incorporated, about 1 minute. With the mixer still on low, gradually add the liquid, and once the dough comes together, increase the speed to medium and mix until the dough is smooth and satiny, stopping the machine 2 or 3 times to scrape the dough from the hook and the sides of the bowl, if necessary, about 10 minutes. (After 5 minutes of kneading, if the dough is still sticking to the sides of the bowl, add flour, 1 tablespoon at a time and up to ¼ cup total, until the dough is no longer sticky.) Turn the dough out onto a lightly floured work surface and knead to form a smooth, round ball, 15 to 30 seconds.

4. Place the dough in a very lightly oiled large mixing bowl, rubbing the dough around the bowl to coat lightly with oil. Cover the bowl with plastic wrap and place in the warmed oven until the dough doubles in size, about 1½ hours.

5. Gently press the dough into a rectangle 1 inch thick and no longer than 9 inches. With a long side facing you, roll the dough firmly into a cylinder, pressing with your fingers to make sure the dough sticks to itself. Place the dough in a greased 9 by 5 by 3-inch loaf pan and press gently so it touches all four sides of the pan. Loosely cover with plastic wrap and set aside in a warm place until the dough almost doubles in size, about 1½ hours.

6. Keep one oven rack at the lowest position and place the other at the middle position and heat the oven to 350 degrees. Place an empty loaf pan on the bottom rack. Bring 2 cups of water to a boil in a small saucepan.

7. Melt the remaining butter in a small saucepan. Remove the plastic wrap from the loaf and carefully brush the top with the melted butter and evenly sprinkle the remaining 2 teaspoons cornmeal across the top. Pour the boiling water into the empty loaf pan in the oven and set the loaf onto the middle rack. Bake until an instant-read thermometer inserted at an angle from the short end just above the pan rim into the center of the loaf reads 195 degrees, 40 to 45 minutes. Remove the bread from the pan, transfer to a wire rack, and cool to room temperature. Slice and serve.

CRESCENT ROLLS

PERHAPS THE MOST POPULAR DINNER ROLL served at holiday tables is the crescent roll. What's a shame is that the crescent rolls most Americans serve come from the supermarket refrigerator case—those diminutive arcs of prefab dough that taste artificial and go stale in minutes. We wanted to make rolls that were tender, rich, and easy enough to accommodate in an already jam-packed holiday schedule.

Our first few attempts turned out rolls that were paunchy, boring, and flat-flavored. They were hard to handle, stuck to the countertop, and had much too much yeast. Many bread recipes try to speed up the rising time of a dough by using an excessive amount of yeast—sometimes as much as 2 tablespoons for 3 or 4 cups of flour. What you get besides speed is a cheesy flavored, lackluster roll that quickly goes stale. So a more modest quantity of yeast was going to be key.

For flour, our options included all-purpose and bread flour. Because crescent rolls should be soft and supple, bread flour, with a high protein content that makes for strong gluten development, would give the rolls more chew and a crustier crust than we wanted. We stuck with our kitchen workhorse, King Arthur unbleached all-purpose flour.

The next variable was the eggs. The working version of our recipe called for one. We compared batches made with one, two, and three eggs, and the latter was the winner. These rolls were soft and pillowy, with a lovely golden crumb.

Although we had been using whole milk in our testing, we wanted to compare three liquids side by side: water, skim milk, and whole milk. The whole milk rolls tasted the richest but were also the most dense. The rolls made with water lacked flavor and tenderness. The rolls made with skim milk were just right—flavorful and rich.

Up until now, we had been adding 8 tablespoons of softened butter in 1 tablespoon increments while the bread dough was kneaded in a standing mixer. Could these rolls absorb more fat without becoming heavy or greasy? We increased the butter in the next two batches by 4 and 8 tablespoons, respectively. It was clear that these rolls liked their fat; they took to 16 tablespoons of butter (two whole sticks) with aplomb.

However, adding the softened butter incrementally to the mixing dough was a messy and

SHAPING CRESCENT ROLLS

1. Roll the dough to a 20 by 13-inch rectangle; use a pizza wheel to trim the edges. Cut the dough in half lengthwise, then cut 16 triangles, as illustrated.

2. Before rolling the crescents, elongate each triangle of dough, stretching it an additional 2 to 3 inches in length.

3. Starting at the wide end, gently roll up each crescent, ending with the pointed tip on the bottom.

drawn-out process. To simplify things, we decided to melt the butter and add it to the dough along with the other ingredients. This worked perfectly. So far, we had developed a better-than-average crescent roll recipe, but the crust was not sufficiently flaky, and we were having difficulty rolling out and shaping the sticky dough.

The easiest way to handle a butter-laden, sticky dough is to let it rest in the refrigerator before rolling it out. This combats two problems. First, the gluten in the dough relaxes, allowing the dough to be rolled without "bucking," or snapping back into shape after rolling. Second, the butter in the dough solidifies, making the dough easier to roll and less sticky to handle.

We had intended to refrigerate the risen and punched-down dough for a couple of hours, but we forgot about it until the next morning. Panic-stricken, we took the dough out of the refrigerator and easily rolled it into a long sheet, cut it, and shaped the pieces into little bundles. After allowing the rolls to rise at room temperature for about an hour, we popped them in the oven. When they were done, we noticed the difference immediately—blisters! When we bit into a roll, the crust snapped and flaked. This was the kind of crescent roll we had been trying to achieve all along, with flavor and a flaky crust.

To find out why an overnight chill had paid off, we called Maggie Glezer, a baker certified by the American Institute of Baking. She explained that when dough is chilled for a long time—a process bakers call retarding—acetic acid builds up in the dough, giving it a richer flavor as well as a blistered crust. Carl Hoseney, professor emeritus in the department of grain science and industry at Kansas State University, added that blisters are also caused by gases escaping from the dough during retardation.

With these points in mind, we set out to see if a longer refrigerator stay would be even better. We made another batch of dough, let it rise at room temperature, punched it down, and put it in the fridge. The next morning, we formed the dough into crescents, then, instead of letting the rolls rise for an hour and baking them, we put them back in the fridge. The following day, we let the rolls lose their chill at room temperature, then baked them. The crust was even more blistered than before. Next we tried chilling the rolls for three nights; these were better still, with an excellent flavor and a stunning, crackled crust. What we also liked about these rolls is that all you need do on the day they are served is to let them rise one last time and bake them—creating no dirty dishes and taking up no precious workspace.

Now we wondered if the rolls could be frozen and baked off as needed. Because raw dough can't be frozen (the cold temperature kills one third of the yeast, affecting both flavor and texture), we prebaked the rolls until they were about three-quarters done,

EQUIPMENT: Food Processor

Spending several hundred dollars on a standing mixer may not be an option. In that case, you may want to buy a good food processor and use it for everything, including bread kneading. An inexpensive hand-held mixer can handle (if not as well) most of the other tasks usually reserved for a standing mixer, including whipping cream or beating cake batter.

So how to go about buying a food processor that can handle pesto as well as bread dough? We evaluated seven food processors based on the results in five general categories: chopping and grinding, slicing, grating, pureeing, and kneading.

We found that most food processors chop, grind, slice, grate, and puree at least minimally well. Of course, there are differences in models, but they were not as dramatic as the results of our bread-kneading tests. A food processor won't really knead bread fully, but the dry and wet ingredients come together beautifully to form the dough. If a recipe calls for a smooth, satiny ball of dough, you will have to knead the dough by hand on the counter after processing; however, the kneading time should be just a few minutes.

We found that successful kneading in a food processor was linked directly to large bowl size as well as to the weight of the base. The 11-cup machines were best because they provided ample space for the ball of dough to move around. A heavy base provided stability, and the nods went to KitchenAid and Cuisinart, with their substantial, 10-pound-plus bases. Luckily, these machines also did the best job on the other basic food processor tests.

then cooled and froze them. One week later, we defrosted them at room temperature and then finished the baking. Not one taster could tell the difference between these rolls and a batch that had been baked from start to finish without freezing.

All we had to do now was tweak the baking method. Up until this point, we had been baking the rolls at 375 degrees from start to finish. But during our research on retarding dough, we learned that boosting the oven temperature to 425 degrees for the initial bake, then lowering it to 350 degrees when the rolls were just starting to color, would improve the rolls' oven spring. (Oven spring, a term used by professional bakers, defines the dramatic increase in size caused when bread gets that initial blast of heat from the oven.) The 425/350 combination worked, making the rolls pleasantly larger and loftier.

We wondered if adding steam to the baking bread would help with oven spring and encourage formation of a thin and delicate crust. After placing the rolls on the lower-middle rack, we poured 1 cup of hot tap water onto a preheated baking sheet on the oven floor. The burst of steam, combined with the high oven temperature, gave the rolls an even higher rise and turned the crust into a thin and still flakier shell. Now we had a dramatic-looking roll with great flavor, a lovely, tender crumb, and a delicate crust. We bit into a crescent roll with the satisfaction of knowing that making it would be just as easy to fit into a busy holiday schedule as popping open a can.

Crescent Rolls

MAKES 16 ROLLS

When you bake the crescent rolls, make sure the light in the oven is switched off. If the light is on after you shut the oven door, the burst of steam may cause the bulb to crack. You can make the dough up to 4 days ahead of time or even partially bake the rolls and freeze them for longer storage. To do this, begin baking the rolls as instructed, but let them bake at 350 degrees for only 4 minutes, or until the tops and bottoms brown slightly. Remove them from the oven and let cool. Place the partially baked rolls in a single layer inside a zipper-lock bag and freeze. When you're ready to serve them, defrost at room temperature and place them in a preheated 350-degree oven for 12 to 16 minutes. You can freeze the rolls for up to 1 month.

DOUGH

¼	cup skim milk
16	tablespoons (2 sticks) unsalted butter, cut into 16 pieces
¼	cup sugar
3	large eggs
3½	cups (17½ ounces) unbleached high-protein all-purpose flour (such as King Arthur) or 4 cups (20 ounces) unbleached all-purpose flour (such as Pillsbury or Gold Medal), plus extra for work surface
1	teaspoon rapid-rise or instant yeast
1½	teaspoons salt

EGG WASH

1	egg white beaten with 1 teaspoon water

1. FOR THE DOUGH: Microwave the milk, butter, and sugar in a 4-cup microwave-safe measuring cup until the butter is mostly melted and the mixture is warm (about 110 degrees on an instant-read thermometer), about 1½ minutes (alternatively, heat the milk, butter, and sugar in a small saucepan over medium heat until warm; remove from heat). Whisk to dissolve the sugar. Beat the eggs lightly in a medium bowl; add about one-third of the warm milk mixture to the eggs, whisking to combine. When the bottom of the bowl feels warm, add the remaining milk mixture, whisking to combine.

2. Combine the flour and yeast in the bowl of a standing mixer fitted with the paddle attachment; mix on lowest speed to blend, about 15 seconds. With the mixer running, add the milk and egg mixture in a steady stream; mix on low speed until a loose, shiny dough forms (you may also see satiny webs as the dough moves in the bowl), about 1 minute. Increase the speed to medium and beat 1 minute; add the salt slowly and continue beating until stronger webs form, about 3 minutes longer. (Note: The dough will remain loose rather than forming a neat, cohesive mass.) Transfer the dough to a large bowl, cover the bowl with plastic wrap, and place in a warm, draft-free spot until the dough doubles in bulk and the surface feels tacky, about 3 hours.

3. Line a rimmed baking sheet with plastic wrap. Sprinkle the dough with flour (no more than 2 tablespoons, to prevent sticking) and punch down.

Is there a supermarket dinner roll worth serving (and eating)? We lined up six readily available brands, plus our homemade roll, and gave them a try. It was no surprise that our crescent roll put the others to shame. Placing a distant second was Pillsbury's crescent roll, defined by tasters as "sweet" and "wheaty" but also "greasy" and "doughy." Almost tying with the Doughboy was our local supermarket's refrigerated crescent roll, judged by tasters as having an "artificial," "movie popcorn" flavor. The other contenders included Rhode's White Roll Dough (called "gummy" and "squishy"), Bread du Jour Italian rolls ("vapid and offensive"), Sunbeam Brown 'n Serve rolls ("sour"), and J. J. Nissen Brown 'n Serve rolls (likened to "cotton balls" and "gym socks").

Turn the dough onto a floured work surface and form into a rough rectangle shape. Transfer the rectangle to a lined baking sheet, cover with plastic wrap, and refrigerate overnight.

4. Line a rimmed baking sheet with parchment paper. Turn the dough rectangle onto a lightly floured work surface and, following the illustrations on page 239, roll and shape. Arrange the crescents in four rows on the parchment-lined baking sheet; wrap the baking sheet with plastic wrap, and refrigerate at least 2 hours or up to 3 days.

5. Remove the baking sheet with the chilled rolls from the refrigerator, unwrap, and cover with an overturned large disposable roasting pan. (Alternatively, place the sheet pan inside a large garbage bag.) Let rise until the crescents feel slightly tacky and soft and have lost their chill, 45 to 60 minutes. Meanwhile, turn off the oven light, place a rimmed baking sheet on the oven floor, adjust one rack to the lower-middle position, and heat the oven to 425 degrees.

6. FOR THE EGG WASH: With a pastry brush, lightly dab the risen crescent rolls with the egg wash. Transfer the baking sheet with rolls to the oven rack and, working quickly, pour 1 cup hot tap water into the hot baking sheet on the oven floor. Close the door immediately and bake 10 minutes; reduce the oven temperature to 350 degrees and continue baking until the tops and bottoms of the rolls are deep golden brown, 12 to 16 minutes longer. Transfer the rolls to a wire rack, cool for 5 minutes, and serve warm.

PARKER HOUSE ROLLS

IN THIS DAY AND AGE OF THICK-CRUSTED, naturally leavened breads, puffy, yeasty rolls are becoming harder and harder to find. But what is more alluring than a hot, golden-domed roll straight from the oven? We have a soft spot for thin-crusted, fluffy-crumbed American rolls.

Parker House rolls are the epitome of this sort of roll: pillowy soft, a little sweet, and packed with butter. Parker House rolls owe their name to Boston's famed Parker House, a hotel that has been a bastion of Brahmin hospitality since the middle of the nineteenth century. Truth be told, the roll is pretty much a standard dinner roll; it's the shape that matters. It starts off as a round roll that is flattened, buttered, and folded in half. For our rolls, we wanted a simple, rich roll that would be ready in the least time possible.

Almost all of the recipes we gathered had the same ingredients in varying proportions. These are fairly rich rolls, loaded with milk, eggs, butter, and a fair amount of sugar. Each recipe also employed a healthy amount of yeast for a quick rise and a big, boozy yeast flavor. We tinkered with proportions until we arrived at a roll that was buttery but not too rich and very tender-crumbed from the large amount of milk and egg.

Selecting the ideal kneading time took some testing. With a soft, billowy, tender crumb as our goal, we knew a reasonably short knead was in order, but how short was short? We tried times of 4 to 10 minutes (in the mixer on medium speed) and were most pleased with a 6-minute knead, followed by a scant minute by hand. With 10 minutes of kneading, the dough's gluten was overdeveloped and too elastic—its texture more like that of a chewy sandwich. With four minutes, the dough lacked structure and collapsed during baking. Six minutes built just enough gluten for support but not enough to detract from the airy crumb.

With a full package of yeast to a scant 4 cups of flour, we knew a quick rise would not be a problem. We also decided to hasten the first rise by setting the dough in a preheated oven. We found that an oven heated to 200 degrees for 10 minutes and then turned off retained just enough heat to speed along the rising dough without having a detrimental effect on the yeast. Within 45 minutes, the dough had doubled in volume.

After we divided the dough, we rounded the individual portions on the countertop until they developed a smooth, tight skin and perfect globe shape—the rounding helps the dough rise by redistributing the yeast and sugars and expunging the carbon dioxide. By the time we rounded all 24 balls of dough, the first to be rounded had relaxed enough to be shaped. We found that the best way to shape the dough was to lightly flatten it with our palms and then roll it into an oval shape with a small French-style rolling pin or short dowel. We found out the hard way that it is important to keep the edges thicker than the center so that they will adhere to each other when the dough is folded and not puff open during baking.

After folding and spacing the rolls on a baking sheet, we gave them a light brushing of butter. They were now ready for their second rise, this time

outside of the oven. Traditional recipes suggest dunking the formed rolls in melted butter, but we thought this would be too much of a good thing.

We tried baking the rolls in baking dishes and sheet pans and were most pleased with the sheet pans. While we liked the height of the rolls baked in a dish, the rolls in the middle were gummy long after the outer rolls were perfectly baked. A metal baking sheet delivered even heat and got the rolls out of the oven in about 20 minutes. Parker House rolls must be eaten warm. After a 10 minute rest once out of the oven, they are ready to serve, preferably with a roast and plenty of gravy.

Parker House Rolls

MAKES 24 ROLLS

When rounding the dough and shaping the rolls, it is important to keep the remaining dough covered, otherwise it will quickly dry out and develop a "skin." Rolling the dough

SHAPING PARKER HOUSE ROLLS

1. Divide the relaxed dough into two equal pieces and, with your hands, pull and shape each piece to a length of 18 inches, with a measure of about 1½ inches across.

2. With a bench scraper, cut each length of dough into twelve 1½-inch-long pieces (each piece will weigh about 1½ ounces). Loosely cover all 24 pieces with plastic wrap.

3. With a cupped palm, roll each piece of dough into a smooth, tight ball, and then loosely cover it with plastic wrap.

4. Beginning with the balls rounded first (because the dough has relaxed), use the palm of your hand to flatten a ball of dough into a ½-inch-thick circle.

5. With a small rolling pin or thick dowel floured to prevent sticking, flatten out the center of the dough until the circle becomes a rough oval. Make sure to keep the edges thicker than the middle.

6. Lightly brush the dough with melted butter, then fold in half and gently seal the edges. Place the roll on the prepared baking sheet. Repeat steps 4 through 6 with the remaining balls of dough, making sure to space the rolls evenly on the baking sheet.

243

into symmetrical rounds takes a little practice, but you will quickly get the hang of it. A dry, unfloured countertop helps because the dough will stick a little. Although we like using a French-style rolling pin for flattening the rolls, a more traditional option is a thin dowel or the handle of a wooden spoon. Whatever your choice, lightly flour it or the dough will stick to it.

1¼	cups whole milk
2	tablespoons sugar
1	package (about 2¼ teaspoons) rapid-rise or instant yeast
1	large egg, lightly beaten
4–4¼	cups (20 to 21¼ ounces) unbleached all-purpose flour, plus extra for work surface
1½	teaspoons salt
14	tablespoons unsalted butter, 8 tablespoons cut into 8 pieces and softened, the remaining 6 tablespoons melted

1. Adjust an oven rack to the lowest position and heat the oven to 200 degrees. Once the oven reaches 200 degrees, maintain the oven temperature for 10 minutes, and then turn off the heat.

2. Microwave (or otherwise warm) the milk and sugar together until the mixture is warm (about 100 degrees). Whisk in the yeast and the egg and set aside. Combine 4 cups of the flour and the salt in the bowl of a standing mixer fitted with a paddle attachment and mix on the lowest speed to blend, about 15 seconds. With the mixer running on low speed, add the liquid mixture in a steady stream and mix until the flour is moistened, about 1 minute. With the mixer still running, slowly begin to add the softened butter, one piece at a time, until incorporated into the dough. Increase the speed to medium and beat until the dough is thoroughly combined and scrappy, about 2 minutes longer. Replace the paddle with a dough hook and knead the dough on medium speed until smooth but still sticky, about 6 minutes, adding more flour in tablespoon increments, if necessary, for the dough to clear the sides of the bowl. Scrape the dough out of the mixing bowl and onto a lightly floured work surface and knead by hand until very smooth and soft, but no longer sticky, about 1 minute. Transfer the dough to a lightly greased large mixing bowl, cover with plastic wrap, and place in the warmed oven until the dough doubles in bulk, about 45 minutes.

3. Once the dough has doubled, punch it down, replace the plastic wrap, and allow the dough to rest for 5 minutes. Meanwhile, with a pastry brush, liberally butter the bottom and sides of a large rimmed baking sheet with 3 tablespoons of the melted butter. Follow the illustrations on page 243 to shape the dough into rolls and place them on the baking sheet. Lightly brush the tops of the rolls with the remaining butter and loosely cover with plastic wrap. Set the rolls in a warm place and let rise until almost doubled, about 45 minutes.

4. When rolls are almost fully risen, adjust an oven rack to the middle position and heat the oven to 375 degrees. Bake the rolls until the tops are dark golden brown, 20 to 22 minutes. Transfer the rolls to a wire rack and cool for 10 minutes. Serve warm.

SWEET POTATO ROLLS

ALTHOUGH WE GENERALLY MAKE YEASTY, quick-rising breads like Parker House rolls for our holiday meals, ruddy-orange sweet potato rolls are another favorite. Their bright color, mellow flavor, and tender crumb complement just about everything on the dinner table. But, as we found, many existing recipes use the sweet potato for little more than color and moistness. When we baked a few sample recipes, the sweet potato flavor was faint at best. We decided that we wanted a moist, tender-crumbed roll packed with the sweet potato's allusive flavor and vivid orange color.

What, exactly, is a sweet potato roll? Basically, it is a soft dinner roll enriched with sweet potato puree. Sweet potatoes add color and flavor, but their starches also help the rolls retain moisture and make for a light, soft crumb. (See our deep-dish pizza recipe on page 252 for more on this phenomenon.) The only trick is balancing the ratio of flour and potato; otherwise, the bread is dense and gummy. We hoped to add as much sweet potato as we could to our roll without compromising a tender crumb. With our favorite milk- and butter-rich dinner roll recipe in hand (the dough for our Parker House rolls, minus the brush of melted butter) and a shopping cart's worth of sweet potatoes, we were ready.

But before starting the rolls, we had to choose a method for making the sweet potato puree. Having worked on a recipe for sweet potato pie (see page 379), we knew that microwaving was the most efficient way to cook this vegetable—the sweet potatoes cook through in about 10 minutes and do not absorb water, as they do if boiled or steamed. We also like baking sweet potatoes for the same reasons, but baking takes significantly longer (it is the best option if you do not have a microwave). After cooking and briefly cooling, it was simple work to scoop the flesh out of the skin and mash it with a fork.

With our puree in hand, we were ready to start working on our roll recipe. Our testing method was simple. We added sweet potato puree in quarter-pound increments to our basic roll recipe (with some of the flour and milk left out to compensate for the puree). A half pound of puree added only a hint of orange to the rolls, and no flavor. With three-quarters of a pound of puree, the rolls were attractively colored but still lacked flavor. At a pound, the flavor was perceptible but still weak, and the color was markedly improved. A pound and a quarter of sweet potato puree, about two medium-sized sweet potatoes, proved perfect. The rolls were moist and deeply flavored with sweet potato while still retaining a dinner roll lightness and a tender crumb. We tried adding more sweet potato puree and were rewarded with dense, gummy rolls. We had reached the tipping point.

A few minor alterations to the recipe improved the overall flavor. We added some molasses, which reinforced the mildly sweet, earthy flavor of the sweet potatoes. A pinch of ground nutmeg also helped. And instead of using an egg or milk wash for the top, we brushed the rolls with melted butter, which helped the crust brown to a deep, autumnal orange hue.

We found that a room-temperature rise, which took about two hours, was necessary for the dough to develop enough structure and the soft yet slightly elastic crumb we desired. When we tried letting the dough rise in a warm oven, we were sorely disappointed. The roll's crumb was too billowy, and it lacked structure. And a strong yeast flavor competed with the delicate sweet potato flavor.

We tried baking the rolls individually on a sheet pan, but nobody liked the thick, chewy crust the rolls developed. Instead, tasters favored the tender rolls cooked in baking dishes. We experimented with different baking dishes, and cake pans proved the most attractive and efficient, as two rounds could easily fit onto one rack in the oven, leaving room for other baked goods.

These rolls stay fresh for a surprisingly long time. The sweet potato's starches and high sugar content retained moisture well, and we enjoyed these rolls upward of four days after baking them. In fact, the older they were, the more the sweet potato flavor came out. The leftovers make great toast—with butter and marmalade—and fabulous sandwiches.

Sweet Potato Rolls

MAKES 16 ROLLS

Sweet potatoes lose some volume when microwaved, so it is important to choose sweet potatoes large enough to compensate for the weight loss. For 20 ounces of puree, we needed 2 sweet potatoes weighing a total of about 24 ounces prior to cooking. While the flour measurement in this recipe seems inexact, we found that the moisture content of sweet potatoes varies from potato to potato and must be compensated for with flour. During kneading, the dough should freely clear the sides of the workbowl; if not, add more flour a tablespoon at a time. This dough has a unique texture that is dense but still soft and moist.

2	medium sweet potatoes (about 12 ounces each)
1/2	cup whole milk
7	tablespoons unsalted butter
2	tablespoons molasses
3	tablespoons granulated sugar
1	large egg
1	package (about 2 1/4 teaspoons) rapid-rise or instant yeast
3 1/2–4	cups (17 1/2 to 20 ounces) unbleached all-purpose flour
2	teaspoons salt
1/8	teaspoon freshly grated nutmeg

1. Prick the sweet potatoes several times with a fork and place on a double layer of paper towels in the microwave. Cook at full power for 5 minutes;

turn each potato over, and continue to cook at full power until tender, but not mushy, about 5 minutes longer. Halve each potato crosswise, insert a small spoon between the skin and flesh, and scoop the flesh into a medium bowl, discarding the skin. (If the potatoes are too hot to comfortably handle, fold a double layer of paper towels into quarters and use to hold each potato half.) Mash the cooked potatoes coarsely with a fork or a spoon (there should be a little more than 1½ cups of puree). Allow the puree to cool to about 100 degrees.

2. Warm the milk, 4 tablespoons butter, molasses, and sugar together in a small saucepan or in the microwave until the butter melts. Stir well and allow the mixture to cool. Once the mixture reaches a temperature of about 100 degrees, whisk in the egg and the yeast and set aside. Place 3½ cups flour, salt, and nutmeg in the bowl of a standing mixer fitted with the paddle attachment and mix on the lowest speed to blend, about 15 seconds. With the mixer running on low speed, add the liquid mixture in a steady stream and mix until the flour is moistened, about 1 minute, then add the potato puree and process until the dough is thoroughly combined and scrappy, about 2 minutes. Replace the paddle with the dough hook and knead the dough on medium speed until smooth but still sticky, about 8 minutes, adding more flour in tablespoon increments if necessary for the dough to clear the sides of the bowl. Scrape the dough out of the mixing bowl and onto a lightly floured work surface and knead by hand until very smooth and soft, but no longer sticky, about 1 minute. Transfer the dough to a lightly greased large bowl, cover with plastic wrap, and place in a draft-free spot until the dough has doubled in bulk, about 2 hours.

3. Once doubled, punch the dough down, replace the plastic wrap, and allow the dough to rest for 5 minutes. Meanwhile, melt the remaining 3 tablespoons butter and, with a pastry brush, liberally butter the inside of two 9-inch cake pans, reserving the remaining butter. With a knife or bench scraper, divide the dough in half and then in half again. Cut each quarter of the dough into 4 pieces to yield a total of 16 equal pieces. Following illustration 3 on page 243, shape each piece of dough until it feels tight and smooth. Evenly space 8 rolls in each cake pan, 7 around the perimeter of the pan and 1 in the middle. Brush the rolls with the remaining butter, loosely cover with plastic wrap, and allow to double in bulk, 1½ to 2 hours.

4. When the rolls are almost fully risen, adjust an oven rack to the middle position and heat the oven to 375 degrees. Bake the rolls until the tops are dark brown, 20 to 22 minutes. Invert the rolls onto a cooling rack, turn the rolls upright, and cool for 10 minutes. Serve warm. (Leftover rolls can be stored in an airtight container at room temperature for several days; warm or toast before serving.)

GLAZED CINNAMON ROLLS

A PUFFY CINNAMON ROLL COATED WITH thick white icing brings out the child in all of us, encouraging even the most mature person to greedily uncoil its tight swirls and dig in. Some of us in the test kitchen have been known to drop by the local mall just to worship at that shrine (which shall remain nameless) to calorie-laden cinnamon rolls. As delicious as those artery-clogging rolls can be, they are too much for all but the rarest hedonistic fit. They are so sweet and so rich, it's nearly impossible to finish one roll.

Our ideal cinnamon roll is a little more reserved. The dough should be soft and rich but not greasy. The filling should be slightly sweet, rather than sugary sweet, and potent with cinnamon. The icing should be creamy and thick and boast a tang sufficient to balance the richness and sweetness elsewhere in the roll.

With our ideal cinnamon roll in mind, we collected recipes and started testing. The recipes we found used a variety of dough types, from lean, sandwich bread dough to buttery brioche dough, a very rich French dough made with huge amounts of egg yolks and butter. While we were inclined toward recipes using brioche-style dough (they would undoubtedly taste better), brioche can be difficult to make, requiring upwards of 15 minutes of kneading and small, patient additions of softened butter. We hoped to develop a dough with a similar richness and texture to brioche, but without all the effort.

We decided to start with our recipe for basic American sandwich bread made with milk and a modest amount of butter (just 2 tablespoons). To develop richness, we tried adding varying amounts of eggs, butter, and cream. With too many whole eggs, the dough turned hard, dry, and almost cakey, though it did have an appealing golden hue. More butter gave the dough more flavor and a softer texture. However, with too much butter, the dough practically oozed off the counter and was difficult to work with. Cream, surprisingly, did little at all. Milk was just fine for this dough.

After many attempts, we settled on a soft dough enriched with a good amount of butter (8 tablespoons) as well as a single whole egg and two egg yolks. When baked, this dough had a tender crumb, buttery richness, slight golden color, and enough gluten development for a little resiliency. (Gluten is the protein formed when flour is mixed with water; it gives bread its structure.) The recipe also allowed for the butter to be added melted rather than in softened pieces, as in brioche.

With our dough ready, we turned our attention to the filling, which came together easily. Our tasters preferred a mix of cinnamon and just enough sugar to temper the cinnamon's bitterness. Tasters liked rolls with a whopping 3 tablespoons of cinnamon.

We tested granulated sugar as well as light and dark brown sugar in the filling. White sugar was too dry and added little flavor. Dark brown sugar proved too wet and turned syrupy, like the filling for a sticky bun. And the strong molasses flavor detracted from the cinnamon. Light brown sugar proved the best sweetener, adding moisture and a light molasses flavor that complemented the cinnamon. Salt mixed with the cinnamon and sugar helped marry the flavors and sharpen the sugar's sweetness.

Shaping the dough into pinwheel spirals could not have been any easier. The soft dough gracefully yielded to a light touch under the rolling pin as we rolled it out. We then sprinkled it with the filling and rolled it up slowly and tightly so that the rolls would not uncoil while cooking. The best tool for cutting the soft dough into rounds proved to be dental floss. Eccentric as it is, dental floss (make sure it's unflavored) smoothly cuts through soft dough without squeezing the filling out of place.

Although a few tasters liked a thin, drizzled powdered sugar and cream glaze, most tasters preferred a thick, tangy cream cheese icing. We altered a standard cream cheese icing by omitting the butter and adding corn syrup for glossiness and smoothness. A judicious smear of icing (rather than a heavy, thick coating) was more appropriate on these civilized rolls.

Glazed Cinnamon Rolls

MAKES 12

Because cinnamon is the predominant flavor in these rolls, make sure to have good-quality, fresh cinnamon on hand. While we rarely grind our own cinnamon, we try to make sure that our ground cinnamon is less than six months old and from a reputable source, like Penzeys or McCormick/Schilling (see page 249 for the results of our tasting). This dough should be very tender and soft, so be stingy with additions of flour. We found only a very light dusting was necessary to prevent the dough from sticking to the counter while rolling it.

DOUGH

1/2 cup milk

8 tablespoons (1 stick) unsalted butter, plus 1 tablespoon for greasing baking dish

1/2 cup warm water (about 110 degrees)

1 package (about 2 1/4 teaspoons) rapid-rise or instant yeast

1/4 cup sugar

1 large egg plus 2 large yolks

1 1/2 teaspoons salt

4–4 1/4 cups (20 to 21 1/4 ounces) unbleached all-purpose flour, plus more for work surface

ICING

8 ounces cream cheese

2 tablespoons corn syrup

2 tablespoons heavy cream

1 cup confectioners' sugar

1 teaspoon vanilla extract
   Pinch salt

FILLING

3/4 cup light brown sugar

3 tablespoons ground cinnamon

1/8 teaspoon salt

1. FOR THE DOUGH: Heat the milk and 8 tablespoons butter in a small saucepan over medium heat until the butter melts. Remove the pan from the heat and set aside until the mixture is warm (about 100 degrees).

2. In the bowl of a standing mixer fitted with the paddle attachment, mix together the water, yeast, sugar, egg, and yolks on low speed until well mixed. Add the salt, warm milk mixture, and 2 cups flour and mix on medium speed until thoroughly blended, about ½ minute. Switch to the hook attachment, add 2 cups flour, and knead on medium speed (adding more flour 1 tablespoon at a time, if necessary) until the dough is smooth and freely clears the sides of the bowl, about 10 minutes. Scrape the dough onto a lightly floured work surface. Shape the dough into a round, place it in a lightly greased large mixing bowl, and cover the bowl with plastic wrap. Leave in a draft-free, warm spot until doubled in bulk, 1½ to 2 hours.

3. FOR THE ICING: While the dough rises, combine all of the icing ingredients in the bowl of a standing mixer fitted with the paddle attachment and blend together on low speed until roughly combined, about 1 minute. Increase the speed to high and mix until the icing is uniformly smooth and free of cream cheese lumps, about 2 minutes. Transfer the icing to a small bowl and refrigerate.

4. TO ROLL AND FILL THE DOUGH: After the dough has doubled, punch it down and turn it out onto a lightly floured work surface. Using a rolling pin, shape the dough into a 16 by 12-inch rectangle, with a long side facing you. Mix together the filling ingredients in a small bowl and sprinkle the filling evenly over the dough, except for the top ½ inch of the dough. Roll the dough, beginning with the long edge closest to you and using both hands to pinch the dough with your fingertips as you roll (see illustration 1 below). Moisten the top border with water and seal the roll (see illustration 2 below). Lightly dust the roll with flour and press on the ends if necessary to make a uniform 16-inch tube. Use the softened butter to grease a 9 by 13-inch baking dish. Cut the roll into 12 pieces using dental floss (see illustration 3 below) and evenly distribute the rolls, cut-side up, in the prepared baking dish. Cover with plastic wrap and place in a draft-free warm spot until doubled in bulk, 1½ to 2 hours.

5. TO BAKE THE ROLLS: When the rolls are almost fully risen, adjust an oven rack to the middle position and heat the oven to 350 degrees. Bake until golden brown and a thermometer inserted into the center of the rolls registers 185 to 188 degrees, 25 to 30 minutes. Invert the rolls onto a cooling rack and allow to cool for 10 minutes. Turn the rolls upright on a large serving plate and use rubber spatula to spread with icing. Serve immediately.

SHAPING CINNAMON ROLLS AND STICKY BUNS

1. Sprinkle the filling evenly over the dough, leaving a border of ½ inch on the far end. Roll up the dough, pinching it gently with your fingertips to keep it tightly rolled.

2. Moisten the top border with water and then pinch the dough ends together to form a secure seam.

3. With dental floss, cut the formed roll in half, cut each half in half again, and then cut each piece into 3 rolls for a total of 12 rolls.

STICKY BUNS

ALTHOUGH BETTER KNOWN FOR CHEESESTEAKS and Rocky films, Philadelphia's best export, in our humble opinion, is the sticky bun. These rich, tender rolls are swirled with sugar and spices and liberally coated with a sticky caramel and pecan glaze. Sticky buns should be over-the-top and sinfully rich. There's no such thing as a "slightly rich" sticky bun.

For the sticky bun dough, we hoped to adapt the dough from our cinnamon roll recipe (the cinnamon roll being the polite, uptown relative of the sticky bun). While not quite as rich as brioche dough, which many recipes appear to use for sticky buns, our cinnamon roll dough was buttery and chewy and much easier to make than brioche. Our intuition proved right: the rich, soft dough was perfectly suited to the job and was as delicious with pecans and caramel as with cinnamon and cream cheese icing. Our only alterations to the dough were the addition of a little extra sugar to make the dough more moist (and more decadent) and a healthy dose of vanilla to complement the caramel glaze.

Most of the flavor in sticky buns comes from the topping, so the filling should be simple and must complement both the caramel and the pecans. A thick smear of butter was a given, as was a coating of sugar. White sugar lent little flavor, so we chose dark brown sugar for its deep, earthy notes. We found a few traditional sticky bun recipes flavored with cardamom (reflecting the once substantial Scandinavian population in the Philadelphia area), and we loved the slightly exotic flavor and aroma of this spice. A

INGREDIENTS: Cinnamon

True cinnamon, which is made from the dried bark of a tropical evergreen tree called *Cinnamomum zeylanicum,* has been all but unavailable in the United States for almost 100 years. Early in the 20th century, this spice became very popular for medicinal uses in Europe, and its cost skyrocketed. A century ago, American merchants began importing cassia, which is the bark of a related tropical evergreen, *Cinnamomum cassia.* Because of this, Americans have grown used to and prefer the stronger, fuller flavors of cassia.

While there is just one true cinnamon, commonly called Ceylon cinnamon, there are a number of different cassias, typically identified by their place of origin. Some spice merchants will indicate this on their labels, but most supermarket brands do not, nor can you tell by appearance which variety you are buying. We decided to hold a blind tasting of all these cinnamons, the true and the not-so-true, to see if we have been missing out on something.

As predicted by our research, the one true cinnamon sample was unlike the cassias. While most tasters did not find anything offensive about it, it was, ironically, often downgraded for not tasting "cinnamon-y." While subdued, its flavor was complex, with notes of citrus and clove.

As for the cassias, almost half of those sampled in our tasting were Indonesian cassia (also known as Korintje cassia), a variety that comprises the overwhelming majority of so-called cinnamon sold in the United States today. While some of these Indonesian cassias were notably spicy and bitter, the common denominator among those which the tasters liked was a solid, familiar cinnamon flavor that was relatively strong and had no off flavors.

The cassia that particularly grabbed the tasters came from China. Chinese cassia tends to have a stronger, sweeter flavor than Indonesian cassia. Both the samples in our tasting were also notably spicy, reminding many tasters of Red Hots candy. Penzeys Chinese cassia, which was anything but meek, secured the top ranking as excellent overall.

The second favorite sample was a Vietnamese cassia. Vietnamese cassias, which only recently became available in the United States with the relaxing of the U.S. trade embargo, tend to be expensive and hold a reputation for being the "world's finest." The two Vietnamese samples in our tasting, though, were quite different from each other. Penzeys Extra Fancy Vietnamese cassia finished second overall with big yet balanced flavors and a subtle complexity. The other Vietnamese cassia in our tasting, McCormick/Schilling Premium cinnamon, was also well-received by tasters, but not for any kind of flavor intensity. Instead, they liked it for being light and sweet, with faint spice notes.

Whether cinnamon or cassia, the characteristic flavors and aromas of these spices come from their essential oils, which in turn are composed of hundreds of chemical compounds. One of the reasons that Ceylon, or "true," cinnamon is so different from cassia is that the main components of its essential oils are different. The chemical compound cinnamaldehyde gives cassia its characteristic flavor. While Ceylon cinnamon contains cinnamaldehyde, it also contains a significant amount of eugenol, the chemical compound that gives cloves their aroma and flavor.

little cinnamon added complexity, and salt tied all the flavors together.

The sticky-sweet sauce is certainly the most important element of a proper sticky bun. We found most recipes make a quick "caramel" sauce by combining brown sugar, corn syrup, and butter. When we tried this sort of sauce, the flavors were one-dimensional and the color was unappealing—sort of thin and transparent. We decided that if we were going to go to all the trouble of making sticky buns, it was worth making a real caramel sauce.

While a lot of home cooks are hesitant to make caramel sauce because of the perceived dangers of molten sugar, there is really nothing to fear. We came up with a foolproof technique that could not be any easier or safer. To prevent unmelted sugar clumps from marring the sauce's supple texture, we dissolved the sugar in water, then brought the mixture to a boil. In a separate pot, we heated the remaining ingredients—cream, butter, vanilla, corn syrup, and salt. It would be crucial to have the liquid being added to the caramelized sugar quite hot to prevent the caramel from clumping and to reduce spattering. We then boiled the sugar syrup, monitoring it with a thermometer, until it reached the dark amber hue we desired, about 350 degrees on the thermometer. As soon as it reached 350 degrees, we removed the caramel from the heat to avert further darkening and added the hot cream mixture. A brief stir combined everything, and our sauce was done.

With our method perfected, we focused on the ratio of ingredients in our caramel sauce. We reduced the amount of cream—traditional caramel sauces have almost the same amount of cream and sugar—so that it would better adhere to the buns. We also wanted the sauce to harden and turn sticky as it cooled, a must for any self-respecting sticky bun. Adding more butter accomplished this goal and improved the sheen of our sauce.

As for the pecans, toasted and coarsely chopped was the way to go, according to all of our tasters. Untoasted nuts tasted bland and steamed. A mere five minutes in a skillet over medium heat dramatically improved their flavor. Whole pecans looked dramatic on top of our sticky buns, but they proved difficult to eat. A coarse chop allowed the nuts to coat the buns evenly and to fall into all the nooks and crannies.

Sticky Buns

MAKES 12

The only tricky part of this recipe is turning out the baked buns from the baking dish; the caramel coating is very hot and gooey. We like the convenient handles on a Pyrex baking dish, which allow for a firm grasp out of harm's way. Cardamom is extremely volatile and quickly loses its flavor once ground. If you have a spice grinder, simply pulse the whole seeds (excluding the pods) until reduced to a fine powder. If using ground cardamom, make sure it is less than six months old.

DOUGH

Dough from Cinnamon Rolls (page 247), with sugar increased to ½ cup and 2 teaspoons vanilla extract beaten with water-yeast mixture in step 2

1   **tablespoon unsalted butter, softened, for greasing baking dish**

CARAMEL SAUCE

2   **cups sugar**
¾   **cup heavy cream**
4   **tablespoons unsalted butter**
1   **teaspoon vanilla extract**
    Pinch salt
2   **tablespoons corn syrup**
2   **cups whole pecans (about 8 ounces), lightly toasted and very coarsely chopped**

FILLING

4   **tablespoons butter, cut into ¼-inch pieces and softened**
¾   **cup packed light brown sugar**
1   **teaspoon ground cardamom**
1   **teaspoon ground cinnamon**
¼   **teaspoon salt**

1. FOR THE DOUGH: Prepare as directed through step 2 of the recipe for Cinnamon Rolls. Use the softened butter to grease a 9 by 13-inch baking dish.

2. FOR THE CARAMEL SAUCE: While the dough rises, combine the sugar and 1 cup water in a heavy-bottomed 2-quart saucepan, placing the sugar in the center of the pan to prevent the sugar crystals from adhering to the sides of the pan. Cover and bring the mixture to a boil over high heat. Once boiling,

uncover and continue to boil until the syrup is thick and straw-colored (it will register 300 degrees on a candy thermometer). Reduce the heat to medium and continue to cook until the sugar is deep amber and begins to smoke (it will be 350 degrees).

3. Meanwhile, bring the cream, butter, vanilla, salt, and corn syrup to a simmer over high heat in a small saucepan. (If the cream mixture reaches a boil before the syrup reaches a deep amber, or 350 degrees, remove from the heat and set aside.)

4. Remove the sugar syrup from the heat, pour about one quarter of the cream mixture into it, and let the bubbling subside. Add the remaining cream mixture and whisk until the sauce is smooth. While still hot, pour the caramel sauce into the prepared baking dish. Sprinkle the pecans over the caramel and set the pan aside.

5. TO ROLL AND FILL THE DOUGH: After the dough has doubled in size, punch it down and turn it out onto a lightly floured work surface. Using a rolling pin, shape the dough into a 16 by 12-inch rectangle with a long side facing you. Combine the filling ingredients in a small bowl, and sprinkle the filling evenly over the dough, except for the top ½ inch of the dough. Roll the dough, beginning with the long edge closest to you and using both hands to pinch the dough with your fingertips as you roll (see illustration 1 on page 248). Moisten the top border with water and seal the roll (see illustration 2 on page 248). Lightly dust the roll with flour and press on the ends if necessary to make a uniform 16-inch tube. Cut the roll into 12 pieces using dental floss (see illustration 3 on page 248) and evenly distribute the rolls, cut-side up, in the prepared baking dish. Cover with plastic wrap and place in a draft-free warm spot until doubled in bulk, 1½ to 2 hours.

6. TO BAKE THE ROLLS: When the rolls are almost fully risen, adjust an oven rack to the middle position and heat the oven to 350 degrees. Bake until golden brown and a thermometer inserted into the center registers 185 to 188 degrees, 25 to 30 minutes. Allow to cool in the pan for 5 minutes. Then very carefully, holding the baking dish by the ends, invert the buns onto a large serving plate. With a rubber spatula, scrape out any caramel remaining in the dish and spread it over the buns. Allow to cool for 10 minutes; serve warm.

DEEP-DISH PIZZA

DEEP-DISH PIZZA (ALSO KNOWN AS CHICAGO-STYLE or pan pizza) may have its roots in Italy, but this recipe is as American as apple pie. In fact, Italians would not recognize this creation—it has no counterpart in Italy.

Deep-dish pizza is about 75 percent crust, so the crust must be great. We wanted that crust to be rich, substantial, and moist, with a tender, yet slightly chewy crumb and a well-developed flavor, like that of a good loaf of bread. We also thought a crust should be crisp and nicely browned without being dry or tough. Knowing how time-consuming pizza making can be, we also wanted a pizza dough that could be made in as little time as possible without sacrificing quality.

After scouring various cookbooks, we made five different pizza doughs and baked them in deep-dish pans. To our disappointment, none delivered the flavorful, crisp brown crust that we felt was needed.

After these initial tests, we tried dozens of variations. We played around with the ratio of water to flour, the amount of oil, the type of flour, and just about every other variable we could think of. But we weren't satisfied until we finally widened the field and tried a recipe for focaccia that used boiled, riced potatoes to add moisture and flavor to the dough. This crust was just what we were hoping for: very wet and yet easy to handle, light, and smooth. When baked, it was soft and moist, yet with a bit of chew, sturdiness, and structure that was not present in the previous doughs. (For more information on this somewhat unusual use of potatoes, see page 252.)

Now that we had found a dough that we liked, the challenge was to come up with a rising and baking method suited to deep-dish pizza. We placed the pizza dough in a barely warmed oven for the first rise, reducing the initial rising time from 1 hour to 35 minutes and producing dough that tasted no different from the dough that rose at room temperature for a full hour.

Next we tried reducing—even eliminating—the amount of time allowed for the second rise. The dough given a full 30 minutes of rising time was vastly better than doughs given a second rise of only 15 minutes or given no second rise at all. The flavor was more complex and the texture of the pizza crust

SCIENCE: The Role of Potatoes in Pizza Dough

The boiled potatoes in our deep-dish pizza dough had a distinct effect on the flavor and texture of the final crust. The result: a moister, more tender, sweeter, and softer dough than one made with just wheat flour. We wanted to know why the boiled potatoes made such a difference in the pizza dough.

According to Dr. Al Bushway, professor of food science at the University of Maine, potatoes contain more starch than wheat flour. Since starch traps moisture during baking, this made for a moister dough. Potatoes also contain less protein than flour. This results in less gluten being formed in the dough, which in turn produces a softer, more tender product. Finally, potatoes add another dimension of flavor in two ways. For one, the free sugars in the potatoes cause faster fermentation, resulting in a more complex flavor in a shorter period of time. Second, the sugars that are not consumed by the yeast in the fermentation process add sweetness to the final dough.

was softer and lighter, making this second rise too important to pass up or shorten.

After some testing, we discovered that a crust baked at 425 degrees on a baking stone was almost perfect; the bottom and sides of the pizza were well-browned, and the interior crumb was moist, light, and evenly cooked through. The exterior of this crust was, however, slightly tough. To combat this, we began lining the pizza pan with oil. After some experimentation, we found that the pizzas made with a generous amount of oil lining the pan (¼ cup was optimal) had a far more desirable crust than those made with little or no oil in the pan. Lightly "frying" the dough in the pan made for a rich, caramelized exterior; this added a good amount of flavor and a secondary texture to the crust, without drying it out or making it tough.

Now it was time for the toppings. On most pizzas, the toppings can simply be placed on raw dough and baked, since the crust bakes in about the same amount of time as the toppings. But we found that the weight of the toppings prevented the crust from rising in the oven, resulting in a dense, heavy crust, especially in the center of the pie. So we tried prebaking crusts from 5 minutes up to 15 minutes to develop some structure before adding the toppings.

The pizza prebaked for 15 minutes, then topped, was perfect. The pizza had a chance to rise in the oven without the weight or moisture of the toppings, and the toppings had just enough time to melt and brown.

Deep-Dish Pizza

MAKES ONE 14-INCH PIZZA, SERVING 4 TO 6

Prepare the topping while the dough is rising so it will be ready when the dough is ready. Baking the pizza in a deep-dish pan on a hot pizza stone will help produce a crisp, well-browned bottom crust. Otherwise, a heavy rimless baking sheet (do not use an insulated cookie sheet) will work almost as well. If you've only got a rimmed baking sheet, turn it upside down and bake the pizza on the flat rimless side. The amount of oil used to grease the pan may seem excessive, but in addition to preventing sticking, the oil helps the crust brown nicely.

1	medium russet (baking) potato (about 9 ounces), peeled and quartered
3½	cups (17½ ounces) unbleached all-purpose flour
1½	teaspoons rapid-rise or instant yeast
1¾	teaspoons salt
1	cup warm water (about 110 degrees)
6	tablespoons extra-virgin olive oil, plus more for oiling bowl
1	recipe topping (see page 254)

1. Bring 1 quart water and the potato to a boil in a small saucepan over medium-high heat; cook until tender, 10 to 15 minutes. Drain and cool until the potato can be handled comfortably; press through the fine disk on a potato ricer or grate through the large holes on a box grater. Measure 1⅓ cups lightly packed potato; discard the remaining potato.

2. Adjust one oven rack to the highest position and the other rack to the lowest position; heat the oven to 200 degrees. Once the temperature reaches 200 degrees, maintain the heat for 10 minutes, then turn off the heat.

3. Combine the flour, yeast, and salt in the workbowl of a food processor fitted with the steel blade. With the motor running, add the water and process until the dough comes together in a shaggy ball. Add

the potato and process for several seconds, then add 2 tablespoons oil and process several more seconds, until the dough is smooth and slightly sticky. Transfer the dough to a lightly oiled medium bowl, turn to coat with oil, and cover tightly with plastic wrap. Place in the warmed oven until the dough is soft and spongy and doubled in size, 30 to 35 minutes.

4. Oil the bottom of a 14-inch deep-dish pizza pan with the remaining 4 tablespoons olive oil. Remove the dough from the oven and gently punch down; turn the dough onto a clean, dry work surface and pat into a 12-inch round. Transfer the round to the oiled pan, cover with plastic wrap, and let rest until the dough no longer resists shaping, about 10 minutes.

5. Place a pizza stone or rimless baking sheet on the lowest oven rack (do not use an insulated cookie sheet; see note), and heat the oven to 500 degrees. Uncover the dough and pull up into the edges and up the sides of the pan to form a 1-inch-high lip. Cover with plastic wrap; let rise in a warm draft-free

---

EQUIPMENT: Box Graters

A box grater is one of those unfortunate kitchen tools—it occupies significant cabinet or counter space, is used infrequently, yet is absolutely essential. While food processors come complete with a grater attachment, not everyone has one, and it's doubtful that those who do would dirty the entire contraption to grate a handful of mozzarella. That said, there are a number of graters on the market, from nonstick to heavy-grade stainless steel. We wanted to find out if there was a significant difference between these models—did we need to spend $20 on a grater, or would a $6 grater do the job?

We tested eight different box graters, ranging in price from $6.48 to $19.99. We grated items of varying texture and firmness: mozzarella cheese, celeriac, carrots, and ginger. The winning box grater would need to rate well in all categories—it would be fast (efficient and sharp, requiring little effort and pressure), stable (no rocking or sliding), comfortable (a good grip on the handle), and easy to clean (a single trip through the dishwasher or a quick scrub with soapy water—all models were dishwasher-safe). With those standards in mind, we grated and rated.

We soon found that most graters had little problem with speed and sharpness—from carrots to cheese, the shreds were clean and uniform, falling quickly from the grater. Ginger proved a problem for two models, which sported only the punched, raised-spike holes for grating smaller items. Those spiked teeth grabbed onto the ginger fibers, leaving juice on the counter and negligible scrapings of actual ginger meat. Graters with miniature versions of the large-holed side were much more successful with ginger.

Stability proved an essential component of a quality box grater. While many models slid a bit if set atop a smooth countertop, testers found sliding to be the lesser of evils. Grated knuckles, the unwelcome result of tipping and rocking, were a common (and unacceptable) occurrence with poorly balanced, flimsy graters. The graters with the largest bases sat firmly on the countertop, allowing fast, safe grating.

Several graters boasted "slipfree" rubber bases, which we found to be both a help and a hindrance. When grating soft items that required little pressure (such as cheese), the bases indeed kept the grater firmly in place. But when grating firmer items (such as carrots) requiring more pressure, the immovable graters tipped, endangering fingers. Additionally, testers preferred a smooth surface for making uninterrupted passes with the cheese or vegetable. The models with rubber or plastic bases and tops were not composed of a single piece of metal, so the grated item had to be lifted over the attached base and top.

Comfort was similarly affected by the size of the grater's base; there was no need for a tight grip as long as the grater was well-balanced. The most stable graters required merely a hand resting on the top. As a bonus, larger bases offered wider openings at the top, enabling a clear view of progress.

Most of the graters were easy to clean. A simple scrub by hand or a single run through the dishwasher removed all traces of cheese or vegetables. However, the two models that trapped the ginger fibers had significant problems. The fibers were thoroughly enmeshed in the teeth, proving a true challenge for washing by hand, and they remained firmly in place after a heavy-duty dishwasher run, quickly drying into an intractable mess. The fibers had to be delicately plucked by hand from the sharp teeth.

On your next trip to the kitchen store, look for box graters with extra wide bases, preferably composed of a single piece of high-grade metal, with one side offering tiny raised holes for smaller items. We found the more expensive graters ($15 to $20) to be the ones that met these requirements. The top-rated graters were the Küchenprofi 6-Sided, Amco Professional Performance, and Progressive International Perfect Prep. You can justify the extra expense and cabinet space with the savings in Band-Aids.

spot until doubled in size, about 30 minutes. Uncover the dough and prick generously with a fork. Reduce the oven temperature to 425 degrees and bake on the preheated stone or baking sheet until dry and lightly browned, about 15 minutes. Add the desired toppings; bake on the stone or baking sheet until the cheese melts, 10 to 15 minutes (5 to 10 minutes for a 10-inch pizza). Move the pizza to the top rack and bake until the cheese is spotty golden brown, about 5 minutes longer. Let cool 5 minutes, then, holding the pizza pan at an angle with one hand, use a wide spatula to slide the pizza from the pan to a cutting board. Cut into wedges and serve.

➤ VARIATIONS

10-Inch Deep-Dish Pizzas

If you don't own a 14-inch deep-dish pizza pan, divide the dough between two 10-inch cake pans.

Follow the recipe for Deep-Dish Pizza through step 3. Grease the bottom of two 10-inch cake pans with 2 tablespoons olive oil each. Turn the dough onto a clean, dry work surface and divide it in half. Pat each half into a 9-inch round; continue with recipe, reducing the initial baking time on the lowest rack to 5 to 10 minutes and dividing the topping evenly in half between pizzas.

Fresh Tomato Topping with Mozzarella and Basil

4	medium ripe tomatoes (about 1½ pounds), cored, seeded, and cut into 1-inch pieces
2	medium cloves garlic, minced
	Salt and ground black pepper
6	ounces mozzarella cheese, shredded (about 1½ cups)
1¼	ounces Parmesan cheese, grated (about ½ cup)
3	tablespoons shredded fresh basil leaves

1. Mix together the tomatoes and garlic in a medium bowl; season to taste with salt and pepper and set aside.

2. Top the partially baked crust evenly with the tomato mixture, followed by the mozzarella, then the Parmesan. Bake as directed in step 5 of the recipe for Deep-Dish Pizza. Scatter the basil over the fully baked pizza before cutting it into wedges.

Four-Cheese Topping with Pesto

½	cup Pesto (see recipe below)
6	ounces mozzarella cheese, shredded (about 1½ cups)
4	ounces provolone cheese, shredded (about 1 cup)
1¼	ounces grated Parmesan cheese (about ½ cup)
1¼	ounces blue cheese (about ¼ cup, crumbled)

Spread the partially baked crust evenly with pesto; sprinkle with the mozzarella, followed by the provolone, Parmesan, and blue cheese. Bake as directed in step 5 of recipe for Deep-Dish Pizza.

Pesto

MAKES ABOUT ¾ CUP

Basil usually darkens in homemade pesto, but you can boost the green color by adding the optional parsley.

¼	cup pine nuts, walnuts, or almonds
3	medium cloves garlic, unpeeled
2	cups packed fresh basil leaves
2	tablespoons fresh flat-leaf parsley leaves (optional)
7	tablespoons extra-virgin olive oil
	Salt
¼	cup finely grated Parmesan cheese

1. Toast the nuts in a small, heavy skillet over medium heat, stirring frequently, until just golden and fragrant, 4 to 5 minutes. Transfer the nuts to a plate.

2. Add the garlic to the empty pan. Toast, shaking the pan occasionally, until fragrant and the color of the cloves deepens slightly, about 7 minutes. Transfer the garlic to a plate, cool, peel, and chop.

3. Place the basil and parsley (if using) in a heavy-duty, quart-size, sealable plastic bag; pound the bag with flat side of a meat pounder or a rolling pin until all the leaves are bruised.

4. Place the nuts, garlic, herbs, oil, and ½ teaspoon salt in the workbowl of a food processor fitted with the steel blade; process until smooth, stopping as necessary to scrape down the sides of the bowl. Transfer the mixture to a small bowl, stir in the cheese, and

adjust the salt. (The surface of the pesto can be covered with a sheet of plastic wrap or thin film of oil and refrigerated for up to 5 days.)

THIN-CRUST PIZZA

ALTHOUGH DEEP-DISH PIZZA HAS ITS adherents in Chicago and elsewhere, many American pizza lovers (including most New Yorkers) prefer something closer to the Italian original, with a thin, crisp crust. To satisfy both camps, we think a pizza should be either thick, soft, and chewy (like our deep-dish pizza) or thin and crisp—and not in between. Our goal for making thin-crust pizza was simple: a shatteringly crisp, wafer-thin crust with a deeply caramelized flavor and no trace of raw yeast or flour and toppings that were sleek, light, and off the charts in flavor.

We knew that this dough must not only taste remarkably good, it must be easy to produce and cooperative as well. Pizza is casual fare and should shape up easily. Our first inclination, therefore, was to advance to the food processor and give it a whirl against the standing mixer and hand methods. It buried the competition for ease and speed, producing gorgeous, supple doughs in about 30 seconds, or faster than you can say "large pepperoni."

We were keen to make a big, free-form pizza, and we knew that a thin crust would need every bit of conventional oven heat it could get in the 10 minutes or so it would take to bake. That meant 500 degrees and a giant pizza stone with an hour's head start to preheat. (Though we tested a slightly lower oven heat as well, the extra minutes the pizza needed to brown left the finished crust more tough than crisp.) Wanting the crackerlike simplicity of a rich burnished crust to prevail, we dressed the pizzas with sauce and mozzarella only.

A handful of the pizza recipes we reviewed offered ideas that contributed significantly to the success of our future recipe. Overnight fermentation (the dough's first long rise) in the refrigerator was a key first precept. The finished dough is put to bed in chilly quarters—where it rises at its leisure—and is then stretched and baked the following day. Granted,

---

INGREDIENTS: **Mozzarella Cheese**

If you're going to the trouble of making your own pizza, you certainly don't want to sabotage your efforts by using inferior mozzarella. Still, we wondered whether premium buffalo mozzarella (made from water buffalo milk and imported from Italy) was worth the added expense. To find out which kinds of mozzarella work best in pizza, we had 16 tasters sample six different brands, including three shrink-wrapped low-moisture cheeses from the supermarket (two made from whole milk, one from part skim milk), a preshredded part-skim cheese also from the supermarket, one salted fresh cow's milk mozzarella made at a local cheese shop, and one salted fresh buffalo mozzarella imported from Italy. We sampled each cheese raw and cooked on a deep-dish pizza. Tasters were asked to rate each cheese on overall flavor (both raw and melted), texture, and melting properties.

When tasted raw, the results were quite clear. Tasters liked the gamey, barnyard flavor of the buffalo mozzarella. The fresh cow's milk mozzarella also performed quite well. Among the supermarket cheeses, there was a clear bias for the whole milk cheeses over those made with part skim milk. The preshredded cheese had a dry, rubbery texture and grainy mouthfeel. (Even

when cooked, most tasters noted that it was chalky or grainy.) Preshredded cheese is coated with powdered cellulose to prevent clumping. Some tasters also felt that the preshredded cheese was drier, attributable to the cellulose or to having been shredded months ago.

On pizzas, the results were the same (at least in terms of flavor), but moisture was now a factor. The fresh cheeses exuded a lot of liquid that flooded the surface of the pizza. Unless the fresh mozzarella is pressed of excess liquid before cooking (we had success weighting the shredded cheese for an hour prior to cooking in a strainer set in a bowl), it is unsuitable for pizza.

Because most cooks (ourselves included) don't want to weight cheese, we think the shrink-wrapped supermarket cheeses make more sense for sprinkling on pizzas. Stick with a whole milk cheese and try to choose a brand with a bit more moisture than the rest of the pack. Our favorite supermarket cheese was Calabro whole milk mozzarella brand (from Connecticut), which was softer and moister than the other rubbery supermarket offerings. Certainly, don't use preshredded cheese. The convenience is simply not worth the sacrifice in taste and texture.

this approach removes home pizza making from the world of whimsy and impulse, but the fact that the dough was so easy to handle and the baked pizza so flavorful and crisp more than made up for the delay.

By letting the dough rest overnight, we were able to use less yeast and gain more flavor from fermentation. The chilled, rested dough also handled easily, having become more pliant and less sticky in the intervening hours. Even better, we could toss the dough into the fridge and forget about it altogether until the next day—we didn't need to wait around to punch it down after a two- to three-hour rise at room temperature. By using warm water to process the dough, the yeast got enough of a jump to take off in the cold climate of the refrigerator; the refrigerated dough holds for up to two days without depleting the energy of just ½ teaspoon of yeast.

The second precept was that a soft, supple, and frankly moist dough produces a light, crisp crust. This proved true time after time. Surprisingly, and to our everlasting relief, moist doughs were also easier to work with than drier ones.

Having long been a fan of the neo-Neapolitan-style pizza, which is just a couple of hairs thinner than the original thin-crust pizza of Naples, we knew the only instrument equal to the task of achieving a crust as thin as a credit card was a rolling pin. Armed with our overnight-rested, food-processor dough and a tapered French rolling pin, we dusted a large sheet of parchment paper lightly with flour and commenced rolling as one would a pie dough.

The dough was fully compliant under the pin until we made an effort to turn it like a regular pie dough. At that point, the dough gripped the parchment for dear life. Though thinner and wider it rolled, we could not shake it loose. A potentially maddening situation morphed into a saving grace when we realized the parchment could accompany the dough to the oven. As the pizza baked, it loosened from the paper automatically, and the stone remained clean. Best yet, the tackiness of the dough against the parchment prevented the dough from shrinking back, eliminating the need for excess flouring when rolling out. Eventually, we refined this technique by positioning an 18-inch piece of plastic wrap directly onto the top surface of the dough

THIN-CRUST PIZZA ON HOLD

Our recipe makes two rail-thin 14-inch pizzas. If you're hungry for just one pizza, make the full recipe anyway. Roll out both doughs, but roll one of them to 15 inches. Dress the dough rolled to the standard 14 inches with sauce and topping and bake it; poke the larger dough everywhere with a fork, but leave it undressed. Bake the undressed dough on the stone for 2 minutes, then remove it from the parchment and cool it on a rack. (The dough will look like a large flour tortilla and will have shrunk to 14 inches.) Wrap well and freeze on a baking sheet (yes, it is pretty big, but the sheet can be balanced on top of other frozen goods). When you're in the mood for pizza, heat up the stone for an hour, defrost and dress the frozen dough, slide it onto parchment, and bake it for nine minutes. Pizzas done this way were so good our tasters could not distinguish them from fresh. A frozen disk will keep nicely for up to three weeks in the freezer—but can you wait that long to have another?

during rolling. Thus insulated, the dough could be rolled effortlessly and flipped about like a sandwich. It did not dry out. Once the dough was rolled, the plastic wrap peeled off without a hitch; the thin round could be dressed and hurried into the oven without further ado.

While Americans have a propensity for using high-protein flour in breads, our research indicated that Italians use fairly soft flour. Here in our test kitchen, King Arthur all-purpose is one of our favorite flours. A fairly strong all-purpose flour with no chemical additives, King Arthur all-purpose has the light yellow color associated with unbleached, untampered-with flour. Its flavor is outstanding. We had been using it throughout testing, occasionally in combination with softer flours such as cake or rye to lighten the dough (these flour combinations produced unexceptional pizzas). But doughs made exclusively with King Arthur were occasionally less than cracker-crisp, especially during damp weather.

At the suggestion of Maggie Glezer, a baker certified by the American Institute of Baking and a wizard with yeast, we switched from King Arthur all-purpose flour at 11.7 percent protein to Gold Medal unbleached all-purpose flour at 10.5 percent protein. Flours with a higher protein content require more vigorous kneading to create structure in the dough and more water to achieve proper hydration. The lower-protein Gold Medal flour yielded uniformly light doughs that were as full-flavored as those made with King Arthur.

Working initially with measures of volume—2 cups flour to ¾ cup water—the results became unpredictable enough to convince us to switch to weights. We discovered stunning discrepancies between liquid measuring cups at that volume (up to a tablespoon), and with our meager dough ball, a few drops of water more or less made quite an impact.

We found that thin-crust pizzas are best simply topped—tomato sauce and good mozzarella are just fine. If you want to get fancier, tread carefully. A thin crust cannot bear the weight and water of raw vegetables or the stifling canopy of four cheeses. During their stay in the oven, the crust and topping must become one, sustaining temperatures that drive off moisture as they toast the crust mahogany, bake the sauce to a lacquer, and graft cheese to the top. If you want to add some embellishments, try caramelized onions, arugula tossed with olive oil, roasted mushrooms, or strips of roasted red peppers before baking. Thin-crust pizza can also be "flavored" after baking, with a thin layer of pesto or thin medallions of goat cheese.

A final note or two. Force of habit persuaded us to transfer the hot, sliced pizza to a cooling rack. Though the pizza seldom survived long enough to underscore the merits of this method, on the occasions that it did, the air circulating under the crust kept it crisp. In fact, the crusts generally became more crisp a few minutes after being removed from the oven—like a cookie might. And although a 14-inch pizza may sound extra-large, one of these will satisfy only two restrained, polite adults. So serve them as snacks, as appetizers, make two, make a salad.

Crisp Thin-Crust Pizza
MAKES TWO 14-INCH PIZZAS

All-purpose unbleached flour with a protein percentage no higher than 10.5, such as Gold Medal, makes the lightest, crispiest pizzas. We recommend weighing the flour and water, but because many factors affect the flour's capacity to absorb water, heed visual and tactile clues to achieve a dough with the proper consistency (that is, adjusting the amount of water added as necessary). For rolling out the dough, we prefer commercial-sized parchment paper sheets, though parchment sold in rolls 14 inches wide also works. Keep in mind that it is more important for the rolled dough to be of even thinness than to be a perfect circle. For topping the pizzas, we recommend buying a chunk of whole milk mozzarella and shredding it by hand with a box grater; do not use fresh or prepackaged shredded mozzarella, and resist the temptation to sprinkle on more cheese than is recommended.

2	cups (10 ounces) unbleached all-purpose flour, preferably Gold Medal, protein content no higher than 10.5 percent
½	teaspoon rapid-rise or instant yeast
½	teaspoon honey
½	teaspoon salt
¾	cup plus 2 teaspoons (6¼ ounces) water, preferably filtered or spring, 100 to 105 degrees
¼	cup olive oil
1	cup Quick Tomato Sauce for Pizza (see page 258)
10	ounces whole milk mozzarella, shredded (about 2 cups)

DAY 1

1. Combine the flour, yeast, honey, and salt in the workbowl of a food processor fitted with the steel blade. With the machine running, add all but 2 teaspoons water through feed tube. With the machine still running, add the olive oil through the feed tube and process until the dough forms a ball, about 30 seconds. Turn the dough out onto a work surface. The dough should look shaggy and stick to the counter. (If the dough forms a clean ball and looks slightly curdy on the surface, it is too dry. Add 1 teaspoon water and throw the dough against

the counter 10 times. Repeat if necessary with another teaspoon of water until the dough is sticky.)

2. Divide the dough in half and place each piece in a gallon-sized, heavy-duty zipper-lock plastic bag and seal. Refrigerate overnight or up to 48 hours.

DAY 2

1. Adjust an oven rack to the lowest position, set a baking stone on the rack, and heat the oven to 500 degrees. Heat the baking stone for 1 hour before proceeding.

2. Remove the dough from the plastic bags. Set each half in the center of a lightly floured large sheet of parchment paper. Cover each with two 18-inch lengths plastic wrap overlapping in the center (alternatively, use one 18-inch length of extra-wide plastic wrap); let the doughs rest for 10 minutes.

3. Setting one dough aside, roll the other into a 14-inch round with an even thinness of $\frac{1}{32}$ inch, using the tackiness of the dough against the parchment to help roll. If the parchment wrinkles, flip the dough sandwich over and smooth the wrinkles with a metal dough scraper.

4. Peel the plastic wrap off the top of the rolled dough. Use a soup spoon to spread and smooth $\frac{1}{2}$ cup tomato sauce to the edges of the dough. Sprinkle with about 1 cup cheese. With scissors, trim excess parchment so that it is just larger than the dough.

5. Slip the dough with the parchment onto a pizza peel, inverted rimmed baking sheet, or rimless cookie sheet. Slide the pizza, parchment and all, onto the hot baking stone. Bake until deep golden brown, about 10 minutes. Remove from the oven with a pizza peel or pull the parchment with the pizza onto a baking sheet. Transfer the pizza to cutting board, slide the parchment out from under the pizza; cut the pizza into wedges and slide onto a wire rack. Let cool 2 minutes until crisp; serve.

6. While the first pizza is baking, repeat steps 3 and 4 to roll and sauce the second pizza; allow the baking stone to reheat 15 minutes after baking the first pizza, then repeat step 5 to bake the second pizza.

➤ VARIATIONS

Crisp Thin-Crust Pizza with Arugula

Since dressed arugula will wilt, it's best to prepare the topping for each pizza as needed. For two pizzas, double the amounts listed below.

Toss 5 ounces arugula, stemmed (about 1 cup lightly packed), with 1 tablespoon extra-virgin olive oil and salt and pepper to taste. Follow the recipe for Crisp Thin-Crust Pizza, preparing the pizza as directed and baking for 8 minutes. Sprinkle the arugula over the pizza and return to the oven for 2 minutes more. Cool and slice as directed.

Crisp Thin-Crust Pizza with Pesto

For best presentation, spoon eight equal portions of pesto (each about 1 teaspoon) evenly over the baked pizza. Cut the pizza so each slice has one portion of pesto.

Follow the recipe for Crisp Thin-Crust Pizza, spooning 8 teaspoons pesto (see page 254) over each pizza as soon as it comes out of the oven.

Quick Tomato Sauce for Pizza

MAKES ABOUT 1½ CUPS

This recipe makes a bit more sauce than needed to sauce two thin-crust pizzas.

1	(14½-ounce) can crushed tomatoes
1	large clove garlic, minced or pressed through garlic press
1	tablespoon olive oil
	Salt and ground black pepper

1. Process the tomatoes in the workbowl of a food processor fitted with the steel blade until smooth, about five 1-second pulses.

2. Heat the garlic and oil in a medium saucepan over medium heat until the garlic is sizzling, about 40 seconds. Stir in the tomatoes; bring to a simmer and cook, uncovered, until the sauce thickens enough to coat a wooden spoon, about 15 minutes. Season to taste with salt and pepper.

10
SANDWICHES

WHAT COULD BE SIMPLER OR MORE American than a sandwich? Each region of the country has its own famous creation—the Reuben from New York, the lobster roll from New England, the cheesesteak from Philadelphia, and the po' boy from New Orleans. Other sandwiches, like the Sloppy Joe and grilled cheese, are family favorites across the nation. Although a sandwich is quick work, that doesn't mean that there aren't plenty of places to make a misstep. Frankly, most sandwiches are fast food that satisfy hunger efficiently but not memorably. Our goal for the recipes in this chapter was to develop truly great sandwiches that were still easy to prepare.

GRILLED CHEESE SANDWICHES

ANYONE WITH KIDS MAKES A LOT OF grilled cheese sandwiches. Rarely are they as good as they could be. Quite simply, most parents are often rushed. We set some time aside to figure out exactly how to make consistently great grilled cheese sandwiches—hot and buttery, with a golden, lacy-crisp exterior and a tender interior oozing with melted cheese.

When it comes to grilled cheese sandwiches, the filling is largely a question of personal taste. What tradition does firmly suggest is that the cheese be cut into thin, even slices for even melting. Unfortunately, achieving such perfectly sliced cheese can be problematic. Cheese planes don't work well on soft, rubbery cheeses. Besides, not everyone has a cheese plane. Achieving thin slices with a knife requires patience, practice, and a relatively hard block of cheese. We usually end up with a pile of small, uneven pieces, suitable for placing together like a mosaic.

With this in mind, we opted for the common box grater. Grating is quick and efficient, and it always delivers a uniform mass of cheese, whether it's hard or soft, from a big hunk or a tiny nub. And grated cheese covers the entire slice of bread in one even layer.

Choosing the right bread is like choosing the right pillow. Some people like soft, while others prefer firm. The test kitchen's favorite is Pepperidge Farm Toasting White Bread for its ½-inch-thick

slices, delicate flavor, tender yet firm texture, and crumb with craterlike pockets that cradle the melted cheese perfectly.

Having tried the full range of fats, from vegetable spray to mayonnaise to clarified butter, we chose to work with (salted) butter for its superior flavor and ability to turn the bread deeply golden. We also preferred buttering the bread instead of adding butter to the skillet, where the butter tends to burn and is absorbed unevenly by the bread. For this approach, melted butter was the logical choice.

A heavy-gauge skillet with a flat bottom is your best choice for cooking grilled cheese sandwiches. The real key when it comes to cooking, though, is low heat. We found we could leave the sandwich in the skillet over low heat for an astonishing 30 minutes on one side before the bread became too dark. Few of us have that kind of time to spend making a simple sandwich. But the fact is, the longer it takes the bread to turn golden, the more developed and crispy the exterior will be. The level of heat can be raised slightly, but no higher than medium-low. The least amount of time you can get away with to achieve a golden-crisp exterior is about 5 minutes per side, though 8 to 10 minutes is optimal.

~≈~

Grilled Cheese Sandwiches
SERVES 2

Classic grilled cheese means mild cheddar cheese, but the technique we use works for most any cheese. Grilled cheese sandwiches are best served hot out of the pan, though in a pinch they can be held, unsliced, for about 20 minutes in a warm oven. The possible variations on the basic grilled cheese sandwich are endless, but the extras are best sandwiched between the cheese. Try a few very thin slices of baked ham, prosciutto, turkey breast, or tomato, or two to three tablespoons of caramelized onions. Condiments such as Dijon mustard, pickle relish, or chutney can be spread on the bread instead of sandwiched in the cheese.

3   ounces cheese (preferably mild cheddar), grated on large holes of box grater (about 1 cup, lightly packed)

4   slices (½ inch thick) firm white sandwich bread, such as Pepperidge Farm Toasting White

2   tablespoons butter (preferably salted), melted

1. Heat a heavy 12-inch skillet over low to medium-low heat. Meanwhile, sprinkle a portion of the cheese over two bread slices. Top each with a remaining bread slice, pressing down gently to set.

2. Brush the sandwich tops with half the melted butter. Place each sandwich, buttered-side down, in the skillet. Brush the remaining side of each sandwich completely with the remaining butter. Cook until crisp and deep golden brown, 5 to 10 minutes per side, flipping the sandwiches back to the first side to reheat and crisp, about 15 seconds. Serve immediately.

REUBEN SANDWICHES

A REUBEN IS A NEW YORK DELI STANDARD. When made well, a towering stack of juicy corned beef is built onto good rye bread, accompanied by Swiss cheese and sauerkraut, and dressed with an ample amount of Thousand Island dressing. Cooked on a buttered griddle, the bread toasts to a dark brown color, the cheese melts into the corned beef and sauerkraut, and the thick pile of corned beef gently heats through. Served with a sour pickle and a root beer, this hefty sandwich is as close to heaven as a sandwich can get.

But when made wrongly, the sandwich can taste awful. At most sandwich counters, the bread turns out greasy and undertoasted, and it is filled with a measly amount of poor-quality corned beef, wet sauerkraut, and stiff pieces of old Swiss cheese. After having one too many of these bad Reubens at our local "New York style" deli, we decided it was about time we learned how to make a proper Reuben.

Good corned beef should have a dusty pink color and should be juicy. Don't bother with corned beef that looks dry or has a slimy or tacky texture. A Reuben, as we quickly found out, tastes only as good as its individual components. After finding some good corned beef (we like Boar's Head), we determined that one sandwich needed 6 ounces of meat, which produces a well-stacked sandwich that is both manageable for the cook and the appetite. Also important is thinly sliced corned beef. When the slices are too thick, the pile of meat becomes overly chewy and dense. On the other hand, thinly sliced meat has many nooks for the dressing, cheese, and sauerkraut.

Putting the sandwich together was fairly straightforward, but we did learn a few tricks. First, the sandwich turned out evenly dressed when the Thousand Island was spread onto both pieces of bread as well as layered into the middle of the stack of corned beef. Also, we found it best to line each piece of bread with a slice of Swiss, so that the cheese would melt into the sandwich from both sides. While most recipes butter the griddle or pan, we found it better to butter the bread. By brushing melted butter directly onto the bread and using a nonstick pan, we were able to use less fat and ensure that the sandwich would not turn out greasy. It took roughly 5 to 10 minutes for each side to brown and toast over medium-low heat. Higher heat simply toasted the bread before the filling had a chance to heat through.

Last, we found that this well-stacked sandwich cooked more evenly when compacted with a little pressure. Placing a heavy object on the sandwiches as they cooked caused the corned beef, Swiss, and sauerkraut to meld together and made it easier to flip the sandwiches over in the pan (and to eat them). We used a heavy stockpot as a sandwich press but also found that a skillet, similar in size to the one in which we cooked the sandwiches, worked well when weighted down with a heavy can.

Reuben Sandwiches
SERVES 4

Four Reubens will fit tightly into a 12-inch nonstick skillet. If using a smaller skillet, the sandwiches will have to be cooked in two batches. Place the first batch of Reubens on a wire rack set over a baking sheet in a 200-degree oven. The wire rack prevents the bread from getting soggy and helps the warm air to circulate evenly around the sandwich.

8	slices hearty rye bread
¾	cup Thousand Island Dressing (page 31)
1	pound sauerkraut, squeezed dry of excess moisture (about 1⅓ cups)
8	slices good-quality deli Swiss cheese, such as Emmenthaler (about 8 ounces)
1½	pounds thinly sliced good-quality corned beef
2	tablespoons unsalted butter, melted

1. Place the bread on a work surface and spread each slice with 1 tablespoon of Thousand Island dressing. Onto 4 slices, stack one slice of Swiss, ⅓ cup sauerkraut, 1 tablespoon dressing, 6 ounces corned beef, and another slice of Swiss. Top with the remaining slices of bread.

2. Heat a heavy 12-inch nonstick skillet over medium heat until fairly hot, 2 to 3 minutes. Brush the sandwich tops with half the melted butter. Place each sandwich, buttered-side down, in the skillet. Using a large stockpot or a skillet holding a heavy can as a weight, weigh the sandwiches down as they cook. Cook until crisp and deep golden brown on the bottom, 5 to 10 minutes. Remove the weight, brush the sandwich tops with the remaining butter, and flip the sandwiches. Weight again and cook until crisp and deep golden brown on the second side, 5 to 10 minutes. Remove the weight and flip the sandwiches back to the first side to reheat and crisp, about 15 seconds. Serve immediately.

PHILLY CHEESESTEAK SANDWICHES

ALTHOUGH MOST PHILADELPHIANS SAY there is no such thing as a bad cheesesteak sandwich, they are (somewhat surprisingly) very difficult to re-create at home. The key to a good Philly cheesesteak sandwich lies ultimately in the unique texture of the meat. Making a quick study of an authentic cheese-steak, we took note of the cooking method used by most cheesesteak stands in Philly. First, a good-sized roast is frozen, then sliced into credit card–thin slices on the deli slicer. The thin slices of raw meat are then thrown onto a hot well-greased griddle over a heap of browned onions. With the help of two heavy-duty spatulas, the meat and onions are chopped together and moved around the hot griddle. As the meat fin-ishes cooking, slices of cheese are draped over the top of the pile and allowed to melt. A few final swipes with the spatula mix the melted cheese into steak, and the whole mixture is then placed in a toasted hoagie bun. It is the texture of this thinly sliced and spatula-chopped meat that makes this recipe so difficult to make at home.

With the texture of the meat an obvious goal, we

began our testing. Our first thought was to get a butcher to do the work for us. But it took only one trip to the supermarket to realize this would not be so easy. To get thin-enough slices, the butcher would have to freeze an appropriately sized roast overnight. Even after we managed to convince a butcher to do this for us, the slices of beef we procured were about ¼ inch thick. Although these steaks were rela-tively thin, they were simply not thin enough. Consequently, we bought several different cuts of meat (we chose steaks since roasts would produce too much meat) to see if we could slice them thinly on our own. When partially frozen, the steaks were easier to slice thin, but our knife skills were not fine enough to cut paper-thin slices. Looking at the food processor on the kitchen counter, we wondered if we couldn't use it like a deli slicer.

Using the slicing blade of the food processor, we processed several frozen steaks with a modicum of

PREPARING MEAT FOR PHILLY CHEESESTEAK SANDWICHES

After preparing blade, sirloin, or round steaks, place the strips of meat on a parchment-lined baking sheet and freeze until the exterior hardens but the interior remains soft and yields to gentle pressure, 25 to 50 minutes.

BLADE STEAKS

1. Cut each steak in half lengthwise, leaving the gristle attached to one half.

2. Cut away the gristle from the half to which it is still attached.

SIRLOIN OR ROUND STEAKS

Trim the fat from the steaks and cut into 1-inch-wide strips.

success. The meat that made it through the slicing disk had the perfect texture. However, not much meat made it through. The solid block of frozen steak was too hard, and the blade had a difficult time cutting the meat neatly. Also, the wide mouth of the food processor opening made it easy for the steak to slip sideways and get caught. Still, knowing we were on to something, we began to fiddle with the technique. First, we tried freezing the steaks only partially, making it easier for the food processor blade to do its work. Second, we tried cutting the steaks into strips and forcing them through the feed tube. The sides of the thin tube supported the steak strips as they were processed, preventing them from falling sideways and getting caught. Using the feed tube plunger, we made quick work of the task.

With the technique nailed down, we tested different types of steaks. Cheesesteaks should not be made with expensive cuts, so we tested blade, top sirloin, round, and chuck steaks as well as sirloin tips. Steaks from the round, blade, and top sirloin all worked well, tasting beefy and tender. Chuck steaks, on the other hand, turned out tough and sinewy, while the sirloin tips were fibrous and livery.

Using a nonstick skillet, we easily brought the remaining sandwich ingredients in line. First, onions were quickly browned. The steak, already in bite-sized pieces, was added. It did not need to be cut using a metal spatula. Once the meat was cooked through, we laid slices of cheese on top, let them melt slightly, and then quickly folded them into the meat and onions. This method worked like a charm, and several tasters native to Philadelphia were amazed at the authenticity of our homemade sandwich. They did, however, quarrel over what type of cheese to use—one claiming only American or provolone should be used, the other promoting Cheese Whiz as the authentic choice. A taste test didn't turn up a winner, so we decided to leave the choice up to the cook. Topped with sautéed peppers, hot peppers, sweet relish, or hot sauce and laid into a long toasted sub roll, this sandwich is by all standards a great Philly cheesesteak.

Philly Cheesesteak Sandwiches
SERVES 4

These sandwiches are great as is, but they can be topped with pickled hot peppers, sautéed bell peppers, sweet relish, or hot sauce.

2	pounds blade, sirloin, or round steak, trimmed and partially frozen according to the illustrations on page 262
2	tablespoons vegetable oil
I	very large onion (about 20 ounces), cut into ¼-inch dice Salt and ground black pepper
6	slices American or deli-style provolone cheese, or 5 tablespoons Cheese Whiz
4	large fresh sub rolls, slit partially open and lightly toasted

SHAVING MEAT FOR PHILLY CHEESESTEAK SANDWICHES

1. Once the meat has been partially frozen, place the strips in the feed tube of a food processor fitted with the slicing disk. Turn on the food processor, and use the plunger to push the meat down into the blade.

2. The food processor will shave the meat into small, paper-thin pieces.

1. Using a food processor fitted with the slicing disk, shave the partially frozen meat (see the illustrations on page 263). Set the shaved meat aside.

2. Heat the oil in a 12-inch nonstick skillet over high heat until shimmering, about 2 minutes. Add the onion and sauté until softened and well browned around the edges, 4 to 5 minutes. Add the meat, ½ teaspoon salt, and ⅛ teaspoon black pepper and cook until the meat is fully cooked, 2 to 3 minutes.

3. Turn the heat to low and place slices of cheese over the meat. Allow the cheese to melt, about 1 minute. Using the tip of a heatproof rubber spatula or a wooden spoon, mix the melted cheese and meat together thoroughly. Remove the pan from the heat and spoon 1 cup of the meat mixture into each toasted bun. Serve immediately, with garnishes (see note), if desired.

SLOPPY JOES

EVERYONE LOVES A GOOD SLOPPY JOE. Spooned into a supermarket hamburger bun, the loose meat filling and ketchup-sweet sauce cause the bottom half of the bun to disintegrate, causing the diner to eat this sandwich with a fork. Sloppy Joe spice packages and canned premade filling can be found in supermarkets everywhere. But this quick-cooking sandwich tastes far better when made from scratch.

Most recipes call for the same few ingredients: ground meat, onions, garlic, some sort of tomato product, and seasonings. After making a few renditions of this recipe, we noted the keys to success include well-cooked but not overdone meat, an ample amount of slightly spicy/slightly sweet sauce, and a minimum of other seasonings. But a few questions remained: Which type of ground meat, which tomato products, and which seasonings?

Starting with the meat, we tried 95 percent, 90 percent, 85 percent, and 80 percent lean ground beef. The 95 percent and 90 percent lean had great meaty flavor but turned out dry and rubbery. At the other extreme, the 80 percent lean meat was too greasy. The 85 percent lean ground beef struck the perfect balance between meat and fat.

Although some recipes call for sauces made entirely from ketchup, we found them tart, vinegary,

and lacking tomato flavor. We then tried combining the ketchup with tomato puree, crushed tomatoes, and tomato paste. The smooth, slightly thickened texture of pureed tomatoes worked well, adding an honest tomato punch to the ketchup. We liked the balance of sweet and vinegar flavors when ½ cup of ketchup was mixed with 1 cup of tomato puree. We added ½ cup of water to the sauce as it cooked, loosening it to the proper "sloppy" consistency.

To this ketchup-tomato puree, we tried adding numerous spices, including chili powder, Tabasco, Worcestershire, celery salt, garlic powder, dried onion, paprika, dry mustard, and sugar. While fresh onion and garlic tasted better than their stale, powdered counterparts, tasters disliked all other spices except small amounts of chili powder, Tabasco, and sugar. A little kick from the chili powder and Tabasco balanced lightly by brown sugar gave our Sloppy Joes a straightforward and simple flavor. The other spices were unanimously deemed out of place in this simple sandwich.

Sloppy Joes
SERVES 4

These sandwiches are sloppy to eat, so serve them on plates with forks and knives.

1	tablespoon vegetable oil
1	medium onion, minced
1	medium clove garlic, minced
½	teaspoon chili powder
¾	pound 85 percent lean ground beef
¼	teaspoon salt
⅛	teaspoon ground black pepper
1	teaspoon brown sugar
1	cup tomato puree
½	cup ketchup
¼	cup water
	Dash hot pepper sauce, such as Tabasco (optional)
4	hamburger buns

1. Heat the oil in a large skillet over high heat until shimmering, about 1 minute. Add the onion and sauté, stirring often, until softened and browned around the edges, about 2 minutes. Add the garlic and chili powder and sauté until aromatic, about

30 seconds. Add the beef, salt, ground black pepper, and brown sugar and reduce the heat to medium. Cook, using a wooden spoon to help break the meat into small pieces, until the meat is no longer pink, about 3 minutes.

2. Add the tomato puree, ketchup, water, and Tabasco (if using). Cook until slightly thickened, about 4 minutes. Adjust the seasonings with salt and pepper to taste. Spoon ½ cup of the meat mixture into each hamburger bun and serve immediately.

TUNA MELTS

TUNA MELTS HAVE BEEN GIVEN A BAD RAP by institutional cafeterias and greasy, second rate diners. Bland, watery tuna salad is typically found hiding underneath an oily, plastic-tasting piece of cheese. Even worse, the bread is usually undertoasted and soggy. But these poor examples should not be cause for the home cook to abandon this 1950s classic.

With great tuna salad at the ready (see recipe on page 43), we looked to turn it into a good melt. Usually, the tuna is placed on the bread, topped with cheese, and placed under the broiler. It is necessary, as we soon found out, to toast the bread first. Toasted bread remains crisp and better supports the tuna salad and melting cheese. Although we thought the type of cheese would make a difference, tasters preferred a wide range of cheeses, with freshness and melting power being the only qualities that mattered. Last, we liked a slice of tomato on top of the tuna, directly under the melting cheese. The tomato added a refreshing, clean flavor and helped keep the sandwich from tasting institutional or musty.

Tuna Melts

SERVES 4

Choose a cheese that melts easily, such as Swiss, provolone, mozzarella, or American.

1	recipe Classic Tuna Salad (page 43)
4	slices high-quality sandwich bread, toasted
4	tomato slices, about ¼ inch thick
4	thin slices cheese

1. Adjust an oven rack so it is 6 inches from the broiler element and heat the broiler. Place the bread on a baking sheet. Spread about ½ cup tuna salad atop each slice of bread and top with a slice of tomato. Place a slice of cheese on top of the tomato.

2. Broil until the cheese has melted and begun to brown in spots, about 2 minutes. Serve immediately.

OYSTER PO' BOYS

THE PO' BOY IS A SANDWICH FROM NEW Orleans. Making one calls for hollowing a crisp baguette and filling it with a variety of sandwich meats and seafood. We especially like a po' boy filled with spicy fried oysters "dressed" with mayonnaise, diced pickle, lettuce, and tomato. As you eat this sandwich, the mayonnaise mixes with the juices from the tomatoes, pickles, and spicy oysters to create the unmistakable flavor of an authentic oyster po' boy.

But not all po' boys are created equal. When made with bland, greasy oysters, a cheap, doughy baguette, or "dressed" with aged, lifeless vegetables, this famous New Orleans lunch turns into a bitter disappointment. While it takes only one bite of a good po' boy to stir a lifelong craving for this sandwich, trips to New Orleans lunch counters are, for most of us, rare. We decided to find a way to re-create an authentic oyster po' boy at home.

Our fried oyster recipe (see page 224) was the natural place to begin. Focusing on the remaining components of the sandwich, we decided we should not skimp on the quality of the baguette, the ripeness of the tomato, or the crispness of the lettuce and pickles. Trying to get the mayonnaise to mingle with the juices of the oysters, tomatoes, and pickles made us understood why many recipes recommend pulling out some of the baguette's spongy interior. When a small channel of the interior crumb is removed, there is less bread to soak up these valuable juices. Finally, we noted how fresh the po' boy tasted when fresh lemon juice, salt, and black pepper were sprinkled onto the sandwich just before eating.

Oyster Po' Boys

SERVES 4

1	baguette, cut into four 6-inch lengths, each length halved to separate top and bottom crusts
½	cup mayonnaise
2	teaspoons lemon juice
	Salt and ground black pepper
½	cup dill pickles, cut into ¼-inch dice
½	pound shucked oysters in their liquor (20 to 24 oysters), breaded and fried according to the recipe on page 224 and drained on a plate lined with paper towels
1	medium tomato, cut into ⅛-inch-thick slices
4	leaves green leaf lettuce, root ends trimmed

Using your fingers, evenly pull out a 1-inch-wide channel of interior crumb from the top and bottom of each length of baguette. Spread 1 tablespoon of mayonnaise over each channel and sprinkle each with ¼ teaspoon lemon juice and salt and pepper to taste. Working with the bottom pieces of bread, evenly sprinkle with 2 tablespoons minced pickle and place 4 or 5 fried oysters on top. Add 2 or 3 slices of tomato and 1 leaf of lettuce. Top with the upper crust of the baguette and slice in half. Serve immediately.

LOBSTER ROLL

FOUND AT ROADSIDE STANDS ALONG THE Northeast coast, this summertime sandwich highlights the delicate flavor of local lobsters. Fresh lobster meat is dressed lightly with mayonnaise and mixed with a few aromatics and herbs. Fitted into a lightly buttered hot dog roll, the recipe is simple enough to let the star ingredient—the lobster—shine.

Although roadside stands steam lobsters for the sole purpose of making this sandwich, it is a time-consuming procedure to do at home. We found several types of cooked lobster meat at the supermarket, but only one of them was good enough to suit our notion of a lobster sandwich. Imitation lobster made from cooked, shredded, pressed, and colored white fish is commonly available but tastes as bad as it sounds. We also came across tubs of promising-looking pasteurized lobster meat. While these tubs are filled with authentic lobster, it tastes like fishy cardboard. At one supermarket, we found freshly steamed lobster meat. Although expensive, this is the best option if you don't want to steam your own.

Working with 8 ounces of lobster meat (to make four rolls), we tried adding various aromatics and herbs to find the perfect combination. Red onions tasted too potent and overpowering, and shallots tasted tart and out of place. We tried both celery and celery seed, preferring the delicate crunch and fresh flavor of finely minced celery.

Next we tested dill, parsley, chervil, and tarragon. Tasters found the flavor of dill too strong, while parsley simply tasted boring and grassy. Chervil was OK, but tarragon was fantastic. Its delicate anise flavor helped bring out and intensify the sweet flavor of the lobster. A spray of fresh lemon juice lightened up the heft of the mayonnaise binder. After making a few batches, we noted the lobster meat, depending on how fresh it is, needs slightly more or less mayonnaise.

Lobster Roll

SERVES 4

If you can't find impeccably fresh cooked lobster meat at your local market, see page 213 for instructions on steaming a single 1½- to 2-pound hard-shell lobster to obtain the meat necessary for this recipe.

8	ounces chilled, freshly cooked lobster meat, cut into ½-inch pieces
2	tablespoons minced celery
½	teaspoon minced fresh tarragon leaves
⅛	teaspoon salt
⅛	teaspoon ground black pepper
1	teaspoon lemon juice
2–3	tablespoons mayonnaise
4	hot dog rolls, lightly toasted
1	tablespoon unsalted butter, melted

Mix the lobster, celery, tarragon, salt, pepper, and lemon juice together in a medium bowl. Fold in 2 tablespoons of the mayonnaise, taste, and add one more tablespoon if the mixture seems dry. Brush the inside of each roll with some butter and fill with roughly ⅓ cup lobster mixture. Serve immediately.

11

QUICK BREADS, MUFFINS, AND BISCUITS

QUICK BREADS, SUCH AS CORNBREAD AND gingerbread, as well as muffins and biscuits have a number of elements in common. All of these baked goods can be quickly prepared (the batter or dough can usually be assembled in the time it takes to preheat the oven) and quickly baked. This sets them far apart from yeast breads, which must rise for hours on the counter. Chemical leaveners (baking soda and baking powder) are speedy and reliable.

Several methods are commonly used to assemble quick breads. The most common, often referred to as the quick bread method, calls for measuring wet and dry ingredients separately, pouring wet into dry, then mixing them together as quickly as possible. Batters for many muffins, quick breads, and pancakes (which are a form of quick bread) typically rely on this approach.

A second technique, often called the creaming method and more common to cake batters, starts with creaming the butter and sugar until light and fluffy. Eggs and flavorings are beaten in, then the dry and liquid ingredients are alternately added.

A third possibility comes from the tradition of biscuit and pie-making, in which cold fat is cut into the dry ingredients with fingertips, forks, a pastry blender, or the blade of a food processor. Once the mixture has achieved a cornmeal-like texture with pea-sized flecks, liquid is added and quickly mixed in.

We have tested these three mixing methods on many of the recipes in this chapter. Often, we have found that the same ingredients will bake up quite differently depending on how they are combined.

In addition to mixing methods, it's also important to pay attention to the choice of flours and leaveners in these recipes. The protein content of the flour can greatly affect the texture in these simple baked goods. (For more information on flour, see page 231.) Chemical leaveners (that is, baking soda and baking powder) are key elements in quick bread recipes. See page 271 for more information on these ingredients.

JALAPEÑO CORNBREAD

CORNBREAD DIVIDES PEOPLE ALONG GEO-graphic lines almost as definitively as barbecue. Southerners swear by unsweetened, crisp-crusted bread baked in a cast-iron skillet, while Northerners are wedded to sweetened, dairy-rich bread. We have kitchen staff from both sides of the Mason-Dixon line who believe that "their" cornbread is "it" and anything else is downright heretical.

INGREDIENTS: Cornmeal

Cornmeal comes in a variety of colors (usually yellow or white, sometimes blue) and grinds. To see if there was a link between color and flavor, we tested 11 different cornmeals in a simple cornbread recipe. Before these tests, we would have bet that color was a regional idiosyncrasy that had little to do with flavor. But the tasting proved otherwise. Cornbreads made with yellow cornmeal were judged to have a more potent corn flavor than those made with white meal.

The way the cornmeal was ground also affected flavor in these tests. Large commercial mills use huge steel rollers to grind dent corn (a hard, dry corn) into cornmeal. This is how Quaker, the leading supermarket brand, is produced. But some smaller mills scattered around the United States grind with millstones; this product is called stone-ground cornmeal. (If water is used as an energy source, the cornmeal may be labeled "water-ground".) Stone-ground cornmeal is usually a bit coarser than cornmeal processed through steel rollers.

Besides differences in milling methods, smaller millers often choose not to degerm, or remove all the germ, cleanly. This makes their product closer to a whole-grain cornmeal. If the color is uniform, the germ has been removed. A stone-ground cornmeal with some germ will have flecks that are both lighter and darker than the predominant color, whether that's yellow or white.

In our tests, we found the texture of cornbreads made with stone-ground meals to be more interesting, since the cornmeals were not of a uniform grind. More important, we found that cornbreads made with stone-ground cornmeal tasted much better than those made with the standard Quaker cornmeal.

The higher moisture and oil content of stone-ground cornmeal causes it to go rancid within weeks. If you buy some, wrap it tightly in plastic or put it into a moisture-proof container, then refrigerate or freeze it. Degerminated cornmeals, such as Quaker, keep for a year if stored in a dry, cool place.

To appease both parties (we attempt to be diplomatic about such regionalized fare), we borrowed from both styles and came up with a cornbread that, we think, represents the best of both worlds: skillet cooking and Southern technique for a crisp crust and intense corn flavor, and a little sugar, dairy, and eggs to bring out the corn's natural flavors. Then, with our perfect cornbread recipe in hand, we went "Texas-style" (Southern or Southwestern, depending on your view) and added peppers—both jalapeño and red bell—as well as cheddar cheese for a little zest and extra flavor.

While Southerners and Northerners disagree about sweeteners and leavening, they do agree that good-quality cornmeal is the foundation for respectable cornbread. If you can find it, stone-ground meal is best (see page 268 for details on our tasting). After tasting both yellow and white cornmeal breads (yellow meal being typically Northern and white typically Southern), we decided to go with yellow meal. Most tasters believed it had a stronger flavor and a more characteristic "corn" color. But white cornmeal will work just as well in the recipe if you prefer it, as many Southerners do.

To achieve a lush, fine-crumbed cornbread, we took a lesson from Southern cornbread and made "mush" with a portion of the meal. Mush is meal that is softened with boiling water before it is combined with the rest of the batter. The mush added moisture and a fine texture to the bread as well as a second dimension of corn flavor. The mush also allowed us to make the bread without any white flour, which can dull the corn's flavor.

Buttermilk was our liquid of choice. Its bright tang accentuated the corn's natural sweetness and lent body without a lot of additional fat. When we tried other dairy products, like whole milk and cream, they merely muted the corn's flavor.

While we knew we wanted a little sweetener in the cornbread, we were not sure what type. Honey was too assertive and contrasted sharply with the jalapeño flavor. White sugar was fine, but light brown sugar proved the best choice. Its subtle earthiness supported the flavor of both the corn and the peppers. Surprisingly, just 2 teaspoons was enough to round things out without causing the bread to taste saccharine.

Choosing peppers was easy. We were after flavor and a mild piquancy, not incendiary heat. Two jalapeño chiles, with their seeds and ribs removed, provided just enough flavor and zip. For more heat, serrano chiles or a habanero chile can be added. For a little additional color, we picked red bell pepper. A quick sauté cooked the peppers and helped to bring the pan up to temperature.

As any Southerner will tell you, an extremely hot cast-iron skillet is the secret to a crisp, golden-brown crust. Cast-iron skillets are readily available at hardware stores, kitchen supply stores, and most garage sales for very reasonable prices. Pick one up, even if only for making cornbread. Cast iron is easy to season and maintain, and you will find it serves well in a variety of situations. Most Southern cornbread recipes instruct you to preheat the pan in the oven, but in this case, the skillet was already heated through from cooking the peppers. To keep it hot while we finished mixing the batter, we set it in the oven. Through experience, we found that if the batter sizzles when it is added to the pan, a perfect, golden crust should result.

Jalapeño Cornbread
SERVES 6

A well-seasoned cast-iron skillet is the best possible pan for baking cornbread. It gets ferociously hot and holds the heat, making for a crisp, golden crust. If your pan is not well seasoned, you may want to coat it lightly with cooking spray before adding the batter so that the bread will not stick after baking. The texture of the cornbread will vary according to your cornmeal. Very fine-grained meal will result in a dense, uniform loaf, while coarser-grained meal with have a bit more of a bite. The stone-ground cornmeal typically sold in the supermarket is the best choice.

2 tablespoons unsalted butter

2 medium jalapeño chiles, stemmed, seeded, and diced fine

1 medium red bell pepper, stemmed, seeded, and diced fine

1 cup (5 1/2 ounces) yellow cornmeal, preferably stone-ground

2 teaspoons packed light brown sugar

3/4 teaspoon salt

1	teaspoon baking powder
¼	teaspoon baking soda
¼	teaspoon ground black pepper
½	cup boiling water
¾	cup buttermilk
⅛	teaspoon hot pepper sauce, such as Tabasco
1	large egg, lightly beaten
2	ounces cheddar cheese, shredded (about ½ cup)

1. Adjust an oven rack to the lower-middle position and heat the oven to 450 degrees. Add the butter to a 10-inch cast-iron skillet and place over medium-high heat until the butter foams. Add the chiles and bell pepper and cook, stirring occasionally, until softened and beginning to brown, about 5 minutes. Transfer the peppers to a small bowl and set aside. Set the skillet, uncleaned, in the oven.

2. Measure ⅓ cup cornmeal into a medium bowl. In a separate larger bowl, whisk together the remaining cornmeal, brown sugar, salt, baking powder, baking soda, and black pepper. While whisking, pour the boiling water in a slow, steady stream into the ⅓ cup cornmeal, followed by the buttermilk, hot pepper sauce, and the egg. Pour the wet mixture into the dry ingredients and stir until just combined. Mix in the cooked peppers and the cheese.

3. Carefully remove the skillet from the oven and quickly pour the batter into the heated skillet. Bake until light golden brown, about 10 minutes. Remove the skillet from the oven, invert the cornbread onto a wire rack, and cool for 5 minutes. Flip the bread right-side up and serve warm or at room temperature. For a moister texture, let the cornbread cool in the skillet.

BANANA BREAD

SOME OVERRIPE BANANAS ON THE KITCHEN counter are an excellent excuse to make banana bread. However, many banana breads are flat, gritty, or heavy. Worse, some loaves taste only remotely of bananas. Good banana bread is soft and tender with plenty of banana flavor and crunchy toasted walnuts. It should be moist and light, something so delicious that you look forward to the bananas on the counter turning soft and mushy.

In our testing, we found it very important to pay close attention to the condition of the bananas. Sweet, older, darkly speckled bananas infused the bread with both moisture and flavor, which meant that the bread, whether still warm or day-old, succeeded with less butter (minus 2 tablespoons) than the amount used in most recipes (½ cup).

We also experimented with the way we prepared the bananas for the batter: slightly mashed, mashed well, and pureed. Loaves with slightly mashed bananas left chunks of fruit. We preferred a smoother texture, but pureeing the bananas turned out to be a bad idea, because the batter did not rise as well. Leavener probably escaped before the thin batter developed enough structure to trap gases. Bananas well-mashed by hand kept the batter thick.

We still wanted more moisture in the bread, so we tried mixing in milk, buttermilk, sour cream, and plain yogurt. Sour cream added richness, but it also made for a heavy texture and an unattractive, pebbly crust. Milk added little flavor and created a slick crust. Buttermilk added a delightful tang, but yogurt let the banana flavor stand out. And because yogurt has more solids than buttermilk, it made for a somewhat more solid loaf, which we preferred.

While the added yogurt softened the bread's crumb, we still sought a more delicate, open grain. So we decided to experiment with various mixing methods to see how they affected the final texture. We considered the quick bread method (dry ingredients mixed in one bowl, liquids in another, with the two then gently stirred together) and the creaming method (butter and sugar creamed together, dry and wet ingredients then alternately mixed in).

The creaming method created a soft texture (reminiscent of butter cake) and good volume from the whipped sugar and butter. However, its lighter color looked less appetizing next to the golden-brown loaf achieved with the quick bread method. The quick bread method produced a delicate texture, too, and the less consistent crumb looked hearty and delicious. It also rose more than the creamed loaf. All in all, it was a better choice.

Take caution when mixing, though. When we stirred the wet and dry ingredients into a smooth batter, the loaves turned out small and tough. Flour contains protein, and when protein mixes with water, gluten develops. The more you stir with a spoon, the more the gluten proteins arrange into long, orderly bundles. These bundles create an elastic batter that resists changing shape and cannot rise as well. To minimize gluten development, fold together the wet and dry ingredients gently, just until the dry ingredients are moistened. The batter should still be thick and chunky, but without any streaks of unincorporated flour.

Banana Bread

MAKES ONE 9-INCH LOAF

Greasing and flouring only the bottom of a regular loaf pan causes the bread to cling to the sides and rise higher. If using a nonstick loaf pan, on which the sides are very slick, grease and flour the sides as well as the bottom. Either way, use a loaf pan that measures 9 inches long, 5 inches across, and 3 inches deep.

2	cups (10 ounces) unbleached all-purpose flour
¾	cup (5¼ ounces) sugar
¾	teaspoon baking soda
½	teaspoon salt
1¼	cups toasted walnuts, chopped coarse (about 1 cup)
3	very ripe, soft, darkly speckled large bananas, mashed well (about 1½ cups)
¼	cup plain yogurt
2	large eggs, beaten lightly
6	tablespoons butter, melted and cooled
1	teaspoon vanilla extract

1. Adjust an oven rack to the lower-middle position and heat the oven to 350 degrees. Grease and flour a 9 by 5-inch loaf pan; set aside.

2. Whisk the flour, sugar, baking soda, salt, and walnuts together in a large bowl; set aside.

3. Mix the mashed bananas, yogurt, eggs, butter, and vanilla with wooden spoon in a medium bowl. Lightly fold the banana mixture into the dry ingredients with a rubber spatula until just combined and batter looks thick and chunky. Scrape the batter into prepared loaf pan and smooth the surface with a rubber spatula.

4. Bake until the loaf is golden brown and a toothpick inserted in the center comes out clean,

---

INGREDIENTS: Baking Soda and Baking Powder

Quick breads, muffins, and biscuits as well as cookies, cakes, pancakes, and waffles get their rise from chemical leaveners—baking soda and baking powder—rather than yeast. Chemical leavenings react with acids to produce carbon dioxide, the gas that causes these baked goods to rise.

To do its work, baking soda relies on an acid in the recipe, such as buttermilk, sour cream, yogurt, or molasses. It's important to use the right amount of baking soda in recipes. Use more baking soda than can be neutralized by the acidic ingredient, and you'll end up with a metallic-tasting, coarse-crumbed quick bread or cake.

Baking powder is nothing more than baking soda (about one-quarter to one-third of the total makeup) mixed with a dry acid and double-dried cornstarch. The cornstarch absorbs moisture and keeps the baking soda and dry acid apart during storage, preventing premature production of the gas. When baking powder becomes wet, the acid comes into contact with the baking soda, producing carbon dioxide. Most commercial baking powders are "double-acting." In other words, they contain two kinds of acids—one that produces a carbon dioxide reaction at room temperature, the other responding only to heat. Baking soda reacts immediately on contact with an acid and is thus "single-acting."

---

about 55 minutes. Cool in the pan for 5 minutes, then transfer to a wire rack. Serve warm or at room temperature.

➤ VARIATIONS

Banana-Chocolate Bread

Follow the recipe for Banana Bread, reducing the sugar to 10 tablespoons and mixing 2½ ounces grated bittersweet chocolate (a heaping ½ cup) into the dry ingredients.

Banana-Coconut Bread with Macadamia Nuts

Adjust an oven rack to the middle position and heat the oven to 350 degrees. Toast ½ cup flaked, sweetened coconut and 1 cup chopped macadamia nuts on a small baking sheet, stirring every 2 minutes, until golden brown, about 6 minutes. Follow the recipe for Banana Bread, substituting the toasted macadamias and coconut for the walnuts.

Orange-Spice Banana Bread

Follow the recipe for Banana Bread, adding 1 teaspoon ground cinnamon, ¼ teaspoon grated nutmeg, and 2 tablespoons grated orange zest to the dry ingredients.

CRANBERRY-NUT BREAD

WE DON'T MAKE CRANBERRY NUT BREAD just for ourselves. We make it for the kindergarten teacher, the mail carrier, and anyone else who deserves something homemade rather than store-bought for the holidays.

The problem is that this simple bread is often sub-par, sunken in the middle, too dense, or so overly sweetened that the contrast between the tart berries and what should be a slightly sweet dough is lost. We wanted to avoid these problems, and we had some

EQUIPMENT: Loaf Pans

A good loaf pan will evenly brown banana bread and other quick breads (as well as yeast breads, such as sandwich bread). In addition, loaves should release cleanly and the pans should be easy to get in and out of the oven, with little chance of sticking an oven mitt into the batter or baked bread.

We tested 10 loaf pans made from a variety of materials, including metal, glass, and stoneware. We found that dark-colored metal loaf pans browned breads more evenly than light-colored metal pans. Most of the dark metal pans were lined with a nonstick coating that also made the release of baked breads especially easy. We found that sweet breads, such as banana bread, were especially prone to burning in glass loaf pans. Sticking was also a problem in these pans. Stoneware loaf pans did a decent job of browning, but we had trouble removing loaves from these pans. Our testers found that pans with handles at either end were easier to work with and kept us from sticking an oven mitt into the edge of a baked loaf.

In the end, we recommend that you buy metal loaf pans with a nonstick coating. Although there's no harm in spending more money on heavier pans, the cheapest, lightest pan in our testing (Ecko Baker's Secret, $4) was the favorite. One final piece of advice: Even with the nonstick coating, we recommend greasing and flouring your loaf pan to ensure easy release.

other goals in mind as well. We were looking for a crust that was golden brown and evenly thin all the way around and a texture that was somewhere between a dense breakfast bread and a light, airy cake. And, for convenience's sake, we wanted a recipe that fit easily into a standard 9 by 5-inch loaf pan. After looking at almost 60 recipes, it seemed evident that the mixing method and the leavening were the most important factors in getting the quick bread we were after.

First we tackled mixing. Some recipes called for the creaming method, others the quick bread method. We made several loaves using each of these methods. While the creaming method did give us a marginally more tender bread, we quickly determined that it was too light and airy. We liked the denser, more compact texture produced by the quick bread method. An added advantage of the quick bread method is that—as its name implies—it can be put together very quickly.

Next we moved on to leavening. When we looked back at our testing, we noted that 75 percent of the recipes combined baking powder with baking soda to leaven the bread. The rest used all baking powder or all baking soda. We tried every option we could think of using these two leaveners, both alone and together. We found that baking powder seemed to enhance the flavor, while baking soda supported the structure; finding the right balance was tricky. Eventually, we came to the decision that ¼ teaspoon of baking soda combined with 1 teaspoon of baking powder gave us the bright flavor and rather dense texture we were looking for.

With our mixing and leavening methods settled, we focused on ingredients. We quickly determined that we liked the flavor that butter provided over that of oil, margarine, or shortening. More than one egg made the bread almost too rich and caused the interior to turn somewhat yellow. After testing different amounts and types of sugar, we stuck with 1 cup of granulated sugar, which provided just the right amount of sweetness. Orange zest added not only to the flavor but to the interior appearance as well.

We also tinkered with the liquid component. Many recipes called for water or even boiling water, but freshly squeezed orange juice was usually mentioned and offered the best flavor. We compared fresh, home-squeezed orange juice with commercially prepared juices made from both fresh oranges and from concentrate; home-squeezed juice was the winner, hands down.

Not every recipe called for dairy, but we tested everything from heavy cream to sour cream. Both buttermilk and yogurt provided the moistness and tang we were looking for, with buttermilk edging out yogurt by a hairbreadth.

Last but not least were the cranberries. The cranberry harvest begins just after Labor Day and continues through early fall, which means that by mid- to late January, no fresh berries are available. Cranberries freeze beautifully, so grab a few extra bags to have on hand and freeze them until ready to use. We found no discernible difference in the finished product whether using fresh or frozen cranberries.

Cranberry Nut Bread

MAKES ONE 9-INCH LOAF

We prefer sweet, mild pecans in this bread, but walnuts can be substituted. Resist the urge to cut into the bread while it is hot out of the oven; the texture improves as it cools, making it easier to slice. To toast pecans, place a skillet over medium heat, add chopped pecans, and toast, shaking the pan frequently, until nuts are fragrant, 3 to 5 minutes.

1	tablespoon grated orange zest
1/3	cup fresh orange juice
2/3	cup buttermilk
6	tablespoons unsalted butter, melted and cooled
1	large egg, beaten lightly
2	cups (10 ounces) unbleached all-purpose flour
1	cup (7 ounces) sugar
1	teaspoon salt
1	teaspoon baking powder
1/4	teaspoon baking soda
1 1/2	cups cranberries (about 6 ounces), chopped coarse
1/2	cup pecans, chopped coarse and toasted

1. Adjust the oven rack to the middle position and heat the oven to 375 degrees. Grease and flour a 9 by 5-inch loaf pan; set aside.

2. Stir together the orange zest, orange juice, buttermilk, butter, and egg in a small bowl. Whisk together the flour, sugar, salt, baking powder, and baking soda in a large bowl. Stir the liquid ingredients into the dry ingredients with a rubber spatula until just moistened. Gently stir in the cranberries and pecans. Do not overmix. Scrape the batter into the prepared pan and smooth the surface with a rubber spatula.

3. Bake 20 minutes, then reduce the heat to 350 degrees; continue to bake until golden brown and a toothpick inserted in the center of the loaf comes out clean, about 45 minutes longer. Cool in the pan 10 minutes, then transfer to a wire rack and cool at least 1 hour before serving. Once cooled, the bread can be wrapped in plastic and stored at room temperature for a couple of days.

BOSTON BROWN BREAD

RARELY EATEN MORE THAN A HUNDRED miles outside of Boston and almost never served without baked beans, "Boston" brown bread is a unique loaf. Characteristically steamed in an old coffee can, this chemically leavened bread is robust, dense, and strongly flavored with earthy grains and the bittersweet tang of molasses. Boston brown bread may be a dying tradition, but, as Boston locals, we love it and wanted to come up with a perfect recipe.

Like Boston baked beans, brown bread is a study in Puritan frugality. Most of the recipes we gathered offered up a simple batter of cornmeal, whole wheat and rye flours, molasses, raisins or currants, and baking soda for leavening. While we appreciated the simple flavors of these uncomplicated recipes, we found most of them to be unbalanced, tasting predominantly of whole wheat. We wanted a recipe in which all the ingredients were on more equal footing.

We knew that altering the basic ingredients was akin to heresy and did not want to stray too far. We did, however, decide that changing the flour mixture—lightening the whole wheat and rye flours with a little unbleached white flour—was a safe change. The addition of the white flour allowed the cornmeal and molasses flavors to come through more clearly. We also tried substituting oat flour for part of the rye flour, but the resulting loaf was gummy and lacked any oat flavor.

We also found that the choice of cornmeal makes a real difference in this simple bread. High-quality stone-ground cornmeal was the tasters' favorite. It had a stronger corn flavor than fine-ground and added a pleasing texture to the loaf. If stone-ground cornmeal is difficult to find, try Goya-brand coarse cornmeal, which proved readily available and delicious.

We experimented with different kinds of molasses and were most pleased with the darker varieties, especially Grandma's Robust molasses. Light, or mild, molasses was fine and provided adequate flavor, but dark molasses imparted a hardier flavor that nicely complemented the earthy whole wheat and rye flours. Blackstrap, the dregs of sugar processing and therefore the strongest-flavored molasses, was too much, giving the loaf a bitter, one-dimensional flavor.

For cooking, there are two schools of thought: steaming and baking. In a side-by-side comparison, tasters favored the steamed loaves over the baked. Most people thought the baked loaves were closer to Irish soda bread in texture and flavor than what they knew as brown bread. While delicious, the baked bread was another species. The steamed loaves were dense, moist, and deeply satisfying.

Traditionally, Boston brown bread is steamed in a large coffee can. Because we buy our coffee in a bag, we resorted to more readily available containers: loaf pans. Small pans, about 8½ by 4 inches, proved the perfect size for even cooking in about two hours. To keep moisture from seeping into the bread, we used a double layer of greased aluminum foil very tightly sealed around the lip of the pan.

Steaming may be a bit of an overstatement. We found that the bread cooked most evenly and had the moistest crumb when the water slowly simmered over very low heat. We cooked the loaves in two 8-quart Dutch ovens (one loaf in each pot), with water reaching halfway up the sides of the loaf pans. With any more water, the loaves became too moist and were unevenly cooked. If you do not have two large Dutch ovens, you can use a deep roasting pan sealed with aluminum foil for one or both of the loaves. We found it important to check the water level every 30 minutes, adding more water whenever the level fell less than halfway up the side of the pan. If your pot has a tight-fitting lid, chances are you will not have to add additional water.

Two hours proved to be the best cooking time. The bread was cooked through—a skewer inserted into the middle came out clean—and had a velvety soft crumb. When we cooked the loaf any longer, it dried out and became tough.

Boston brown bread's robust flavors stand up well to baked beans and pot roasts as well as hearty soups and stews. If you have any leftover bread (an unlikely proposition), try it toasted with butter and jam, especially marmalade. Cream cheese is good, too.

Boston Bread

MAKES 2 SMALL LOAVES

Low and steady heat is the key to a tender, moist brown bread. If your burner's flame is too high to allow for a slow, barely bubbling simmer, use a heat diffuser. If you choose to go the classic route and steam the bread in coffee cans, use two 1-pound cans and make sure to liberally grease the insides of the cans. As with the loaf pans, coffee cans should be tightly wrapped with buttered aluminum foil. We like dark molasses, especially Grandma's Robust, in this recipe; see page 92 for more information on types of molasses. This bread is best served warm.

2	tablespoons unsalted butter, softened
1	cup (5½ ounces) cornmeal, preferably stone-ground
1	cup (3½ ounces) rye flour
½	cup (2¼ ounces) whole wheat flour
½	cup (2½ ounces) unbleached all-purpose flour
2	teaspoons baking soda
1	teaspoon salt
1	cup raisins
2	cups buttermilk
¾	cup molasses, preferably dark or robust

1. Fold two 16 by 12-inch pieces of foil in half to yield two foil rectangles, each measuring 12 by 8 inches. With the butter, liberally grease two 8½ by 4-inch loaf pans as well as the center portion of each piece of foil (see illustration 1 on page 275).

2. In the bowl of a standing mixer fitted with a paddle attachment, combine all of the dry ingredients. Mix on low speed until blended, about 30 seconds. Add the raisins and mix until uniformly dispersed, about 15 seconds longer. With the

machine still on low speed, slowly pour in the buttermilk and molasses and mix until fully combined, about 30 seconds. Stir the batter with a rubber spatula for several strokes, scraping the bottom of the bowl to mix in any unincorporated ingredients. Evenly divide the batter between the greased loaf pans and wrap very tightly with the buttered foil (see illustration 2 below).

3. Set each loaf pan in a large Dutch oven or a roasting pan and fill each vessel with enough water to reach halfway up the side of each loaf pan. (If your roasting pan is large enough, you may be able to fit both loaves in one pan.) Bring to a simmer over medium-high heat, reduce the heat to low, and cover with a lid. (If using a roasting pan, wrap tightly with foil.) Check the water level every 30 minutes to make sure the water still reaches halfway up the sides of the loaf pans. Cook until a skewer inserted in the middle of the loaves comes out clean, about 2 hours. Carefully remove the loaves from the pans and transfer them a cooling rack. Cool for 10 minutes. Slice and serve.

MAKING BROWN BREAD

1. Fold a 16 by 12-inch piece of aluminum foil in half to yield a rectangle that measures 12 by 8 inches. Liberally grease the center portion of the foil with butter. Repeat with a second piece of foil.

2. Scrape the batter into a greased loaf pan, place the foil buttered-side down over the batter, and then seal the edges tightly. Use the second piece of foil on the second loaf pan.

GINGERBREAD

GINGERBREAD SHOULD BE TENDER, MOIST, and several inches thick. It should be easy enough to assemble just before dinner so squares of warm gingerbread can be enjoyed for dessert. As our early tests proved, these goals are rarely met. Gingerbread has a tendency to be dry and tough, and many recipes are unnecessarily complicated. Yes, you will probably need a lot of ingredients (mostly spices already in your pantry), but the mixing method should be simple. Gingerbread is a quick bread, after all.

To start our kitchen tests, we chose a milk-based gingerbread. Many recipes call for water, but in our initial tests tasters found these breads considerably drier and less rich than those made with milk. Milk fat adds tenderness and flavor; it is a must. With that decision made, we focused next on sweeteners. Most recipes include a dry sweetener—granulated sugar, light brown sugar, or dark brown sugar—as well as a liquid sweetener—molasses most often, but sometimes honey, maple syrup, or corn syrup.

We quickly discovered that molasses is the right liquid sweetener. Honey and corn syrup were judged too bland and boring. Maple syrup had some partisans, but most tasters thought the maple flavor clashed with the spices. Maple syrup also made a very sweet gingerbread. We preferred the gentler flavor of light or mild molasses as compared with dark or robust molasses or blackstrap molasses. (See page 92 for more information on types of molasses.)

Brown sugar is more commonly used in gingerbread recipes than white. We expected to like its heartier, richer flavor. However, tasters preferred samples prepared with granulated sugar. With brown sugar added to the mix, the molasses flavor overwhelmed the spices. Granulated sugar let the spices shine through.

As for the spices, tasters liked a combination of ground ginger, cinnamon, cloves, nutmeg, and allspice. Cardamom was rejected for its strong methanol flavor, and mace was deemed too timid in this setting. We tested and liked both crystallized and grated fresh ginger, but everyone in the test kitchen agreed that regular ground ginger (something most cooks are likely to have in the pantry) delivered excellent results. If you like a stronger ginger flavor, you can replace the ground ginger with a mixture of grated fresh and crystallized ginger as directed in the note preceding our recipe. Finally, we found that a pinch of cocoa, which is sometimes added to gingerbread, added earthiness and complexity to our recipe.

In kitchen tests, butter was the hands-down favorite over vegetable oil and shortening. We found that melting the butter yielded a denser, moister cake. When we creamed the butter and sugar, the result was lighter, fluffier, and more cakelike. As for the eggs, we found that two added too much moisture to the batter, which tended to sink in the middle near the end of the baking time. A single egg ensured sufficient tenderness and proper height.

Although we had been using milk in our recipe, we were intrigued by some old-fashioned recipes that called for sour cream, yogurt, or buttermilk instead. Sour cream and yogurt gave gingerbread too much tang and we quickly dropped them from contention. Buttermilk, however, had some nice effects on our recipe. The color was darker and the texture slightly moister. However, buttermilk also made the crumb coarser and the flavor was a bit too strong. By comparison, the gingerbread made with milk had a better rise and finer texture. In the end, we found that a 50/50 ratio of buttermilk and milk offered the best traits of each.

With buttermilk added to the recipe, we found that baking soda was the best leavener. We tested both cake and all-purpose flours and discovered that cake flour was too soft for this recipe—it made gingerbread with an unappealingly doughy texture. All-purpose flour gave gingerbread the proper structure.

We tested several methods for combining the wet and dry ingredients, including adding the melted fat to the dry ingredients before the liquids as well as beating the butter, sugar, and eggs, then alternately adding wet and dry ingredients. In the end, the simplest method proved best. We combined all the dry ingredients in one bowl, all the wet ingredients (including the melted butter, egg, and sugar) in another bowl, and then beat the dry ingredients into the wet ingredients, giving ourselves gingerbread that went into the oven in less than 10 minutes and was great tasting when it came out.

Gingerbread
SERVES 8

For a stronger ginger flavor, replace the ground ginger with 3 tablespoons grated fresh ginger and 3 tablespoons minced crystallized ginger. If you don't own an 11 by 7-inch pan, you can also bake the batter in a 9-inch square pan. This gingerbread is moist and delicious on its own, but it can be served with a dollop of lightly sweetened whipped cream.

2¼	cups sifted (9 ounces) unbleached all-purpose flour
½	teaspoon baking soda
½	teaspoon salt
2	teaspoons ground ginger
I	teaspoon ground cinnamon
½	teaspoon ground cloves
½	teaspoon ground nutmeg
½	teaspoon ground allspice
I	teaspoon Dutch-processed cocoa
8	tablespoons unsalted butter, melted and cooled to room temperature
¾	cup mild or light molasses
¾	cup (5¼ ounces) sugar
½	cup buttermilk
½	cup milk
I	large egg

1. Adjust an oven rack to the middle position and heat the oven to 350 degrees. Grease and flour an 11 by 7-inch baking pan.

2. Whisk together the flour, baking soda, salt, ginger, cinnamon, cloves, nutmeg, allspice, and cocoa in a medium bowl.

3. Beat the butter, molasses, sugar, buttermilk, milk, and egg in a large bowl with an electric mixer on low speed. Add the dry ingredients and beat on medium speed until the batter is smooth and thick, about 1 minute, scraping down the sides of the bowl with a rubber spatula as needed. Scrape the batter into the prepared pan and smooth the surface.

4. Bake until the top springs back when lightly touched and the edges have pulled away from the pan sides, about 40 minutes. Set the pan on a wire rack and cool for at least 10 minutes. Serve warm or at room temperature. (Gingerbread can be wrapped in plastic, then foil, and refrigerated up to 5 days.)

Gingerbread with Dried Fruit

Follow the recipe for Gingerbread, folding ¾ cup raisins, dried cranberries, or chopped prunes into the finished batter.

BLUEBERRY MUFFINS

THE OXFORD COMPANION TO FOOD defines American muffins as "small, squat, round cakes," yet today's deli muffins are, by comparison, big and buxom, inflated by chemical leavening and tattooed with everything from chocolate chips to sunflower seeds. We wanted a blueberry muffin with a daintier stature, a moist, delicate little cake that would support the blueberries both physically, and, if we may say so, spiritually (in terms of flavor).

Despite the easy promise of a gingham-lined basket of warm, cuddly blueberry muffins, much can go wrong from kitchen to table. We made a half-dozen recipes, producing muffins that ranged from rough and tough to dense, sweet, and heavy to the typical lackluster coffee shop cake with too few blueberries and too little flavor. It was clear that blueberry muffins came in no one style, flavor, or size, so we asked tasters to state which basic style of muffin they fancied: round tea cake or craggy biscuit. Of the 15 tasters, all but one said tea cake.

Because minor fluctuations in ingredients occasioned seismic differences in the resulting muffins, we thought it best to hold fast to a recipe whose proportions landed in between the two extremes in the original tests. That meant we would be working with 1 stick of butter, 1 cup sugar, 2 cups flour, and ½ cup milk. It was not a perfect recipe, but would be a serviceable springboard for future testing.

The two principal methods available to the muffin baker are the quick bread method and creaming. In side-by-side tests using our control recipe, we got a firsthand taste of both methods. Had we been merely licking batter off our fingers, there would have been no contest: The creamed version was like a cake batter you could suck through a straw. But the two baked muffins were nearly identical. Though the mixed muffin was slightly squatter than its creamed companion, its texture was not inferior. We were

pretty sure this more easily executed technique was one we could work with—or around.

For flour we remained true to unbleached all-purpose; cake flour produced a batter that was too light to hold the blueberries aloft. Bleached flour lacked the flavor spectrum of unbleached. We set off next in pursuit of the perfect amount of butter to turn out a moister, richer muffin, more like the tea cake our tasters had preferred. Increasing the butter in the control recipe simply weighed down the crumb without making the muffins any more moist. We also increased the liquid (we tested both milk and buttermilk) and added extra egg yolks. Neither approach brought improvement. When we substituted yogurt for milk, the muffins had the springiness of an old camp mattress.

Knowing that sour cream is often used in quick breads, we decided to give it a try. We also wondered if the egg white protein from two eggs might be too much of the wrong type of liquid—adding structure rather than tenderness. Our new recipe, then, called for 1 egg, 1 cup sour cream, no milk, and only half a stick of butter. It was a great success—the muffins were tender and rich, and the sour cream played up to the blueberries' flavor. An additional ¼ cup sour cream made even nicer muffins.

Through additional testing, we discovered that this rather heavy batter required a full tablespoon of baking powder to rise and shine, but tasters noted no off chemical flavor. (If too much chemical leavener is added, some of it will fail to react and will give the baked good a bitter, soapy flavor.) Next, we refined the mixing method. Hoping to get more lift into the picture, we whisked the egg and sugar together by hand until the sugar began to melt, whisked in the melted butter, then the sour cream, and poured them into the dry ingredients. This method of mixing promised to deliver more air—and lift—to the egg, sugar, and butter. We folded everything together using the gentlest strokes possible. (We found that these muffins, like most others, became tough when overmixed.) This modified technique produced lovely muffins with a nice rise and beautifully domed crowns.

Until now, the major player in this muffin had been not only off-stage but out of season. Our winter testing left us with a choice between pricey fresh blueberries the size of marbles and tiny frozen wild berries. The flavor and sweetness of the frozen berries gave them a big edge over the puckery, flavorless fresh berries. In addition, the tiny wild berries distributed themselves in the batter nicely, like well-mannered guests, whereas the cultivated berries took the muffin by storm, leaving huge pockets of sour fruit pulp. So impressed were we by the superiority of these little berries that we resolved to offer them top billing in the recipe. (You shouldn't have to be vacationing in Maine to make a decent blueberry muffin.) We came across one last trick. Frozen blueberries tend to be bleeders—and gummy when tossed with flour—so we discovered that they must remain completely frozen until they are stirred into the batter.

These were perfect workaday muffins, but we wanted to give them a chance to play dress-up, to be more like little cakes. With that in mind we considered a couple of options. A big fan of pebbly streusel topping dusted with confectioner's sugar, we picked up the recipe from our Dutch apple pie topping and pared it down to meet the demands of a dozen muffins. The streusel weighed heavily on the muffins and diminished their lift.

Our next topping idea came from Marion Cunningham's *Breakfast Book* (Knopf, 1987), in which she rolls whole baked muffins in melted butter and then dips them in cinnamon-sugar. The concept was a winning one. The melted butter seeped into the muffin's crown, the sugar stuck, and the muffin was transformed into a tender, sugar-tufted pillow.

We also made a simple syrup glaze with lemon juice. Brushed on the muffin tops, it made a nice adhesive for granulated sugar (which we mixed with either finely grated lemon zest or fresh ginger). Finally, muffins to take to the ball.

EQUIPMENT: Muffin Papers

Do you need to line muffin tins with ruffled paper cups? To find out, we baked muffins with and without paper liners. Those baked in liners were shorter than those baked right in the cup, but they also had a more rounded, filled-out look. When peeling off the paper, though, we lost a good portion of the muffin. Muffin papers also keep the muffin's sides from browning as well as those baked right in the cup. We prefer to grease muffin tins instead of using paper liners.

Blueberry Muffins
MAKES 12 MUFFINS

When making the batter, be sure to whisk vigorously in step 2, then fold carefully in step 3. You should not see large pockets of flour in the finished batter, but small occasional sprays may remain. A spring-loaded ice cream scoop ensures uniform muffin size and clean dispensing when transferring the dough to the holes in a muffin tin.

2	cups (10 ounces) unbleached all-purpose flour
1	tablespoon baking powder
½	teaspoon salt
1	large egg
1	cup (7 ounces) sugar
4	tablespoons unsalted butter, melted and cooled slightly
1¼	cups (10 ounces) sour cream
1½	cup frozen blueberries, preferably wild

1. Adjust an oven rack to the middle position and heat the oven to 350 degrees. Spray a standard muffin tin with nonstick vegetable cooking spray.

2. Whisk the flour, baking powder, and salt in a medium bowl until combined. Whisk the egg in a second medium bowl until well-combined and light-colored, about 20 seconds. Add the sugar and whisk vigorously until thick and homogenous, about 30 seconds; add the melted butter in 2 or 3 additions, whisking to combine after each addition. Add the sour cream in 2 additions, whisking just to combine.

3. Add the frozen berries to the dry ingredients and gently toss just to combine. Add the sour cream mixture and fold with a rubber spatula until the batter comes together and the berries are evenly distributed, 25 to 30 seconds. (Small spots of flour may remain and batter will be thick. Do not overmix.)

4. Use an ice cream scoop or large spoon to drop the batter into the greased muffin tin. Bake until light golden brown and a toothpick or skewer inserted into the center of a muffin comes out clean, 25 to 30 minutes, rotating the pan from front to back halfway through the baking time. Invert the muffins onto a wire rack, stand the muffins upright, and cool 5 minutes. Serve as is or use one of the toppings on page 279.

➤ VARIATIONS

Cinnamon-Sugar-Dipped Blueberry Muffins

While the muffins are cooling, mix ½ cup sugar and ½ teaspoon ground cinnamon in a small bowl and melt 4 tablespoons butter in small saucepan. After the baked muffins have cooled 5 minutes, and working one at a time, dip the top of each muffin in melted butter and then cinnamon-sugar. Set the muffins upright on a wire rack; serve.

Ginger- or Lemon-Glazed Blueberry Muffins

While the muffins are baking, mix 1 teaspoon grated fresh ginger or grated lemon zest and ½ cup sugar in a small bowl. Bring ¼ cup lemon juice and ¼ cup sugar to a simmer in a small saucepan over medium heat; simmer until the mixture is thick and syrupy and reduced to about 4 tablespoons. After the baked muffins have cooled 5 minutes, brush the tops with glaze, then, working one at a time, dip the tops in lemon sugar or ginger sugar. Set the muffins upright on a wire rack; serve.

CORN MUFFINS

CORN MUFFINS ARE EASILY THE MOST MIS-understood muffin on the breakfast table. They suffer from an identity crisis, never knowing if they are cornbread in a cup or corn cake. And there seems to be little consensus as to what a good corn muffin is (a reflection of the eternal debate between the Northern and Southern parts of the country over what constitutes good cornbread: sweet and tender versus savory, well crusted, and a bit coarse). After baking an array of corn muffin recipes and sampling muffins from several local bakeries, we found that we favored a muffin with a moist and tender crumb, a pronounced corn flavor, and just enough sugar to round out the corn's savory edge. In other words, we wanted a sweeter and cakier version of our skillet-baked jalapeño cornbread (see page 269), minus the chiles and cheddar.

To achieve our desired muffin, we knew we would be, at a minimum, introducing flour to the recipe and adding more eggs and sugar. Incorporating flour proved a delicate balancing act.

EQUIPMENT: Muffin Tins

The majority of muffin tins on the market are made of coated aluminum and are lightweight. We purchased two tins of this type as well as two heavy-gauge "professional" aluminum tins and one "air-cushioned" aluminum tin. Three had a nonstick coating. The tins ranged in price from $5 to $26.

We baked up two different varieties of muffins to test the two things that really matter—browning and sticking. We wanted the muffins to brown uniformly and to be easily plucked from the tin. Corn muffins were ideal for the browning test, blueberry for the sticking test—no one wants a sweet, sticky berry left in the tin rather than the muffin.

Browning ended up being the deciding factor in these tests. Sticking was not an issue as long as the tins were sprayed with cooking oil. The best tins browned the muffins evenly, the worst browned them on the top but left them pallid and underbaked on the bottom. As we had observed in other bakeware tests, darker coated metals, which absorb heat, do the best job of browning baked goods. The air-cushioned tin produced pale muffins that were also small (the cushioning made for a smaller cup capacity, about ⅓ cup rather than the standard ½ cup).

We found the heavier-gauged aluminum tins to have no advantage—they are much more expensive than other tins, weigh twice as much, and do not produce superior muffins. Their heft may make them durable, but unless you bake commercially, the lightweight models will last a lifetime. The $5 Ecko Baker's Secret tin took top honors, besting tins that cost five times as much.

When we added too much flour, the subtleties of the cornmeal were masked and the muffin tasted bland—a problem that plagues many corn muffins. With too little flour, the muffins were squat and too dense. A half cup of flour proved perfect. The structure of this muffin was lighter and looser than that of our cornbread but retained the moist, tight crumb we desired. And the corn flavor was not compromised. To see if we could improve on the texture, we tried cake flour, which yielded a nominally softer crumb. However, most tasters thought that the difference was insignificant, so we went with all-purpose flour.

While the muffins tasted OK, they were in dire need of leavening and structure. Adding another egg helped a little, but the muffins were still low and flat-topped. We increased the baking powder and baking soda incrementally in successive batches and found that it took double the amount of the leavening in the cornbread to achieve high, rounded muffins.

While Southerners cringe at the thought of sweetener in cornbread, we believed that these muffins needed a healthy dose of sugar. Light brown sugar had given the skillet cornbread a slight earthiness, but it was overwhelming in the muffins. White sugar proved the best choice because it allowed for a clean, unmitigated corn flavor.

So, with just minor alterations to our cornbread recipe, we had the moist, flavorful muffins we hoped for. While ideal for breakfast, these muffins will also work as a lunch or dinner accompaniment, especially if you have a Northern crowd attuned to sweet cornbread.

❦

Corn Muffins
MAKES 12 MUFFINS

As the batter is quite thin, we found that the easiest way to portion it was to transfer it to a large Pyrex measuring cup and pour it. A ladle will work well too.

INGREDIENTS: Butter

Butter is a key ingredient in muffins and biscuits, and there's no reason you can't slather more butter over both when they come warm from the oven. For this purpose (and so many others), we wondered if the brand of butter makes a difference. To answer this question, we embarked on a two-month odyssey, testing eight brands of butter in six different applications. We tasted the butters plain (both at room temperature and melted), in pie crust, in yellow cake, in buttercream frosting, and in sautéed turkey cutlets.

All butter must consist of at least 80 percent milk fat, according to U.S. Department of Agriculture standards. Most commercial butters do not exceed this. European butters and Hotel Bar's Plugrá are exceptions, with 82 to 88 percent milk fat. All butters contain about 2 percent milk solids, and the remainder is water.

The results of our extensive testing were surprising. Although the two high-fat butters in the tasting (Plugrá and Celles Sur Belle, a French brand sold in many gourmet stores) performed well in most tests, they were not runaway winners. In fact, most tasters felt that all the cakes, pie crusts, and sautéed turkey cutlets tasted pretty much the same, no matter which brand of butter was used. Even tasted plain the results were fairly close.

One test did reveal some discernible differences. In a rich buttercream frosting made with softened butter, confectioners' sugar, and a little milk, the Plugrá was head and shoulders above the others for both a pleasant, delicate butter flavor and an airy texture. The other high-fat butter, Celles Sur Belle, scored well but was not judged to have as light a texture as the Plugrá. In this one instance, the butter is such an important ingredient and the recipe is so simple that a higher-fat butter created a noticeable difference in both flavor and texture.

Overall, however, we recommend that you pay more attention to the condition in which you buy the butter and the conditions under which you store it than to the particular brand. Throughout the testing, we ran across sticks of butter that were rancid or stale-tasting. We attributed these problems to improper shipping or poor storage at the market, not the manufacturer. We recommend that you purchase butter from a store you can depend on that has a high turnover of products.

Butter can also spoil in your refrigerator, turning rancid from the oxidation of fatty acids. Exposure to air or light is particularly damaging, which explains why Land O'Lakes takes the precaution of wrapping its unsalted butter in foil. We find that the best way to store butter is sealed in an airtight plastic bag in your freezer, pulling out sticks as you need them. Butter will keep in the freezer for several months and in the refrigerator for no more than two to three weeks.

The fat in butter is vulnerable not only to oxidation but also to picking up odors. While butter is particularly susceptible at warmer temperatures, it can take on odors even when chilled or frozen. For this reason, we advise against storing butter in your refrigerator's butter compartment, which tends to be warmer because it's inside the door. To find out how much of a difference this made, we stored one stick of butter in its original wrapper in the butter compartment and one in the center of the refrigerator. After one week, the butter in the compartment had begun to pick up off flavors, while the one stored in the center still tasted fresh.

One final note about butter. We use unsalted butter in our test kitchen. We like its sweet, delicate flavor and prefer to add our own salt to recipes. We find that the quality of salted butter is often inferior and that each manufacturer adds a different amount of salt, which makes recipe writing difficult. While you can certainly get away with using salted butter in some savory recipes (as long as you adjust the total amount of salt in the recipe), we strongly recommend using unsalted butter when baking.

1³⁄₄ cups (9¹⁄₂ ounces) yellow cornmeal, preferably stone-ground

¹⁄₂ cup (2¹⁄₂ ounces) unbleached all-purpose flour

¹⁄₂ cup (3¹⁄₂ ounces) sugar

³⁄₄ teaspoon salt

2 teaspoons baking powder

¹⁄₂ teaspoon baking soda

³⁄₄ cup rapidly boiling water

1¹⁄₄ cups buttermilk

2 large eggs, beaten lightly

2 tablespoons unsalted butter, melted

1. Adjust an oven rack to the lower-middle position and heat the oven to 425 degrees. Spray a standard muffin tin with nonstick vegetable cooking spray.

2. Measure ¹⁄₂ cup cornmeal into a medium bowl. In a separate larger bowl, whisk together the remaining cornmeal, flour, sugar, salt, baking powder, and baking soda. While whisking, pour the boiling water in a slow, steady stream into the ¹⁄₂ cup of cornmeal, followed by the buttermilk and the eggs. Pour the wet mixture into the dry ingredients and stir until just combined. Stir in the melted butter until incorporated.

3. Transfer the mixture to a large Pyrex measuring cup and pour the batter into the greased muffin tins, filling the holes almost to the rim. Bake until the muffins are golden brown, about 18 to 20 minutes. Set the tin onto a wire rack to cool slightly, about 5 minutes. Remove the muffins from the tin and serve warm or at room temperature.

BUTTERMILK BISCUITS

BISCUITS SHARE WITH MUFFINS THE DISTINCTION of being among the simplest of all breads. They are made from a mixture of flour, leavener (baking powder or soda), salt, fat (usually butter or vegetable shortening), and liquid (milk, buttermilk, sour milk, yogurt, or cream). To make them, one cuts fat into the dry ingredients, as when making pie dough; the liquid is then stirred in until a dough forms. Biscuits are usually rolled out and cut, although they can also be shaped by hand or dropped onto a baking sheet by the spoonful.

We began our testing by focusing on the flour. We found that the kind of flour you choose has a great effect on the biscuit you end up with. The main factor here is the proportion of protein in the flour. Low-protein, or "soft," flour (such as cake flour or White Lily, a favored brand in the South) encourages a tender, cakelike texture as well as a more moist crumb. Higher-protein, or "strong," flour (such as all-purpose flour) promotes a crispier crust and a drier, denser crumb.

Tasters liked the crispier crust of the biscuits made with all-purpose flour and the tender, airy crumb of the biscuits made with cake flour. We found that a combination of half cake flour and half all-purpose flour delivered the best results—a crisp crust and a tender crumb. If you don't have cake flour, all-purpose flour makes a fine biscuit as long as you add more liquid to the batter.

Fat makes biscuits (and other pastries) tender, moist, smooth, and tasty. Butter, of course, delivers the best flavor, while vegetable shortening makes a slightly flakier biscuit with better holding powers. However, we don't think this gain in shelf life is worth the loss in flavor. Stick with unsalted butter when making biscuits.

We discovered that a proportion of ¹⁄₂ cup fat to 2 cups flour provides the best balance of tenderness and richness with structure. The way in which the fat and flour are combined is nearly as important as their proportions. The fat must be "rubbed" into the dry ingredients, making a dry, coarse mixture akin to large bread crumbs or rolled oats, with some slightly bigger lumps mixed in. This rubbing may seem unimportant, but in fact it is crucial to the proper rising of the biscuits. Gas released by the leavening during baking must have a space in which to collect; if the texture of the dough is homogeneous, the gas will simply dissipate. Melting fat particles create convenient spaces in which the gas can collect, form bubbles, and produce a rise. Proper rubbing breaks the fat into tiny bits and disperses it throughout the dough. As the fat melts during baking, its place is taken up by gas and steam, which expand and push the dough up. The wider the dispersal of the fat, the more even the rising of the dough.

If, however, the fat softens and binds with the dry ingredients during rubbing, it forms a pasty goo, the spaces collapse, and the biscuits become leaden. To produce light, airy biscuits, the fat must remain cold and firm, which means rubbing must be deft and quick. Traditionally, biscuit makers pinch the cut-up fat into the dry ingredients, using only their fingertips—never the whole hand, which is too warm—and they pinch hard and fast, practically flinging the little bits of flour and fat into the bowl after each pinch. Less experienced cooks sometimes cut in the fat by scraping two knives in opposite directions or by using a bow-shaped pastry blender. We found, however, that the easiest way to go about this task is with the help of a food processor. Pulsing the dry ingredients and the fat is fast and almost foolproof.

After cutting in the fat, liquid is added and the dough is stirred, just until the ingredients are bound, using a light hand so the gluten will not become activated. We found that buttermilk (or plain yogurt) gives biscuits the best flavor. It also creates a lighter, airier texture than regular milk. That's because the acid in the buttermilk reacts with the leaveners to increase the rise.

Biscuits are best formed by gently patting gobs of dough between your hands. If the work surface, the dough, and the cutter are generously floured, fluffy biscuits can be rolled and cut; but the softness of the dough makes this a tricky procedure, and the extra flour and handling will make the biscuits heavier and somewhat dense.

SHAPING BUTTERMILK BISCUIT DOUGH

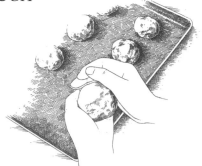

Our buttermilk biscuit dough is too soft to roll and cut. Using a sharp knife or dough cutter, divide the dough in quarters and then cut each quarter into thirds. With lightly cupped hands, gently shape each piece into a ball.

Because they need quick heat, biscuits are best baked in the middle of the oven. Placed too close to the bottom, they burn on the underside and remain pale on top; set too near the oven roof, they do not rise well because the outside hardens into a shell before the inside has had a chance to rise properly. As soon as they are light brown, they are done. Be careful, as overcooking will dry them out. Biscuits are always at their best when served as soon as they come out of the oven. The dough, however, may be made some hours in advance and baked when needed; the biscuits will still rise well.

Buttermilk Biscuits
MAKES 12

Mixing the butter and dry ingredients quickly so the butter remains cold and firm is crucial to producing light, tender biscuits. The easiest and most reliable approach is to use a food processor fitted with a steel blade. Expect a soft and slightly sticky dough. The wet dough creates steam when the biscuits bake and promotes the light airy texture. If the dough is too wet for you to shape the biscuits by hand, lightly flour your hands and then shape the biscuits.

1	cup (5 ounces) unbleached all-purpose flour
1	cup (4 ounces) plain cake flour
2	teaspoons baking powder
½	teaspoon baking soda
1	teaspoon sugar
½	teaspoon salt
8	tablespoons unsalted butter, chilled, cut into ¼-inch cubes
¾	cup cold buttermilk, or ¾ cup plus 2 tablespoons plain yogurt

1. Adjust an oven rack to the middle position and heat the oven to 450 degrees.

2. Place the flours, baking powder, baking soda, sugar, and salt in a large bowl or the workbowl of a food processor fitted with the steel blade. Whisk together or pulse six times.

3. If making by hand, use two knives, a pastry blender, or your fingertips to quickly cut in the butter until the mixture resembles coarse meal with a few slightly larger butter lumps. If using a food processor, remove the cover and distribute the butter

evenly over the dry ingredients. Cover and pulse 12 times, each pulse lasting 1 second.

4. If making by hand, stir in the buttermilk with a rubber spatula or fork until the mixture forms a soft, slightly sticky ball. If using a food processor, remove the cover and pour the buttermilk evenly over the dough. Pulse until the dough gathers into moist clumps, about eight 1-second pulses.

5. Transfer the dough to a lightly floured surface and quickly form into a rough ball. Be careful not to overmix. Using a sharp knife or dough cutter, divide the dough in quarters and then cut each quarter into the thirds. Quickly and gently shape each piece into a rough ball (see illustration on page 282), and place on an ungreased cookie sheet. (The baking sheet can be wrapped in plastic and refrigerated for up to 2 hours.)

6. Bake until the biscuit tops are light brown, 10 to 12 minutes. Serve immediately.

➤ VARIATION

Buttermilk Biscuits with All Purpose Flour

Follow the recipe for Buttermilk Biscuits, replacing the cake flour with an extra cup of all-purpose flour. Increase the buttermilk or yogurt by 2 tablespoons.

CREAM BISCUITS

OUR BUTTERMILK BISCUITS ARE EASY TO prepare; you can have biscuits on the table in 20 minutes. But many cooks are intimidated by this kind of biscuit because they are not comfortable with the traditional process of cutting butter into flour. We wondered if we could come up with a recipe for homemade biscuits that could be made quickly and easily and that would not require cutting fat into flour. In short, was it possible to take the guesswork out of making biscuits to create a fool-proof recipe?

First, we tried varying the dairy. The biscuits made with yogurt and sour cream were a bit sodden in texture, those with a milk and milk/butter combination were tough and lifeless, and a whipped cream biscuit was too light. This last approach also required whipping the cream, which seemed like too much trouble for a simple recipe. So we tried using plain heavy cream, without whipping, and this biscuit was the best of the lot.

Next we decided to do a blind tasting, pitting the cream biscuits against our conventional buttermilk biscuit recipe, which requires cutting butter into the flour. The result? Both biscuits had their partisans. The cream biscuits were lighter and more tender. They were also richer tasting. The buttermilk biscuits were flakier and had the distinctive tang that many people associate with good biscuits. Although neither biscuit was sweet, the buttermilk version seemed more savory.

At this point, we decided that cream biscuits were a worthy (and easier) alternative to traditional buttermilk biscuits. Still, we were running into a problem with the shape of the biscuits, as they were spreading far too much during baking; they needed more structure. When making biscuits, we have always followed the conventional advice about not overworking the dough. Kneading the dough encourages the development of gluten, a protein that gives baked products structure but that when overdeveloped can also make them tough. In our experience, the best biscuits are generally made from dough that is handled lightly. This is certainly true of buttermilk biscuits. But cream biscuits, being less sturdy than those made with butter, become soft and "melt" during baking. In this case, we thought, a little more structure produced by a little more handling might not be such a bad thing. So we baked up two batches. The first dough we patted out gingerly; the second dough we kneaded for 30 seconds until it was smooth and uniform in appearance. The results were remarkable. The more heavily worked dough produced much higher, fluffier biscuits than the lightly handled dough, which looked short and bedraggled.

We ran into a problem, though, when one batch of biscuits had to sit for a few minutes while we waited for the oven to heat up. During baking, the dough spread, resulting in biscuits with bottoms that were too wide and tops that were too narrow. Clearly, the biscuits had to be popped into the oven immediately after cutting. As for dough thickness, 1 inch provides a remarkably high rise, more appealing than biscuits that start out ½ inch thick. We also discovered that it was best to add just enough cream to hold the dough together. A wet dough does not hold its shape as well during baking.

Although we find it easy enough to quickly roll out this dough and then cut it into rounds with a biscuit cutter, you can simply shape the dough with your hands or push it into the bottom of an 8-inch cake pan. The dough can then be flipped onto the work surface and cut into wedges with a knife or dough scraper.

Now we had the simplest of biscuit recipes: Whisk together the dry ingredients, add heavy cream, form the dough, knead it, cut it, and bake it. Serve these biscuits with a savory bowl of soup or stew. The rich reward will surprise you.

~

Cream Biscuits

MAKES 8

Bake the biscuits immediately after cutting them; letting them stand for any length of time can decrease the leavening power and prevent the biscuits from rising in the oven.

2	cups (10 ounces) unbleached all-purpose flour
2	teaspoons sugar
2	teaspoons baking powder
½	teaspoon salt
1½	cups heavy cream

1. Adjust the oven rack to the upper-middle position and heat the oven to 425 degrees. Line a rimmed baking sheet with parchment paper.

2. Whisk together the flour, sugar, baking powder, and salt in a medium bowl. Add 1¼ cups cream and stir with a wooden spoon until the dough forms, about 30 seconds. Transfer the dough to the countertop, leaving all dry, floury bits behind in the bowl. In 1 tablespoon increments, add up to ¼ cup cream to the dry bits in the bowl, mixing with a wooden spoon after each addition, until moistened. Add these moistened bits to the rest of the dough and knead by hand just until smooth, about 30 seconds.

3. Following the illustrations below, cut the biscuits into rounds or wedges. Place the biscuits on the parchment-lined baking sheet and bake until golden brown, about 15 minutes. Serve immediately.

➤ VARIATIONS

Cream Biscuits with Fresh Herbs
Follow the recipe for Cream Biscuits, whisking 2 tablespoons minced fresh herbs into the flour along with the sugar, baking powder, and salt.

Cream Biscuits with Cheddar Cheese
Follow the recipe for Cream Biscuits, stirring ½ cup (2 ounces) cheddar cheese cut into ¼-inch pieces into the flour along with the sugar, baking powder, and salt. Increase the baking time to 18 minutes.

TWO WAYS TO SHAPE CREAM BISCUIT DOUGH

  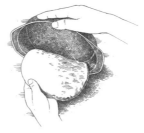 

ROUND BISCUITS
1a. Pat the dough on a lightly floured work surface into a ¾-inch-thick circle.

1b. Punch out dough rounds with a biscuit cutter. Push together the remaining pieces of dough, pat into a ¾-inch-thick round, and punch out several more biscuits. Discard the remaining scraps.

WEDGE BISCUITS
2a. Press the dough into an 8-inch cake pan, then turn the dough out onto a lightly floured work surface.

2b. With a knife or bench scraper, cut the dough into 8 wedges.

12

EGGS AND BREAKFAST

EGGS ARE AN ESSENTIAL INGREDIENT IN most desserts and are used in numerous savory recipes, everything from egg salad (see page 45) to stuffings for the holiday turkey. But more often than not, we think of breakfast when we think of eggs. Simply prepared (typically scrambled or fried) or used as an ingredient in pancakes or waffles, eggs are at the heart of an American breakfast.

Depending on the breed of the hen and her size, an egg can weigh as much as 3 ounces or as little as 1 ounce. Size is not necessarily a reflection of quality, nor is the color of the shell. The average weight of one egg for each of the common sizes is as follows: jumbo (2½ ounces), extra-large (2¼ ounces), large (2 ounces), and medium (1¾ ounces). We generally use large eggs in our recipes, but you can use other sizes if you approximate the total weight by relying on the preceding figures. For instance, you would replace four large eggs (which weigh 8 ounces), with three jumbo eggs (7½ ounces) rather than four jumbo eggs (10 ounces).

No matter the size, the egg consists of two parts that can function quite differently in recipes. The white, or albumin, consists primarily of water (about 90 percent) and layers of protein. It begins to coagulate at 144 degrees, ahead of the yolk. The yolk is where most of the fat and cholesterol in the egg are located. The yolk also contains most of the vitamins and nutrients, as well as lecithin, the emulsifier that gives sauces with eggs their smooth texture. The yolk begins to coagulate at 149 degrees.

In recent years, numerous outbreaks of intestinal illness have been traced to eggs contaminated with salmonella. Although the odds of getting a bad egg are quite low (some experts estimate that 1 in 10,000 eggs is contaminated with the bacteria), it makes sense to take some precautions. This is especially true if you are cooking for the young, the elderly, women who are pregnant, or for people with compromised immune systems.

Thorough cooking of eggs, to at least 160 degrees, will kill any salmonella that may be present. Because it is hard to use an instant-read thermometer on scrambled eggs, you have to rely on visual clues. Given the thickening temperatures mentioned above, if you are concerned about salmonella, you should cook all eggs until fully set; for fried eggs, that means avoiding runny yolks.

Eggs should always be refrigerated to prolong their shelf life. Since the door is actually the warmest spot in most refrigerators, you should keep eggs in their container and store them on one of the shelves. The shelves are likely to be colder, and the box acts as a layer of insulation around the eggs.

Of course, there is more to breakfast than just plain eggs. Bacon is a must for many cooks, as are home fries or hash browns. Others prefer to build the first meal of the day around oatmeal or corned beef hash rather than eggs. This chapter contains all these favorites in addition to recipes for blueberry pancakes and buttermilk waffles.

SCRAMBLED EGGS

SCRAMBLED EGGS SHOULD BE A DREAMY mound of big, softly wobbling curds, yellow as a legal pad, glistening, a hairbreadth away from being undercooked. (If you are concerned about salmonella, see the chapter introduction.) When cut, the eggs should be cooked enough to hold their shape but soft enough to eat with a spoon.

We first tested beating the eggs to see if this made a difference in the final outcome. Our advice is to stop muscling the raw eggs into a tight froth. We found that overbeating can cause premature coagulation of the eggs' protein—even without heat! Too much beating can make eggs tough before they hit the pan. For a smooth yellow color and no streaks of white, we whip eggs in a medium-sized bowl with a fork and stop while the bubbles are large. For 10 or 12 eggs, we've found that a balloon whisk works well.

Before beating, the eggs get a few additions—salt, pepper, and either milk or water. Compared side by side, we found that scrambled eggs made with water are less flavorful, don't fluff as nicely, form wrinkled curds, and aren't as soft as those made with milk. With its traces of sugar, proteins, and fats, milk has a wonderful pillowy effect and helps create large curds— the bigger you can get the curds, the more steam you'll trap inside, for puff all the way to the table.

We tried most of the pans in our kitchen and discovered that a nonstick surface is best for scrambled eggs. As always, a heavy-bottomed skillet is preferable.

We tested the major brands of nonstick skillets and particularly liked pans from All-Clad and Calphalon. Both pans are sturdy but not overly heavy. For instance, many enameled cast-iron pans weigh close to five pounds and are hard to maneuver. A pan that weighs two to three pounds is much easier to control and still heavy enough to heat evenly. When shopping, make sure the handle is comfortable and preferably heat-resistant.

Cheap, thin pans overheat and are difficult to control on high heat. Thicker pans may take longer to heat up, but they hold heat evenly without hot spots.

Pan size is important, too. While a 10-inch skillet worked best for eight eggs, it was too big for two eggs. The batter spread out so thin that while we were busy moving one area of the eggs, another area overcooked. We found that the more the eggs are contained, the bigger the curds. An 8-inch skillet kept the two-egg batter at a depth of about ¼ inch, and the curds came out nice and plump.

We've tried cooking scrambled eggs over medium heat, but the eggs got tough, dried out, and overcoagulated, like a badly made meringue that "weeps." A hot pan will begin to cook eggs instantaneously, for the quickest coagulation. The tradeoff for using high heat is making sure the eggs are off the heat before serious damage is done.

Keeping the eggs in constant, steady motion also helps keep them from overcooking. You don't want to beat the eggs, but they should be gently stirred as they cook. A wooden or plastic spatula works best; use the flat edge to snowplow a 2- to 3-inch swath of eggs across the pan in one pass. The idea is to slowly push, lift, and fold. Two eggs should cook into big curds in about 30 seconds.

When are the eggs done? The idea behind big voluptuous curds is to trap steam. The larger the curds, the more steam is pocketed inside, and the more the eggs will continue to cook once off the heat. We like scrambled eggs soft and juicy, so they look positively underdone when we make that final fold and push them out of the pan. But if you get the eggs off the heat when they're still juicy, you'll always get lush scrambled eggs with big curds that melt in your mouth.

Fluffy Scrambled Eggs
SERVES 4

These eggs cook very quickly, so it's important to be ready to eat before you start to cook them.

8	large eggs
½	teaspoon salt
	Several grinds of ground black pepper
½	cup milk
1	tablespoon butter

1. Crack the eggs into a medium bowl. Add the salt, pepper, and milk. Whip with a fork until the streaks are gone and color is pure yellow; stop beating while the bubbles are still large.

2. Meanwhile, put the butter in a 10-inch nonstick skillet, then set the pan over high heat. When the butter foams, swirl it around and up the sides of the pan. Before the foam completely subsides, pour in the beaten eggs. With a wooden or plastic spatula, push the eggs from one side of the pan to the other, slowly and deliberately, lifting and folding the eggs as they form into curds, until the eggs are nicely clumped into a single mound but remain shiny and wet, 1½ to 2 minutes. Serve immediately.

➤ VARIATIONS
Two Scrambled Eggs
Season 2 eggs with ⅛ teaspoon salt, 1 grind of pepper, and 2 tablespoons milk. Heat 1½ teaspoons butter in an 8-inch skillet. Cooking time is 30 to 45 seconds.

Four Scrambled Eggs
Season 4 eggs with ¼ teaspoon salt, 2 grinds of pepper, and ¼ cup milk. Heat ¾ tablespoon butter in a 10-inch skillet. Cooking time is about 1 minute.

Twelve Scrambled Eggs
Season 12 eggs with ¾ teaspoon salt, 6 grinds of pepper, and ¾ cup milk, and mix using a balloon whisk. Heat 1½ tablespoons butter in a 12-inch skillet. Cooking time is 2½ to 3 minutes.

FRIED EGGS

ANYONE CAN MAKE FRIED EGGS—BUT FEW and far between are the cooks who can make them perfectly every time. For most of us, they are sometimes great and sometimes second rate. While our efforts are usually at least passable, we decided to eliminate the guesswork and figure out how to best and most easily fry the perfect egg every time. For our taste, this means an egg with a white that is firm, not runny, and a yolk that sets up high and is thick but still runny.

For starters, we thought it made sense to investigate the hardware. After testing skillets made from aluminum, hard-anodized aluminum, stainless steel, and well-seasoned cast iron in addition to one with a nonstick coating, our initial feeling was confirmed: There is no point in frying eggs in anything but a nonstick pan.

Next we examined the degree to which the pan should be heated before the eggs are added. We learned that there is a point at which the temperature of the pan causes the egg to behave just as we want it to. When an egg lands in a pan that's at the correct temperature, it neither runs all over the place nor sputters or bubbles; instead, it just sizzles and sets up into a thick, restrained oval. Getting the taste and texture of the white just right depends on achieving this correct set point. A white that's too spread out becomes overcooked, rubbery, and tough, while a white that browns at the edges as soon as it hits the pan ends up tasting metallic—at least to us.

We needed to devise a plan that would incorporate this crucial setting temperature, no matter what type of pan or what cooktop a cook was using. To begin, we placed the pan on a low setting and let it heat for a full five minutes. We had discovered that while eggs might set up well initially if a pan is not completely heated, they then tend to overcook at the finish; five minutes ensures a thorough preheating of the pan. Next we added the butter, which we allowed to melt and foam, waiting for the foaming to subside before adding the egg. We knew immediately that the pan was too hot—the white sputtered into huge bubbles, and the butter had even started to brown. Fast-forward to the next egg. This time we again put the pan on the burner for five minutes but set the heat below the low setting. And this time we hit the mark: We added the egg just as the butter foam subsided, and it set up perfectly. On this perfect setting the butter took exactly one minute to melt, foam, and subside.

Now that the egg was sitting pretty, we moved on to the next part of the cooking process. Thumbing through cookbooks, we found directions for basting with butter, adjusting the temperature, and covering the eggs as techniques to get the desired thick and runny yolk. Eggs basted with butter were too rich, and the process was fussy. Adjusting the heat to get both white and yolk to cook properly was actually pretty difficult. In all cases we ended up with the bottom too browned and the yolk too runny.

We moved on to using a cover during the cooking process. After putting two eggs in the skillet, we put on the lid and allowed the eggs to cook for two minutes. One of the eggs was cooked perfectly, but the other was slightly undercooked. We realized that with such a short cooking time, we had to get the eggs into the pan at the same time. We tried the covered skillet method one more time, but in this case broke each of the eggs into a cup before starting the process. This allowed us to empty the eggs into the skillet simultaneously. This method worked beautifully. The steam created when the pan was covered produced whites that were firm but not at all rubbery and yolks that were thick yet still runny.

Since not all folks want a runny egg, we also experimented with other stages of doneness. It took 2½ minutes for a set but soft yolk, and 3 minutes for a light-colored, cooked-through yolk.

It's worth mentioning at this point that the fat used is meant to be a flavoring agent as well as lubricant. We tried several kinds. Canola oil had too little flavor, olive oil had too much, but both bacon fat and butter were delicious. For four eggs in a 10-inch skillet, we found that 1 tablespoon of either fat works well. A quick sprinkle of salt and freshly ground pepper before throwing on the cover is also recommended—the seasonings don't impart as much flavor if added after the eggs are cooked.

Perfect Fried Eggs

SERVES 4

A nonstick skillet is essential because it ensures an easy release of the eggs. Since burners vary, it may take an egg or two before you determine the ideal setting for frying eggs on your stovetop. Follow the visual clue in the recipe and increase the heat if necessary. If you've just fried up some bacon or happen to have some bacon grease around, use it in place of the butter for really tasty fried eggs. Unlike butter, however, bacon grease will not go through visual changes that you can use to gauge the pan's heat.

4   large eggs
1   tablespoon cold unsalted butter
     Salt and ground black pepper

1. Heat a 10-inch heavy-bottomed nonstick skillet over the lowest possible heat for 5 minutes. Meanwhile, crack 2 eggs into a cup or small bowl; crack the remaining 2 eggs into a second cup or small bowl. Add the butter to the skillet; let it melt and foam. When the foam subsides (this should take about 1 minute; if the butter browns in 1 minute, the pan is too hot), swirl to coat the pan.

2. Working quickly, pour two eggs on one side of the pan and the other two eggs on the other side. Season the eggs with salt and pepper; cover and cook about 2½ minutes for runny yolks, 3 minutes for soft but set yolks, and 3½ minutes for firmly set yolks. Slide the eggs onto a plate and serve immediately.

GETTING THE EGGS INTO THE PAN

Crack the eggs into two small bowls or cups, then let the eggs slide into the hot skillet simultaneously from opposite sides of the pan.

> VARIATION
Two Fried Eggs

Follow the recipe for Perfect Fried Eggs, using an 8- or 9-inch heavy-bottomed nonstick skillet, cracking 1 egg into each cup, and decreasing the butter to 1½ teaspoons. Decrease the cooking times to about 2 minutes for runny yolks, 2½ minutes for soft but set yolks, and 3 minutes for firmly set yolks.

DENVER OMELET

WHILE WE LOVE SOFT, DELICATELY FLAVORED French omelets, we also have a weakness for lightly browned diner-style omelets bursting at the seams with filling. And our favorite is the Denver omelet, a mixture of sautéed bell peppers, onions, and ham with a generous portion of melted Monterey Jack cheese. Unfortunately, like too much diner food, Denver omelets are often ill-prepared and lacking in flavor. We set out to remedy this problem and make a refined Denver omelet worth cooking at home.

As we see it, the two biggest problems facing Denver omelets are undercooked filling and overcooked eggs. And the two together can be quite off-putting—crunchy, vegetal-tasting peppers sandwiched between layers of tough eggs. The filling proved the easiest place to start. We wanted a well-cooked, slightly browned filling that brought out the natural sweetness in the peppers. And we wanted the ham's smokiness to cut through the rich creaminess of the eggs and cheese. To emphasize the pepper's sweetness and build complexity of flavor, we used both red and green peppers, which also made for a more attractive filling. We first tried julienning the vegetables, as done in many diners, but tasters complained that the vegetables were hard to eat and the peppers' skins added an unpleasant, fibrous quality to the filling. So we switched to a dice, which was easier to eat, and the peppers' thick skins no longer marred the texture. To keep the cooking time short, we diced everything fairly small. The vegetables softened and lightly browned with about six minutes of cooking over medium-high heat.

After trying several different kinds of ham, including ham steaks, canned ham, and sliced deli ham, we found they all worked fine, but ham steaks proved the easiest to dice and provided the deepest, smokiest flavor. We first tried adding the ham to the vegetables long enough to just warm through, but the filling did not take on the ham's potent flavor. When the ham was added midway through cooking, however, the smokiness infused the vegetables and the diced ham browned at the edges.

Although we had overcome the hurdle of undercooked vegetables, the filling tasted one-dimensional. Borrowing from the classic Basque dish of piperade—a mixture of ham, peppers, and onions from which the Denver filling is clearly derived—we added a hint of garlic and parsley. The garlic sharpened the robust flavors, and the parsley added some freshness. The final touch was a dash of hot pepper sauce, which accented the flavors without necessarily tasting spicy.

With our filling perfected, we moved on to the eggs. There are probably more techniques for cooking omelets than for any other dish under the sun. We tested a variety and came up with a relatively foolproof method. First off, a good-quality, nonstick pan is crucial; otherwise you are guaranteed to produce scrambled eggs instead of an omelet. For these big, overstuffed omelets, we found that a 10-inch pan worked best, allowing the eggs to spread out to provide plenty of surface area for the filling. After experimenting with different heat levels, medium-high seemed to work the best because the eggs set quickly. At lower heat, they tended to get rubbery. The sizzling of the butter when added to the pan

proved a good indicator of when the pan was hot enough to receive the eggs (the butter added great flavor as well).

With the eggs in the pan, we quickly stirred them with a heat-safe rubber spatula until they just began to set, a matter of a few seconds. Then, gingerly, we lifted up the edges of the set eggs with the spatula and tilted the pan, allowing the uncooked eggs to run underneath and cook. When the eggs were almost fully set—just a little runny on top—we added the cheese. We discovered that once the cheese was almost melted, the bottom had lightly browned and was ready to come out of the pan. We quickly covered half the omelet with the warm pepper filling, slid the omelet onto a plate, filled-side first, and, with a slight twist of the wrist, flipped the empty half over the filled half. (We tried folding the omelet in the pan with the spatula, but this method occasionally ripped the omelet.)

We were pleased with the technique and the egg's light browning, but the omelet itself was a little dense and tough. Because the omelet cooked longer than a French-style omelet, the eggs were robbed of moisture. To increase the moisture, we tried adding milk, cream, and water to the beaten eggs. Milk and cream worked equally well, but water diluted the omelet's subtle flavor. As little as 1 tablespoon of cream or milk to 3 eggs was just right. The interior stayed fluffy and moist, while the exterior was lightly browned.

FOLDING A DENVER OMELET

1. Pull the cooked eggs in along the edges of the pan toward the center, tilting the pan so that any uncooked egg runs to the pan's edges.

2. Sprinkle the cheese evenly across the surface of the omelet and let it melt slightly. With the handle of the pan facing you, spoon the filling over the left side of omelet.

3. Slide the filled half of the omelet onto a warm plate. With a slight turn of the wrist, slightly invert the pan so the other side of the omelet folds over the filling.

Denver Omelet

SERVES 1

Prepare the filling (recipe follows) and then begin making the omelet. Beat the egg mixture for a second omelet in a separate bowl. Once first omelet is done, heat another ½ tablespoon butter in an empty pan, add egg mixture and proceed to make second omelet. The filling recipe makes enough for two omelets. See the illustrations on page 290 for tips on making an omelet.

3	large eggs
1	tablespoon cream or milk
	Salt and ground black pepper
½	tablespoon unsalted butter
2	ounces Monterey Jack cheese, shredded (about ½ cup)
½	recipe filling for Denver Omelet

1. Beat the eggs, cream or milk, and salt and pepper to taste with a fork in a small bowl until thoroughly combined. Heat the butter in a 10-inch nonstick skillet over medium-high heat. When the foaming subsides and the butter just begins to turn color, pour in the eggs. Cook until the edges begin to set, about 2 to 3 seconds, then, with a rubber spatula, stir in a circular motion until slightly thickened, about 10 seconds. Use the spatula to pull the cooked edges in to the center, then tilt the pan to one side so that the uncooked egg runs to the edge of the pan. Repeat until the omelet is just set but still moist on the surface, 1 to 2 minutes

2. Sprinkle the cheese evenly across the omelet and allow to partially melt, 15 to 20 seconds. With the handle of the pan facing you, spoon the filling over the left side of the omelet. Slide the omelet onto a warmed plate, filled-side first, and, with a slight twist of the wrist, invert the pan so that the other side folds over the filling. Serve immediately.

Filling for Denver Omelet

MAKES ENOUGH TO FILL 2 OMELETS

A ham steak is our top choice for this recipe, although canned ham and sliced deli ham will work. If using sliced deli ham, add it with the garlic, parsley, and hot sauce.

1	tablespoon unsalted butter
½	medium red bell pepper, stemmed, seeded, and diced
½	medium green bell pepper, stemmed, seeded, and diced
1	small onion, diced
¼	teaspoon salt
4	ounces ham steak, diced (about 1 cup)
1	medium clove garlic, minced
1	tablespoon minced fresh parsley leaves
½	teaspoon hot pepper sauce, such as Tabasco

Heat the butter in a medium nonstick skillet over medium-high heat. When the foaming subsides, add the peppers, onion, and salt. Cook, stirring occasionally, until the onion softens, about 4 minutes. Add the ham and cook until the peppers begin to brown lightly, about 2 minutes. Add the garlic, parsley, and hot pepper sauce and cook for 30 seconds. Transfer to a small bowl and cover to keep warm.

BLUEBERRY PANCAKES

A TALL STACK OF FLUFFY BUTTERMILK PANCAKES polka-dotted with fresh blueberries is a hard breakfast to beat. But how often are they really memorable? Most of time the pancakes are leaden or burnt and the berries are flavorless or have burst and stained the pancakes a lurid purple. Determined to come up with a foolproof recipe, we picked up several quarts of blueberries and set to work.

First off, we needed a pancake recipe. In our opinion, the best pancakes are airy, tender, and tangy with buttermilk. And they need to be quick to prepare—no whipped egg whites for us. We started off by making a variety of recipes and picking and choosing what we liked best in each. Buttermilk was a given, but we discovered that too much made for an ungainly batter. We found that a little regular milk helped thin the batter out to a more workable, pourable consistency.

In subtle-flavored baked goods like pancakes, where the metallic bitterness of chemical leavening can be detected easily, it is imperative to use a minimal amount of leavening so that it is fully consumed during rising. While the use of baking soda alone would have made things easy, these pancakes were thin in flavor, lacking buttermilk's tang. The soda was neutralizing all the acid in the buttermilk and stripping it of flavor. Baking powder and buttermilk yielded tough pancakes that tasted sour. The baking powder has its own built-in acid and was leaving the buttermilk alone; the resulting buttermilk tang was too much. After a bit more testing, we discovered that a combination of baking soda and baking powder was best. A small amount of baking soda made the pancakes light and tender and tamed the buttermilk tang slightly. The baking powder provided rise without neutralizing the remaining buttermilk tang.

As far as flour, we tried both all-purpose and cake flour. When made with cake flour, the pancakes were almost as thin as crepes and turned leaden under the syrup's weight. All-purpose flour provided enough structure for an airy pancake that was sturdy enough to absorb a thorough soaking of syrup. We also chose to include a little cornmeal for a contrast in texture; the slight grittiness of the cornmeal makes a point of how light and fluffy the pancakes are.

There are two schools of thought regarding the best way to incorporate the blueberries into the pancakes: add them to the pancakes as they cook, or fold them into the batter. While adding the berries during cooking generally prevents the berries from breaking and releasing their juices, it is a hassle to stand over the skillet and drop the berries one by one onto the circles of batter. Cooking breakfast can be enough of a chore without adding a hurdle like that. So we went with folding the berries into the batter, doing so as gently as we could with a rubber spatula. After seeing the berries in several batches burst during cooking, we realized that a slightly thicker batter would insulate the berries from the pan's high heat. A slight reduction in the amount of buttermilk in the batter was all that was needed.

As an extra bit of security, we tossed the blueberries with a portion of the flour prior to incorporating them into the batter. If any of the blueberries burst, the flour soaked up the juices before they had a chance to stain the batter. The flour coating also helped to further protect the berries from the griddle's heat.

While we had succeeded in preventing the berries from bursting, we had not done anything about flavor. Even at their very best, blueberries can have an allusive flavor that dissipates quickly when cooked. Tiny, sweet wild blueberries from Maine are our favorite to cook with because they are packed with bright flavor and have a low moisture content, but it's hard to find these berries fresh outside of New England. We experimented with frozen Maine blueberries, but their high moisture content colored the pancakes a ghastly shade of bruise.

We decided to go with conventional fresh blueberries but looked at ways to improve their flavor. Lemon zest and vanilla proved to be the ingredients we were looking for. The lemon zest added tartness to the already tangy berries, and the vanilla emphasized the berries' floral notes.

Blueberry Pancakes
SERVES 3 TO 4
(MAKES ABOUT 8 PANCAKES)

Although tiny wild blueberries are our favorite, feel free to use whatever blueberries you may have on hand. To achieve an even distribution of blueberries in the batter, give it a quick but gentle stir with a rubber spatula before ladling each batch onto the griddle. To keep the first batch of pancakes warm while the rest finish cooking, line a rimmed baking sheet with a dish towel, place the pancakes in a single layer, cover with another clean dish towel, and set the baking sheet in a 200-degree oven. The pancakes should keep without deteriorating for about 15 minutes.

½	pint fresh blueberries (I cup)
I	cup (5 ounces) unbleached all-purpose flour
½	teaspoon grated lemon zest
2	teaspoons sugar
I	tablespoon stone-ground cornmeal
½	teaspoon salt
½	teaspoon baking powder
¼	teaspoon baking soda
¾	cup buttermilk
¼	cup milk (plus I to 2 tablespoons more if the batter is too thick)
I	large egg, separated
2	tablespoons unsalted butter, melted
½	teaspoon vanilla extract
	Vegetable oil for brushing griddle

1. In a small bowl, gently toss the blueberries and 2 teaspoons flour; set aside. In a larger bowl, mix

together the lemon zest and the remaining dry ingredients. Pour the buttermilk and the milk into a 2-cup Pyrex measuring cup and whisk in the egg white. Separately whisk together the egg yolk and the melted butter, and then combine with the other wet ingredients. Add the wet ingredients to the dry ingredients and stir together with a rubber spatula until just mixed. Carefully fold in the blueberries until evenly distributed throughout the batter.

2. Meanwhile, heat a griddle or large skillet over medium-high heat. Brush the pan liberally with vegetable oil. When water splashed on the surface sizzles, pour or ladle the batter, about ¼ cup at a time, onto the griddle, making certain not to overcrowd the pan. When bubbles appear in the top of the pancake and the pancake bottoms are brown (this should take 2 to 3 minutes), carefully flip the pancakes over and cook until the remaining side has browned, 1 to 2 minutes longer. Re-oil the skillet and repeat for the next batch of pancakes. Serve hot.

GERMAN APPLE PANCAKE

FOUND UNDER A VARIETY OF ALIASES, INCLUding Dutch pancake, Dutch baby, and puff pancake (to name just a few), a German apple pancake is a crisp, puffy baked pancake packed with apples. A few renowned pancake houses around the country have daily lines of hungry breakfast goers snaking out the door waiting for this simple yet deeply satisfying breakfast treat. But, as we found out, apple pancakes worth waiting for are few and far between. The average pancake falls far short of what we consider ideal: a crisp, brittle top, a rich but neutral-flavored pancake, and well caramelized apples.

German apple pancake batter is a simple affair, closer in composition and consistency to thin crepe batter than thicker conventional pancake batter. It should be a very loose mixture of eggs, milk or cream, flour, and a pinch of salt. The secret to the batter is balancing the amount of eggs with the milk or cream. Many of the batters we tested yielded pancakes that were far too eggy. For a 10-inch pancake, tasters agreed that two eggs was just enough for structure and flavor. Three eggs made a dense, gummy pancake predominately flavored with egg.

As for the dairy component, we tried milk, cream, and half-and-half. Milk alone made a loose, relatively flavorless pancake dominated by the eggs. All cream was over-the-top in richness—almost resembling a custard in texture. Half-and-half proved a great compromise between milk and cream. It gave the pancake body and depth without being too rich.

To round out the pancake's flavors, we added vanilla extract and a small amount of white sugar. The apples provide the sweetening for this pancake, but sugar in the batter wedded the flavors.

Unlike stovetop pancakes that are packed with chemical leavening and buttermilk, oven-baked pancakes rely on heat and eggs for an explosive rise. While a very high heat—500 degrees—guaranteed a dramatic rise and golden crust, it failed to fully cook the pancake's interior. Leaving the pancake in the oven for more time at this high temperature caused the crust to burn, so, to remedy the problem, we tried starting the pancake at a high temperature and quickly reduced the heat to finish cooking. We discovered that if the oven temperature is brought too low, the pancake needs to bake too long and the exterior dries out by the time the interior is set. After several tests, we found it best to preheat the oven to 500 degrees and to lower the temperature to 425 degrees when the pancake goes into the oven.

Much to our surprise, cooking the apples proved to be a bigger issue than assembling the batter. We wanted well-caramelized apples for the best flavor, but we also wanted the apples to retain a bit of bite for contrast with the soft and creamy pancake. We knew firm Granny Smith apples would be the best choice because they stand up well to cooking. These tart apples would also keep the dish from becoming too sweet.

We started with the simplest method—cooking the apples in some butter until they turned golden brown and the apples' natural sugars caramelized. Our first few attempts at cooking the apples were frustrating. Over medium heat, the apples verged on chunky applesauce before they caramelized; over high heat, they scorched before the apples' sugars browned.

One of the test cooks then suggested an eccentric method—sautéing the apples in caramel, a common technique in Vietnamese cooking. In this manner, the caramel flavor is already developed, and the apples are cooked until the desired texture is reached. The technique worked beautifully, but making a caramel prior to cooking the apples was time-consuming and a bit daunting for early morning cooking.

Hoping to avoid making caramel, we tried adding sugar to the apples as they cooked over high heat in the hope that the sugar would caramelize as the apples cooked. It was close, but not quite there. The apples were slightly overcooked by the time the sugars had caramelized. When we switched to light brown sugar, the technique worked beautifully; the apple slices were uniformly golden and retained some body. This technique works well, but we found that it is crucial to cut the apples into even slices; otherwise they cooked unevenly and the smaller slices burned.

Straight from the oven, German apple pancake is quite dramatic and will certainly impress your breakfast companions. Get to the table fast though—the pancake sinks within a couple of minutes. A dusting of confectioners' sugar and warm maple syrup are the classic accompaniments.

German Apple Pancake

SERVES 4

Tradition dictates that this supersized pancake should be cooked in a cast-iron skillet, but we found that an oven-safe, nonstick skillet worked significantly better. If you want to use cast-iron, reduce the heat to medium-high after five minutes when cooking the apples; otherwise they may burn in the oven because the cast iron retains so much heat. And be careful removing the pancake from a cast-iron skillet; it may stick unless your pan is very well seasoned. We chose Granny Smith apples for their tartness and firm texture and their availability, but if you have access to similar, more interesting varieties, such as Rhode Island Greening or Mutsus, by all means try them.

- 2 large eggs
- ¾ cup half-and-half
- 1 teaspoon vanilla extract
- ½ teaspoon salt
- 1 tablespoon granulated sugar
- ½ cup (2½ ounces) unbleached all-purpose flour
- 1 tablespoon unsalted butter
- 3 medium Granny Smith apples (about 1¼ pounds), peeled, cored, and cut into ¼-inch slices
- ¼ cup packed light brown sugar
- 2 tablespoons confectioners' sugar
  Maple syrup, warmed

1. Adjust an oven rack to the middle position and heat the oven to 500 degrees. Combine the eggs, half-and-half, vanilla, salt, and granulated sugar in the workbowl of a food processor or a blender jar and process until well combined, about 15 seconds. Add the flour and process until thoroughly mixed and free of lumps, about 30 seconds; set the batter aside.

2. Add the butter to a 10-inch ovenproof nonstick skillet and heat over medium-high heat until the butter foams. Add the apples and sprinkle the brown sugar evenly over them. Cook, stirring occasionally, until the apples begin to turn light brown, about 5 minutes. Continue to cook over medium-high heat, stirring constantly, until the apples are golden brown, 4 to 5 minutes.

3. Remove the pan from the heat. Quickly pour the batter into the pan and place the pan in the oven. Reduce the heat to 425 degrees and cook until browned and puffed, 16 to 17 minutes. With a rubber spatula, slide the pancake out of the skillet onto a serving platter, dust it with confectioners' sugar, and serve immediately, accompanied by warmed maple syrup.

➤ VARIATION

German Apple Pancake with Caramel Sauce

On a lark, we tried the pancake with caramel sauce, and everyone loved it. So, for a rustic dessert or a truly hedonistic breakfast experience, make a batch of the caramel sauce from the Sticky Buns recipe on page 250. You will have extra caramel sauce, but it keeps well in the refrigerator for up to 2 weeks.

Follow the recipe for German Apple Pancake, replacing the maple syrup with Caramel Sauce (page 250), increasing the cream in the sauce to 2 cups and decreasing butter to 2 tablespoons.

WAFFLES

AFTER TESTING MORE THAN 15 RECIPES, we realized that our ideal waffle requires a thick batter, so the outside can become crisp while the inside remains custardy. We also learned that a good waffle must be quickly cooked; slow cooking evens out the cooking rate, causing the center to overcook by the time the exterior is crisp and brown.

Many waffle batters are too thin, usually because the proportion of milk to flour—at 1 cup each—is too high. Such thin batter results in disappointing, gummy-textured waffles with dry, unappealing interiors. We found that ⅞ cup buttermilk, or ¾ cup sweet milk, to 1 cup flour is a far better proportion.

Most recipes omit buttermilk entirely or, at best, list it as an option. Yet we found that buttermilk is absolutely crucial. Why? Because buttermilk, when teamed up with baking soda, creates a much thicker batter than the alternative, sweet milk paired with baking powder. We eventually found a way to make good waffles with sweet milk (reduce the amount of liquid and use homemade baking powder for a thicker batter), but buttermilk waffles will always taste better.

Although many recipes for buttermilk waffles call for baking powder, it's not necessary. All that's required is baking soda, which reacts with the acid in the buttermilk to give the batter lift. Baking powder is essentially baking soda plus cream of tartar, an acidic ingredient. Baking powder is useful when the batter itself contains no other source of acid. We eliminated the baking powder from our working recipe and found not only that it wasn't necessary but that it wasn't all that helpful; these waffles cooked up crispier. Out of curiosity, we also tried to make a waffle with buttermilk and baking powder, eliminating the baking soda. The waffle was inedible. (See page 271 for more information on how baking powder and soda work.)

Because crispness is so important in waffles, we tried substituting cornmeal for a bit of the flour and found that 1 tablespoon per cup of flour adds extra crackle. We also experimented with the addition of cake flour and found that it produces a finer crumb and a more tender product. This waffle lacked that desirable contrast between a crisp exterior and creamy interior.

Some waffle recipes call for separating the egg and then whipping the white and folding it into the mixed batter. We made waffles this way and found that this extra step does improve things. The beaten whites make the batter glossier and the waffle fluffier inside. If you cut through a cooked waffle made with beaten egg whites, you can actually see pockets of air trapped inside. The same examination of a whole-egg waffle revealed a flatter, more consistent texture.

EQUIPMENT: Waffle Irons

No matter how foolproof the recipe, all waffles will be rubbery and flaccid if cooked in the wrong waffle iron. To find out which waffle irons work the best, we gathered six traditional (not Belgian) waffle makers, with prices ranging from $20 to $50. We narrowed our selection to include only round models, as they account for 60 percent of waffle iron sales.

The differences in brands were dramatic. The top-rated models turned out crisp, well-browned waffles in just three minutes. The worst models produced rubbery or hard waffles that took nearly twice as long to cook.

What makes the difference? The critical issue is how hot the waffle iron can get. We tested each waffle maker with an infrared thermometer, measuring the temperature of each quadrant and then averaging the results for each machine. The models producing the rubbery waffles had an average temperature of 330 degrees, while the highly rated models averaged 380 degrees. That difference is enough to sear and crisp the exterior without drying out the interior. The weaker models didn't have enough heat to set up the contrasting textures—crisp on the outside, creamy in the middle—that we wanted.

All models tested had lights indicating when the iron was ready to use, but many of these lights were inconveniently placed and difficult to see. Only a few models also had a "done" light, indicating when the waffles were fully cooked. This feature effectively eliminated all guesswork—simply set the degree of doneness, and voilà, a perfectly browned, crisp waffle.

Our favorite waffle irons were the Farberware Millennium Deluxe ($30) and the Cuisinart Classic Round ($50). The Villaware Perfect Waffler ($40) also received high marks, but testers soon wearied of the piercing chirp this model emitted when the waffles were done.

Look at a number of waffle recipes and you'll see a wide range of recommendations as to how to combine ingredients. But most have this in common: They add all of the liquid ingredients at once. This practice necessitates overmixing and usually results in clumps of unmoistened flour. When we used a whisk to combine the ingredients until they were smooth, the batter was thin and the waffle tough.

The objective is to moisten the flour thoroughly, not to create a smooth batter, and for this there is no question that a gentle hand is crucial. This is the technique that worked best for us: Pour the liquid ingredients into the dry ingredients very slowly, mixing gently with a rubber spatula. When most of the liquid has been added, the batter becomes thicker; switch to a folding motion, similar to that used in folding egg whites, to finally combine and moisten the batter. Then continue folding as you add the beaten egg white.

When you bake them, remember that darker waffles taste better than lighter ones. The browning reaction promotes flavor development. Waffles should be cooked until medium-brown, not lightly tanned. Toasty brown waffles will also stay crispier longer than manila-colored waffles, which are likely to be soggy by the time they get to the table.

Buttermilk Waffles

MAKES 3 TO 4,
DEPENDING ON SIZE OF WAFFLE IRON

The secret to great waffles is a thick batter, so don't expect a pourable batter. The optional dash of cornmeal adds a pleasant crunch to the finished waffle. This recipe can be doubled or tripled. Make toaster waffles out of leftover batter—undercook the waffles a bit, cool them on a wire rack, wrap them in plastic wrap, and freeze. Then pop them in the toaster as you like for a quick breakfast.

I	cup (5 ounces) unbleached all-purpose flour
I	tablespoon cornmeal (optional)
½	teaspoon salt
¼	teaspoon baking soda
I	egg, separated
⅞	cup buttermilk
2	tablespoons unsalted butter, melted and cooled

1. Heat a waffle iron. Whisk the dry ingredients together in a medium bowl. Whisk the egg yolk with the buttermilk and butter.

2. Beat the egg white until it just holds a 2-inch peak.

3. Add the liquid ingredients to the dry ingredients in a thin, steady stream while mixing gently with a rubber spatula. (Do not add liquid faster than you can incorporate it into the batter.) Toward the end of mixing, use a folding motion to incorporate the ingredients. Gently fold the egg white into the batter.

4. Spread an appropriate amount of batter onto the hot waffle iron. Following the manufacturer's

---

SCIENCE: Why Commercial Baking Powder Doesn't Work in Waffles

Baking powder is made from two major elements: an acid (such as cream of tartar) and baking soda. The cream of tartar provides the acidity the baking soda needs to produce a rise. Baking powder is used when there is no natural acidity in the batter, as in a batter made with sweet milk and without the addition of an acidic ingredient such as yogurt or buttermilk.

When baking soda comes in contact with a moist, acidic environment, carbon dioxide gas is produced, which in turn provides rise. This chemical reaction is quite pronounced in a buttermilk batter. Buttermilk contains lactic acid, which reacts strongly with the soda, generating a thick, spongy batter in seconds.

Because sweet milk reacts less strongly with baking powder, the batter remains thin. This is partially because most baking powder is double-acting, which means that it produces a rise once at room temperature, when added to the batter, and once in the oven, when the temperature climbs above 120 degrees. Baking powder is designed to create gas slowly, so that a cake, for example, will have time plenty of time to rise in the oven before the bubbles dissipate and the cake sets.

In our tests, it was clear that most of the rise with baking powder occurs at oven temperatures. Since waffles are cooked so quickly, baking powder is not ideally suited to this type of batter; the amount of "room-temperature" acid it can provide is insufficient. With waffles you want a lot of room-temperature reaction, and therefore it's best, when using sweet milk, to make your own recipe for baking powder, using cream of tartar (which works at room temperature) and baking soda.

---

instructions, cook the waffle until golden brown, 2 to 5 minutes. Serve immediately. (In a pinch, you can keep waffles warm on a wire rack in a 200-degree oven for up to 5 minutes.)

➤ VARIATION

Almost As Good As Buttermilk Waffles

MAKES 3 TO 4

If you're out of buttermilk, try this sweet-milk variation. By making your own baking powder (using baking soda and cream of tartar; for more information see page 271) and by cutting back on the quantity of milk, you can make a thick, quite respectable batter. The result is a waffle with a crisp crust and moist interior.

Follow recipe for Buttermilk Waffles, adding ½ teaspoon cream of tartar to the dry ingredients and substituting a scant ¾ cup milk for buttermilk.

OATMEAL

THE MIDWINTER MUSE OF BELLY-WARMING oatmeal has been a source of bewitchment for us over the years. We've all had pasty mounds of oatmeal better suited as glue for arts and crafts projects than for breakfast. But some of us in the test kitchen have also had great bowls of steaming oatmeal, and we wanted to have some more. There was much to explore, from the kind of oats used to the cooking technique to the method of stirring. We began by first considering the oats.

Oats are a cool-climate grain crop that make for excellent animal feed but must be cleaned, toasted, hulled, and then cleaned again if they are to be used for human consumption. This process makes what are called oat groats. Similar in appearance to brown rice, oat groats are not readily available in stores and make more of a nutty rice-type dish than a creamy cereal food.

The oat cereal product most familiar to American households—next to Cheerios—is rolled oats, an American innovation of the late 19th century. Rolled oats are made by steaming oat groats and flattening them with large rollers. In supermarkets you will find two types of rolled oats—quick-cooking and regular, also known as old-fashioned. Quick-cooking are cut into smaller pieces before rolling and are rolled thinner than the regular variety, so the cereal takes just one minute to cook versus five. In the test kitchen, we tried making hot cereal with both.

The quick-cooking were a bit powdery and had no real flavor, but they did have a pleasant mushy consistency. In a matter of minutes, however, the bowl of oatmeal cooled and gelled into a flabby paste. Hot oatmeal from Quaker old-fashioned oats turned out a slightly more bulky bowl of cereal but was still insubstantial, drab, and flecky in texture. We did try regular rolled oats purchased in the bulk section of a natural foods store. They were noticeably more golden in color than the Quaker variety and had better flavor. As we later learned, the rolled oats sold in natural foods store bulk bins are often flash-toasted during processing.

Instant oats, often sold in individual flavor packets, are a slightly different species, made with cut groats that have been precooked and dried before being rolled. So, amazingly, all you must do is stir a packet into boiling water and you've got breakfast—if you want to call it that. What we really ended up with was a bowl of gelled oat chaff that was quick to lose its moisture and heat.

As it turns out, many Scottish and Irish cooks scorn American rolled oats, saying they make a sloppy bowl of "porridge." We figured we should carefully consider the opinion of these renowned oat eaters. In these countries, oatmeal is made from steel-cut oats-groats that have been cut into a few pieces but have not been otherwise processed or rolled. Also known as Scotch oats, Irish oatmeal, or pinhead oats, they can typically be found in the bulk foods section of natural foods stores. Supermarkets carry pricey canned varieties, but all of the tins we tried were stale.

Making hot oatmeal from steel-cut oats took considerably longer than making it with regular rolled oats (about 25 to 30 minutes total), but the outcome was very much worth the wait. The hot cereal had a faint nutty flavor, and, while its consistency was surprisingly creamy, it was also toothsome; there was a firm core to the soft oat granules that whimsically popped between our teeth when chewed. Now we had to do some fine-tuning to determine how to bring out the best texture and flavor of these oats.

Taking a clue from the flash-toasting technique of the natural foods store's rolled oats, we tried toasting the steel-cut oats. This definitely helped to accent the nutty flavor. Because oats are high in oil content and thus quick to burn, we found toasting them in a skillet as opposed to the oven provided better control. And, to no great surprise, toasting the oats with a little butter in the skillet lent them a sweet, rounded nutty flavor, with an aroma like butterscotch.

As for the cooking method, we tried a variety of approaches: adding to boiling water then dropping to a simmer, boiling constantly, simmering only, starting in cold water, covered versus uncovered, and so on. The ultimate goal was to determine which method would create the creamiest bowl of oatmeal without being too mushy.

Starting in cold water is supposed to make the creamiest oatmeal. It did, but it was mushy, too. There was no kernel pop. Tasters agreed that the cereal needed to be more toothsome. Starting in boiling water and dropping to a simmer did just that—but so did simmering only, and that made for a creamier oatmeal, too, with just five or so more minutes in cooking time.

We did try simmering with the pot covered to see if that might speed up the process. The outcome was disappointingly gummy. And cooking over a double boiler, as recommended in many cookbooks produced early in the 20th century, made for a soupy, loose consistency and an even longer cooking time. In sum, the best method seemed to be a steady uncovered simmer on medium-low heat.

Many cookbooks suggest soaking the oats before cooking, anywhere from five minutes to overnight. Because we were planning on toasting the oats, we had to factor this in. Soaking the oats for five minutes before toasting caused them to clump up in the skillet, and the final outcome was a less creamy oatmeal. Soaking for five minutes after toasting made for a thick, creamy bowl of oatmeal, but no more thick and creamy than that made from the toasted oats that had not been soaked—and the cooking time was no different, either. Just to see what would happen, we did try presoaking without toasting. Made this way, the oatmeal was quite pasty.

With the cooking technique down, all we needed to test was the cooking medium. We had been using water only. A few recipes used milk, but our oatmeal was so creamy with just water we thought milk would push it over the top. When completely replacing the water, milk was indeed over the top, as well as quick to burn the pan bottom. A ratio of 3 parts water to 1 part milk, however, added a pleasant roundness in texture and flavor to the oatmeal.

Many oatmeal recipes require frequent stirring. Surprisingly, we found that when oats are cooked slowly at a moderate simmer they do not need constant attention for the first 20 minutes of cooking time. It is in the final five to eight minutes, when the hot cereal has swelled and just a bit of liquid remains on top that the pot must be stirred to blend the liquid and oats and to prevent sticking. We found that the last eight minutes is also the best time to stir in the salt (see below for details) and, if they are to be added, raisins, so that they plump. Following an old tradition, we confirmed that the rounded handle end of a wooden spoon is the best stirring tool. Stirring with the usual end of a spoon, like stirring early in the cooking process or stirring frequently, results in a mushier, less toothsome oatmeal.

Finally, we found that a rest period is essential

SCIENCE: Hold the Salt, Please

Almost all of the recipes we found for making oatmeal from steel-cut oats also called for the addition of salt only after the oatmeal had cooked for at least 10 minutes. After trying a batch in which we added the salt to the water before adding the oats, we found there was good reason for this practice— salt added beforehand hardened the meal and prevented the grains from swelling.

To find out why, we contacted Professor Chuck Walker, who teaches a course on breakfast cereal technology at Kansas State University. He explained that under slow-cooking conditions and without the addition of salt, a lot of starch and pentosans, a group of naturally occurring gums, leach out through the oats' cell walls. While all cereal grains contain pentosans, oats have an unusually large amount. These gums love water, so they prefer to leach out into the cooking water, which is why oats make for such a creamy hot cereal. Like the pentosans, salt is also strongly attracted to water. So if added at the beginning of cooking, it essentially will compete with the starch and gums for the water. This is why you get a less creamy cereal.

---

after cooking because the consistency changes significantly with just slight cooling. The creamy grains pull together like a pudding. For this reason it's important that the oatmeal still be a bit liquidy when it is pulled off the heat. It holds its heat well during the resting period, but much liquid evaporates. If you cover the pot during the five-minute rest period, moisture condenses on the lid and drips back down on the hot cereal, so it's better without the lid.

Perfect Oatmeal
SERVES 3 TO 4

Many supermarkets sell prepackaged steel-cut oats, but we found they were often stale and always expensive. A better option is to buy them in bulk at a natural foods store. To double the recipe, use a large skillet to toast the oats; increase the cooking time to 10 to 15 minutes once the salt has been added. If desired, pass maple syrup or brown sugar separately when serving, or try the topping at right.

    3   cups water
    1   cup whole milk
    1   tablespoon unsalted butter
    1   cup steel-cut oats
    ¼   teaspoon salt

1. Bring the water and milk to a simmer in a large saucepan over medium heat. Meanwhile, heat the butter in a medium skillet over medium heat until just beginning to foam; add the oats and toast, stirring constantly with a wooden spoon, until golden and fragrant with a butterscotch-like aroma, 1½ to 2 minutes.

2. Stir the toasted oats into the simmering liquid, and reduce the heat to medium-low; simmer gently, until the mixture thickens and resembles gravy, about 20 minutes. Add the salt and stir lightly with a wooden spoon handle. Continue simmering, stirring occasionally with the spoon handle, until the oats absorb almost all the liquid and the oatmeal is thick and creamy, with a pudding-like consistency, 7 to 10 minutes. Off heat, let the oatmeal stand uncovered for 5 minutes. Serve immediately, with topping if desired.

Honeyed Fig Topping with Vanilla and Cinnamon
MAKES ABOUT 1 CUP, ENOUGH FOR 4 SERVINGS OF OATMEAL

    5   ounces dried figs (about 1 cup), each fig
         quartered and stemmed
    1½   tablespoons honey
    ⅛   teaspoon vanilla extract
    1½   tablespoons water
    ⅛   teaspoon ground cinnamon

Bring the figs, honey, water, vanilla, and cinnamon to a simmer in a small saucepan over medium-high heat; cook until the liquid reduces to a glaze, about 4 minutes. Spoon a portion over the individual bowls of hot oatmeal; serve immediately.

BACON

MANY HOME COOKS NOW USE THE MICROwave to cook bacon, while others still fry bacon in a skillet. In restaurants, many chefs "fry" bacon in the oven. We decided to try each of these methods to find out which worked best.

For each cooking technique, we varied temperature, timing, and material, cooking both a typical store-bought bacon and a thick-cut mail-order bacon. The finished strips were compared in terms of flavor, texture, and appearance, while the techniques were compared for consistency, safety, and ease.

While the microwave would seem to have the apparent advantage of ease—stick the pieces in and forget about them—this turned out not to be the case. The bacon was still raw at 90 seconds; at two minutes it was medium-well-done in most spots, but still uneven; but by two minutes and 30 seconds the strips of bacon were hard and flat and definitely overcooked. The finished product didn't warrant the investment of time it would take to figure out the perfect number of seconds. Microwaved bacon is not crisp, it is an unappetizing pink/gray in color even when well-done, and it lacks flavor.

The skillet made for a significantly better product. The bacon flavors were much more pronounced than in the nuked version, the finished color of the meat was a more appealing brick red, and the meat had a pleasing crispness. There were, however, a number of drawbacks to pan-frying. In addition to the functional problems of grease splatter and the number of 11-inch strips you can fit into a 12-inch round pan, there are problems of consistency and convenience. Because all of the heat comes from below the meat, the strips brown on one side before the other. Moreover, even when using a cast-iron pan, as we did, heat is not distributed perfectly evenly across the bottom of the pan. This means that to get consistently cooked strips of bacon you have to turn them over and rotate them in the pan. In addition, when more strips are added to an already-hot pan, they tend to wrinkle up, making for raw or burnt spots in the finished product.

The best results from stovetop cooking came when we lowered the heat from medium to medium-low, just hot enough to sizzle. The lower temperature allowed the strips to render their grease more slowly, with a lot less curling and spitting out of the pan. Of course, this added to the cooking time, and it did not alleviate the need for vigilance.

Oven-frying seemed to combine the advantages of microwaving and pan-frying while eliminating most of the disadvantages. We tried cooking three strips in a preheated 400-degree oven on a 12 by 9-inch rimmed baking sheet that would contain the grease. The bacon was medium-well-done after 9 to 10 minutes and crispy after 11 to 12 minutes. The texture was more like a seared piece of meat than a brittle cracker, the color was that nice brick red, and all of the flavors were just as bright and clear as when pan-fried. Oven-frying also provided a greater margin of error when it came to timing than either of the other methods, and, surprisingly, it was just about as easy as microwaving, adding only the steps of preheating the oven and draining the cooked bacon on paper towels. Finally, the oven-fried strips of bacon were more consistently cooked throughout, showing no raw spots and requiring no turning or flipping during cooking. Because the heat hits the strip from all sides, there is no reason for the bacon strips to curl in one direction or another, and when the strips do curl, the ruffled edges cook as quickly as the flat areas.

Our last test was to try 12 strips of bacon—a pretty full tray—in a preheated oven. This test was also quite successful. The pieces cooked consistently, the only difference being between those in the back and those in the front of the oven; we corrected for this by rotating the tray once from front to back during cooking. That was about the limit of our contact with the hot grease.

Oven-Fried Bacon
SERVES 4 TO 6
Use a large, rimmed baking sheet that is shallow enough to promote browning, yet tall enough (at least ¾ inch in height) to contain the rendered bacon fat. If cooking more than one tray of bacon, exchange their oven positions once about halfway through the cooking process.

INGREDIENTS: Bacon
We tested a range of bacons, including nine leading supermarket brands, a preservative-free "natural" brand, and two premium mail-order brands. Tasters were asked to rate all 12 brands based on flavor, balance of lean to fat, and overall quality. Our tasting showed that both the flavor of the meat itself and the flavors provided by the curing process were crucial factors in judging bacon.

We found a surprising difference in the "pork" flavor of the brands tested. Different manufacturers use different parts of the pork belly to make their bacon. Once the spareribs have been removed, the entire remaining belly can be used for bacon, but the best bacon comes from the center of the belly. The top portion of the belly is quite lean, while the bottom portion is very fatty.

In terms of flavors provided by curing, tasters preferred a strong balance of salt and sugar. We found that most bacons have only a mild smoky flavor, no doubt because the smoking process in most modern processing plants takes just six to eight hours. The one bacon with a real smoked flavor was one of the mail-order varieties. This bacon was smoked for 24 hours and was clearly in a class by itself. Among supermarket brands, Oscar Mayer took top honors, followed by John Morrell and Hillshire Farm. The one brand cured without preservatives landed at the bottom of the rankings owing to its rubbery texture and excessive sweetness.

12	slices bacon, thin- or thick-cut

Adjust an oven rack to the middle position and heat the oven to 400 degrees. Arrange the bacon slices in a rimmed baking sheet or other shallow baking pan. Roast until the fat begins to render, 5 to 6 minutes; rotate the pan front to back. Continue roasting until the bacon is crisp and brown, 5 to 6 minutes longer for thin-sliced bacon, 8 to 10 minutes for thick-cut. Transfer with tongs to a paper towel-lined plate, drain, and serve.

CORNED BEEF HASH

CORNED BEEF HASH IS NOT A BREAKFAST for those who fear fat or like to start the day with yogurt and wheat germ. By its very nature, hash is a hearty, stick-to-your-ribs meal. Legends abound as to the origins of fried meat and potato hash. "Hash house" was a colloquial term in the late-19th century for any cheap eating establishment—hash being a fry-up of questionable meat.

Corned beef hash, in particular, can be traced back to New England ingenuity and frugality. What was served as boiled dinner the night before was recycled as hash the next morning. All the leftovers—meat, potatoes, carrots, and sometimes cabbage—would be fried up in a skillet and capped with an egg. This being a dish of leftovers, we found traditional recipes to be few and far between, as if corned beef hash were a common-sense dish, unworthy of a recipe. And the recipes we did find produced starchy, one-dimensional hash that was light on flavor. Knowing most people do not have leftovers from a boiled dinner sitting in their refrigerator, we set out to create a flavorful hash with fresh ingredients that was easy to prepare.

Meat and potatoes are the heart and soul of this dish—everything else is just seasoning. While leftover beef from the boiled dinner on page 157 is ideal, we found that deli-style corned beef can be just as satisfying. At first, we diced the meat into pieces equivalent in size to the potatoes, but this led to tough and chewy meat that sharply contrasted with the potato's velvety softness. Mincing the beef kept it tender and imparted a meatier flavor to the hash. There is no need for a uniform mince; we coarsely chopped the meat and then worked our knife back and forth across the rough dice until the meat was reduced to ¼-inch or smaller pieces.

Potatoes were an easy choice. Texture being foremost, we knew we wanted starchy potatoes that would retain some character but that would soften and crumble about the edges to bind the hash together. We quickly ruled out anything waxy, such as red potatoes, because they remained too firm. Russets were our top choice.

Prior to being combined with the beef, the potatoes must be parboiled. While we generally boil our potatoes whole and unpeeled so they don't absorb too much liquid, we discovered that dicing the potatoes prior to cooking worked fine in this instance. And they cooked more quickly, too. To echo the flavors of the corned beef, we added a couple of bay leaves and a bit of salt to the cooking water. About four minutes of cooking after the potatoes had come to a boil yielded perfect potatoes—soft but not falling apart.

As far as other vegetables, tasters quickly ruled out anything but onions. Carrots may be traditional, but tasters agreed that their sweetness compromised the simplicity of the hash. Onions, on the other hand, added characteristic body and roundness that supported the meat and potatoes rather than detracting from it. We liked them best cooked slow and steady until lightly browned and meltingly soft. Along with the onions, we chose garlic and thyme to flavor the hash. Garlic sharpened the dish and a minimum of thyme added an earthiness that paired well with the beef.

Although the potatoes loosely bound this mixture, most recipes call for either stock or cream to hold the ingredients more firmly together. We tested both and preferred the richness of the cream. A little hot pepper sauce added with the cream brought some spice to the dish.

After cooking several batches of hash at varying temperatures and with differing techniques, we realized that a fairly lengthy cooking time was crucial to flavor. The golden crust of browned meat and potatoes deepened the flavor of the hash depth. Recipes we tried dealt differently with the crust. Some preserved the crust in one piece, cooking both sides by flipping the hash or sliding it onto a plate and inverting it back into the skillet; and other recipes suggested breaking up the crust and folding it back into the hash. After trying both styles, tasters preferred the latter, for its better overall flavor. And it's a lot easier than trying to flip the heavy, unwieldy hash. We lightly packed the hash into the skillet with the back of a wooden spoon, allowed the bottom to crisp up, and then folded the bottom over the top and repeated the process several times. In this way, the crisp browned bits get evenly distributed throughout the hash.

Tasters agreed that the eggs served with hash need to be just barely set, so that the yolks break and moisten the potatoes. While poaching is the easiest technique for preserving a lightly cooked yolk, it can be something of a hassle. We found that we could "poach" the eggs in the same pan as the hash by nestling the eggs into indentations in the hash, covering the pan, and cooking them over low heat. The results were perfect: runny yolks with the eggs conveniently set in the hash and ready to be served.

EQUIPMENT: Coffee Makers

Making coffee is the first task of the day in most American kitchens. But what's the best means of brewing it? To find out, we assembled a group of appliances representing the major methods used to brew coffee: a percolator, an expensive automatic-drip machine with thermos, an inexpensive automatic-drip machine with burner plate, a manual plastic drip cone that fits over a glass carafe, a flip pot (also known as a Napoletana), a plunger pot (also called a French press), and a vacuum coffee maker.

We ran a series of experiments to determine the best grind of coffee to use for each method, then proceeded to the actual testing. We rated each coffee maker on the basis of the temperature, flavor, and body of the coffee it produced as well as on ease of use.

We quickly dismissed several methods based on the poor quality of the coffee or the hassle involved in getting the device to work. A flip pot can brew only one or two cups at a time, takes 20 minutes to get the job done, seems excessively dangerous (you must flip the burning hot metal pot), and makes gritty, slightly burnt coffee.

A plunger pot is easier to use, but tasters felt that too much sediment passed through the mesh filter that separates the spent grounds from the coffee, even when coarsely ground beans were used. If you don't mind slightly gritty coffee, make sure to fill the glass pot with hot tap water before adding the boiling water and grounds. If you skip this step, the brewed coffee will be cold.

The percolator performed as expected. It worked quickly and delivered very hot coffee, but tasters complained about weak flavor. That's because the water doesn't spend much time in contact with the coffee—it's too busy being recycled through the inner tubing in this device.

Our two automatic-drip machines were easy to use, but the coffee tasted bitter, especially when we tried to make a full pot.

According to experts we spoke with, the water and grounds should stay in contact for four to six minutes. If this period stretches beyond the six-minute mark, the grounds start to release bitter compounds that will harm the flavor of the coffee. We found that automatic drip machines can turn out two or three cups of coffee within the proper time frame but that it often takes 10 minutes to yield six cups. The model tested with the burner had an added problem—coffee that was so-so right after brewing quickly developed a horrible burnt flavor. The drip machine with the thermos did not have this problem.

Two brewing methods stand out as superior, at least in terms of quality. Coffee brewed in a vacuum pot has much to offer—properly hot temperature, a rich flavor that captures the nuances in expensive beans without any bitterness, and a full body without sediment. The real problem here is convenience. This showy device relies on a vacuum created between two glass bowls. Although not hard to use, the glass bowls are wobbly and liable to break. As an intriguing finale to an occasional meal, this conversation piece makes sense, but not every day at six in the morning.

Our favorite coffee brewing method is the manual drip. The convenience factor is second only to an automatic drip: Grind and measure the coffee into the filter-lined cone, then add water just off a boil in batches. You can't leave the kitchen, but the coffee tastes great, without the bitterness associated with an automatic drip machine. That's because the plastic cones on manual drip models are larger than the cones inside automatic drip machines, so the water runs through the grounds more quickly.

If you let the coffee drip into an insulated thermos (prewarmed by rinsing it with hot tap water) rather than a glass carafe, the coffee will stay hot and fresh-tasting for hours. Best of all, you can pick up a plastic cone for $5 and a thermos for $25.

Corned Beef Hash

SERVES 4

A well-seasoned cast-iron skillet is traditional for this recipe, but we prefer a 12-inch nonstick skillet. The nonstick surface leaves little chance of anything sticking and burning. Our favorite tool for flipping the hash is a flat wooden spatula, although a stiff plastic spatula will suffice. We like our hash served with ketchup.

2	pounds russet potatoes, peeled and cut into $\frac{1}{2}$-inch dice
$\frac{1}{2}$	teaspoon salt
2	bay leaves
4	ounces (4 slices) bacon, diced
I	medium onion, diced
2	medium cloves garlic, minced
$\frac{1}{2}$	teaspoon minced fresh thyme leaves
I	pound corned beef, minced (pieces should be $\frac{1}{4}$ inch or smaller)
$\frac{1}{2}$	cup heavy cream
$\frac{1}{4}$	teaspoon hot pepper sauce, such as Tabasco
4	large eggs
	Salt and ground black pepper

1. Bring the potatoes, 5 cups of water, salt, and bay leaves to a boil in a medium saucepan over medium-high heat. Once boiling, cook the potatoes for 4 minutes, then drain and set the potatoes aside.

2. Place the bacon in a 12-inch nonstick skillet over medium-high heat and cook until the fat is partially rendered, about 2 minutes. Add the onion and cook, stirring occasionally, until softened and browned at the edges, about 8 minutes. Add the garlic and thyme and cook until fragrant, 30 seconds. Add the corned beef and stir until thoroughly combined with the onion mixture. Mix in the potatoes and lightly pack the mixture into the pan with a spatula. Reduce the heat to medium and pour the heavy cream and hot pepper sauce evenly over the hash. Cook undisturbed for 4 minutes, then, with the spatula, invert the hash, a portion at a time, and fold the browned bits back into the hash. Lightly pack the hash into the pan. Repeat the process every minute or two until the potatoes are thoroughly cooked, about 8 minutes longer.

3. Make four indentations (each measuring about 2 inches across) equally spaced on the surface of the hash. Crack one egg into each indentation and sprinkle the egg with salt and pepper to taste. Reduce the heat to medium-low, cover the pan, and cook until the eggs are just set, about 6 minutes. Cut into four wedges, each wedge containing one egg, and serve immediately.

HOME FRIES

WHEN WE BEGAN TRYING TO UNCOVER THE secret of the ultimate home fries, we went right to the source—diners. But soon we learned that the problems with this dish are often the same, no matter where they are cooked and consumed. Frequently, the potatoes are not crisp, they are greasy, and the flavorings are either too bland or too spicy.

Our first step was to define home fries—individual pieces of potato cooked in fat in a frying pan on top of the stove and mixed with caramelized onions. We also knew what they should look and taste like. They should have a deep golden brown crust and a tender interior with a full potato flavor. The potatoes should not be greasy but instead feel crisp and moist in your mouth.

We knew the potatoes would end up in a skillet with fat, but would it be necessary to precook them, as our research suggested? We began testing with the simplest approach: dice the potatoes raw and cook them in a hot skillet with fat. But in test after test, no matter how small we cut them, it proved challenging to cook raw potatoes all the way through and obtain a crisp brown crust at the same time. Low temperatures helped cook the inside, but the outside didn't crisp. High temperatures crisped the outside, but the potatoes had to be taken off the heat so early to prevent scorching that the insides were left raw. We decided to precook the potatoes before frying them in a skillet.

Because a common approach to home fries is to use leftover baked potatoes, we baked some of each type, stored them in the refrigerator overnight, then diced them and put them in a skillet with fat. These tests were disappointing. None of the resulting home fries had great potato flavor. They all tasted like leftovers, and their texture was somewhat gummy. The exterior of the red potatoes was not crisp, although they looked very good, and the starchier russet potatoes fell apart.

Next we tried starting with freshly boiled potatoes. Potatoes that were boiled until tender broke down in the skillet, and the inside was overcooked by the time the exterior was crisp. So we tried dicing and then braising the potatoes, figuring we could cook them through in a covered pan with some water and fat, remove the cover, let the water evaporate, and then crisp up the potatoes in the remaining fat. Although this sounded like a good idea, the potatoes stuck horribly to the skillet.

Finally, we considered a technique in Lydie Marshall's *Passion for Potatoes* (HarperPerennial, 1992). Marshall instructs the cook to cover diced raw potatoes with water, bring the water to a boil, then immediately drain the potatoes well and sauté them. This treatment allows the potatoes to cook briefly without absorbing too much water, which is what makes them susceptible to overcooking and breaking down.

We tested this technique with russets, Red Bliss potatoes, and Yukon Golds. Eureka! It worked better with all three varieties of potato than any of the other methods we had tried. The Yukon Golds, though, were the clear favorite. Each individual piece of potato had a crisp exterior, and the inner flesh was tender, moist, and rich in potato flavor. The appearance of each was superior as well, the golden yellow color of the flesh complementing the crispy brown exterior. The russets were drier and not as full flavored but were preferred over the Red Bliss, which all tasters found to be somewhat mushy and disappointingly bland.

We decided to test another medium-starch potato. All-purpose potatoes also browned well and were tender and moist on the inside, but they lacked the rich buttery flavor and appealing yellow color of the Yukon Golds, which remained the favorite.

Having discovered the ideal cooking method and the preferred potato variety, we moved on to the best way to cut the potatoes. We found sliced potatoes much harder to cook than diced ones. A pound of sliced potatoes stacks up three or four layers deep in a large skillet. The result is uneven cooking, with some slices burning and others remaining undercooked. Countless tests had convinced us that one of the keys to success in cooking home fries is to cook the potatoes in a single layer. When a pound of potatoes is diced, one cut side of each potato piece can have contact with the skillet at all times. We tested

---

INGREDIENTS: Orange Juice

Can anything rival the juice you squeeze at home? To find out, we gathered 34 tasters to evaluate 10 brands of supermarket orange juice as well as juice we squeezed in the test kitchen and juice fresh-squeezed at the supermarket.

Our top choice had been squeezed the day before at a local supermarket, closely followed by the juice we squeezed ourselves. Cartons of chilled, not-from-concentrate juices took third and seventh places, with three brands of frozen concentrate squeezed in the middle. Chilled juices made from concentrate landed at the bottom of the rankings.

How could juice squeezed the day before at a supermarket beat out juice squeezed minutes before the tasting? And how could frozen concentrate beat out more expensive chilled juices from concentrate?

The produce manager at the store where we bought fresh-squeezed juice told us he blends oranges to produce good-tasting juice. This can be a real advantage, especially when compared with juice squeezed at home from one kind of orange. Any loss in freshness can be offset by the more complex and balanced flavor of a blended fresh juice, as was the case in our tasting.

Although no one was surprised that the two fresh juices took top honors, the strong showing of the frozen concentrates was a shock. It seems that frozen concentrate doesn't deserve its dowdy, old-fashioned reputation.

Why does juice made at home from frozen concentrate taste better than prepackaged chilled juice made from concentrate? Heat is the biggest enemy of orange juice. Frozen concentrates and chilled juices not made from concentrate are both pasteurized once at around 195 degrees to eliminate microorganisms and neutralize enzymes that will shorten shelf life. Chilled juices made from concentrate are pasteurized twice, once when the concentrate is made and again when the juice is reconstituted and packaged. This accounts for the lack of fresh-squeezed flavor in chilled juices made from concentrate.

dices of various size and found the ½-inch cube to be ideal—easy to turn and to eat, characterized by that pleasing combination of crispy outside and soft fleshy inside.

Deciding whether or not to peel the potatoes was easy. All tasters preferred the texture and flavor contributed by the skin. Leaving it on also saved time and effort.

Thus far we had determined that letting the potatoes sit undisturbed in hot fat to brown each side was critical to a crisp exterior. We found it best to let the potatoes brown undisturbed for four to five minutes before the first turn, then to turn them a total of three or four times. Three tablespoons turned out to be the ideal amount of fat for 1 pound of potatoes. When sampling potatoes cooked in different frying mediums, we found that a 50/50 combination of butter and oil offered the best of both worlds, providing a buttery flavor with a decreased risk of burning (butter burns more easily than vegetable oils). Refined corn and peanut oils, with their nutty overtones, were our first choices.

Soft, sweet, and moist, onions are the perfect counterpoint to crispy potatoes, but we had to determine the best way to include them. Tests showed the easiest and most efficient way also produced the best results: dice the onions and cook them before cooking the potatoes. More flavor can be added with help from parsley, red or green bell peppers (sautéed with the onion), or cayenne pepper, as you wish. Whatever your choice, these are home fries worth staying home for.

Diner-Style Home Fries

SERVES 2 OR 3

If you need to double this recipe, instead of crowding the skillet, cook two batches of home fries separately. While making the second batch, you can keep the first batch hot and crisp by spreading the potatoes on a rimmed baking sheet placed in a 300-degree oven. The paprika adds a warm, deep color, but it can be omitted. An alternative is to toss in 1 tablespoon minced parsley just before serving the potatoes.

2½ tablespoons corn or peanut oil
1   medium onion, chopped small

1   pound (2 medium) Yukon Gold or all-purpose
      potatoes, cut into ½-inch cubes
1¼   teaspoons salt
1   tablespoon unsalted butter
1   teaspoon paprika
      Ground black pepper

1. Heat 1 tablespoon oil in a 12-inch heavy-bottomed skillet over medium-high heat until hot but not smoking. Add the onion and sauté, stirring frequently, until browned, 8 to 10 minutes. Transfer the onion to a small bowl and set aside.

2. Meanwhile, place the diced potatoes in a large saucepan, cover with ½ inch water, add 1 teaspoon salt, and place over high heat. As soon as the water begins to boil, after about 6 minutes, drain the potatoes thoroughly in a colander.

3. Heat the butter and remaining 1½ tablespoons oil in the now-empty skillet over medium-high heat until the butter foams. Add the potatoes and shake the skillet to evenly distribute the potatoes in a single layer; make sure that one side of each piece is touching the surface of the skillet. Cook without stirring until one side of the potatoes is golden brown, 4 to 5 minutes, then carefully turn the potatoes with a wooden or heatproof plastic spatula. Spread the potatoes in a single layer in the skillet again and repeat the process until the potatoes are tender and browned on most sides, turning three or four times, 10 to 15 minutes longer. Add the onions, paprika, ¼ teaspoon salt, and pepper to taste; stir to blend and serve immediately.

➤ VARIATIONS

Spicy Home Fries

Follow the recipe for Diner-Style Home Fries, adding a pinch of two of cayenne pepper to potatoes along with paprika.

Home Fries with Bell Pepper and Cumin

Follow the recipe for Diner-Style Home Fries, cooking 1 finely chopped red or green bell pepper with the onion. Remove the pepper with onion and add both back to the pan along with the paprika and 1 teaspoon ground cumin.

HASH BROWNS

FOR BREAKFAST, MANY PEOPLE LIKE HOME fries—sautéed chunks of potato that retain their shape and individuality when cooked. Others prefer hash browns, which are thin, crisply sautéed potato cakes made with grated or chopped potatoes, raw or precooked. Unlike other potato cakes, hash browns do not contain eggs. The starch from the grated or finely chopped potatoes provides the binder needed to hold the cake together. With just salt and pepper added for seasoning, the focus remains on the potato flavor.

We were pretty sure that high-starch potatoes would be necessary for this recipe but decided to test low-starch red potatoes and medium-starch Yukon Golds as well as high-starch russets just to make sure. As expected, we found that the high-starch russets yielded the best overall results. They adhered well, browned beautifully, and had the most pronounced potato flavor.

Our next challenge was to decide between raw and precooked potatoes. Precooked potatoes tasted good, but when cut into chunks they did not stay together in a cohesive cake, and when grated they needed to be pressed very hard to form a cake. Unfortunately, this meant they ended up having the mouthfeel of fried mashed potatoes. Although this is an acceptable alternative if you have leftover cooked potatoes, we preferred using raw, grated potatoes. We also liked the more textured interior, the pronounced potato taste, and the way the raw shreds of potatoes formed an attractive, deeply browned crust.

Choosing the best method for cutting the potatoes was easy. Grating on the large-hole side of a box grater or with the shredding disk on a food processor yielded hash browns that formed a coherent cake when cooked. Chopped potatoes, even when finely chopped, did not hold together as well.

We found that cooking hash browns with butter provided good color and a very rich flavor. We tested bacon fat (figuring that many cooks might have some in the kitchen at breakfast time) and were disappointed. The color was a bit anemic and the potato flavor was lacking. Vegetable oil could not produce the same rich golden brown color that butter did, and the flavor was lacking. Butter is clearly the best choice.

Hash browns can be made into one or more individual servings or one large portion that can be cut into wedges. No matter how you choose to present the hash browns, make sure you serve them steaming hot.

Hash Browns
SERVES 4

To keep the potatoes from turning brown, grate them just before cooking. This recipe cooks the potatoes in one large cake. For individual servings, simply divide the raw grated potatoes into four equal-sized patties and reduce the cooking time to 5 minutes per side. To vary flavor, add 2 tablespoons grated onion, 1 to 2 tablespoons of an herb of your choice, or roasted garlic to taste to the raw grated potatoes. You can also garnish the cooked hash browns with snipped chives or scallion tops just before serving.

I   pound high-starch potatoes, such as russets, peeled, washed, dried, grated coarse, and squeezed dry in kitchen towel (I ½ cups loosely packed grated potatoes)

¼   teaspoon salt
     Ground black pepper

I   tablespoon butter

1. Toss the fully dried grated potatoes with the salt and pepper to taste in a medium bowl.

2. Heat half the butter in a 10-inch skillet over medium-high heat until it just starts to brown, then scatter the potatoes evenly over the entire pan bottom. Using a wide spatula, firmly press the potatoes to flatten; reduce the heat to medium and continue cooking until dark golden brown and crisp, 7 to 8 minutes.

3. Invert the hash browns, browned-side up, onto a large plate; add the remaining butter to the pan. Once the butter has melted, slide the hash browns back into the pan. Continue to cook over medium heat until the remaining side is dark golden brown and crisp, 5 to 6 minutes longer.

4. Slide the hash browns onto a plate or cutting board, cut into wedges, and serve immediately.

13

COOKIES, BROWNIES, AND BARS

MAKING COOKIES, BROWNIES, AND BARS is America's favorite kind of baking project. Not only are the results usually quite good, but the time, effort, and skills required are usually minimal. Ingredient lists draw heavily on pantry staples as well as refrigerated items (like butter and eggs) that can be found in most reasonably stocked kitchens.

Most cookie doughs are prepared in the same fashion. The butter is creamed with the sugar until light and creamy. The eggs and other liquids (vanilla or other extracts) are added. Finally, the flour and other dry ingredients, which have been sifted or stirred together, are added.

This process sounds easy (and it is), but there is some important science going on here. The butter must be properly creamed to incorporate the right amount of air into the fat. In our tests, we've consistently found that cookies made with creamed butter bake higher and have a lighter texture than those made with butter that is not creamed. (Brownies are meant to be dense and fudgy, so melted butter is fine in this case.) We also found that creaming the butter with sugar adds more air than beating the butter alone. That's because the sharp edges of the sugar crystals physically aerate the butter by cutting small air pockets into the fat.

In most cases, the first step is to soften the butter. Chilled butter (at 35 degrees, the temperature of most refrigerators) is too cold to combine with other ingredients. We found that cookies made with cold butter are often flat because not enough air is whipped into the butter during creaming. Ideally, an hour or two before you want to make cookies, remove the butter from the refrigerator and let it warm to about 65 degrees. Butter starts to melt at 68 degrees, so the stick should still be a bit firm when pressed.

If you have forgotten to soften the butter, don't use the microwave to bring it up to room temperature. The microwave will melt the butter in places. Instead, we found it best to cut the butter into very small bits so they will warm up quickly. By the time you have preheated the oven and assembled and measured the remaining ingredients, the butter should be close to 65 degrees.

A standing mixer (see page 237 for information on our tests of specific brands) produces the best results when creaming butter and sugar, although a hand-held mixer will often suffice. Once the butter and sugar have been creamed, most recipes call for the addition of eggs and vanilla or other liquids. Because cold eggs have a tendency to curdle the batter, it's best to make sure the eggs are at room temperature before being added to the mix. (Eggs can be brought to room temperature by letting them sit out on the counter for an hour or two or by placing them in a bowl of hot tap water for just five minutes.) At this point, the dry ingredients can be stirred into the batter. Although many recipes call for combining the ingredients by hand at this stage, we found it is perfectly fine to use an electric mixer if the speed is set to low.

In many old-fashioned recipes, the flour, leavener, and salt are sifted together before being added to the batter. This was necessary when flour was often lumpy straight from the bag. Because modern flour is presifted, however, we find this step to be unnecessary when making cookies. (Cakes are a different matter.) We simply mix the dry ingredients together in a bowl (a whisk does this well) to make sure that the leavener and salt will be evenly distributed in the batter. When making cookies there are two dry ingredients that we like to sift. Cocoa powder and confectioners' sugar often have small lumps. We find that sifting breaks up these lumps and does an excellent job of helping the cocoa and powdered sugar to mix with the other dry ingredients.

The final step in the dough-making process is to add solid ingredients such as chocolate chips and nuts. These can be stirred in by hand or with a standing mixer. If using the mixer, keep the speed low and beat just long enough (five seconds should be enough time) to incorporate the solid ingredients evenly into the dough.

Once the dough is finished, it can be shaped (or not) in a number of ways to change the appearance or texture of the baked cookies. (No matter how the dough is shaped, you can inhibit spreading in the oven—and thus prevent the cookies from becoming too thin—by chilling the dough in the refrigerator for at least one hour.)

The quickest way to get the dough into the oven is to drop it from a spoon directly onto a cookie sheet. Because the pieces of dough are not round, they spread unevenly in the oven. The result is cookies with thin, crisp edges and thicker centers.

For molded or shaped cookies, each piece of dough is rolled into a ball or otherwise manipulated by hand before being placed on a cookie sheet. When rolled into a ball, the dough is often also rolled in sugar before being baked. Shaping the dough into a ball promotes even spreading and thickness in the baked cookies.

The third option is rolling and cutting. This method is used to guarantee a thin, crisp cookie suitable for decorating. Rolled-and-cut cookies have an even thickness from edge to edge and usually snap rather than bend.

Whether dropping the cookies or shaping them, measuring the batter will ensure that all of the cookies will be the same size and will bake at the same rate. And be sure to leave enough room between pieces of dough to allow the cookies to spread in the oven without touching. Two inches is usually a safe distance.

Once cookies are in the oven, we find it best to reverse the top and bottom sheets and also rotate each sheet from back to front at the halfway point of the baking time to promote even baking. If you like your cookies soft and chewy, underbake them slightly and allow the cookies to firm up on the baking sheets for several minutes before transferring them to a cooling rack.

When making second and third batches, do not place dough directly onto hot cookie sheets. This causes excess spreading and uneven baking because it will probably take you a few minutes to get all the dough on the sheet.

Most cookies taste best the day they are made. That said, most cookies can also be stored with only minimal loss in freshness. Soft, chewy cookies may dry out a bit and harden after a few days, but they will retain their flavor.

If you want to keep cookies for several days, we suggest storing them in an airtight container at room temperature. In our testing, we found that you can restore just-baked freshness to chewy cookies by wrapping a single cookie in a sheet of paper towel and microwaving it until soft, 15 to 25 seconds. Cool microwaved cookies before serving. This technique works best with oversized cookies like peanut butter

and oatmeal that should be chewy and a bit soft. Do not try this with cookies that should be crisp.

CRISP CHOCOLATE CHIP COOKIES

RICH AND BUTTERY, WITH SOFT, TENDER cores and crispy edges, Toll House cookies are the American cookie jar standard. As such, they serve as the springboard for all other versions of the chocolate chip cookie. The two most popular variations, thick and chewy and thin and crispy, embody the Toll House cookie's textural extremes. Given the popularity of chocolate chip cookies in America (and the number of partisans for each style), we decided to develop recipes for cookies at either end of the textural spectrum. We would tackle thin and crispy first, followed by thick and chewy.

We could see the thin, crisp cookies clearly. They would be very flat, almost praline in appearance, and would pack a big crunch without either breaking teeth or shattering into a million pieces when eaten. They'd have the simple, gratifying flavors of deeply caramelized sugar and rich butter, along with agreeable amounts of salt and vanilla. The chips—always tender and super chocolaty—would not overwhelm but leave plenty of room for enjoyment of the surrounding cookie. Finally, these cookies would be resilient enough for pantry storage and worthy of five consecutive appearances in a school lunchbox.

To get our bearings, we first surveyed a handful of recipes for thin and crispy chocolate chip cookies, taking inventory of the ingredient lists and ratios. We were hoping to find the key to what might make these cookies thinner and crispier than the classic Toll House. Our collection of test recipes featured the same basic ingredients—butter, flour, sugar, flavorings, and chocolate chips—but widely varying ratios and yields. As a result, the cookies were all quite different when baked. While all of the cookies tasted good, tasters were dissatisfied with the various textures, which they found too brittle, too crumbly, too dense, or too greasy. Believe it or not, we were pleased with the mixed reactions. The ingredients we had to work with held promise; we just needed to understand the role of each one and tweak the proportions to arrive at a cookie with the texture we wanted.

Whether chewy or crispy, nearly all chocolate chip cookies contain a mixture of granulated and brown sugars. Aside from contributing sweetness, sugar also affects the texture, flavor, and color of the cookies. Doughs high in granulated sugar yield crispy cookies. As the cookies cool, the sugar crystallizes and the cookies harden. Brown sugar is quite different from granulated. It contains 35 percent more moisture and is also more hygroscopic (that is, it more readily absorbs moisture from the atmosphere). Consequently, cookies made with brown sugar come out of the oven tender and pliable and often soften further as they stand. These characteristics were the opposite of what we were looking for. Nevertheless, we knew the recipe had to include some brown sugar, because it alone is responsible for the irresistible butterscotch flavor we associate with chocolate chip cookies.

With this understanding, we went on to test various proportions of sugar. Too much granulated sugar produced cookies with no butterscotch flavor. Too much brown sugar produced cookies that were delicious but too soft. Desperate to retain the flavor of the brown sugar, we shifted from dark brown to light brown. Light brown sugar, we knew, had the potential to crisp the cookies because it contains half the molasses that dark brown sugar does and, therefore, less moisture. But we were skeptical because its flavor is weaker. We needn't have worried; the cookies were much improved, producing a flavor that fully satisfied tasters. After a little more tinkering, we settled on ⅓ cup light brown sugar and ½ cup granulated sugar, yielding cookies with a notable butterscotch flavor and sufficient crunch.

Satisfied with the crispness of the cookies, we turned our attention to their thickness. Throughout earlier testing, we hadn't been totally happy with the cookies' "spread" in the oven—they never became thin enough to achieve the praline-like look we were after. This was important not just for appearance's sake but because we had noticed that the flatter the cookies were, the more delicate and tender they became; we wanted them crisp, without being tough.

After some research, we returned to the kitchen

armed with the understanding that a cookie's spread is determined largely by the type, treatment, and melting properties of fat in the dough. Butter, which is key in this recipe, has both a low melting point and outstanding flavor. Initial test recipes advised creaming butter and sugar, but we noticed that cookies made with this technique came out of the oven with a slight lift. We were certain that creaming was the culprit.

When butter and sugar are creamed, rigid sugar crystals cut into the butterfat and create air cells. As the remaining ingredients are incorporated into the airy mixture, the air cells get locked up in the dough and capture moisture from the butter (and other ingredients) as it vaporizes in the oven. The cells expand, and the cookies rise. Our other option, melting the butter, was much more successful. Because melted butter, unlike creamed, does not accommodate air cells, the moisture from various ingredients has nowhere to go except out. Working our way down from 12 tablespoons, we found that the cookies spread evenly and effortlessly at 8 tablespoons (one stick) of melted butter. To get them thinner still, we added a couple tablespoons of milk, working on a tip from Shirley Corriher, author of *Cookwise* (Morrow, 1997). As Corriher explains, adding a small amount of liquid to a low-moisture dough thins the dough and enhances its spread. The cookies were flatter than pancakes.

Having spent all of our time thus far perfecting the cookies' texture and spread, we were surprised to notice that they were looking slightly pallid and dull. The light brown sugar we had introduced to the recipe was the problem (it has less browning power than dark brown sugar). Knowing that corn syrup browns at a lower temperature than sugar, we tried adding a few tablespoons. As it happened, the corn syrup made the surface of the cookies shiny and crackly. Despite their new spiffy, dressed-up look, though, they remained a little on the pale side. We rectified the situation by adding a bit of baking soda, which enhances browning reactions in doughs. With only a few tests at various amounts, the cookies went from washed out to a beautiful deep golden brown.

Finally, after a few last-minute adjustments to the amount of salt and vanilla, we spooned a full recipe of the dough onto two parchment-lined baking sheets and tested baking times and temperatures. Much to our disappointment, these cookies were slightly chewy, because they did not spread properly. After a few batches, we found that these cookies, like Greta Garbo, wanted to be alone, baked one sheet at a time. In 12 uninterrupted minutes at 375 degrees, they spread, flattened, caramelized, and came out to cool into thin, crispy, and delicious chocolate chip cookies.

Now we just had to find out if these cookies had staying power. We stored a batch of the finished cookies in an airtight container for a week to test their longevity. After the wait, tasters gathered to give them a final critique. The cookies were still a hit, as crisp and flavorful as they had been on day one. In fact, some commented that the crunch had improved with time.

Thin, Crispy Chocolate Chip Cookies

MAKES ABOUT 4 DOZEN 2-INCH COOKIES

The dough, en masse or shaped into balls and wrapped well, can be refrigerated up to 2 days or frozen up to 1 month. Be sure to bring it to room temperature before baking.

1½	cups (7½ ounces) unbleached all-purpose flour
¾	teaspoon baking soda
¼	teaspoon salt
8	tablespoons (1 stick) unsalted butter, melted and cooled
½	cup (3½ ounces) granulated sugar
⅓	cup packed (2¾ ounces) light brown sugar
3	tablespoons light corn syrup
1	large egg yolk
2	tablespoons milk
1	tablespoon vanilla extract
¾	cup (4½ ounces) semisweet chocolate chips

1. Adjust an oven rack to the middle position and heat the oven to 375 degrees. Line two baking sheets with parchment paper.

2. Whisk the flour, baking soda, and salt in a medium bowl until thoroughly combined; set aside.

3. In the bowl of a standing mixer fitted with the paddle attachment, beat the melted butter, granulated sugar, light brown sugar, and corn syrup at low speed until thoroughly blended, about 1 minute. Add the yolk, milk, and vanilla; mix until fully incorporated and smooth, about 1 minute, scraping the bottom and sides of the bowl with a rubber spatula as necessary. With the mixer running on low speed, slowly add the dry ingredients and mix until just combined. Do not overbeat. Add chips and mix on low speed until distributed evenly throughout the batter, about 5 seconds.

4. Leaving about 2 inches between each ball, scoop the dough onto the parchment-lined baking sheets with a 1¼-inch (1 tablespoon capacity) ice cream scoop. Bake, one sheet at a time, until the cookies are deep golden brown and flat, about 12 minutes.

5. Cool the cookies on the baking sheet for 3 minutes. Using a wide metal spatula, transfer the cookies to a wire rack and let sit until crisped and cooled to room temperature.

CHEWY CHOCOLATE CHIP COOKIES

AN ATTRACTIVE VARIATION ON THE TRADITIONAL chocolate chip cookie that some bake shops and cookie stores have recently made their reputations on—not to mention a lot of money—is the over-sized cookie. Unlike the traditional cookies made at home, these cookies are thick right from the edge to the center. They are also chewy, even a bit soft. Although we knew at the outset that molding the dough rather than dropping it into uneven blobs would be essential to achieving an even thickness, we didn't realize how much of a challenge making a truly chewy cookie would be.

We added more flour or ground oats (as some recipes suggest), which helped the cookies hold their shape and remain thick but also made the texture cakey and dry rather than chewy. When we tried liquid sweeteners, such as molasses and corn syrup, the dough spread too much in the oven and the cookies baked up thin.

At this point in our testing, we decided to experiment with the butter. Some chewy cookies start with melted rather than creamed butter. In its solid state, butter is an emulsion of butter and water. When butter is melted, the fat and water molecules separate. When melted butter is added to a dough, the proteins in the flour immediately grab onto the freed water molecules to form elastic sheets of gluten. The gluten makes a cookie chewy.

Our first attempt with melted butter was disappointing. The dough was very soft from all the liquid, and the cookies baked up greasy. Because the dough was having a hard time absorbing the liquid fat, we reduced the amount of butter from 16 to 12 tablespoons. We also reduced the number of eggs from 2 to 1 to stiffen the dough.

The cookies were chewy at this point, but they became somewhat tough as they cooled, and after a few hours they were hard. Fat acts as a tenderizer, and by reducing the amount of butter in the recipe we had limited its ability to keep the cookies soft. The only other source of fat is the egg. Since our dough was already soft enough and probably could not stand the addition of too much more liquid, we

decided to add another yolk (which contains all the fat) and leave out the white. This dough was still stiff enough to shape, and, when baked, the cookies were thick and chewy, and they remained that way when they cooled. Finally, we had the perfect recipe.

Thick and Chewy Chocolate Chip Cookies
MAKES ABOUT 18 LARGE COOKIES

These oversized cookies are chewy and thick, like many of the chocolate chip cookies sold in gourmet shops and cookie stores. They rely on melted butter and an extra yolk to keep their texture soft. These cookies are best served warm from the oven but will retain their texture even when cooled. To ensure the proper texture, cool the cookies on the cookie sheet. Oversized baking sheets allow you to get all the dough into the oven at one time. If you're using smaller baking sheets, put fewer cookies on each sheet and bake them

---

INGREDIENTS: Chocolate Chips

Chips have a lower cocoa butter content than chocolate bars, which keeps them from becoming too liquidy when baked. Often the cocoa butter is replaced by sugar, which is why we found many chocolate chips in our tasting of various brands to be quite sweet. We also found that the chips we liked best straight out of the bag tasted best in cookies. Nestlé, Guittard, Ghirardelli, and Tropical Source (a brand sold in natural foods stores) all received high marks. The chips that excelled were noted for a balance of bitterness, sweetness, and smoothness, and, as we discovered, these chips hold a few curious secrets.

In the spectrum of chocolates, chips are generally considered the least refined. The most refined would be a coating chocolate, also known as couverture, an extremely glossy chocolate usually found only in specialty candy-making shops and used by pastry chefs in various confections. Chocolate chips lack the fluidity necessary to meet the technical demands of the work turned out by a pastry chef, such as molds and truffles or even the seemingly simple chocolate-dipped strawberry. For example, a bowl of melted couverture will pour out smoothly, like cream, but a bowl of melted chips will slide sluggishly like glue. This high viscosity and low fluidity are what make the chip shape possible. When squeezed through a nozzle onto a moving belt in the factory, the chocolate quickly sets up into a pert morsel rather than collapsing into a small blob.

The chip that rated second in our tasting defied the unspoken standard for chip shape. Guittard grinds and blends its chip chocolate in the same way that it does its couverture. This helps to develop the flavor. The tradeoff, however, is that the chip is too fluid to hold the tightly pointed shape of a typical chip. Even so, some of our tasters liked the larger size and unorthodox disk-like shape of the chip in a thick, chewy cookie. However, this shape does not work well in a thin, crisp cookie.

The top-rated chip, Tropical Source, did showcase the typical pointed shape, but, like the Guittard chip, it had an unusually high cocoa butter content. The average chip is 27 percent cocoa butter, but both Guittard and Tropical Source chips contain 30 percent. Cocoa butter is renowned for providing the melt-in-your-mouth lusciousness of chocolate. Because it is costly, though, most chocolate chip manufacturers limit the cocoa butter content. Tasters typically had to agitate chips between their tongue and the roof of their mouth or even bite into some to break them down. Guittard and Tropical Source stood out because they melted more smoothly than the rest. Tropical Source worked well in both our thin and thick cookies.

Finally, what about the classic Nestlé Toll House Morsels? These chips taste good, but they are ultragooey when cooled, which makes them better suited to a thick, chewy cookie than a thin, crisp one.

in batches. See the illustrations below for tips on shaping these cookies.

2	cups plus 2 tablespoons (10½ ounces) unbleached all-purpose flour
½	teaspoon baking soda
½	teaspoon salt
12	tablespoons (1½ sticks) unsalted butter, melted and cooled
½	cup (3½ ounces) granulated sugar
1	cup packed (7 ounces) light or dark brown sugar
1	large egg plus 1 egg yolk
2	teaspoons vanilla extract
1–1½	cups (6 to 9 ounces) semisweet chocolate chips

1. Adjust the oven racks to the upper- and lower-middle positions and heat the oven to 325 degrees. Line two large baking sheets with parchment paper.

2. Whisk the flour, baking soda, and salt together in a medium bowl; set aside.

3. In the bowl of a standing mixer fitted with the paddle attachment, beat the melted butter, granulated sugar, and brown sugar at low speed until thoroughly blended, about 1 minute. Add the egg, yolk, and vanilla; mix until fully incorporated and smooth, about 1 minute, scraping the bottom and sides of the bowl with a rubber spatula as necessary. With the mixer running on low speed, slowly add the dry ingredients and mix until just combined, about 2 minutes. Do not overbeat. Add chips and mix on low speed until distributed evenly throughout the batter, about 5 seconds.

4. Roll a scant ¼ cup dough into a ball. Holding a dough ball in the fingertips of both hands, pull it into two equal halves. Rotate the halves 90 degrees and, with the two jagged surfaces facing up, join the halves together at their base, again forming a single ball, being careful not to smooth the dough's uneven surface. Place the formed dough onto the cookie sheet, leaving 2½ inches between each ball.

5. Bake, reversing the position of the baking sheets halfway through baking (from top to bottom and front to back), until the cookies are light golden brown and the outer edges start to harden yet the centers are still soft and puffy, 15 to 18 minutes. Cool the cookies on the sheets. When cooled, peel cookies from the parchment.

➤ VARIATIONS

Chocolate Chip Cookies with Coconut and Toasted Almonds

Follow the recipe for Thick and Chewy Chocolate Chip Cookies, adding 1½ cups sweetened dried coconut and 1 cup toasted sliced almonds along with chips.

Black and White Chocolate Chip Cookies with Pecans

Follow the recipe for Thick and Chewy Chocolate Chip Cookies, substituting ½ cup white chocolate chips for ½ cup of semisweet chips. Add 1 cup chopped pecans with chips.

SHAPING THICK CHOCOLATE CHIP COOKIES

1. Creating a jagged surface on each dough ball gives the finished cookies an attractive appearance. Start by rolling a scant ¼ cup of dough into a smooth ball.

2. Holding the dough ball in the fingertips of both hands, pull the dough apart into two equal halves.

3. Each half will have a jagged surface where it was ripped from the other. Rotate each piece 90 degrees so that the jagged surfaces face up.

4. Jam the halves back together into one ball so that the top surface remains jagged.

CHOCOLATE COOKIES

OBSESSIONS OFTEN BEGIN WITH CHANCE encounters, a wry, fetching smile glanced out of the corner of an eye or perhaps one's first taste of a homegrown tomato. One of our greatest obsessions, however, has been the first transcendent bite of the perfect chocolate cookie, still warm out of the oven. That first bite would reveal a center of hot fudge sauce, and the texture would call to mind chocolate bread pudding with a deep, complex chocolate flavor. This would be the sort of confection that creates intense focus while it is consumed, sights and sounds subordinate to taste, overloading the other senses to the point of dysfunction.

The problem is that we have, for years, been trying to perfect this cookie. We have created large, dense cookies that were rich and decadent, but the chocolate flavor was dull and overwhelming, and the texture was, well, on the dry side. We have also experimented with thin, crisp cookies (nice but not intense), chewy cookies (good but not showstoppers), and cakelike chocolate cookies, which tend to be dry and uninspiring. The test kitchen also made a half-dozen recipes from various cookbooks and discovered a world of difference in texture, flavor, and appearance, from soft mocha-colored disks to thick mounds of pure fudge. This panoply of outcomes gave us pause, since the ingredient lists seemed to have more in common than the cookies themselves.

Figuring out what makes a chocolate cookie tick was going to require weeks of testing and a great deal of detective work.

Our first step was to strip the recipes down to their basics to understand the fundamentals. A chocolate cookie is a mixture of melted chocolate, sugar, eggs, butter, flour, baking soda or powder, and salt. Vanilla, coffee, and nuts are extras.

The key issues were how to handle the butter and eggs. The butter can be melted or creamed, and the eggs can be beaten or just whisked into the batter. For the first test batch, we melted the butter and whipped the eggs. The results were good, but the cookies were a bit cakey and loose, without any chew. For the next batch we melted the butter and did not beat the eggs. These cookies were a bit dry and cakey. When we started creaming the butter and beating the eggs into it after creaming, we noticed an immediate improvement. However, we finally settled on a modified creaming method with minimal beating to produce moist cookies that were not cakey.

The next issue was one of proportions, that is, the ratio of flour to butter to eggs to sugar to chocolate. This was going to be crucial to the thickness of the cookie, its texture, and the degree to which the taste of chocolate would dominate. Looking over the recipes we had tested, we saw so many permutations that we felt like the British trying to crack the German secret code in World War II.

EQUIPMENT: Baking Sheets

Most baking sheets (also called cookie sheets) have the same basic design. They are a piece of metal that is usually slightly longer than it is wide. (A standard size is 16 inches long and 14 inches across.) Some are dark, some are light. Some have rims on all four sides. Others have rims on one or two sides but otherwise have flat edges. We tested 11 sheets in a variety of materials and came to some surprising conclusions.

First of all, shiny light-colored sheets do a better job of evenly browning the bottoms of cookies than dark sheets. Most of the dark sheets are nonstick, and we found that these pans tend to over-brown cookies. Shiny, silver sheets heat much more evenly, and if sticking is a concern we simply use parchment paper. Parchment paper also keeps the bottom of the cookies from overbrowning.

In our testing, we also came to prefer sheets with at least one rimless edge. This way we could slide a whole sheet of parchment paper onto a cooling rack without actually touching the hot paper. (When cooled, the cookies can be peeled away from the paper.) The open edge also makes it possible to slide cookies on a rack, rather than lifting them onto the rack and possibly dropping them. Our favorite cookie sheet is made of tinned steel and is manufactured by Kaiser. At just $7, it was also the cheapest sheet we tested.

A final note about lining baking sheets with parchment. Even when sticking is not an issue, we like to use parchment paper. It makes cleanup a snap, and we can reuse baking sheets for subsequent batches without having to wash them first. When parchment is essential, the recipes in this chapter call for it. Otherwise, use parchment at your discretion.

To organize the facts, we made a chart of the various ratios of eggs, sugar, chocolate, and butter to flour, with related comments on the taste, texture, and shape of each cookie we had tested. We quickly noted that the ratio of eggs and butter to flour was less important than the ratio of sugar and chocolate to flour. The driest cookie used less than ½ cup of sugar per cup of flour; the richest, wettest cookie used 3 cups. The cookie with the faintest chocolate flavor and a relatively firm, dry texture used only 2 ounces of chocolate per cup of flour, whereas other recipes used up to a pound of chocolate with only ½ cup of flour.

After many tests designed to balance sweetness and moisture, we settled on 1 cup of sugar and 8 ounces of chocolate to 1 cup of flour. Finally, we had a moist cookie with good chocolate flavor. Nonetheless, we thought the flavor and texture could be better, so we moved on to other ingredients.

We started the cookie with all white granulated sugar and then tested a mixture of brown sugar and granulated, which seemed to improve the flavor and added just a bit more moisture. We also tried corn syrup, which had little effect. A small amount of vanilla extract and instant coffee powder rounded out the flavors. Throughout the testing, we had been using all-purpose flour. We decided to try cake flour, but the resulting cookie was a bit too delicate. We also varied the quantity of flour throughout the testing process, starting at 3 cups and eventually working our way down to 2 cups. To create a thicker, more stable cookie, we tried replacing some of the butter with vegetable shortening (Crisco), but this created an unattractive, greasy-looking cookie with a pale white sheen. We thought that the choice of leavener might be important, so we tested baking powder against baking soda and found that the cookies with the powder were slightly thicker.

At this point our cookie was thick and very good, but still not the sort of thing that would reduce the average adult to tears of joy. The flavor remained a bit dull, and the texture was moist but monochromatic. We wondered if we could solve this problem by varying the type of chocolate. We found that unsweetened chocolate, an ingredient often called for in chocolate cookie recipes, added a bit of intensity to the flavor. Unfortunately, we also discovered an aggressive sour note in these cookies, even when the sugar level was adjusted for the bitterness of the chocolate. Semisweet and bittersweet chocolate turned out to be better choices owing to their rounder, less overwhelming flavors. These chocolates undergo more processing than unsweetened, and they also get other flavorings; this no doubt gives them a smoother, richer flavor overall. (For more information on types of chocolate, see page 316.)

Our hunt was almost over, but now we wondered if a bit of cocoa powder might add more depth of flavor to our cookie. One-half cup of Dutch-processed cocoa was substituted for the same amount of flour, and the chocolate flavor became smoother and deeper. (We also tried a batch of cookies made only with cocoa powder—no chocolate—and they were disappointing, having just a faint chocolate flavor.) At last, we had brought our fantasy to life: a double-chocolate cookie that was rich and soft, with an intense chocolatey center that could drive anyone to distraction.

Thick and Chewy Double-Chocolate Cookies

MAKES ABOUT 3½ DOZEN COOKIES

To melt the chocolate in a microwave, heat at 50 percent power for 2 minutes, stir, then continue heating at 50 percent power for 1 more minute. If not completely melted, heat an additional 30 to 45 seconds at 50 percent power. We recommend using a spring-loaded ice cream scoop to scoop the dough. Resist the urge to bake the cookies longer than indicated; they may appear underbaked at first but will firm up as they cool.

2	cups (10 ounces) unbleached all-purpose flour
½	cup Dutch-processed cocoa powder
2	teaspoons baking powder
1	teaspoon salt
16	ounces semisweet chocolate, chopped
4	large eggs
2	teaspoons vanilla extract
2	teaspoons instant coffee or espresso powder
10	tablespoons (1¼ sticks) unsalted butter, softened
1½	cups packed (10½ ounces) light brown sugar
½	cup (3½ ounces) granulated sugar

1. Sift together the flour, cocoa, baking powder, and salt in a medium bowl; set aside.

2. Melt the chocolate in a medium heatproof bowl set over a pan of almost-simmering water, stirring once or twice, until smooth; remove from the heat. Beat the eggs and vanilla lightly with a fork, sprinkle the coffee powder over to dissolve, and set aside.

3. In the bowl of a standing mixer fitted with the paddle attachment, beat the butter at medium speed until smooth and creamy, about 5 seconds. Beat in the sugars until combined, about 45 seconds; the mixture will look granular. Reduce the speed to low and gradually beat in the egg mixture until incorporated, about 45 seconds. Add the chocolate in a steady stream and beat until combined, about 40 seconds. Scrape the bottom and sides of the bowl with a rubber spatula. With the mixer at low speed, add the dry ingredients and mix until just combined. Do not overbeat. Cover with plastic wrap and let stand at room temperature until consistency is scoopable and fudgelike, about 30 minutes.

4. Meanwhile, adjust the oven racks to the upper-middle and lower-middle positions and heat the oven to 350 degrees. Line two baking sheets with parchment paper. Leaving about 1½ inches between each ball, scoop the dough onto the parchment-lined cookie sheets with a 1¾-inch ice cream scoop.

5. Bake, reversing the position of the baking sheets halfway through baking (from top to bottom and front to back), until the edges of the cookies have just begun to set but the centers are still very soft, about 10 minutes. Cool the cookies on the sheets about 10 minutes, slide the parchment with the cookies onto a wire rack, and cool to room temperature; remove with a wide metal spatula.

➤ VARIATION

Thick and Chewy Triple-Chocolate Cookies

If you like bursts of warm melted chocolate in your cookies, include chocolate chips in the batter.

Follow the recipe for Thick and Chew Double-Chocolate Cookies, using a wooden spoon to stir 12

INGREDIENTS: **Types of Chocolate**

There are many options when it comes to chocolate: unsweetened, bittersweet, semisweet, cocoa powder, and chips. The question is, how are they different?

Unsweetened chocolate, often called baking chocolate or chocolate liquor, is made from roasted cocoa beans and contains about 50 percent solids from the beans and 50 percent cocoa butter. Bittersweet and semisweet chocolates (also called dark chocolates) are made from unsweetened chocolate that is ground with sugar and then further refined. Since bittersweet and semisweet chocolates are about 50 percent sugar, they have less chocolate flavor than unsweetened, which has no added sugar. (Although individual brands may vary, bittersweet averages around 46 percent sugar by weight; semisweet is about 57 percent sugar.) The chocolate flavor they do have, however, is less bitter and more complex, features appreciated by many bakers.

Chocolate chips are made from chocolate with relatively little cocoa butter, about 30 percent or even less. (Dark chocolates, by comparison, must have at least 35 percent cocoa butter.) This is because the chips will not hold their shape with more fat. This lower percentage of cocoa butter makes for a less buttery flavor and a grainier texture.

Cocoa powder is made from unsweetened chocolate. Much of the fat is removed by pressing, leaving behind the solids. These leftover solids are then fluffed up and packaged. Dutch-processed cocoa is less acidic than regular cocoa, and many people feel that this results in a stronger, more interesting chocolate flavor.

Another factor that affects the quality of one brand of chocolate over another is the use of additives. Most processed dark chocolates include vanilla, lecithin (which makes chocolate smoother when poured), and other flavorings, often including soy. In addition, some manufacturers roast their beans for a shorter time on the theory that when the chocolate is baked by consumers it will undergo additional processing.

As for which type of semisweet chocolate is best for a chocolate cookie, we tested four major brands head to head: Nestlé, Baker's, Ghirardelli, and Callebaut. The Baker's turned out a gritty cookie that received low marks, Nestlé had an off, somewhat fruity taste, and the Ghirardelli had a muted but pure chocolate flavor that was quite pleasant. But the Callebaut was our favorite, with a big chocolate flavor that was clean, direct, and full of punch.

---

ounces (about 2 cups) of semisweet chocolate chips into the batter after the dry ingredients are incorporated. The addition of the chips will slightly increase the yield of the cookies.

OATMEAL COOKIES

WHEN WE DECIDED TO DEVELOP A RECIPE for oatmeal cookies, we also decided that we wanted an oversized cookie that was chewy and moist. Most oatmeal cookies seem dry to us, and the flavor of the oats weak. Many recipes don't call for enough oats, and spices often overwhelm the flavor of the oats that are there.

The flavor issues were easily solved with some testing. We experimented with various amounts of oats and found that to establish a real oat flavor we needed a ratio of 2 cups oats to 1 cup flour—far more oats than in most recipes.

To keep the focus on the oats, we decided to eliminate the cinnamon, a common ingredient in these cookies, because it overpowered the oats. We wanted some spice, however, and chose nutmeg, which has a cleaner, subtler flavor that we liked with oats.

Our cookies tasted good at this point, but we needed to work on the texture. In our tests, we found that a high proportion of butter to flour helped to keep the cookies moist. We settled on 2 parts butter (1 cup) to 3 parts flour (1½ cups).

We found that shaping the dough into 2-inch balls (rather than dropping it by the meager rounded tablespoon called for in most recipes) helped keep the cookies more moist and chewy, especially in the center, which remains a bit underbaked in an oversized cookie. Smaller cookies are considerably drier and more cakelike, something we did not want in an oatmeal cookie.

Our final tests involved the sugar. We experimented with various amounts and found that adding a full cup each of both brown and granulated sugar delivered the best results, a cookie that was especially moist and rich. Sugar makes baked goods more moist and tender because it helps them hold onto water during baking process. In addition, sugar encourages exterior browning, which promotes crispness.

Big and Chewy Oatmeal-Raisin Cookies

MAKES ABOUT 18 LARGE COOKIES

If you prefer a less sweet cookie, you can reduce the white sugar by one-quarter cup, but you will lose some crispness. Do not overbake these cookies. The edges should be brown, but the rest of the cookie should be very light in color. Parchment paper makes for easy cookie removal and cleanup, but it is not a necessity. If you don't use parchment, cool the cookies on the baking sheet for two minutes before transferring them to a cooling rack.

1½	cups (7½ ounces) unbleached all-purpose flour
½	teaspoon salt
½	teaspoon baking powder
¼	teaspoon freshly grated nutmeg
½	pound (2 sticks) unsalted butter, softened
1	cup packed (7 ounces) light brown sugar
1	cup (7 ounces) granulated sugar
2	large eggs
3	cups old-fashioned rolled oats
1½	cups raisins (optional)

1. Adjust the oven racks to the low and middle positions, and heat the oven to 350 degrees. Line two large baking sheets with parchment paper.

2. Whisk the flour, salt, baking powder, and nutmeg together in a medium bowl; set aside.

3. In the bowl of a standing mixer fitted with the paddle attachment, beat the butter at medium speed until creamy, about 1 minute. Add the sugars and beat until fluffy, about 3 minutes. Beat in the eggs one at a time. With the mixer running on low speed, slowly add the dry ingredients and mix until just combined.

4. Stir in the oats and raisins, if using.

5. Working with a generous 2 tablespoons of dough each time, roll the dough into 2-inch balls. Place the balls on the parchment-lined cookie sheets, leaving at least 2 inches between balls.

6. Bake, reversing the position of the baking sheets halfway through baking (from top to bottom and front to back), until the edges of the cookies turn golden brown, 22 to 25 minutes. Slide the cookies, on the parchment, to a cooling rack. Let cool at least 30 minutes before peeling the cookies from the parchment.

➤ VARIATIONS

Date Oatmeal Cookies

Follow the recipe for Big and Chewy Oatmeal Cookies, substituting 1½ cups chopped dates for the raisins.

Ginger Oatmeal Cookies

Follow the recipe for Big and Chewy Oatmeal Cookies, adding ¾ teaspoon ground ginger to the flour and other dry ingredients and omitting the raisins.

Chocolate Chip Oatmeal Cookies

Follow the recipe for Big and Chewy Oatmeal Cookies, omitting the nutmeg and substituting 1½ cups semisweet chocolate chips for the raisins.

Nut Oatmeal Cookies

Follow the recipe for Big and Chewy Oatmeal Cookies, decreasing the flour to 1⅓ cups and adding ¼ cup ground almonds and 1 cup chopped walnut pieces along with the oats. (The almonds can be ground in a food processor or blender.) Omit the raisins.

Orange and Almond Oatmeal Cookies

Follow the recipe for Big and Chewy Oatmeal Cookies, omitting the raisins and adding 2 tablespoons minced orange zest and 1 cup toasted chopped almonds (toast the nuts in 350-degree oven for 5 minutes) along with the oats.

MOLASSES SPICE COOKIES

MOLASSES COOKIES ARE THE COOKIE pariahs, the dowdy group in the cookie crowd—permanently out of style and hopelessly old-fashioned. But we've come to appreciate good molasses cookies for their honesty and simplicity. On the outside, their cracks and crinkles give them a humble, charming countenance. Inside, an uncommonly moist, soft yet chewy, tooth-sinking texture is half the appeal; the other is a warm, tingling spiciness paired with the dark, bittersweet flavor of molasses. Unfortunately, molasses spice cookies are often miserable specimens, no more than flat, tasteless cardboard rounds of gingerbread. They can be dry and cakey without the requisite chew; others are timidly flavored with molasses and are either recklessly or vacantly spiced.

We started by testing a half-dozen different recipes, using a variety of fats, flours, and mixing methods. Although these early experiments yielded vastly different cookies in terms of flavor and appearance, a few things were clear. The full, rich flavor of butter was in, flat-tasting shortening was out. Flour required no fussing over—unbleached all-purpose flour was perfectly suited to the task. The mixing technique was a standard one: Cream the butter and sugar, add any eggs, then the molasses, and, finally, stir in the dry ingredients.

Molasses is at the core of these cookies. Enough must be used to give them a dark, smoky, bittersweet flavor, but we found that a surfeit of molasses creates a sticky, unworkable dough. For the amount of butter (12 tablespoons) and flour (2½ cups) we were using, the molasses ceiling was ½ cup. We had been using mild (also called light) molasses up to this point, but in an attempt to boost flavor, we baked batches with dark and blackstrap molasses. Cookies made with dark molasses were filled with bold flavor and rich color, and they garnered much praise. Those made with blackstrap molasses had a few fans, but, for most of us, the wicked brew overtook the spices and embittered the cookies.

Molasses alone cannot supply the cookies with enough sweetness, so either granulated or brown sugar would be required. Dark brown sugar (we chose dark over light for its stronger molasses flavor) yielded cookies that were surprisingly puffy and cakey, and they spread too little on the baking sheet. Granulated sugar yielded cookies that were pale both in color and flavor. A combination of granulated and brown sugars was the ticket. The brown sugar fortified the molasses flavor while the granulated sugar, a spreading agent, allowed the cookies to attain a good, even thickness in the oven without much puff. After some fiddling, we found equal amounts of brown and granulated sugar to be ideal.

Most molasses cookie recipes call for no more than a single egg to bind things together. The white of a whole egg—harmless as it may seem—made the dough sticky. The difference was subtle, but the white also caused the baked cookie to have a slightly cake-like crumb and a firmer, drier feel than we cared for. A lone yolk was all the cookies needed.

Molasses is a mildly acidic ingredient, so baking soda, an alkali that reacts with the acidity of the molasses to provide lift, is the logical leavener for these cookies. In our testing, cookies with too little baking soda were flat and failed to develop those attractive fault lines. The proper amount of baking soda (1 teaspoon) gave the cookies nice height—a pleasure to sink your teeth into—and a winsome appearance, with large, meandering fissures.

It was time to refine the flavor of the cookies. A teaspoon of vanilla extract complemented generous amounts of sharp, spicy ground ginger and warm, soothing cinnamon. Cloves, rich and fragrant, and allspice, sweet and mysterious, were added, but in more judicious quantities. Nutmeg was pedestrian and had little to offer. Finely and freshly ground black pepper, however, added some intrigue—a soupçon of heat against the deep, bittersweet flavor of the molasses.

To shape the molasses cookies, we rolled generous heaping tablespoons of dough into balls, coating them with granulated sugar, which, after baking, gave the cookies a frosted sparkle. Out of a 375-degree oven, the cookies were perfect—the edges were slightly crisped and the interiors soft and chewy. We determined that the cookies must be baked one sheet at a time since cookies baked on the lower rack inevitably baked up puffed and smooth rather than craggy and cracked.

Most important, we noted that the cookies must come out of the oven when they appear substantially underdone, otherwise their soft, moist, chewy texture will harden upon cooling. Whisk them out when the edges are hardly set, the centers are still soft and puffy, and the dough looks shiny and raw between the cracks. The cookies finish baking with residual heat, so don't shortchange them of a five-minute repose on the baking sheet before removal to the cooling rack.

While the spicy aroma lingers in the kitchen, be the first to bite into a warm, soft, chewy molasses spice cookie. These cookies may be out of style, but they are definitely not out of favor.

Molasses-Spice Cookies
MAKES ABOUT 22 COOKIES

For best flavor, make sure that your spices are fresh. Light or mild molasses gives the cookies a milder flavor; for a stronger flavor, use dark molasses. (See page 92 for more information about molasses.) Either way, measure molasses in a liquid measure. If you find that the dough sticks to your palms as you shape the balls, moisten your hands occasionally in a bowl filled with cold tap water and shake off the excess. Bake the cookies one sheet at a time; if baked two at a time, the cookies started on the bottom rack won't develop the attractive cracks. Remove the cookies from the oven when they still look slightly raw and underbaked. If you plan to glaze the cookies (see recipes on page 320), save the parchment paper that they were baked on.

⅓	cup (about 2½ ounces) granulated sugar, plus ½ cup for dipping
2¼	cups (11¼ ounces) unbleached all-purpose flour
1	teaspoon baking soda
1½	teaspoons ground cinnamon
1½	teaspoons ground ginger
½	teaspoon ground cloves
¼	teaspoon ground allspice
¼	teaspoon finely ground black pepper
¼	teaspoon salt
12	tablespoons (1½ sticks) unsalted butter, softened
⅓	cup packed (2¾ ounces) dark brown sugar
1	large egg yolk
1	teaspoon vanilla extract
½	cup (about 6 ounces) light or dark molasses

1. Adjust an oven rack to the middle position and heat the oven to 375 degrees. Line two baking sheets with parchment paper. Place ½ cup sugar for dipping in a 8- or 9-inch cake pan.

2. Whisk the flour, baking soda, spices, and salt in a medium bowl until thoroughly combined; set aside.

3. In a standing mixer fitted with the paddle attachment, beat the butter with brown and granulated sugars at medium-high speed until light and fluffy, about 3 minutes. Reduce the speed to medium-low and add the yolk and vanilla; increase the

GLAZING COOKIES

When completely cool, return the cookies to the parchment-lined baking sheets. Dip a spoon into the glaze and then move the spoon over the cookies so that glaze drizzles down onto them.

speed to medium and beat until incorporated, about 20 seconds. Reduce the speed to medium-low and add the molasses; beat until fully incorporated, about 20 seconds, scraping the bottom and sides of the bowl once with a rubber spatula. Reduce the speed to the lowest setting; add the flour mixture and beat until just incorporated, about 30 seconds, scraping the bowl down once. Give the dough a final stir by hand to ensure that no pockets of flour remain at the bottom. The dough will be soft.

4. Using a tablespoon measure, scoop a heaping tablespoon of dough and roll it between your palms into a 1¼- to 1½-inch ball; drop the ball into the cake pan with the sugar and repeat to form about 4 balls. Toss the balls in sugar to coat and set on a prepared baking sheet, spacing them about 2 inches apart. Repeat with the remaining dough.

5. Bake, one sheet at a time and reversing the position of the baking sheet halfway through baking (from front to back), until the cookies are browned, still puffy, and the edges have begun to set, but the centers are still soft (the cookies will look raw between the cracks and seem underdone), about 11 minutes. Do not overbake.

6. Cool the cookies on the baking sheet for 5 minutes, then use a wide metal spatula to transfer the cookies to a wire rack; cool the cookies to room temperature and serve.

➤ VARIATIONS

Molasses Spice Cookies with Dark Rum Glaze

For the glaze, start by adding the smaller amount of rum; if the glaze is too thick to drizzle, whisk in up to an additional ½ tablespoon rum.

Follow the recipe for Molasses-Spice Cookies. When completely cool, return the cookies to the cooled parchment-lined baking sheets. Whisk 1 cup confectioners' sugar (about 4 ounces) and 2½ to 3 tablespoons dark rum in a medium bowl until smooth. Drizzle the glaze over the cookies with a soup spoon (see the illustration at left), dipping the spoon into the glaze as necessary. Transfer the cookies to a wire rack and allow the glaze to dry, 10 to 15 minutes.

Molasses Spice Cookies with Orange Essence

The orange zest in the sugar coating causes the sugar to become sticky and take on a light orange hue, giving the baked cookies a unique frosty look.

In the workbowl of a food processor, process ⅔ cup granulated sugar and 2 teaspoons grated orange zest until pale orange, about 10 seconds; transfer the sugar to an 8- or 9-inch cake pan and set aside. Follow the recipe for Molasses-Spice cookies, adding 1 teaspoon grated orange zest to the butter and sugar along with the molasses and substituting the orange sugar for granulated sugar when coating the dough balls in step 4.

HERMITS

HERMITS ARE A COOKIE CERTAINLY WORTHY of their eccentric name. Depending on who you ask, they can be a bar or drop cookie; soft and spongy or dry and biscuit-like; packed with dried fruit and nuts or free of both; and heavily seasoned with warm spices like ginger, cloves, and nutmeg or flavored only with molasses. Whatever the particular recipe, most sources trace the hermit's origin to colonial New England. The name is supposedly derived from the fact that the cookies were better after several days hidden away, which allowed for the flavors to blend and intensify.

After a taste test that included cookies we baked in-house and commercially produced hermits from local and national bakeries, tasters agreed that an ideal hermit should have a texture in between cake and brownie—that is, it should be soft, moist, and dense. We decided that hermits should be studded with raisins and taste predominantly of molasses, but with warm spices lingering in the background. And tasters favored thick-sliced biscotti-like cookies over both bar and drop cookies because they had more crust than bar cookies and a softer crumb than either bar or drop cookies.

From the outset, we knew that attaining the right texture would be tricky. Most hermit recipes we tried relied on two eggs as well as some baking soda and baking powder for their rise. The result is a puffy cookie that was dry and too cakey for our taste. We found that omitting baking powder from the batter limited the cookies' spread and height, but they were still too loose-crumbed and fluffy. Leaving out one of the two eggs made them too dense, but we realized we were on the right track. In the next batch, we omitted the egg white of one of the eggs, and the resulting cookies were everything we wanted—soft and rich, but with a slightly cakey crumb. The cakey crumb is the secret to their longevity. We enjoyed these cookies up to a week after baking them. And, as the story of how they got their name suggests, the flavors were better after a couple of days of storage.

For both sweetening and flavor, hermits depend on molasses. We tried light, dark, and blackstrap molasses and found that most tasters favored mild, although some liked the stronger-flavored dark molasses. Molasses alone was not enough to fully sweeten the cookies, so we included light brown sugar. Dark brown pushed the bittersweet flavor of the molasses over the edge, while granulated white sugar seemed a bit dull.

A healthy amount of raisins also helped sweeten the cookies and rounded out the flavors. Raisins also lent the cookies a pleasing toothsome quality that contrasted nicely with the crisp crust and soft crumb.

Since the hermit is a not-very-distant relation of the spice cookie, we felt it appropriate to borrow the spice mixture from our favorite molasses-spice cookie (page 319) and revise it to best suit the hermits. We decided to keep the unlikely spice—black pepper—which contributes a kick that heightens the piquancy of the other spices. Tasters agreed that it significantly improved the flavor of our hermits.

Hermits

MAKES ABOUT 16 COOKIES

The dusting of confectioners' sugar is optional, but it does improve the cookies' appearance. It is important to wait until the cookies are completely cooled before dusting them, otherwise the sugar can melt and turn gummy. We like to keep hermits around during the holidays because they store well, and the flavors sit well with both eggnog and mulled cider. See page 92 for information that will help you choose between light and dark molasses.

2	cups (about 10 ounces) unbleached all-purpose flour
½	teaspoon baking soda
½	teaspoon ground cinnamon
½	teaspoon ground cloves
¼	teaspoon ground allspice
¼	teaspoon ground ginger
⅛	teaspoon finely ground black pepper
½	teaspoon salt
8	tablespoons (1 stick) unsalted butter, melted and cooled
½	cup packed (3½ ounces) light brown sugar
2	large eggs, 1 whole and 1 separated, white lightly beaten
½	cup (about 6 ounces) light or dark molasses
1½	cups raisins
2	tablespoons confectioners' sugar (optional)

1. Whisk the flour, baking soda, spices, and salt together in a medium bowl; set aside.

2. Whisk the melted butter and brown sugar together in another medium bowl until just combined. Add the whole egg, egg yolk, and molasses and whisk thoroughly. Using a rubber spatula, fold the dry ingredients into the molasses mixture until combined. Stir in the raisins. Cover the bowl with plastic wrap and refrigerate for at least 1 hour.

3. Adjust an oven rack to the middle position and heat the oven to 350 degrees. Line a baking sheet with parchment paper.

4. Using a rubber spatula, form the dough into

two logs on the prepared pan, as shown in illustration 1 below. Brush the logs with the beaten egg white.

5. Bake until the tops of the logs have browned and spring back when touched, 20 to 25 minutes. Set the pan on a cooling rack and cool for 15 minutes. Using two spatulas, transfer the logs to a cutting board, and follow the directions in illustration 2 below to slice. When the cookies have completely cooled, dust with confectioners' sugar if desired.

SHAPING HERMITS

1. Divide the dough in half and shape each half on a parchment-lined baking sheet into a log that measures 14 inches long, 2 inches across, and 2 inches high. The logs should be at least 4 inches apart because they will spread during baking.

2. Cool the baked logs (still on the pan) on a wire rack for 15 minutes. Using two spatulas, transfer the logs to a cutting board. With a sharp chef's knife or serrated bread knife, cut the logs crosswise into cookies about 2 inches thick

PECAN SANDIES

TAKE SHORTBREAD, A SCOTTISH COOKIE, and give it a dose of Americana—namely pecans and brown sugar—and it is transformed into a nutty, buttery cookie with a hint of caramel flavor. The texture: tender but crisp and sandy with a slow melt-in-your-mouth character. Call them "pecan sandies," after their noteworthy texture. Indeed, pecan sandies can be purchased in any grocery store cookie aisle, but for the richest, purest butter, pecan, and brown sugar flavors they are best—and easily—made at home.

Recipes for pecan sandies run the gamut. Sometimes called pecan or brown sugar pecan shortbread, pecan sandies are rich in butter like shortbread. And because a crisp, sandy texture—not a puffy or cakey crumb—is the goal, they do not contain chemical leaveners for lift (also like shortbread). We made cookies similar to simple sugar cookies, with pecans, that are dropped onto a baking sheet; we baked basic roll-and-cut cookies made with cake flour; we sampled cookies made with vegetable oil and a duo of ground nuts and chopped nuts; we sliced cookies from a refrigerator cookie log. We concluded quickly that cake flour is unnecessary. A tender cookie could be made with unbleached all-purpose flour, our kitchen standard. Oil does make for a sandy texture, but it falls pitifully short in flavor—the rich, sweet flavor of pure butter is paramount. Last, we learned that a dropped cookie doesn't have the neat, clean edges that pecan sandies should have. A rolled cookie or a refrigerator cookie (formed in a sliceable log) would be the way to create a perfect-looking cookie.

The type and amount of sugar best for pecan sandies needed to be determined. In a working recipe that we assembled, we tried light brown sugar, dark brown sugar, granulated sugar, confectioners' sugar, and different combinations of each. Confectioners' sugar, with its small amount of cornstarch, had a noticeable tenderizing effect on the cookies. Too much, however, and the cookies turned pasty and gummy—a ¼ cup was all that was needed. Granulated sugar had little to offer in the way of flavor; dark brown sugar offered too much. Light brown sugar, tinged with molasses, gave the cookies a gentle caramel flavor that complemented—not overwhelmed—the nuttiness of the pecans and richness of the butter.

Next, we made batches of pecan sandies with a whole egg and without. A whole egg was excessive—the dough was sticky and difficult to work with. Without an egg, however, the cookies baked up with a texture more like pie pastry, and they lost their attractive sharp edges in the oven. A single yolk was what the dough needed. By comparison, these cookies were fine-pored and stalwart, keeping their crisp, clean look even after baking.

So far, we had been using a good amount of finely chopped nuts for flavor. We tried grinding a portion of those nuts, leaving the other portion chopped, and found the cookies made with ground nuts to be finer-textured, more tender, and nuttier than those made exclusively with chopped nuts. The oils in the nuts released during grinding contributed to the tenderness and flavor of the cookies. But tasters demanded an even finer cookie, one in which chopped nuts didn't mar the delicate sandy texture, so we ground all of the pecans. Tasters were pleased.

As for flavor refinements, a bit of salt helped to boost flavor. Vanilla extract, even the smallest amount of it, was too perfumed and distracting. Tasters did like a hint of cinnamon, however; its flavor could not be singled out, but it added nuance and a layer of warmth.

A matter of mechanics: We were grinding the pecans in a food processor, but we were making the cookie dough using the typical creamed butter method in a standing mixer. It occurred to us that these cookies were not a far cry from pâte sucrée, or French tart pastry, which is made entirely in the food processor, so we gave it a whirl, taking it from start to finish in the processor. We ground the nuts with the sugars to help prevent the nuts from going greasy and clumpy as they broke down, added the flour, cut in the butter, and finally added the egg. The dough quantity was large and resisted being perfectly combined, so we emptied it onto the counter and kneaded it gently until it came together into an even, cohesive dough. It worked faster and more cleanly than we could have hoped—and now we didn't have to take out the butter ahead of time to soften it for creaming and we didn't have to haul out and dirty the standing mixer.

For baking, rolling the dough out into sheets and stamping out cookies with a cutter was one option, but this technique generates scraps, which we preferred to do without. Instead, we treated the dough as we would for refrigerator cookies, shaping the just-made dough into one 12-inch log, cutting it in half, wrapping each in plastic wrap, and putting them into the freezer only long enough to firm up their exteriors. At this point, we took them out, rolled them along the counter surface to round out the flat side they had rested on while soft, then put them into the refrigerator until thoroughly chilled. After a couple of hours, we sliced the logs into ¼-inch coins, accessorized with a pecan half pressed into each slice (for presentation, otherwise the cookies look homely), and they were ready to bake.

Pecan sandies should become only modestly brown with baking—the edges should begin to deepen to golden brown, but the bulk of the cookie should be blond. They need to be thoroughly baked, however, even under the pecan adornment, to obtain their characteristic crisp, sandy texture. A 325-degree oven was ideal—a cooler oven took longer than necessary, and a hotter one gave the cookies too much color. Once on the cooling rack, pecan sandies must cool completely, lest their texture fail to live up to their name.

~≈~

Pecan Sandies
MAKES ABOUT 32 COOKIES

Once the dough is shaped into logs, it should be frozen for 30 minutes (to speed chilling), and then refrigerated for at least 2 hours to finish chilling. The chilled dough can be refrigerated for up to 3 days before being sliced and baked.

- 1½ cups pecan halves, plus about 32 pecan halves for pressing onto unbaked cookies
- ¼ cup (1 ounce) confectioners' sugar
- ½ cup packed (3½ ounces) light brown sugar
- 1½ cups (7½ ounces) unbleached all-purpose flour
- ¼ teaspoon salt
- 12 tablespoons (1½ sticks) cold unsalted butter, cut into ½-inch cubes
- 1 large egg yolk

1. Combine 1½ cups pecans and sugars in the bowl of a food processor. Pulse the pecans and sugars until the nuts are ground, about twenty 1-second pulses. Add the flour and salt and pulse to combine, about twelve 1-second pulses. Scatter the butter pieces over the dry ingredients and pulse until the mixture resembles damp sand and rides up the sides of the bowl, about eighteen 1-second pulses. With

the machine running, add the yolk and process until the dough comes together in a rough ball, about 20 seconds.

2. Turn out the dough (it will look scrappy and uneven) onto a clean, dry work surface and gently knead until it is evenly moistened and cohesive. Using the palms of your hands, roll the dough into an even 12-inch log, cut the log in half with a chef's knife, and wrap each half in plastic wrap. Freeze the dough logs until very cold but still malleable, about 30 minutes; remove them from the freezer, unwrap and roll them on the work surface to round off the flat sides. Rewrap the logs in plastic wrap and refrigerate the dough logs until thoroughly chilled and completely firm, about 2 hours.

3. Adjust the oven racks to the upper- and lower-middle positions and heat the oven to 325 degrees. Line two baking sheets with parchment paper. Unwrap the dough logs and, using a sharp chef's knife, slice the logs into coins ¼ inch thick, slightly rotating the log after each slice so that it does not develop a markedly flat side. Place slices on prepared baking sheets, spacing them about ¾ inch apart. Press a pecan half in the center of each slice.

4. Bake, reversing the position of the baking sheets in the oven halfway through the baking time (from top rack to bottom and front to back), until the edges of the cookies are golden brown, about 24 minutes. Cool the cookies 3 minutes on the baking sheets, then transfer them to a wire rack with a wide metal spatula and let them cool to room temperature.

Fudgy Brownies

MOST AMERICANS ARE PASSIONATE ABOUT brownies. Some are passionate about eating them, indulging in a brownie's rich, chocolatey decadence. Others are passionate about a recipe, scrawled on a stained index card bequeathed to them by their mother, guaranteeing everyone they meet that this family heirloom produces the best brownie of all.

We've sampled good brownies, but rarely have we ever encountered the brownie to beat all others. And yet somehow we know exactly how the perfect brownie ought to taste and look. Those light cakey versions are not for us. We imagine a moist, dark, luscious interior with a firm, smooth, velvety texture that your teeth glide through easily, meeting just a little resistance in chewing. Our perfect brownie must pack an intense chocolate punch and have deep, resonant chocolate flavor, but it must fall just short of overwhelming the palate. It must not be so sweet as to make your teeth ache, and it must certainly have a thin, shiny, papery crust and edges that crisp during baking, offering a contrast with the brownie's moist center. With all of this in mind, we began our quest, determined to meet our brownie ideal.

Our baking sense told us that the taste and texture of the brownie we sought lay in a delicate balance of the five ingredients basic to all brownie recipes: chocolate, flour, sugar, butter, and eggs. After gathering a number of recipes that promised to deliver a fudgy brownie, we made a select six that confirmed our expectations. The varying proportions of these five ingredients produced batches of brownies that were soft and pasty; dry and cakey; or chewy, like a Tootsie Roll. Chocolate flavor was divergent, too, ranging from intense but one-dimensional jolts to weak, muted passings on the palate. Our next step was to cobble together a composite recipe that would incorporate the best traits of these six recipes. It would serve as the foundation for all of our testing.

The two essential qualities we were looking for in these brownies were a chewy, fudgy texture and a rich chocolate flavor. We went to work on flavor first. After making the six initial test recipes, we knew that unsweetened chocolate was a good source of assertive chocolate flavor. Semisweet and bittersweet chocolates don't have as much chocolate punch because of the large amount of sugar they contain. But this is also why they are smoother and milder. One of our favorite recipes from the initial test yielded a brownie with exceptional chocolate flavor; this recipe combined unsweetened and bittersweet chocolates, so to the composite recipe we tried adding varying amounts of the two chocolates. (Semisweet and bittersweet chocolates are not identical but can be exchanged for one another in many recipes depending on what's available at the supermarket; we'll refer to semisweet from here on because it's what we used when testing the recipes.)

Too much unsweetened chocolate and the

COOKIES, BROWNIES, AND BARS

brownies were sour and acrid, too much semisweet chocolate and they were one dimensional and boring. We found that 5 ounces of semisweet and 2 ounces of unsweetened created just the right flavor balance. Next we thought to add some cocoa powder, which typically adds flavor but no harshness. We were pleased with this combination. The unsweetened chocolate laid a solid, intense chocolate foundation, the semisweet provided a mellow, even, sweet flavor, and the cocoa smoothed any rough edges and added depth and complexity. We tried both Dutch-processed cocoa and natural cocoa and found them to work equally well.

We then fiddled with the type and quantity of sugar needed to sweeten the brownies, given the amount and types of chocolate and cocoa they contained. In addition to white sugar, we tried brown sugar to see if it might add flavor, but it didn't. We also tried a bit of corn syrup, thinking it might add moistness and chew, but it only made the brownies wet and gummy and the crust dull. Satisfied that white sugar was the best sweetener for the job, we tested varying amounts. We knew we didn't want overly sweet brownies. Too little sugar, though, left the brownies with a chocolate flavor that was dull, muted, and flat, much like mashed potatoes without salt. Just the right degree of sweetness was provided by 1¼ cups sugar; the flavor of the brownies was now spot-on.

Satisfied with the flavor of the brownies, we moved on to refining the texture, starting with flour. Our composite recipe contained ¾ cup flour, but wanting to exhaust all reasonable quantities, we baked brownies with as little as ¼ cup and up to 1¼ cups, increasing the quantity in ¼ cup increments. The batch with the least amount of flour was like goopy, sticky, chocolate-flavored Spackle, so pasty it cemented your mouth shut. The one with 1¼ cups flour had good chew, but it verged on dry, and the chocolate flavor was light and muted. One cup was perfect. The chocolate flavor remained deep and rich, and the texture was fudgy, smooth, and dense, the moist crumb putting up a gentle resistance when chewed.

Butter was up next. Melting butter, rather than creaming it with sugar and eggs, makes for a dense, fudgy texture. Creaming produces an aerated batter,

which bakes into lighter, cakier brownies. Had we questioned this baker's axiom after the initial test, in which all of the six recipes employ the melted butter technique, any doubts would have been dispelled. But now the question of how much butter remained.

Semisweet chocolate contains more fat than unsweetened chocolate, yet many recipes that call exclusively for one type of chocolate frequently call for the same amount of butter (some 16 tablespoons) per cup of flour. As it stood, our working recipe used semisweet and unsweetened chocolate, cocoa, 1 cup flour, and 10 tablespoons butter. The texture of the brownies this recipe produced was moist and dense, albeit a bit sodden and pasty. Improvement came with less butter. Minus 2 tablespoons, the brownies shed their soggy, sodden quality but still remained moist and velvety.

With butter and flour set, we went to work on eggs. We tried as few as two and as many as six. Two eggs left the brownies dry and gritty and compromised the chocolate flavor. With four or more eggs, the brownies baked into cakey rubber erasers with an unattractive, high-domed, dull matte crust. Three was the magic number—the brownies were moist and smooth, with great flavor and delicate chew.

We finalized the recipe by making adjustments to vanilla and salt and then began to examine other factors that might have an impact on the brownies. First we tried baking in a water bath, a technique used for delicate custards, reasoning that gentle heat might somehow improve texture. Not so. We got a grainy, sticky, puddinglike brownie.

We experimented with midrange oven temperatures. Three-hundred-fifty degrees did the job and did it relatively quickly, in about 35 minutes (many brownies bake for nearly an hour). As is the case with most other brownies, if baked too long, these brownies run the risk of drying out; they must be pulled from the oven when a toothpick inserted into the center comes out with some sticky crumbs clinging to it.

After making more than 50 batches, we really began to appreciate an aspect of brownies quite beside their rich flavor and texture—with only a couple of bowls, a whisk, and a spatula, the batter can be mixed and in the oven in 10 minutes.

Chewy, Fudgy Triple-Chocolate Brownies

MAKES SIXTY-FOUR 1-INCH BROWNIES

Either Dutch-processed or natural cocoa works well in this recipe. These brownies are very rich, so we prefer to cut them into small squares for serving.

5	ounces semisweet or bittersweet chocolate, chopped
2	ounces unsweetened chocolate, chopped
8	tablespoons (1 stick) unsalted butter, cut into quarters
3	tablespoons cocoa powder
3	large eggs
1¼	cups (8¾ ounces) sugar
2	teaspoons vanilla extract
½	teaspoon salt
1	cup (5 ounces) unbleached all-purpose flour

1. Adjust the oven rack to the lower-middle position and heat the oven to 350 degrees. Spray an 8-inch-square baking pan with nonstick cooking spray. Fold two 16-inch pieces of foil lengthwise to measure 7 inches wide. Fit one sheet in the bottom of the greased pan, pushing it into the corners and up the sides of the pan (overhang will help in removal of baked brownies). Fit the second sheet in the pan in the same manner, perpendicular to the first sheet. Spray the foil with nonstick cooking spray.

2. In a medium heatproof bowl set over pan of almost-simmering water, melt the chocolates and butter, stirring occasionally until mixture is smooth. Whisk in the cocoa until smooth. Set aside to cool slightly.

3. Whisk together the eggs, sugar, vanilla, and salt in a medium bowl until combined, about 15 seconds. Whisk the warm chocolate mixture into the egg mixture; then stir in the flour with a wooden spoon until just combined. Pour the mixture into the prepared pan, spread into corners, and level surface with a rubber spatula; bake until slightly puffed and a toothpick inserted in the center comes out with small amount of sticky crumbs clinging to it, 35 to 40 minutes. Cool on a wire rack to room temperature, about 2 hours. Remove the brownies from the pan using the foil handles and transfer to a cutting board. Cut into 1-inch squares. (Do not cut brownies until ready to serve; brownies can be wrapped in plastic and refrigerated up to 5 days.)

➤ VARIATION

Triple-Chocolate Espresso Brownies

Follow the recipe for Chewy, Fudgy Triple-Chocolate Brownies, whisking in 1½ tablespoons instant espresso or coffee powder along with cocoa in step 2.

SCIENCE: Chocolate Flavor Diffusion

One of the more interesting ideas we heard about the dos and don'ts of working with chocolate desserts was proposed to us by famed New York chef Jean-Georges Vongerichten, who stated that the less one cooks chocolate, the better it tastes. We decided to check this out with Tom Lehmann, director of bakery assistance at the American Institute of Baking. He agreed.

Chocolate, Lehman explained, is a very delicate substance, full of highly sensitive, volatile compounds that give chocolate much of its flavor. When chocolate is heated, the liquids in it turn to steam and carry away these volatile compounds. That's what makes the kitchen smell so good when brownies are in the oven. The bad news is that these volatile compounds are no longer in the brownies—which is where you really want them to be. This situation is made even more acute by the fact that unwanted volatile compounds have already been driven off during the processes of roasting and conching (kneading, grinding, and smoothing the chocolate) by the manufacturer, both of which improve the flavor of chocolate beans. Additional exposure to heat, therefore, has no benefits; it simply makes the chocolate more bitter and less complex tasting.

So, what are the lessons to be learned for home cooks who bake with chocolate? First, underbaking is always better than overbaking. Dry chocolate desserts will have much less flavor and tend to be bitter. Second, use as much fat as possible. Fat increases the retention of volatile compounds. That's why low-fat chocolate desserts usually taste like sugar but not chocolate.

BLONDIES

BLONDIES ARE A FIRST COUSIN TO BOTH brownies and chocolate chip cookies. Although blondies are baked in a pan like brownies, the flavorings are similar to those in chocolate chip cookies—vanilla, butter, and brown sugar, otherwise known as butterscotch. Blondies are sometimes laced with nuts and chocolate chips or butterscotch chips. Most of the time, blondies are pretty bland and need all the help they can get from additional ingredients. Dry, floury, flavorless—we have eaten them all. What does it take to make a good blondie?

The majority of the recipes we found had essentially the same ingredients but in different proportions that yielded blondies with dramatically different textures—from light and cakey to dense and buttery. Tasters preferred the latter, but with reservations. They felt that blondies could be too dense, as were some of the ones we tried. Super-dense blondies tasted of little more than raw flour and butter.

After baking a variety of blondie recipes, we found that the key to dense blondies that did not taste raw lay in how the butter was incorporated into the batter and the amount of flour in the batter. Melted butter produced a much denser blondie than creamed butter because the creaming process incorporates air into the batter. Melting the butter also meant that we could make the batter in a mixing bowl rather than dirtying a food processor or standing mixer.

While we knew all-purpose flour would give us the chewiest, densest texture, the exact amount of flour was tricky to determine. Too much flour resulted in a dense, flavorless cookie and too little produced a greasy cookie that oozed butter. After a dozen batches with the slightest of variations in the amounts of flour, we finally settled on one-and-a-half cups of all-purpose flour leavened with a small amount of baking powder. These cookies were definitely dense and very chewy, but they had risen just enough to prevent them from being "gooey."

For sweetening and flavor, tasters favored light brown sugar, which lent the right amount of earthy, molasses flavor; dark brown sugar was overpowering. And combined with a substantial amount of vanilla extract and salt (to sharpen the sweetness), the light brown sugar developed a rich butterscotch flavor.

To add both texture and flavor to the cookies, we included chocolate chips and pecans. While the chips are traditional, pecans are not. Most recipes suggest walnuts, but tasters thought the pecans better complemented the butterscotch flavor.

We also tried butterscotch chips, but most tasters found that they did little for this recipe. On a whim, we included white chocolate chips with the semisweet chips and we were surprised that they produced the best blondie yet. While white chocolate does not have cocoa, it does have cocoa butter, which highlighted both the vanilla and caramel flavors. These blondies now had a significantly deeper and richer flavor.

Blondies

MAKES ABOUT 36 BARS

If you have trouble finding white chocolate chips, feel free to chop a bar of white chocolate into small chunks.

1 1/2	cups (7 1/2 ounces) unbleached all-purpose flour
1	teaspoon baking powder
1/2	teaspoon salt
12	tablespoons (1 1/2 sticks) unsalted butter, melted and cooled
1 1/2	cups packed (10 1/2 ounces) light brown sugar
2	large eggs
1 1/2	teaspoons vanilla extract
1/2	cup semisweet chocolate chips
1/2	cup white chocolate chips
1	cup pecans, toasted and chopped coarse

1. Adjust an oven rack to the middle position and heat the oven to 350 degrees. Spray a 9 by 13-inch pan with nonstick vegetable cooking spray. Fold two 16-inch pieces of foil lengthwise so that one measures 13 inches wide and the other measures 9 inches wide. Fit one sheet in the bottom of the greased pan, pushing it into the corners and up the sides of the pan (overhang will help in removal of baked bars). Fit the second sheet in the pan in the same manner, perpendicular to the first sheet. Spray the foil with nonstick cooking spray.

2. Whisk the flour, baking powder, and salt together in a medium bowl; set aside.

3. Whisk the melted butter and brown sugar together in a medium bowl until combined. Add the

eggs and vanilla and mix well. Using a rubber spatula, fold the dry ingredients into the egg mixture until just combined. Do not overmix. Fold in the chocolate chips and nuts and turn the batter into the prepared pan, smoothing the top with a rubber spatula.

4. Bake until the top is shiny and cracked and feels firm to the touch, 22 to 25 minutes. Place the pan on a rack and cool completely. Cut into rectangles that measure about 1½ inches by 2 inches.

SEVEN-LAYER BARS

SEVEN-LAYER BARS, ALSO KNOWN AS MAGIC bars, are indeed made in seven layers and, you could say, come together like magic. Seven-layer bars are a jumble of chips (chocolate and otherwise), nuts, and coconut layered over a crust of crumbled graham crackers. The magic is the sweetened condensed milk, which when poured over these ingredients and baked, brings them together to create a cohesive bar cookie. Seven-layer bars are rich, supremely decadent, and sticky-sweet.

Simplicity in construction aside, seven-layer bars are not without their share of problems. They are most often flavor-related (the medley of chips tend to be mismatched, and at times overpowering), but sometimes poor construction can cause problems. Seven-layer bars can be too delicate and fall apart at the first bite, can have too thin a graham cracker crust, or can be insufficiently gooey so the ingredients won't stay together. We were after a solid bar cookie loaded with sweet, rich flavors and a chewy-crunchy texture.

Starting at the bottom, we tested our graham cracker crust options. Most graham cracker crusts are made by combining graham crumbs with melted butter. This crust would be no exception. Although store-bought crumbs are convenient, the crust they formed was far too delicate to support all the ingredients that would be layered on them. In order to produce a more substantial crust, we found it was necessary to hand-crush whole graham crackers into coarser crumbs. We placed whole crackers in a large zipper-lock bag and pounded them with whatever blunt instrument was handy (the underside of a measuring cup, a rolling pin). The result was a motley crew of crumbs, bits, and chunks. When brought together with the butter and then the condensed milk, these coarse crumbs created a sturdy crust packed with graham cracker flavor.

Next we tested every "chip" combination imaginable and let our tasters determine which options were worthy and which needed reconsidering. Toffee chips were the biggest loser of the bunch. The small nuggets of toffee melted away into nothing but a thin, sticky, almost flavorless layer, and did little to contribute to the structure of the bar. Since bar structure was indeed an important factor, it became clear that we would have to stick to the standard morsel-shaped chip as they tended to keep shape better than smaller "bits" or mini-chips. When baked, morsels became soft and luxurious, but retained enough shape to help add more bulk to this bar cookie.

The least favorite type of chip turned out to be peanut butter. They were salty and somewhat artificial-tasting, and the combination of peanut butter, coconut, and graham crackers seemed to turn tasters off. Chocolate chips—both semisweet and white chocolate—were well liked. Butterscotch chips also made the cut. They were buttery, slightly spicy, and offered a nice flavor change from the chocolate. In the end, we found that two cups of chips was the perfect amount. Tasters liked semisweet chocolate chips more than any of the others, so we settled on one cup of semisweet morsels and split the second cup between the white chocolate and butterscotch chips.

Next it was time to concentrate on the coconut. Some of the recipes we initially tested were overly coconut-y, and tasters were quite clear that they expected less. When we found the optimum amount—one cup—there was still something missing. The coconut flavor was flat and somewhat uninteresting. So we decided to toast the coconut to enhance its flavor. Fully toasted coconut, which was then baked on top of the seven layers for 25 minutes, came out of the oven in shards—too brown and overly crunchy. But without any toasting, the flavor was insipid. The solution was to toast the coconut ever so slightly. On top of the seven layers, the slightly toasted coconut browned evenly without becoming hard, and its flavor was much improved.

When it came to nuts, we tested all the usual suspects: pecans, walnuts, almonds, and macadamia nuts. Because of their meaty texture and big flavor, tasters preferred walnuts. We tried toasting the nuts to enhance their flavor, but the differences were marginal and not worth the extra effort.

Sweetened condensed milk is a mixture of whole milk and sugar (up to 45 percent of its content) that is heated until 60 percent of the water content evaporates. What's left behind is an ooey-gooey, light tan liquid, which acts as the "glue" in seven-layer bars. The technique couldn't be simpler. Just open the can and pour it all over the top, as evenly as possible. We tested several ways of spreading the condensed milk evenly over the layers. Running a spatula over the condensed milk unearthed the layers below and made a mess of the whole thing. In the end, we just poured the condensed milk as evenly as we could over the layers and then let the heat of the oven do the rest.

Seven-Layer Bars

MAKES ABOUT 25 BARS

Place the graham crackers in a large zipper-lock plastic bag and pound them with the underside of a measuring cup, a rolling pin, or a smooth meat mallet. The result should be an assortment of crumbs, bits, and chunks that measures about 1½ cups.

1	cup sweetened flaked coconut
8	tablespoons (1 stick) unsalted butter
8	whole graham crackers (4 ounces), crushed (see note)
1	cup finely chopped walnuts
1	cup semisweet chocolate chips
½	cup white chocolate chips
½	cup butterscotch-flavored chips
1	(14-ounce) can sweetened condensed milk

1. Adjust an oven rack to the lower-middle position and heat the oven to 350 degrees. Spray a 9 by 13-inch pan with nonstick vegetable cooking spray. Fold two 16-inch pieces of foil lengthwise so that one measures 13 inches wide and the other measures 9 inches wide. Fit one sheet in the bottom of the greased pan, pushing it into the corners and up the sides of the pan (overhang will help in removal of baked bars). Fit the second sheet in the pan in the same manner, perpendicular to the first sheet. Spray the foil with nonstick cooking spray.

2. Spread the coconut on a baking sheet and bake until the outer flakes just begin to brown, about 8 minutes; set aside. At the same time, place the stick of butter into the lined baking pan and put it in the oven to melt, about 6 minutes.

3. When the butter has melted, remove the pan from the oven and sprinkle the graham cracker crumbs over the melted butter. Toss lightly until all the butter is absorbed and the crumbs are evenly distributed. In order, sprinkle the walnuts, chocolate chips, white chocolate chips, butterscotch chips, and coconut over the graham crackers. Pour the condensed milk evenly over the entire dish.

4. Return the pan to the oven and bake until the top is golden brown, about 25 minutes. Cool on a wire rack to room temperature, about 2 hours. Remove the bars from the pan using the foil handles and transfer to a cutting board. Using a sharp knife, cut into 2 by 3-inch bars.

LEMON BARS

TO MAKE LEMON BARS, A BOTTOM LAYER or "crust" is pressed into a pan, prebaked, and then topped with a filling. The cookies are baked again, and then cut into bars. They are pretty easy to make, but that doesn't mean it's easy to get them just the way you want them. Whether from bakeries or home recipes, the crust is often quite soggy, and many versions are too sweet and lack true lemon flavor.

We started with the crust, knowing that flour, butter, and sugar would be the main ingredients of the bottom layer. We also knew that since we wanted a cookie or shortbread texture rather than a pastry-type crust, we would need a fair amount of sugar. No liquid would be necessary because we weren't trying to create the little pockets of steam that produce flakiness and layering in pastry.

Our first challenge was to decide the proportion of flour to butter and the amount, as well as the type, of sugar. We decided, after several taste tests, that a crust made with ½ cup of butter per 1¼ cups of flour proved to be just right—it was neither too greasy nor too dry. Since sugar affects tenderness as well as sweetness, the amount and type of sugar needed to be determined along with the butter. Brown sugar proved too rich for our tasters' palates, while granulated sugar produced a crust that was a bit brittle and gritty. The best, most tender texture came from confectioners' sugar.

Having decided on the basic ingredients, we began to investigate ways to combine and bake them. For most cookies and one type of pastry, the fat and sugar are creamed together in the first step. The alternative is to start by cutting the fat into the flour with your fingertips or a food processor, which is common in most pastry crusts. After testing both methods, we decided that because of the proportion of flour to butter and the absence of liquid, the second method was best suited for this crust. Cutting the butter into the flour created a crumbly mixture that could be pressed into the pan. The standard temperature of 350 degrees worked best to produce a golden brown, crisp crust.

Lemon bars are traditionally made by pre-baking the crust, then adding a raw mixture of eggs, sugar, flour, lemon juice and lemon zest before baking to set the filling. Once we had settled on our crust, we tried a number of recipes using this technique, and regardless of ingredient portions, we turned out consistently soggy crusts. We wanted a crust that would stay crisp even after it was topped with a filling, and concluded that the only way to achieve this would be to abandon tradition and precook a lemon filling (lemon curd) on the stove before adding it to the crust.

For a 9-inch square pan, we estimated that we would need about 3 cups of lemon curd. The traditional lemon curds all contained between 1 and 1½ cups sugar, but the amount of lemon juice varied widely, between ½ and 1½ cups. There was also quite a bit of play between whole eggs and yolks, with the average falling between 8 and 10 eggs total. Though the recipes were divided on the matter of using direct heat versus a double boiler, most were quite cavalier about cooking time, with visual descriptions of the desired final texture ranging from "thick" to "very thick" to "like whipped cream." Only two mentioned cooking temperatures: 160 and 180 degrees, a rather wide range

when dealing with eggs. Some recipes added butter at the beginning of the cooking time; others preferred to whisk it in later.

During our early experiments, certain proportions emerged easily. The balance of sweetness and tartness we sought came in at roughly two parts sugar to one part lemon juice. Four full tablespoons of finely grated lemon zest (strained out after cooking along with any hardened bits of egg whites from the eggs) packed enough lemon punch without having to linger in the final custard, where it would become bitter or usurp the silky texture. A pinch of salt brightened the flavor. Four tablespoons of butter were perfect, smoothing taste and refining texture. Adding cold butter chunks to the still-liquid curd proved superior to whisking the butter in after stovetop cooking.

Holding the proportions of the above ingredients constant, we made a number of lemon curds testing various combinations of whole eggs and yolks. Somewhat surprisingly, the curds that tasted great in a spoon were not always the ones that tasted best baked. The curd made with whole eggs alone had a light texture in the spoon and a gorgeous sheen, but it had a muted color and a texture most tasters described as "mayonnaise-like" when baked. The curd made with whole eggs and whites had a smooth, translucent surface but firmed up too much, while the curd made with an equal ratio of whole eggs to yolks was faulted for being cloyingly rich. In the end, most tasters preferred a curd made principally with yolks and only a couple of whole eggs for structure. Creamy and dense with a vibrant color, it did not become gelatinous when baked, as did those curds made with whole eggs, but it did set up enough to slice. Its flavor also lingered and teased. This made sense to us because fats carry flavors and hold them on the palate. Egg yolks are high in fat.

But the most interesting discovery was still to come. Remembering a lemon mousse we'd made, we wanted to see what a softening splash of cream might do to the curd. Adding cream before cooking the curd on the stovetop gave it a cheesy flavor. But three tablespoons of cold, raw cream stirred in just before baking proved a winning touch. It cooled the just-cooked curd, blunted its acidity, and lightened its final baked texture to a celestial creaminess.

When added to the crust and baked just to set, the curd maintained a celestial creaminess, and the crust stayed perfectly crispy.

~❧~

Lemon Bars

MAKES ABOUT 16 BARS

The warm filling must be added to a warm crust. Start preparing the filling when the crust goes into the oven.

CRUST .

1¼	cups (6¼ ounces) unbleached all-purpose flour
½	cup (2 ounces) confectioners' sugar, plus extra to decorate the finished bars
½	teaspoon salt
8	tablespoons (1 stick) unsalted butter, at very cool room temperature, cut into 1-inch pieces

LEMON FILLING

7	large egg yolks, plus 2 large eggs
1	cup plus 2 tablespoons (8 ounces) sugar
⅔	cup juice from 4 to 5 medium lemons, plus ¼ cup finely grated zest
	Pinch salt
4	tablespoons unsalted butter, cut into 4 pieces
3	tablespoons heavy cream

1. FOR THE CRUST: Spray a 9-inch square baking pan with nonstick vegetable cooking spray. Fold two 16-inch pieces of foil lengthwise to measure 9 inches wide. Fit one sheet in the bottom of the greased pan, pushing it into the corners and up the sides of the pan (overhang will help in removal of baked bars). Fit the second sheet in the pan in the same manner, perpendicular to the first sheet. Spray the foil with nonstick cooking spray.

2. Pulse the flour, confectioners' sugar, and salt in a food processor workbowl fitted with the steel blade. Add the butter and process to blend, 8 to 10 seconds, then pulse until the mixture is pale yellow and resembles coarse meal, about three 1-second pulses. (To do this by hand, mix the flour, confectioners' sugar, cornstarch, and salt in a medium bowl. Freeze the butter and grate it on the large holes of a box grater into the flour mixture. Toss the butter pieces to coat. Rub the pieces between your fingers for a minute, until the flour turns pale

yellow and coarse.) Sprinkle the mixture into the lined pan and press firmly with fingers into an even layer over entire pan bottom. Refrigerate for 30 minutes.

3. Adjust the oven rack to the middle position and heat the oven to 350 degrees. Bake the crust until golden brown, about 20 minutes.

4. FOR THE FILLING: In a medium nonreactive bowl, whisk together the yolks and whole eggs until combined, about 5 seconds. Add the sugar and whisk until just combined, about 5 seconds. Add the lemon juice, zest, and salt; whisk until combined, about 5 seconds. Transfer the mixture to a medium nonreactive saucepan, add the butter pieces, and cook over medium-low heat, stirring constantly with a wooden spoon, until the curd thickens to a thin saucelike consistency and registers 170 degrees on an instant-read thermometer, about 5 minutes. Immediately pour the curd through a single-mesh stainless steel strainer set over a clean nonreactive bowl. Stir in the heavy cream; pour the curd into the warm crust immediately.

5. Bake until the filling is shiny and opaque and the center 3 inches jiggle slightly when shaken, 10 to 15 minutes. Cool on a wire rack to room temperature, about 45 minutes. Grab the edges of the foil to lift onto a cutting board. Cut into serving-size bars, wiping the knife clean between cuts, as necessary. Sieve confectioners' sugar over the bars, if desired.

~~~~~~~~~~~~~~~~~~~~~~

PECAN BARS

PECAN BARS ARE BASICALLY PECAN PIE baked into small, manageable rectangles or squares. The filling is a bit firmer so that it can be neatly cut. And instead of a pastry crust, most pecan bars call for a cookie-type crust, akin to shortbread.

Starting from the bottom up, we wanted a short-bread-like crust that would be substantial enough to support the filling. But the crust has to be tender and buttery. Unlike pie, bar cookies must have enough structural integrity to be eaten out of hand. Nothing is worse than a bar cookie that fractures into pieces upon the first bite. From our experience, the crust is usually the fatal flaw of a bar cookie; it is often soggy and undercooked or rock hard and tough.

We tested several shortbread recipes until we found one close to what we wanted—buttery and rich but still strong enough to slice and support the filling—and then hammered out the finer points. We had the best results processing the dough in a food processor, which quickly cuts the butter into the flour without overheating it, and it is an easy method to boot. It took under two minutes to process the crust and gently pack it into a lined baking pan. We found that a crust baked three-quarters of the way or until it was just beginning to brown resulted in the most flavor and best texture.

Although we were pleased with the crust's flavor and texture—buttery and just firm enough—one of the tasters made a suggestion that would change our opinion. She proposed adding ground pecans, bringing it more into "pecan sandy" territory. With a couple of minor adjustments to the flour and butter amounts to accommodate the nuts, the crust was markedly improved. The nut's sandy texture pleasingly contrasted with the silky filling, and the nuts also prevented the crust from becoming too tough.

As the crust bakes, the filling can be assembled. Since there is less filling in a pecan bar than in a pie, the flavors must be more concentrated. Working with our favorite pecan pie filling recipe, we cut back on both wet and dry ingredients until we hit the delicate balance of sweetness and gooeyness we desired.

To boost the flavor, we added a substantial amount of vanilla extract and bourbon or rum— both common to many Southern-style pecan pie recipes. The liquor cut through the sweetness and intensified the flavor of the nuts. We also included a healthy dose of salt, which sharpened the sweetness and also intensified the pecan flavor.

While it may sound like a minor issue, the size of the pecans proved to be important. Tasters definitely had opinions—some favored whole pecans, and some favored finely chopped. The whole pecans were attractive, floating on top of the cookie, but they did not cut easily and made the bars hard to eat out of hand. Finely chopped nuts were not as visually appealing but were easier to eat. We decided to chop the pecans coarsely and managed to please everyone.

Pecan Bars

MAKES 2 DOZEN BARS

Assemble the pecan filling while the crust bakes. Once the crust is lightly browned, spread the filling on top and continue baking. Because of their high sugar content, pecan bars store well and taste great up to five days after baking. They also freeze well if wrapped tightly in plastic wrap. While we liked bourbon the best, dark rum is quite good. For a very boozy tasting cookie, add another tablespoon of liquor.

CRUST

1	cup (5 ounces) unbleached all-purpose flour
1/4	teaspoon baking powder
1/3	cup packed (2⅓ ounces) light brown sugar
1	teaspoon salt
1/4	cup pecans, toasted and chopped coarse
6	tablespoons cold unsalted butter, cut into small pieces

FILLING

4	tablespoons unsalted butter, melted
1/2	cup packed (3½ ounces) light brown sugar
1/3	cup light corn syrup
2	teaspoons vanilla extract
1	tablespoon bourbon or dark rum
1/2	teaspoon salt
1	large egg, lightly beaten
2	cups pecans, toasted and chopped coarse

1. FOR THE CRUST: Adjust an oven rack to the middle position and heat the oven to 350 degrees. Spray a 9-inch square baking pan with nonstick vegetable cooking spray. Fold two 16-inch pieces of foil lengthwise to measure 9 inches wide. Fit one sheet in the bottom of the greased pan, pushing it into the corners and up the sides of the pan (overhang will help in removal of baked bars). Fit the second sheet in the pan in the same manner, perpendicular to the first sheet. Spray the foil with nonstick cooking spray.

2. Place flour, baking powder, brown sugar, salt, and pecans in the bowl of a food processor fitted with the steel blade. Process the mixture until it resembles coarse cornmeal, about five 1-second pulses. Add the butter and pulse until the mixture resembles sand, about 8 times. Pat the mixture evenly into the prepared pan and bake until the crust is light brown and

springs back when touched, about 20 minutes.

3. FOR THE FILLING: While the crust is in the oven, whisk together the melted butter, brown sugar, corn syrup, vanilla, bourbon, and salt in a medium bowl until just combined. Add the egg and whisk until incorporated.

4. Pour the filling on top of the hot crust and sprinkle the pecans evenly over the top. Bake until the top is brown and cracks start to form across the surface, 22 to 25 minutes. Cool on a wire rack for 1 hour. Remove the bars from the pan using the foil handles and transfer to a cutting board. Cut into bars that measure about 1½ inches by 2 inches.

RASPBERRY SQUARES

RASPBERRY SQUARES ARE ONE OF THE BEST and easiest bar cookies to prepare. With raspberry squares, the filling is ready-made (it comes straight from a jar of raspberry preserves). And these homey bars have textural interest created by the layering of filling on crust.

Bar cookies can be loosely divided into two camps. There's the cakelike version, which includes the chocolate brownie, and the cookielike version, which, stripped down to the basics, is what bakers call a "short" pastry, such as raspberry squares. A short pastry has a tender, almost sandy crumb that it gets by way of the right combination of flour, fat, sugar, and salt—with an emphasis on the fat and the flour. In a short pastry (think of shortbread), a generous amount of fat is required to coat the particles of flour, the purpose of this coating being to restrict the flour's access to liquid. Flour contains proteins that when combined with water form gluten—a substance that is desirable in bread, where you want chew, but not in a raspberry square, where you want tenderness.

In the many recipes for all manner of "short" bar cookies we looked at, the amount of butter ranged from ½ cup to 1 cup for about 2½ cups of flour. We found that a whole cup of butter made the raspberry squares greasy, whereas ½ cup left them on the dry side; ¾ cup butter was just right.

The sugar in many of the recipes also ranged from ½ cup to 1 cup, with some calling for white sugar, some for brown, some for a mix of the two. Here, too, we went for the midway, deciding on equal amounts of white and light brown sugar, which made for a deeper flavor than white alone, and on a total of ⅔ cup, which was sweet enough to be pleasing but not cloying.

INGREDIENTS: Raspberry Preserves

Jelly, jam, preserve, fruit spread—what's the difference, and is any one of these products better than the others for baking or spreading on toast? We put eight leading brands to a taste test to find out. But before we give you the results, some definitions are in order.

A jelly is a clear, bright mixture made from fruit juice, sugar, and often pectin or acid. No less than 45 pounds of fruit must be used for each 55 pounds of sugar.

A jam is a thick mixture of fruit and sugar (and often pectin) that is cooked until the pieces of fruit are very soft and almost formless—the texture of a thick puree. It is also made with 45 pounds of fruit solids combined with 55 pounds of sugar. Preserves are almost identical to jams, but preserves may contain large chunks of fruit or whole fruit.

Fruit spreads, which have become common grocery store stock over the last 10 years, do not fall under the labeling standards applied to jellies and jams—hence the generic name, fruit spreads. These products are usually made with concentrated grape and/or pear juice or low-calorie sweeteners, which replace all or part of the sugar

In our tasting, we tried all of the above in our raspberry square recipe and also sampled each on toast. Brands that tasted good on toast also worked best in raspberry squares, so there's no need to buy a special jam for baking. Although tasters preferred preserves and jams to jellies (they liked bits of fruit), they were most concerned with flavor. Too many brands were overly sweet—so sweet it was hard to taste the raspberries. The top two brands were Trappist Jam and Smucker's Preserves. Interestingly, both of these preserves are made with corn syrup, yet tasters felt these brands had the strongest raspberry flavor.

Although fruit spreads are less sweet than traditional jams and jellies, tasters felt that the concentrated fruit juices obscured the flavor of the raspberries. The result was a generic "fruit roll-up flavor."

Although we weren't interested in tampering too much with the flavor of our crust by adding things like vanilla, cinnamon, or lemon zest, as called for in some recipes, we did find it a bit plain as it was and were attracted by the idea of adding some oats or nuts, which would make a more subtle contribution to flavor while also adding some textural interest. The oats, with their bulk and absorbency, would have to displace some of the flour. After trying various proportions we found that we liked the combination of 1¼ cups oats to 1½ cups flour. We played around with the nuts and found ourselves preferring a pairing of sweet almonds with nutty pecans (although either also works on its own).

We were now pretty pleased with our crust except for one nagging problem. It was rather pale, not golden brown. We wanted that golden brown color not only for appearance's sake but for flavor; we knew that a deeply colored crust would have a more developed, nutty flavor.

The procedure we had been following to prepare the squares for baking was recommended in a number of recipes. It involved lining the bottom of the pan with most of the dough, spreading the preserves on top, and then covering the preserves with the rest of the dough. One or two recipes had recommended baking the bottom crust alone first to brown it and firm it up, but we had rejected this option as being a bit fussy. Now we tried this procedure and were happy to learn that it effectively colored—and flavored—the crust.

These squares can easily be put together in 15 minutes. The only inconvenience is having to wait for them to bake and cool before digging in.

~≻

Raspberry Squares
MAKES 25 SQUARES

Lining the pan with foil is helpful on two counts. It makes removal of the squares for cutting very easy (just lift out the entire block and place it on a cutting board to cut), and it makes for easy cleanup. For a nice presentation, trim ¼ inch off the outer rim of the uncut baked block. The outside edges of all the cut squares will then be neat.

1½ cups (7½ ounces) unbleached all-purpose flour
1¼ cups quick-cooking oats
⅓   cup (2¾ ounces) granulated sugar
⅓   cup packed (2¾ ounces) light brown sugar
¼   teaspoon baking soda
¼   teaspoon salt
½   cup finely chopped pecans or almonds, or a combination
12 tablespoons (1½ sticks) unsalted butter, cut into 12 pieces and softened but still cool
1   cup raspberry preserves

1. Adjust the oven rack to the lower-middle position and heat the oven to 350 degrees. Spray a 9-inch-square baking pan with nonstick cooking spray. Fold two 16-inch pieces of foil lengthwise to measure 8 inches wide. Fit one sheet in the bottom of the greased pan, pushing it into corners and up the sides of the pan (overhang will help in removal of baked squares). Fit the second sheet in the pan in the same manner, perpendicular to the first sheet. Spray foil with nonstick cooking spray.

2. In a bowl of a standing mixer, mix the flour, oats, sugars, baking soda, salt, and nuts at low speed until combined, about 30 seconds. With the mixer running at low speed, add the butter pieces; continue to beat until the mixture is well-blended and resembles wet sand, about 2 minutes.

3. Transfer ⅔ of the mixture to the prepared pan and use hands to press the crumbs evenly into the bottom. Bake until starting to brown, about 20 minutes. Using a rubber spatula, spread preserves evenly over the hot bottom crust; sprinkle the remaining oat/nut mixture evenly over the preserves. Bake until the preserves bubble around the edges and the top is golden brown, about 30 minutes, rotating the pan from front to back halfway through baking time. Cool on a wire rack to room temperature, about 1½ hours. Remove the squares from the pan using the foil handles and transfer to a cutting board. Cut into 1¼- to 1½-inch squares.

14

CAKES

WE ARE A CAKE-LOVING NATION. WE MAKE cakes to celebrate birthdays, weddings, anniversaries, and almost any other holiday you can think of. Cakes can be as simple as sheet cake sprinkled with confectioners' sugar or as complicated as a multitiered affair with filling, frosting, and nuts. This chapter examines favorite cakes, with emphasis on the simpler cakes most home cooks are likely to make.

Cake making requires precision and careful attention to detail. A slight mismeasurement of ingredients or the failure to follow a specific beating instruction can have drastic consequences in terms of flavor and texture. Over the years, we have developed a list of general tips designed to head off the mistakes home cooks are most likely to make.

Proper oven temperature is always important, especially when baking a cake, so periodically check your oven temperature with an oven thermometer. If your oven is too hot, the sides of the cake will set before the middle does, and the cake will hump or crack. If your oven is too cold, the air will escape from the batter before the batter begins to set, and the cake will have a coarse texture and may even fall.

You should own two sets of cake pans—two pans that measure 8 inches across and two that measure 9 across. Some recipes call for 8-inch cake pans, others for 9-inch pans. Use the correct size. If the pans are too large, they overheat the rim of the cake, causing the same sorts of problems as an overheated oven. If the pans are too small, batter may rise right out of them. Choose sturdy aluminum pans with absolutely vertical sides. Do not use disposable foil pans, which often produce misshapen cakes. (For information about what to look for when buying cake pans, see page 348.)

Generously grease the pans with shortening (such as Crisco) or butter and coat them well with flour. The flour holds the fat in place and keeps the batter from seeping through to the pan bottom. We find that shiny cake pans are almost always nonstick, so there is no need for parchment paper liners. If you are using an older pan with a dull finish, as an extra precaution you may want to grease the pan, line the bottom with a piece of parchment or waxed paper, grease the paper, and then flour the pan and paper.

Have all ingredients, especially butter, eggs, and milk, at room temperature. Chilled ingredients do not emulsify well, which leads to a dense cake, and cold butter won't even mix into a batter. Very warm ingredients may cause air cells in creamed butter to dissolve. Unless specified otherwise in a recipe, all ingredients should register between 65 and 70 degrees on an instant-read thermometer. Let butter soften on the counter for about an hour before creaming. The sticks should give when pressed but still hold their shape with no signs of melting.

To bring eggs to room temperature quickly, submerge uncracked eggs in a bowl of warm water for 5 to 10 minutes. Since separating eggs is somewhat easier when they are cold, you may want to separate the eggs first and then let them warm up while you assemble and measure the remaining ingredients. You may also place a bowl or measuring cup filled with yolks or whites in a bowl of warm water if necessary.

Unless otherwise noted, measure flour carefully by the dip-and-sweep method. Dip the measuring cup into the container of flour, scoop out a heaping cupful, and then level the top with the straight edge of a butter knife or icing spatula. Do not shake, tap, or pack the cup. If the cup is not completely filled

---

SCIENCE: To Sift or Not to Sift?

Sifting flour is a chore. This is especially true when sifting into a measuring cup, since you inevitably end up sifting twice as much as you need to fill the cup. Many bakers skip this step, thinking it insignificant. Here's why you shouldn't.

Sifting reduces the overall amount of flour (in weight) that goes into the recipe. Because sifting aerates the flour, 1 cup of sifted cake flour weighs in at about 3 ounces, whereas 1 cup of cake flour measured with the dip-and-sweep method weighs around 4 ounces.

To see what kind of differences this makes, we baked two cakes—one with sifted flour, one with unsifted. The cake made with sifted flour baked up perfectly flat, a dream to frost and layer since it required no trimming or leveling. The cake made with unsifted flour, however, mounded in the center and, though still very tasty, was also a bit drier.

Recipes with cocoa powder, such as our chocolate cake, often call for sifting. In this case, sifting breaks up small clumps of cocoa that form as the powder sits in the package. Sifted cocoa can be evenly distributed throughout a cake batter; with unsifted cocoa this isn't always the case.

---

on the first try, dump the flour back into the container and dip again.

Give pans enough space in the oven. Cakes placed too close together will rise toward each other and end up lopsided. Cakes placed too close to the oven walls won't rise as high on the side nearest the wall. Keep pans at least 3 inches from each other and the oven walls and on the middle rack of the oven. If your oven is small, stagger the pans on racks set at the upper-middle and lower-middle positions to allow for proper air circulation.

Use your finger and a cake tester to judge when layers are done. Cakes should be baked until firm in the center when lightly pressed and a toothpick or skewer inserted in the center comes out clean or with just a crumb or two adhering. If the tester comes out perfectly clean, the cake is probably overcooked and dry.

CHOCOLATE SHEET CAKE

A SHEET CAKE IS LIKE A TWO-LAYER CAKE with training wheels—it's hard to fall off. Unlike regular cakes, which often require trimming and decorating skills to make sure the cake doesn't turn out lopsided, domed, or altogether amateurish, sheet cakes are single-story and easy to frost. These are the sorts of cakes made for church suppers, old home days, bake sales, and Fourth of July picnics, decorated with red, white, and blue frosting.

But sheet cakes are still cakes. They can still turn out dry, sticky, or flavorless and, on occasion, can even sink in the middle. So we set out to find the simplest, most dependable recipe for a chocolate sheet cake, one that was moist yet also light and chocolatey.

First off, a sheet cake is nothing more than cake batter baked in one layer, usually in a square or rectangular pan. A basic chocolate sheet cake is used as the foundation for Mississippi mud cake (just add a layer of marshmallow cream and chocolate frosting) and is also referred to as Texas sheet cake. We started with a test batch of five different recipes that required a variety of mixing techniques, everything from creaming butter to beating yolks, whipping whites, and gently folding everything together at the end. The best of the lot was the most complicated to make. But we were taken with another recipe that simply whisked together the ingredients without beating, creaming, or whipping. Although the recipe needed work, its approach was clearly a good match for the simple, all-purpose nature of a sheet cake.

The recipe called for 2 sticks of butter, 4 eggs, 1½ cups flour, 2 cups sugar, ½ cup cocoa, 1 teaspoon vanilla, and ⅛ teaspoon salt. Our first change was to add buttermilk, baking powder, and baking soda to lighten the batter, as the cake had been dense and chewy in its original form. To increase the chocolate flavor, we reduced the sugar and flour, increased the cocoa, and decreased the butter. To further deepen the chocolate taste, we also decided to use semisweet chocolate in addition to the cocoa. With this revised recipe and our simple mixing method, we actually had a cake that was superior to those whose recipes called for creaming butter or whipping eggs.

The only significant problem came when we tested natural versus Dutch-processed cocoa and discovered that the cake fell a bit in the center when we used the former. A few tests later, we eliminated the baking powder entirely, relying instead on baking soda alone, and the problem was fixed. (Natural cocoa is more acidic than Dutch-processed, and when it was combined with baking powder, which also contains acid, it produced an excess of carbon dioxide gas. This in turn caused the cake to rise very fast and then fall like a deflated balloon that pops.)

Also of note is the low oven temperature—325 degrees—which, combined with a relatively long baking time of 40 minutes, produced a perfectly baked cake with a lovely flat top. Using a microwave oven rather than a double boiler to melt the chocolate and butter also saved time and hassle.

This cake can be frosted with almost anything—a buttercream, an Italian meringue, a sour cream or whipped cream frosting—but we developed a classic American milk chocolate frosting that pairs well with the darker flavor of the cake. Unlike a regular two-layer cake, this cake is a snap to frost.

Chocolate Sheet Cake

SERVES 10 TO 12

Melting the chocolate and butter in the microwave is quick and neat, but it can also be done in a heatproof bowl set over a saucepan containing 2 inches of simmering water. We prefer Dutch-processed cocoa (see page 352) for the deeper chocolate flavor it gives the cake. The baked and cooled cake can be simply served with lightly sweetened whipped cream or topped with any frosting you like.

12	tablespoons (1½ sticks) unsalted butter, plus 1 tablespoon for greasing baking pan
¾	cup cocoa, preferably Dutch-processed
1¼	cups (6¼ ounces) unbleached all-purpose flour
¼	teaspoon salt
8	ounces semisweet chocolate, chopped
4	large eggs
1½	cups sugar
1	teaspoon vanilla extract
1	cup buttermilk
½	teaspoon baking soda

1. Adjust an oven rack to the middle position and heat the oven to 325 degrees. Grease the bottom and sides of a 9 by 13-inch baking pan with 1 tablespoon butter.

2. Sift together the cocoa, flour, and salt in a medium bowl; set aside. Heat the chocolate and remaining 12 tablespoons butter in microwave-safe bowl covered with plastic wrap for 2 minutes at 50 percent power; stir until smooth. (If not fully melted, heat 1 minute longer at 50 percent power.) Whisk together the eggs, sugar, and vanilla in a medium bowl.

3. Whisk the chocolate into the egg mixture until combined. Combine the buttermilk and baking soda; whisk into the chocolate mixture, then whisk in the dry ingredients until the batter is smooth and glossy. Pour the batter into the prepared pan; bake until firm in the center when lightly pressed and a toothpick inserted in the center comes out clean, about 40 minutes. Cool on a wire rack until room temperature, at least 1 hour; ice with frosting, if desired, and serve. (Cake can be covered in plastic and stored at room temperature for up to 2 days.)

Creamy Milk Chocolate Frosting

MAKES ABOUT 2 CUPS, ENOUGH TO ICE ONE 9 BY 13-INCH CAKE

This frosting needs about an hour to cool before it can be used, so begin making it when the cake comes out of the oven.

½	cup heavy cream
	Pinch salt
1	tablespoon light or dark corn syrup
10	ounces milk chocolate, chopped
½	cup (2 ounces) confectioners' sugar
8	tablespoons (1 stick) cold unsalted butter, cut into 8 pieces

1. Heat the cream, salt, and corn syrup in a microwave-safe measuring cup on high until simmering, about 1 minute, or bring to a simmer in a small saucepan over medium heat.

2. Place the chocolate in the workbowl of a food processor fitted with the steel blade. With the machine running, gradually add the hot cream mixture through the feed tube; process 1 minute after the cream has been added. Stop the machine; add the confectioners' sugar to the workbowl and process to combine, about 30 seconds. With the machine running, add the butter through the feed tube one piece at a time; process until incorporated and smooth, about 20 seconds longer.

3. Transfer the frosting to a medium bowl and cool at room temperature, stirring frequently, until thick and spreadable, about 1 hour.

LEMON POPPY SEED POUND CAKE

LEMON POPPY SEED POUND CAKE SHOULD be easy to make, right? No tricky melted chocolate or whipped egg whites to deal with—just eggs, butter, flour, sugar, lemon flavoring, and poppy seeds. But if it's so easy, why does it often turn out spongy, rubbery, heavy, dry, and disappointing, with the poppy seeds sinking to the bottom? What we wanted was a fine-crumbed, rich, moist, and buttery cake with evenly dispersed poppy seeds. And not only did we want it to taste great, we wanted it to be easy to make, too.

We started with the traditional method of creaming the butter, sugar, and lemon zest until fluffy and light in color, adding the beaten eggs and vanilla slowly, then sifting and folding cake flour in by hand (all-purpose flour provides for a stout, rubbery cake, making cake flour critical in a pound cake), then adding the poppy seeds. The cake was very good, with a submissive crumb, golden buttery interior, and a subtle hint of lemon. But the method was tricky and time-consuming. It required us to bring all of the ingredients to room temperature, beat the butter and sugar for five minutes, and then incorporate the eggs into the fat over a three- to five-minute time period to make sure the batter wouldn't curdle (a curdled batter can make the crust look mottled and leave the cake's interior dense, with a disjointed crumb). In addition, the poppy seeds sank to the bottom. There had to be an easier way to make a great lemon poppy seed pound cake.

We turned to cookbooks looking for shortcuts. First we tried cutting softened butter into the flour using a standing mixer. A lot like making pie dough, we've found this method provides a velvety texture and superfine crumb when making some cakes. Although the batter was great, the baked-off cake was too open-grained (caused by too much air incorporated into the batter) and too tender, tasting more like a tender yellow cake than a pound cake.

Next we tried mixing the eggs, sugar, and zest by hand, then whisking in the melted butter and finally the flour. Since we were melting the butter, we didn't have to worry about curdling the batter or plan ahead by bringing any of the ingredients to room temperature an hour or two before mixing the cake. Best of all, we were able to put the batter together and get it in the oven in less than five minutes.

Although this cake had a tight grain and nicely browned exterior, some problems still existed. During testing, this method was not yielding consistent results. Some cakes swelled and split nicely down the center, but others didn't. There was also the problem of the zest and poppy seeds clumping or sinking to the bottom of the pan. We had to figure out how

to keep them suspended within the cake's crumb.

We thought about our method and tried to come up with ways to somehow make the cake less likely to vary from batch to batch. It hit us—making this cake batter was not unlike making mayonnaise. We were essentially using the principle of emulsification, where two otherwise unagreeable liquids are coaxed together into one unified form. In mayonnaise, emulsification concerns incorporating oil into egg yolks; in mixing the cake, the emulsification is between the melted butter and the eggs and sugar. The easy and technologically savvy way to make a mayonnaise is to use a food processor, so why not try the same tool to make the cake?

The method was a success. The cake had a split dome that gave us a peek into its marvelously yellow interior. Knowing that not everyone has a food processor, we tried the method in a blender. Although the cake was a bit more dense, the differences were so minimal that we felt confident recommending the blender as a reasonable alternative. With our method nailed down, we went on to see how we might improve the cake's texture and flavor.

When we tried changing the amount of butter in the cake, it came out either too greasy or too dry. And when we played around with the amount of eggs, the cake became either too spongy or too dense. We found the answer in a can of baking powder. With just 1 teaspoon, we instilled the cake with enough breath to produce a really nice and consistent crumb, without making the cake tough.

In our next test, we pulsed the sugar and zest together before adding the eggs to the food processor bowl. We figured that if we could integrate the zest into the sugar and turn the two into one ingredient, the zest might stand a fighting chance at staying suspended within the cake.

As for poppy seeds, we added them to the batter tossed with some of the dry ingredients so they wouldn't sink to the bottom of the cake as it baked. We also tried soaking the poppy seeds in milk to bring out their flavor, but since the poppy seeds are present more for crunch and appearance than for flavor, we decided to bypass this step.

Dense, rich, and speckled with poppy seed polka dots, this was a cake that delivered a pound cake attitude but was as easy to make as a quick bread.

Lemon Poppy Seed Pound Cake

SERVES 8

A blender can be substituted for the food processor in mixing the cake—just be wary of splattering when adding the melted butter. If you like a lot of lemon flavor, make the lemon glaze (recipe follows) to brush over the cake.

½	pound (2 sticks) unsalted butter, plus 1 tablespoon, softened, for greasing pan
1 ½	cups (6 ounces) plain cake flour, plus 1 tablespoon for pan
1	teaspoon baking powder
½	teaspoon salt
1 ¼	cups (8¾ ounces) sugar
2	tablespoons grated zest plus 2 teaspoons juice from 2 medium lemons
4	large eggs
1 ½	teaspoons vanilla extract
⅓	cup poppy seeds

1. Adjust an oven rack to the middle position and heat the oven to 325 degrees. Grease a 9 by 5-inch loaf pan with 1 tablespoon softened butter; dust with 1 tablespoon flour, tapping out the excess.

2. Whisk the flour, baking powder, and salt together in a medium bowl. In a glass measuring cup, melt the butter in the microwave. Once melted, whisk thoroughly to reincorporate the separated milk solids. In the bowl of a food processor fitted with the steel blade, combine the sugar and zest in five 1-second pulses. Add the eggs, vanilla, and lemon juice and blend for 5 seconds.

3. With the food processor running, add the melted butter in a steady stream (this should take about 20 seconds). Transfer the mixture to a large bowl.

4. In a small bowl, combine the poppy seeds and 1 tablespoon of the flour mixture. Set aside. Sift one-third of the remaining flour mixture into the egg mixture; whisk gently to combine. Sift the remaining flour into the egg mixture in two more additions, whisking just to incorporate, adding and incorporating the flour-tossed poppy seeds at the end.

5. Pour the batter into the prepared pan and bake, rotating the pan halfway through baking, until a toothpick or skewer inserted into the split on the top

of the cake comes out clean (the cake may still look slightly wet in the opening), 50 to 60 minutes. If glazing, follow the instructions below. Otherwise, cool the cake in the pan for 10 minutes, invert the cake onto a metal cooling rack, then turn the cake right-side up. Cool at least 1 hour or overnight. (The cake can be wrapped in plastic and stored at room temperature for up to 5 days.)

VARIATION

Lemon Pound Cake

The cake is also delicious without poppy seeds.

Follow the recipe for Lemon Poppy Seed Pound Cake, omitting the poppy seeds. In step 4, sift the flour mixture into the batter in three batches.

Lemon Glaze

MAKES ENOUGH TO GLAZE ONE POUND CAKE

To help the glaze penetrate into the cake, poke the top and sides of the just-baked cake with a toothpick.

½	cup sugar
¼	cup lemon juice

While the cake is cooling, bring the sugar and lemon juice to a boil in a small nonreactive saucepan, whisking occasionally to dissolve the sugar. Turn the heat to low and simmer until thickened slightly, about 2 minutes. Immediately after taking the cake out of the pan, poke the top and sides of the cake with a toothpick. Brush the warm glaze all over the cake. Cool the cake to room temperature.

SOUR CREAM COFFEE CAKE

A STATUESQUE SOUR CREAM COFFEE CAKE with delicate streusel swirls and mounds of streusel topping is the king of coffee cakes. Not only does it taste fabulously rich and hearty, but it is easy to make, looks impressive on a cake stand, is apropos morning through night, and has the potential to last well beyond its first day out of the oven.

But in the recipes we tried, the coffee cakes were

either too stout or too sweet, too spicy or too bland, and sometimes even too tough. The streusel inside of the cake was most often wet and pasty, and the streusel topping sometimes melted into the cake, while other times it stayed sandy and granular.

In our efforts to revamp sour cream coffee cake, we decided to first isolate what was important to us. We all agreed that a tube pan lent the most handsome presentation to the cake shape and that we liked streusel so much that we wanted two layers of it—plus the crowning topping.

Because this cake is a behemoth, with hefty amounts of sour cream, butter, eggs, and streusel, a strong flour like all-purpose is required. For the traditional buttery-yellow cake color, we decided on four eggs, enough to give structure to the cake and provide for a tight crumb. We also added a generous amount of baking powder to help lighten the cake's load and baking soda to react with the acidity of the sour cream. As far as fat goes, the more the better, since this is what gives the strong cake its sensitive side and its ability to stay moist for days. One-and-a-half sticks of butter and 1½ cups of sour cream seemed to do the trick. To keep the cake from being too heavy, we chose to use only granulated sugar in the cake base.

Crispy, crunchy, yet melt-in-your-mouth streusel requires a careful agreement between sugar, flour, and butter; nuts and spices also warrant careful scrutiny. Our first discovery was to treat the top streusel and the interior streusel separately. We enjoyed the contrast of tender cake to crunchy topping and so decided to use nuts only in the topping. One cup was just the right amount. We also found that the interior layers of streusel became pasty when we included butter in the mix, so butter, like nuts, would be reserved for the topping. We did like the appearance and flavor from the combined use of granulated and dark brown sugar for both the topping and the inner layers of streusel. In both cases we also found flour necessary to keep the sugar in the streusel from melting or congealing in cement-like shards. Cinnamon—and a hefty dose of it at 2 tablespoons—was the only spice needed to lend warmth to the streusel's flavor.

One hour in the oven at 350 degrees proved to be the best and easiest option for baking; at higher temperatures the streusel became too dark, requiring an aluminum foil shield to protect it from the heat. Because the recipe is quite saturated with fat, we found it best to let the cake cool in the pan for at least one hour to become crack-proof before unmolding. Best of all, if stored well, this cake actually improves with age.

Sour Cream Coffee Cake

SERVES 16

To store the cake, wrap it securely in aluminum foil. If your tube pan has a removable bottom (in which case it is also called an angel food cake pan), wrap the outside portion of the bottom of the pan with aluminum foil before baking the cake. For this sort of cake, though, it's actually easier to use a pan made from a single piece of metal.

STREUSEL

- ¾ cup (3¾ ounces) unbleached all-purpose flour
- ¾ cup (5¼ ounces) granulated sugar
- ½ cup packed (3½ ounces) dark brown sugar
- 2 tablespoons ground cinnamon
- 2 tablespoons unsalted butter, cold
- 1 cup pecans, chopped

CAKE

- 12 tablespoons (1½ sticks) unsalted butter, softened but still cool, cut into 1-inch cubes, plus 2 tablespoons for greasing pan
- 4 large eggs
- 1½ cups sour cream
- 1 tablespoon vanilla extract
- 2¼ cups (11½ ounces) unbleached all-purpose flour
- 1¼ cups (8¾ ounces) granulated sugar
- 1 tablespoon baking powder
- ¾ teaspoon baking soda
- ¾ teaspoon salt

1. FOR THE STREUSEL: Combine the flour, granulated sugar, ¼ cup dark brown sugar, and cinnamon in the workbowl of a food processor. Transfer 1¼ cups of this mixture to a small bowl; stir in the remaining ¼ cup brown sugar and set aside (this will be the streusel for the inside of the cake). Add the butter and pecans to the remaining dry ingredients

in the food processor bowl. Pulse the mixture until the nuts and butter have been broken down into small pebbly pieces, about ten 1-second pulses. Set aside. (The streusel with the butter and nuts will be for the top of the cake).

2. **FOR THE CAKE:** Adjust the oven rack to the bottom position and heat the oven to 350 degrees. Grease a 10-inch tube pan (with 10-cup capacity) with 2 tablespoons softened butter. Combine the eggs, 1 cup sour cream, and vanilla in a medium bowl.

3. Place the flour, sugar, baking powder, baking soda, and salt in the bowl of a standing mixer and mix on low speed for 30 seconds to blend. Add the butter and remaining ½ cup sour cream and mix on low speed until the dry ingredients are moistened. Increase to medium speed and beat 30 seconds. Scrape down the sides of the bowl. Decrease mixer speed to medium-low and slowly incorporate the egg mixture in three additions, beating for 20 seconds after each addition and scraping the sides of the bowl as necessary. Increase the speed to medium-high and beat for 1 minute (the batter should increase in size and become aerated and pale in color).

4. Add 3 cups of batter to the prepared pan. With an offset metal spatula or rubber spatula, smooth the surface of the batter. Sprinkle with ¾ cup streusel filling (without butter or nuts). Drop 1 cup of batter over the streusel, spread evenly, and then add the remaining streusel filling. Top with remaining batter and the streusel topping (with the butter and nuts).

5. Bake until the cake feels firm to the touch and a toothpick or skewer inserted into the center comes out clean (although there may be bits of sugar from the streusel clinging to the tester), 50 to 60 minutes. Cool the cake in the pan for 30 minutes. Place a rimmed baking sheet over the top of the cake and invert the cake onto the pan (cake should now be upside down, with the streusel on the bottom). Remove the tube pan, place a wire rack on top of the cake, and reinvert so the streusel is facing up. Cool for 2 hours and serve, or cool completely and wrap cake in aluminum foil. (Cake can be stored at room temperature for up to 5 days.)

➤ VARIATIONS

Chocolate Chip Sour Cream Coffee Cake
Follow the recipe for Sour Cream Coffee Cake, sprinkling ½ cup chocolate chips on top of the cake batter before adding the first and second streusel layers, for a total of 1 cup chips. Finish the assembly and bake as instructed.

Lemon-Blueberry Sour Cream Coffee Cake
Toss 1 cup frozen blueberries with 1 teaspoon grated lemon zest in a small bowl. Follow the recipe for Sour Cream Coffee Cake, sprinkling ½ cup blueberries on top of the cake batter before adding the first and second streusel layers for a total of 1 cup blueberries. Finish the assembly and bake as instructed.

Almond-Apricot Sour Cream Coffee Cake
Follow the recipe for Sour Cream Coffee Cake, substituting slivered almonds for the pecans and ½ teaspoon almond extract for the vanilla extract. Spoon ½ cup apricot preserves into zipper-lock bag. Cut off a corner tip. Squeeze out 6 dollops of apricot preserves on top of cake batter before adding the first and second streusel layers, for a total of 12 dollops. Finish the assembly and bake as instructed.

APPLE CAKE

EASIER TO BAKE THAN A HOMEMADE APPLE pie but more refined than a quick-cooking apple crisp, an apple cake serves up sweet-tart apples married to a gracious, buttery cake. It can be baked in many forms—loaf pan, cake pan, glass baking dish, even cast-iron skillet. Another part of the apple cake's changing wardrobe is the placement of the apples. They can be found inside, on top of, or underneath the cake. In fact, the only constant in the apple cake recipes we explored was the apples themselves.

We began our tests by gathering a small mountain of apple cake recipes and baked off five that were representative of the group. Most were disappointing. One cake tasted like an overly spiced apple muffin, with flavorless apple chunks suspended in a grainy, gingerbread-colored interior. A loaf-pan cake made by layering McIntosh apples in the batter came out heavy and eggy, with wet pockets of cake and steamed, supersoft apples. We tried an apple upside-down cake consisting of partially cooked apples arranged in a round cake pan with the cake batter poured on top. This one turned out like a third-grade craft project, shellacked, inedible, and ready to hang on the wall. The fourth recipe sounded easy—toss sliced apples in a baking dish and pour batter on top—but it resulted in a loose apple crisp–like dessert. The fifth cake showed some promise. Baked in a springform pan, it consisted of a stiff layer of batter topped with raw chopped apples. Although tasters found the cake too tightly bound and the apples too heavily spiced, we took a shine to its stand-up presentation. The cake was clean-edged and pretty, with a ring of apples jutting up above its crown.

From these initial tests, we gathered our wish list: We wanted the apples to retain their sweet character and to refrain from exuding so much juice as to affect the cake. The cake should contribute a subtle backdrop in flavor, not a barrage of overwhelming spices, and its texture should be sturdy enough to support the apples without being firm and dense, the way a quick bread is.

To find a cake suitable to serve as the foundation for the apples, we turned to our recipe for yellow cake (see page 349). While it was buttery, tender, and rich, this cake was also too delicate to stand up to the weight and released juices from the sliced apples, which we had shingled across the top.

To give the cake base more muscle, we increased the ratio of flour to liquids and added a bit more baking powder for greater lift. We then topped the cake with raw sliced apples coated in sugar. Although improved, this cake was too spongy. It was also a touch sodden from the exuded apple liquid, and it dipped slightly in the center from the apples' weight and juices.

We found a partial solution in the choice of apples: Granny Smith. While Grannies don't have superior flavor, they hold their shape nicely during baking and don't give off much juice. Even better choices, if you can find them, are Pink Lady, Cameo, and Gala. Even with the Grannies, however, the cake was still unable to fully support the fruit. After a host of additional tests, including broiling the apple slices ahead of time, fiddling with ingredient ratios, and

baking the cake at different temperatures and on different rack levels in the oven, the center still sank. How could we produce a stand-up cake with a thick top layer of richly flavored apples?

The solution dawned on us when we noticed a Bundt pan sitting inconspicuously on a corner shelf. With this pan, we wouldn't have a sinking problem—there would be no center to sink. What's more, the hollow center of the pan might knock down the baking time (which until this point had been 1½ hours). And if we placed the apples in the bottom of the pan and then inverted it after baking, the fruit could still be perched on top. We happily dusted off the Bundt pan and increased our working recipe by one-half to fill its larger size.

To prevent sticking, we greased the pan with 2 tablespoons of softened butter, then tossed raw, cubed apples in brown sugar and laid them in the pan. (Cubes fit better than slices in the Bundt's fluted shape.) We topped the apples with batter and popped the pan in the oven. Forty-five minutes later, we pulled out the cake and inverted it onto a cake stand. Although perfectly baked, the cake was no show-stopper, with some apples hugging the cake and others glued to the pan.

To solve this problem, we tried sprinkling 6 tablespoons of sugar over the bottom of the pan before adding the brown sugar–tossed apples, hoping that the sugar would melt and trap the apples' juices before they hit and then stuck to the pan. This apple cake fell out of the pan without any coaxing, and the chopped apples clung to the swells of the cake—not the valleys of the pan.

But this cake wasn't without fault. It was pale and gummy at its apex. When we tested dark brown sugar in the pan instead of white, the apples looked bruised, a result we attributed to uneven melting of the brown sugar. But the cake wasn't gummy anymore, as the brown sugar had created a semicrisp shell around the apples. Next, we gave a combination of white and brown sugars a try. We sprinkled 6 tablespoons of white sugar in the pan. Then, as evenly as possible, we added 2 tablespoons of dark brown sugar on top of the white. We added the sugared apples and, finally, the batter. This version was still mottled in color—light patch, dark patch, light patch—a problem that was easily solved by substituting light brown sugar for dark. When unmolded, the cake practically glowed with a haloed ring of apples of a lovely, flaxen gold. This apple cake was the one—tall, bountiful, and proud not to be an apple pie.

Apple Cake

SERVES 10 TO 12

Cake flour does this cake the most justice (see below for more details), but if there's none available, use a lower-protein, unbleached all-purpose flour instead. Pillsbury and Gold Medal are good options. The cake must be unmolded right after baking. If bits of apple or caramelized sugar stick to the pan, use a toothpick to remove them and return them to their rightful spots on the cake while still warm. Try Pink Lady, Cameo, or Gala apples rather than Grannies if you can find them. This cake is best served the day it is made, with a dusting of powdered sugar, if you like.

CAKE

- ½ pound (2 sticks) unsalted butter, cut into 16 pieces, softened but still cool, plus 2 tablespoons for greasing pan
- 1¼ cups (8¾ ounces) granulated sugar, plus 6 tablespoons for pan
- 2 tablespoons light brown sugar for pan
- 3 large eggs plus 2 large egg yolks

- ½ cup heavy cream
- 2 teaspoons vanilla extract
- 2¼ cups (9 ounces) plain cake flour
- 1 tablespoon baking powder
- ¾ teaspoon salt

APPLES

- 2 Granny Smith apples (about 1 pound), peeled, cored, and cut into ½-inch cubes
- 2 tablespoons light brown sugar

1. FOR THE CAKE: Adjust an oven rack to the lower-middle position and heat the oven to 350 degrees. Grease a standard nonstick 12-cup Bundt pan with 2 tablespoons softened butter; dust the sides with 2 tablespoons granulated sugar, then evenly distribute the remaining 4 tablespoons granulated sugar in the bottom of the pan. Evenly sprinkle the brown sugar on top of the granulated sugar, breaking up large lumps with fingers.

2. Whisk the eggs and yolks in a 2-cup measuring cup to combine. Add the cream and vanilla and beat until thoroughly combined.

3. In the bowl of a standing mixer fitted with the paddle attachment, combine the flour, 1¼ cups sugar, baking powder, and salt. Mix on the lowest speed until combined, about 30 seconds. With the mixer

---

INGREDIENTS: Cake Flour

Although most home cooks use all-purpose flour for everything, even cakes, the Cook's test kitchen is inclined to use lower-protein flours when a delicate texture and fine crumb are in order. In an effort to find out if the type of flour used in these situations really makes a difference, we used our apple cake recipe (above) to perform head-to-head tests.

First, a bit about the theory of low- and high-protein flours. All-purpose flour has a relatively high protein content (10 to 11.7 percent, depending on the brand: King Arthur is in the 11.7 percent range, Pillsbury and Gold Medal around 10 percent), whereas cake flour runs in the 8 to 9 percent range. When water and flour are mixed, gluten is formed. The higher the protein content, the higher the gluten production. For cakes, biscuits, and other chemically leavened baked goods, lower gluten levels usually translate into a softer, more tender crumb.

There is one additional complication. Cake flour is bleached, whereas one can easily find unbleached all-purpose flour.

Bleaching affects the starches in flour such that it can absorb greater amounts of liquid and fat. While this results in a finer crumb, many people can taste an "off" flavor when bleached flour is used owing to the residual hydrochloric acid left behind from bleaching.

Our understanding of different flours was confirmed when we baked two apple cakes, one with unbleached all-purpose and one with bleached cake flour. The former was a bit tough, the latter much more delicate, albeit with a slightly off flavor. Clearly, the cake flour was the winner, even when taking flavor into account. We also tested Pillsbury's lower-protein all-purpose flour against the higher-protein King Arthur (both unbleached). Of these two, Pillsbury was preferable, but, all-in-all, the cake flour still produced a more delicate, fine-textured cake. The conclusion? Use cake flour if you have it. If not, choose the lowest protein, unbleached all-purpose flour you can find, Pillsbury and Gold Medal being two widely available brands.

still running on the lowest speed, add the butter 1 piece at a time in 1-second intervals, beating until the mixture resembles coarse meal, with butter bits no larger than small peas, 1 to 1½ minutes.

4. With the mixer still running, add ½ cup liquid; mix at the lowest speed until incorporated, 5 to 10 seconds. Increase the speed to medium-high and beat until light and fluffy, about 1 minute. With the mixer still running, add the remaining liquid in a steady stream (this should take about 30 seconds). Stop the mixer and scrape down the bowl with a rubber spatula, then beat at medium-high speed to combine, about 30 seconds.

5. FOR THE APPLES: Toss the cubed apples with 2 tablespoons light brown sugar and distribute in an even layer over the sugar in the pan. Add the batter in 4 portions, and gently level with an offset spatula or the back of a soup spoon.

6. Bake until the cake begins to pull away from the sides of the pan, springs back when pressed with a finger, and a toothpick or skewer inserted into the center of cake comes out clean, 35 to 45 minutes. Meanwhile, line a wire rack with a 12-inch square of foil. Immediately invert the cake onto the foil-lined rack. Cool at least 1 hour, then slide onto a serving plate; cut into slices and serve.

BOSTON CREAM PIE

SPONGE CAKE IS THE BEST CHOICE FOR Boston cream pie, that misnamed yellow layer cake filled with custard and drizzled with chocolate icing. Ideally, sponge cake is lighter than the standard butter-based layer cake, with a springy but delicate texture that stands up nicely to a rich custard filling and a sweet chocolate glaze. It should not be dry or tough, the curse of many classic sponge cakes, nor should it be difficult to make.

Why is this cake called Boston cream pie? It seems that the cake does indeed have its roots in Boston, dating back to the middle of the nineteenth century. Modern baking experts believe that since pies predated cakes in the American kitchen, pie pans were simply more common kitchen equipment than cake pans. Hence the name pie was originally given to this layer cake.

Because the cake layers are the trickiest part of Boston cream pie to get right, we decided to start there. There are several kinds of sponge or "foam" cakes, so named because they depend on eggs (whole or separated) beaten to a foam to provide lift and structure. They all use egg foam for structure, but they differ in two ways: whether fat (butter or milk) is added and whether the foam is made from whole eggs, egg whites, or a combination.

We started by making a classic American sponge cake, which adds no fat in the form of butter or milk and calls for eight beaten egg whites folded into four beaten egg yolks. The cake certainly was light, but it lacked flavor, and the texture was dry and a bit chewy. To solve these problems, we turned to a recipe for a hot-milk sponge cake, in which a small amount of melted butter and hot milk are added to the whole-egg foam. This cake turned out much better on all counts. The added fat provided not only flavor but also tenderized the crumb. This particular recipe also used fewer eggs than our original sponge cake recipe.

We were now working with a master recipe that used ¾ cup cake flour, 1 teaspoon baking powder, ¾ cup sugar, and 5 eggs. We started by separating out all five whites and found that the cake was too light, its insufficient structure resulting in a slightly sunken center. We then separated out and beat just three of the whites, and the resulting cake was excellent. When all-purpose flour was substituted for cake flour, the cake had more body and was a bit tougher than the version with cake flour. We then tried different proportions of the two flours, finally settling on a 2–1 ratio of cake flour to all-purpose. We also did some tests to find the proper ratio of eggs to flour and found that 5 eggs to ¾ cup flour (we tested ½ cup and a full cup) was best. Five eggs also turned out to be appropriate: Six eggs produced an "eggy" cake, while four eggs resulted in a lower rise and a cake with a bit less flavor.

We had thought that the baking powder might be optional, but it turned out to be essential to a properly risen cake. Although angel food and classic sponge cakes, which use no added fat, do not require chemical leavening, in this sponge cake—given the addition of milk and melted butter combined with the relatively small amount of beaten egg whites in proportion to the flour—baking powder was necessary.

Two tablespoons of melted butter was just the right amount; 3 tablespoons made the cake a bit oily and the butter flavor too prominent. As for the milk, 3 tablespoons was best; larger quantities resulted in a wet, mushy texture.

With our basic recipe in hand, we played with the order of the steps. Beating the whole-egg foam first, and then the whites, allowed the relatively fragile foam to deteriorate, producing less rise. We found that beating the whites first was vastly better. After much experimentation, we also found it best to fold together, all at the same time, the beaten whole eggs, the beaten whites, and the flour, and then, once the mixture was about half-mixed, to add the warm butter and milk. This eliminated the possibility that the liquid would damage the egg foam and also made the temperature of the butter/milk mixture less important than it was in other sponge cakes.

Determining when a sponge cake is properly cooked is a little more difficult than it is with a regular American layer cake. A sponge cake should provide some resistance and not feel as if one just touched the top of a soufflé. Another good test is color. The top of the cake should be a nice light brown, not pale golden or a dark, rich brown.

We also tested the best way to handle the cake once out of the oven. When left to cool in a baking pan, the cake shrinks away from the sides and the edges become uneven. Quickly removing it onto a cooling rack works well, but it's tricky, because the cake pan is very hot. We discovered that the best method is to place the hot cake pan on a kitchen towel, cover it with a plate, and then use the towel to invert the cake. Finally, reinvert the cake and slip it back onto a cooling rack.

With the cake layers baked, Boston cream pie comes together rather easily. A classic pastry cream filling works perfectly, while a thin chocolate glaze is the ideal frosting.

Boston Cream Pie

SERVES 8 TO 10

Make the pastry cream, followed by the cake layers. Start the glaze when the cake layers have cooled.

PASTRY CREAM

2	cups milk
6	large egg yolks
½	cup (2½ ounces) sugar
¼	teaspoon salt
¼	cup cornstarch, sifted
1	teaspoon vanilla extract
1	tablespoon rum
2	tablespoons unsalted butter, optional

GLAZE

1	cup heavy cream
¼	cup light corn syrup
8	ounces semisweet chocolate, chopped into small pieces
½	teaspoon vanilla extract

1	recipe Foolproof Sponge Cake (see recipe on page 347)

1. FOR THE PASTRY CREAM: Heat the milk in a small saucepan until hot but not simmering. Whisk the yolks, sugar, and salt in a large saucepan until the mixture is thick and lemon-colored, 3 to 4 minutes. Add the cornstarch; whisk to combine. Slowly whisk in the hot milk. Cook the milk mixture over medium-low heat, whisking constantly and scraping the pan bottom and sides as you stir, until the mixture reaches the consistency of a thick pudding and loses all traces of raw cornstarch flavor, about 10 minutes. Off heat, stir in the vanilla, rum, and butter (if using) and transfer to another container to cool to room temperature, placing a piece of plastic wrap directly on the surface of the mixture to prevent a skin from forming. Refrigerate the pastry cream until firm. (Can be refrigerated overnight.) To ensure that the pastry cream does not thin out, do not whisk once it has set.

2. FOR THE GLAZE: Bring the cream and corn syrup to a full simmer over medium heat in a medium saucepan. Off heat, add the chocolate; cover

and let stand for 8 minutes. (If the chocolate has not completely melted, return the saucepan to low heat; stir constantly until melted.) Add the vanilla; stir very gently until the mixture is smooth. Cool until tepid so that a spoonful drizzled back into the pan mounds slightly. (Glaze can be refrigerated to speed up the cooling process, stirring every few minutes to ensure even cooling.)

3. TO ASSEMBLE PIE: While the glaze is cooling, place one cake layer on a cardboard round on a cooling rack set over wax paper. Carefully spoon the pastry cream over the cake and spread it evenly up to the edge of the cake. Place the second layer on top, making sure the layers line up properly.

4. Pour the glaze over the middle of the top layer and let it flow down the cake sides. Use a metal spatula, if necessary, to completely coat the cake. Use a small needle to puncture any air bubbles. Let sit until the glaze fully sets, about 1 hour. Serve that day, preferably within a couple of hours.

Foolproof Sponge Cake

MAKES TWO 8- OR 9-INCH CAKES

The egg whites should be beaten to soft, glossy, billowy peaks. If beaten until too stiff, they will be very difficult to fold into the whole-egg mixture.

½	cup (2 ounces) plain cake flour
¼	cup (1½ ounces) unbleached all-purpose flour
1	teaspoon baking powder
¼	teaspoon salt
3	tablespoons milk
2	tablespoons unsalted butter
½	teaspoon vanilla extract
5	large eggs, room temperature
¾	cup (3¾ ounces) sugar

1. Adjust an oven rack to the lower-middle position and heat the oven to 350 degrees. Grease two 8- or 9-inch cake pans and cover the pan bottoms with rounds of parchment paper. Whisk the flours, baking powder, and salt in a medium bowl (or sift onto wax paper). Heat the milk and butter in a small saucepan over low heat until the butter melts. Remove from the heat and add the vanilla; cover and keep warm.

2. Separate three of the eggs, placing the whites in the bowl of a standing mixer fitted with the whisk attachment and reserving the 3 yolks plus the remaining 2 whole eggs in another mixing bowl. Beat the 3 whites on low speed until foamy. Increase the mixer speed to medium and gradually add 6 tablespoons sugar; continue to beat the whites to soft, moist peaks. (Do not overbeat.) Transfer the egg whites to a large bowl and add yolk/whole-egg mixture to the mixer bowl.

3. Beat the yolk/whole-egg mixture with the remaining 6 tablespoons sugar. Beat on medium-high speed until the eggs are very thick and a pale yellow color, about 5 minutes. Add the beaten eggs to the whites.

4. Sprinkle the flour mixture over the beaten eggs and whites; fold very gently 12 times with a large rubber spatula. Make a well in one side of the batter and pour the milk mixture into the bowl. Continue folding until the batter shows no trace of flour and the whites and whole eggs are evenly mixed, about 8 additional strokes.

5. Immediately pour the batter into the prepared cake pans; bake until the cake tops are light brown and feel firm and spring back when touched, about 16 minutes for 9-inch cake pans and 20 minutes for 8-inch cake pans.

6. Immediately run a knife around the pan perimeters to loosen the cakes. Cover one pan with a large plate. Using a towel, invert the pan and remove the pan from the cake. Peel off the parchment. Reinvert the cake from the plate onto the rack. Repeat with the remaining cake. Cool cake layers to room temperature before assembling Boston cream pie.

YELLOW LAYER CAKE

YELLOW CAKE HAS ALWAYS BEEN A BROAD category, but most of the recipes for making it are very similar. For example, in *The Boston Cook Book*, published in 1884, Mary Lincoln, one of Fannie Farmer's colleagues at the Boston Cooking School, outlined several recipes for yellow cake. But she singled out one as "the foundation for countless varieties of cake, which are often given in cookbooks under different names." Mrs. Lincoln's master cake formula turns out to be similar to what we today call a 1-2-3-4 cake, made with 1 cup butter, 2 cups sugar, 3 cups (sifted) cake flour, and 4 eggs, plus milk and small amounts of baking powder, vanilla, and salt. As it turns out, things have not changed much since more than a century ago. When analyzed, most of the yellow cake recipes in today's cookbooks are 1-2-3-4 cakes or something very similar.

So when we set out in search of the perfect yellow cake, the first thing we did was bake a 1-2-3-4 cake. It wasn't a bad cake, it just wasn't very interesting. Instead of melting in the mouth, the cake seemed crumbly, sugary, and a little hard. The crust was tacky and separated from the underlying cake. Above all, the cake lacked flavor. It did not taste of butter and eggs, as all plain cakes ought to, but instead seemed merely sweet.

Before tinkering with the ingredients, we decided to try a different mixing method. We had mixed our 1-2-3-4 cake in the classic way, first beating the butter and sugar until light and fluffy, then adding the eggs one at a time, and finally adding the dry ingredients and milk alternately. Now we wanted to try mixing the batter by the so-called two-stage method, developed by General Mills and Pillsbury in the 1940s and later popularized by Rose Levy Beranbaum in *The Cake Bible* (Morrow, 1988).

In the two-stage method, the flour, sugar, baking powder, and salt are combined, the butter and about two-thirds of the milk and eggs are added, and the batter is beaten until thick and fluffy, about a minute. Then, in the second stage, the rest of the milk and eggs are poured in and the batter is beaten about half a minute more. The two-stage method is simpler, quicker, and more nearly foolproof than the

---

EQUIPMENT: Cake Pans

If you want to make a layer cake (even once a year for someone's birthday), you must own good cake pans. There's no sense doing all that work only to have the cake stick to flimsy disposable aluminum pans. When shopping, make sure to buy two sets of cake pans, preferably two 8-inch pans and two 9-inch pans. Different pans will produce cake layers of varying sizes, and layers that are the same size are easier to assemble and frost.

We baked both plain and chocolate butter cakes in 11 different pans. We found that cakes released perfectly from pans lined with nonstick or "stick-resistant" coatings. Most cakes released adequately from uncoated pans, with one exception. The flexible fiberglass pans we tested repeatedly held onto large chunks of cake. Because these pans also gave the cakes a faint rubbery flavor, they quickly fell to the bottom of the ratings.

When it came to browning the crust, we found dramatic differences in the pans. In general, the darker the pan, the darker the crust. Some bakers advise against using pans with dark finishes, such as nonstick coatings, because they worry about overbrowning. We found that dark pans created a darker crust but not one that was "overbrowned" or undesirable. In fact, we enjoyed the richer flavor of dark crusts when eating these cakes unfrosted, and we also found that their sturdiness and resistance to crumbling made them easier to frost.

We determined that pans with light-colored or shiny finishes could produce well-browned cakes, as long as the pans were made from aluminum. That's because aluminum conducts evenly and quickly. In contrast, stainless steel is a poor conductor of heat and pans made from this material produced pale-looking cakes. In general, we prefer aluminum or tinned steel pans, preferably with a nonstick coating and/or a dark finish.

As for the other variables, all pans produced cakes of similar height, despite differences in pan depth. Since we preferred cakes with darker crusts, the insulated pans fell to the bottom of our ratings—two layers of metal separated by airspace slowed down the browning process. While we liked most of the heavier "commercial" pans, our favorite pan was one of the lightest. In the end, the metal used and the finish are more important than the weight.

Finally, the issue of handles proved to be decisive in our testing. Pans with handles (or wings) on either side are much easier to transfer to the oven when filled with batter and to rotate once in the oven. Handles make it much easier to grab the pan without landing the corner of a pot holder in a finished cake. Simply put, we love handles.

The bottom line: The most important factor when buying a cake pan is the finish. Dark nonstick or stick-resistant coatings ensure easy release and also promote deep browning of the crust, which means more flavor and no crumbs marring the frosting. If you have a choice, buy cake pans with handles on either side. Handles will prevent even the klutziest cook from sticking an oven mitt into a just-baked cake.

conventional creaming method.

The results exceeded our expectations. The two-stage method is often touted for the tender texture it promotes in cakes, and our two-stage 1-2-3-4 cake was indeed tender. But, more important, its consistency was improved. Whereas the conventionally mixed 1-2-3-4 cake had been crumbly, this cake was fine-grained and melting, and, interestingly enough, it did not seem overly sweet. Even the crust was improved. It was still a bit coarse, but only slightly sticky. This was a cake with a texture that we truly liked.

The problem was the taste. The cake still didn't have any. In fact, oddly enough, it seemed to have less taste than the conventionally mixed version. Certainly it had less color. The 1-2-3-4 cake, it seemed, conformed to a typical cake pattern—as the texture lightened, the taste and color faded.

After trying to remedy the taste deficit by playing around with the ingredients in many ways—primarily adjusting the amounts and proportions of the sugar and eggs—we finally recalled a recipe called Bride's Cake in *Mrs. Rorer's New Cook Book*, published in 1902. This is basically an egg-white pound cake—made of a pound each of flour, sugar, butter, and egg whites—with a cup of milk and a little chemical leavening added. What would happen, we wondered, if we made Mrs. Rorer's cake with whole eggs instead of egg whites? It seemed worth a try.

We cut all of Mrs. Rorer's ingredients by half—that is, we made a half-pound cake, so that the batter would fit into two standard 9-inch round cake pans—and when mixing the batter we followed the two-stage method. The resulting cake was richer, more flavorful, and generally more interesting than any of the 1-2-3-4 cakes we had baked, but it was not perfect. The layers were low, and the cake was just a tad dense and rough on the tongue (though not rubbery, thank goodness). We had several options. We could try to open up the crumb by adding more milk and baking powder; we could try to lighten the cake up with an extra egg or a couple of extra yolks; or we could try to increase the volume and tenderize the texture by adding a few more ounces of sugar. We tried all three strategies. The last one—the extra sugar—did the trick. This cake was fine-grained, soft, and melting, and it tasted of butter

and eggs. It had elegance and finesse and yet was still sturdy enough to withstand the frosting process.

Both the 1-2-3-4 cake and our improved yellow cake based on Mrs. Rorer's recipe are made with a half pound each of butter and eggs. But while the 1-2-3-4 cake contains 3 cups of sifted cake flour and 1 cup of milk, our improved yellow cake contains just 2¼ cups of sifted cake flour and only ½ cup of milk. So, while the 1-2-3-4 cake contains, by weight, 3 ounces more flour and milk than butter and eggs, our yellow cake contains 3 ounces less flour and milk than butter and eggs. This difference in basic proportions, as it turns out, makes a tremendous difference in texture and taste.

Yellow Layer Cake

SERVES 8 TO 10

Adding the butter pieces to the mixing bowl one at a time prevents the dry ingredients from flying up and out of the bowl. This yellow cake works with any of the frostings that follow.

4	large eggs, room temperature
½	cup whole milk, room temperature
2	teaspoons vanilla extract
2¼	cups sifted (6¾ ounces) plain cake flour
1½	cups (10½ ounces) sugar
2	teaspoons baking powder
¾	teaspoon salt
½	pound (2 sticks) unsalted butter, softened, each stick cut into 8 pieces
1	recipe Coffee Buttercream or Chocolate Cream Frosting (see pages 350 to 351)

1. Adjust an oven rack to the lower-middle position and heat the oven to 350 degrees. Generously grease two 9-inch cake pans with vegetable shortening and cover the pan bottoms with rounds of parchment paper or wax paper. Grease the parchment rounds, dust the cake pans with flour, and tap out excess.

2. Beat the eggs, milk, and vanilla with a fork in a small bowl; measure out 1 cup of this mixture and set aside. Combine the flour, sugar, baking powder, and salt in the bowl of a standing mixer fitted with the

paddle attachment; mix on the lowest speed to blend, about 30 seconds. With the mixer still running at the lowest speed, add the butter one piece at a time; mix until the butter and flour begin to clump together and look sandy and pebbly, with pieces about the size of peas, 30 to 40 seconds after all the butter is added. Add reserved 1 cup of egg mixture and mix at the lowest speed until incorporated, 5 to 10 seconds. Increase the speed to medium-high and beat until light and fluffy, about 1 minute. Add the remaining egg mixture (about ½ cup) in a slow steady stream, about 30 seconds. Stop the mixer and scrape the sides and bottom of bowl. Beat on medium-high until thoroughly combined and the batter looks slightly curdled, about 15 seconds.

3. Divide the batter equally between the prepared cake pans; spread to the sides of the pan and smooth with a rubber spatula. Bake until the cake tops are light gold and a toothpick or skewer inserted in the center comes out clean, 20 to 25 minutes. (Cakes may mound slightly but will level

when cooled.) Cool on a rack for 10 minutes. Run a knife around the pan perimeters to loosen. Invert one cake onto a large plate, peel off the parchment, and reinvert onto a lightly greased rack. Repeat with the other cake. Cool completely before icing.

4. Assemble and frost the cake according to the illustrations below. Cut the cake into slices and serve. (Cover leftover cake with plastic and refrigerate; bring to room temperature before serving.)

Vanilla Buttercream Frosting

MAKES ABOUT 4 CUPS, ENOUGH TO ICE ONE 8- OR 9-INCH TWO-LAYER CAKE OR ONE 8-INCH THREE-LAYER CAKE

The whole eggs, whipped until airy, give this buttercream a light, satiny smooth texture that melts on the tongue.

| 4 | large eggs |
| I | cup (7 ounces) sugar |

FROSTING A LAYER CAKE

1. To anchor the cake, spread a dab of frosting in the center of a cardboard round cut slightly larger than the cake. Center a cake layer on the cardboard round.

2. Place a large blob of icing in the center of the layer and spread it to the edges with an icing spatula. Imagine you are pushing the icing into place rather than scraping it on.

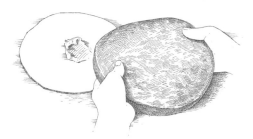

3. Hold the spatula at a 45-degree angle to the cake and drag it across the surface to level the icing.

4. Using a second cardboard round, slide the next cake layer into place. Repeat steps 2 and 3 with each new cake layer.

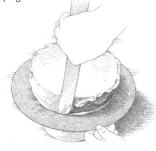

5. To ice the sides of the cake, scoop up a large dab of icing on the tip of the spatula and spread it on the sides with short side-to-side strokes.

2 teaspoons vanilla extract
Pinch salt
1 pound (4 sticks) unsalted butter, softened,
each stick cut into quarters

1. Combine the eggs, sugar, vanilla, and salt in the bowl of a standing mixer; place the bowl over a pan of simmering water. Whisking gently but constantly, heat the mixture until it is thin and foamy and registers 160 degrees on instant-read thermometer.

2. Beat the egg mixture on medium-high speed with the whisk attachment until light, airy, and cooled to room temperature, about 5 minutes. Reduce the speed to medium and add butter, one piece at a time. (After adding half the butter, the buttercream may look curdled; it will smooth with additional butter.) Once all the butter is added, increase the speed to high and beat 1 minute until light, fluffy, and thoroughly combined. (Can be covered and refrigerated up to 5 days.)

> VARIATION

Coffee Buttercream Frosting

Dissolve 3 tablespoons instant espresso in 3 tablespoons warm water. Follow the recipe for Vanilla Buttercream Frosting, omitting the vanilla and beating the dissolved coffee into the buttercream after the butter has been added.

Chocolate Cream Frosting

MAKES ABOUT 3 CUPS, ENOUGH TO ICE
ONE 8- OR 9-INCH TWO-LAYER CAKE

This soft, rich frosting is the perfect companion to a tender yellow layer cake.

16 ounces bittersweet or semisweet chocolate,
chopped fine
1½ cups heavy cream
⅓ cup light corn syrup
1 teaspoon vanilla extract

Place the chocolate in a heatproof bowl. Bring the heavy cream to a boil in a small saucepan over medium-high heat; pour over the chocolate. Add the corn syrup and let stand 3 minutes. Whisk gently until smooth; stir in the vanilla. Refrigerate 1 to 1½

hours, stirring every 15 minutes, until the mixture reaches a spreadable consistency.

DEVIL'S FOOD CAKE

THE CRAZE FOR FANCY CAKE NAMES DATES back to the latter part of the nineteenth century. But only one of these cakes has truly survived from that period to ours—the devil's food cake. Its success is a testament to its utter simplicity and, being a moist chocolate cake, it has had lasting appeal.

The obvious question is, "Just what is this cake?" The short answer is that the name refers to the color of the cake, not the texture, taste, shape, or fancy decorations. One group of food historians would argue that devil's food is a black cake; others would point to a reddish hue—cocoa naturally contains red pigments—as the distinguishing characteristic.

The problem with defining the devil's food cake, beyond the obvious issue of color, is that over time the recipe has been changed and embellished to the point where different recipes have little in common. To get a better handle on the situation, we pulled together two dozen or so recipes from cookbooks and the Internet, and our test kitchen baked the most promising five. The blind tasting that followed helped us put together a good working definition of our ideal devil's food cake. Although some of the recipes were similar to a regular chocolate cake (crumbly, a bit dry, and milder in flavor), we found the essence of devil's food to be a very moist, velvety texture combined with an intense chocolate experience. In addition, the better cakes were very dark, almost black. Here was a chocolate cake that was rich in both color and texture.

The next question was how to construct the ideal recipe. Despite their several differences, we first noted that all the recipes were constructed using the basic layer cake method. Butter and sugar were creamed, and then eggs were beaten in, followed by flour, cocoa, milk or water, and other ingredients. The next things we noticed were that the majority of recipes for this cake called for both cocoa and baking soda (not baking powder) and that many also suggested the addition of melted chocolate. Almost all of them used boiling water as the liquid of choice, although recipes from the early 1900s preferred milk, sour milk, or buttermilk. So the four key ingredients—those which really stood out in our research—were chocolate, cocoa, baking soda, and water.

The first issue was whether both chocolate and cocoa were necessary for the best flavor. The one cake out of five that used only cocoa was the driest and least flavorful. Clearly, a bit of chocolate was a must, and we finally settled on 4 ounces after testing smaller and larger amounts. As expected, the cake that used milk instead of water had less flavor, since milk tends to dull the flavor of chocolate (think of milk versus dark chocolate).

Baking soda was the leavener of choice in virtually every recipe we found, but we tested this anyway. To our great surprise, the baking powder cake produced a totally different product. It was much lighter in color, and, more to the point, it was fudgy, almost like a brownie. It shared none of the delicate, velvety texture that we had come to expect of a classic devil's food. We also tested the proper amount of baking soda and settled on 1 teaspoon. More caused the cake to fall in the center, and any less didn't provide enough lift.

We continued our testing to refine the recipe and found that a mixture of cake flour and all-purpose was best. The all-purpose flour provided structure, while the addition of the cake flour made the cake a bit more delicate. On a lark, we made one cake by whipping the egg whites separately from the yolks, but the result was a much too flimsy cake that could not support the large amount of water called for in most recipes—so it sank. We played with the number of eggs, trying two, three, and then four. The middle road proved best—three eggs was just right. White sugar was tested against brown sugar and the latter won, improving the flavor. Many devil's food recipes do indeed call for brown sugar, whereas those for regular chocolate cakes tend to use regular white sugar.

Although we had tested milk and buttermilk against water—the water produced a more intense chocolate experience—we tried adding sour cream to the recipe and were impressed. It deepened the flavor, added substance to the texture, and provided a richer taste experience, the chocolate flavor lingering in the mouth and coating the tongue.

Finally, we wondered if boiling water was really necessary. To find out, we made a cake with room-temperature water and found that it made virtually no difference. But when we tested dissolving the cocoa in the boiling water (as opposed to simply mixing it in with the flour), we found that this significantly enhanced the cocoa's flavor.

We had finally discovered the essence of a great devil's food cake. Unlike chocolate cake, which is

---

INGREDIENTS: **Two Types of Cocoa**

Dutch-processed cocoa is less acidic (or more alkaline) than a regular cocoa such as Hershey's. The theory is that reducing the acidity of natural cocoa enhances browning reactions, which in turn result in a darker color. Because the red pigments in cocoa become more visible in a more acidic environment, the more acidic natural cocoa is supposed to produce a redder cake. Manufacturers also claim that the process of Dutching cocoa results in a smoother, less bitter chocolate flavor.

To determine the veracity of these claims, we conducted a head-to-head test of three Dutch-processed cocoas—Droste, King Arthur Flour's "black" cocoa (made from beans that are roasted until they are almost burnt), and Pernigotti, a very expensive brand sold at Williams-Sonoma stores—against Hershey's natural cocoa.

All three Dutch-processed cocoas produced darker cakes with more chocolate flavor than the Hershey's did, bearing out our research. The Hershey's cocoa also produced a much redder cake, just as promised. But we also noticed textural differences in the cakes. The cake made with Hershey's was dry and airy without much complexity of flavor. Among the cakes made with Dutch-processed cocoa, the cake made with the expensive Pernigotti produced a very moist, soft crumb; that made with Droste was a bit dry with a more open crumb; and the "black" cocoa cake was very dense, almost spongy, although incredibly chocolatey as well.

So if you want a richer-tasting, darker, more velvety cake, use Dutch-processed cocoa, keeping in mind that quality matters. Those who must have a reddish color can go with regular cocoa, but the taste and texture will suffer somewhat.

---

usually made from milk and has a higher proportion of fat (butter), devil's food provides a velvety, more intense chocolate experience. And it is a particularly dark cake when made with Dutch-processed cocoa; supermarket cocoa will give it a redder hue. (See "Two Types of Cocoa" on page 352.) It is, ultimately, a singular cake in its devotion to a pure chocolate experience, subordinating everything to this simple but tasty proposition.

Devil's Food Cake

SERVES 8 TO 10

Regular, or natural, cocoa like Hershey's can be used with good results, though the cakes will bake up a bit drier, redder, and with slightly less chocolate flavor.

½	pound (2 sticks) unsalted butter, softened, plus extra for greasing pans
4	ounces unsweetened chocolate, chopped
¼	cup Dutch-processed cocoa
1¼	cups boiling water
¾	cup (3¾ ounces) unbleached all-purpose flour
¾	cup (3 ounces) plain cake flour
1	teaspoon baking soda
¼	teaspoon salt
1½	cups packed (10½ ounces) dark brown sugar
3	large eggs, room temperature
½	cup sour cream
1	teaspoon vanilla extract
1	recipe Vanilla or Coffee Buttercream Frosting (page 350 to 351)

1. Adjust the oven racks to the upper- and lower-middle positions; heat the oven to 350 degrees. Meanwhile, grease three 8-inch cake pans with butter and line the bottom of each pan with a round of parchment or wax paper. Combine the chocolate and cocoa in a medium bowl; pour the boiling water over and whisk until smooth. Sift together the flours, baking soda, and salt onto a large sheet of parchment or wax paper; set aside.

2. Place the butter in the bowl of a standing mixer and beat at medium-high speed until creamy, about 1 minute. Add the brown sugar and beat on high until light and fluffy, about 3 minutes. Stop the mixer and scrape down the bowl with a rubber spatula. Increase the speed to medium-high and add the eggs one at a time, beating 30 seconds after each addition. Reduce the speed to medium; add the sour cream and vanilla and beat until combined, about 10 seconds. Stop the mixer and scrape down the bowl. With the mixer on low, add about one-third of the flour mixture, followed by about one half of the chocolate mixture. Repeat, ending with the flour mixture; beat until just combined, about 15 seconds. Do not overbeat. Remove the bowl from the mixer; scrape the bottom and sides of the bowl with a rubber spatula and mix gently to thoroughly combine.

3. Divide the batter evenly among the cake pans and smooth the batter to the edges of each pan with a rubber spatula. Place two pans on the lower-middle rack and one on the upper-middle rack. Bake until a toothpick or skewer inserted in the center comes out clean, 20 to 23 minutes. Cool on a wire rack 15 to 20 minutes. Run a knife around each pan perimeter to loosen. Invert the cakes onto a large plate; peel off the parchment, and reinvert onto a lightly greased rack. Cool completely.

4. Assemble and frost the cake according to the illustrations on page 350. Cut the cake into slices and serve. (Cover leftover cake with plastic and refrigerate; bring to room temperature before serving.)

COCONUT LAYER CAKE

COCONUT CAKE SHOULD BE PERFUMED inside and out with the cool, subtle, mysterious essence of coconut. Its layers of snowy white cake should be moist and tender, with a delicate, yielding crumb, and the icing a silky, gently sweetened coat covered with a deep drift of downy coconut. So it's irksome and disappointing that coconut cakes are often frauds, no more than plain white cakes with plain white icing slapped with shredded coconut. We decided to pursue a coconut cake that lived up to our dreams.

With a roundup of cakes baked according to different recipes, likes and dislikes among the members of the tasting panel surfaced. Cakes baked in a 9 by 13-inch baking pan defied the archetypal sky-high layer-cake form. Coarse, crumbly textured cakes did not fit the bill, nor did cakes tinted yellow from yolks or whole eggs. Light, spongy, cottony cakes were too dry and too toothsome for a coconut cake. Doctored with coconut milk and a bit of coconut extract and tweaked ever so slightly, a basic white cake garnered the most praise for its buttery flavor and its tender, fine crumb.

The cake doctored with coconut milk and extract was good, but it wasn't perfect. We found that from batch to batch, coconut milk could produce mystifyingly different results—sometimes a flat cake, sometimes a mounded cake, sometimes a heavy, greasy cake. We discovered that the source of the problem was variation in the fat content of coconut milk, which can be as much as 33 percent from brand to brand. Cream of coconut, a sweetened coconut product that contains a few inscrutable emulsifiers, seemed to be a more consistent product, perhaps because there appear to be fewer brands, Coco López being the best known. So we cut back on some of the sugar that went into the batter and used cream of coconut instead of coconut milk. These cakes baked up beautifully, their exteriors an appealing burnished brown color that the coconut milk versions lacked, and they tasted more strongly of coconut as well.

Unfortunately, these cakes also baked up with a giant mound at their centers, which made them look more like desert turtles than dessert. Because the batter was a very thick one that could use gentler heat (which would facilitate a more even rise in the oven), we were able to lower the mounds by reducing the oven temperature to 325 degrees. The resulting cakes were significantly improved. Then, to level things out even more, we manipulated the quantity of eggs. During these trials, we discovered that one yolk in addition to six egg whites gave the cakes a richer, fuller flavor without tainting their saintly color. This did nothing to alleviate the remaining slight mounding problem, however, so we tried scaling back on the cream of coconut and diluting the batter with a bit of water. This thinner batter baked into nice, even cakes.

It was time to work on the icing. Cream cheese frosting—not uncommon on coconut cakes—was unanimously rejected for its heavy texture and a distinct, distracting tang that obscured the delicate coconut flavor. Whipped cream met with just as much opposition; lifeless and uninteresting, it was patently unsuited to a coconut cake. Most tasters acknowledged that seven-minute meringue icing is what they'd expect, but we found this icing to be painfully sweet and devoid of appealing texture. So we assembled one coconut cake with a butter and confectioners' sugar icing and one with an egg white buttercream that was an offshoot of the whole-egg buttercream we like to use with our yellow layer cake and devil's food cake. Both icings garnered applause, but the egg white buttercream was the favorite. Not only was it incredibly lithe, but it was also less sweet, significantly more silky and smooth, and much more fluffy and light than its competitor. In some ways, it was reminiscent of the traditional seven-minute icing, just not as sweet or as sticky, and with a creamier consistency.

This buttercream begins life as a meringue, with softened butter eventually beaten in. We tried two approaches to building the meringue. In the first, the whites and sugar are simply beaten to soft peaks in a standing mixer. In the second, the whites and sugar

INGREDIENTS: Coconut Extract

Pure extracts are essential oils extracted from natural flavoring agents such as fruit rinds, nuts, and herbs and then dissolved in alcohol. Imitation extracts are fabricated from chemical compounds that mimic natural flavors; these compounds are then also dissolved in alcohol. As with most things natural and synthetic, natural extracts cost more. When it came to coconut extract, we wanted to know whether "pure" was worth the price. So we made our buttercream frosting using three extracts—McCormick Imitation Coconut Extract, Spices Etc. Natural Coconut Flavoring, and LorAnn Gourmet Coconut Flavor—and put them to the test.

LorAnn Gourmet Coconut Flavor was uniformly rejected, bringing new meaning to the word artificial. One taster commented, "I feel like I'm eating suntan lotion." McCormick Imitation Coconut Extract came in second. Tasters didn't note any off flavors and considered this extract "subtle" and "good." Spices Etc. Natural Coconut Flavoring, made from the pulp of coconuts, was the most "deeply coconutty" and highly praised of the group. Ringing in at $3.25 for a 1-ounce bottle compared with $2.42 for the McCormick, the natural is worth the extra 80 cents.

are whisked together over a hot water bath until the sugar dissolves and the mixture is warm to the touch. The former straightforward meringue fell quickly as the butter was added, and the resulting buttercream was incredibly heavy and stiff, almost no better than the butter and confectioners' sugar icing. The meringue that went over heat was much more stable. Although it did fall when butter was added, the completed icing was soft, supple, and dreamy. (Note that this temperature is not hot enough to eliminate the unlikely presence of salmonella bacteria in the eggs.)

The textural coup de grace of a coconut cake is its woolly coconut coat. Indeed, pure white shredded coconut straight from the bag makes for a maidenly cake. Toasted coconut, however, has both chew and crunch as well as a much more intense flavor. And when toasted not to the point of even brownness but to that where it resembles a toss of white and bronze confetti, it dresses this cake to be belle of the ball.

Coconut Layer Cake

SERVES 8 TO 10

Cream of coconut is often found in the soda and drink-mix aisle in the grocery store. One 15-ounce can is enough for both the cake and the buttercream; make sure to stir it well before using because it separates upon standing.

CAKE

1	large egg plus 5 large egg whites
¾	cup cream of coconut
¼	cup water
1	teaspoon vanilla extract
1	teaspoon coconut extract
2¼	cups (9 ounces) plain cake flour, sifted
1	cup (7 ounces) sugar
1	tablespoon baking powder
¾	teaspoon salt
12	tablespoons (1½ sticks) unsalted butter, cut into 12 pieces, softened, but still cool
2	cups packed (about 8 ounces) sweetened shredded coconut

BUTTERCREAM

4	large egg whites
1	cup (7 ounces) sugar
	Pinch salt
1	pound (4 sticks) unsalted butter, each stick cut into 6 pieces, softened, but still cool
¼	cup cream of coconut
1	teaspoon coconut extract
1	teaspoon vanilla extract

1. FOR THE CAKE: Adjust the oven rack to the lower-middle position and heat the oven to 325 degrees. Grease two 9-inch round cake pans with shortening and dust with flour.

2. Beat the egg whites and whole egg in a large measuring cup with a fork to combine. Add the cream of coconut, water, vanilla, and coconut extract and beat with a fork until thoroughly combined.

3. Combine the flour, sugar, baking powder, and salt in the bowl of a standing mixer fitted with the paddle attachment. Mix on the lowest speed to combine, about 30 seconds. With the mixer still running on the lowest speed, add the butter 1 piece at a time, then beat until the mixture resembles coarse meal, with butter bits no larger than small peas, 2 to 2½ minutes.

4. With the mixer still running, add 1 cup liquid. Increase the speed to medium-high and beat until light and fluffy, about 45 seconds. With the mixer still running, add the remaining 1 cup liquid in a steady stream (this should take about 15 seconds). Stop the mixer and scrape down the bowl with a rubber spatula, then beat at medium-high speed to combine, about 15 seconds. (Batter will be thick.)

5. Divide the batter between the cake pans and level with an offset or rubber spatula. Bake until deep golden brown, the cakes pull away from sides of pans, and a toothpick inserted into the center of the cakes comes out clean, about 30 minutes (rotate the cakes after about 20 minutes). Do not turn off the oven.

6. Cool in the pans on wire racks for about 10 minutes, then loosen the cakes from the sides of the pans with a paring knife, invert the cakes onto racks, and reinvert them so the top sides face up; cool to room temperature.

7. TO TOAST THE COCONUT: While the cakes are cooling, spread the shredded coconut on a rimmed baking sheet; toast in the oven until the shreds are a

mix of golden brown and white, 15 to 20 minutes, stirring 2 or 3 times. Cool to room temperature.

8. FOR THE BUTTERCREAM: Combine the egg whites, sugar, and salt in the bowl of a standing mixer; set the bowl over a saucepan containing 1½ inches of barely simmering water. Whisk constantly until this mixture is opaque and warm to the touch and registers about 120 degrees on an instant-read thermometer, about 2 minutes.

9. Transfer the bowl to the mixer and beat the whites on high speed with the whisk attachment until barely warm (about 80 degrees) and the whites are glossy and sticky, about 7 minutes. Reduce the speed to medium-high and beat in the butter 1 piece at a time. Beat in the cream of coconut and coconut and vanilla extracts. Stop the mixer and scrape the bottom and sides of bowl. Continue to beat at medium-high speed until well-combined, about 1 minute.

10. TO ASSEMBLE CAKE: With a long serrated knife, cut both cakes in half horizontally so that each cake forms two layers. Assemble and frost the cake according to the illustrations on page 350. Sprinkle

---

SCIENCE: Baking Soda's Double Role

In addition to leavening, baking soda plays a second important role in carrot cakes—it is responsible for breaking down the carrots so they are sufficiently cooked to complement the flavors of the cake. We discovered this while testing leavening agents. The carrots came out just right when we used a combination of baking soda and baking powder, but when we used only baking powder the carrots were crisp and undercooked. Curious, we decided to investigate.

We found out that, like other vegetables, carrots get their crispness from water-filled cells. The cell walls retain the water in the cells, just as the plastic walls of a zipper-lock bag hold water in the bag. But instead of plastic, a plant's cell walls are made of carbohydrate chains of cellulose. M. Susan Brewer, associate professor of food science and human nutrition at the University of Illinois, explained that cellulose breaks down when it is exposed to heat in the presence of an alkali such as baking soda. This disintegration of the carrots' cell walls permits water to leak out, much as it would out of a baggie that has been pricked with a pin. It is this water leakage that causes the softening effect, according to Brewer.

---

the top of the cake with coconut. Then press the coconut into the sides of the cake with your hand, letting the excess fall back onto a baking sheet or piece of parchment paper. Cut the cake into slices and serve. (Cover leftover cake with plastic and refrigerate; bring to room temperature before serving.)

CARROT CAKE

CARROT CAKE CAME OF AGE IN THE '70S, along with platform shoes and bell bottoms. Seeing those wide-legged pants in vogue again got us to thinking about that old standard that can still be found almost everywhere. Unfortunately, though, today's carrot cakes are more often than not too dense and oily, overwhelmed by spices, and topped with a cloyingly sweet frosting that drowns out whatever carrot taste the cake had to begin with. We wanted something very different. Our goal from the start was maximum carrot flavor that didn't overpower or compromise the taste and texture of the finished cake.

We began by looking through cookbooks to see just how various authors defined carrot cake. Choosing a basic middle-of-the-road recipe, we pared it down to its essentials. Our original recipe called for 3 cups of raw carrots to 2 cups of flour. After just one taste, we knew that we wanted more carrots in our version. When we increased the amount to 4 cups, we were still unsatisfied with the taste. Rather than increasing the amount of carrots just yet, we decided to experiment with cooking the carrots, because some recipes called for this technique. The cake we made with 4 cups of grated, cooked carrots had a soft, dull carrot flavor, not our ideal. Next, we tried cooking the carrots and mashing them before adding them to the cake. This cake had an overwhelming carrot flavor with a distracting orange color.

Cooking the carrots clearly was not the answer, so we returned to increasing the amount of raw, grated carrots in our basic recipe. With 7 cups, the cake had just the right amount of carrot flavor, but we now had a problem: The texture of the cake had become gummy.

To solve the problem of our gummy-textured

cake, we tried some tests to remove excess liquid from the carrots. Because liquid cannot be easily drained directly from the carrots, we had to come up with a way to draw it out. We began by sautéing the carrots in butter until there was no liquid in the pan. As with our previous tests with cooked carrots, the taste was overwhelming and a disappointment.

Trying another tack, we remembered our coleslaw recipe, which solves the moisture problem by salting the cabbage and draining it until sufficient liquid has been extracted. Because we were making something sweet rather than savory, we wanted to accomplish this without adding extra salt to our recipe. In the past, we had often added sugar to fruits to draw out their liquid to make a dessert sauce. We decided to try tossing the carrots with sugar and then draining them to see what resulted.

After 20 minutes, about a cup of liquid had drained from the carrots. Subsequent tests with varying draining times showed that, while anything more than five minutes extracted enough liquid to improve the texture of the finished cake, 20 to 30 minutes provided the best results. Before we discarded the drained liquid, we tasted it and found it to be very sweet. To compensate for this loss of sugar, we added ⅔ cup white sugar back to our recipe. The original cake, made with the carrots that had not been drained, seemed undercooked when compared with the cake made with drained carrots. Even though it added an extra step to the recipe, the results were worth it. At this point, we turned to the question of flour and found that adding an extra ⅔ cup balanced the flavor and texture of the drained carrots perfectly.

Traditionally, carrot cakes are made with vegetable oil, perhaps because of health concerns associated with the consumption of animal fats (why pollute an otherwise healthful carrot cake with butterfat?) or simply because vegetable oil cake is easier to make than a conventional creamed butter and sugar cake. Being big fans of the taste of butter, however, we suspected that we would prefer it to oil. One taste and our suspicions were confirmed. When contrasted with the cake made with oil, the cake made with melted butter had a clean, buttery taste that was appealing to us. As a further test, we decided to cream the butter with sugar as in conventional

cake-making methods. The resulting cake had a light, creamy flavor that was good for some purposes but not appealing in a carrot cake, which should have some real substance.

Finding the cake we were now making a little too greasy for our tastes, we began cutting back on the amount of butter. Cutting back from 2½ sticks to 2 sticks produced a cake that was less greasy yet retained the pleasing butter flavor.

We have always loved the flavor of browned butter in baked goods, which gave us the idea to test its effect on our carrot cake. As a final move, we browned the butter lightly before adding it to the sugar. This cake was our clear favorite, having a depth of flavor lacking in our other trials.

Even though we knew that we wanted a carrot cake that could stand on its own, the image of a richly frosted carrot cake proved too tempting to resist. We decided our carrot cake deserved a cream cheese frosting that was creamy and sweet but not cloying. We also wanted a frosting that had a bit of tang to it. When we researched recipes for frosting, we found that almost all of the recipes consisted of confectioners' sugar, cream cheese, and butter in varying ratios. After settling on the right proportions of these ingredients, we had frosting with a great texture and flavor but not enough tang. We tried adding sour cream to the frosting and got a frosting that, when combined with the balanced flavors of the cake, produced exactly what we envisioned in our ideal carrot cake.

Carrot Cake with Tangy Cream Cheese Frosting
SERVES 12

The carrots for this cake can be grated quickly if your food processor has a fine shredding or grating disk. Otherwise, use the fine holes on a box grater. Serve the cake the same day you make it.

CARROT CAKE
2⅔ cups (13¾ ounces) unbleached all-purpose flour
4 teaspoons baking powder
½ teaspoon baking soda
2 teaspoons ground cinnamon

1	teaspoon salt
2	pounds carrots, grated fine (7 cups)
1⅔	cups (11½ ounces) granulated sugar
½	pound (2 sticks) unsalted butter
1	cup packed (7 ounces) light brown sugar
5	eggs
1½	teaspoons vanilla extract

FROSTING

1	pound cream cheese, softened
10	tablespoons (1¼ sticks) unsalted butter, softened
2½	cups (10 ounces) confectioners' sugar
2½	tablespoons sour cream

1. FOR THE CAKE: Adjust an oven rack to the center position and heat the oven to 350 degrees. Generously grease and flour the bottoms and sides of two 9-inch round cake pans. Invert the pans and rap sharply to remove excess flour.

2. Whisk the flour, baking powder, baking soda, cinnamon, and salt in a large bowl; set aside. Toss the grated carrots with 1 cup granulated sugar in a colander set over a large bowl; drain until 1 cup liquid has collected, 20 to 30 minutes.

3. Meanwhile, melt the butter in a large skillet over medium-low heat, stirring frequently; cook until golden brown, 8 to 10 minutes. Transfer to a large bowl; cool for 10 minutes, then whisk in the remaining ⅔ granulated sugar and the brown sugar. Add the eggs one at a time, whisking thoroughly before adding the next; add the vanilla. Add the flour mixture, stirring until almost combined, then mix in the carrots.

4. Divide the batter evenly between the pans; smooth the surfaces with a rubber spatula. Bake until the cakes feel firm in the center when pressed lightly and a toothpick or skewer inserted in the center comes out perfectly clean, 40 to 50 minutes. Transfer the pans to wire racks; cool for 10 minutes. Run a knife around the perimeter of each pan, invert the cakes onto racks. Reinvert onto additional racks; cool completely before frosting.

5. FOR THE FROSTING: Beat the cream cheese and butter in the bowl of standing mixer on low speed until homogenous, 3 to 4 minutes. Add the confectioners' sugar and sour cream; beat until well

blended, 1 to 2 minutes longer.

6. Assemble and frost the cake according to the illustrations on page 350. Cut the cake into slices and serve. (Cover leftover cake with plastic and refrigerate; bring to room temperature before serving.)

➤ VARIATIONS

Carrot Cake with Pineapple and Pecans
Strain one 20-ounce can crushed pineapple packed in its own juice into a medium bowl, pressing the pineapple against the strainer with a wooden spoon to drain thoroughly. Toast ¾ cup chopped pecans in a medium skillet set over medium heat, shaking the pan occasionally to move the nuts, until fragrant, 5 to 7 minutes. Follow the recipe for Carrot Cake with Tangy Cream Cheese Frosting, adding ¾ cup drained pineapple and toasted pecans along with the carrots.

Carrot Cake with Raisins and Walnuts
Toast ¾ cup chopped walnuts in a medium skillet set over medium heat, shaking the pan occasionally to move the nuts, until fragrant, 5 to 7 minutes. Follow the recipe for Carrot Cake with Tangy Cream Cheese Frosting, adding ¾ cup raisins and toasted walnuts along with the carrots.

NEW YORK CHEESECAKE

CHEESECAKE HAS TAKEN A TAWDRY TWIST these days. It's available in flavors like Irish coffee, cappuccino crunch, and Key lime. These frauds may masquerade as cheesecakes, but there is only one true cheesecake: the New York cheesecake.

An orchestration of different textures and an exercise in flavor restraint, New York cheesecake should be a tall, bronze-skinned, and dense affair. At the core, it should be cool, thick, smooth, satiny, and creamy; radiating outward, it goes gradually from velvety to suede-like, then, finally, about the edges, it is cake-like and fine-pored. The flavor should be simple and pure and minimalist, sweet and tangy, and rich to boot. It should not be citrusy, vanilla-scented, fluffy, mousse-like, leaden, gummy, chewy, or starchy. It should not be so dry as to make you gag, and it definitely should not bake up with a fault as large as the San Andreas (we're talking New York, after all).

We decided to start with the crust and work our way up. Some recipes claim that a pastry crust was the crust of choice for the original New York cheesecake. We tried one, but, after a lot of expended effort, a pastry crust only became soggy beneath the filling. Cookie and cracker crumbs were tasty and more practical options. Every taster considered a mere dusting of crumbs on the bottom of the cheesecake insufficient. We wanted a crust with more presence.

A graham cracker crust made with a cup of crumbs, some sugar, and melted butter, pressed into the bottom of the springform pan and pre-baked until it was fragrant and browning around the edges was ideal at a thickness of about ⅜ inch. If served within a day of baking, it retained crispness. If the cheesecake was held for a couple days, the crust softened, but tasters didn't seem to mind—the graham cracker crumbs still offered their sweet toasty flavor. We tried sprucing up the basic graham cracker crust with additions like brown sugar and ground cinnamon, but a basic crust always proved best.

A gingersnap crust, potent with molasses and spices, overwhelmed the flavors of the cheesecake—a no-go. Chocolate wafers made a crust that a couple tasters called bitter, but most others found the dark bittersweet cocoa flavor a nice match for the sweet cheesy filling. That the chocolate crust retained more of its crispness was another thing going for it. But since a chocolate wafer crust was somewhat unorthodox, we carried on with the graham cracker version, noting the chocolate crust as a good alternative.

A great New York cheesecake should be of great stature. One made with 2 pounds (four bars) of cream cheese was not tall enough. We threw in another half pound—the springform pan reached maximum capacity, but the cheesecake stood tall and looked right. The amount of sugar was quickly settled—1½ cups. The cheesecake struck a perfect balance of sweet and tangy.

Cheesecakes always require a dairy supplement to the cream cheese—usually either heavy cream or sour cream, or sometimes both. We made a cheesecake without any additional dairy and found out why this is true. Though the all-cream-cheese cheesecake tasted undeniably like cream cheese, the texture was gluey and pasty, akin to mortar, and much like a bar of cream cheese straight out of its wrapper. Additional dairy loosens up the texture of the cream cheese, giving the cake a smoother, more luxurious feel.

We found that heavy cream, even when used in the smallest amounts, dulled and flattened the flavor of the cream cheese. Sour cream, with a tartness of its own, supplemented the tangy quality of the cream

---

INGREDIENTS: Commercial Cheesecakes

Could it be possible that even good cooks might be better off simply defrosting a store-bought frozen cheesecake instead of baking a fresh one at home? We wanted to make sure our efforts (and possibly yours) weren't in vain, so we thawed four commercial cheesecakes and assembled a taste test, adding our homemade version as one of the contenders.

The commercial contestants were Trader Joe's New York Style Cheesecake; Sara Lee Original Cream Cheesecake; Original Cheesecake from The Cheesecake Factory, a chain of eateries featuring more than 30 flavors of cheesecake; and The Ultimate New York Cheesecake from David Glass, a gourmet dessert company.

It was a landslide, with the Cook's cheesecake winning an easy victory—tasters prized its "fresh," "tangy" flavor and "dense but creamy" texture. The "crispy" crust with "true graham flavor"

beat out commercial cheesecakes with crusts that were more "reminiscent of cardboard" than graham crackers.

The Sara Lee cheesecake took second place for its "soft," "smooth" texture, though a few tasters remarked that it left a "burning sensation" in the back of their throats. In a tie for third place were the David Glass and Cheesecake Factory entries, striking tasters as "artificially vanilla-tasting with an overly cinnamon-y crust" (the former) and "acidic and sour" (the latter). Each and every taster put the Trader Joe's cheesecake in last place, uniformly rejecting it for being not only "pasty" and "floury" but also "absolutely tasteless."

The lesson here is clear: Don't be lured in by the ease of store-bought cheesecake. Take the time to make it at home, and you won't be disappointed.

cheese, but an overabundance made the cheesecake taste sour and acidic. What tasters preferred was a relatively small amount of sour cream—⅓ cup. It was enough to offer a twang of tartness and help give the cheesecake a smoother, creamier texture without advertising its presence.

Eggs help bind the cheesecake, make it cohesive, and give it structure. They also help achieve a smooth, creamy texture. Whole eggs are often called for in cheesecakes of non–New York persuasions. We tried as few as four and as many as six whole eggs—these cheesecakes had textures that were called "light," "fluffy," and even "whipped." Recipes for New York cheesecake seem to agree that a few yolks in addition to whole eggs help to get the velvety, lush texture of a proper New York cheesecake. Our testing bore this out, and, ultimately, we concluded that a generous amount of eggs—six whole and two yolks—yield a cheesecake of unparalleled texture: dense but not heavy, firm but not rigid, and perfectly rich.

Some kind of starch—usually either flour or cornstarch—makes a regular appearance in cheesecake recipes. Starch helps to thicken the texture and to guard against the cracking that results from overbaking, but as evidenced by the half-dozen or so starch-laced cakes we made, even in small amounts, a gummy, starchy presence can be detected. Tasters noticed a dry, pasty mouthfeel in cheesecakes made with only a tablespoon of flour and cornstarch. They much preferred the meltingly luxurious quality of a completely starch-free cheesecake.

Perfecting the flavor of the cheesecake was easy. Tasters complained that the orange zest that recipes often call for made the cheesecake taste like a creamsicle, so it was out of there in a New York minute. Next to go was lemon zest because its flavor was distracting. A couple of teaspoons of lemon juice, however, helped to perk up the flavors without adding a lemon-flavored hit. Just a bit of salt (cream cheese already contains a good dose of sodium) and a couple teaspoons of vanilla extract rounded out the flavors. Everyone in the test kitchen appreciated this minimalist cheesecake.

On the part of the cook, cheesecake is well loved for the fact that it goes together easily. However, care must be used when mixing the ingredients lest the batter contain small nodules of unmixed cream cheese that can mar the smoothness of the baked cake. Frequent and thorough scraping of the bowl during mixing is key to ensuring that every spot of cream cheese is incorporated, but starting with semisoftened cream cheese is certainly helpful. It doesn't need to be at room temperature, nor does it need to be nuked. Simply cutting it into chunks and letting it stand while the crust is prepared and the other ingredients assembled—30 to 45 minutes—made mixing easier.

There are many ways to bake a cheesecake—in a moderate oven, in a low oven, in a water bath, and in accordance with the New York method—500 degrees for about 10 minutes, then 200 degrees for about an hour—which appears to be a standard technique. We tried them all, but the New York method was the only one that yielded the nut-brown surface that is a distinguishing mark of an exemplary New York cheesecake. This dual-temperature, no-water-bath baking method also produced a lovely graded texture—soft and creamy at the center and firm and

PRESSING THE CRUMBS INTO THE PAN

1. Use the bottom of a ramekin or drinking glass to press the crumbs into the bottom of a buttered springform pan. Press the crumbs as far as possible into the edges of the pan.

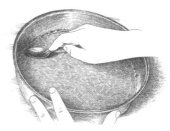

2. Use a teaspoon to neatly press the crumbs into the corners of the pan to create a clean edge.

dry at the periphery.

The New York baking method was not without flaws, however. After an hour at 200 degrees, the very center of the cheesecake—even after chilling—was loose and slurpy, a result of underbaking. Some recipes leave the cheesecake in the still-warm, turned-off, propped-open oven for about 30 minutes to finish "baking." As such, the cheesecake was marginally better, but still insufficiently baked.

We tried extending the hour-long baking time to get the center of the cheesecake to set up to the right consistency. We took it 15 and 30 minutes past an hour. The cheesecake baked for 1½ hours to an internal temperature of about 150 degrees was whisked out of the oven. Chilled, it was cheesecake perfection. It sliced into a neat slab with a cleanly set center texture—not a wet, sloppy one. Each slice kept its shape and each bite felt satiny on the tongue. Though this prolonged New York baking method was relatively foolproof, we do caution against taking the cheesecake beyond an internal temperature of 160 degrees. The few that we did were hideously and hopelessly cracked. Uptight though it may seem, an instant-read thermometer inserted into the cake is the most reliable means of judging the doneness of the cheesecake.

Cheesecake is also well-loved (by the sweet tooth, not the waistline) because it lasts longer in the refrigerator than a dessert should. After a day or two, the crust is a little soggy, but the cake tastes every bit as good.

New York Cheesecake

SERVES 12 TO 16

For the crust, chocolate wafers (Nabisco Famous) may be substituted for graham crackers; you will need about 14 wafers. The flavor and texture of the cheesecake is best if the cake is allowed to stand at room temperature for about 30 minutes before serving. When cutting the cake, have a pitcher of hot tap water ready; dipping the blade of the knife into the water and wiping it after each slice helps make clean slices.

GRAHAM CRACKER CRUST

8 whole graham crackers (4 ounces), broken into rough pieces and processed in food processor until uniformly fine

1 tablespoon sugar
5 tablespoons butter, melted, plus additional 1 tablespoon melted butter for greasing pan

FILLING

2½ pounds cream cheese, cut into rough 1-inch chunks and left to stand at room temperature for 45 minutes
⅛ teaspoon salt
1½ cups (10½ ounces) sugar
⅓ cup (2½ ounces) sour cream
2 teaspoons juice from 1 lemon
2 teaspoons vanilla extract
2 large egg yolks plus 6 large eggs

1. FOR THE CRUST: Adjust an oven rack to the lower-middle position and heat the oven to 325 degrees. Brush the bottom and sides of a 9-inch springform pan with ½ tablespoon melted butter. Combine the graham cracker crumbs and sugar in a medium bowl; add 5 tablespoons melted butter and toss with a fork until evenly moistened. Empty the crumbs into the springform pan and, following the illustrations on page 360, press evenly into the pan bottom. Bake until fragrant and beginning to brown around edges, about 13 minutes. Cool on a wire rack while making the filling.

2. FOR THE CHEESECAKE FILLING: Increase the oven temperature to 500 degrees. In a standing mixer fitted with the paddle attachment, beat the cream cheese at medium-low speed to break up and soften it slightly, about 1 minute. Scrape the beater and the bottom and sides of bowl well with a rubber spatula; add the salt and about half of the sugar and beat at medium-low speed until combined, about 1 minute. Scrape the bowl; beat in the remaining sugar until combined, about 1 minute. Scrape the bowl; add the sour cream, lemon juice, and vanilla, and beat at low speed until combined, about 1 minute. Scrape the bowl; add the yolks and beat at medium-low speed until thoroughly combined, about 1 minute. Scrape the bowl; add the remaining eggs two at a time, beating until thoroughly combined, about 1 minute, and scraping the bowl between additions.

3. Brush the sides of the springform pan with the remaining ½ tablespoon melted butter. Set the

springform pan on a rimmed baking sheet (to catch any spills if the springform pan leaks). Pour the filling into the cooled crust and bake 10 minutes; without opening the oven door, reduce the oven temperature to 200 degrees and continue to bake until the cheesecake registers about 150 degrees on an instant-read thermometer inserted in the center, about 1½ hours. Transfer the cake to a wire rack and cool until barely warm, 2½ to 3 hours. Run a paring knife between the cake and springform pan sides. Wrap tightly in plastic wrap and refrigerate until cold, at least 3 hours. (The cheesecake can be refrigerated up to 4 days.)

4. To unmold the cheesecake, remove the sides of the pan. Slide a thin metal spatula between the crust and springform pan bottom to loosen, then slide the cake onto a serving plate. Let the cheesecake stand at room temperature about 30 minutes, then cut into wedges and serve with topping, if desired.

FRESH STRAWBERRY TOPPING

THE DENSE, CREAMY RICHNESS OF A NEW York cheesecake makes it the perfect candidate for some kind of fruity foil. A ruby-colored, glazed strawberry topping is the classic fruit accompaniment to New York cheesecake.

We tried to make one out of frozen strawberries, but, once thawed, the berries looked ragged and unattractive. We tried gently poaching fresh slivered berries in sugar syrup, but the syrup was weak in flavor and color. We tried cooking berries with sugar until they released their juices, but they never released enough to make much of a sauce, so we supplemented their juices with strawberry liqueur and thickened the liquid with cornstarch. Sadly, the strawberry flavor from the liqueur was not pure, and the heat killed the fresh flavor and texture of the berries, making them shaggy and dull.

We shifted gears. This time we macerated slivered berries in some sugar and a pinch of salt for about 30 minutes to soften them and cause them to exude some of their juices. We then pureed a cup of strawberry jam in a food processor until it was smooth. The pureeing made the jam frothy, so we simmered it for a few minutes until it was again dark, clear, and free of froth. We stirred in some lemon juice to add liveliness, then poured the molten mixture over the berries, tossed them, and chilled them for a few hours. The maceration and the heat of the jam gave the berries just enough coaxing to transform them from their raw rigid state to a yielding texture. The syrup they sat in had a clean strawberry flavor and draped nicely over a slice of cheesecake.

Fresh Strawberry Topping

MAKES ABOUT 1½ QUARTS

This accompaniment to cheesecake is best served the same day it is made.

2	pounds strawberries, cleaned, hulled, and cut lengthwise into ¼- to ⅜-inch wedges
½	cup (3½ ounces) sugar
	Pinch salt
1	cup (about 11 ounces) strawberry jam
2	tablespoons juice from 1 lemon

1. Toss the berries, sugar, and salt in a medium bowl; let stand until the berries have released some juice and the sugar has dissolved, about 30 minutes, tossing occasionally to combine.

2. Process the jam in a food processor until smooth, about 8 seconds; transfer to a small saucepan. Bring the jam to a simmer over medium-high heat; simmer, stirring frequently, until dark and no longer frothy, about 3 minutes. Stir in the lemon juice; pour the warm jam over the strawberries and stir to combine. Cover with plastic wrap and refrigerate until cold, at least 2 hours or up to 12. To serve, spoon a portion of sauce over individual slices of cheesecake.

15

PIES

IF THERE IS ONE ALL-AMERICAN DESSERT, it is probably pie. There were pies on the Mayflower, and pies have continued to be a source of American pride and ingenuity ever since. This chapter begins with the crust—the hardest part of pie making for many cooks. But with the right ingredients, mixing technique, and rolling method, pie dough doesn't have to be a challenge.

The chapter continues with a selection of all-time favorite pies, such as Dutch apple, peach, lemon meringue, and blueberry, as well as some old-fashioned pies we think are worth reconsidering, including custard pie, coconut cream pie, and sweet potato pie. All of these pies are honest fare, suited to special occasions and holidays as well as weeknight suppers and family picnics.

PIE DOUGH

MAKING GOOD PIE CRUST CAN BE A SIMPLE procedure, but almost everyone who has tried can tell horror stories of crusts that turned out hard, soggy, flavorless, oversalted, underbaked, too crumbly, or unworkable. Advice is easy to come by: One expert says that butter is the secret to perfect crust; others swear by vegetable shortening, lard, even canola oil. Some omit salt, some omit sugar, some insist that working the dough by hand is essential, some use cake flour in addition to all-purpose flour, some freeze the dough, some do away with the rolling pin . . . and so on.

Simple as it can be, pie crust—essentially a combination of flour, water, and fat—raises numerous questions: What are the ideal proportions of the main ingredients? What else should be added for character? What methods should be used to combine these ingredients?

The most controversial ingredient in pastry is fat. We've found that all-butter crusts have good taste, but they are not as flaky and fine-textured as those made with some shortening, which are our favorites. All-shortening crusts have great texture but lack flavor; oil-based crusts are flat and entirely unappealing; and those made with lard are not only heavy and strongly flavored but out of favor owing to concerns about the effects of animal fat on health. After experimenting

with a variety of combinations, we ultimately settled on a proportion of 3 parts butter to 2 parts shortening as optimal for both flavor and texture.

Vegetable shortenings such as Crisco are made from vegetable oil that has been hydrogenated, a process in which hydrogen gas is pumped into the molecules of a vegetable oil to incorporate air and to raise its melting point above room temperature. Unhydrogenated (or regular) vegetable oil holds no more air than water and so makes for poor pie doughs. Crisco, on the other hand, is about 10 percent gas and does a good job of lightening and tenderizing. (The way the butter is incorporated into the flour also contributes to flakiness. See "What Makes Pastry Flaky?" on page 367 for details.)

We experimented with the relative proportions of fat and flour and finally settled on a ratio of 2 parts flour to 1 part fat, which produces crusts that are easy to work and, when baked, more tender and flavorful than any other.

Pie crusts are usually made with all-purpose flour. No matter what we've tried—substituting cornstarch for part of the all-purpose flour (a cookie-baking trick that increases tenderness), adding ¼ teaspoon baking powder to increase rise and flakiness, and mixing cake flour or pastry flour with the all-purpose flour (again, to increase tenderness)—we always come back to plain old all-purpose flour.

We also tackled the proportions of salt and sugar, which were much easier to resolve. After testing amounts ranging from ¼ teaspoon to as much as 2 tablespoons, we settled on 1 teaspoon salt and 2 tablespoons sugar for a double-crust pie, amounts that enhance the flavor of the dough without shouting out their presence.

We experimented with a variety of liquid ingredients, such as buttermilk, milk, and cider vinegar, a common ingredient in many pastry recipes. No liquid additions improved our basic recipe, so we recommend that you stick with ice water.

Pie dough can be made by hand, but we've found that the food processor is faster and easier and does the best job of cutting the fat into the flour. Proper mixing is important. If you undermix, the crust will shrink when baked and became hard and crackly. If you overprocess, you'll get a crumbly, cookie-like dough. The shortening should be pulsed with the flour until the mixture is sandy; butter is then pulsed in until the mixture looks like coarse crumbs, with butter bits no larger than the size of a pea.

Once the flour and fat have been combined, the dough can be transferred to a bowl, and the ice water can be added and mixed in. We've come to favor a rubber spatula and a folding motion to mix in the water, which exposes all of the dough to moisture without overworking it, something that can happen if the dough is left in the food processor and the water is pulsed in. Using a spatula to incorporate water allows for the least amount of water to be used (less water means a more tender dough) and reduces the likelihood of overworking the dough. Still, we've also learned that it doesn't pay to be too stingy with the water. If there isn't enough, the dough will be crumbly and hard to roll.

Finally, we found that pie dough need not be difficult to roll out if you remember two basic guidelines: Make sure the dough is well chilled before rolling, and add a minimum of flour to the work surface. Flour added during rolling will be absorbed by the dough, and too much flour will cause the dough to toughen. If the dough seems too soft to roll, it's best to refrigerate it rather than adding more flour.

Basic Pie Dough

FOR ONE DOUBLE-CRUST 9-INCH PIE

2½	cups (12½ ounces) unbleached all-purpose flour
1	teaspoon salt
2	tablespoons sugar
8	tablespoons all-vegetable shortening, chilled
12	tablespoons unsalted butter, chilled, cut into ¼-inch pieces
6–8	tablespoons ice water

1. Pulse the flour, salt, and sugar in a food processor fitted with the steel blade until combined. Add the shortening and process until the mixture has the texture of coarse sand, about 10 seconds. Scatter the butter pieces over the flour mixture; cut the butter into the flour until the mixture is pale yellow and resembles coarse crumbs, with butter bits no larger than small peas, about ten 1-second pulses. Turn the mixture into a medium bowl.

2. Sprinkle 6 tablespoons ice water over the mixture. With the blade of a rubber spatula, use a folding motion to mix. Press down on the dough with the broad side of spatula until the dough sticks together, adding up to 2 tablespoons more ice water if the dough will not come together. Divide the dough into two balls and flatten each into a 4-inch-wide disk. Wrap each in plastic and refrigerate at least 1 hour, or up to 2 days, before rolling.

➤ VARIATION

Pie Dough for Lattice-Top Pie

This crust has a firmer texture than the basic recipe, making it easier to work with when creating a lattice top for peach pie (see page 371).

Follow the recipe for Basic Pie Dough, increasing the flour to 3 cups (15 ounces), reducing the shortening to 7 tablespoons, reducing the butter to 10 tablespoons, and increasing the ice water to 10 tablespoons. Divide the dough into two pieces, one slightly larger than the other. (If possible, weigh the pieces; they should register 16 ounces and 14 ounces.) Flatten the larger piece into a rough 5-inch square and the smaller piece into a 4-inch disk; wrap separately in plastic and chill as directed.

PIE DOUGH FOR PREBAKED PIE SHELL

BAKING AN UNFILLED PIE PASTRY, COMMONLY called blind baking, can turn out to be the ultimate culinary nightmare. Without the weight of a filling, a pastry shell set into a hot oven can shrink dramatically, fill with air pockets, and puff up like a linoleum floor after a flood. The result? A shrunken, uneven shell that can hold only part of the filling intended for it.

We started with our favorite pie dough recipe (see left) and began to investigate the effects of resting the dough (in the refrigerator or the freezer), docking it (pricking the dough before it bakes), and weighting the crust as it bakes to keep it anchored in place. All three tricks are used by professional bakers to prevent common problems encountered when blind-baking a crust.

We found that refrigeration does the best job of preventing shrinkage. Pastry shrinkage is caused by gluten. Simply put, when you add water to the proteins in flour, elastic strands of gluten are formed. The strands of gluten in the dough get stretched during the rolling process, and if they are not allowed to relax after rolling, the pastry will snap back like a rubber band when baked, resulting in a shrunken, misshapen shell. Resting allows the tension in the taut strands of dough to ease so that they remain stretched and do not shrink back when heated.

This process does not occur, however, when the dough is immediately placed in the freezer to rest after rolling. When frozen, the water in the crust solidifies, freezing the gluten in place so it is not free to relax. As a result, when you bake the dough, the tense, stretched strands of gluten snap back, causing the crust to shrink.

We might have concluded that pie dough should be refrigerated and not frozen if we hadn't noticed that the frozen crusts, although shrunken, were much flakier than the refrigerated crusts. Pastry is made up of layers of dough (protein and starch from the flour combined with water) and fat. Dough and fat have different heat capacities. When you place the pastry in the oven after freezing it (rather than just

ROLLING OUT PIE DOUGH

No matter what kind of pie crust you are making (single, double, or lattice top), follow these directions before proceeding to the specific directions on that type of crust.

1. Sprinkle a couple of tablespoons of flour over the work surface and the top of the dough. To roll, apply light pressure to the dough with a rolling pin and work from the center outward to avoid rolling over the same area more than necessary.

2. Every 30 seconds or so, slide a bench scraper under the dough to make sure it is not sticking to the work surface. Rotate the dough a quarter turn and continue rolling out. Rotating the dough ensures that it will be thinned to a uniform thickness and form a circle.

3. To make sure that you've rolled the dough to the right size, place the pie plate you are using upside down on top of it; the diameter of the dough should be 2 inches greater than that of the pie plate.

4. When the dough has reached the correct size, fold it into quarters. Place the folded dough in the empty pie plate, with the folded point of the dough in the center of the plate. Unfold gently.

5. Lift the edge of the dough with one hand and ease the pastry along the bottom into the corners with the other hand; continue around the circumference of the pan. Do not stretch the dough. For a double-crust or lattice top pie, leave the dough as is. For a single-crust prebaked pie shell, trim the dough edges to extend about $1/2$ inch beyond the rim of the pan, fold the overhang under itself, and either flute the dough or press the tines of a fork against the dough to flatten it against the rim of the pie plate.

refrigerating it), the dough heats up and starts to set relatively quickly in comparison with the time it takes for the butter to melt and then vaporize, as butter has a much higher proportion of water than the dough. As a result, by the time the water in the butter starts to turn to steam, the dough is well into its setting phase. The air spaces occupied by the frozen butter, now that it has largely turned to steam, hold their shape because the dough is far along in the baking process.

Dough that you have refrigerated, on the other hand, is not as well set by the time the butter vaporizes; hence the air pockets disappear, the soft dough simply sinking into the spaces left by the butter. We came to a simple conclusion: First refrigerate the pie shell to relax the gluten, thus solving the problem of shrinkage during baking, then pop the dough in the freezer to improve flakiness.

This bit of science led to one other fascinating discovery. It is common knowledge that lard or vegetable shortening such as Crisco produces very flaky doughs. In fact, we use a combination of butter and shortening in our recipe because of the improvement in texture over an all-butter crust. The explanation for this phenomenon is simple. Lard and Crisco don't melt as quickly as butter when heated. Therefore, they retain their shape as the dough sets up, keeping the layers of pastry separated.

While this combination chilling method prevents shrinkage, ballooning can occur when air pockets form beneath the crust. Typically, bakers dock (or prick) the dough with the tines of a fork before it goes into the oven. However, we found that docking was not necessary as long as the dough is weighted. Since weighting is a must—it not only prevents ballooning but keeps the shell, especially the sides, in place as it bakes—we do not bother to dock pastry dough. Some professional bakers swear by "official" pie weights, while others make do with rice or dried beans. We found that metal or ceramic pie weights do a better job than rice or beans. They are heavier and therefore more effective at preventing the pastry from puffing. Pie weights are also better heat conductors and promote more thorough browning of the pastry.

We got the most consistent results and even browning by baking in the middle rack at a constant

SCIENCE: What Makes Pastry Flaky?

Why is it that some cooks produce pie crusts that are consistently tender and flaky, while others, despite the best of intentions, repeatedly deliver tough, cookie-like crusts? Part of the answer has to do with butter and the degree to which it is incorporated in the dough. While shortening makes a big contribution to the flakiness of our pie crust, it also benefits from relatively large pieces of butter. As the butter melts during baking, evaporation produces steam. The steam creates pockets in the dough that help to make it flaky.

When a dough is overprocessed and the butter is dispersed too evenly, it coats the flour and prevents it from absorbing liquid; the same thing happens when a dough is made with oil. The result is a crumbly dough rather than a flaky one. Underprocessing, however, will create a tough dough, because the fat has failed to coat the flour enough.

375 degrees. At higher temperatures the pastry was prone to overbrowning and burned in spots, while lower temperatures caused the edges to brown well before the bottom did. More important than temperature and placement, though, was cooking time.

There are two stages in prebaking. In the first stage, the dough is baked with a lining and weights. This stage usually takes about 25 minutes; the objective is to cook the dough until it sets, at which point it can hold its shape without assistance. When the dough loses its wet look, turns off-white from its original pale yellow, and the edges just start to take on a very light brown color, the dough is set. If you have any doubts, carefully (the dough is hot) touch the side of the shell to make sure that the crust is firm. If you remove the pie weights too soon, the sides of the dough will slip down, ruining the pie shell.

For the second stage, the foil and weights are removed, and the baking continues. At this point, if you are going to fill the pie shell and then bake it again, as for pumpkin or pecan pie or quiches, you should bake it until it is just lightly browned, about 5 minutes. Pie shells destined for fillings that require little or no further cooking, such as cream and lemon meringue pies, should be baked for about 12 more minutes.

Pie Dough for Prebaked Pie Shell

FOR A SINGLE-CRUST 9-INCH PIE

See the illustrations on page 366 for tips on rolling out pie dough. We prefer ceramic or metal pie weights for prebaking the pie shell. If you don't own any weights, rice or dried beans can stand in, but since they're lighter than pie weights, be sure to fill up the foil-lined pie shell completely.

1¼	cups (6¼ ounces) unbleached all-purpose flour, plus extra for dusting dough and work surface
½	teaspoon salt
1	tablespoon sugar
3	tablespoons all-vegetable shortening, chilled
4	tablespoons unsalted butter, chilled, cut into ¼-inch pieces
4–5	tablespoons ice water

1. Pulse the flour, salt, and sugar in a food processor fitted with the steel blade until combined. Add the shortening and process until the mixture has the texture of coarse sand, about 10 seconds. Scatter the butter pieces over the flour mixture; cut the butter into the flour until the mixture is pale yellow and resembles coarse crumbs, with butter bits no larger than small peas, about ten 1-second pulses. Turn the mixture into a medium bowl.

2. Sprinkle 4 tablespoons ice water over the mixture. With the blade of a rubber spatula, use a folding motion to mix. Press down on the dough with the broad side of the spatula until the dough sticks together, adding up to 1 tablespoon more ice water if the dough will not come together. Flatten the dough into a 4-inch disk. Wrap in plastic and refrigerate at least 1 hour, or up to 2 days, before rolling.

3. If the dough has been refrigerated longer than 1 hour, let it stand at room temperature until malleable. Roll the dough on a lightly floured work surface or between two large sheets of plastic wrap to a 12-inch disk. Transfer the dough to a pie plate by rolling the dough around a rolling pin and unrolling over a 9-inch pie plate or by folding the dough in quarters, then placing the dough point in the center of the pie plate and unfolding. Working around the circumference of the pie plate, ease the dough into the pan corners by gently lifting the dough edges with one hand while pressing around the pan bottom with the other hand. Trim the dough edges to extend about ½ inch beyond the rim of the pan. Fold the overhang under itself; flute the dough or press the tines of a fork against the dough to flatten it against the rim of the pie plate. Refrigerate the dough-lined pie plate until firm, about 40 minutes, then freeze until very cold, about 20 minutes.

4. Adjust the oven rack to the lower-middle position and heat the oven to 375 degrees. Remove the dough-lined pie plate from the freezer and press a doubled 12-inch piece of heavy-duty foil inside the pie shell and fold the edges of the foil to shield the fluted edge; distribute 2 cups ceramic or metal pie weights over the foil. Bake, leaving the foil and

---

EQUIPMENT: Pie Plates

Pie plates come in a variety of shapes and sizes as well as materials. We tested the three main types of pie plate—glass, ceramic, and metal—and found that a Pyrex glass pie plate did the best job of browning the crust, both when filled and baked blind (the bottom crust is baked alone, filled with pie weights to hold its shape). Several metal pie plates also browned quite well, but the glass pie plate has a number of other advantages.

Because you can see through a Pyrex plate, it's easy to judge just how brown the bottom crust has become during baking. With a metal pie plate, it's easy to pull the pie out of the oven too soon, when the bottom crust is still quite pale. A second feature

we like about the traditional Pyrex plate is the wide rim, which makes the plate easier to take in and out of the oven and also supports fluted edges better than thin rims. Finally, because glass is nonreactive, you can store a pie filled with acidic fruit and not worry about metal giving the fruit an off flavor.

Pyrex pie plates do heat up more quickly than metal pie plates, so pies may be done a bit sooner than you think, especially if you are following a recipe that was tested in a metal plate. All the times in our recipes are based on baking in a glass pie plate; if baking in metal, you may need to add two to three minutes for empty crusts and five minutes for filled pies.

weights in place until the dough looks dry and is light in color, 25 to 30 minutes. Carefully remove the foil and weights by gathering the corners of the foil and pulling up and out. For a partially baked crust, continue baking until light golden brown, 5 to 6 minutes; for a fully baked crust, continue baking until deep golden brown, about 12 minutes more. Transfer to a wire rack.

➤ VARIATION

Prebaked Pie Dough Coated with Graham Cracker Crumbs

Custard fillings, such as those used in lemon meringue pie and cream pies, are tough on crisp crusts. After much experimentation, we found that rolling out the pie dough in graham cracker crumbs promotes browning and crisps the crust. It also adds a wonderful graham flavor that complements the lemon and cream pie fillings without masking the character of the dough itself.

Follow the recipe for Pie Dough for Prebaked Pie Shell, sprinkling the work surface with 2 tablespoons graham cracker crumbs when rolling out the dough. Sprinkle more crumbs over the dough itself. Continue sprinkling additional crumbs underneath and on top of the dough as it is rolled, coating the dough heavily with crumbs. You will use a total of about ½ cup crumbs. Fit the graham cracker–coated dough into a pie plate as directed and bake fully.

BLUEBERRY PIE

BLUEBERRY PIES TRADITIONALLY RELY ON flour or cornstarch to thicken the fresh fruit filling. We find these thickeners to be problematic. Cornstarch thickens well, but at a price. In our tests, it yielded dull fruit, lacking in bright flavor and noticeably less tart. As a result, the mixture tasted sweeter and heavier.

The flour resulted in fruit that was similarly unsatisfying in appearance and taste, and it also had another failing—two tablespoons was not enough to firm up the fruit well. To give flour another chance, we ran a test using 4 tablespoons. This time, the fruit was gummy and almost inedible. As it turns out, this is because flour, unlike the other thickeners, contains proteins and other components as well as starch. As

a result, it takes at least twice as much flour by volume to create the same degree of thickening as cornstarch. This amount of flour will adversely affect your blueberry pie—you can taste it.

Given our experience with peach pie (see page 370), we expected tapioca and potato starch to perform much better, and they did. Tasters slightly preferred the potato starch; however, the tapioca, when pulverized in a food processor, did an admirable job.

During additional testing we found that the amount of potato starch or tapioca should be varied depending on the juiciness of the berries. If you like a juicier pie, 3 tablespoons of potato starch or tapioca is an adequate amount for 6 cups of fresh blueberries. If you like a really firm pie with no juices, 4 tablespoons is the correct amount.

Blueberries and lemon are a natural combination, and a little zest and juice enhanced the flavor of the berries. Allspice and nutmeg were also good, being a welcome change of pace from the traditional cinnamon, which can overwhelm the delicate flavor of the berries. Finally, we found that 2 tablespoons of butter, cut into small bits and scattered over the filling just before the top crust was put in place, gave the berry filling a lush mouthfeel that everyone enjoyed.

With our filling done, the rest of this pie went together quickly. The double crust produced by our Basic Pie Dough (page 365) worked perfectly with blueberries. Tasters liked the effect of brushing the top crust with egg white and sprinkling it with sugar just before the pie went into the oven.

Unlike other fruit pies, for which the fruit must be peeled and sliced, blueberry pie goes together rather quickly, especially if you have the dough on hand in the refrigerator or freezer. Even with the rolling steps, you can have a blueberry pie in the oven in about 20 minutes.

➤

Blueberry Pie
SERVES 8

See the illustrations on page 366 for tips on rolling out pie dough. The amount of sugar and potato starch can vary, depending on the quality of the fruit and personal taste. If you prefer a less sweet pie or if the fruit is especially sweet, use the lower sugar amount. (Save the 1 tablespoon sugar for sprinkling on the pie just before it goes into the oven.) If you like your pie juices fairly thick or if the fruit is really juicy, then opt for the higher amount of starch. If you don't have or can't find potato starch, substitute an equal amount of pulverized Minute tapioca ground for about 1 minute in a food processor or spice grinder. Serve the pie with vanilla ice cream or Whipped Cream (page 382).

I	recipe Basic Pie Dough (page 365)
3	pints (6 cups) blueberries, rinsed and picked over
¾–I	cup (5¼ to 7 ounces) plus I tablespoon sugar
2	teaspoons juice and I teaspoon grated zest from I lemon
¼	teaspoon ground allspice
	Pinch nutmeg
3–4	tablespoons potato starch (see note)
2	tablespoons unsalted butter, cut into small pieces
I	egg white, lightly beaten

1. Adjust an oven rack to the lowest position and heat a rimmed baking sheet and the oven to 500 degrees. Remove one piece of dough from the refrigerator (if refrigerated longer than 1 hour, let stand at room temperature until malleable).

2. Roll the dough on a lightly floured work surface or between two large sheets of plastic wrap to a 12-inch disk. Transfer the dough to a pie plate by rolling the dough around a rolling pin and unrolling over a 9-inch pie plate or by folding the dough in quarters, then placing the dough point in the center of the pie plate and unfolding. Working around the circumference of the pie plate, ease the dough into the pan corners by gently lifting the dough edges with one hand while pressing around the pan bottom with the other hand. Leave the dough that overhangs the lip of the pie plate in place; refrigerate the dough-lined pie plate.

3. Toss the berries, sugar, lemon juice and zest, spices, and potato starch in a medium bowl; let stand for 15 minutes.

4. Roll out the second piece of dough to a 12-inch disk. Spoon the berries into the pie shell and scatter the butter pieces over the filling. Place the second piece of dough over the filling. Trim the top and bottom edges to ½ inch beyond the pan lip. Tuck this rim of dough underneath itself so that the folded edge is flush with the pan lip. Flute the edging or press with fork tines to seal. Cut four slits on the dough top. If the pie dough is very soft, place in the freezer for 10 minutes. Brush the egg white onto the top of the crust and sprinkle evenly with the remaining 1 tablespoon sugar.

5. Place the pie on the baking sheet and lower the oven temperature to 425 degrees. Bake until the top crust is golden, about 25 minutes. Rotate the pie and reduce the oven temperature to 375 degrees; continue baking until the juices bubble and the crust is deep golden brown, 30 to 35 minutes longer.

6. Transfer the pie to a wire rack; cool to room temperature, at least 4 hours.

PEACH PIE

OUR OCCASIONAL DISAPPOINTMENT WITH peach pies in the past has taught us to wait for peach season and then buy only intoxicatingly fragrant peaches, ripe enough when squeezed to make you swoon. But even ripe peaches vary in juiciness from season to season and from peach to peach, making it difficult to know just how much thickener or sweetener a pie will need. Because fresh peaches are so welcome, we are inclined to forgive them if the pie they make is soupy or overly sweet or has a bottom crust that didn't bake properly.

But we wanted to remove the guesswork from this anthem to summer. We wanted to create a filling that was juicy but not swimming in liquid, its flavors neither muscled out by spices nor overwhelmed by thickeners. The crust would be buttery, flaky, and well browned on the bottom, with a handsome, peekaboo lattice on the top.

Our standard recipe for pie dough is ultrarich, made with butter for flavor and shortening for flakiness (see Basic Pie Dough on page 365). But when we used this recipe for our first tests with peaches and a lattice-weave top crust, we were confronted with melting lattice strips. We realized that the crust on this particular pie would demand certain adjustments. We needed a sturdier dough, which meant less fat and more flour (see Pie Dough for Lattice-

Top Pie on page 365).

Our second challenge was to find a thickener that would leave the fruit's color and flavor uncompromised. A fruit pie should appear to be self-thickening, producing clear, syrupy juices, even when it is not. Early tests demonstrated that flour and cornstarch were both too noticeable; what's wanted is a thickener that does the job without calling attention to itself. Then we found an old recipe that suggested potato starch as a thickener. We had never thought to try it in a pie. Tapioca is another option advocated by some bakers.

We conducted side-by-side tests with flour, cornstarch, pulverized Minute tapioca (so no undissolved beads would remain in the baked pie), and potato starch. Flour and cornstarch fared no better than expected. The ground tapioca performed admirably, having no lumps, but pulverizing the tapioca seemed like an unnecessary bother for a simple pie. The potato starch scored big: Its clarity outshone flour but was less cosmetically glossy than cornstarch; its thickening Oqualities rivaled tapioca in strength and neutrality; and, still better, there was no need for pulverizing.

Next we turned our attention to the peaches themselves. After attempting to shave a ripe peach with a vegetable peeler, we resorted to traditional blanching and found that two full minutes in boiling water were necessary to humble even the ripest of peaches. A quick dip in an ice bath stabilized the temperature of the fruit and got the peels moving.

Experimenting with different sugars, we were surprised to discover that both light and dark brown sugar bullied the peaches, while white sugar complemented them. As in most fruit pies, lemon juice brightened the flavor of the peaches; it also kept the peach slices from browning before they went into the pan. A whisper of ground cinnamon and nutmeg and a dash of salt upped the peach flavor and added a note of complexity.

Trying different oven rack levels and temperatures to satisfy the browning requirements of both the top and bottom crust brought us back to our blueberry pie recipe (page 370), which recommends a low rack, initial high heat (425 degrees), and moderately high heat (375 degrees) to finish. We found that a glass pie dish and preheated baking sheet gave us a pleasantly firm and browned bottom crust. A quick prebaking spritz of the lattice top with water and a sprinkle of sugar brought this pie home.

Lattice-Top Fresh Peach Pie
SERVES 8

See the illustrations on page 366 for tips on rolling out pie dough. If your peaches are larger than tennis balls, you will probably need five or six; if they're smaller, you will need seven or eight. Cling and freestone peaches look identical; try to buy freestones, because the flesh will fall away from the pits easily. Use the higher amount of potato starch if the peaches are very juicy, less if they are not terribly juicy. If you don't have or can't find potato starch, substitute an equal amount of pulverized Minute tapioca ground for about 1 minute in a food processor or spice grinder. Serve the pie with vanilla ice cream or Whipped Cream (page 382).

MAKING THE LATTICE TOP

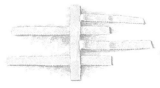 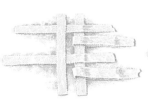 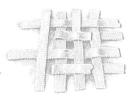 

1. Lay out 4 strips of dough on parchment paper. Fold the first and third strips back, then place a long strip of dough slightly to the right of the center, as shown.

2. Unfold the first and third strips over the perpendicular strips and fold the second and fourth strips back. Add a second perpendicular strip of dough. Now unfold the second and fourth strips.

3. Repeat this process with two more perpendicular strips (you will have a total of eight strips of dough, four running in each direction). Freeze the lattice until firm, about 15 minutes.

4. Place the lattice on top of the filled pie. Trim off the excess lattice ends, fold the rim of the shell up over the lattice strips, and crimp.

I	recipe Pie Dough for Lattice-Top Pie (page 365)
6–7	ripe, medium-sized peaches (about 7 cups when sliced)
I	tablespoon juice from I lemon
I	cup (7 ounces) plus I tablespoon sugar
	Pinch ground cinnamon
	Pinch ground nutmeg
	Pinch salt
3–5	tablespoons potato starch (see note)

1. Remove the dough from the refrigerator (if refrigerated longer than 1 hour, let stand at room temperature until malleable). Roll the larger dough piece to a 15 by 11-inch rectangle, about ⅛ inch thick; transfer the dough rectangle to a baking sheet lined with parchment paper. With a pizza wheel, fluted pastry wheel, or paring knife, trim to even out the long sides of the rectangle, then cut the rectangle lengthwise into eight strips, 15 inches long by 1¼ inches wide. Freeze the strips on a baking sheet until firm, about 30 minutes.

2. Roll the smaller dough piece on a lightly floured work surface or between two large sheets of plastic wrap to a 12-inch disk. Transfer the dough to a pie plate by rolling the dough around a rolling pin and unrolling over a 9-inch pie plate or by folding the dough in quarters, then placing the dough point in the center of the pie plate and unfolding. Working around the circumference of the pie plate, ease the dough into the pan corners by gently lifting the dough edges with one hand while pressing around the pan bottom with the other hand. Leave the dough that overhangs the lip of the pie plate in place; refrigerate the dough-lined pie plate.

3. Remove the dough strips from the freezer; if too stiff to be workable, let stand at room temperature until malleable and softened slightly but still very cold. Following the illustrations on page 371, form the lattice top and place in the freezer until firm, about 15 minutes.

4. Meanwhile, adjust an oven rack to the lowest position and heat a rimmed baking sheet and the oven to 500 degrees. Bring 3 quarts water to a boil in a large saucepan and fill a large bowl with 2 quarts cold water and 2 trays ice cubes. Peel the peaches according to the illustrations below. Halve, pit, and cut each peeled peach into ⅜-inch slices.

5. Toss the peach slices, lemon juice, 1 cup sugar, cinnamon, nutmeg, salt, and potato starch in a medium bowl.

6. Turn the peach mixture into the dough-lined pie plate. Remove the lattice from the freezer and place on top of the filled pie. Trim the lattice strips and crimp the pie edges (see illustration 4 on page 371). Lightly brush or spray the lattice top with 1 tablespoon water and sprinkle with the remaining 1 tablespoon sugar.

7. Lower the oven temperature to 425 degrees. Place the pie on the baking sheet and bake until the crust is set and begins to brown, 25 to 30 minutes. Rotate the pie and reduce the oven temperature to 375 degrees; continue baking until the crust is deep golden brown and juices bubble, 25 to 30 minutes longer. Cool the pie on a wire rack for at least 2 hours before serving.

PEELING PEACHES

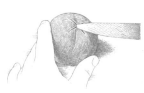   

1. With a paring knife, score a small x at the base of each peach.

2. Lower the peaches into a pan of boiling water with a slotted spoon. Cover and blanch until their skins loosen, about 2 minutes.

3. Using the slotted spoon, transfer the peaches to a bowl of ice water. Let stand to stop cooking, about I minute.

4. Cool the peaches, then, starting from the scored x, peel each peach.

DUTCH APPLE PIE

DUTCH APPLE PIE IS COMPOSED OF TENDER, creamy apple filling, flaky pie crust, and buttery mounds of streusel. To get our bearings, we began by making five Dutch apple pies, each with a different recipe and technique. Surely one had to come close to our ideal. Not so. Each pie was a miserable failure. Variously soupy and void of crust, filled with undercooked apples or dotted with greasy, melted pools of butter, these pies were bad enough to induce laughter in the test kitchen. But we were stymied—why had they failed? What makes baking a Dutch apple pie any different from baking a standard American-style apple pie?

Before we could begin to solve the problems of Dutch apple pie, we needed to define just what it was. As it turns out, there are three components and one major omission that convert an ordinary apple pie into a Dutch apple pie. The additions consist of dried fruit (such as currants or raisins), dairy in the filling, and a streusel topping in lieu of the standard top crust. The major omission is lemon juice.

This omission was far from incidental, as it turned out. A standard apple pie is baked from start to finish with lemon juice, which helps to break down the apples and allows them to release their juices, making for a juicy as well as tender pie filling. But most of the recipes for Dutch apple pie that we had unearthed called for the addition of only one liquid ingredient—usually heavy cream—five minutes before the pie was done baking. When we sliced into these pies, we noticed two things. First, the interior was not creamy and golden; it was greasy and runny. Second, the apples didn't seem to have cooked through, despite the 45-minute-plus baking times.

Knowing something was amiss, we made a call to Barry Swanson, a professor of food science at Washington State University. He explained that when the cream came into contact with the hot, acidic apples, the fat and water in the cream separated, giving the pies their lumpy, greasy, runny interiors. In addition, because these pies were undergoing dry-heat cooking (since there was no liquid, such as lemon juice, providing the apples with moisture), a much slower process than wet-heat cooking, the apples were remaining too crunchy. While a few recipes call for adding the dairy at the beginning of the baking sequence, they, too, produced pies with a coagulated filling.

At first we thought we might doctor the situation by heating the cream before adding it to the almost-finished pie. But even if the cream didn't separate, five minutes in the oven wouldn't provide enough baking time for the cream to set amidst the layers of apples, and we would still be stuck with unevenly distributed amounts of cream in the pie. Our next thought was to try adding some lemon juice and zest to the pie prior to adding the cream. But the lemon-cream combination sent tasters running for cover. The quickest fix we came up with was to cook off the water by reducing the cream, thereby preventing the fat from separating when it encountered the hot pie filling. This effectively remedied our dairy dilemma, but the apples were still too crunchy.

It occurred to us that sautéing the apples with some butter and sugar before they went into the pie might solve the crunch problem. So we prepared for a new experiment: precooking the apples as well as prebaking the pie shell.

Choosing a Dutch oven for its size (as well as apropos name), we sautéed the apples until they were tender from exterior to interior and some of the softer pieces began to break down. We strained the apples of their juices, packed them into the prebaked pie shell, and reduced ½ cup of heavy cream with the remaining apple juices (to give the cream reduction a flavor boost). The cream reduction was thick, glossy, and redolent with appley undertones. We spooned the sauce over the filling and topped the pie with streusel. After a mere 10 minutes in the oven, the filling was just right, and we had a perfectly crisp and flaky pie crust to boot.

Now that the filling and crust met our expectations, we moved on to the streusel. We wanted it to be just crunchy enough on the outside to allow for some textural deviation from the flush and tender filling, but it also had to have enough fat to create a melt-in-your-mouth sensation. After trying almost all possible combinations of brown sugar, light brown sugar, white sugar, honey, cornmeal, baking powder, flour, salt, spices, and butter, we found the perfect streusel to be a composition of melted butter with a touch of salt, just enough cornmeal to give it some crunch, a combination of light brown sugar and white sugar, and enough flour to bind everything together. By tossing the melted butter into the dry ingredients with a fork, we were able to create large chunks of streusel surrounded by smaller pea-sized morsels.

Now the only thing standing between us and a real Dutch apple pie was the dried fruit. The earliest recipe we found was published in 1667 and included currants. While currants far surpassed shriveled black raisins in terms of beauty, they did not contribute much flavor or chew. Dried cherries and cranberries were too sweet and too bold a shade of red for the subtle, wheaty hue of the pie interior. We finally found solace in golden raisins, both sweet and plump, yet not too showy.

Dutch Apple Pie
SERVES 8

The most efficient way to make this pie is to use the dough's chill times to peel and core the apples and prepare the streusel, then cook the apples while the dough prebakes. For a finished look, dust the pie with confectioners' sugar just before serving.

1	recipe Pie Dough for Prebaked Pie Shell (page 368), fully baked

APPLE FILLING

2½	pounds (about 5 medium) Granny Smith apples
2	pounds (about 4 medium) McIntosh apples
¼	cup (1¾ ounces) sugar
½	teaspoon ground cinnamon
⅛	teaspoon salt
2	tablespoons unsalted butter
¾	cup golden raisins
½	cup heavy cream

STREUSEL TOPPING

1¼	cups (6¼ ounces) unbleached all-purpose flour
⅓	cup packed light brown sugar
⅓	cup granulated sugar
1	tablespoon cornmeal
7	tablespoons unsalted butter, melted

1. FOR THE PIE SHELL: Prepare as directed, baking the crust until deep golden brown. Remove the

baked crust from the oven and increase the oven temperature to 425 degrees.

2. FOR THE APPLE FILLING: Meanwhile, peel, quarter, and core the apples; slice each quarter crosswise into pieces ¼ inch thick. Toss the apples, sugar, cinnamon, and salt in a large bowl to combine. Heat the butter in a large Dutch oven over high heat until foaming subsides; add the apples and toss to coat. Reduce the heat to medium-high and cook, covered, stirring occasionally, until the apples are softened, about 5 minutes. Stir in the raisins; cook, covered, stirring occasionally, until the Granny Smith apple slices are tender and the McIntosh apple slices are softened and beginning to break down, about 5 minutes longer.

3. Set a large colander over a large bowl; transfer the cooked apples to the colander. Shake the colander and toss the apples to drain off as much juice as possible. Bring the drained juice and cream to a boil in the now-empty Dutch oven over high heat; cook, stirring occasionally, until thickened and a wooden spoon leaves a trail in the mixture, about 5 minutes. Transfer the apples to the prebaked pie shell; pour the reduced juice mixture over and smooth with a rubber spatula.

4. FOR THE STREUSEL TOPPING: Combine the flour, sugars, and cornmeal in a medium bowl; drizzle with the melted butter and toss with a fork until evenly moistened and the mixture forms many large chunks with pea-sized pieces mixed throughout. Line a rimmed baking sheet with parchment paper and spread the streusel in an even layer on the paper. Bake the streusel until golden brown, about 5 minutes; cool the baking sheet with the streusel on a wire rack until cool enough to handle, about 5 minutes.

5. TO FINISH THE PIE: Sprinkle the streusel evenly over the pie filling. Set the pie plate on the now-empty baking sheet and bake until the streusel topping is deep golden brown, about 10 minutes. Cool on a wire rack to room temperature and serve.

➤ VARIATION
Quick Dutch Apple Crisp
SERVES 8

This quick variation on our Dutch apple pie eliminates the pie crust, allowing you to have dessert on the table in less than an hour.

Follow the recipe for Dutch Apple Pie, omitting the pie dough and beginning with step 2. In step 3, pack the cooked apples into an 8-inch square baking dish and pour the reduced juice mixture over. Continue with recipe at step 4.

CUSTARD PIE

AN OLD-FASHIONED CUSTARD PIE IS MADE with fresh cream, sugar, nutmeg, and eggs. The custard should be extraordinarily delicate and light, with a rich cream flavor. But when we baked up a sampling of custard pies in our test kitchen, we were quickly reminded of their shortcomings. Many had a tough, overbaked outer ring of custard (the perimeter overbakes by the time the center is set), a soggy, milk-soaked pie crust, and an eggy taste that is less than delightful for a dessert.

Although this dessert was relatively simple to make, clearly it was not foolproof. After these early tests, we were clear about what we wanted—a custard pie recipe with a crisp crust, a tender yet flavorful filling, and a relatively foolproof cooking method.

The first question was, which type of liquid is best? We tried, in order of ascending cholesterol count, skim milk, whole milk, half-and-half, light cream, and heavy cream. The skim milk gave the custard a hollow taste and a thin texture; the whole milk provided good flavor but did not set up well; the half-and-half was good; the light cream was a bit fatty; and the heavy cream was much too much of a good thing. We played a bit more with proportions and settled on 2 cups milk to 1 cup heavy cream.

Before we pursued this recipe any further, however, we had to deal with the issue of the crust. When making other custard-based pies, such as pumpkin, the test kitchen has found the best method is to prebake the crust, add a hot filling, and then finish the baking in the oven as quickly as possible. Since we wanted to prebake the crust as much as possible (to prevent sogginess), we had to get the filled pie in and out of the oven fast (so the fully baked crust wouldn't color further). So the question became, how could we speed up the thickening process?

We naturally turned to the issue of the thickener itself. After some reflection, we thought that a combination of cornstarch and eggs might be best. The reason for this pairing lies in understanding the science of thickeners. When cornstarch is added to an egg custard mixture, the viscosity is greater—in other words, the mixture becomes thicker. This causes heat to be transmitted more evenly throughout the custard, which neatly solves the problem of the overcooked perimeter. At the same time, eggs also add flavor and provide emulsification, which ensures a longer-lasting custard mixture less likely to "weep" the next day. Finally, it is a well-known fact among bakers that cornstarch helps prevent eggs from curdling. One theory is that swelling starch granules make it more difficult for egg proteins to bond, the immediate cause of curdling. A good balance between cornstarch and eggs should therefore produce the best and most foolproof custard pie.

Having thought this through, we started a new round of tests using cornstarch along with the eggs. (We later discovered that custard pies that use both eggs and cornstarch do exist; most often from the South, they are referred to simply as custard pies or sometimes silk pies.) At first, we added 2 tablespoons of cornstarch to 2 cups of milk, 1 cup of cream, and 3 whole eggs. The pie had difficulty setting up properly, so we increased the cornstarch to 3 tablespoons, which worked fine. The pie was evenly cooked throughout, including the edges, and had a delicate, light texture, a major improvement on a standard eggs-only custard pie. We also tried 4 tablespoons, which produced a gloppy, Jell-O-like product.

Now the issue was finding the best way to assemble the filling. We thought that preheating the milk/cream mixture made a lot of sense since it could be done quickly without fear of overcooking the eggs. The hot milk/cream mixture could be slowly whisked into the eggs, and the custard could then be heated until thick. We used a medium-low heat until the custard reached 155 degrees. We stirred occasionally but not constantly. Once the mixture reached that temperature, we stirred constantly but gently with a wooden spoon. At 170 degrees, the custard on the edge of our wooden spoon thickened to a loose paste; this meant that the custard in contact with the bottom of the saucepan was starting to set up. At this point, we noticed that the custard looked a bit clumpy, with small curds in the mix. At first we thought that the mixture had curdled, but in fact it was not a problem. The pie came out just fine. We poured the hot, thickening custard into the hot prebaked pie shell and found that it took only 12 to 15 minutes at 375 degrees to finish the baking. We removed the pie from the oven when the custard still wobbled a bit when lightly shaken but felt mostly set, not very loose.

To finish off the testing, we fiddled with the sugar and settled on ⅔ cup—this was enough to add flavor but less than the ¾ cup or more called for in most recipes. We liked the addition of nutmeg, but only ¼ teaspoon. After experimenting to find the best lemon and orange variations, we were done.

Custard Pie

SERVES 8

The prebaked pie shell can be made ahead, but it should be heated in a 375-degree oven until hot, about 5 minutes, before the custard filling is poured into it. Or, if you prefer to prebake the pie shell and make the pie in one continuous process, begin heating the milk and cream for the custard when the foil and pie weights are removed; the filling should be ready at the same time that the shell is ready to be filled. (The oven rack position and temperature for prebaking the pie shell remain the same for the filled pie.)

1	recipe Pie Dough for Prebaked Pie Shell (page 368), fully baked

CUSTARD FILLING

2	cups whole milk
1	cup heavy cream
3	large eggs
⅔	cup (4 ¾ ounces) sugar
3	tablespoons cornstarch
2	teaspoons vanilla extract
¼	teaspoon fresh grated nutmeg
⅛	teaspoon salt

1. FOR THE PIE SHELL: Prepare as directed, baking the crust until deep golden brown. Remove the baked crust from the oven and leave the oven on.

2. FOR THE CUSTARD FILLING: Heat the milk and cream in a medium saucepan over medium-low heat until steaming, about 6 minutes. Meanwhile, whisk together the eggs, sugar, cornstarch, vanilla, nutmeg, and salt in a medium bowl until thoroughly combined and smooth.

3. (If necessary, heat the prebaked pie shell in the oven until hot, about 5 minutes.) Whisk the steaming milk and cream into the egg and cornstarch mixture in a slow, steady stream. Return the egg and milk mixture to the saucepan and cook over medium-low heat, stirring constantly with a wooden spoon and occasionally scraping the bottom of the pan, until the custard begins to thicken and forms a ridge on the tip of the spoon when the bottom of the pan is scraped and the spoon is lifted, 6 to 8 minutes. (If using a thermometer, stir occasionally until the custard reaches 160 degrees, then constantly.)

4. TO FINISH AND BAKE THE PIE: Pour the custard into the hot pie shell. Bake in a 375-degree oven until the custard has set around the edges but jiggles slightly in the center when shaken, 12 to 15 minutes. Cool to room temperature, about 2 hours. Cut into wedges and serve.

VARIATIONS

Lemon Custard Pie

Follow the recipe for Custard Pie, decreasing the vanilla to 1 teaspoon, substituting 1½ tablespoons grated lemon zest for the nutmeg, and whisking 1½ tablespoons lemon juice into the egg and cornstarch mixture.

Orange Custard Pie

Follow the recipe for Custard Pie, decreasing the vanilla to 1 teaspoon, substituting 1½ tablespoons grated orange zest for the nutmeg, and whisking 1½ tablespoons orange juice into the egg and cornstarch mixture.

LEMON MERINGUE PIE

THE IDEAL LEMON MERINGUE PIE HAS A RICH filling that balances the airy meringue without detracting from the flavor of lemon. The lemon filling should be soft but not runny, firm enough to cut but not stiff and gelatinous. Finally, the meringue itself should not break down and puddle on the bottom or "weep" on top—not even on rainy days.

The ingredients in lemon meringue pie have remained constant for some time: sugar, water (or sometimes milk), cornstarch (sometimes mixed with flour), egg yolks, lemon juice (and usually zest), and a little butter. To our tastes, the straightforward lemon flavor of the water-based filling is pleasant, but it is also one-dimensional, lacking depth. Milk, however, subdues the lemon flavor. The solution is to rely primarily on water and a lot of egg yolks (we use six rather than the usual three), eliminating the milk altogether. This has another benefit: The addition of egg yolks allows you to cut back on both sugar (which acts as a softener at a certain level) and cornstarch and still achieve a firm yet tender filling.

The meringue is much more tricky. On any given day it can shrink, bead, puddle, deflate, burn, sweat, break down, or turn rubbery. Most cookbooks don't even attempt to deal with the problems of meringue. They follow the standard recipe—granulated sugar and cream of tartar beaten slowly into the egg whites—assuming, apparently, that there is no way around the flaws. After making 30-something lemon meringue pies, we're not sure we blame anyone for skirting the issue. For as easy as it was to figure out the perfect lemon filling, the meringue remains, finally, only a manageable mystery.

The puddling underneath the meringue is from undercooking. Undercooked whites break down and return to their liquid state. The beading on top of the pie is from overcooking. This near-the-surface overcooking of the meringue causes the proteins in the egg white to coagulate, squeezing out moisture, which then surfaces as tears or beads.

This double dilemma might seem insurmountable, but we hit upon a solution. If the filling is piping hot when the meringue is applied, the underside of the meringue will not undercook; if the oven temperature is relatively low, the top of the meringue won't overcook. A relatively cool oven also produces the best-looking, most evenly browned meringue. To further stabilize the meringue, we like to beat in a tiny bit of cornstarch; if you do this, the meringue will not weep, even on hot, humid days.

Lemon Meringue Pie

SERVES 8

As soon as the filling is made, cover it with plastic wrap to keep it hot and then start working on the meringue topping. You want to add hot filling to the pie shell, apply the meringue topping, and then quickly get the pie into the oven.

LEMON FILLING

1	cup (7 ounces) sugar
1/4	cup (1 ounce) cornstarch
1/8	teaspoon salt
1 1/2	cups cold water
6	large egg yolks
1	tablespoon grated zest and 1/2 cup juice from 2 or 3 lemons
2	tablespoons unsalted butter

MERINGUE TOPPING

1	tablespoon cornstarch
1/3	cup water
1/4	teaspoon cream of tartar
1/2	cup (3 1/2 ounces) sugar
4	large egg whites
1/2	teaspoon vanilla extract

1	recipe Prebaked Pie Dough Coated with Graham Cracker Crumbs (page 369), fully baked and cooled completely

APPLYING A MERINGUE TOPPING

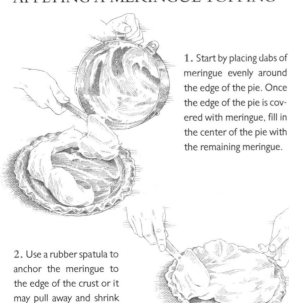

1. Start by placing dabs of meringue evenly around the edge of the pie. Once the edge of the pie is covered with meringue, fill in the center of the pie with the remaining meringue.

2. Use a rubber spatula to anchor the meringue to the edge of the crust or it may pull away and shrink in the oven.

1. FOR THE FILLING: Mix sugar, cornstarch, salt, and water in a large, nonreactive saucepan. Bring mixture to simmer over medium heat, whisking occasionally at beginning of the process and more frequently as mixture begins to thicken. When mixture starts to simmer and turn translucent, whisk in egg yolks, two at a time. Whisk in zest, then lemon juice, and finally butter. Bring mixture to a good simmer, whisking constantly. Remove from heat, place plastic wrap directly on surface of filling to keep hot and prevent skin from forming.

2. FOR THE MERINGUE: Mix cornstarch with water in small saucepan; bring to simmer, whisking occasionally at beginning and more frequently as mixture thickens. When mixture starts to simmer and turn translucent, remove from heat. Let cool while beating egg whites.

3. Heat oven to 325 degrees. Mix cream of tartar and sugar together. Beat egg whites and vanilla until frothy. Beat in sugar mixture, 1 tablespoon at a time, until sugar is incorporated and mixture forms soft peaks. Add cornstarch mixture, 1 tablespoon at a time; continue to beat meringue to stiff peaks. Remove plastic from lemon filling and return to very low heat during last minute or so of beating meringue (to ensure filling is hot).

4. TO FINISH THE PIE: Pour hot filling into pie shell. Using a rubber spatula, immediately distribute meringue evenly around edge and then center of pie to keep it from sinking into filling (see figure 1 on page 377). Make sure meringue attaches to pie crust to prevent shrinking (see figure 2 on page 377). Use back of spoon to create peaks all over meringue. Bake pie until meringue is golden brown, about 20 minutes. Transfer to wire rack and cool to room temperature. Serve that day.

SWEET POTATO PIE

THERE ARE TWO KINDS OF SOUTHERN cooking: lady food and down-home food. In the former category are such treats as Coconut Layer Cake (see page 355). Sweet potato pie was from the start in the latter category, since sweet potatoes have always been cheap and available and the recipes for this dessert are traditionally short on eggs, milk, and white sugar. Instead of scarce white sugar, country cooks relied more heavily on the natural sweetness and texture of the sweet potatoes themselves, combined with sorghum syrup or molasses. This resulted not in the custard-like pie we know today but in a toothier pie, something more akin to a delicate version of mashed sweet potatoes.

But all that is history. The question for our test kitchen was how to create a distinctive sweet potato pie, a recipe that honored the texture and flavor of sweet potatoes while being sufficiently recognizable as a dessert. Neither a custardy, pumpkin-style pie nor mashed-potatoes-in-a-crust pie would do.

A review of more than 30 recipes led us to five distinctive approaches to this dish, ranging from mashed sweet potatoes with a modicum of milk and eggs to Paul Prudhomme's syrup-soaked Sweet Potato Pecan Pie to a typical pumpkin pie, with sweet potatoes substituted for the pumpkin. Some recipes separated the eggs and whipped the whites, some used evaporated or condensed milk, others used a combination of white and sweet potatoes, and most of them used a profusion of spices. To our surprise, all of them had abandoned molasses or sorghum for either white or brown sugar.

Although the classic pumpkin-pie style was good, our tasters were drawn to more authentic recipes, especially one published in Dori Sanders's *Country Cooking* (Algonquin Books of Chapel Hill, 1995), which had more sweet potato flavor. One problem with all such recipes, however, was their mashed-potatoes-in-a-crust quality. We wanted a recipe that would work as a dessert, not a savory side dish to a turkey dinner. This would require fiddling with the amount of milk, eggs, and sugar as well as with the method of preparing the potatoes. Another problem with these recipes was the likelihood they had been modernized (using white sugar, for example), and we wondered if we could bring the sweet potato pie back to its roots, making it a dessert with more character than the white-tablecloth pie it had become.

The first step was to determine the best method of preparing the sweet potatoes. One group of tasters was keen on slicing cooked potatoes and then layering them in the pie shell. This method was quickly discarded, since its product bore little resemblance to a dessert. We also gave up on using a food processor to beat the cooked potatoes; this resulted in a very smooth, custardy texture. We finally settled on coarsely mashing the potatoes, leaving a few small lumps. This also simplified the recipe, precluding the need to pass the potatoes through a sieve to remove fibrous strings, a step called for in some of the more refined recipes. We also decided on microwaving as the easiest method of precooking the sweet potatoes. It took just 10 minutes, without having to first boil water or preheat an oven.

Next, we discarded the notion of using a bit of white potato in the recipe (a technique often used by traditional Southern cooks to lighten the texture). This made the pie more complicated and a bit grainy as well. Separating the eggs and whipping the whites, another common procedure, produced an anemic, fluffy dessert lacking in moisture and flavor. Sweetened condensed milk did not improve the flavor, and we ended up preferring regular milk over half-and-half. We added two yolks to three whole eggs to properly moisten the texture. Orange zest and lemon juice were tried and discarded because they detracted from the delicate flavor of the sweet potato itself; a bit of bourbon helped to accentuate the flavor.

A major problem with modern sweet potato pies is that they call for the usual pumpkin pie spices, which overwhelm the taste of the sweet potato. The solution was to use only a modest amount of nutmeg. White sugar was fine, but since older recipes often call for molasses (or sorghum syrup, cane syrup, dark corn syrup, and even maple syrup), we decided to test it. The results were mixed, so we settled on 1 tablespoon of molasses as optional. This boosts flavor without overpowering the pie with the distinctive malt taste of molasses. (Even 2 tablespoons of molasses were too many.)

At this point we had a pie that we liked a lot, with real sweet potato flavor and enough custardy richness to place it firmly in the dessert category. But something was still lacking. The pie tasted a bit vegetal; it needed more oomph. Based on Paul Prudhomme's notion of adding pecan pie flavorings to the mix, we made a few pies to see if we could create two layers—one of sweet potato filling and one similar to the sweet filling in a pecan pie—to jazz things up. Creating two separate layers presented a challenge until we came upon the idea of baking the pecan pie filling first, until it set in the shell, about 20 minutes,

and then adding the sweet potato filling on top. This worked like a charm and made a stupendous pie. Even so, many tasters found the process a little unwieldy. After more experiments, we came up with an easy-as-pie technique for adding a separate bottom layer: We simply sprinkled the bottom of the crust with brown sugar before adding the filling.

Now we had something really special, a pie with an intense, thick, pure-sweet-potato filling, perfectly complemented by a layer of melted brown sugar just beneath. Its unique nature is reflected in the color of the filling, which is a fantastic orange rather than the dull brown that results from the use of too much molasses and too many spices. This was a sweet potato pie that any Southern cook would be proud of.

~≺

Sweet Potato Pie
SERVES 8 TO 10

Prepare the sweet potato filling while the crust is baking so that it will be ready soon after the pie shell comes out of the oven. (The crust should still be warm when you add the brown sugar layer and sweet potato filling.) The sweet potatoes cook quickly in the microwave but can also be pricked with a fork and baked uncovered in a 400-degree oven until tender, 40 to 50 minutes. Some tasters preferred a stronger bourbon flavor in the filling, so we give a range below. If you like molasses, use the optional tablespoon; a few tasters felt it deepened the sweet potato flavor. Serve the pie with our Whipped Cream (page 382).

1	recipe Pie Dough for Prebaked Pie Shell (page 368), partially baked

SWEET POTATO FILLING

2	pounds sweet potatoes (about 5 small to medium)
2	tablespoons unsalted butter, softened
3	large eggs plus 2 yolks
1	cup (7 ounces) sugar
½	teaspoon grated nutmeg
¼	teaspoon salt
2–3	tablespoons bourbon
1	tablespoon molasses (optional)
1	teaspoon vanilla extract
⅔	cup whole milk
¼	cup (1¾ ounces) packed dark brown sugar

1. FOR THE PIE SHELL: Prepare as directed, baking the crust until light golden brown. Remove the baked crust from the oven and reduce the oven temperature to 350 degrees.

2. FOR THE SWEET POTATO FILLING: Meanwhile, prick sweet potatoes several times with a fork and place on a double layer of paper towels in a microwave. Cook at full power for 5 minutes; turn each potato over and continue to cook at full power until tender, but not mushy, about 5 minutes longer. Cool 10 minutes. Halve a potato crosswise; insert a small spoon between the skin and flesh, and scoop the flesh into a medium bowl; discard the skin. (If the potato is too hot to handle comfortably, fold a double layer of paper towels into quarters and use this to hold each potato half.) Repeat with the remaining sweet potatoes; you should have about 2 cups. While the potatoes are still hot, add the butter and mash with a fork or wooden spoon; small lumps of potato should remain.

3. Whisk together the eggs, yolks, sugar, nutmeg, and salt in a medium bowl; stir in the bourbon, molasses (if using), and vanilla, then whisk in the milk. Gradually add the egg mixture to the sweet potatoes, whisking gently to combine.

4. TO FINISH AND BAKE THE PIE: Sprinkle the bottom of the warm pie shell evenly with the brown sugar. Pour the sweet potato mixture into the pie shell over the brown sugar layer. Bake until the filling is set around the edges but the center jiggles slightly when shaken, about 45 minutes. Transfer the pie to a wire rack; cool to room temperature, about 2 hours, and serve.

COCONUT CREAM PIE

COCONUT CREAM PIE EVOKES HAPPY thoughts—a fluffy cloud of a dessert, a sweet finish to a satisfying home-cooked meal. But to imagine the taste of a coconut cream pie and to taste one on the plate in front of you are likely to be discordant experiences. We discovered this first-hand when we whipped up a few recipes. These coconut cream pies were not the dreamily soft, smooth and satiny, delicately perfumed, luscious cream pie fillings floating in crisp crusts we had hoped for. Instead, they were disappointingly heavy, leaden, pasty, noxiously sweet, bland vanilla puddings in soggy pie shells.

First we went to work on the crust. Though a plain pastry crust is typical of a coconut cream pie, we were not the least bit wowed—the crust was fully prebaked and started out perfectly crisp, but when the filling went in, it quickly became soggy. It was a graham cracker crust—a somewhat unorthodox but not completely odd option—that was the crowd-pleaser. Its crisp, sandy texture, sturdy build, and substantial presence was the perfect contrast to the creamy smooth filling. Its sweet, toasty flavor also complemented the filling's gentle flavors.

It occurred to us, though, that the flavor of the graham crust could be heightened and made to better fit its role by adding some coconut to it. In our next attempts, we toasted some shredded coconut until it was golden brown, then processed it along with the graham crackers so that it could be broken down into the finest bits. The coconut was a welcomed addition; though it offered only a little flavor, ¼ cup of it dispersed throughout the cracker crumbs gave the crust that characteristic fibrous, nubby coconut crunch.

Coconuts are exotic tropical nuts (seeds, actually). They hail from lands of balmy breezes, palm trees, and ocean air, but recipes for coconut cream pie fillings are boring and domesticated. They consist of no more than eggs, sugar, cornstarch or flour, and cream or milk. In a nutshell, they are vanilla cream pies garnished with a spray of toasted shredded coconut. We wanted to breathe some life into this downtrodden pie by pumping the filling full of true coconut flavor.

As with other cream pies, the filling for coconut cream pie is made on the stovetop in the same manner as a home-cooked pudding. In developing a filling, the first thing we needed to do was find the right kind of cream or "milk" to use. We made versions with half-and-half, milk, and coconut milk. As we expected, the first two were boring, bland puddings. The coconut milk filling had a delicate coconut flavor and aroma, but it was far too rich to be palatable. We pulled back on the coconut milk and tried a filling made with one 14-ounce can of coconut milk cut with a cup of whole milk. Much better, but still we felt we needed to work in more coconut flavor.

We stirred some toasted shredded coconut into the filling, but the long stringy shreds suspended in the otherwise smooth filling were unappealing. Next, we took the advice of a recipe that suggested steeping unsweetened shredded coconut (which comes shredded in fine flecks and is available in natural foods and Asian grocery stores) in the milk to extract some of its flavor; the coconut was then strained out and pressed to remove any liquid that it was withholding. Though this technique didn't yield the results expected—the steeped mixture didn't have much more flavor and was a nuisance to boot—we did make the fortuitous discovery that the unsweetened shredded coconut itself had good, pure coconut flavor. We captured this delicate coconut flavor by leaving the tiny bits in the filling. The coconut also offered up their gritty coconut crunch. One-half cup of coconut in the filling was good; any more and it overran the smoothness of the filling.

Next, we tasted side-by-side a filling thickened with cornstarch and one with flour. The cornstarch, as we expected, made a filling with a lighter, more natural feel; the flour made a heavy and starchy goo. One-quarter cup of cornstarch was just the right amount to allow the filling to set up into a firm texture. When chilled, the pie sliced neatly and cleanly. The filling had just enough resistance to keep it from slipping and sliding onto the plate.

As for eggs, some recipes called for whole eggs, some for just yolks, and a few for both. The number called for ranged from two to six. Our preference was for five yolks. This number made a filling with a smooth, lush, supple mouthfeel and a full, deep flavor. By comparison, fillings with whole eggs—even with whole eggs plus yolks—had a leaner, gummier texture and a hollow flavor. In addition, their color wasn't as appealing as an all-yolk filling.

We were now very close to a final recipe. The last adjustments were to add some salt and vanilla to heighten and round out the flavors. Some butter whisked into the hot filling just before pouring it into its shell was the finale that smoothed out any rough edges and made the coconut cream feel and taste superbly creamy, rich, and silky, but not so unctuous as to make one slice—topped with a puff of whipped cream—a challenge to eat.

Coconut Cream Pie
SERVES 8 TO 10

Unsweetened shredded coconut is available in natural foods stores as well as in Asian grocery stores. When toasting the coconut, keep a close eye on it because it burns quite easily.

CRUST

5	tablespoons unsweetened shredded coconut
10	graham crackers (5 ounces, or 1 package), broken into rough pieces
2	tablespoons sugar
5	tablespoons unsalted butter, melted

FILLING

1	(14-ounce) can coconut milk, well-stirred
1	cup whole milk
½	cup (1¼ ounces) unsweetened shredded coconut
⅔	cup (4¾ ounces) sugar
¼	teaspoon salt
5	large egg yolks
¼	cup (1 ounce) cornstarch
1½	teaspoons vanilla extract
2	tablespoons unsalted butter, cut into 4 pieces

3	cups Whipped Cream (page 382), with 1½ teaspoons dark rum added with vanilla extract, if desired, and whipped to soft peaks

1. FOR THE CRUST: Adjust an oven rack to the middle position and heat the oven to 325 degrees. Spread the 5 tablespoons coconut in a 9-inch Pyrex glass pie plate and toast in the oven until golden brown, about 9 minutes, stirring 2 or 3 times. When cool enough to handle, reserve 1 tablespoon for garnishing the finished pie.

2. Pulse the graham crackers and the remaining 4 tablespoons toasted coconut in a food processor until the crackers are broken down into coarse crumbs, about 10 one-second pulses. Process the mixture until evenly fine crumbs form, about 12 seconds. Transfer the crumbs to a medium bowl and stir in the sugar to combine; add the melted butter and toss with a fork until the crumbs are evenly moistened. Wipe out the now-empty pie plate and empty the crumb mixture into it. Using the bottom of a

WHIPPING CREAM TO SOFT AND STIFF PEAKS

SOFT PEAKS
Cream whipped to soft peaks will droop slightly from the ends of the beaters or whisk.

STIFF PEAKS
Cream whipped to stiff peaks will cling tightly to the ends of the beaters or whisk and will hold its shape.

ramekin or measuring cup, press the crumbs evenly into the bottom and up the sides. Bake the crust until deep golden brown and fragrant, about 22 minutes. Cool the crust on a wire rack while making the filling.

3. FOR THE FILLING: Bring the coconut milk, milk, shredded coconut, ⅓ cup sugar, and salt to a simmer in a medium saucepan over medium-high heat, stirring occasionally with a wooden spoon to dissolve the sugar. When the mixture reaches a simmer, whisk the egg yolks in a medium bowl to break them up, then whisk in the remaining ⅓ cup sugar and cornstarch until well-combined and no lumps remain. Gradually whisk the simmering liquid into the yolk mixture to temper it, then return the mixture to the saucepan, scraping the bowl with a rubber spatula. Bring the mixture to a simmer over medium heat, whisking constantly, until 3 or 4 bubbles burst on the surface and the mixture is thickened, about 30 seconds. Off heat, whisk in the vanilla and butter. Pour the filling into the cooled

crust, press a sheet of plastic wrap directly on the surface of the filling, and refrigerate until the filling is cold and firm, at least 3 hours.

4. Just before serving, spread or pipe the whipped cream over the chilled pie filling. Sprinkle the reserved 1 tablespoon toasted coconut over the whipped cream. Cut the pie into wedges and serve.

Whipped Cream
MAKES ABOUT 3 CUPS

For the maximum volume and best flavor, use pasteurized (not ultrapasteurized) heavy cream. When you think the cream is almost properly whipped, you may want to switch from an electric mixer to a whisk for greater control. Cream can go from properly whipped to overwhipped in a matter of seconds. If cream becomes granular and curdled-looking, you've beaten it too long and must start over with a new batch of cream. This recipe makes enough to thickly cover a cream pie. If you want to dollop a little whipped cream over individual slices of other pies, cut this recipe by half or by one-third.

1½	**cups heavy cream, chilled, preferably pasteurized or pasteurized organic**
1½	**tablespoons sugar**
½	**teaspoon vanilla extract**

1. Chill a nonreactive, deep bowl and the beaters of an electric mixer in the freezer for at least 20 minutes. (If the freezer is too crowded to accommodate the bowl, place the beaters in a bowl, fill with ice water, and chill on the counter. When the bowl and beaters are well chilled, dump out the ice water and dry thoroughly.)

2. Add the cream, sugar, and vanilla to the chilled bowl. Beat on low speed until small bubbles form, about 30 seconds. Increase the speed to medium and continue beating until the beaters leave a trail, about 30 seconds. Increase the speed to high and continue beating until the cream is smooth, thick, and nearly doubled in volume, about 20 seconds for soft peaks or about 30 seconds for stiff peaks (see the illustrations at left). If necessary, finish beating with a whisk to adjust consistency. Serve immediately or spoon into a fine sieve or strainer set over a measuring cup and refrigerate for up to 8 hours.

16

CRISPS, COBBLER,
AND OTHER FRUIT DESSERTS

THERE IS AN ASTONISHING ARRAY OF OLD-fashioned American desserts that consist of fruit baked with bread, cake crumbs, flour and butter, oats, crackers, and the like. In the days when home cooks were frugal, these desserts were an easy way to use up stale leftovers while providing a bit of variety in terms of texture and flavor. Most of these simple desserts have funny names that are hard to keep straight. While regional differences exist, most American cookbooks agree on the following formulations:

BETTY Fruit is combined with buttered bread (or sometimes cake) crumbs and baked. Similar to a crisp, except that crumbs are usually layered with fruit instead of placed all on top. Also called a brown betty.

BUCKLE Fruit is mixed with simple yellow cake batter and baked. Cake batter can be topped with streusel crumbs.

COBBLER Fruit is topped with a crust, which can be made from cookie dough, pie pastry, or biscuit topping, and baked. If made from biscuit or cookie dough, the topping can be dropped over the fruit for a cobbled appearance.

CRISP Fruit is topped with a "rubbed" mixture of butter, sugar, and flour, then baked. The topping often includes nuts or oats.

CRUMBLE An English term for crisp, usually made with oats.

GRUNT Fruit is topped with biscuit dough, covered, and baked so that biscuits steam rather than bake. The texture is akin to dumplings and is often gummy. Sometimes made on top of the stove. Also called a slump.

PANDOWDY Fruit is covered with pastry dough and baked. The dough is cut, scored, and pressed into fruit. Sometimes the crust is pressed into the fruit during baking; other recipes "dowdy" the crust after baking.

PLATE CAKE Fruit is topped with rolled biscuit dough and baked. When done, the dessert is flipped, and the biscuit topping becomes the bottom crust.

SHORTCAKE Often grouped with crisps, cobblers, and such, this dessert is made with fruit that has not been baked. Rather, the fruit is macerated and then layered between split biscuits with whipped cream.

SLUMP See Grunt.

The following pages contain recipes for our favorite American fruit desserts.

BROWN BETTY

A BROWN BETTY (ALSO CALLED A BETTY) IS a simple, frugal fruit dessert that dates back to the late 1800s. Betties are usually made by layering buttered bread crumbs between layers of sweetened and sometimes spiced apples or other fruits.

We started our recipe development by testing three classic apple betty recipes. Two out of the three were horrid. They instructed the cook to pour hot water over layers of apples and buttered bread crumbs before baking, resulting in soggy, watery apples and pasty bread crumbs. The clear winner was a recipe that called for putting the crumbs on the top only. The result was a very crisp topping, though any apple pieces that happened to peek out through the bread crumbs were dried out and leathery.

After this primary round of testing, we came to some conclusions. First, we would abandon the common technique of pouring water over the dessert. Second, we would aim for a pleasantly crunchy (but not dry) topping and forgo layering the apples and bread crumbs to avoid sogginess.

We focused on the topping first. We made sure that we had a sufficient amount of bread crumb topping to completely cover the fruit to protect it from the dry heat of the oven. Three cups of bread crumbs turned out to be just the right amount to cover a 9-inch square pan full of fruit, and this amount of crumbs eliminated the problem of dried-out apples. We see apple betty as a modest, home-style dessert and therefore chose to use store-bought white bread to make crumbs. A firm sandwich bread holds up well and is our choice for this dessert. We kept the melted butter to a minimum so that the topping wouldn't be greasy and added brown sugar for flavor, with a touch of granulated sugar for gentle sweetness. Though many apple betty recipes use a heavy hand with spices, we determined that just a small amount of cinnamon was necessary to complement the pure flavor of the apples.

As for the filling, we borrowed an idea from our Dutch apple pie recipe, which calls for a combination of Granny Smith apples (for tartness and firm texture) and McIntosh (for sweetness and moisture). When cooked, the Grannies hold their shape, while the McIntosh break down and release their juices. The apples are cut into substantial chunks, which tasters preferred over thin slices. A mere tablespoon of flour was all that was needed to thicken the juices to a sauce-like consistency. Lemon juice was added to perk up the flavor and prevent the apples from discoloring while we prepared the topping. A very small amount (¼ cup) of sugar was all that was needed to make a mildly sweet but not overly sugary filling.

We were fairly happy with the betties we were turning out at this point, but after almost an hour in the oven, the toppings dried out too much and became hard and tough rather than pleasantly crisp. The solution was to cover the betty with foil during most of the baking time and then remove the foil and increase the heat at the end to allow for a final browning.

Firm, relatively dry fruits work best in brown betties. (Juicier fruits make the crumbs soggy). We had the best luck with apples and pears. Plums are an especially good, if a bit juicy, alternative. We found that quick-cooking tapioca does a better job than flour of thickening the bountiful plum juices and keeping the crumbs crisp.

Apple Brown Betty

SERVES 4 TO 6

This dessert should be served warm, ideally with a scoop of vanilla ice cream.

FILLING

1½	pounds Granny Smith apples (about 3 medium)
1½	pounds McIntosh apples (about 3 medium)
1½	tablespoons lemon juice
¼	cup (1¾ ounces) granulated sugar
1	tablespoon all-purpose flour

TOPPING

6	slices (about 6 ounces) firm white sandwich bread (such as Pepperidge Farm)
¼	cup packed (1¾ ounces) plus 2 tablespoons packed dark brown sugar
2	tablespoons granulated sugar
¼	teaspoon ground cinnamon
5	tablespoons unsalted butter, melted

1. FOR THE FILLING: Adjust an oven rack to the middle position and heat the oven to 375 degrees. Peel, quarter, core, and cut the apples into 1-inch chunks. Mix the apples with the lemon juice, sugar, and flour in a medium bowl.

2. FOR THE TOPPING: Tear the bread into large pieces and pulse in a food processor to yield 3 cups of very coarse crumbs. (Most pieces should be about the size of a peanut.) Toss the bread crumbs, sugars, cinnamon, and melted butter in a medium bowl. Rub with your fingers to combine.

3. TO ASSEMBLE AND BAKE THE BETTY: Place the apple filling in a 9-inch square pan. Sprinkle the topping evenly over the fruit, making sure that all the fruit is covered. Cover with aluminum foil and bake until the apples in the center of the pan are tender when pierced with the tip of a knife, 45 to 50 minutes. Remove the foil and increase the oven temperature to 400 degrees. Bake until the topping is browned and the juices bubble, about 10 minutes. Cool slightly on a rack and serve warm.

➤ VARIATIONS

Pear Brown Betty

One half teaspoon of grated fresh ginger makes a nice addition to this variation and the one that follows.

Follow the recipe for Apple Brown Betty, replacing the apples with 2½ to 3 pounds firm ripe pears that have been peeled, cored, and cut into 1-inch chunks.

Plum Brown Betty

Follow the recipe for Apple Brown Betty, replacing the apples with 2½ to 3 pounds firm plums that have been pitted and cut into 1-inch chunks. Add 1 extra tablespoon granulated sugar to the filling if the plums are particularly tart. Replace the flour with 1 tablespoon quick-cooking tapioca.

CRISP

THERE IS SELDOM ANYTHING CRISP ABOUT most crisps. This simple baked dessert, made from sweetened fruit topped with a combination of sugar, butter, and flour, almost invariably comes out of the oven with a soggy top crust. A few recipes go so far as to refer to this classic dish as a crunch, a term that does little to suggest the flat, dull, overly sweetened crumble that serves as a streusel topping for the fruit.

We tried covering fruit with sweetened and buttered oats (for a British take on a crisp, called a crumble) as well as plain toppings without oats or nuts and were unimpressed. None of these toppings merited the name "crisp." We found that spices (we recommend cinnamon and nutmeg) and nuts (particularly whole almonds or pecans) are essential. The spices add flavor to the topping, while the nuts give it some texture and much-needed crunch. We also found that the food processor does the best job of making the topping, although you can also use your fingers or a fork.

Firm fruits, such as apples, pears, nectarines, peaches, and plums, work best in crisps. Berries are quite watery and will make the topping soggy if used alone. However, they will work in combination with firmer fruits. If you like, replace up to one cup of the fruit in the fillings with an equal amount of berries. We think that raspberries are especially good with apples, while blueberries work nicely with peaches.

Our tests revealed that when using apples, a combination of Granny Smith and McIntosh apples works best. The McIntosh apples have good flavor and cook down to form a thick sauce. The Granny Smiths cut some of the sweetness and hold their shape.

We found it unnecessary to thicken the fruit in all but two cases. Plums are a bit watery and benefit from the addition of a little quick-cooking tapioca. Peaches will thicken up on their own but need some help when blueberries are added to the mix. Juices thrown off by any of the other fruits will evaporate or thicken nicely without causing the topping to become soft.

As for flavoring the fruit, we found ¼ cup sugar to be adequate, especially since the toppings are fairly sweet. We also like to add some lemon juice and zest. One half teaspoon of grated ginger makes a nice addition to any of the fillings.

Apple Crisp
SERVES 4 TO 6

A dollop of whipped cream or vanilla ice cream is always welcome, especially if serving the crisp warm. To double the recipe, place the ingredients in a 9 by 13-inch baking dish and bake for 55 minutes at 375 degrees without increasing the oven temperature.

TOPPING

6	tablespoons unbleached all-purpose flour
¼	cup packed (1¾ ounces) light brown sugar
¼	cup (1¾ ounces) granulated sugar
¼	teaspoon ground cinnamon
¼	teaspoon ground nutmeg
¼	teaspoon salt
5	tablespoons unsalted butter, chilled, cut into ½-inch pieces
¾	cup coarsely chopped nuts

FILLING

3	medium Granny Smith apples (1¼ to 1½ pounds)
3	medium McIntosh apples (1¼ to 1½ pounds)
½	teaspoon grated zest and 1½ tablespoons juice from 1 lemon
¼	cup (1¾ ounces) granulated sugar

1. FOR THE TOPPING: Pulse the flour, sugars, spices, and salt in the workbowl of a food processor. Add the butter and pulse 10 times, about 4 seconds for each pulse. The mixture will first look like dry sand, with large lumps of butter, then like coarse cornmeal. Add the nuts, then pulse again, four to five times, about 1 second for each pulse. The topping should look like slightly clumpy wet sand. Be sure not to overmix or the mixture will become too wet and homogeneous. Refrigerate the topping while preparing the fruit, at least 15 minutes.

2. Adjust an oven rack to the lower-middle position and heat the oven to 375 degrees.

3. FOR THE FILLING: Peel, quarter, core, and cut the apples into 1-inch chunks. (You should have 6 cups.) Toss the apples, zest, juice, and sugar in a medium bowl. Scrape the fruit mixture with a rubber spatula into an 8-inch square (2-quart) baking pan or 9-inch deep dish pie plate.

4. **To assemble and bake the crisp:** Distribute the chilled topping evenly over the fruit. Bake for 40 minutes. Increase the oven temperature to 400 degrees and continue baking until the fruit is bubbling and the topping turns deep golden brown, about 5 minutes more. Serve warm. (The crisp can be set aside at room temperature for a few hours and then reheated in a warm oven just before serving.)

➤ VARIATIONS

Apple-Raspberry Crisp

Follow the recipe for Apple Crisp, using two rather than three McIntosh apples and adding 1 cup fresh raspberries to the fruit mixture.

Pear Crisp

Follow the recipe for Apple Crisp, replacing the apples with 2½ to 3 pounds pears.

Peach Crisp

Nectarines can be used in place of peaches if desired. For peach-blueberry crisp, reduce the cut peaches to 5 cups and add 1 cup fresh blueberries and 1 tablespoon quick-cooking tapioca to the fruit mixture.

Follow the recipe for Apple Crisp, replacing the apples with 2½ to 3 pound peaches, peeled, pitted, and cut into ⅓-inch wedges.

Plum Crisp

Follow the recipe for Apple Crisp, replacing the apples with 2½ to 3 pounds plums, pitted and cut into ⅓-inch wedges and adding 1 tablespoon quick-cooking tapioca to the fruit mixture.

APPLE PANDOWDY

PANDOWDY IS A SORT OF DEEP-DISH PIE, originally made with sweetened apples covered with a very thick piece of pastry and baked. Some time before serving, the pastry is scored and pushed into the fruit so it absorbs their juices. Like its fruit dessert cousins, which may be described according to how they look when served or even how they sound when eaten, pandowdy got its name for being just that—"dowdy," or on the homely side.

When we began our recipe development by making five pandowdies from various sources, we realized that making this dessert was not without its pitfalls. Though "soggy" is not too far off in describing the texture of the submerged pastry in a good pandowdy, we considered doughs that qualified as "waterlogged," "saturated," or "total mush" to be failures. We wanted to produce a crust that preserved some of its baked structure, one that was at once both soggy and crispy/flaky. Likewise, some of our first attempts at apple fillings fell short of acceptable, ranging from "overspiced" to "tasteless." We knew our charge would be to develop something in between.

We started with the apples, not only concentrating on their flavor and texture but also knowing that the variety we used would determine the amount of juices released during baking. As with other apple desserts (including apple pie), we found that a combination of Granny Smith and McIntosh apples delivered the best results. An all–Granny Smith pandowdy left a lot to be desired. In the short time that the dowdy is in the oven, the apples held their shape, retained most of their firm texture, and shed only a minimal amount of juices. While we liked their tart assertive flavor, we could not "dowdy" the pastry—there were no juices for it to soak up—and crunchy apples were not the tasters' ideal. The all-McIntosh version came out of the oven on the other end of the spectrum. The apples were broken down and listless—like applesauce—and there was too much juice. The pastry crust, which had already been steamed in the oven, soaked the juices right up and turned into a waterlogged mess. A 50/50 ratio of the two apple varieties yielded a perfect balance of delicate apple juices and yielding yet sturdy apple chunks.

Seasoning the filling came next. A traditional dowdy is not a fancy dish. We decided to keep it simple and limited the flavorings to brown sugar for a caramel-like sweetness, vanilla extract for roundness, and lemon zest for brightness. Although the combination of these ingredients with two types of apples was pleasing, tasters were looking for a hint of cinnamon. In the end, a sprinkling of cinnamon-sugar on the pastry's surface added cinnamon flavor without compromising the freshness of the apples.

It was time to focus on the pastry. We found that

387

our standard pie pastry, with both butter and shortening, yielded good results. The most pressing problem was the overrun of dough around the 8-inch dish in which we were baking the dowdy. When we tucked the excess pastry around the sides of the pan (as recommended in a few recipes), the pastry dropped below the apple layer and "boiled" into a mass of unappealing mush. To avoid such oversaturated dough, especially on the sides and in the corners, we found that it was best to trim the dough to size, avoiding the potential of boiling the dough altogether. Cutting air vents into the surface of the raw dough before baking also helped to prevent excessive steaming and subsequent rubberizing of the pastry. With the edges untucked and the vents opened, the pastry came out of the oven crisp, tender, and flaky, perfect for dunking in the fruit and soaking up its juices.

A few recipes suggested dowdying the crust

MAKING A PANDOWDY

1. As soon as it emerges from the oven, score the pastry with a sharp knife by running the knife lengthwise and crosswise to form 2-inch squares.

2. Use the edge of a spoon or metal spatula to press the edges of the crust squares down into the fruit. Don't completely submerge the pieces or they will become exceedingly soggy.

during baking. We quickly rejected this notion, as it made the crust unbearably soggy. Scoring the crust when it emerged from the oven and then pressing the crust down into the juices was a far better option.

Apple Pandowdy
SERVES 4 TO 6

See the illustrations at left for tips on "dowdying" the crust. Serve the pandowdy warm in deep bowls with scoops of vanilla ice cream.

CRUST

1	cup (5 ounces) unbleached all-purpose flour
½	teaspoon salt
2	tablespoons sugar
2	tablespoons all-vegetable shortening, chilled
6	tablespoons unsalted butter, chilled, cut into ¼-inch pieces
3–4	tablespoons ice water
½	teaspoon ground cinnamon
1	tablespoon milk

FILLING

2	medium Granny Smith apples (about 1 pound), peeled, cored, and cut into ¼-inch slices
2	large McIntosh apples (about 1 pound), peeled, cored, and cut into ¼-inch slices
⅓	cup packed (2⅓ ounces) light brown sugar
1	teaspoon grated lemon zest
½	teaspoon vanilla extract

1. FOR THE CRUST: Pulse the flour, salt, and 1 tablespoon sugar in a food processor fitted with the steel blade until combined. Add the shortening and process until the mixture has the texture of coarse sand, about 10 seconds. Scatter the butter pieces over the flour mixture; cut the butter into the flour until the mixture is pale yellow and resembles coarse crumbs, with butter bits no larger than small peas, about ten 1-second pulses. Turn the mixture into a medium bowl.

2. Sprinkle 3 tablespoons ice water over the mixture. With the blade of a rubber spatula, use a folding motion to mix. Press down on the dough with the broad side of spatula until the dough sticks together, adding up to 1 tablespoon more ice water if the

dough will not come together. Place the dough on a sheet of plastic wrap and press into either a square or a circle, depending on whether you are using a square or round pan. Wrap the dough in plastic and refrigerate at least 1 hour, or up to 2 days, before rolling out.

3. FOR THE FILLING: Preheat the oven to 425 degrees. Toss the apple slices, brown sugar, lemon zest, and vanilla together in a large bowl until the apples are evenly coated with the sugar. Place the apples in an 8-inch square or 9-inch round glass baking dish. Mix together the remaining tablespoon of granulated sugar and the cinnamon in a small bowl and set aside.

4. TO ASSEMBLE AND BAKE THE PANDOWDY: If dough has been refrigerated longer than 1 hour, let it stand at room temperature until malleable. Roll the dough on a lightly floured work surface or between two large sheets of plastic wrap to a 10-inch square or circle. Trim the dough to the exact size of the baking dish. Place the dough over the apples. Brush the dough with milk and sprinkle with the cinnamon-sugar mixture. Cut four 1-inch vents into the dough. Bake until golden brown, 35 to 40 minutes.

5. Score the pastry with a knife as soon as it emerges from the oven. Use the edge of a spoon or spatula to press the edges of the crust squares down into the fruit without completely submerging them. (See the illustrations on page 388.) Because the crust will soften quickly, serve pandowdy warm.

➤ VARIATION

Pear Pandowdy

It's important to use perfectly ripe pears in this recipe. Firm pears don't exude enough juice, and overly ripe pears will break down into mush when baked.

Follow the recipe for Apple Pandowdy, replacing the apples with 2 pounds ripe pears and replacing the lemon zest with 1 teaspoon grated fresh ginger.

CHERRY COBBLER

NO MORE THAN A FLEET OF TENDER BISCUITS on a sea of sweet fruit, good cobblers hold their own against fancy fruit desserts. But unlike fancy fruit desserts, cobblers come together in a couple of quick steps and can be dished up hot, ready to hit the dance floor with a scoop of vanilla ice cream.

Picking fresh sour cherries one summer in Vermont and cooking them up into a compote for crêpes acquainted us with their virtues. Sour cherries have sufficient acidity to cook up well and become truly expressive with a touch of sugar and some heat. (Sweet eating cherries, like Bings, lose their flavor when cooked.) Until then, the only sour, or baking, cherries we had known of were the canned variety. And however plump and lacquered their depiction on the label, those that slid from under a lattice were so pale, so limp and exhausted, that their flavor barely registered. But we knew sour cherries would feel at home in a cobbler—if we could find good ones.

Though sour cherries are grown in relatively large quantities in Michigan, here in the Northeast our grocery shelves are bereft of sour cherry products, save the crayon-red canned gravy with lumps called "pie filling." So we were grateful to find two different kinds of jarred sour cherries at our local Trader Joe's during the off season (all 11 months of it). In addition, the Cherry Marketing Institute of Michigan provided us with variously processed sour cherries—frozen, canned, and dried. Since it would be months before we could try making cobbler with fresh cherries, we began our tests with processed.

Early tests in which we prepared quick fruit fillings elicited unenthusiastic comments from tasters. While frozen Michigan sour cherries maintained their color well, flavor was left largely to the imagination. Both canned and jarred sour cherries from Michigan were flaccid and developed an anemic pallor when cooked. Adding a handful of dried cherries did little to heighten their impact. Only Trader Joe's jarred Morello cherries drew a crowd. Deep ruby red, plump, meaty, and tart, they delivered bracing flavor and a great chew right out of the jar.

This experience prompted us to do a little research. Sour cherries, we learned, are classified in two groups, amarelles and griottes. The former have lighter flesh—tan on the inside—and clear juices; the latter are dark—even black—with deep red juice. The best known examples of each group are Montmorency (an amarelle) and Morello (a griotte). Most tart cherries grown in the United States are Montmorency. Those from Eastern Europe are Morello. With a couple of us remembering the stellar cherries we had tasted in baked goods in Germany, we decided to base our recipe on jarred Morellos.

A cobbler should be juicy, but not swimming in juice, and it should taste like the fruit whose name it bears. Jarred and canned cherries come awash in juices, which we would use to produce the sauce. Since jarred and canned cherries have already been processed, they are already cooked—the less heat they're exposed to thereafter, the better. Straining off the juice, we dumped the drained contents of four 24-ounce jars of Morellos into a 9 by 13-inch baking dish, then thickened and sweetened 3 cups of the juice. The resulting flavor was a bit flat. We replaced 1 cup of the cherry juice with red wine and added a cinnamon stick, a pinch of salt, and a whiff of almond extract. Much better. Red wine and sour cherries have a natural affinity; the cinnamon stick added a fragrant woody depth; and, as with all fruits, salt performed its usual minor miracle. The almond extract brought the entire flavor experience up a couple of notches. For thickener we resolved to go with cornstarch. It could be mixed in with the sugar and brought directly to a simmer with the reserved cherry juices, then poured over the waiting cherries and baked. Lightly thickened fruit is best; a cobbler shouldn't be thick enough to spread on toast.

We also had some requirements for the cobbles. We wanted them feather-light but deeply browned and crisp. This said a number of things to us. The first was: no eggs. Eggs would make our biscuits too heavy and substantial. The second thing it said was buttermilk. Buttermilk biscuits are famously light and tender. The third precept came by way of a number of Southern recipes, which said a wet dough makes a nice light biscuit. We baked several biscuit variations to confirm these notions, settling on all-purpose flour, a moderate amount of butter, small amounts of baking powder and soda, a touch of sugar, a wave of buttermilk, and a nice hot oven. Dispensing with rolling, we dropped the biscuits onto the fruit with an ice cream scoop. The biscuits had a buttery lightness, a mild tang, and a crunchy, sugary top.

Not quite satisfied with their pale bellies touching the fruit, we undertook to bake the biscuits for 15 minutes on a baking sheet while the filling was coming together on the stove. We then wedded them to the fruit for only 10 minutes in the oven. By then the fruit (already hot from the cooked sauce)

was bubbling around the biscuits, which were deeply browned on top and baked through underneath. Heaven in about a half-hour.

Jarred Morellos made a fine cobbler, but we wanted more, and, finally, summer came. We used both Morellos and Montmorency cherries. And how were the fresh cobblers? Both varieties of fresh cherries graced the recipe, yielding cobblers with plump, gorgeous, deeply flavorful fruit. The Montmorency cherries bore a candy apple red and a flavor resonant with almond accents; the fresh Morellos were transcendent, with a smooth richness and complex flavor notes. If you can get your hands on fresh sour cherries during their brief season in July, buy them—quickly—and start baking. And take heart. When the brief sour-cherry season is over, jarred Morello cherries will create a cobbler that is almost as wonderful.

⌁

Sour Cherry Cobbler
SERVES 12

Use the smaller amount of sugar in the filling if you prefer your fruit desserts on the tart side and the larger amount if you like them sweet. Serve with vanilla ice cream or lightly sweetened whipped cream (see page 382).

BISCUIT TOPPING

2	cups (10 ounces) unbleached all-purpose flour
6	tablespoons (2⅔ ounces) sugar plus additional 2 tablespoons for sprinkling
½	teaspoon baking powder
½	teaspoon baking soda
½	teaspoon salt
6	tablespoons unsalted butter, chilled, cut into ½-inch cubes
1	cup buttermilk

FILLING

4	(24-ounce) jars Morello cherries, drained (about 8 cups drained cherries), 2 cups juice reserved
¾–1	cup (5¼ to 7 ounces) sugar
3	tablespoons plus 1 teaspoon cornstarch
	Pinch salt
1	cup dry red wine
1	(3-inch) stick cinnamon
¼	teaspoon almond extract

1. FOR THE BISCUIT TOPPING: Adjust an oven rack to the middle position and heat the oven to 425 degrees. Line a baking sheet with parchment paper.

2. In the workbowl of a food processor fitted with the steel blade, pulse the flour, 6 tablespoons sugar, baking powder, baking soda, and salt to combine. Scatter the butter pieces over and process until the mixture resembles coarse meal, about fifteen 1-second pulses. Transfer to a medium bowl; add the buttermilk and toss with a rubber spatula to combine. Using a 1½- to 1¾-inch spring-loaded ice cream scoop, scoop 12 biscuits onto the baking sheet, spacing them 1½ to 2 inches apart. Sprinkle the biscuits evenly with 2 tablespoons sugar and bake until lightly browned on tops and bottoms, about 15 minutes. (Do not turn off oven.)

3. FOR THE FILLING: Meanwhile, spread the drained cherries in an even layer in a 9 by 13-inch glass baking dish. Stir the sugar, cornstarch, and salt together in a medium nonreactive saucepan. Whisk in the reserved cherry juice and wine, and add the cinnamon stick; set the saucepan over medium high heat, and cook, whisking frequently, until the mixture simmers and thickens, about 5 minutes. Discard the cinnamon stick, stir in the almond extract, and pour the hot liquid over the cherries in the baking dish.

4. TO ASSEMBLE AND BAKE THE COBBLER: Arrange the hot biscuits in 3 rows of 4 over the warm filling. Bake the cobbler until the filling is bubbling and the biscuits are deep golden brown, about 10 minutes. Cool on a wire rack 10 minutes; serve warm.

➤ VARIATION
Fresh Sour Cherry Cobbler
Morello or Montmorency cherries can be used in this cobbler. Do not use sweet Bing cherries. If the cherries do not release enough juice after macerating for 30 minutes, use cranberry juice to make up the difference.

FILLING

1¼ cups (8¾ ounces) sugar
3 tablespoons plus 1 teaspoon cornstarch
 Pinch salt
4 pounds fresh sour cherries, pitted (about 8 cups), juices reserved
1 cup dry red wine
 Cranberry juice (if needed)

1 (3-inch) cinnamon stick
¼ teaspoon almond extract

1 recipe Biscuit Topping (see page 390)

1. FOR THE FILLING: Stir together the sugar, cornstarch, and salt in a large bowl; add the cherries and toss well to combine. Pour the wine over the cherries; let stand 30 minutes. Drain the cherries in a colander set over a medium bowl. Combine the drained and reserved juices (from pitting the cherries); you should have 3 cups. If not, add enough cranberry juice to equal 3 cups.

2. FOR THE BISCUIT TOPPING: While the cherries macerate, prepare and bake the biscuit topping.

3. TO ASSEMBLE AND BAKE THE COBBLER: Spread the drained cherries in an even layer in a 9 by 13-inch glass baking dish. Bring the juices and cinnamon stick to a simmer in a medium nonreactive saucepan over medium-high heat, whisking frequently, until the mixture thickens, about 5 minutes. Discard the cinnamon stick, stir in the almond extract, and pour the hot juices over the cherries in the baking dish.

4. Arrange the hot biscuits in 3 rows of 4 over the warm filling. Bake the cobbler until the filling is bubbling and the biscuits are deep golden brown, about 10 minutes. Cool on a wire rack 10 minutes; serve warm.

BLUEBERRY BUCKLE

BUCKLE IS A SIMPLE DESSERT OF CAKE BATTER and fresh fruit, traditionally blueberries, sometimes covered with a streusel topping. The flavors are straightforward and unadulterated, and the combination of warm, fresh fruit and soft, moist cake is easy to appreciate. But as with any dessert, especially a fruit dessert, buckle has its share of problems. The cake can be dry and uninteresting or fruit-saturated and overly sweet. The trick is to create a moist cake that doesn't collapse under the weight of the berries.

We started our testing with the main component of the dish, the yellow cake. Our first yellow cakes were made in the traditional manner of creaming the butter, sugar, and eggs (whole or yolks) together.

When tasters tried the traditional cakes, they found them a little too "airy" and wanted a denser, moister variation. The first thing we did was abandon creaming the butter and begin melting it. This way we were not incorporating air into the fat. Melted butter yielded a denser cake.

Next we experimented with the number of eggs in the batter. The more we used, the fluffier the cake, so we started scaling back. We started with three, went to two, then down to one, and still the tasters were unsatisfied. With little confidence, we omitted the eggs altogether and baked off a batter of flour, butter, sugar, a pinch of salt, leavener, and milk. The cake came out of the oven closer to the ideal of the tasters. It was soft, moist, and dense and offered good contrast with the fruit.

Blueberries were the next order of business. Blueberries are native to North America, and when colonists first arrived, they quickly discovered the low-growing wild blueberry bush, dense with tiny blue fruit. The cultivated blueberries we commonly find in the grocery store are fatter and paler in color than the tiny, purplish-blue wild blueberries. Though many people love the plump cultivated berries, in the past we have found that wild blueberries have a more complex flavor and tend to hold their shape and color better in baked goods. Tested side by side, tasters preferred wild berries to their fatter cousins, but either will do in a buckle.

Some recipes called for tossing the berries with a small amount of flour to more easily incorporate them into the batter. We found this step unnecessary; in fact, it actually complicated the process, since the flour became gluey and held the fruit together in clumps. We also found that frozen berries do not work well in this recipe. They shed too much liquid and dampen the cake batter. Buckle is a true summer dessert.

Next we tried other sorts of berries, but tasters felt that blueberries were really the best choice. Raspberries and blackberries fell apart during the relatively long cooking time for this dessert. Sliced peaches and nectarines were better, but in the end blueberries carried the day.

The last point to concentrate on was the streusel topping. To add streusel topping or not to add streusel topping? When tested side by side, tasters surprisingly rejected the buckle topped with streusel.

They found that it cluttered the simple flavors of the cake and berries, making the buckle more akin to a coffee cake than a simple fruit dessert. At the same time, they enjoyed the slight crunch provided by the topping. The streusel-less buckle had a browned but still pliable surface. Tasters wanted something, though nothing extreme, to plow their fork or spoon through. Reaching back to a technique we'd read about in an old cookbook, we tried taking the melted butter out of the cake batter entirely. Instead, we melted the butter in the cake pan itself and poured the butterless batter over it. As the batter is poured into the buttered pan, the butter rises around the sides and spreads over the top of the buckle. When baked, the butter crisps the surface and creates an interesting, toothy crust. This buckle was a hit. Sprinkling a little granulated sugar over the butter-topped batter made the crust even crunchier.

Blueberry Buckle

SERVES 6

A buckle is best served in bowls with vanilla ice cream.

4	tablespoons unsalted butter
¾	cup (3¾ ounces) unbleached all-purpose flour
¾	cup (5¼ ounces) plus 1 tablespoon sugar
1	teaspoon baking powder
¼	teaspoon salt
¾	cup milk
2	cups blueberries, preferably wild

1. Adjust an oven rack to the lower-middle position and heat the oven to 350 degrees. Put the butter in an 8-inch square or 9-inch round pan, and place the pan in the oven to melt the butter.

2. Meanwhile, whisk the flour, ¾ cup sugar, baking powder, and salt together in a small bowl. Add the milk and whisk until just incorporated into the dry ingredients.

3. When the butter has melted, remove the pan from the oven. Pour the batter into the pan without stirring it into the butter. Arrange the fruit over the batter. Sprinkle with the remaining tablespoon of sugar. Bake until the surface is golden brown and the edges begin to pull away from the sides of the pan, 40 to 50 minutes. Serve warm.

STRAWBERRY SHORTCAKE

SHORTCAKES MAY SEEM SIMILAR TO CRISPS and cobblers, but there is one important difference—the fruit is not cooked. For a true shortcake, sweetened fruit, usually strawberries, is spread between a split biscuit. A dollop or two of whipped cream is also added. The contrast of the cool fruit, warm and crisp biscuit halves, and chilled whipped cream places this dessert in a category by itself.

Because the fruit is not cooked, frozen fruit is not an option. The fruit must be ripe as well. Half-ripe berries will bake up fine in a pandowdy but will make a second-rate shortcake. Also, because the fruit is not baked, only softer fruits are appropriate. A pear or apple shortcake does not make sense. Strawberries are soft enough and have enough flavor to be used uncooked.

We don't like quartered or sliced strawberries in shortcakes—they often slide off the split biscuit—but we don't like the look of a crushed fruit shortcake either. So we found a happy compromise by slicing most of the strawberries and then crushing the remaining portion of the berry mixture to unify the sliced fruit. The thick puree anchors the remaining whole or sliced fruit so that it won't slip off the split biscuit.

Our testing for this recipe revolved mostly around the biscuit. Strawberry shortcake requires something different from the biscuit topping used in our cherry cobbler recipe. There, the fruit is so juicy and sweet that a light, tender biscuit works best. Shortcake, on the other hand, must be substantial enough to withstand splitting and layering with juicy fruit and whipped cream. It should be more dense and cakey. We assumed that a richer biscuit—that is, one made with eggs—would work best.

To make sure, we tried four very different sweetened biscuits—a baking powder version with fat cut into flour, baking powder, salt, and sugar and then moistened with milk; buttermilk biscuits, with buttermilk in place of milk and baking soda substituted for part of the baking powder; cream biscuits, with heavy cream standing in for the milk and some of the fat; and egg-enriched cream biscuits, with an egg and half-and-half replacing the milk. After sampling each, we felt that the egg-enriched biscuits had the advantage. The baking powder and buttermilk biscuits

weren't rich enough. The cream biscuits were good looking but gummy inside. The egg and half-and-half biscuits were finer-textured and more cakelike.

With our general direction settled, we began to test individual ingredients. Because biscuits should be tender, we assumed that low-protein cake flour would deliver the best results. Defying our predictions, the cake flour biscuit came in last, with a meltingly tender yet powdery and dry texture that was too much like shortbread. There was not enough gluten in this flour to support all the fat. Shortcakes made with all-purpose flour were tender, moist, and cakey. They were our clear favorites, besting a combination of cake and all-purpose flours as well as the plain cake flour.

We then experimented with liquids, figuring that the egg might be crucial but maybe not the half-and-half, which had won in our initial test. Buttermilk made the biscuits too savory, while heavy cream made them squat and dense. Milk was fine, but the richer flavor of half-and-half makes it our first choice.

The food processor is foolproof and is our preferred method for mixing biscuits. For cooks without a food processor, we suggest freezing the butter and then using a box grater to shave the butter into bits before cutting it into the flour.

When testing dough shaping, we made an interesting discovery. Although hand-formed biscuits look attractive and rustic, we found they were fairly easy to overwork, since warm hands can cause the dough's surface butter to melt. Using a biscuit cutter requires less handling, and dough rounds cut this way develop a natural crack around the circumference during baking, making them easy to split by hand. We also realized we didn't need a rolling pin. Patting the dough to a thickness of ¾ inch on a floured work surface was fast and simple.

After cutting six perfect rounds of dough, we found that the scraps could be pulled together, kneaded, and cut to get one or two more rounds. These shortcakes will be a little tougher and less attractive than those from the first cutting.

Strawberry Shortcake

SERVES 6

Start the recipe by preparing the fruit, then set the fruit aside while preparing the biscuits to allow the juices to become syrupy.

FRUIT

8   cups hulled strawberries

6   tablespoons (2⅔ ounces) sugar

SHORTCAKES

2   cups (10 ounces) unbleached all-purpose flour, plus more for work surface and biscuit cutter

5   tablespoons (about 2¼ ounces) sugar

1   tablespoon baking powder

½   teaspoon salt

8   tablespoons unsalted butter, chilled, cut into ½-inch cubes

1   large egg, lightly beaten

½   cup plus 1 tablespoon half-and-half or milk

1   large egg white, lightly beaten

2   cups Whipped Cream (page 382)

1. **FOR THE FRUIT:** Place 3 cups hulled berries in a large bowl and crush with a potato masher. Slice the remaining 5 cups berries and stir into the crushed berries along with the sugar. Set the fruit aside to macerate for at least 30 minutes and up to 2 hours.

2. **FOR THE SHORTCAKES:** Adjust an oven rack to the lower-middle position and heat the oven to 425

SPLITTING SHORTCAKES

When the shortcakes have cooled, look for a natural crack around the circumference. Gently insert your fingers into the crack and split the shortcake in half.

degrees. In the workbowl of a food processor fitted with the steel blade, pulse the flour, 3 tablespoons sugar, baking powder, and salt to combine. Scatter the butter pieces over and process until the mixture resembles coarse meal, about fifteen 1-second pulses. Transfer to a medium bowl.

3. Mix the beaten egg with the half-and-half in a measuring cup. Pour the egg mixture into the bowl with the flour mixture. Combine with a rubber spatula until large clumps form. Turn the mixture onto a floured work surface and lightly knead until it comes together.

4. Use your fingertips to pat the dough into a 6 by 9-inch rectangle about ¾ inch thick, being careful not to overwork the dough. Flour a 2¾-inch biscuit cutter and cut out 6 dough rounds. Place the rounds 1 inch apart on a small baking sheet, brush the tops with egg white, and sprinkle with the remaining 2 tablespoons sugar. (Can be covered and refrigerated for up to 2 hours before baking.)

5. Bake until the shortcakes are golden brown, 12 to 14 minutes. Place the baking sheet on a wire rack and cool the cakes until warm, about 10 minutes.

6. **TO ASSEMBLE:** When the shortcakes have cooled slightly, split them in half (see the illustration at left). Place each cake bottom on an individual serving plate. Spoon a portion of the fruit and then dollop of whipped cream over each cake bottom. Cap with the cake top and serve immediately.

RHUBARB FOOL

"FOOL" IS A QUICK, EVERYDAY DESSERT that originated—along with its quaint and quirky name—in Britain. When we decided to try our hand at this simple dessert—essentially cooked fruit with sweetened whipped cream folded in—we sided with tradition and used rhubarb as the cooked fruit foundation.

Although fool is in itself no culinary feat, working with rhubarb can prove tricky. First, its sourness can be overpowering. Second, if boiled or cooked too hard and fast, it breaks down into a watery, porridge-like mass. Finally, its vivacious red color leaches out easily, leaving the rhubarb a drab gray. We knew that before we could finalize a fool, we would have to tame the rhubarb.

To begin our testing we tried baking the rhubarb, stewing it for a long time, sautéing it in butter, and simmering it for a short time. Baking and sautéing turned the rhubarb pulpy, chalky, and bland, while stewing produced a watery cream-of-rhubarb soup. And in each case the rhubarb lost its attractive red color, presenting instead hues that varied from gray-lavender in the baked version to pale, watery yellow in the stewed. The simmered batch, on the other hand, had a nice pinkish red color, a sweet/tart flavor, and a thick, toothsome texture.

The simmered rhubarb was not ideal, though; it was still too tart for most tasters. Looking further, we found an interesting precooking approach that purported to subdue its acidity: soaking 6-inch pieces in cold water for 20 minutes prior to cutting and simmering. When we gave this trick a try, we were surprised to find the rhubarb much less acidic, with a flavor that was more round and full. But this approach had one drawback—the color had dulled to a pale mauve.

To figure out what happened, we called Barry Swanson, a confirmed rhubarb enthusiast who is a professor of food science at Washington State University in Pullman. Swanson explained that a water-soluble pigment called anthocyanin is responsible for rhubarb's somewhat chalky, tannic mouthfeel as well as its bright pinkish red color. When we presoaked the rhubarb, a portion of the anthocyanin escaped from the rhubarb's cut ends into the water, muting the color as well as the harsh bite.

Swanson also explained that anthocyanin is sensitive to the acidity of its environment. When the pH is high (low acidity), the color shifts to the bluish gray range; when the pH is low (high acidity), the color is red. Thinking about this, we wondered what would happen if we reintroduced an acid with no bitter or tannic qualities, such as the citric acid in orange juice, while the rhubarb simmered. This test was successful. The juice added just enough acidity to restore the rhubarb red without having any ill effects on flavor. Fifty pounds later, we had finally figured out how to cook rhubarb.

Fool-making tradition dictates that the cream be folded into the fruit, but this gave the dessert a somewhat dull, monochromatic texture and flavor.

Arranging the fruit and cream in layers produced a more interesting result. The natural tanginess of the rhubarb played off the sweetness of the cream, and the alternating texture of fruit and cream made for a pleasing contrast.

Rhubarb Fool

SERVES 8

For more information about whipping heavy cream, see page 382. For a fancier presentation, use a pastry bag to pipe the whipped cream into individual glasses. To make one large fool, double the recipe and layer the rhubarb and whipped cream in a 12-cup glass bowl.

2¼	pounds rhubarb, trimmed of ends and cut into 6-inch lengths
⅓	cup juice from 1 large orange
1	cup plus 2 tablespoons (about 8 ounces) sugar Pinch salt
2	cups heavy cream, chilled, preferably pasteurized or pasteurized organic

1. Soak the rhubarb in 1 gallon cold water for 20 minutes. Drain, pat dry with paper towels, and cut the rhubarb crosswise into slices ½-inch thick.

2. Bring the orange juice, ¾ cup sugar, and salt to a boil in a medium nonreactive saucepan over medium-high heat. Add the rhubarb and return to a boil, then reduce the heat to medium-low and simmer, stirring only 2 or 3 times (frequent stirring causes rhubarb to become mushy), until the rhubarb begins to break down and is tender, 7 to 10 minutes. Transfer the rhubarb to a nonreactive bowl, cool to room temperature, then cover with plastic and refrigerate until cold, at least 1 hour or up to 24.

3. Beat the cream and remaining 6 tablespoons sugar in the chilled bowl of a standing mixer on low speed until small bubbles form, about 45 seconds. Increase the speed to medium; continue beating until the beaters leave a trail, about 45 seconds longer. Increase the speed to high; continue beating until the cream is smooth, thick, and nearly doubled in volume and forms soft peaks, about 30 seconds.

4. To assemble the fool, spoon ¼ cup rhubarb into each of eight 8-ounce glasses, then spoon in a layer of ¼ cup whipped cream. Repeat, ending with a

dollop of cream; serve. (Can be covered with plastic wrap and refrigerated up to 6 hours.)

➤ VARIATION

Strawberry-Rhubarb Fool

Clean and hull 2 pints strawberries; quarter each berry. Follow the recipe for Rhubarb Fool, substituting strawberries for 1¼ pounds rhubarb.

BANANAS FOSTER

BANANAS FOSTER IS A CLASSIC, SIMPLE dessert that hails from New Orleans. The recipe was made famous by Brennan's restaurant, which has been serving it since 1951. The dish is often made tableside at restaurants (or at home, for guests) in a chafing dish. Bananas are cooked in a caramel-type sauce of melted butter and brown sugar, then flambéed with rum, brandy, banana liqueur, or a combination of liquors. The luscious mixture is then spooned over scoops of vanilla ice cream.

Although bananas Foster is quick and simple, with very few ingredients, it can go wrong. Sometimes the bananas are overcooked and mushy. The sauce can be too thin, overly sweet, or taste too strongly of alcohol. We wanted a quick, reliable dessert with tender but not mushy bananas and a flavorful but not too potent sauce.

First we settled on the amounts of dark brown sugar and butter. Sauces made with high ratios of butter to sugar were thin, greasy, and not sweet enough, while too little butter made a sauce that was sugary and sticky. Four tablespoons of butter to ½ cup of brown sugar created a slightly thickened, buttery (but not greasy) sauce.

We pulled brandy, rum, and banana liqueur from the test kitchen liquor cabinet to determine which would be best for this dish. Brandy didn't seem to complement the bananas very well, and tasters quickly dismissed it. And while a touch of banana liqueur added a pleasant banana flavor, it lacked the depth and complexity of rum. We chose to use dark rum—its full-bodied flavor was a perfect foil for the sweetness of the bananas and brown sugar.

The recipes we had uncovered called for anywhere from 1 tablespoon to 2 cups of spirits. We started with 1 tablespoon of dark rum and worked our way up to 4 tablespoons, which was just enough to impart a definite rum flavor but not so much as to turn the dessert into an after-dinner drink.

Our final experiments were with flavorings. Tasters agreed that a cinnamon stick and a strip of lemon zest gave the sugary sauce a welcome depth and brightness.

Bananas Foster

SERVES 4

While the bananas cook, scoop the ice cream into individual bowls so they are ready to go once the sauce has been flambéed. Before flambéing, make sure to roll up long shirt sleeves, tie back long hair, turn off the exhaust fan (otherwise the fan may pull the flames up), and turn off any lit burners (this is critical if you have a gas stove).

4	tablespoons unsalted butter
½	cup packed (3½ ounces) dark brown sugar
1	cinnamon stick
1	strip lemon zest, 1 to 2 inches long by about 1½ inch wide
2	large, firm, ripe bananas, peeled and halved lengthwise and then crosswise
4	tablespoons dark rum
1	pint vanilla ice cream, divided among four bowls

1. Melt the butter in a heavy-bottomed 12-inch skillet over medium heat. Add the brown sugar, cinnamon stick, and lemon zest; stir to dissolve the sugar, about 1 minute. (If the heat is too high, the butter and sugar will separate instead of combining to form a sauce.)

2. Add the bananas and spoon some sauce over each piece. Cook until the bananas are glossy and golden on the bottom, about 1½ minutes. Turn the bananas and continue cooking until very soft but not mushy or falling apart, about 1½ minutes longer.

3. Remove the skillet from the heat. Add the rum and wait until the rum has warmed slightly, about 5 seconds. Wave a lit match over the pan until the rum ignites, shaking the pan to distribute the flame over the entire pan. When the flames subside (this will take 15 to 30 seconds), divide the bananas and sauce among the four bowls of ice cream and serve.

17

PUDDINGS

MOST PUDDINGS ARE MADE WITH EGGS, sugar and some sort of dairy—milk, half-and-half, and/or cream. They are basically chilled custards. Although custards contain few ingredients and come together quickly, they are far from foolproof. As custards are heated, individual protein molecules in the eggs begin to unfold and stretch out. (Think of a bird's nest of dried pasta; when it is cooked, the individual strands of pasta unwind and stretch out.) Once unfolded, the molecules form new bonds, and as they form these bonds, water molecules become trapped between them, causing the custard to thicken. The problem with egg custards is that overcooking results in tighter bonding that forces the water molecules out of this network and causes the proteins to clump. This process is called curdling.

There are several ways to prevent curdling. The first is the judicious use of heat. When a custard reaches 185 to 190 degrees, the proteins bond so extensively that they form clumps and the eggs curdle—in effect, they become scrambled eggs. Slow, gentle heat, then, is one way to succeed with custards. This is especially true of custards made without cornstarch, such as crème brûlée or the custard base of an ice cream. The use of cornstarch is another way to guard against curdling, and American custards generally contain it. Cornstarch gives the cook greater leeway when it comes to the application of heat. Cornstarch molecules in a custard are very large and therefore come between unwound egg proteins during cooking, in effect blocking, at least temporarily, their attempts to bond. Puddings with cornstarch can be heated well above 180 degrees without any curdling; that's because the starch molecules are incredibly effective at keeping the unwound egg proteins from joining up.

CHOCOLATE PUDDING

ON A MAP OF DESSERTS, CHOCOLATE PUDDING can be located as the chocolate version of a classic cornstarch custard. Typically, a cornstarch custard is made by cooking a mixture of sugar, cornstarch, eggs (or egg yolks), a bit of salt, and a dairy liquid in a saucepan on the stovetop until thickened. Vanilla, and sometimes butter, is added off the heat.

The choicest chocolate pudding should taste deeply of chocolate and dairy ingredients, be thickened to a soft suppleness, and sweetened just enough to support the chocolate bouquet. The correct balance of dairy and chocolate should make the dessert rich but not cloying and exceptionally smooth on the tongue. Taking voluptuous as our keyword, we set out to create a pudding that would bring together all of these factors. We determined that a pudding based on three cups of liquid would yield enough for six ramekin-size servings.

From early tests, we concluded that a pudding mixture needs to be pampered by sifting the dry ingredients (sugar, cornstarch, and cocoa powder) before combining them with the liquids to make the liquid-thickener amalgamation as smooth as possible from the start. We also learned that to achieve a gorgeous texture, it is important to monitor the strength of the heat beneath the saucepan and to use a reasonably slow hand to stir (not whisk or beat) the pudding mixture as it approaches the thickening point, then continue to stir slowly as it cooks for two minutes. Vigorous beating can break down the starch granules built up during the thickening process. We also found that it helped to strain the finished pudding through a fine-meshed sieve to ensure a suave, smooth texture.

With these points in mind, we began to test individual ingredients. We made puddings with all milk, 2 parts milk and 1 part heavy cream, 2 parts milk and 1 part light cream, half milk and half heavy cream, half milk and half light cream, and all light cream. The clear winner was the leaner blend of milk and light cream, which was rich but not overwhelming and mixed well with the chocolate.

Now we were ready to begin building the chocolate flavor. We started with 3 ounces of unsweetened chocolate alone, but that proved inadequate. An ounce or two more of semisweet chocolate added only a nuance of flavor; an ounce or two of bittersweet chocolate raised the chocolate meter slightly, but not enough. At this point, we turned to cocoa powder to see if it would develop, sharpen, and polish the chocolate flavor. Fortunately, it did. We eventually settled on 2 tablespoons cocoa powder, along with a combination of unsweetened and bittersweet chocolate.

One nagging problem remained. Although the density, dairy ingredients, and chocolate intensity were right on the mark, the pudding left a trace of chalkiness on the tongue. To remedy this problem, we eliminated the unsweetened chocolate, replacing it with bittersweet and adjusting the amount of sugar in the recipe to balance out the sweetness. Now the pudding was smooth and silky. There are two reasons for the pudding's successful textural change with the use of bittersweet chocolate. First, unsweetened chocolate has a lower percentage of cocoa butter than the bittersweet variety. Second, bittersweet chocolate contains some milk solids and lecithin (an emulsifier), both of which create a smoother, creamier texture and mouthfeel.

Double-Chocolate Pudding

SERVES 4 TO 6

To melt the chocolate, chop and place it in a heatproof bowl set over a pan of almost simmering water, stirring once or twice until smooth. You can also melt the chocolate in a microwave at 50 percent power for 3½ minutes, stopping to stir after 2 minutes. If the chocolate is not yet completely melted, heat up to 30 seconds more at 50 percent power. While we prefer the slightly less sweet bittersweet chocolate for this pudding, semisweet chocolate can be substituted for it with success.

    2   tablespoons Dutch-processed cocoa powder
    2   tablespoons cornstarch
    ⅔   cup (2⅓ ounces) sugar
    ⅛   teaspoon salt
    1   cup light cream
    3   large egg yolks
    2   cups whole milk
    6   ounces bittersweet or semisweet chocolate, melted (see note) and cooled slightly
    1   tablespoon unsalted butter, softened
    2   teaspoons vanilla extract
    1   cup Whipped Cream (page 382), whipped to soft peaks

1. Sift the cocoa powder, cornstarch, sugar, and salt into a medium heavy-bottomed saucepan (preferably nonstick). Slowly whisk in the light cream, followed by the yolks, then the milk. Stir in the chocolate. (Chocolate will form clumps that smooth with cooking.)

2. Bring the mixture to a boil over medium-high heat, stirring constantly with a whisk and scraping the bottom and sides of the pot. The pudding will gradually darken and thicken. Reduce the heat to medium and cook, stirring gently but constantly with a wooden spoon until the pudding very thickly coats the spoon, 1½ to 2 minutes.

3. Pass the pudding through a fine-mesh strainer into a medium bowl, pressing with a rubber spatula. Stir in the butter and vanilla. Press plastic wrap directly on the surface and refrigerate until cold and set, at least 3 hours or up to 48 hours. Spoon the pudding into serving dishes and top each with a dollop of whipped cream.

EQUIPMENT: Fine-Mesh Strainers

If you want to dust cocoa over a cake, remove bits of curdled egg from pudding, or turn cooked raspberries into a seedless sauce, you need a fine-mesh strainer. Unlike a regular strainer (which has relatively large holes), a fine-mesh strainer is covered with the same material used in window screens. This mesh will trap solid material and break up lumps in dry ingredients such as cocoa powder and flour. (We often use a fine-mesh strainer to sift these ingredients.)

We put five fine-mesh strainers through a series of tests. We poured pureed pea soup through the strainers to test their ability to remove large solid bits. We pushed a raspberry puree through them to see how they would withstand scraping and moderate pressure. Finally, we passed pastry cream through the strainers to test their ability to catch small particles. (All fine-mesh strainers can sift dry ingredients like cocoa and flour, so we did not run this test.)

Based on these tests, we think it's imperative to buy a stainless steel strainer (aluminum can discolor acidic foods) with some heft. You don't want the strainer to buckle under moderate pressure, as several did in our tests. The finer the mesh, the better. Several strainers let solids pass through, which is unacceptable. Other strainers had handles that were uncomfortable, another no-no in our book.

In the end, testers preferred the Williams-Sonoma Piazza 18cm Strainer ($26), which yielded perfectly smooth soup, raspberry puree, and pastry cream. The Küchenprofi 22cm Classic Strainer ($29.99) was the second choice in the test kitchen.

BUTTERSCOTCH PUDDING

GRADE-SCHOOL CAFETERIAS REGULARLY serve up dishes of butterscotch pudding that are sweet and satisfying—but only to children. Kids love pudding in any form, but to adults this kind of pudding (which invariably comes from a box) can taste gluey, artificial, and one-dimensional. We knew that butterscotch pudding made from scratch would be altogether different. We wanted a perfectly fresh and creamy pudding with a deep, rich brown sugar flavor that would satisfy children and adults alike.

Typically, pudding is made with just a few basic ingredients: some kind of dairy—milk, cream, or half-and-half—plus eggs, sugar, and cornstarch. As for the butterscotch flavor, we knew that brown sugar would be a key player. It appeared on the ingredient list of every recipe we consulted. In addition, we found recipes that called for healthy doses of butter, vanilla, rum, and even molasses to provide that much-wanted taste of butterscotch.

After mixing puddings with each of these flavoring agents in various combinations, we uncovered the essence of butterscotch. A caramel made from butter and brown sugar plus a generous amount of vanilla gave us what we were looking for—an intense caramel/vanilla taste with buttery undertones. Dark brown sugar produced a stronger butterscotch flavor than light brown sugar, but molasses was overpowering and thus swiftly rejected. A spoonful of rum kept the sweetness in check and added complexity to the pudding.

Although the flavor elements of the recipe went together quickly, we had a lot of trouble achieving a desirable texture. Time after time, we produced puddings that were quite grainy. When we added hot cream to the butter–brown sugar mixture, it seized up. Although these bits of sugar would dissolve with further cooking, evidently some residual grittiness was being imparted. Clearly, we needed to prevent the sugar from seizing up in the first place. When we switched from hot cream to cold cream, we avoided the problem altogether, and the texture was silky and smooth.

Once we'd refined our technique, we made puddings with various combinations of dairy. We settled on a light, but not-too light combination of 1 part heavy cream to 2 parts whole milk. Three egg yolks and ¼ cup cornstarch provided enough thickening power to make a pudding that was nicely thickened without being stiff or gluey.

Butterscotch Pudding

SERVES 6

To ensure a smooth texture, make sure to add the cream and milk gradually. See the illustration below for a tip on measuring brown sugar.

6	tablespoons unsalted butter
1¼	cups packed (8¾ ounces) dark brown sugar
1	cup heavy cream
2	cups whole milk
3	large egg yolks
¼	cup cornstarch
2	teaspoons vanilla extract
1	teaspoon dark rum, optional
1	cup Whipped Cream (page 382), whipped to soft peaks

1. Melt the butter in a medium heavy-bottomed saucepan (preferably nonstick) over medium heat. Add the brown sugar and cook, stirring occasionally, until the mixture bubbles and becomes lighter in color, 3 to 4 minutes.

2. Gradually whisk the heavy cream into the butter and sugar mixture; whisk until the sugar is

MEASURING BROWN SUGAR

When a recipe calls for some quantity of packed brown sugar, fill the correct dry measure with the brown sugar and use the next smallest cup to pack it.

completely dissolved, about 1 minute. Gradually whisk in the milk and bring the mixture to a simmer.

3. Whisk the egg yolks in a medium bowl until thoroughly combined. Gradually whisk about ½ cup of the milk mixture into the egg yolks to temper. Whisk in the cornstarch until completely dissolved. Whisk the cornstarch mixture back into the hot milk mixture. Return to a simmer over medium heat, stirring gently but constantly with a wooden spoon until 3 or 4 bubbles burst on the surface and the mixture is thickened and glossy, 2 to 3 minutes.

4. Pass the pudding through a fine-mesh strainer into a medium bowl, pressing with a rubber spatula. Whisk in the vanilla and rum, if using. Press plastic wrap directly on the surface and refrigerate until cold and set, at least 3 hours or up to 48 hours. Spoon the pudding into serving dishes and top each with a dollop of whipped cream.

Banana Pudding

BANANA PUDDING IS A CLASSIC SOUTHERN recipe that combines homemade vanilla pudding with Nilla Wafers, sliced bananas, and, often, a meringue topping. Disappointing versions of this dessert couple pudding that is too sweet, bland, or starchy with cookies that are dissolved and pasty. We wanted a creamy, fresh pudding with lightly softened cookies and pure banana flavor.

We started by pulling a number of banana pudding recipes from our library, including the recipe from the back of the Nilla Wafer box. The first conclusion tasters came to was that they weren't especially fond of meringue-topped puddings. While beautiful, puddings topped with meringue struck our (mostly Yankee) tasters as odd—they all preferred a whipped cream topping. So we set out to develop a recipe for individual puddings topped with whipped cream, but, in a nod to Southern tradition, we would include a variation with a meringue topping.

With our focus on the pudding, we noted a few variables to test: Should we use whole eggs, egg yolks, or no eggs at all? What type of dairy product would make the creamiest, smoothest pudding?

What about the ratio of sugar to dairy? Should we include butter?

When comparing puddings made with whole eggs, egg yolks, and no eggs, the pudding made with yolks was the clear favorite. Pudding made with whole eggs wasn't rich enough—tasters described it as "light." Without any eggs, the pudding tasted bland and was loose in texture. It also had a ghastly white color. The pudding made with yolks was not only luscious, but it had a pleasant yellow hue.

As for the dairy, we tested whole milk, heavy cream, half-and-half, and even 2 percent milk. Puddings made with 2 percent and whole milk weren't thick and creamy enough, while those made with heavy cream were over the top. We settled on half-and-half for a pudding that was supercreamy but not so heavy that it was difficult to finish a serving. A ratio of ¼ cup sugar to 3 cups half-and-half made a pleasantly sweet pudding, and a few tablespoons of butter swirled in at the end gave it a glossy sheen.

The technique used to make the pudding was also an important factor. When we made the pudding by heating a mixture of half-and-half, sugar, cornstarch, and egg yolks, we ended up with a slightly grainy finished product. A smooth, fine-textured pudding was produced by first heating the half-and-half, then slowly mixing it with egg yolks that had been beaten with sugar and cornstarch.

With our pudding set, we turned our attention to the bananas. Only bananas that were just ripe (not speckled with brown spots) did the pudding justice—overripe bananas were too mushy and got lost in the silky pudding. Tasters also rejected banana chunks, preferring thinner, more refined slices.

The last step was to figure out how to deal with the cookies. While Nilla Wafers are the cookie of choice for this dessert, we ran across a recipe that substituted gingersnaps and gave it a try. A minority of tasters enjoyed the contrast of spicy ginger against the mellow flavors of banana and vanilla, but most thought that the combination strayed too far from the customary flavors. We decided to stick with Nilla Wafers, but we had to determine if they should be left whole or crushed.

Tradition fell by the wayside when tasters preferred crushed Nilla Wafers layered in the pudding over whole cookies. Crushed cookies had more visual appeal (they made a more distinctive layer in a parfait glass, which is our favorite way to serve the pudding), and tasters didn't like having to "cut" whole cookies with a spoon. To add some crunch, we garnished the finished puddings with a whole cookie.

Banana Pudding

SERVES 4

We like the way the pudding looks in individual parfait glasses, but the recipe can be doubled, assembled in a 10-cup glass bowl, and then garnished with whipped cream just before serving.

PUDDING

3	cups half-and-half
¾	cup (5¼ ounces) sugar
¼	teaspoon salt
4	large egg yolks
3	tablespoons cornstarch
3	tablespoons unsalted butter, chilled, cut into 3 pieces
1½	teaspoons vanilla extract
24	Nilla Wafers, plus 4 more for garnish
2	large ripe bananas, cut into ¼-inch slices
1	cup Whipped Cream (page 382), whipped to soft peaks

1. FOR THE PUDDING: Place the half-and-half, ½ cup sugar, and salt in a heavy-bottomed medium saucepan over medium heat and bring to a simmer, stirring to completely dissolve sugar.

2. Meanwhile, whisk the egg yolks in a medium bowl until thoroughly combined. Whisk in the remaining ¼ cup sugar, and continue whisking until the sugar has begun to dissolve and the mixture is creamy, about 15 seconds. Whisk in the cornstarch until combined and the mixture is pale yellow and thick, about 30 seconds.

3. When the half-and-half mixture reaches a full simmer, gradually whisk ½ cups of the simmering half-and-half mixture into the yolk mixture to temper. Return the egg mixture to the saucepan, scraping the bowl with a rubber spatula. Return to a simmer over medium heat, stirring gently but constantly with a wooden spoon until 3 or 4 bubbles burst on the surface and the mixture is thickened and glossy, 2 to 3 minutes.

4. Pass the pudding through a fine-mesh strainer into a medium bowl, pressing with a rubber spatula. Whisk in the butter and vanilla. Set the pudding aside.

5. TO ASSEMBLE THE PUDDINGS: Place the Nilla Wafers in a sealed zipper-lock plastic bag and break them into pieces by tapping the cookies with a wooden spoon. Tap only a few times, so that mostly large pieces remain.

6. Gently stir the pudding and then spoon a generous ¼ cup pudding into each of four 8-ounce parfait or wine glasses (the pudding will seem too thin—it sets up when refrigerated). Top with several banana slices and then sprinkle with a thin layer of wafer pieces. Repeat once more, ending with a final layer of pudding. Press a piece of plastic wrap directly on the surface of each pudding and refrigerate until well chilled, at least 4 hours or overnight.

7. TO SERVE: Top each pudding with a dollop of whipped cream and garnish with a whole Nilla Wafer. Serve immediately.

➤ VARIATION

Banana Pudding with Meringue

SERVES 6 TO 8

Reserve the egg whites when separating the yolks for the pudding and use them to make the meringue topping.

Follow the recipe for Banana Pudding through step 4, pressing plastic wrap directly on the surface of the pudding in the bowl. Prepare Meringue Topping according to the recipe on page 377 and the heat oven to 325 degrees. Remove the plastic wrap from the pudding and pour half of pudding into a buttered 9-inch square baking dish. Evenly distribute all of the banana slices over the pudding, then top with crushed Nilla Wafer pieces (crushing all 28 pieces). Cover with remaining pudding. Using a rubber spatula, immediately distribute meringue evenly around the edge and then the center of the pudding. Make sure the meringue attaches to the edge of the baking dish to prevent shrinking. Use the back of a soup spoon to create peaks all over the meringue. Bake the pudding until the meringue is golden brown, about 20 minutes. Transfer to a wire rack and cool to room temperature, then refrigerate 4 hours before serving. (Do not refrigerate overnight or the meringue will become soggy and spongy.)

RICE PUDDING

AT ITS BEST, RICE PUDDING IS SIMPLE AND
lightly sweet, and it tastes of its primary component:
rice. At its worst, the rice flavor is lost to cloying
sweetness, condensed dairy, and a pasty, leaden
consistency.

Right from the start we agreed on the qualities
of the ideal candidate: intact, tender grains bound
loosely in a subtly sweet, milky sauce. We were
looking for a straightforward stovetop rice pudding,
in which the texture and the flavor of the primary
ingredient would stand out.

We decided to check out the cooking medium
and method first. For our first experiment, we prepared and tasted eight existing recipes for rice pudding, each using a different combination of water,
milk, and cream and each with varying ratios of rice
to liquid. The tasting revealed that cooking the rice
in milk or cream obscured the rice flavor, while
cooking the rice in water emphasized it. The most
appealing balance of rice flavor and satisfying yet not
too rich consistency was achieved when we cooked
1 cup of rice in 2 cups of water until it was absorbed
and then added equal parts (2½ cups each) of whole
milk and half-and-half to make the pudding. Whole
milk alone made the pudding too thin, but the milk
and half-and-half together imparted just the right
degree of richness. Eggs, butter, whipped cream, and
heavy cream—on their own or in combination—
overpowered the flavor of the rice.

We also tried a couple of variations in the cooking method, such as covering the pot or not, and
using a double boiler. The double boiler lengthened
the cooking time by 25 minutes and turned out a
pudding that was gummy and too sweet. By far the
best results came from cooking the rice and water in
a covered pot simmering the cooked rice and dairy
mixture uncovered. This technique gave us just what
we wanted—distinct, tender grains of rice in a
smooth sauce that tasted of milk rather than reduced
cream. We found we could cut 10 minutes off the
total cooking time by simmering the rice in the
water and dairy mixture together from the start, but
this approach sacrificed the texture of the grains and
resulted in a pudding that our tasters described as
overly dense and sweet.

Now it was time to try different kinds of rice. We

tested the readily available varieties: supermarket
brands of long- and medium-grain white (such as
Goya, which distributes both of these types nationally), Arborio (a superstarchy Italian short-grain
white used to make risotto), and basmati (an aromatic long-grain white).

All rice contains two types of starch, called amylose and amylopectin, but they are present in different concentrations in different kinds of rice. Arborio,
with its high level of amylopectin, made a stiff, gritty
pudding. On the other end of the starch scale, long-
grain rice, which is high in amylose, cooked up
separate and fluffy. But the puddings made with
long-grain rice were a little too thin for our liking,
and the flavor of the basmati rice was too perfumey,
overwhelming the milk. Medium-grain rice, which
has a high proportion of amylopectin (but less than
short-grain), cooked up a little more moist and
sticky than long-grain. This type proved ideal for our
rice pudding, which had a creamy texture and tasted
distinctly of rice and milk. As a final test, we made a
pudding with cooked rice that had been refrigerated
overnight. Unfortunately, the result was liquidy and
grainy, without discernible rice flavor.

Simple Stovetop Rice Pudding

SERVES 6 TO 8

*We prefer pudding made from medium-grain rice, but long-
grain is perfectly acceptable if that's what you happen to have
on hand.*

¼ teaspoon salt
1 cup medium-grain rice
2½ cups whole milk
2½ cups half-and-half
⅔ cup (4⅔ ounces) sugar
1¼ teaspoons vanilla extract

1. Bring 2 cups water to a boil in a large, heavy-
bottomed saucepan (at least 3 quarts). Stir in the salt
and rice; cover and simmer over low heat, stirring
once or twice, until the water is almost fully
absorbed, 15 to 20 minutes.

2. Add the milk, half-and-half, and sugar. Increase
the heat to medium-high and bring to a simmer,

then reduce the heat to maintain a simmer. Cook, uncovered and stirring frequently, until the mixture starts to thicken, about 30 minutes. Reduce the heat to low and continue to cook, stirring every couple of minutes to prevent sticking and scorching, until a spoon is just able to stand up in the pudding, about 15 minutes longer.

3. Remove from the heat and stir in the vanilla extract. Cool and serve at room temperature or chilled. (Can be covered by placing plastic wrap directly on the surface of the pudding and then refrigerating for up to 2 days.)

➤ VARIATIONS

Rice Pudding with Orange and Toasted Almonds

Follow the recipe for Simple Stovetop Rice Pudding, adding ⅓ cup slivered almonds that have been toasted until just golden and fragrant in small heavy skillet over medium heat (4 to 5 minutes, with frequent stirring) and 2 teaspoons grated orange zest along with vanilla extract.

Rice Pudding with Cinnamon and Dried Fruit

Follow the recipe for Simple Stovetop Rice Pudding, adding ½ cup dried fruit (such as raisins, cranberries, cherries, or chopped prunes or apricots) and 1 teaspoon ground cinnamon along with vanilla extract.

TAPIOCA PUDDING

TAPIOCA PUDDING, WITHOUT QUESTION, is as much about texture as flavor. People react strongly to it—they either love it or loathe it. Most of us in the test kitchen happen to love it.

At its worst, tapioca is a gelatinous, gluey custard resilient enough to resist the assault of a spoon. At its best, tapioca pudding is simple, honest food, free of pretense and complicated cooking. With simplicity in mind, we sifted through a stack of recipes to come up with a recipe that would deliver the best combination of texture and flavor.

The first step to tackle was the cooking method. Many recipes we tried had intricate directions for cooking the tapioca that, unsurprisingly, failed to produce anything special. We had the best luck with the easiest method; all of the ingredients were combined in a saucepan for five minutes at room temperature (to soften the tapioca), brought slowly to a boil, and removed from the heat. That's it—the pudding thickened as it cooled. We could not make it any easier or faster. We tried batches with varying amounts of tapioca to arrive at a firm yet supple texture and found that as little as ¼ cup provided just the right amount of thickening for 2½ cups of milk.

Most of the recipes we tried included egg yolks in the pudding but reserved the egg whites to lighten it; the whites were beaten to stiff peaks and folded into the pudding just before serving. Judicious in our use of raw eggs these days, we decided to cook the whole egg with the pudding and turned to whipped cream to lighten it. Just a small amount of cream was necessary to yield a texture similar to that of a pudding lightened with egg whites, and, as a bonus, the flavor was markedly improved. The pudding now had a rich, creamy flavor and supple texture that offset the tapioca's tackiness.

Tradition dictates that tapioca pudding should be flavored only with sugar and vanilla. While granulated sugar kept the flavors clean, it was a little flat to our tastes. Maple syrup and dark brown sugar muddied the flavors and tinted the pudding's snowy white color an unappetizing beige. A small amount of light brown sugar in conjunction with granulated sugar contributed a faint earthiness that supported the vanilla's floral notes and did not affect the pure whiteness of the pudding.

We were not thrilled with the use of vanilla extract in the pudding. Even when we dramatically increased the amount of extract, the flavor tasted one-dimensional and commercial—like cheap vanilla ice cream. While we rarely use whole vanilla beans because of the expense and extra work involved, we found this was one instance where it was definitely worth it. The simplicity of the pudding provided a good platform for the nuances of the vanilla, and the specks of seed in the pudding visually emphasized the vanilla, much as they do in ice cream.

To emphasize the vanilla bean's presence, we added vanilla extract to the whipped cream that was folded in, which gave us the heady vanilla aroma and slight boozy accent the vanilla bean lacked. The pudding now had the flavor of a rich vanilla sauce but with tapioca's alluring texture.

Tapioca Pudding

SERVES 4

This is an instance where a vanilla bean can make a big impression and is well worth the cost and effort. After scraping the bean for the seeds, the bean pod can be added to the pudding for extra flavor. Serve the pudding slightly warm, at room temperature, or chilled, but do wait until just before serving to fold in the whipped cream.

2½	cups whole milk
1	large egg, plus 1 large yolk, lightly beaten
¼	cup (1¾ ounces) plus 1 tablespoon granulated sugar
1	tablespoon light brown sugar
	Salt
¼	cup quick-cooking tapioca
½	vanilla bean, split in half lengthwise and seeds scraped out
½	cup heavy cream
½	teaspoon vanilla extract

1. Combine the milk, egg and yolk, sugars (reserving 1 tablespoon granulated sugar), ¼ teaspoon salt, tapioca, and the vanilla seeds and pod in a medium saucepan and allow to sit for 5 minutes. Bring the mixture to a boil over medium heat, and, once boiling, stir constantly for 2 minutes. Remove the pan from the heat and scrape the pudding into a medium bowl. Cover with plastic wrap and place in the refrigerator until set, at least 1 hour or up to 2 days.

2. While the pudding chills, combine the heavy cream, vanilla extract, remaining 1 tablespoon sugar, and a pinch of salt in the bowl of a standing mixer fitted with a whisk attachment and mix on medium speed until the cream holds soft peaks. Cover and refrigerate until needed.

3. When ready to serve, remove the vanilla pod from the pudding and discard. Fold half the whipped cream into the pudding. Divide the pudding among individual cups or bowls and top each with a dollop of the remaining cream. Serve immediately.

INDIAN PUDDING

INDIAN PUDDING, A CORNMEAL-THICKENED custard assertively flavored with molasses, is the sort of dessert that could only have originated in New England, where molasses was once as common a seasoning as salt. What may sound like an odd dessert is actually quite delicious. Long baking at a low heat makes for a silky textured yet hearty pudding, deeply flavored with bittersweet molasses and warm spices.

But outside of a few restaurants in the Boston area known for traditional New England cookery, Indian pudding is hard to find these days. Admittedly, it is labor-intensive and time-consuming, requiring attentive stirring while it cooks on the stovetop and then lengthy baking time. Determined to make a pudding that would be worth all of this effort, we set to work to create a recipe that would taste great and cook faster than most.

After making and tasting many batches of Indian pudding, we decided that the major problems associated with it were poor flavor, a curdled or "broken" texture after baking, and an extremely long cooking time—most recipes requiring upward of three hours in the oven. We decided to tackle each of these issues separately.

The flavor of good Indian pudding has a complexity that belies its brief ingredient list. The molasses, in conjunction with the spices, imparts a mysterious depth to the pudding. The trick is balancing the flavors; too many recipes we tried produced a pudding that was either overwhelmingly molasses-flavored or too heavily spiced and reminiscent of pumpkin pie. We made batch after batch with varying amounts of molasses and spices until we hit on the ideal amount of each—balanced enough that each component in the pudding could still be tasted. We also limited the spices to cinnamon and ginger because most tasters felt that additional spices, like nutmeg and mace, just muddied the pudding's flavor. To round out the flavors and add more sweetness (using only molasses for sweetening overwhelmed the spices), we added maple syrup, which is a little untraditional, but it greatly improved the pudding.

While most Indian pudding recipes call for fine-ground cornmeal, we discovered that coarser, stone-ground meal made for a more richly flavored pudding. Fine-textured, commercially produced cornmeal is usually so overprocessed that it has lost most of its flavor, whereas coarser stone-ground meal retains its sweet, characteristic corn flavor. (For more information on cornmeal, see page 268.) While not quite toothsome, the pudding had an appealing texture when made with stone-ground meal.

We quickly discovered that Indian pudding "breaks" or curdles for one of two reasons: too much fat in the mix or too high a baking temperature. The fat issue was easy enough to overcome by excluding butter and adding a little cornstarch to stabilize the milk fat. Because the pudding is so heavily seasoned, tasters did not miss the fat. And a dollop of whipped cream or scoop of ice cream on top of the pudding adequately replaced any missing fat. As for the baking temperature, we found that anything over 275 degrees was too hot and that a water bath was essential to prevent curdling. A pudding baked at 300 degrees without a water bath cooked incompletely and had the texture of cottage cheese. The water bath insulates the pudding from overheating and ensures that the pudding cooks evenly. Unfortunately, the low temperature necessitated a longer cooking time than we hoped—a full two hours. But this is still a good hour shorter than most recipes required.

Indian Pudding

SERVES 6

Toasting the spices in the saucepan prior to adding the liquid brings out their volatile oils and sharpens their flavor. Humble-looking Indian pudding requires some sort of embellishment. We like to add a dollop of whipped cream that has been flavored with rum, vanilla extract, and maple syrup instead of sugar. Vanilla ice cream is another option.

1/2	teaspoon ground ginger
1/2	teaspoon ground cinnamon
4	cups whole milk
1	teaspoon vanilla extract
1/4	cup maple syrup
1/2	cup molasses
1/2	teaspoon salt
3/4	cup (about 4 ounces) yellow cornmeal, preferably stone-ground
1	teaspoon cornstarch
2	large eggs, lightly beaten
	Whipped Cream (page 382) or vanilla ice cream

1. Adjust an oven rack to the lower-middle position and heat the oven to 275 degrees. In a medium saucepan over medium-high heat, toast the cinnamon and ginger until fragrant, about 1½ minutes. Add the milk (reserving 2 tablespoons), vanilla, maple syrup, molasses, and salt and heat to just below boiling. Stirring constantly with a whisk, slowly pour the cornmeal into the milk mixture and reduce the heat to low. Cook, stirring frequently, until the mush has thickened and the whisk leaves furrows across the surface of the mixture, about 30 minutes.

2. Meanwhile, whisk together the reserved 2 tablespoons milk and the cornstarch in a small bowl until free of lumps. Whisk in the eggs and set the mixture aside. Bring several quarts of water to a boil in a tea kettle and keep hot.

3. When the cornmeal mush has thickened (after 30 minutes of cooking), pour the egg mixture into the cornmeal mush in a slow, steady stream while constantly stirring with a whisk. Once completely mixed, increase the heat to medium-high and cook, stirring constantly, until large bubbles rise to the surface, 1 to 2 minutes.

4. Remove the pan from the heat and pour the mixture into a greased 9-inch soufflé dish or 2-quart casserole dish. Cover tightly with aluminum foil and set the dish inside a deep roasting pan. Carefully pour the boiling water into the roasting pan, adding enough water to reach halfway up the sides of the dish. Carefully place the roasting pan in the oven and bake until the center of the pudding is no longer runny and has gently set, about 2 hours. Remove the soufflé dish from the water bath and cool on a wire rack for at least 20 minutes or up to 2 hours. Spoon the warm pudding into individual bowls and top with whipped cream or vanilla ice cream. Serve immediately.

INDEX

SAVE $5

Three books no kitchen in America should be without.

PLUS a special savings offer when you order all 3!

The Best Recipe

"If the Joy of Cooking is the first step for cooks, then The Best Recipe is the entire staircase." — New York

The Best Recipe presents our 700 favorite recipes taken from the pages of *Cook's Illustrated* from 1993 through 1999. The recipes have been organized and annotated with information on the science of cooking, cookware buying recommendations, suggestions on which food products are best, plus over 200 illustrations demonstrating techniques from making pie dough to boning chicken. Now you can have all of your favorite *Cook's* recipes in one handy volume, indexed for quick reference. *560 pages; hardcover; $24.95 (Save $5.00 off the bookstore price.)*

The Best Recipe: Grilling & Barbecue

"Serious outdoor cooks will find this an invaluable guide." — The Daily Oklahoman

Over 400 recipes, with both charcoal and gas grill variations, cover just about everything that has ever been grilled, from steaks and chops to ribs and pulled pork. 300 illustrations show you preparation techniques in step-by-step detail, and testing results provide you with equipment buying recommendations and suggestions on which food products are best. *336 pages; hardcover; $24.95 (Save $5.00 off the bookstore price.)*

JUST $67.50 SAVE 25% WHEN YOU BUY ALL 3 BOOKS

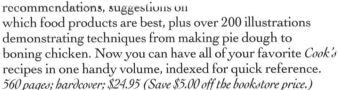

The Best Recipe: Soups & Stews

"As always, the editors' search for perfection, with multiple tested recipes, provides real wisdom for cooks." — Dayton Daily News

The editors of *Cook's Illustrated* tested 23 chicken noodle soups, 40 cioppinos, and 54 beef burgundies to find the absolute best methods for making more than 200 soups and stews. Now you can have the very best versions of these recipes, and much more, in **The Best Recipe: Soups & Stews.** Over 200 recipes cover just about every soup and stew imaginable — from American classics, such as Manhattan Clam Chowder, Chicken Noodle Soup, and Gumbo, to international favorites, such as Coq au Vin, Hot and Sour Soup, Irish Stew, and Beef Goulash. 200 step-by-step illustrations clarify preparation methods, and no-nonsense testing results provide you with equipment buying recommendations. *368 pages; hardcover; $24.95 (Save $5.00 off the bookstore price.)*

About The Best Recipe

"This gastronomic classic belongs on every serious cook's shelf." – The Christian Science Monitor

"The Best Recipe is without question one of the best cooking books published this year." – The Houston Chronicle

What they're saying

About The Best Recipe: Grilling & Barbecue

"A comprehensive guide for grilling and barbecuing that answers everything from how to grill a whole bluefish to making barbecued chicken that isn't dry." – Lincoln Star Journal

About The Best Recipe: Soups & Stews

"Not only 200 exemplary recipes but an armament of technical information, tips, and equipment recommendations all cooks will welcome." – Amazon.com's "Best of 2001" Review

To order call 1-800-611-0759 or visit our online bookstore at
www.cooksillustrated.com

(reference code CACBS1)